ENCYCLOPEDIA OF AFRICAN-AMERICAN CULTURE AND HISTORY,
SUPPLEMENT

ENCYCLOPEDIA OF AFRICAN-AMERICAN CULTURE AND HISTORY, SUPPLEMENT

General Editor

Jack Salzman

Associate Editors

Greg Robinson
Thaddeus Russell

Macmillan Reference USA

an imprint of the Gale Group

New York • Detroit • San Francisco • London • Boston • Woodbridge, CT

Macmillan Reference USA
1633 Broadway
New York, NY 10019

Macmillan Reference USA
27500 Drake Rd.
Farmington Hills, MI 48331-3535

PRINTED IN THE UNITED STATES OF AMERICA
Printing number
1   2   3   4   5   6   7   8   9   10

Library of Congress Cataloging-in-Publication Data
Encyclopedia of African-American culture and history. Supplement / edited by Jack
Salzman.
      p. cm.
    Includes bibliographical references and index.
    ISBN 0-02-865441-2 (hc.:alk. paper)
      1. Afro-Americans—Encyclopedias. 2. Afro-Americans—History—Encyclopedias. I.
Salzman, Jack. II. Encyclopedia of African-American culture and
history.

E185 .E54 1996 Suppl.
973'.0496073'003—dc21
                                                            00-063833

CONTENTS

———

EDITORIAL AND PRODUCTION STAFF

PREFACE

The original 5-volume *Encyclopedia of African American Culture and History (EAACH)* was published in 1996. It took more than five years to complete the work, which runs to 1.8 million words and contains slightly more than 2,200 entries. When the original set was published, the reviews were glowing: "This encyclopedia," wrote *American Libraries* in May of 1997, "is of enduring value and destined to become a standard reference source." And so it has; EAACH almost immediately established itself as a core reference work on the culture and history of African Americans.

As gratifying as the response to EAACH has been, the set was not published without some trepidation. After all, although we had almost two million words to work with, our intent was to bring the reader as much expert knowledge as we could about all aspects of the African-American experience. A great deal of information can be conveyed with 1.8 million words. But the history and culture of African Americans is so rich and complex that we knew from the outset that EAACH could not be as comprehensive as we wanted it to be. Difficult choices would have to be made, and they were. Although we were able to include a vast number of biographies (almost two-thirds of the original entries are biographies)—as well as a substantial number of entries devoted to events, historical eras, legal cases, areas of cultural achievement, professions, sports, and places—there was so much that could not be included because of space limitations. This Supplement is intended in large part to make up for some of the omissions from the original set. This new volume, which henceforth should be considered an integral part of the original set, contains 455 entries, of which 365 are totally new; there are 378 biographies and 77 topical entries. In addition, the Supplement contains 90 updates on material included in EAACH; 9 of the state articles have been updated as have 53 biographies. In addition, immediately following this Preface the reader will find a table of "Deaths since 1996," which contains a list of African Americans featured in the original set who have died since EAACH's publication. A cumulative index at the end of this volume along with a system of cross-references is designed to integrate the Supplement and the *Encyclopedia of African-American Culture and History*. Cross-references at the end of most articles refer to articles in the original encyclopedia as well as other articles in the Supplement. The volume number in which an article appears is indicated within brackets after the reference.

No doubt some users of the now 6-volume EAACH will still be concerned about a missing subject. Hopefully, when the next Supplement appears a few years hence, those concerns will be lessened. But one cannot be too sure. Our knowledge of the past of people of African descent in the United States continues to grow, as do the number of African Americans who deserve recognition in our contemporary world. As a result, the list in our data base of potential entries for the next Supplement continues to grow at a rather unnerving rate. But it is unnerving only because of the amount of work that will need to be done; that we know as much as we now do about the history and culture of African Americans to make such work necessary is most gratifying.

As always, there are a number of people whose efforts on behalf of the current work should be acknowledged. It is with considerable pleasure that I can here note the efforts of Greg Robinson and Thad Russell in helping me establish the basic list of entries for the Supplement. To the 63 contributors who wrote the entries, my thanks. My thanks, too, to AP/ Wide World Photos, Archive Photos, Inc., Corbis Corporation, Fisk University Library, Yorkin Publications, and the Library of Congress for providing us with the photographs that are such an integral part of the encyclopedia. In addition, it is a pleasure to acknowledge the efforts of Jill Lectka and Shirelle Phelps of Gale. And finally—as always—there is Cecily, my wife, who for more than forty years has made possible whatever good work I have been able to do.

JACK SALZMAN
NEW YORK CITY

Deaths Since First Publication

Daisy Gaston. Bates   *November 11, 1914-November 4, 1999*

Clayton "Peg Leg" Bates   *October 11, 1907-December 6, 1998*

Lester Bowie   *October 11, 1941-November 8, 1998*

Thomas Bradley   *December 29, 1917-September 9, 1998*

Herman Russell Branson   *August 14, 1914-June 7, 1995*

Ronald H. Brown   *August 1, 1941-April 3, 1996*

Samuel Joseph Brown   *April 16, 1907-October 23, 1994*

Charles Wesley Buggs   *August 6, 1906-September 13, 1991*

Selma Hortense Burke   *December 31, 1900-August 29, 1995*

Stokely Carmichael   *July 29, 1941-November 15, 1998*

Betty Carter   *May 16, 1930-September 26, 1998*

Wilton Norman Chamberlain   *August 21, 1936-October 12, 1999*

Alice Childress   *October 12, 1920-August 14, 1994*

Albert Cleage   *June 13, 1911-February 20, 2000*

Eldridge Leroy Cleaver   *August 31, 1935-May 1, 1998*

Sarah Delany   *September 19, 1889-January 25, 1999*

Thomas Covington Dent   *March 20, 1932-June 6, 1998*

Charles Coles Diggs, Jr.   *December 2, 1922-August 24, 1998*

Ulysses Dove   *January 17, 1947-June 11, 1996*

Robert Todd Duncan   *February 12, 1903-February 28, 1998*

Harry "Sweets" Edison   *October 10, 1915-July 27, 1999*

Lonne Elder III   *December 26, 1931-June 11, 1996*

Francine Everett   *April 13, 1917-May 27, 1999*

James Farmer   *January 12, 1920-July 9, 1999*

Leon Forrest   *January 8, 1937-November 6, 1997*

Florence D. Griffith-Joyner   *December 21, 1959-September 21, 1998*

Jester Hairston   *July 9, 1901-January 18, 2000*

Chester Higgins   *May 10, 1917-May 25, 2000*

Jean Blackwell Hutson   *September 7, 1914-February 4, 1998*

Lois Mailou Jones   *November 3, 1905-June 9, 1998*

Barbara C. Jordan   *February 21, 1936-January 17, 1996*

Jacob A. Lawrence	*September 7, 1917-June 9, 2000*
Hughie Lee-Smith	*September 20, 1915-February 22, 1999*
Louis E. Martin	*November 18, 1912-January 27, 1997*
Curtis Mayfield	*June 3, 1942-December 26, 1999*
Dorothy Maynor	*September 3, 1910-February 19, 1996*
Henry Cecil Ransom McBay	*May 29, 1914-June 23, 1995*
Claudia McNeil	*August 13, 1917-November 25, 1993*
Thelma "Butterfly" McQueen	*January 8, 1911-December 22, 1995*
Archibald Lee "Archie" Moore	*December 13, 1916-December 9, 1998*
Everett Frederick Morrow	*April 20, 1909-July 19, 1994*
Marion "Tank" Motley	*June 5, 1920-June 27, 1999*
James Madison Nabrit	*September 4, 1900-December 27, 1997*
Harold Nicholas	*March 17, 1921-July 3, 2000*
Walter Payton	*July 25, 1954-November 1, 1999*
Ann Lane Petry	*October 12, 1908-April 28, 1997*
Benjamin Quarles	*January 28, 1904-November 16, 1996*
Wilson Camanza Riles	*June 27, 1917-April 1, 1999*
Monetta J. Sleet, Jr.	*February 14, 1926-September 30, 1996*
Carl Burton Stokes	*June 21, 1927-April 3, 1996*
Valores J. "Val" Washington	*September 18, 1903-1995*
Robert Clifton Weaver	*December 29, 1907-July 17, 1997*
James Lesesne Wells	*November 2, 1902-January 20, 1993*
Dorothy West	*June 2,1907-August 16, 1998*
Joseph Goreedd "Joe" Williams	*December 12, 1918-March 29, 1999*
Marion Williams	*August 19, 1927-July 2, 1994*
Robert Franklin Williams	*February 26, 1925-October 15, 1996*
Sherley Anne Williams	*August 25, 1944-July 6, 1999*
Coleman Alexander Young	*May 24, 1918-November 29, 1997*

A list of African Americans featured in the *Encyclopedia of African-American Culture and History* who have died since publication.

ALPHABETICAL LIST OF ARTICLES

―――――――

DIRECTORY OF CONTRIBUTORS

A

Omar Ali
Columbia University
CAREY, MARY ANN SHADD
COLORED FARMERS' ALLIANCE
CROMWELL, OLIVER
DELLUMS, C(OTTRELL) L(AWRENCE)
FULANI, LENORA BRANCH
LATIMER, LEWIS HOWARD
MFUME, KWEISI

B

Abel Bartley
Akron, Ohio
JACKSONVILLE, FLORIDA

Kathleen Benson
Museum of the City of New York
BLACK MAGICIANS
BULLARD, EUGENE

William W. Boyer
Newark, Delaware
VIRGIN ISLANDS

James Bradley
Brooklyn, New York
DINKINS, DAVID NORMAN (UPDATE)
O'LEARY, HAZEL ROLLINS (UPDATE)

Carol Brennan
Grosse Pointe Park, Michigan
JONES, GRACE
SANDERS, BARRY

Roderick Bush
St. Johns University
BLACK NATIONALISM

C

Patrick J. Carroll
Corpus Christi State University
MEXICO (UPDATE)

Jeffrey J. Crow
State of North Carolina
NORTH CAROLINA (UPDATE)

D

Elly Dickason
JACKSON, SHIRLEY ANN

Patrick Dickson
Curry College
ASSOCIATION OF SOUTHERN WOMEN FOR
    THE PREVENTION OF LYNCHING
COMMISSION ON INTERRACIAL
    COOPERATION

Kenya Dilday
Columbia University
WINFREY, OPRAH GAIL (UPDATE)

Jill Dupont
Chicago, Illinois
JOHNSON, EARVIN, JR. "MAGIC" (UPDATE)
LEWIS, CARL (UPDATE)

Mervyn Dymally
United States Congress
DEMOCRATIC PARTY (UPDATE)

Michael Eric Dyson
Providence, Rhode Island
JACKSON, JESSE LOUIS (UPDATE)

E

Gerald Early
Washington University
ALI, MUHAMMAD (UPDATE)

F

Michel Fabre
Paris, France
EXPATRIATES (UPDATE)

Harris Friedberg
New Haven, Connecticut
JACKSON, MICHAEL, AND THE JACKSON
    FAMILY (UPDATE)

Michael Wade Fuquay
George Mason University
FELLOWSHIP OF RECONCILIATION, THE
GRANDMASTER FLASH (JOSEPH SADDLER)
GRIFFEY, KEN, JR.
GWYNN, ANTHONY KEITH "TONY"
NEVILLE BROTHERS, THE
RICE, JERRY

G

Jessica L. Graham
Cornell University
FREEDOM RIDES

H

Richard C. Hanes
Eugene, Oregon
BLACK UPPER CLASS

JUMPING
LOWNDES COUNTY FREEDOM ORGANIZATION
SHARECROPPER/SHARECROPPING UNION

John A. Hardin
Western Kentucky University
KENTUCKY (UPDATE)
LOUISVILLE, KENTUCKY (UPDATE)

F. Zeal Harris
Washington, D.C.
ANDERSON, GARLAND
ARMISTEAD, JAMES
BLACKFACE
CHILDRESS, ALVIN
CLEAGE, PEARL
DOWNING, HENRY F.
GORDONE, CHARLES
GREGORY, THOMAS MONTGOMERY
HAMPTON, HENRY
HUGHES, ALBERT AND ALLEN
JACKSON, SAMUEL LEROY
NICHOLS, NICHELLE (GRACE NICHOLS)
RICHARDSON, WILLIS
SMITH, ANNA DEAVERE
WALTON, LESTER A.
WHITAKER, FOREST

James Haskins
University of Florida
BLACK MAGICIANS
BULLARD, EUGENE

Antonio F. Holland
Lincoln University
MISSOURI (UPDATE)

Carrell P. Horton
Fisk University
BOWMAN, SISTER THEA
BROWN, ARTHUR MCKIMMON
BUSH, JOHN EDWARD
CLARK, MAMIE PHIPPS
COOK, GEORGE F. T.
COOK, JOHN FRANCIS, JR.
COOK, JOHN FRANCIS, SR.
DAVIS, HARRY E.
DURHAM, JOHN STEPHENS
ELLIS, GEORGE WASHINGTON
FARLEY, JAMES CONWAY
FLETCHER, BENJAMIN HARRISON
FRANCIS, MILTON A.
GANDY, JOHN MANUEL
GARDINER, LEON
HIGHTOWER, DENNIS F.
JACKSON, ALEXINE CLEMENT

JONES, MARION
JONES, ROY, JR.
MORGAN, CLEMENT GARNETT
WHEAT, ALAN

Helen R. Houston
Tennessee State University
BENJAMIN, R(OBERT) C(HARLES) O('HARA)
CANNON, NOAH CALWELL W.
COCHRAN, JOHNNIE L., JR.
CORROTHERS, JAMES DAVID
COTTER, JOSEPH SEAMON, JR.
COTTER, JOSEPH SEAMON, SR.
DAVIS, DANIEL WEBSTER
EMANUEL, JAMES A., SR.
MCGIRT, JAMES EPHRIAM
PHYLON
RANGER, JOSEPH
ROWE, GEORGE CLINTON
SIMPSON, JOSHUA MCCARTER
TEAGUE, ROBERT
THOMPSON, AARON BELFORD
VROMAN, MARY ELIZABETH

J

Robert L. Johns
Fisk University
ALBERT, OCTAVIA
ALEXANDER, JOHN HANKS
BARÉS, BASILE JEAN
BERRY, EDWIN C.
BIVINS, HORACE C.
BROOKS, WALTER HENDERSON
BROWN, SOLOMON G.
BROWN, WESLEY A(NTHONY)
BUSH, GEORGE WASHINGTON
BUTLER, THOMAS C.
CAILLOUX, ANDRÉ
CARTER, LOUIS
CHASE, WILLIAM CALVIN
CLARKE, LEWIS G.
CLARK, JOSEPH SAMUEL
CLEAGE, ALBERT B., JR. (JARAMOGI ABEBE
    AGYEMAN)
CLEM, CHARLES DOUGLASS
CLOUGH, INEZ
CROCKETT, GEORGE WILLIAM, JR.
CROGMAN, WILLIAM H.
CROTHERS, SCATMAN
DAVIS, ARTHUR PAUL
DAVIS, JOHN HENRY "BLIND JOHN"
DEAN, WILLIAM H., JR.
DICKENSON, SPENCER C.
DIXON, JULIAN
DORMAN, ISAIAH

DUDLEY, SHERMAN H.
EASTON, HOSEA
ELLISON, WILLIAM
EVERETT, FRANCINE (FRANCEINE
    WILLIAMSON)
FAUNTROY, WALTER E.
FISHER, ADA (LOIS) SIPUEL
FLAKE, FLOYD H.
FLETCHER, ALPHONSE, JR.
FRANK, FREE (FRANK MCWORTER)
FREEMAN, ELIZABETH (MUM BETT,
    MUMBET)
GARDNER, NEWPORT (OCCRAMER
    MARYCOO)
GRAVELY, SAMUEL L., JR.
GUILLAUME, ROBERT
HENDRICKS, BARBARA
JACKSON LEE, SHEILA
JEFFERSON, WILLIAM JENNINGS
JOHNSON, EDWARD AUSTIN
JOHNSON, WILLIAM
JONES, FREDERICK M.
KEYES, ALAN
LAFAYETTE PLAYERS
LAYTON, JOHN TURNER
LEMUS, RIENZI B(ROCK)
LEWIS, DELANO EUGENE
LEWIS, THEOPHILUS
LUCAS, SAM
MACARTY, VICTOR-EUGÉNE
MCCLELLAN, GEORGE MARION
MCGHEE, FREDERICK LAMAR
MCJUNKIN, GEORGE
MÉTOYER, LOUIS
MÉTOYER, MARIE-THÉRÉSE (COINCOIN)
MITCHELL, PARREN J.
NASH, CHARLES EDMUND
NATIONAL MEDICAL ASSOCIATION
NORTH STAR
PERRY, HEMAN EDWARD
PICKENS, WILLIAM
PLEDGER, WILLIAM ANDERSON
REASON, CHARLES (LEWIS)
REASON, PATRICK HENRY
ROPER, MOSES
SCARBOROUGH, WILLIAM SANDERS
SCHMOKE, KURT
SHAW, EARL D.
SMITH, JOSHUA BOWEN
SMITH, STEPHEN
SUMNER, FRANCIS CECIL
THOMPSON, ELOISE (ALBERTA VERONIC)
    BIBB
THOMPSON, JOHN W.
VASHON, GEORGE BOYER
WARFIELD, WILLIAM (CAESAR)

WASOW, OMAR
WEBB, WELLINGTON (EDWARD)
WHITMAN, ALBERY
WILLIAMS, JUAN
WILSON, FLIP (CLEROW WILSON)

K

Randall Kennedy
Harvard Law School
MARSHALL, THURGOOD (UPDATE)

Kevin C. Kretschmer
Des Moines, Iowa
BADGER, ROBERT AND RODERICK
BASEBALL
BOXING
CONNERLY, WARD
MARTIN, LOUIS EMANUEL
PARSONS, RICHARD DEAN
REDMAN, JOSHUA
SHAW, ALAN
SOWELL, THOMAS
STRAKER, DAVID AUGUSTUS

L

Wahneema Lubiano
Princeton, New Jersey
MORRISON, TONI (UPDATE)

M

James Manheim
Ann Arbor, Michigan
ATLANTA, GEORGIA (UPDATE)
BIRMINGHAM, ALABAMA (UPDATE)
DALLAS, TEXAS (UPDATE)
DETROIT, MICHIGAN (UPDATE)
FLORIDA (UPDATE)
LOS ANGELES, CALIFORNIA (UPDATE)
NEW YORK CITY (UPDATE)
PHILADELPHIA, PENNSYLVANIA (UPDATE)
TEXAS (UPDATE)
WASHINGTON, D.C. (UPDATE)

Louise P. Maxwell
Columbia University
WATERS, MAXINE MOORE (UPDATE)

Eddie S. Meadows
University of California, Los Angeles
MARSALIS, WYNTON (UPDATE)

Susan McIntosh
Columbia University
DAVIS, OSSIE (UPDATE)
MURPHY, EDDIE (UPDATE)

James A. Miller
Trinity College, Hartford, Connecticut
GREGORY, RICHARD CLAXTON "DICK"
(UPDATE)

Sally Myers
Defiance, Ohio
PITTSBURGH, PENNSYLVANIA (UPDATE)

N

Jim Naughton
Washington, D.C.
JORDAN, MICHAEL JEFFREY (UPDATE)

Richard Newman
Harvard University
GATES, HENRY LOUIS, JR.
WEST, CORNEL RONALD

Dolores Nicholson
Metropolitan Nashville Public Schools
DAY, WILLIAM HOWARD
DENBY, CHARLES
FORD, BARNEY LAUNCELOT
HENRY, AARON "DOC"
JONES, SCIPIO AFRICANUS
MORIAL, ERNEST NATHAN "DUTCH"
SCOTT, ROBERT CORTEZ "BOBBY"
WEEMS, RENITA

P

Michael Paller
Columbia University
WOLFE, GEORGE C. (UPDATE)

Mary Pattillo-McCoy
Northwestern University
BLACK MIDDLE CLASS

Sandra Patton
St. Paul, Minnesota
ADOPTION

Marcus D. Pohlmann
Rhodes College
DEINDUSTRIALIZATION
FORD, HAROLD EUGENE, SR. (UPDATE)
MEMPHIS, TENNESSEE (UPDATE)

Valencia Price
Tennessee State University
BAKER, GWENDOLYN CALVERT
BELTON, SHARON SAYLES
BRANDON, BARBARA
BROWNE, HUGH M.
BRUNSON, DOROTHY

BURCH, CHARLES EATON
GAYNOR, FLORENCE S.
GREGG, JOHN ANDREW
HOLLAND, WILLIAM H.
KOONTZ, ELIZABETH DUNCAN
SAMPSON, EDITH SPURLOCK
SKLAREK, NORMA MERRICK
SMYTHE-HAITHE, MABEL MURPHY
TILLMAN, NATHANIEL PATRICK "TIC," SR.
WALLACE, PHYLLIS ANN

R

Robert Reid-Pharr
City University of New York
GAY MEN (UPDATE)

Greg Robinson
George Mason University
AFFIRMATIVE ACTION (UPDATE)
ALBANY, GEORGIA
ALI, MUHAMMAD (UPDATE)
ASHE, ARTHUR ROBERT, JR. (UPDATE)
BARRY, MARION SHEPILOV, JR. (UPDATE)
BEREA COLLEGE
BETHUNE-COOKMAN COLLEGE
BLAXPLOITATION FILM (UPDATE)
BOND, JULIAN (UPDATE)
BOWE, RIDDICK (UPDATE)
BROWN, LEE PATRICK
BROWN, RONALD H. (UPDATE)
BROYARD, ANATOLE PAUL
BUTTS, CALVIN O. I., III (UPDATE)
CARMICHAEL, STOKELY (UPDATE)
CHASE-RIBOUD, BARBARA DEWAYNE
(UPDATE)
CHAVIS, BENJAMIN FRANKLIN, JR.,
(MUHAMMAD) (UPDATE)
CLARK ATLANTA UNIVERSITY
CLARKE, JOHN HENRIK
CLEVELAND, OHIO (UPDATE)
CONYERS, JOHN, JR. (UPDATE)
COSBY, WILLIAM HENRY, JR. "BILL"
(UPDATE)
CROUCH, STANLEY
CROWN HEIGHTS RIOT
DAVIS, ANGELA YVONNE (UPDATE)
DAVIS, OSSIE (UPDATE)
DELANY, SARAH LOUISE "SADIE" AND ANNIE
ELIZABETH "BESSIE"
DEMOCRATIC PARTY (UPDATE)
DILLARD UNIVERSITY
DINKINS, DAVID NORMAN (UPDATE)
ESPY, MICHAEL
EXPATRIATES (UPDATE).
FARRAKHAN, LOUIS ABDUL (UPDATE)
FORD, HAROLD EUGENE, JR.

FORD, HAROLD EUGENE, SR. (UPDATE)

FOREMAN, GEORGE EDWARD (UPDATE)

FRANKLIN, JOHN HOPE (UPDATE)

GAY MEN (UPDATE)

GOLDBERG, WHOOPI (UPDATE)

GOLF (UPDATE)

GOMES, PETER JOHN

GREGORY, RICHARD CLAXTON "DICK" (UPDATE)

GRIFFITH-JOYNER, FLORENCE DELOREZ (UPDATE)

HEIGHT, DOROTHY (UPDATE)

HEMINGS, SALLY (UPDATE)

HERMAN, ALEXIS MARGARET

HIGGINBOTHAM, A. LEON, JR.

HOLYFIELD, EVANDER (UPDATE)

HUSTON-TILLOTSON COLLEGE

JACKSON, JESSE LOUIS (UPDATE)

JACKSON, MICHAEL, AND THE JACKSON FAMILY (UPDATE)

JOHNSON, EARVIN, JR. "MAGIC" (UPDATE)

JORDAN, BARBARA CHARLINE (UPDATE)

JORDAN, MICHAEL JEFFREY (UPDATE)

JORDAN, VERNON EULION, JR. (UPDATE)

JULIUS ROSENWALD FUND

LEE, SHELTON JACKSON "SPIKE" (UPDATE)

LEONARD, RAY CHARLES "SUGAR RAY" (UPDATE)

LEWIS, CARL (UPDATE)

LEWIS, HENRY, JR.

MARSALIS, WYNTON (UPDATE)

MARSHALL, THURGOOD (UPDATE)

MAYORS (UPDATE)

MCCALL, H. CARL

MCMILLAN, TERRY (UPDATE)

MILITARY (UPDATE)

MILLION MAN MARCH

MORRISON, TONI (UPDATE)

MOSELEY-BRAUN, CAROL (UPDATE)

MOSLEY, WALTER (UPDATE)

MURPHY, EDDIE (UPDATE)

NATIONAL ASSOCIATION FOR THE ADVANCEMENT OF COLORED PEOPLE (UPDATE)

NATION OF ISLAM (UPDATE)

O.J. SIMPSON TRIAL

PARKS, ROSA LOUISE MCCAULEY (UPDATE)

POWELL, COLIN LUTHER (UPDATE)

PRESIDENTS OF THE UNITED STATES (UPDATE)

REPUBLICAN PARTY (UPDATE)

ROBINSON, JACK ROOSEVELT "JACKIE" (UPDATE)

RUSTIN, BAYARD (UPDATE)

SAN FRANCISCO AND OAKLAND, CALIFORNIA (UPDATE)

SATCHER, DAVID

SHABAZZ, BETTY

SHARPTON, ALFRED, JR. (UPDATE)

ST. LOUIS, MISSOURI (UPDATE)

TYSON, MICHAEL GERALD "MIKE" (UPDATE)

WASHINGTON, DENZEL (UPDATE)

WATERS, MAXINE MOORE (UPDATE)

WATSON, ROBERT JOSE

WATTS, JULIUS CAESAR, JR. "J.C."

WINFREY, OPRAH GAIL (UPDATE)

WOLFE, GEORGE C. (UPDATE)

Elmer R. Rusco
University of Nevada, Reno

NEVADA (UPDATE)

Thaddeus Russell
Columbia University

BROWN, WILLIE LEWIS, JR. (UPDATE)

LEONARD, RAY CHARLES "SUGAR RAY" (UPDATE)

S

Evan A. Shore
Columbia University

BOND, JULIAN (UPDATE)

Amritjit Singh
Lincoln, Rhode Island

MCMILLAN, TERRY (UPDATE)

Frederick D. Smith, Jr.
Fisk University

ADAMS, EUGENE WILLIAM

BELLAMY, SHERRY F.

CASSELL, ALBERT IRVIN

DERHAM, JAMES, ALSO SPELLED DURHAM

FISHBURNE, LAURENCE

GOURDIN, EDWARD ORVAL

GREENE, MAURICE

HANNAH, MARC

JOHNSON, MICHAEL DUANE

MORTON, FERDINAND QUINTON

PARKS, HENRY GREEN

RICE, NORMAN BLANN

WASHINGTON, KENNETH "KENNY" WILLIAM

Jessie Carney Smith
Fisk University

ADGER, ROBERT MARA

ASSOCIATED NEGRO PRESS

BARROW, WILLIE B. TAPLIN

BERRY, MARY FRANCIS

BINGA, JESSE

BINGA STATE BANK

BOWDEN, ARTEMISIA

BRANTON, WILEY AUSTIN

CALIVER, AMBROSE

CARDOZO, W(ILLIAM) WARRICK

CHAPPELL, EMMA CAROLYN BAYTON

CHENAULT, KENNETH IRVINE

CHESTER, THOMAS MORRIS

COLLINS, CARDISS ROBERTSON

CRUMPLER, REBECCA DAVIS LEE

CULP, DANIEL WALLACE

DE BAPTISTE, RICHARD

DELANY, HUBERT T.

EAGLESON, WILLIAM LEWIS

EVERS-WILLIAMS, MYRLIE BEASLEY

FUDGE, ANN

FULLER, SAMUEL B.

FUTRELL, MARY HATWOOD

GASTON, ARTHUR GEORGE

GILBERT, JOHN WESLEY

GRIER, PAMELA SUZETTE "PAM"

HAMILTON, THOMAS

HARVARD, BEVERLY

HILYER, AMANDA GRAY

HOLSTEIN, CASPAR A.

HOUSTON, WHITNEY

JACKMAN, HAROLD

JOHNSON, HAZEL WINIFRED

JONES, CAROLINE ROBINSON

JONES, ELAINE R.

JONES, LAURENCE CLIFTON

JOYNER, MARJORIE STEWART

KEMP, MAIDA SPRINGER

LAFON, THOMY

LEMOYNE-OWEN COLLEGE

LEWIS, ELMA

MAHONEY, MARY ELIZA

MCAFEE, CHARLES

MCHENRY, DONALD F.

MORGAN, ROSE META

MOTEN, LUCY ELLEN

NABRIT, SAMUEL MILTON

NAIL, JOHN E. (JACK)

OWENS, MAJOR ROBERT

PELHAM, BENJAMIN B.

POSTON, TED

PROCTOR, BARBARA GARDNER

RICHARDS, FANNIE MOORE

ROMAN, CHARLES VICTOR

SHEPARD, JAMES EDWARDS

SIMMONS, RUTH J.

SMITH, BARBARA (B. 1949)

TYLER, RALPH WALDO

WADDY, HARRIET M.

WASHINGTON, AUGUSTUS

WATSON, BARBARA MAE

WEBSTER, MILTON PRICE

WILLIAMS, PAUL REVERE
WILSON, WILLIAM JULIUS

Eric Ledell Smith
Pennsylvania Historical Museum Commission
PENNSYLVANIA (UPDATE)

T

Darius L. Thieme
Fisk University
BURRELL COMMUNICATIONS GROUP
DANIELS, WILLIAM BOONE "BILLY"
EDISON, HARRY "SWEETS"
HAMID, SUFI ABDUL
HAYES, ISAAC
HILL, ANDREW
LOURY, GLENN CARTMAN
MINGO-JONES ADVERTISING AGENCY
NATIONAL BLACK NETWORK
PRATT, AWADAGIN
TATUM, WILBER ARNOLD
TOWNS, EDOLPHUS
WALDEN, AUSTIN T.
WALLER, JOHN L.

Daniel B. Thorp
Virginia Tech
MORAVIAN CHURCH

V

Sheila Velazquez
Knoxville, Tennessee
TENNESSEE (UPDATE)

Ben Vinson III
Barnard College
MEXICO (UPDATE)

W

Hanes Walton, Jr.
University of Michigan
DEMOCRATIC PARTY (UPDATE)

Randy F. Weinstein
The North Star
BLACK COACHES ASSOCIATION
HARRISON, SAMUEL
PRICE, HUGH BERNARD
SAMPSON, JOHN PATTERSON

Pamela Wilkinson
Columbia University
CHASE-RIBOUD, BARBARA DEWAYNE (UPDATE)
MOSLEY, WALTER (UPDATE)

Raymond Winbush
Fisk University
BLACKWELL, RANDOLPH TALMADGE
CLARK, ALEXANDER G.
DANCY, JOHN CAMPBELL, JR.
DAVIS, RICHARD L.
DUDLEY, EDWARD RICHARD
DYMALLY, MERVYN MALCOLM
FRANKS, GARY
HART, WILLIAM HENRY HARRISON
HILLIARD, EARL FREDERICK
LELAND, GEORGE THOMAS "MICKEY"
LINDSAY, INABEL BURNS
MCKINNEY, CYNTHIA ANN
MEEK, CARRIE P.
PAGE, CLARENCE
PAYNE, DONALD MILFORD
PERKINS, EDWARD JOSEPH
RAINES, FRANKLIN D.

Giles R. Wright
New Jersey Historical Commission
NEW JERSEY (UPDATE)

Linda T. Wynn
Tennessee Historical Commission
CAESAR, JOHN
HOLMES, DWIGHT OLIVER WENDELL
JACKSON, JESSE LOUIS, JR.
MCFERREN, VIOLA HUGHES
MIAMI, FLORIDA
NAPIER, JAMES CARROLL
RODNEY KING RIOT
WASHINGTON, SARAH (SARA) SPENCER
WILLIAMS, AVON N., JR

Y

Nancy Yousef
Columbia University
LEONARD, RAY CHARLES "SUGAR RAY" (UPDATE)

Z

Rachel Zellars
Los Angeles, California
BLACK ENTERTAINMENT TELEVISION (BET)
COMBS, SEAN "PUFFY"
GILLESPIE, MARCIA ANN
GLOVER, SAVION
HARRIS, E. LYNN
HEMPHILL, ESSEX
JACKSON, JANET
JOHNSON, MORDECAI WYATT
L L COOL J
PUBLIC ENEMY
QUEEN LATIFAH (OWENS, DANA ELAINE)
RUN-D.M.C.
SINGLETON, JOHN DANIEL
SMITH, BARBARA (B. 1946)
TAYLOR, SUSAN

A

Adams, Eugene William (January 12, 1920–), veterinarian, veterinary educator, pathologist. Eugene Adams was born in Guthrie, Oklahoma, the son of Clarence Leon and Lucille Evelyn Owens Adams. He studied at Wichita State University from 1938 to 1941, then at Kansas State University where he received the D.V.M. degree in 1944. Five years later, he became a captain in the U.S. Air Force Reserve, ending his service in 1956. The following year Adams earned his M.S. degree from Cornell University, and a Ph.D. from that institution in 1962.

After receiving his doctorate in veterinary medicine in 1944, Adams became a public health veterinarian in St. Louis with the U.S. Department of Agriculture. He left in 1951 for Tuskegee Institute, the only historically black college with a school of veterinary medicine. There he served as a professor and later vice provost for nearly forty years, while also spending two years on the faculty of Ahmadu Bello University in Zaria, Nigeria, beginning in 1970. He retired in 1989 and became professor emeritus. In addition to his academic work, Adams has been active on national panels and councils, including the National Resources Research Council of the National Institutes of Health; the Africa Bureau Steering Committee on Agricultural Education, USAID, Africa Bureau; and on the board of directors of the Institute for Alternative Agriculture.

Honored widely for his work, Adams received the Distinguished Teaching Award from the Norden Drug Company in 1956. He became board-certified by the College of Veterinary Pathologists in 1964, and in 1979 earned recognition for his considerable achievements from Tuskegee University with his acceptance of the Distinguished Faculty Achievement Award. *See also* TUSKEGEE INSTITUTE [5]; VETERINARY MEDICINE [5].

REFERENCES

Tuskegee University Press Release. "The Legacy of Dr. Eugene W. Adams, D.V.M., Ph.D." http://svme107.tusk.edu/Tu/Adams1.html.

Henderson, Ashyia N. and Shirelle Phelps, eds. *Who's Who Among African Americans, 12th ed.* 1999.

FREDERICK D. SMITH, JR.

Adger, Robert Mara (1837–June 10, 1910), bibliophile, political activist, entrepreneur. Robert Adger followed in his father's abolitionist and entrepreneurial footsteps as a young man. Educated at the Bird School, an early institution for training black youth, he assisted in his father's three furniture stores as a store manager for most of his life. In 1854 he also became associated with the literary and debating society his father founded, the Banneker Literary Institute, becoming its president in 1863.

Adger supported the cause of fugitive slaves, which brought him into contact with the martyr John Brown.

As a member of the Black Enlistment Committee, he recruited blacks to fight in the Union Army. When the war was over, he continued to fight for African American rights through the Pennsylvania State Equal Rights League, which he served as a corresponding secretary. In 1860 he organized the Fraternal Society to assist refugees from South Carolina, and nine years later sought to promote economic growth in Philadelphia's black community as director of the Philadelphia Building and Loan Association. Adger also took a position as a postal clerk in the early 1880s. In 1897, he organized the Afro-American Historical Society and became its first president.

In addition to these activities, Adger's love of books led him to build an impressive collection of rare books and pamphlets, and he also became a dealer in paintings and prints. He published the first catalog of his collection in 1894 and the second in 1906. This collection became property of Wellesley College and is now housed in the Rare Book Room.

See also ABOLITION [1]; BOOK COLLECTORS AND COLLECTIONS [1]; SLAVERY [5].

REFERENCES

Ball, Wendy, and Tony Martin. *Rare Afro-Americana: A Reconstruction of the Adger Library.* 1981.

Logan, Rayford W., and Michael R. Winston, eds. *Dictionary of American Negro Biography.* 1982.

Martin, Tony. "Bibliophiles, Activists, and Race Men." In *Black Bibliophiles and Collectors*, edited by Elinor Des Verney Sinnette, et al. 1990.

JESSIE CARNEY SMITH

Adoption. The number of children in foster care has grown dramatically since the 1980s, and a disproportionate percentage of those children are African-American. The question of why so many children of color enter foster enter care is complex, relating to the history of racism and economic discrimination of African-American families have endured in the United States. Yet, the institutional history of adoption and race in the United States also reveals that the adoption system itself has contributed to the difficulties of placing black children for adoption.

Adoption was created by statute in the United States in the mid-nineteenth century in response to urbanization and changes in the relationship between work and family that accompanied the industrial revolution. An unmanageable increase in the number of homeless children led to the establishment of public almshouses and asylums in burgeoning eastern cities. From its inception, the U.S. adoption movement has been organized along ideological intertwined racial-ethnic and class lines. African-American children were not served by the social welfare system that emerged in the late 19th and early 20th centuries, and thus, the practice of informal adoption continued to be practiced among black Americans through extended kinship networks of support.

The first public adoption agencies were established following World War I, but the adoption agency structure was expanded following World War II, in response to a dramatic rise in the demand for healthy infants on the part of white middle class couples. Consequently, adoption guidelines were routed toward this specific group. In the 1950s few black couples met the stringent policy requirements for adoption eligibility. The screening policies employed by most adoption agencies through the early 1970s enforced criteria that were inappropriate for most African-American families. Large numbers of prospective black adopters were turned away from agencies for failing to meet such requirements as economic stability, home ownership (with a separate bedroom for the child), and full-time wife and mother. The resulting difficulties in placing children of color, older children, and those with disabilities in adoptive homes led these groups of children to be labeled "unadoptable," and thus agency resources focused on placing healthy, white infants.

The Civil Rights Movement raised public awareness of the large number of black children relegated to foster homes, and the integrationist spirit of the movement made transracial adoption a new consideration for many social workers and prospective white parents. As the number of black children adopted by whites increased in the late 1960s, transracial adoption became a controversial public issue. The questions at the heart of the debate between those for and those against transracial adoptions concern the importance of maintaining African-American cultural identity and white parents' ability to transmit survival skills to black children in a racially oppressive society. While those in favor of transracial adoption offer it as the solution to the large number of black children in foster care, opponents encourage the recruitment of African-American adoptive families.

REFERENCES

Boris, Eileen and Peter Bardaglio. "Gender, Race, and Class: The Impact of the State on the Family and the

Economy, 1790–1945." In *Families and Work*. Edited by Naomi Gerstel and Harriet Engel Gross. 1987.

Cole, Elizabeth S. and Kathryn S. Donley. "History, Values, and Placement Policy Issues in Adoption." In *The Psychology of Adoption*. Edited by David M. Brodzinsky and Marshall D. Schechter. 1990.

Day, Dawn. *The Adoption of Black Children: Counteracting Institutional Discrimination*. 1979.

Dill, Bonnie Thornton. "Our Mothers' Grief: Racial-Ethnic Women and the Maintenance of Families." *Journal of Family History* 13(4): 415-431. 1988.

Ladner, Joyce A. *Mixed Families: Adopting Across Racial Boundaries*. 1977.

Patton, Sandra. *BirthMarks: Transracial Adoption in Contemporary America*. 2000.

SANDRA PATTON

Affirmative Action (Update).

Outside the courts, controversy continued. In June of 1995, the Supreme Court ruled that all race-based programs would be subject to "strict scrutiny" and must be narrowly tailored to suit specific goals. The following month, President Bill Clinton, responding to congressional pressure to roll back minority preferences, proposed a new initiative on affirmative action that would "mend it, not end it." Despite continued support from Clinton, support for affirmative action nationwide continued to erode. In July of 1995, following a lengthy campaign by California Governor Pete Wilson, the Trustees of the University of California voted to end minority preferences in state college admissions. The following year, a coalition led by Wilson and African-American businessman WARD CONNERLY introduced Proposition 209, which barred affirmative action programs under the guise of promoting equal rights for all racial groups.

The enactment of Proposition 209 by California voters in November 1996 (and the U.S. Supreme Court's subsequent dismissal of legal challenges to it) paved the way for similar measures in other states. Although in 1997 Houston's voters defeated a challenge to the city's affirmative action program, the vote was suspended after a court fight, while voters in the state of Washington approved a measure similar to California's in 1998. Despite the efforts of influential educators such as Nathan Glazer and Derek Bok to defend the social impact of minority preferences, by the late 1990s, the future of affirmative action was in doubt more than ever.

REFERENCES

Belz, Herman. *Affirmative Action from Kennedy to Reagan: Redefining American Equality*. 1984.

Horne, Gerald. *Reverse Discrimination: the Case for Affirmative Action*. 1992. http://www.auaa.org/ (homepage of Americans United for Affirmative Action).

GREG ROBINSON

Albany, Georgia.

The birthplace of the Albany Movement, holds a special place in African American history. Albany was founded in 1836 as seat of Dougherty County and commercial center for the flourishing cotton plantations of the Southwest Georgia Black Belt. By 1860 six thousand enslaved blacks, eighty-three percent of the local population, lived in Dougherty County. Following Emancipation, some seven hundred freedmen, most from surrounding areas, settled in Albany's south side. They formed churches and schools and engaged in community action. However, black progress was checked by discrimination and by violent attacks by the Ku Klux Klan and other terrorist groups. In 1868, a convention of Albany blacks led by State Representative Philip Joiner sent a petition to Congress asserting that state officials refused to protect them from attack and urging funds to relocate elsewhere. As many as one thousand blacks fled the Albany area during these years.

In the decades that followed Reconstruction, Albany's blacks were politically disfranchised and economically exploited. A few African Americans, notably Deal Jackson and Bartlow Powell, secured title to large tracts of land, while others such as druggist M. O. Lee operated successful businesses. A community of teachers was employed at the Albany Bible and Manual Training Institute, founded in 1904, which later grew into Albany State College. However, most blacks were forced into sharecropping, turpentine production or domestic service, and faced destitution. In a study published in 1901, the renowned scholar W. E. B. DuBois found that only six percent of blacks in Dougherty County owned any property at all.

Albany's blacks were further embittered by near-total segregation. Although African Americans founded a local branch of the NAACP in 1918 and a Voter's League in 1947–48 to protest Albany's racial caste system, it remained largely untouched. So difficult was life in Albany that 4,500 African Americans left the area in a ten-month period during the Great Migration of 1916–1917, and many more left in the second migration after World War II. By 1960, blacks represented only 40% of the local population.

In fall 1961, Charles Sherrod and Cordell Reagon from the Student Nonviolent Coordinating Committee (SNCC) came to Albany to organize a civil rights protest. On November 1, they led a demonstration at the Trailways bus terminal. Encouraged by their success, on November 17 the NAACP Youth Council, Black Ministers Alliance, and other groups formed the Albany Movement to coordinate civil rights activities. Five days later, five students were arrested at the Trailways bus station. Their trial and conviction sparked protest marches by hundreds of activists, many of them Albany State students who marched despite disciplinary action by college officials. On December 15, the Rev. Dr. Martin Luther King, Jr. was invited to Albany, and he reluctantly agreed to take command of the protest campaign.

Over the following nine months, Albany became the central battlefield of the Civil Rights Movement. King's presence attracted nationwide news coverage and support. The Albany Movement launched dozens of actions, including boycotts, court suits, and voter registration. Over twelve hundred demonstrators were arrested in direct actions. Despite the pressure, the movement was largely unsuccessful. Segregationist local officials refused to bargain in good faith or keep repeated pledges of a biracial commission to review Movement demands. City leaders closed Albany's libraries and parks rather than desegregate them and refused to desegregate city buses even when a boycott by black riders cut into profits. Meanwhile, Albany police chief Laurie Pritchett checked the effectiveness of protests by avoiding violent attacks on nonviolent protestors, by arresting demonstrators on charges other than violating segregation ordinances, and by requisitioning jails in surrounding areas to hold arrestees indefinitely without bail. King's presence alienated both SNCC activists, who resented his assumption of leadership, and NAACP leaders. In August 1962, after city officials, prodded by the Justice Department, admitted in court that city segregation ordinances were unconstitutional, King and his associates declared victory and retired from Albany. Despite its admission, however, the city did not abandon Jim Crow until March 1963. Even then, *de facto* enforcement of segregation and police harassment of activists sparked continued protests, which flared into racial rioting in June 1963. Meanwhile, nine Movement members were indicted by the Justice Department on charges of threatening a juror. The unjust treatment accorded the "Albany Nine" drew na-

tionwide coverage. Their convictions were overturned in 1965.

Since 1963, Albany has integrated its schools and public facilities. Many city employees, including the city manager and four city councilors, are African American. Its rich history is preserved at the Albany Civil Rights Museum housed at Old Mt. Zion Church. *See also* BEVEL, JAMES [1]; CHARLES, RAY [1]; DAWSON, WILLIAM LEVI [2]; FORMAN, JAMES [2]; SHERROD, CHARLES [5]; SOUTHERN CHRISTIAN LEADERSHIP COUNCIL (SCLC) [5]; SOUTHERN REGIONAL COUNCIL [5]; STUDENT NONVIOLENT COORDINATING COMMITTEE [5].

REFERENCES

Chalfen, Michael "'The Way Out May Lead In'": The Albany Movement Beyond Martin Luther King, Jr.," *Georgia Historical Quarterly* Vol. 79 (3), Fall 1995, 561-598.

Drago, Edmund L. *Black Politicians and Reconstruction in Georgia: A Splendid Failure Baton Rouge*. 1982.

Grant, Donald L. *The Way It Was in the South: The Black Experience in Georgia*. 1993.

GREG ROBINSON

Albert, Octavia (December 24, 1853–c. 1889),

writer. Octavia Victoria Rogers Albert, a writer, produced an early account of slavery in Louisiana. *The House of Bondage* brings together the narratives of seven former slaves collected by Rogers after she and her family moved to Louisiana. The accounts first appeared as a serial in the *Southwest Christian Advocate* some months after her early death and then, in response to the requests of readers, in book form.

Very little information about Albert's life is available. She was born a slave in Oglethorpe, Georgia. There, under the influence of Bishop Henry M. Turner, she became a dedicated member of the African Methodist Episcopal Church. After study at Atlanta University, she became a teacher in Montezuma, Georgia. In 1874 she married a fellow teacher, A. E. P. Albert. The only child, Laura T., was born soon after A. E. P. Albert was ordained in the Methodist Episcopal Church in 1877. His duties took the family to Louisiana, where he became editor of *The Southwest Christian Advocate*. Octavia Albert joined her husband's denomination in 1878 and was baptized by him in Houma, Louisiana.

The materials for *The House of Bondage* seem to be based on informal conversations but make no attempt to present dialect. Much of the narrative is based on the accounts of "Aunt" Charlotte Brooks, whose faith sustained her through many trying times. Another striking account tells of Jane Lee's reunion with her long-lost son, Dr. Coleman Lee. There is also some account of the progress of African Americans since Emancipation. The work remains an important and moving document.

See also LITERATURE [3]; SLAVE NARRATIVES [5].

REFERENCES

Albert, Octavia V. Rogers. *The House of Bondage*, or *Charlotte Brooks and Other Stories*. 1890.

Cliff-Pellow, Arlene. "Octavia Albert." In *Notable Black American Women*, edited by Jessie Carney Smith. 1992.

Fleming, John E. "Octavia Victoria Rogers Albert." In *Dictionary of American Negro Biography*, edited by Rayford W. Logan and Michael R. Winston, 1982.

Foster, Frances Smith. "Octavia Victoria Rogers Albert." In *American National Biography*, edited by John A. Garraty and Mark C. Carnes, 1999.

ROBERT L. JOHNS

Alexander, John Hanks

Alexander, John Hanks (January 6, 1864–March 26, 1894), soldier. John H. Alexander was born in Helena, Arkansas, to slave parents. He enrolled in Oberlin College in 1882. There the freshman student won praise from his teachers. In May 1883 he was appointed as an alternate to the U.S. Military Academy at West Point. Friends raised enough money to send him to West Point to take the entrance examination, nonetheless. He won his appointment when his rival failed the examination.

At West Point he did well in spite of ostracism by the white students, although his class rankings were pulled down by a high number of demerits. In 1887 he graduated 32nd in a class of 64 and was commissioned a second lieutenant.

On Alexander's arrival at his assigned post with the black-but white-officered-9th Cavalry Regiment at Fort Robinson, Nebraska, he found himself in limbo since the promotion of the man he was to replace had been delayed. When the mix-up was resolved, he began his career with the regiment. Alexander also served at Fort Washakie, Wyoming, and Fort Duchesne, Utah. He received good efficiency reports, and in October 1893 passed the examinations to qualify for promotion.

On January 6, 1894, Alexander was appointed professor of military science and tactics at Wilberforce College in Xenia, Ohio. His death occurred shortly after he began this tour of duty.

See also INDIAN WARS [3]; MILITARY [4]; UTAH [5].

REFERENCES

"John H. Alexander." *Cleveland Gazette*, 31 March 1894. [Portrait]

http://sites.netscape.net/jrmtnbs/hanks.htm (biography of Alexander).

Marzalek, John F., Jr. "John H[anks] Alexander." In *Dictionary of American Negro Biography*, edited by Rayford W. Logan and Michael R. Winston. 1982.

Schubert, Frank N. *On the Trail of the Buffalo Soldier: Biographies of African Americans in the U.S. Army, 1866–1917*. 1995.

ROBERT L. JOHNS

Ali, Muhammad (Update)

Ali, Muhammad (Update) (January 17, 1942–), professional boxer. During the late 1990s, Ali became the object of renewed public interest. In 1996, in tribute to his travels for peace, Ali was chosen to light the Olympic torch in Atlanta. The same year, Ali was featured in *When We Were Kings,* a documentary movie about his 1974 defeat of George Foreman in Kinshasa.

His personal life has been turbulent. He has been married four times and has had several children as well as numerous affairs, especially during his heyday as a fighter. His oldest daughter, Maryum, is a rap artist, following in her father's footsteps as a poet. Ali made a poetry recording for Columbia Records in 1963 called *The Greatest.* Maryum has recorded a popular rap dedicated to her father. Another daughter, Laila, is a prominent female boxer, likewise following in her father's footsteps.

It would be difficult to overestimate Ali's impact on boxing and on the United States as both a cultural and political figure. He became one of the most recognized men in the world, an enduring, if not always appropriate, stylistic influence on young boxers, and a man who showed the world that it was possible for a black to speak his mind publicly and live to tell the tale.

REFERENCES

http://espn.go.com/sportscentury/features/00014063.html (ESPN tribute to Ali's career)

Muhammad Ali. (AP/Wide World Photos)

Hauser, Thomas. *Muhammad Ali: His Life and Time.* 1991.

Remnick, David. *Still Champion.* 1998.

GERALD EARLY
UPDATED BY GREG ROBINSON

Anderson, Garland (c. 1886–May 31, 1939), playwright. Born in Wichita, Kansas, Anderson, who completed only the fourth grade, wrote *Appearances* (1925) one of the first plays by an African American to be produced on Broadway. A bellhop in his thirties in San Francisco, Anderson managed to complete in three weeks, while working at a busy hotel switchboard, what became a historically valuable dramatic work.

Appearances tells the story of a black bellhop who cleverly escapes persecution after being falsely accused of rape. To get his play produced, Anderson sought the aid of Al Jolsen, a popular white vaudevillian comedian of the 1920s who performed in blackface. Jolsen initially told Anderson that "the American public was not ready to accommodate black and white performers on the same stage." However, Jolsen later contributed money to Anderson's cause, financing Anderson's relocation from San Francisco to New York City.

For months, Anderson searched for sponsors who would produce his play. Facing mounting rejections, Anderson convinced the then-governor of New York, Al Smith, to commit to attending a staged reading of *Appearances*. The honored guest's name lured an audience of approximately seven hundred of the city's most culturally, politically and socially significant persons to hear the actor Richard B. Harrison read from Anderson's play. Despite the successful coordination of the assembly, Anderson received no serious proposals for the production of his script. Still determined, Anderson went to Washington, D.C., and managed to be granted a brief meeting with President Calvin Coolidge. Publicity from this meeting directly led to the production of *Appearances*, which opened at the Frolic Theater, on October 13, 1925.

See also DRAMA [2].

REFERENCES

Anderson, Garland. "How I Became a Playwright." In *Anthology of the American Negro in the Theater*, edited by Lindsay Patterson. 1968.

Ethnic NewsWatch Contempora Magazine 6 (1997): 16.

Hatch, James Vernon and Ted Shine. *Black Theater USA: plays by African-Americans 1847 to Today.* 1996.

Woll, Allen. *Dictionary of the Black Theater: Broadway, Off-Broadway, and selected Harlem Theater.* 1983.

F. ZEAL HARRIS

Armistead, James (1760–1832), spy. Armistead was a slave who spied on British forces led by General Charles Cornwallis, collecting information for the French Major General, Marquis De Lafayette, that became critical in the United States victory in the American War for Independence from Britain (1785–1783).

In Williamsburg, VA, Lafayette was under the orders of General George Washington, to impede the advance of the British Troops. Desperately needing to know about the enemy's movements, equipment, and personnel, Lafayette, in March 1881, hired James Armistead, a slave of William Armistead of Kent County, Virginia, to infiltrate enemy headquarters. Of the spies whom Lafayette sent into the British camp, only Armistead was successful at writing and delivering explicit intelligence reports, passing them through other spies until they reached Lafayette. The first report was received on July 13, 1781. Confidential correspondance between Armistead and Lafayette continued for several more months until Lafayette could minimize and trap the British forces. When Cornwallis surrendered to Lafayette, he was "shocked to find in [Lafayette's] headquarters, a Negro he had [also] hired to spy."

The Virginia Legislature, in appreciation of his heroic deeds, emancipated Armistead in 1786, stating that "Armistead kept open a channel of the most useful information to the army of the state." Three decades later, Armistead bought forty acres of land in Kent County, Virginia, while drawing a pension from the state. In 1824, when Lafayette returned to the United States, he personally greeted Armistead, his former compatriot, who by then had changed his name to James Lafayette.

See also AMERICAN REVOLUTION [1].

REFERENCES

Abdul-Jabbar, Kareem. *Black Profiles in Courage: A Legacy of African-American Achievement*. 1996.

Logan, W. Rayford and Michael R. Winston, eds. *Dictionary of American Negro Biography*. 1982.

Robinson, Wilhelmena S. *International Library of Afro-American Life and History*. 1978.

F. ZEAL HARRIS

Ashe, Arthur Robert, Jr. (Update) (July 10, 1943–February 6, 1993).

Following his death, Ashe was honored in his native Richmond by the raising in 1996 of a statue on Monument Avenue, the city's central thoroughfare. Meanwhile, the Flushing Meadows Tennis Stadium, home of the U.S. Open, was rededicated Arthur Ashe Stadium in 1997.

REFERENCES

Ashe, Arthur, and Arnold Rampersad. *Days of Grace: A Memoir*. 1993.

http://www.cmgww.com/articles/stadium.html (stadium naming in Ashe's honor).

Arthur Ashe, holding trophy. (AP/Wide World Photos)

http://www.cnn.com/US/9607/11/ashe/ (dedication of Ashe statue in Richmond).

GREG ROBINSON

Associated Negro Press. The Associated Negro Press (ANP) officially began operation in Chicago on March 21, 1919, with 80 charter members. Its founder, Claude Barnett (1889?–1967), then an advertising salesman for the *Chicago Defender*, traveled around the country both for the newspaper and to promote Kashmir Chemical Company, of which he was part owner. He found that the paper needed more news about black people; thus, he persuaded his partners in the company to invest in the new publishing venture. Barnett headed the ANP from its founding until around 1964. The service used as its symbol an owl holding a scroll inscribed with the slogan "Progress, Loyalty, Truth."

ANP, a mail service available to subscribers, soon attracted a number of organizations. It operated from small quarters until 1951 when it moved to 3531 South Parkway. Although Barnett devoted much of his time to administrative duties, recruiting reporters and columnists, and soliciting new subscribers, he also wrote many of the news releases, sometimes under the pen name Albert Anderson. In March 1931 Barnett incorporated ANP under the laws of Illinois, defining its purpose in broad terms as gathering and distributing news, features, articles, and books; serving as distributor of advertising matter; and providing data relating to blacks in their social, individual, and economic roles. At its peak, ANP's subscribers numbered over 200 newspapers, mostly from the black press. After World War II, Barnett began a series of 15 trips to Africa and was able to secure 100 new ANP subscribers.

The ANP provided a place for women in its fold, both in the Chicago home office and in some of its bureaus located in metropolitan areas. Alice Allison Dunnigan, reporter and columnist, was notable among this group, serving for 14 years, beginning in 1947 as chief of ANP's Washington bureau (Dunnigan replaced Alvin White, who had headed the bureau since 1939). ANP also used a number of writers who often worked without pay. They included Frederick D. Patterson of Tuskegee Institute and Charles S. Johnson of Fisk University. Notable black journalists and editors who were hired and who represented ANP in high places included William L. Pickens of the NAACP, Percival Prattis, poet and jazz expert Frank Marshall Davis, and journalist Ida Wells Barnett.

Throughout its existence, the ANP was able to expand but continued to struggle for funds to improve service, to pay staff, and to support larger quarters. In the early 1940s, the Negro Newspaper Publishers Association and the ANP discussed a possible merger or even embarking on cooperative efforts in advertising; however, negotiations failed. After then, ANP looked for more support from membership and elsewhere. By the late 1950s, fortunes of the national black weeklies declined and black national magazines such as *Ebony* brought new competition, as did the white daily newspapers. Black publishers no longer had a need for a national black news agency. Barnett retired from active control of ANP in 1964 and sold the agency to Alfred Duckett, a New York public relations company. ANP's headquarters moved to Manhattan, with Barnett as consultant. After Barnett died in 1967, Duckett's features continued for a while, but by the early 1970s ANP's logo had all but disappeared.

See also BARNETT, CLAUDE [1]; DUNNIGAN, ALICE ALLISON [2]; HANCOCK, GORDON BLAINE [3]; JOURNALISM [3].

REFERENCES

Hogan, Lawrence D. *A Black National News Service: The Associated Negro Press and Claude Barnett, 1919–1945*. 1984.

Smith, Jessie Carney, ed. *Notable Black American Men*. 1999.

Wolseley, Roland E. *The Black Press, U.S.A.* 1990.

JESSIE CARNEY SMITH

Association of Southern Women for the Prevention of Lynching.

The Association of Southern Women for the Prevention of Lynching (ASWPL) was a group of white women, organized through the Commission on Interracial Cooperation (CIC), which was committed to ending lynching through active intervention and public education. Jessie Daniel Ames, director of the CIC's women's committee, served as Executive Director of the Central Council of the ASWPL. In establishing the ASWPL, Ames shifted her focus from interracial cooperation toward a white women's campaign devoted entirely to ending lynching. Her intention in forming an organization comprised solely of white women was to attack the myth that lynching was necessary to protect the purity of white womanhood.

Beginning in 1930, the ASWPL built a network of women against lynching through existing women's groups, such as the YWCA, the PTA, the Federation of Women's clubs, and the women's associations of the Southern Baptist and Methodist Episcopal Churches. In all, 109 white women's organizations officially endorsed the ASWPL's platform while more than 43,000 individual members signed anti-lynching pledges. The ASWPL also attempted to prevent possible lynchings through local intervention and investigated a number of lynchings that had occurred. In addition, Ames and the ASWPL carried on a public campaign to force southern newspaper editors, sheriffs, and other officials to commit to the anti-lynching platform.

By 1938, the number of lynchings was decreasing, and the influence of the ASWPL began to wane. The organization was officially dissolved in 1942. Although its effect was limited by the exclusion of African American women and its objection to federal anti-lynching legislation, the ASWPL played a crucial role in reducing the occurrence of lynching in the South.

See also COMMISSION ON INTERRACIAL COOPERATION [S]; LYNCHING [3].

REFERENCES

Ames, Jessie Daniel. "Editorial Treatment of Lynchings." *Public Opinion Quarterly 2* (1938): 77- 84.

Barber, Henry E. "The Association of Southern Women for the Prevention of Lynching, 1930–1942." *Phylon* 34 (1973): 378-389.

Hall, Jacquelyn Dowd. *Revolt Against Chivalry: Jessie Daniel Ames and the Women's Campaign Against Lynching.* Revised Edition. 1993.

PATRICK DICKSON

Atlanta, Georgia (Update).

Ever since African-American assistant George Curtwright worked side by side with Coca-Cola founder Asa Candler to manufacture that soft drink in the early 1890s, Atlanta has tried to project the image of a city where racial conflict has been minimized in the service of the greater goal of prosperity. That image, though, seemed seriously distorted in the early 1990s. Atlanta's population fell as white residents endured long commutes and fled the city for an ever-expanding ring of suburbs. The election in 1993 of mayor Bill Campbell seemed to inaugurate a test of whether a new generation of African-American political leadership in this long majority-black city could combat the risk that Atlanta might become a southern counterpart to the nearly vacant inner cities of the northern Rust Belt. Campbell moved decisively to rebuild the city in his early years in office, winning passage of a 1994 infrastructure bond referendum and cutting the city's sky-high crime rate. In 1995, Campbell named Beverly Harvard as Atlanta's chief of police; she was the first female African-American police chief of a major U.S. city. The 1996 Summer Olympic Games presented the Campbell administration and Atlantans in general with enormous logistical challenges but also with great opportunities. An estimate on the eve of the Games suggested that African Americans would reap about 30 percent of the more than $5 billion that flowed into the local economy. Although Atlantans of all races were shocked by the downtown Olympic Centennial Park bombing that marred the Games, Atlanta won high marks for its ability to move huge crowds through the city's notorious traffic and summer heat. Another mark of prosperity for Atlanta's black population was cemented in place as a $20 million gift from comedian Bill Cosby began to flow into the coffers of Spelman College, one of Atlanta's two highly regarded historically black institutions of higher education. At the time, the gift was the largest single donation ever made to a U.S. college or university.

REFERENCES

Allen, Frederick. *Secret Formula*. 1994.

Chappell, Kevin. "The Three Mayors Who Made It Happen." *Ebony* (July, 1996), 66.

"Campbell, Bill." *Current Biography Yearbook*. 1996.

JAMES MANHEIM

B

Badger, Robert (c.1829–?) and Badger, Roderick (July 4, 1834–December 27, 1890), dentists. Half-brothers Robert and Roderick Badger were born in DeKalb County, Georgia, to the same white master father. Despite the climate of the time, the boys were educated and taught dentistry. It is known that Roderick received dental training from J.B. Badger, a DeKalb County dentist and probable relative; it is likely that Robert's instruction came from the same source.

Robert worked as a traveling dentist in rural Georgia, but made Atlanta his home. As early as the late 1860s, Robert owned property in the state capital and is thought to be among the first blacks to own property there. He married a woman named Caroline and they had nine children, six of whom reached maturity.

Roderick moved to Atlanta in 1856, becoming Atlanta's first black dentist while managing to create a practice that included members of some of the city's most prominent families as patients. He married Mary A. Murphey, the daughter of a wealthy Decatur, Georgia, lawyer, and they had eight children, seven of whom reached maturity.

During the Civil War, Roderick is said to have served as an aide to a Confederate Army colonel. Sometime during the war, both brothers worked as assistant professors at an African-American church that had become an academy for educating blacks. Both Badger brothers were well known and well respected throughout the black community. In 1879, Roderick was elected to the Clark College (University) Board of Trustees, possibly becoming the first black to serve in that capacity. Robert and Roderick Badger are buried in Atlanta's Oakland Cemetery. *See also* ATLANTA, GEORGIA [1]; DENTISTRY [2].

REFERENCES

Howard, W.P. "Destruction of Atlanta," http://www.cviog.uga.edu/Projects/gainfo/atldstr.htm.

Robinson, Henry S. "Robert and Roderick Badger, Pioneer Georgia Dentists." *The Negro History Bulletin* (January 1961): 77-80.

KEVIN C. KRETSCHMER

Baker, Gwendolyn Calvert (December 31, 1931–), administrator, educator, activist. Baker is recognized for leadership in academics and in organizations, particularly for her demonstrated interest in children, women, and people of different ethnic groups. Born in Ann Arbor, Michigan, to Burgess Edward and Viola Lee Calvert, she received B.S., M.A., and Ph.D degrees from the University of Michigan, finishing her dissertation in 1972. She taught in Ann Arbor's public schools from 1964 to 1969 and at the University of Michigan from 1969 to 1976, then becoming the university's director of affirmative action. Baker was the only woman and the second African American to sit on the president's executive cabinet. She helped reduce racism and gender bias on campus by encouraging the university to change its policies and to develop the first multicultural education programs in the nation.

Baker was chief of the Minorities and Women's Programs for the National Institute of Education in Washington, D.C., from 1978 to 1981, which enabled her to continue to concentrate on multicultural education. She held administrative posts at the Bank Street College of Education in New York City from 1981 to 1984. Upon leaving Bank Street College in 1984, she became national executive director of the YWCA of the United States. In 1986, she added membership on the New York City Board of Education, where she continued to work in the interests of different ethnic groups.

In September 1993, Baker left the YWCA and was named president of the United States Committee for UNICEF, where she continues to expand her goals in multicultural education.

See also EDUCATION [2].

REFERENCES

Baker, Gwendolyn C. Taped interview with Dona L. Irvin, September 8, 1993.

Mabunda, L. Mpho, ed. *Contemporary Black Biography, vol. 9.* 1995.

Smith, Jessie Carney, ed. *Notable Black American Women, Book II.* 1996.

VALENCIA PRICE

Barès, Basile Jean

Barès, Basile Jean (January 9, 1845–September 4, 1902), musician, composer. Basile Barès was born a slave and brought up in the business establishment of his owner, Adolphe Périer, who ran one of the leading music stores in New Orleans. Barès's origins were obscured in post-war New Orleans, and his being a slave was never mentioned.

Barès became an excellent pianist and published his first piano piece when he was sixteen and still a slave. Details of his formal music training are sparse. He studied piano with Eugène Prévost and harmony and composition with C. A. Predegam. Barès continued to work for the Périer firm after the war and made several trips to Paris for it. There he had the opportunity to perform and may also have taken further private lessons. In 1866 Barès published six more piano pieces and was active in concerts organized by the Creoles of Color.

Until about the end of the 1880s Barès was very popular with both black and white audiences, who made the sheet music of his dances for the piano into best-sellers. There are some nineteen known compositions from this period. Barès formed a wind and string ensemble that performed at white carnival balls. He continued to work in music stores-for Louis Grunewald in the 1870s and then for Junius Hart. Both firms published some of his music. After the appearance of two pieces in 1884, Barès published no more music. There is no clear explanation for this silence. Suggestions include failure of inspiration, growth of racism, and changes in musical taste. He died in New Orleans.

See also CONCERT MUSIC [2].

REFERENCES

Christian, Marcus B. "Basile Barès." In *Dictionary of American Negro Biography*, edited by Rayford W. Logan and Michael R. Winston. 1982.

Sullivan, Lester, and Ann Sears. "Basile Jean Barès." In *International Dictionary of Black Composers*, edited by Samuel A. Floyd Jr. 1999.

ROBERT L. JOHNS

Barrow, Willie B. Taplin

Barrow, Willie B. Taplin (December 7, 1927–), religious leader, organization executive. Born in Burton, Texas, Barrow grew up in a rural community where her father, Nelson Taplin, pastored a church. Influenced by his work, by age 17 Barrow had become a minister. She attended high school in Texas, studied at the Warner Pacific School of Theology in Portland, Oregon, and organized Portland's first black Church of God. Barrow studied later at the Moody Bible Institute in Chicago and received the doctorate of divinity degree from the University of Monrovia in Liberia.

Barrow has held numerous local and national offices in the Church of God. She did much of her ministry for social action in her work with Jesse Jackson, both in his campaign for the U.S. presidency and in their fight against hunger in Chicago and elsewhere. She was a state coordinator for the Illinois Coalition Against Hunger, leader of a Special Hunger Task Force, and fought hunger as Special Projects Director for the Southern Christian Leadership Conference's Operation Breadbasket.

In the mid-1970s, Barrow became the first woman to be named national vice-president of Operation PUSH (originally People United to Save Humanity, then renamed People United to Serve Humanity), founded on December 25, 1971. After Jackson left the presidency of PUSH to run for national office, Barrow first shared the organization's leadership with others, then assumed the position full-time. She retired in 1989 but continued service to the organization, as chairwoman of the board. She continues to preach in Chicago.

See also JACKSON, JESSE [3]; OPERATION PUSH [4].

REFERENCES

Ginsburg, Jane. "Willie Barrow." *Ms.* 2 (January 1974): 75.

Smith, Jessie Carney, ed. *Notable Black American Women*. 1992.

Who's Who Among African Americans, 12th ed. 1999.

JESSIE CARNEY SMITH

Barry, Marion Shepilov, Jr. (Update)

(March 6, 1936–), politician. Following a controversial comeback campaign that played heavily on themes of "redemption," Barry was reelected Mayor of Washington, D.C. in November of 1994, despite heavy opposition by whites and middle-class blacks. His last term was marked by scandals over political favoritism and the city's near-bankruptcy. Barry's authority was drastically reduced in 1995 when Congress appointed a fiscal control commission to supervise city administration. Barry retired following the end of his term in 1998.

Marion Barry testifying on Capitol Hill, 1989. (AP/Wide World Photos)

REFERENCE

"Barry, Marion." In *Encyclopedia of World Biography* 2nd Ed. 1998.

GREG ROBINSON

Baseball (Update).

Although baseball's popularity as a sport has waned among modern black sports fans, its role in the desegregation of America maintains its importance as an element of black culture. The early history of blacks and baseball mirrors the country at large, dating roughly from 1850 when white middle-class populations in eastern cities adopted the sport as a favorite pastime. The Civil War spread baseball throughout the United States, and black semipro and college teams transformed games into popular community events among blacks in the rural South.

Before the sport became commercialized, it was not uncommon for black and white players to participate together in sanctioned contests. After the onset of Jim Crow laws, however, athletic segregation became the rule. Though written policies never formally excluded blacks from professional baseball, so-called "gentlemen's agreements" precluded black players from competing. As black teams were excluded from organized baseball, they were forced to barnstorm the country seeking opponents. Harlem's Cuban X Giants, founded in 1885, was the first successful black professional team. For decades, countless players also played in Central America, where they were treated as equals on and off the diamond.

A form of parity began in 1920, when Andrew "Rube" Foster founded the Negro National League with teams in six Midwestern cities. It became the first of several successful black leagues that existed between 1920 and 1960. The caliber of play was high, but the schedules were grueling. To ensure solvency, teams routinely played exhibition games with minor league and local teams as they barnstormed through league cities. Stars of the period included James "Cool Papa" Bell, Oscar Charleston, Josh Gibson, LeRoy "Satchel" Paige, and "Smokey" Joe Williams.

The color barrier finally fell in 1947, when Jackie Robinson debuted as a Brooklyn Dodger. Robinson was handpicked by Dodgers general manager/part-owner Branch Rickey to be the first black player in Major League history, due to his background and even temperament. Robinson proved a good choice, as he battled constant harassment (even from teammates) to win the inaugural Rookie of the Year award. Other black players followed, but integration was a slow process, with final team to integrate doing so in 1959. The infusion of Negro Leagues talent proved a boon for teams both on and off the field, as gate receipts jumped due to black fans switching allegiance from Negro League to Major League teams with black players. That shift spelled doom for organized black baseball, as the last black league closed in 1960.

In the half-century since integration, hundreds of black players have donned major league uniforms, and in 1997, Major League Baseball unilaterally retired Jackie Robinson's number "42" in recognition of the fiftieth anniversary of his breaking the color barrier. Nevertheless, baseball has increasingly lost black fans to other sports, particularly football and basketball, which have higher percentages of black athletes. Over fifty years after integration, Major League Baseball still has yet to welcome its first black owner into the sport and currently has only three black managers.

REFERENCES

Holway, John. *Black Diamonds: Life in the Negro Leagues from the Men Who Lived It.* 1989.

MajorLeagueBaseball.com. A History & Records. http://majorleaguebaseball.com/u/baseball/mlbcom/history/mainpage.html.

Peterson, Robert. *Only the Ball Was White.* 1969.

KEVIN C. KRETSCHMER

Bellamy, Sherry F. (October 13, 1952–), lawyer, corporate executive. Sherry Bellamy is a trailblazer in the telecommunications industry and works in support of fair competition in the market. Born and raised in Harlem, Bellamy is the youngest of seven children. Her father was an officer in the Tuskegee Airmen, the African American unit that served the air corps in World War II. She attended elementary and high school in East Harlem. Ignoring the claim of her high school counselor that she could not attend Swarthmore College, Bellamy was admitted to Swarthmore with academic scholarships and graduated in 1974 with a B.A. degree in political science. She credits affirmative action for her scholarship awards. Bellamy continued her studies and in 1977 graduated from Yale Law School. She became a specialist in communications law.

Bellamy's first position as an attorney was with the New Haven Legal Assistance Association, where she established a specialized civil litigation section to represent the interests of children. Following that, she had stints with law firms of Chadbourne & Parke and with Jones, Day, Reavis & Pogue. In 1991 she joined Bell Atlantic Corporation in Washington, D.C., and a few months later was promoted to vice-president and general counsel. When the president and chief executive officer of Bell Atlantic in Maryland retired, Bellamy was named to succeed him and took office on March 1, 1997. She became the first African American woman to hold that position. She and her husband, architect George Bumbray, Jr., have four children.
See also BLACK BUSINESS COMMUNITY [1].

REFERENCES

"Bell Atlantic Names New Presidents in Maryland and Pennsylvania." News Release. http://www.ba.com/nr/97/dex/bellamy2.htm.

"Speaking of People." *Ebony 53* (February 1998): 13.

White, Kelly. "Sherry Bellamy, President and CEO, Bell Atlantic-Maryland." http://www.baltimoresun.com/news/special/blackhistory/profiles/bellamy.shtml.

FREDERICK D. SMITH, JR.

Belton, Sharon Sayles (May 13, 1951–), mayor. Born in St. Paul, Sharon Sales Belton is both the first woman and the first African American to be mayor of Minneapolis. With scholarship aid, she was a student at Macalester College from 1969 to 1973. While in college she was active in civil rights and traveled to Jackson, Mississippi, to assist in the voter registration projects for African Americans. Belton left college when she became pregnant during her senior year. Her daughter was mentally retarded, and Belton insisted on raising her at home rather than having her institutionalized. Subsequently, she married trial attorney and law firm partner, Steve Belton, and they have two sons. In 1986 she completed Harvard University's Program for Senior Executives in the John F. Kennedy School of Government. Her experiences included parole officer (1973–1983) and associate director of the Minneapolis program for victims of sexual assault (1983–1984). Belton was a member of the Minneapolis city council for the eighth ward (1984–1993) and was president of the council (1989–1993). While on the council, she authored a successful resolution mandating the divestment of city funds in South Africa.

In 1993 Belton defeated her white male opponent to become mayor of Minneapolis-a city with a pre-

Minneapolis Mayor Sharon Belton. (AP/Wide World Photos)

dominantly white population. As mayor, Belton continued a style that she followed while serving on the city council; that is, she created a consensus, thus enabling her to share her power. She also set new priorities for the city, increased resources for public safety, reduced personnel in government, streamlined services, and limited tax increases.
See also MINNESOTA [4].

REFERENCES

"New Wave of Black Mayors." *Ebony* 49 (February 1994): 92-96.

Phelps, Shirelle, ed. In *Contemporary Black Biography*, 16 (1998): 12-14.

Who's Who Among African Americans, 1988–99. 10th ed. 1997.

VALENCIA PRICE

Benjamin, R[obert] C[harles] O['Hara]

(March 31, 1855–1900), politician, teacher, lawyer, lecturer, and journalist. Benjamin was born on St. Kitts, British West Indies, sent to England at the age of eleven to study with a private tutor, and attended Trinity College, Oxford for three years. He sailed to various places and finally settled in New York (1869) where he remained until around 1877; around 1875, he became a naturalized U. S. citizen.

In America, Benjamin met such personalities as Highland Garnet and Joe Howard, Jr. (editor of the *New York Star*). He became city editor of *The Progressive American*; later, he was corresponding editor of *The Nashville Free Lance*. In Nashville, he wrote under the name "Cicero." He edited several other papers, including *The Negro American* (Birmingham, Alabama) and *The San Francisco Sentinel*. Benjamin's book publications include *The Adventures of Obediah Kuff, Poetic Gems* (1833), *Don't: A Book for Girls* (1891), and *Benjamin's Pocket History of the American Negro: A Story of Thirty-One Years from 1863–1894* (1894).

At some point, Benjamin moved South to study law, taught school to finance his studies, studied under Josiah Patterson (an eminent Memphis lawyer) and was admitted to the Tennessee Bar (January 1880); he subsequently practiced in twelve states. Based on the petitions from the Southern California Bar Association, President Harrison offered him a consulship in Haiti.

Benjamin was the presiding elder of the California conference of the AME Zion Church.
See also AMBASSADORS AND DIPLOMATS [1]; JOURNALISM [3].

REFERENCES

Logan, Rayford W., and Michael R. Winston, eds. *Dictionary of American Negro Biography*. 1982.

Penn, I. Garland. *The Afro-American Press and Its Editors*. 1891.

Simmons, William J. *Men of Mark*. 1887.

HELEN R. HOUSTON

Berea College.

Berea College, a historic experiment in Southern interracialism, was founded in Berea, Kentucky. In 1853, Cassius M. Clay, a local landowner and abolitionist leader, invited John Fee, a Kentucky preacher, to establish an anti-slavery church. In 1855, Fee opened a one-room school/church whose constitution promised a "cheap and thorough" education to people of all classes and colors. All students were to be assigned jobs in order to cover their tuition and dignify manual labor, which slavery had stigmatized. The project was immediately halted by pro-slavery forces, who drove Fee from the region. Fee then spent the years of the Civil War traveling and raising funds for the school.

In 1866, Fee returned to Kentucky, reopened his school, and obtained a charter from the state legislature establishing Berea College as an interracial institution. Three years later, Berea opened a college department, and offered its first bachelor's degrees in 1873. By 1886, ninety-six African Americans and ninety-one whites were enrolled in Berea's Primary, Intermediate, and Academic (college) departments.

Soon after, however, the college's interracial charter became the target of attacks by segregationists. In 1904, the Kentucky legislature enacted the Day Law, forbidding black and white students from studying together. Berea challenged the law, but the United States Supreme Court upheld it. Berea's trustees thereafter set up Lincoln Institute for its black students. In 1950, changes in the Day Law allowed to Kentucky integrate its colleges, and Berea again welcomed African Americans. Berea chose in 1968 to disband the Primary and Intermediate branches of the school, choosing to focus on undergraduate education. In 1998, *U.S. News & World Report* cited Berea as the number one regional college in the American South for its work program, full-tuition scholarships to all students (of whom eighty percent are from the Southern Appalachian region) and community service. *See also* AMERICAN MISSIONARY ASSOCIATION [1]; KENTUCKY [3]; WOODSON, CARTER GODWIN [5].

REFERENCES

"A Brief History of Berea College." www.berea.edu/Publications/History-of-Berea.html.

Apple, R.W., Jr. "A College of Few Parties and Fewer Complaints," *The New York Times*, September 10, 1998.

GREG ROBINSON

Berry, Edwin C. (December 10, 1854–March 12, 1931), hotel proprietor. Edwin C. Berry is noted as the proprietor of one of the finest small town hotels of his era. The hotel conformed to the customs of its era and catered exclusively to a white clientele. Berry was born to free parents in Oberlin, Ohio. The family moved to Athens, Ohio, in 1856. There he attended Albany Enterprise Academy, a black-founded and operated school. After working as a brick maker, he undertook a five-year apprenticeship as a cook in 1868. In 1878 Berry opened his own restaurant. He success was such that he had to move several times to new locations. In 1892 he built a twenty-room hotel next to his restaurant. The hotel's fine meals and service ensured its success. When Berry retired in

1921, additions had enlarged the hotel to fifty-five rooms.

Berry was involved in Republican politics, but his only attempt to secure a government appointment was frustrated in 1889. Berry was much involved in his work for the Baptist church. In Athens he played a major role in the building of Mount Zion Baptist Church, and he was a delegate to the Ohio Baptist Convention for almost fifty years. He also did much to advocate the cause of temperance. After 1900 Berry served several terms on the board of trustees of Wilberforce University. Berry was recognized as one of the leading African American businessmen in the latter part of the nineteenth century. He left an estate of $55,000 at his death.

See also ENTREPRENEURS [2]; REPUBLICAN PARTY [4].

REFERENCES

Levstik, Frank R. "Edwin C. Berry." In *Dictionary of American Negro Biography*, edited by Rayford W. Logan and Michael R. Winston. 1982.

Richings, G. F. *Evidences of Progress Among Colored People*. 1911.

ROBERT L. JOHNS

Berry, Mary Frances (February 17, 1938–), educator, historian, lawyer, government official, civil rights activist. Mary Frances Berry was born in Nashville to a family beset with hardships, so much so that

Mary Berry. (The Library of Congress)

she was placed in an orphanage for a while. Educated in segregated public schools, she demonstrated such drive and ability that one of her teachers became her mentor and helped bring direction to her life. Working her way through school, Berry received her B.A. from Howard University in 1961 and her M.A. in 1962. She studied at the University of Michigan, earning a Ph.D. in 1966 and the J.D. from Michigan's law school in 1970.

Since 1966, Berry has held numerous academic positions. She has taught at Central Michigan University, Eastern Michigan University, and the University of Maryland (where she directed the Afro-American Studies program from 1974–76). Berry was both chancellor and a professor at the University of Colorado, Boulder, from 1976–80. She then taught at Howard University, and since 1987, she has been the Geraldine R. Segal Professor of American Social Thought at the University of Pennsylvania.

Away from academia, Berry served as assistant secretary of education in the U.S. Department of Health, Education, and Welfare (1977–1980) and was the first black woman to serve as chief educational officer of the United States. Berry was appointed to the U.S. Commission on Civil Rights in 1980, gaining prominence for her outspokenness. She has published widely, often mixing race and gender in her articles and books, such as *The Politics of Parenthood* (1993) and *The Pig Farmer's Daughter and Other Tales of American Justice* (1999).

See also EDUCATION [2]; UNITED STATES COMMISSION ON CIVIL RIGHTS [5].

REFERENCES

Bigelow, Barbara Carlisle, ed. *Contemporary Black Biography*, vol. 7. 1994.

Hine, Darlene Clark, ed. *Black Women in America*, vol. 1. 1993.

Smith, Jessie Carney, ed. *Notable Black American Women*. 1992.

JESSIE CARNEY SMITH

BET. *See* Black Entertainment Television.

Bethune-Cookman College. Bethune-Cookman College is a historically black college and a pioneer in the education of African American women. The legendary African American educator Mary McLeod Bethune founded the school in Daytona Beach, Florida. In 1904, Bethune opened the Daytona Literary and Industrial Training School for Negro Girls in a rented house with 5 students and $1.50 in capital. Originally a modified elementary school, by 1915 the school began offering high school classes and shortly afterwards began a teacher's education program. Although Bethune raised large sums of money for the school from wealthy white donors—by 1923, its physical plant was valued at $250,000—she sought to assure long-term financial support. Thus, in 1923, Bethune's school merged with Cookman Institute, a coeducational African American school in Jacksonville, Florida whose most noted alumnus was labor leader A. Philip Randolph, and affiliated the new institution with the United Methodist Church. In 1931, the school, renamed Bethune-Cookman College, began offering a junior college curriculum. Even during the 1930s, when Bethune was based in Washington as the head of the National Council of Negro Women and a leading figure in President Franklin Roosevelt's "Black Cabinet," she remained president of Bethune-Cookman, and tirelessly solicited funds for the school. In 1941, the year before Bethune retired from Bethune-Cookman, the college established its first 4-year liberal arts degree program, in teacher education.

Bethune-Cookman continued to expand in the decades after World War II. By the year 2000, the college was home to 2557 students and 120 full-time faculty, and offered Bachelor's degrees in 39 fields.

REFERENCES

Sheila Y. Flemming, *Bethune-Cookman College, 1904–1994: The Answered Prayer to a Dream*, 1995.

GREG ROBINSON

Binga, Jesse (April 10, 1865–June 13, 1950), banker, realtor, entrepreneur, philanthropist. Binga was born in Detroit to free parents who relocated there in the 1840s. After three years in high school, Binga dropped out to work in an attorney's office and to study law. He left Detroit in 1855, roaming through Missouri, Minnesota, and Montana, using his barber skills to support himself. He opened barbershops in Tacoma and Seattle, relocated to Oakland, California, and finally settled in Chicago in the mid-1890s.

Binga opened a real estate business in Chicago in 1898, soon becoming one of Chicago's wealthiest African Americans. As the black community grew, particularly during the Great Migration of 1917–1921, so Binga's business grew. He owned a group of storefront apartments known as the Binga Block, considered the city's longest tenement row. Binga diversified by opening the Binga Bank in 1908, the first Northern bank owned and run by African Americans. It, too, grew rapidly during the Great Migration, and in 1919 Binga obtained a charter converting it into a state bank. He moved the bank into larger quarters in 1924 and also opened the Binga Safe Deposit Company and organized an insurance firm.

Binga's enterprises continued growing, building in 1929 an office building called the Binga Arcade. However, the Great Depression took its toll on Binga the next year, when his bank collapsed. He was arrested in 1931 for banking irregularities, of which he was acquitted. He was convicted of embezzlement in a second trial held in 1933. After he was freed in 1938, Binga worked as a church handyman for the rest of his life.

See also BANKING [1]; ENTREPRENEURS [2].

REFERENCES

Ingham, John, and Lynne B. Feldman. *African-American Business Leaders*. 1994.

Osthaus, Carl R. "The Rise and Fall of Jesse Binga, Black Financier." *Journal of Negro History* 58 (January 1973): 39-60.

Smith, Jessie Carney, ed. *Notable Black American Men*. 1999.

JESSIE CARNEY SMITH

Binga State Bank.

Binga State Bank was the first bank owned, managed, and controlled by blacks in the North, and for ten years it was one of the most celebrated black businesses in the country. Established in 1908, its founder—realtor and entrepreneur Jesse Binga (1865–1950)—saw the bank as a necessary financial service for Chicago's black South Side. At first a private enterprise, the small bank grew impressively between 1917 and 1921, during the Great Migration. Binga then took out a charter for the business to become the Binga State Bank and hired several talented blacks to run it. Using funds from his other businesses, Binga became the bank's largest shareholder. Binga worked so that prominent African Americans were associated with the business; for example, *Chicago Defender* editor Robert S. Abbott was a stockholder and on the board of directors.

African Americans embraced the bank, as an alternative to other banks with discriminatory practices and to loan sharks. As the bank grew, it needed more space, and in 1924 Binga built larger, more impressive quarters for it. The new structure became the first bank building constructed by an African American.

The economic collapse of 1929 took its toll on the banking industry, forcing Binga's bank to close in 1930. Binga lost his fortune of $400,000, and thousands of black Chicagoans lost their savings as well. The bank also held an excessive number of first mortgage real estate loans. Many of Binga's financial decisions were declared illegal, leading to his imprisonment. The bank's failure ended an era in the history of black enterprise for that time.

See also BANKING [1]; ENTREPRENEURS [2].

REFERENCES

Drake, St. Clair, and Horace R. Cayton. *Black Metropolis*. 1945.

Osthaus, Carl R. "The Rise and Fall of Jesse Binga, Black Financier." *Journal of Negro History* 58 (January 1973): 39-60.

Spear, Allan H. *Black Chicago: The Making of a Negro Ghetto 1890–1920*. 1967.

JESSIE CARNEY SMITH

Birmingham, Alabama (Update).

Even before the Ku Klux Klan killed four young girls with a bomb placed inside the city's Sixteenth Street Baptist Church in 1963, Birmingham had a long history as one of the most racially divided cities in the U.S. By the 1990s, however, Birmingham had much to show for the efforts of the African-American officials who had come to dominate city government. By the time he retired in 1999, five-term mayor Richard Arrington had increased the city payroll's black representation to approximately fifty percent, and a black presence was especially noticeable on the police force that had terrorized civil-rights demonstrators in the 1960s. Popular with business leaders, Arrington oversaw an impressive transformation of Birmingham's economy, and flourishing health-care and banking industries replaced the city's steel mills as employers of black residents. The city did not escape the changes in family structure that affected African Americans nationwide; by one 1995 estimate, more than fifty percent of the families in Birmingham's central city were headed by single women. Birmingham's significance in African-American history resulted in its emergence as a major travel destination in the 1990s, as tourists and historians flocked to the city in hopes of understanding its vibrant and violent past. The city steered visitors toward a new Birmingham Civil Rights District, which includes the Sixteenth Street Baptist Church, Kelly Ingram Park (the scene of clashes between demonstrators and police in the 1960s), the Fourth Avenue Business District (a historic black commercial hub), and a new Alabama Jazz Hall of Fame that commemorated the work of Birmingham musician Erskine Hawkins, among others. Arrington's hand-picked successor, William Bell, was defeated by maverick candidate Bernard Kincaid in the 1999 mayoral election. The following year, Birmingham took a step toward healing the wounds inflicted by the most painful episode in its history as two men with ties to the Klan were charged and indicted in connection with the 1963 church bombing.

REFERENCES

Edmondsen, Brad. "Birmingham without Fathers." *American Demographics* (July, 1995): 13.

"Major Museums Attract Visitors." *Travel Weekly* (October 11, 1993): S10.

Manheim, James M. "Richard Arrington." In *Contemporary Black Biography*, volume 24. 1999.

Tucker, Cynthia. "In Birmingham, Justice Is Late for Four Little Girls." *Atlanta Journal/Atlanta Constitution* (May 21, 2000): B5.

JAMES MANHEIM

Bivins, Horace C. (May 8, 1862–1937), soldier.

Horace C. Bivins was an enlisted man who served with distinction in the Spanish American War, where he won a commendation for conspicuous bravery. He was one of the best marksmen in the army, winning first place in the all-army carbine contest in 1894. He turned down an offer in 1897 to perform with Buffalo Bill Cody's Wild West Show in favor of remaining in the army.

Bivins was born at Pungoteague in Accomack County, Virginia. He joined the army in 1887, serving with the tenth cavalry. Near the end of the Apache wars in Arizona, during the storming of San Juan Hill on July 1, 1898, Bivins was assigned to a three-man Hotchkiss mountain gun crew. The other two men received wounds early on in the day, but Bivins operated the gun alone in the face of heavy fire and a slight head wound.

In 1900 Bivins was promoted to squadron sergeant major, and the following year he led patrols in pursuit of insurgents in the Philippines. He left the tenth cavalry in December 1901 to take up an appointment as ordinance sergeant, serving at numerous posts before his retirement to live in Billings, Montana. During World War I the government declined his offer to raise a regiment of volunteers. However, Bivins did receive a commission as an officer, and in 1918 he served for six months at Fort Dix, New Jersey. He then returned to Montana. Bivins wrote a thirty-page account of his experiences in Cuba during the Spanish American War for Hershel Cashin's *Under Fire with the Tenth Cavalry* (1899).

See also MILITARY [4]; SPANISH-AMERICAN WAR [5]; WEST, BLACKS IN THE [5].

REFERENCES

Cashin, Hershel. *Under Fire with the Tenth Cavalry*. 1899.

Schubert, Frank N. "Horace C. Bivins." In *Dictionary of American Negro Biography*. eds. Rayford W. Logan and Michael R. Winston. 1982.

ROBERT L. JOHNS

Black Coaches Association. In 1987 a group of African-American assistant basketball coaches gathered in Las Vegas to wrestle with the lack of head coaching opportunities available to minorities. Elsewhere, similar discussions among black assistant football coaches confronted issues surrounding minority education and employment. Eventually, both groups merged to form the Black Coaches Association (BCA), a non-profit organization whose primary purpose was to foster the growth and development of minorities at national and international levels of sports. Membership was extended to all coaches.

The association's mission was straightforward and timely. While addressing issues pertaining to participation and employment of minorities in sports, the association vowed to assist minorities aspiring to inaugurate careers as coaches and administrators at the high school, collegiate, and professional levels. According to the *BCA Journal*, the association embraced commitments 1) to strengthen diversity within the NCAA membership, 2) to create professional development workshops and seminars for BCA members, 3) to vitalize support for the enhancement of opportunities for minorities in athletics from other sports and non-sports organizations, 4) to assist members through career development strategies, and 5) to keep the membership and the general public informed of relevant BCA activities.

The BCA reached its apogee during the 1993–1994 season, when it called for coaches and players to boycott games in protest of an NCAA vote against restoring one of the two men's basketball scholarships eliminated in 1991, a measure that reduced each school's scholarship limit from 15 to 13. The BCA also called for the NCAA to add minorities to its staff and to reconsider the academic restrictions of Propositions 42 and 48, which the association saw as discriminatory toward black athletes. The Congressional Black Caucus stepped in to help mediate, and the boycott was averted.

Recently, however, the BCA has faced turbulent times. In addition to dwindling membership and the disassociation of a number of prominent black coaches, allegations of financial improprieties and inattentive mismanagement led to the resignation of Rudy Washington, the association's founder and chief executive. A change of leadership was forthcoming, with Philadelphia lawyer Tim Stoner being elected executive director of the association and Marianna Freeman, coach of the women's basketball team at Syracuse University, chosen as its president. Both Stoner and Freeman vowed to be more open about the BCA's board selection policies and the use of funds by the leadership, essential issues that have plagued the association for some time.

See also BASKETBALL [1]; THOMPSON, JOHN ROBERT, JR. [5].

REFERENCES

Crothers, Tim. "Inside College Basketball" at: http://sportsillustrated.cnn.com/features/1999/weekly/990111/cb0111.

Freeman, Marianna. "The History of the Black Coaches Association" at: http://www.ironlight.net/bca/journal1.html.

Katz, Andy. "Legal Turmoil Mars BCA Future" at: http://archive.espn.go.com/ncb/features/01289789.html.

RANDY F. WEINSTEIN

Black Entertainment Television (BET).

Black Entertainment Television (BET), a Washington, D.C.-based, twenty-four hour television station and entertainment company, targets African Americans by offering original programming and diverse Black musical videos programming. BET was founded in 1979 by Robert Johnson and aired its first movie, *A Visit to the Chief's Son*, on January 25, 1980. The station is a subsidiary and the primary business of BET Holdings, Inc. and boasts a subscriber membership of over 45,000,000 worldwide.

A graduate of Princeton University and past vice-president of government relations for the National Cable and Television Association (NCTA) from 1976–1979, Johnson secured a consulting contract with the NCTA and then used the contract to secure a loan from the National Bank of Washington. He also secured a $320,000 loan from John C. Malone, head of the Tele-Communications Inc (TCI). After Malone and TCI also paid him $180,000 for a twenty-percent share in the network, Johnson created BET. In 1984, Johnson also formed District Cablevision Inc. to serve Washington D.C. residents. TCI owned seventy-five percent of the new company, and Johnson encountered several lawsuits by competitors. Yet, by 1989 Johnson was able to repay his investors. On October 30, 1991, BET became the first black-controlled company to be listed on the New York Stock Exchange (NYSE). In the first day of its listing, the stock value grew from $9 million to $475 million dollars. In 1995, the company relocated to a new $15 million facility. In 1996, BET added a BET/ Starz! Channel 3, a premium movie channel. In the same year, Johnson pledged $100,000 to Howard University's School of Communication and was awarded the university's Messenger Award for Excellence in Communication.

BET Holdings Inc. publishes *Emerge*, *Heart and Soul*, and *BET Weekend* and owns three other cable channels. The company formed a radio network in 1994 to provide news to urban market radio stations. In 1996, the company formed a partnership with Microsoft to form MSBET, an online service with entertainment news and information.

See also TELEVISION [5]; WASHINGTON, D.C. [5].

REFERENCES

"Johnson, Robert L." *African American.* Ed. Kenneth Estell. 1994.

"Johnson, Robert L." *Who's Who in Black America.* Ed. Shirelle Phelps. 1997.

Smith, Jessie Carney. "Robert L. Johnson." *Black Heroes of the 20th Century* . Ed. Jessie Carney Smith. 1998.

RACHEL ZELLARS

Blackface.
Blackface refers to the make-up worn by actors of the 19th and early 20th century, who smeared burnt cork mixed with greasepaint on their

faces, and in a larger context to Negro Minstrelsy, the first indigenously American form of theatrical entertainment, used to describe the formal act of burlesquing African Americans while wearing blackface makeup.

Blackface began in New York City in the 1820s on the street, in saloons, circuses, and vaudevilles or as sideshows and aftershows to traditional European theater. The actors offered an urban, working class audience a farcical variety show in which they "blacked up" their faces, painted on thick, wide, white or red clown-like lips, and donned wooly wigs, colorful tattered clothing, and oversized shoes to sing, tell jokes, and perform skits using corrupted black vernacular. Performances emphasized parody of the dance and gestures of African Americans. The success of the minstrel show was so great that worldwide performances were demanded.

Between 1850 and 1870, the height in popularity of minstrelsy, the commercial theater began to open to black actors. Excluded from performing "legitimate" theater, talented African-American actors such as Sam Lucas, Dan Lewis, and James A. Bland were left the nominal option of performing in blackface. By 1870, the majority of blackface performers were African American, although producers remained white. Innovative minstrel performer-composers at the turn of the century, such as Bert Williams and George Walker, struggled to dignify the African-American image while cultivating black theater-going audiences through plays such as *The Policy Players* (1899) and *In Dahomey* (1902). In the early 20th century, the rise of groups like the NAACP, and the development of the Harlem Renaissance and the Little Theater Movement, aiming at producing art that uplifted and celebrated Negroes, made blackface start to vanish. By the 1930s, performance in blackface was an outdated mode of entertainment.

Still, by the 1940s, blackface troupes (such as the Christy Minstrels) consisting of five to eight white male actors offered full-scale productions, with classic stock characters and standard ensemble tunes in a fixed two-act format. The show itself was built around traditional stereotypes of blacks as wanting to be white, or as tricksters or foolish/contented slaves.

Despite having largely passed into history, blackface remains a controversial issue, as blackface memorabilia has become hotly pursued by both black and white collectors. Award winning photographer David Levinthal presented a book of photos using his collection of blackface toys, titled *Blackface* (1999). In 1993, white actor Ted Danson caused controversy by appearing in blackface at a Friar's Club roast. In 1999, Missouri Republicans made national news by distributing a photograph of Democratic Governor Mel Carnahan appearing in blackface during a 1960 Kiwanis charity show.

African-American scholars continue to debate blackface, its meanings, and its renewed popularity. If blackface is a means by which white racism can deny the essential humanity of blacks, then some see the recent appropriation by some blacks of blackface and its attendant culture as a way of taking away its power to injure. Regardless of how one views it, blackface will continue to elicit strong reactions as it remains a symbol not only of a dark element of American popular culture, but of American history and racial conflict.

See also BUBBLES, JOHN [1]; COMEDIANS [2]; HOGAN, ERNEST [3]; MINSTRELS/MINSTRELSY [4].

REFERENCES

Bean, Annemarie, James V. Hatch, and Brooks McNamara, editors. *Inside the Minstrel Mask: Readings in Nineteeth Century Blackface Minstrelsy*. 1996.

Bogle, Donald. *Toms, Coons, Mulattoes, Mammies & Bucks*. 1992.

Brockett, Oscar G. *History of the Theater*, seventh edition. 1995.

Lhamon, W.T. *Raising Cain: Blackface Performance from Jim Crow to Hip Hop*. 1998.

Lott, Eric. *Love and Theft: Blackface Minstrelsy and the American Working Class*. 1993.

Toll, Robert. *Blacking Up: The Minstrel Show in Nineteenth Century America*. 1974.

F. ZEAL HARRIS

Black Magicians.

Throughout American history, black magicians have achieved great skill both in the magician's tricks of the trade and in the psychology of magic. Slavery and, later, racial segregation and discrimination prevented many black magicians from plying their trade professionally. But a unique few persevered and overcame the barriers placed before them. In fact, the first recorded magician born in the United States was a black man: Richard Potter (1783–1835). Not only was Richard Potter America's "First Negro Magician," he may have been the first American-born magician.

The name of only one other black born in slavery has come down in the annals of magic in the United

States: Henry "Box" Brown (1816–after 1878), who received his nickname after he escaped from the South by having himself shipped North in a wooden packing crate. In the course of making public appearances on the abolitionist circuit in England, Brown picked up knowledge of various escape tricks from magicians he met and created his own program of "Mesmeric Entertainments." Back in the United States, he continued his magician's career, and in later years performed with his wife and daughter. His last public performance took place in 1878 when he was sixty-two years old.

After the Civil War and the abolition of slavery, it was easier for black entertainers to participate in minstrelsy. Magic and ventriloquism had long been part of the olio portion of the minstrel show, and several blacks made names for themselves as assistants to white magicians. Among them was M.H. Everett, who learned magic from the white musician, Hermann the Great. After his mentor's death, Everett went out on his own as Boomsky the Magician. Alonzo Moore was another successful black minstrel magician. One of Moore's disciples, Benjamin Rucker, also known as Black Herman, became wealthy and famous by focusing on numerology and lucky numbers. His most famous trick was to be buried alive, which he would stage elaborately in cities where he performed. In fact, when he collapsed on stage and died in 1934, many believed it was just another one of his tricks.

William Carl, also known as Black Carl, was among the black entertainers who spearheaded the transition from minstrelsy to vaudeville. But the anti-black sentiment that swept the country in the early years of the twentieth century infected vaudeville, and most black magicians were forced to "go underground" and pose as foreigners. Any number of black magicians—as well as some whites—posed as "Hindu Fakirs." Arthur Dowling, who billed himself as Prince Jovedah de Rajah, the East Indian Psychic, was among the most successful. Another was Marcellus R. Clark, who used the stage name Rhadolph Marcelliee. He was reportedly the first black to perform at an International Brotherhood of Magicians convention when he did his act for that group in Philadelphia in 1952.

Two other distinctly American entertainment arenas, the Lyceum and Chautauqua circuits, arose in the middle nineteenth century. The Lyceum originated as a study group, Chautauqua as a religious movement. Both offered cultural enrichment, which included music and magic acts by late in the century. Blacks formed their own such circuits, where Professor J.

Hartford Armstrong (1886?–1939) had great success. He was one of the few black magicians to perform outside of a minstrel show without pretending to be another nationality. After her father's death, Ellen Armstrong carried on the show, probably the only female magician touring the United States at that time.

Fetaque Sanders' (1915–1992) career bridged the eras of discrimination and equal rights for blacks. While most of his work was before black audiences, he occasionally performed with white shows. Among his claims to fame was being the youngest performer at the Chicago World's Fair of 1933. Frank Brents (b. 1926) was the first African-American magician to appear on television, performing on the "Captain Kangaroo Show, ""Bozo the Clown, "and "The Jerry Lewis Show."

Since the 1970s, many black magicians have been able to make a living at their art. Goldfinger and Dove, a popular husband-and-wife team whose stage act emphasizes glamour and special effects; Lamont Haskins of the Big Apple Circus, whose specialty is close-up magic; and Charles Greene, who has adapted his skills to the uniquely twentieth-century phenomenon, the business trade show. He carries on the tradition of a long line of African-American magicians—many of whom are not mentioned in these pages—who persisted in fighting the barriers that confronted them and passing on their lore.

See also BROWN, HENRY BOX [1].

REFERENCES

Alligood, Leon. "Past Has Been Magic for The Great Fetaque," *The Nashville Banner*, September 17, 1991, pp. B-1+.

Christopher, Milbourne. "Potter the Magician." *MUM*, Vol. 43, No. 5, October 1953, pp. 176-178.

Fletcher, Tom. *100 Years of the Negro in Show Business*. 1954.

McCain, Diana Ross "A Nineteenth-Century Magician." *Early American Life*, Vol. 26, December 1995, p. 42.

Magus, Jim. *Magical Heroes: The Lives and Legends of Great African American Magicians*. 1995.

Moulton, H.J. *Houdini's History of Magic in Boston*, 1792–1915. 1983.

Sampson, Henry T. *Blacks in Blackface: A Source Book on Early Black Musical Shows*. 1980.

———. *The Ghost Walks: A Chronological History of Blacks in Show Business*, 1865–1910. 1983.

Toll, Robert C. "Behind the Blackface: Minstrel Men and Minstrel Myths." *American Heritage*, Vol. 29 (April 1978), pp. 93-105.

JAMES HASKINS
KATHLEEN BENSON

Black Middle Class. Classical notions of class are related to economic stratification. Because racism has historically relegated much of the African American population to poverty, blacks employed other, non-economic bases for stratification. Thus, the black middle class is a segment of the African American community distinguished by economic as well as social characteristics. Economic dimensions include income, occupation, and wealth, while social characteristics may include education, skin tone, respectability, church affiliation, or social club membership. However, substantial upward mobility in the second half of the twentieth century increased the importance of economic characteristics for defining the black middle class.

In the antebellum period there was no group that could be called the black middle class. Yet slavery's racial and skin color hierarchy constituted an early foundation and became part of blacks' evaluation of each other. Slaves with lighter skin had particular advantages because of their position in the slave economy as house or skilled servants. Their sustained and close contact with the slave owning white upper class allowed for direct observation and knowledge of dominant lifestyles. After Emancipation and during Reconstruction, these mulatto house and skilled slaves, along with free Negroes who were also disproportionately of mixed-race, constituted the first black middle class. Aside from a small black intelligentsia, of which figures like W. E. B. DuBois would have been a part, the first black middle class earned its living primarily through service to whites as caterers, barbers, tailors, and other skilled workers.

At the end of the nineteenth century, southern Jim Crow laws and the Great Migration of southern blacks to northern cities altered inter-racial relations and, hence, the configuration of the black middle class. Growing residential segregation in the north and south created all-black ghettos. The second black middle class formed to serve these racially separate communities. Entrepreneurs and professionals—doctors, dentists, teachers, social workers, etc.—formed the core of this new black middle class, indicating the growing importance of economic factors like occupa-

tion. Skin color and connections to whites receded as markers of black middle class status but did not disappear. Also, blacks in lower status occupations could distinguish themselves as middle class by joining the right church (often Episcopal or a more reserved Baptist congregation), gaining membership in the right social clubs (with names like "Amethyst Girls" or "Kool Kustomers" in Chicago), or working for the right causes (often framed in general terms like "race pride" or "social betterment").

National economic prosperity after World War II followed by progressive racial attitudes and policies of the civil rights era marked another change in the size and composition of the black middle class. Predominantly white educational institutions admitted black students, firms recruited at black colleges, affirmative action policies held employers accountable, and unions yielded to the pressure of their formerly excluded black coworkers. Until 1960, less than ten percent of blacks were in white-collar occupations. At the end of the 1990s, half of all blacks worked as professionals, managers, administrators, technicians, salespeople, or clerics. Residential segregation began a slow decline in the 1970s, and blacks began to move to the suburbs. The late twentieth century black middle class is a much more diverse population of secretaries and executives, suburbanites and inner city residents, Catholics and Apostolics.

Throughout these historical transformations debates have focused on the responsibilities of the black middle class to "the race." DuBois argued in the early 1900s that the "talented tenth"—i.e., blacks who had received a liberal education and were politically astute—would lead the black masses out of poverty and despair. He later became disenchanted with their apparent apathy. Sociologist E. Franklin Frazier incited debate in the 1950s with his scathing account of the social life and psychology of the black middle class, stressing their foolish imitation of the white upper class and the rejection of and disdain for black folk culture. Such portrayals continue into contemporary discussions but have been countered by evidence of enduring racial consciousness among the black middle class and solidarity with the black poor, especially in the realms of culture and politics.

The large black middle class cohort formed after World War II is now begetting a second and third generation. These new members were born after southern Jim Crow and with the benefits of affirmative action, however imperiled. The reproduction, growth, and entrenchment of the black middle class, and the concurrent decline in black poverty, signal a significant shift in the composition of the African American community, that will likely have consequences for many other arenas of black American life. *See also* CLASS AND SOCIETY [2]; DUBOIS, W.E.B. [2]; ECONOMICS [2]; FRAZIER, EDWARD FRANKLIN [3]; MIGRATION/POPULATION [4]; RACE, CASTE, AND CLASS [4].

REFERENCES

Billingsley, Andrew. *Climbing Jacob's Ladder: The Enduring Legacy of African American Families*. 1992.

Dawson, Michael C. *Behind the Mule: Race and Class in African-American Politics*. 1994.

Drake, St. Clair, and Horace Cayton. *Black Metropolis: A Study of Negro Life in a Northern City*. 1945.

Du Bois, W. E. B. *The Philadelphia Negro: A Social Study*. Rev. ed. 1996.

Frazier, E. Franklin. *The Negro Family in the United States*. 1939.

Frazier, E. Franklin. *The Black Bourgeoisie*. 1957.

Landry, Bart. *The New Black Middle Class*. 1987.

Pattillo-McCoy, Mary. *Black Picket Fences: Privilege and Peril Among the Black Middle Class*. 1999.

MARY PATTILLO-MCCOY

Black Nationalism.

Black nationalism can be viewed as the reaction of formerly disparate groups of African descent to a sense of mutual oppression and humiliation. Prior to the African slave trade African people like their European counterparts were organized around local cultural loyalties and traditions. In such societies, tradition as embodied in the wisdom of living elders or revered ancestors, is sacred. In areas where enslaved Africans were a minority of the population within the slave states of the United States, expressions of African culture were stringently prohibited. Some scholars argue that such practices destroyed the traditions of those whom they enslaved within a generation or two. Other scholars argue that the traditions were driven underground giving rise to a kind of surreptitious pan Africanization of the culture of the ordinary field hands, which persisted despite the formal adoption of Christianity by the overwhelming majority of Africans within the United States. Both narratives recognize that this experience endowed them with a sense of common experience and identity, the root of nationalist consciousness.

The identity developed in the seventeenth century between Africans and slavery was the edifice upon which a racial division of labor was constructed. This near absolute correlation between Blackness and this most sordid social rank played havoc with the social psychology of whites who dreaded themselves falling into this unenviable social status. For this reason the lines were starkly drawn and reinforced with all of the power that racial myths could muster. Following slavery many whites fought to maintain the prerogatives of racial privilege with respect to the Black population. These practices led to the restriction of Black people from certain desirable jobs, neighborhoods, social activities, etc. The dehumanization of Blacks became the preoccupation of scientists and scholars following the precepts of social Darwinism to a coherent explanation and justification of the relegation of Black people to a subordinate status.

Black nationalism as an ideology has long been an element in the structuring of political action and cultural standpoint. It was both an affirmation of the humanity, strength, and dignity of Black people and an opposition to the degrading myths fashioned by whites It is generally believed to have emerged during the eighteenth century as a challenge to racist ideology which sought to justify the enslavement of people of African descent within the labor force of a presumably democratic country. Until the establishment of the American Colonization Society in 1816, free blacks in the North were called Africans and regarded themselves as Africans (despite the fact that educated blacks were quite distinct culturally from Africans on the continent). Uneducated blacks, on the other hand, because of their isolation from whites, their contacts with slaves from the West Indies, and new salt water slaves (directly from Africa), were substantially African. Free blacks felt the American Colonization society was a scheme to strengthen slavery by sending free blacks back to Africa.

By the 1850s emigration appeals were echoed by several black leaders: Martin Delaney, Henry Highland Garnett, and Alexander Crumwell. The desire to establish an independent nation outside of the control of the United States of America was a consequence of the belief of large numbers of free Black people that their experience outside of the slave states were marked by racist treatment, almost tantamount to the treatment of their enslaved brethren. Slavery required the integration of the enslaved Africans with the white slave owners. But it was the non-slave north which took the lead in the establishment of segregated institutions. These institutions existed in practically every sphere: schools, churches, hospitals, jails, hotels, and public conveyances. Blacks in the north were also subject to pogroms, not to mention the possibility of being enslaved because of the stipulations of the 1850 fugitive slave act.

The Negro Convention Movement was the most effective forum for Afro-American protest in the antebellum period, and the debates within the Convention reflected the shifting tides of the black struggle. Until the 1850s the advocates of moral suasion and the absorption of blacks into the larger society predominated within the Convention movement. With the fugitive slave law of 1850, the Kansas-Nebraska Bill of 1854, the Dred Scott Decision of 1857, and the general proliferation of scientific racist theories the attitude of blacks about strategies and tactics for liberation from North American racist oppression were transformed. Frederick Douglass, who had opposed Henry Highland Garnett's call for insurrection in 1843, by the 1850s began to believe that liberation could only be obtained by resort to violence.

Underneath these debates, however, was the resistance of the slaves themselves, ranging from the Denmark Vessey conspiracy of 1822 to the Nat Turner rebellion of 1831, and the resistance exemplified by thousands of runaway slaves. Such resistance ultimately inspired John Brown's bold assault on Harper's Ferry in 1859, which indicated that the die had been cast. North American civil society could no longer live with the contradiction of enslavement.

With the defeat of Reconstruction the threat of a non-racial democracy was buried beneath a system of racist terror institutionalized throughout the south. This was the context for the emergence of Booker T. Washington as the most distinguished black leader of this period (1895–1915). Washington did not mount a frontal attack on white supremacy but counseled blacks to learn the value of manual labor, hard work and thrift, and to practice the Christian virtues of being clean and quiet. These values rather than empty rhetoric and flashy protest would enable blacks to win acceptance. Although Washington's strategy would be called a comprador strategy by the terms that came to be used in the middle twentieth century, his strategy was essentially a nationalist one.

In the 20th century the New Negro movement was part of the revolutionary anti-colonial movements which shook the capitalist world. This movement argued that the race must be the first concern of people of African descent. The numerous betrayals at the hands of white allies had etched this concern into their collective conscience. This is not to say that there could not be principled alliances, but such alliances

had to be constructed on the basis of independent Black leadership, and the insistence that opposition to racism be a fundamental principle of all members of the alliance. For the most radical among the New Negro militants represented by the African Blood Brotherhood, Cyril Briggs, Richard Moore, and Hubert Harrison, race first made sense in the context of an anti-capitalist and socialist perspective because they understood that the class structure was constructed on the basis of race. That is, the subordinate status of Black people and white supremacy were inextricably intertwined with the formation and consolidation of capitalist civilization, and no progress was possible unless anti-racism and respect for the self-determination of Black people were central to the grievances of all the movements.

During World War I and its aftermath, the new Negro movement fueled the flame of revolt. In 1921 a State Department official by the name of Charles Latham argued that the Garvey movement was considered dangerous because its agitation would find a more fertile filed of class divergence than Bolshevism would likely find in the United States. Garvey's organization, the Universal Negro Improvement Association (UNIA) is the largest organization in the history of the Black Freedom Struggle.

The African Blood Brotherhood had been the most sophisticated of the Black radicals of the New Negro Movement, but they liquidated the issue of independent leadership by joining the CPUSA and allowing the CPUSA to disband the ABB. Yet the former ABB leadership were instrumental in pushing the CPUSA toward a revolutionary perspective and in enrolling it in the fight for racial justice to an extent unmatched by any other predominantly white organization.

In the 1930s the Moorish American Science Temple was prominent on the streets of many Black communities, providing a milieu from which much of the leadership of the early Nation of Islam emerged. Later the NOI would become the largest of the Black nationalist organizations after the UNIA. During the 1930s the movement to stop Mussolini's invasion of Ethiopia was one of the broadest manifestations of nationalism in the African Diaspora. W.E.B. DuBois was ousted from his position in the NAACP because he advocated the development of Black economic power within the existing Black communities, taking advantage of the racial solidarity and sense of common destiny already existing. Du Bois also wrote his masterpiece *Black Reconstruction in America* during this period, which took the revolutionary nationalism of the New Negro militants to a new level and articulated the most sophisticated class analysis of the world system to be known until the 1970s.

During the 1940s Carlos Cooks carried forward the mantle of Garveyism and an oppositional culture flowered among Black and Latino youth which would provide a milieu for the education of Malcolm Little on the streets of Harlem. Malcolm would build on the legacies of Marcus Garvey, Carlos Cooks, and others. Malcolm X called for unity with Black nationalists, the radicals in the civil rights movement, and with revolutionary movements throughout the three continents. This included Dr. Martin Luther King, Jr., who had agreed to enter into a coalition with Malcolm X just before Malcolm was assassinated. Later King articulated a position that called for a global redistribution of wealth and power to all of those who had been victims of U.S. global power. He called on Blacks in the U.S. and all freedom loving people to unite with the barefoot people of the world.

There are many who attempted to carry this legacy forward: The Black Arts Movement, The Revolutionary Action Movement, The Student Nonviolent Coordinating Committee (SNCC), the Black Panther Party (BPP), US, the League of Revolutionary Black Workers, the Congress of African People, the Youth Organization for Black Unity, the Republic of New Africa, the African People's Socialist Party, the African People's Party, the All African People's Revolutionary Party, the Third World Women's Alliance, the Black Workers Congress, the National Black United Front, the National Black Independent Political Party, the December 12th Movement, the Patrice Lumumba Coalition, Malcolm X Liberation University, People's College, the Institute for Positive Education, the Black Workers for Justice, the Black Radical Congress, and many many others.

In the late 1960s and early 1970s the revolutionary thrust was hegemonic within the overall Black Freedom Struggle, but it was fiercely and viciously repressed. J. Edgar Hoover had said in 1963 that the FBI should destroy the civil rights movement because it was the leading edge of a social revolution. In 1968 he said that the BPP was the biggest threat to the national security since the civil war. The BPP was deemed such a threat that more was spent on destroying the BPP than was spent on organized crime during that period. The FBI instigated a process of cold blooded murder of BPP members including Little Bobby Hutton, Fred Hampton, Bunchy Carter, John Huggins, and George Jackson.

Historically, revolutionary forces have involved themselves in center left coalitions as foot soldiers and organizers, but almost always in a subordinate role to the more established liberal forces. In the 1960s and 1970s the Black revolutionaries often dominated such alliances with the liberal Black forces. But they were forced from the leadership in the 1970s. This same trajectory was reflected within the nationalist movement itself as Malcolm X was forced to split with the conservative leadership of the NOI after articulating the revolutionary tradition in an unprecedented manner. Never had an American revolutionary been so central to the expression of a world revolutionary movement.

The revolutionary movements of the 1970s sought to draw lessons from the setbacks dealt the movement in the loss of Malcolm, Martin Luther King, Jr., and the BPP. The League of Revolutionary Black Workers seemed the most likely model. Like the BPP, the League studied Marx, Lenin, and Mao and argued for the necessity of participation in the world socialist movement. Many others followed suit, adopting a variety of positions from classical Marxism-Leninism to variations of Maoism. In this new scientific socialist guise, many rearticulated their Black nationalist viewpoints in terms of a correct position on the national question. Again the organizations varied on their interpretation of the national question. Most used some version of the CPUSA position adopted from the Comintern in 1928–1930. This was problematic as Cruse argued in 1967 because it wanted a national question without nationalists. In this sense the revolutionary subject was undermined by stringent application of a scientific analysis. Black revolutionaries were now preoccupied by the strange lack of class consciousness among American workers, whereas before they understood it clearly. By the 1980s most of these Black left formations had gone the way of the rest of the white Left.

The nationalists of course survived because they did not succumb to the lure of the white Left, as had the African Blood Brotherhood in the 1920s. While organizations such as the Black Workers for Justice, the African People's Socialist Party, the New Afrikan Peoples Organization, the December 12th Movement, the Nation of Islam, etc. continued into the 1990s, all of the Black Leninist had ceased to exist (with the sole exception of elements of the Freedom Road Socialist Organization). FRSO was instrumental in the formation of the Black Radical Congress in the late 1990s. The Nation of Islam is by far the strongest of these organizations, as demonstrated in the Million Man March in October of 1995, but is not trusted by some radicals because of Minister Farrakhan's role in the assassination of Malcolm X.

See also AMERICAN COLONIZATION SOCIETY [1]; BLACK ARTS MOVEMENT, THE [1]; BLACK PANTHER PARTY, THE [1]; BROWN, WILLIAM ANTHONY "TONY" [1]; CARRINGTON, WALTER C. [1]; CUFFE, PAUL [2]; GARVEY, MARCUS [2]; HAYWOOD, HARRY [3]; INNIS, ROY [3]; MALCOLM X [3]; REVOLUTIONARY ACTION MOVEMENT [4]; SIMMONS, JAKE, JR. [5]; STUDENT NONVIOLENT COORDINATING COMMITTEE (SNCC) [5]; UNIVERSAL NEGRO IMPROVEMENT ASSOCIATION [5].

REFERENCES

Adeleke, Tunde. *Unafrican Americans: Nineteenth-Century Black Nationalists and the Civilizing Mission.* 1998.

Bush, Rod. *We Are Not What We Seem: Black Nationalism and Class Struggle in the American Century.* 1999.

Jones, Charles, ed. *The Black Panther Party Reconsidered.* 1998.

Painter, Nell Irvin. *Exodusters: Black Migration to Kansas after Reconstruction.* 1976.

Tyson, Timothy. *Radio Free Dixie: Robert F. Williams and the Roots of Black Power.* 1999.

Woodard, Komozi. *A Nation Within a Nation: Amiri Baraka (LeRoi Jones) and Black Power Politics.* 1999.

RODERICK BUSH

Black Upper Class. A long-standing myth that persisted through the first half of the twentieth century was that black society represented a homogeneous mass exhibiting few distinctions of background, prestige, attitude, power, and behavior. The idea of a black upper class most often met ridicule since the notion was so foreign to most whites

During the years following the Revolutionary War (1775–1783), a growing number of black individuals gained an elevated status within the black population. They were commonly intellectuals, organizers, soldiers, and activists. Some were house servants for influential white families. Also, mixed-race mulattos, particularly offspring or descendants of white gentry with money, were attending the finest schools in the United States and Europe and becoming professionals including educators, lawyers, and doctors. These earliest celebrities included Crispus Attucks, Peter Salem, Brazillai Lew, Phillis Wheatley, and Prince Hall who established the Black Masons.

An actual class of such black elites did not firmly take shape until the 1830s. With most limited in wealth, the key traits were personal achievement, family heritage, education, and light skin color. The black elites were aristocracy relative to black society, but not to white society, though adopting values drawn from American white upper class. Normally not welcomed in white literary organizations, they began organizing numerous self-improvement societies of their own, such as the Adelphic Union for the Promotion of Literature and Science in Boston.

By the mid-nineteenth century, the newly emergent black upper class, populated by a preponderance of fair complexioned people, formed a bond with abolitionists. However, some abolitionists bemoaned the black aristocrats' elitist attitudes toward less fortunate blacks. Some few black elites who held substantial wealth also owned slaves, such as Richard and Joseph Dereof of Charleston. Other notables from this period were St. Louis author Cyprian Clamorgan, aristocrat Samuel Mordecai, the William Johnson family of Natchez, Mississippi, and noted abolitionist orator Frederick Douglass.

Following the Civil War (1861–1865), the social classes within black communities became more defined, consisting of a large lower class, an expanding middle class, and a miniscule upper class. With extensive migration of blacks particularly from the South to northern cities, a nationwide network of black aristocrats evolved with many upper class families personally acquainted and often kin-related. Washington, D.C. became the center of black aristocracy with a concentration of elite families.

This very small upper class was composed of two groups, the "old families" of several generations and newcomers. The old families considered themselves as superior in family heritage, sophistication, and achievement. The newcomers could not gain entry through wealth alone. They often had to demonstrate good standing, education, refinement, and proper light skin pigmentation. The acceptance of such a black upper class by a large part of the black population further legitimized their existence. Prominent families and individuals from this period included U.S. Senator Blauch K. Bruce of Mississippi, Washington, D.C. minister Sterling N. Brown, the family of Cleveland dentist Dr. Joseph Wilson, scholar W.E.B. DuBois, politicians Lewis Hayden and John Redmond, Boston merchant John H. Lewis, Washington activist Mary Church Terrell, Catholic clergyman John H. Dorsey, wealthy Boston businesswoman Phoebe Whitehurst Glover, and Congressman John R. Lynch.

For over half a century following the Civil War black aristocracy exercised considerable influence in Black America. Though most were politically conservative, they used their access to U.S. institutional power to help lay a foundation for the civil rights movement of the 1950s. Despite preoccupation with maintenance of their class status, they persistently served the less fortunate and were committed to racial uplift. Those influential during this period included J. H. Holloway, Boston newspaper editor William Monroe Trotter, Atlanta minister Henry Hugh Proctor, and Boston activist Josephine St. Pierre Ruffin.

The old upper class gradually dwindled in influence. By the 1970s a new black elite representing a broad spectrum of professions took shape with greater wealth and integration into mainstream American society.

See also CLASS AND SOCIETY [2]; ECONOMICS [2]; RACE, CASTE, AND CLASS [4].

REFERENCES

Benjamin, Lois. *The Black Elite: Facing the Color Line in the Twilight of the Twentieth Century.* 1991.

Birmingham, Stephen. *Certain People: America's Black Elite.* 1977.

Cromwell, Adelaide M. *The Other Brahmins: Boston's Black Upper Class, 1750–1950.* 1994.

Gatewood, Willard B. *Aristocrats of Color: The Black Elite, 1880–1920.* 1990.

Graham, Lawrence O. *Our Kind of People: Inside America's Black Upper Class.* 1998.

RICHARD HANES

Blackwell, Randolph Talmadge

Blackwell, Randolph Talmadge (March 10, 1927–May 21, 1981), lawyer, educator, civil rights worker. Born in Greensboro, North Carolina, to Joe Blackwell and Blanche Mary Donnell, Blackwell received his B.S. degree in sociology in 1949 from North Carolina Agricultural and Technical College. He received his J.D. degree from Howard University's law school in 1953.

Blackwell taught at two black colleges-Alabama Agricultural and Mechanical College and Winston-Salem State Teachers College-before director Wiley Branton named him field director for the Voter Education Project in 1962. The VEP was tax-sheltered under the Southern Regional Council, which re-granted funds to civil rights organizations in order to support their voter registration efforts among blacks. During a trip from Greenwood toward Greenville,

Mississippi, with activist Robert Moses, white night riders shot Blackwell. The act spurred Wiley Branton to wire Attorney General Robert Kennedy for federal involvement in Greenwood. After that, the Southern Christian Leadership Conference sent trained voter education workers to Greenwood.

Blackwell became program director of SCLC in 1964 and held the post during the Alabama voting rights campaign in Selma that led to a march across the Edmund Pettus Bridge. After the marchers were attacked on March 17, 1965, or "Bloody Sunday," Blackwell, under Martin Luther King's name, invited religious leaders from across the country to join the Selma to Montgomery March.

Blackwell left the SCLC in 1966 and founded Southern Rural Action, Incorporated, based in Atlanta. In 1977 he moved to Washington, D.C., as director of the Minority Business Enterprise for the Department of Commerce. He returned to Atlanta in 1979 to direct the Office of Minority Enterprise Program and Development, where he remained until he died of cancer.

See also CIVIL RIGHTS MOVEMENT [2]; SOUTHERN CHRISTIAN LEADERSHIP CONFERENCE [5]; VOTER EDUCATION PROJECT [5].

REFERENCES

Branch, Taylor. *Parting the Waters: America in the King Years, 1954–1963.* 1988.

Garraty, John A., and Mark C. Carnes, general eds. *American National Biography*, vol. 2. 1999.

Garrow, David J. *Bearing the Cross: Martin Luther King, Jr., and the Southern Christian Leadership Conference.* 1986.

RAYMOND WINBUSH

Blaxploitation films (Update).

Blaxploitation films (Update). Interest in Blaxploitation films and actors revived following Keenan Ivory Wayans's affectionate spoof *I'm Gonna Git You Sucka* (1989), and the genre enjoyed a popular renaissance in the 1990s, a development influenced by such diverse factors as nostalgia for the 1970s and the popularity of hip-hop films. In particular, Quentin Tarentino, a white director, openly acknowledged the influence of the Blaxploitation film on his scenarios, dialogue, and directorial style, and he paid tribute to the genre with his film *Jackie Brown* (1998), which provided a comeback for actress Pam Grier.

In summary, the achievements of blaxploitation films have included: (1) to prove that black audiences would support black films; (2) to revitalize white studios and urban theaters during the late 1960s to mid '70s; (3) to develop a genre of black action film; (4) to stimulate the integration of mainstream feature films; and (5) to broaden the range of character for black actors and actresses; and (6) to provide an opportunity for new black talent, in front of the camera and behind it.

REFERENCES

Nesteby, James R. *Black Images in American Films: The Interplay Between Civil Rights and Film Culture.* 1982.

Parish, James Robert, and George H. Hill. *Black Action Films: Plots, Critiques, Casts and Credits for 235 Theatrical and Made-for-Television Releases.* 1989.

GREG ROBINSON

Bond, Julian (Update) (January 14, 1940–),
politician. In 1986 Bond ran for U.S. Congress from Georgia and narrowly lost in a bitter contest with John Lewis, his former civil rights colleague. In the early 1990s Bond served as visiting professor and fellow at various colleges, including the University of Pennsylvania, Drexel University, Harvard University, and the University of Virginia, and was a frequent essayist and commentator on political issues. He also was, in the early 1990s, the host of a syndicated television program, *TV's Black Forum.* In February 1998, Bond was

A young Julian Bond, at a press conference. (Corbis Corporation)

elected Chair of the Board of the National Association for the Advancement of Colored People.

REFERENCES

Lewis, Amy. "Julian Bond." In *American Social Leaders.* William McGuire and Leslie Wheeler, eds. 1993.

Neary, John. *Julian Bond: Black Rebel.* 1971.

EVAN A. SHORE
UPDATED BY GREG ROBINSON

Bowden, Artemisia (January 1, 1879–August 18, 1969), educator. Bowden was born in Albany, Georgia, to Milas and Mary Molette Bowden. In 1896, at sixteen, she entered St. Augustine's College in Raleigh, North Carolina. After completing the normal department in 1900, Bowden taught at St. Joseph's Parish School in Fayetteville. The next year she moved to the Normal and Industrial School in High Point.

Bowden was appointed head teacher at St. Philip's School, an Episcopal mission school in San Antonio, Texas. In 1902 she began her long career there. She was dedicated to educating young black people, particularly women who, in her view, had the destiny of their race in their hands. Without church support, Bowden received money from the Women's Auxiliary and raised other monies for St. Philips on her own.

In 1917 Bowden sold the property adjacent to St. Philips Church and bought four acres outside the city. The school was incorporated as St. Philips Junior College and Industrial School, and Bowden became its president-the first woman to head a college in Texas. It was known simply as "Miss Bowden's School." Financial problems during the Depression caused the school in 1942 to be transferred to the local school board. The institution became the St. Phillips Branch of the San Antonio Junior College. Bowden became the dean. After fifty-two years at St. Philips, Bowden retired in 1954. St. Augustine's College awarded her an honorary degree and maintains a student loan fund in her name; in 1971 San Antonio named an elementary school in her honor; and in 1976 an historical marker was placed at the college's original site. Her bust is located on the new campus, and the administration building bears her name. *See also* EDUCATION [2]; TEXAS [5].

REFERENCES

Fleming, G. James, and Christian E. Burckel, eds. *Who's Who in Colored America,* 7th ed. 1950.

Hayden, J. Carleton. "Artemisia Bowden" *Linkage* (Artemisia Bowden Issue, September 1987): 6, 16.

Winegarten, Ruthe. *Black Texas Women*. 1995.

JESSIE CARNEY SMITH

Bowe, Riddick (Update) (1967–), professional boxer. In 1996, Riddick Bowe returned to the ring and was twice awarded decisions over Andrew Golota following illegal low punches by Golota. His troubled personal life continued after he retired from the ring in 1997. In February 1997, he joined the U.S. Marine Corps but resigned after only three days in basic training. In June 1998, Bowe pleaded guilty to abduction after kidnapping his estranged wife and children from their home in North Carolina. During the kidnapping, Bowe also stabbed his wife. Bowe was sentenced in February 2000 to thirty days in prison, six months' house arrest, four years' probation, and ordered not to box during his probation. His lawyers argued his sentence down by presenting evidence that Bowe had suffered brain damage from his boxing career and that it had impaired his judgment, causing the kidnapping.

REFERENCE

Frazier, Eric. "Bowe Gets Break As Judge Cuts Sentence; Boxer Ordered To Quit Sport, Serve 30 Days." *The Charlotte Observer*. March 1, 2000: 1A.

GREG ROBINSON

Bowman, Sister Thea (December 29, 1937– March 30, 1990), evangelist and teacher. Sister Thea Bowman was born in Yazoo City, Mississippi. Named Bertha by her parents, she became a Catholic at age nine and was christened Sister Thea when she became the first black novitiate of the Franciscan Sisters in 1956.

Bowman obtained her undergraduate degree in English from Viterbo College (LaCrosse, Wisconsin) and an M.A. and Ph.D. in linguistics and English literature from Catholic University of America (Washington, D. C.). She taught in Mississippi public schools during the 1960s and at Viterbo from 1971–1978. While teaching at Viterbo, she founded the Hallelujah Singers, a touring group that performed black spirituals.

In 1978, Bowman, whose teaching always included emphasis on different races and cultures, became the consultant on interracial awareness for the Franciscan diocese of Jackson, Mississippi, while also teaching at

Riddick Bowe. (AP/Wide World Photos)

Xavier University (New Orleans). She was honored for her work with the LaCrosse Diocese Justice and Peace Award in 1982. In 1987, she was featured in a story on 60 Minutes and in 1989, she received four awards from government officials, including one from former President Ronald Reagan.

A cancer sufferer since 1984, she was given the American Cancer Society's Courage Award in 1988. She was the first recipient (1989) of the Sister Thea Bowman Justice Award, created by the Bishop Topel Ministries in Spokane, Washington. Bowman was an author and editor of several religious books, including Families: Black and Catholic, Catholic and Black, and *Songs of My People*. Her activities reflected her appreciation and pride in her own heritage while trying to promote intercultural awareness and reciprocal appreciation.

See also RELIGION [4].

REFERENCES

Hine, Darlene Clark, ed. *Black Women in America*, vol. I, A-L. 1993.

Hine, Darlene Clark, ed. *Facts on File Encyclopedia of Black Women in America*, vol. 7. 1997.

Hornsby, Alton, Jr. *Chronology of African-American History*. 1991.

CARRELL P. HORTON

Boxing (Update). Prior to the 1900s, few blacks, foreign or U.S.-born, gained prominence, let alone dominance in prizefighting. Until professional boxing was divided into weight divisions in the late nineteenth century and well after, white promoters conspired to deny African-American fighters opportunities to obtain title fights. For decades, black fighters typically fought more often and for less money than their white counterparts; many black pugilists died young and penniless for their efforts. Among the few notable American-born boxers was George Dixon, champion of the bantamweight featherweight in the late 1800s.

African-American boxers only entered the sport successfully during the twentieth century. Black boxers of note in the century's first half were regarded as trailblazers, earning a celebrity status; for example, Joe Gans, a lightweight, reigned as champion for six years just after the turn of the century. Others to gain prominence were middleweight-heavyweight Sam Langford, light heavyweight-heavyweight Joe Jeannette, and heavyweight Harry Wills. Their fame, however,

paled considerably to that of Jack Johnson, the first black heavyweight titleholder. Johnson was arrogant and outspoken at a time when Jim Crow laws and racist attitudes, generally, were at their zenith in the United States. That public persona (also hurt considerably by his preference for white women) soon infuriated whites, regardless of their interest in boxing. Trouble with American authorities were a constant for Johnson and he only managed to hold his title for as long as he did by fighting in Europe during much of his reign. Due to Johnson's notoriety, it again became more difficult for black boxers to gain title shots.

African-American fighters continued to have greater luck rising through the ranks of the lower weight divisions. Among those who managed to make that journey was Henry Armstrong, who many consider to be among the best boxers of all time. Armstrong held the featherweight, lightweight, and welterweight titles simultaneously in the late 1930s. A considerable cultural shift in the glamour division of heavyweight came with the success of Joe Louis, who won the title in 1937 and held it until 1949. Louis was everything that Johnson had not been: humble, soft spoken, gracious. The key moment in his career was one for which he even had white America solidly in his corner. Louis' 1938 rematch with former champion Max Schmeling—set up by Schmeling's second-round knockout of Louis in 1936—pitted an American and a German (and possible Nazi) against each other in the early days of Hitler's conquest of Europe. His first-round knockout of Schmeling made Louis a national hero across race lines. Louis increased his standing among whites by serving in the U.S. Army during World War II.

In the decade after the second world war, black boxers went from being exceptions to becoming regulars among the ranks of contenders. In the late 1940s, boxing proved a natural sport for coverage by the still-limited technology used in the production of live television. An immensely popular fighter of the time was Sugar Ray Robinson, a flashy and fluid welterweight-middleweight who enjoyed a long career in the spotlight. Robinson won a combined six titles covering three weight classifications. Other champion boxers who were seen routinely on weekly, nationally televised fights were welterweight Kid Gavilan, light heavyweight Archie Moore, and heavyweight Floyd Patterson.

In the early 1960s, welterweight-junior middleweight Emile Griffith was conspicuous as a combined six-time titleholder in that range of three divisions.

Television, however, was increasingly devoting its decreasing boxing coverage to the heavyweight division. Boosted by his earlier gold medal—winning light heavyweight performance in the 1960 Olympic Games, Cassius Clay, Jr. really burst on the national scene with his 1964 upset of feared heavyweight champ Sonny Liston. Combining poetry and braggadocio, Clay knew how to use the television medium to his advantage—and television was only too happy to provide him the forum. Later, when he fought induction into the army during the Vietnam War on religious grounds as a Black Muslim, he became a pariah for a time, escalated by the fact that he publically changed his name to Muhammad Ali. Within a few years, after sentiment turned against the war, Ali was forgiven, even embraced, by the American public. Ali held the heavyweight title an unprecedented three times, accounting for about 11 years of a 15-year period; at the height of his fame he may well have been the most recognizable person on the planet. Ali was just one of several gifted black heavyweights active during the sixties and seventies—Joe Frazier, Ken Norton and George Foreman (who would regain the title 20 years later), for example, but none of the others compared to Ali in terms of personality and popularity.

The biggest names in boxing during the 1980s may have been those fighting in the middle divisions. The most successful of these was Sugar Ray Leonard, who won titles in five weight classifications. Leonard combined uncommon grace and speed to outbox his opponents, often ending a fight, however, with a flurry of punches resulting in a knockout. Leonard, however, was joined by Thomas Hearns, who also piled up titles in five divisions. Like Leonard, Hearns started as a welterweight and moved up through several divisions as he matured and added weight. Unlike Leonard, however, Hearns' strength was unquestioned put-away power that he used to end many a fight with an early knockout. Both Leonard and Hearns were joined in those divisions by such other notables as Marvin Hagler and Dwight (Braxton) Qawi. The heavyweight division was dominated in the early to mid-eighties by Larry Holmes, but later fell into disarray as a number of fighters claimed the title for short periods. Among those was Mike Tyson, a ferocious fighter who seemed invincible in the late-eighties before personal problems outside the ring began to disastrously affect his performances inside the ring.

In the 1990s, the most notable heavyweight champion was Evander Holyfield, a former cruiserweight champ, who stepped up in weight to face many of the top contenders. He twice won the championship and recorded a pair of decisive victories over Tyson, who continued to be a top challenger for much of the decade. Perhaps the best fighter in the world at the beginning of the 21st century is Roy Jones, Jr., who has fought in the middleweight to light heavyweight divisions. Jones has won titles in three weight divisions and is still active.

See also ALI, MUHAMMAD [1]; FOREMAN, GEORGE [2]; HOLYFIELD, EVANDER [3]; JONES JR., ROY [S]; LEONARD, SUGAR RAY [3]; LOUIS, JOE [3]; ROBINSON, SUGAR RAY [4].

REFERENCES

Ashe, Arthur. *A Hard Road to Glory - Boxing: The African-American Athlete in Boxing*. 1993.

The Cyber Boxing Zone Encyclopedia. http://www.cyberboxingzone.com/boxing/hist-idx.htm.

Fleischer, Nathaniel S. *Black Dynamite: The Story of the Negro in the Prize Ring from 1782–1938*. 1938.

KEVIN C. KRETSCHMER

Brandon, Barbara

Brandon, Barbara (1958–), cartoonist. Barbara Brandon reaches a wide national audience through the comic strip to portray life situations among the African American woman from the black perspective. Brandon grew up in New Cassel, Long Island, the daughter of cartoonist Brumsic Brandon, Jr., who was among the first African American cartoonists to be syndicated. He created the strip "Luther," which ran for seventeen years beginning in the late 1960s. Barbara Brandon studied illustration at Syracuse University and, after graduation, took her comic strips called "Where I'm Coming From" to *Elan* magazine. The magazine hired her, but *Elan* folded before the cartoons were published. Brandon then approached *Essence*, but the magazine had no space for cartoons and hired her as a beauty and fashion writer instead.

In 1988 Brandon was hired by the *Detroit Free Press*, which had become interested in featuring more black cartoonists. Her strip "Where I'm Coming From" was first published in June 1989. Her series features women characters, depicted as talking heads, that she calls "the girls." The strip reached 1.5 million readers and became a weekly Sunday addition. Universal Press Syndicate picked up the strip in September 1991, enabling Brandon to become the first African American woman cartoonist to appear in national

Barbara Brandon. (The Gamma Liaison Network)

syndication. Since her sketches focus on women, some critics accuse her of male bashing, but Brandon views her characters as reflections of common experiences in life, who are able to reflect cultural differences that race imposes.

See also COMIC STRIPS [2].

REFERENCES

"Barbara Brandon is First Black Female Cartoonist Nationally Syndicated." *Jet* 80 (August 26, 1991):32.

Bigelow, Barbara Carlisle, ed. *Contemporary Black Biography*, vol. 3. 1993.

Hine, Darlene Clark, ed. *Black Women in America*, vol. I. 1993.

Linden, Amy. "Barbara Brandon: A Comic Strip About Us." *Essence* 20 (March 1990): 46.

VALENCIA PRICE

Branton, Wiley Austin (December 13, 1923–December 15, 1988), lawyer, educator, civil rights worker. Wiley Branton was a prominent lawyer during the Civil Rights Movement of the 1950s and 1960s. His defense of nine black students during the desegregation of Little Rock's Central High School catapulted him into prominence. In the summer 1948 he and a group of friends held voter education clinics for Arkansas blacks; Branton was convicted and fined for violating a state law that governed the printing of ballots. After getting his B.A. in 1950, Branton decided to get a law degree and provide better law service in the state than he had received. In 1953 he received a J.D. degree from the University of Arkansas, Fayetteville.

From 1957 to 1958, during the desegregation of public schools in Arkansas, Branton was chief counsel for the Little Rock Nine with Thurgood Marshall. Still concerned with black voting rights, in 1962 Branton was named director of the Voter Education Project in Atlanta where he helped to register over 600,000 black voters between 1962 and 1965. He was also lawyer for the Freedom Riders. From 1965 to 1967 Branton was special assistant to U.S. attorneys-general Nicholas Katzenbach and Ramsey Clark.

From 1978 to 1983, Branton was dean of the Howard University Law School and then became a partner in the Washington law office of Sidney and Austin. He remained active in civil rights and legal organizations and was recognized for his uncompromising stance.

See also CIVIL RIGHTS MOVEMENT [2]; VOTER EDUCATION PROJECT [5].

REFERENCES

Anderson, Susan Heller. "Wiley Branton, Early Desegregation Lawyer, Dies." *New York Times*, December 17, 1988.

Editors of *Ebony*. *The Ebony Success Library*. 1973.

"Wiley Branton, Famed Civil Rights Attorney, 65, Dies. *Jet* 75 (January 9, 1989): 12-14.

JESSIE CARNEY SMITH

Brooks, Walter Henderson (August 30, 1851–July 6, 1945), clergyman, poet.

Walter Brooks Henderson was a Baptist clergyman, poet, and temperance leader. He was born a slave in Richmond, Virginia. His father, Albert R. Brooks, hired himself out and was involved in an eating house business and a livery stable, but the father and his children became free in 1865.

In 1866 Brooks entered the preparatory school of Lincoln University (Pennsylvania); there he earned a B.A. degree in 1872 and a B.D. the following year. He worked as a clerk in the Richmond post office, and in 1874 he became a Sunday school missionary for the American Baptist Publication society. Brooks was ordained in 1876. After serving as pastor of the Second African Baptist Church of Richmond from 1877 to 1880, he went to Louisiana as a Sunday school missionary. In 1882 he became pastor of the Nineteenth Street Baptist Church, Washington, D.C., where he remained until his death.

As pastor, Brooks had an important role in the community. He campaigned against drunkenness, supported the social gospel, and was recognized as a leading member of the Washington intellectual elite. He won fame for his scholarly sermons, and he also wrote articles for magazines, including the *Journal of Negro History*. His poems are collected in his *Original Poems* (1932).

See also LINCOLN UNIVERSITY [3]; RELIGION [4].

REFERENCES

Biggs, Adam. "Walter Henderson Brooks." In *American National Biography*, edited by John A. Garraty and Mark C. Carnes. 1999.

Brooks, Walter Henderson. *Original Poems*. 1932.

Logan, Rayford W. "Walter Henderson Brooks." In *Dictionary of American Negro Biography*, edited by Rayford W. Logan and Michael R. Winston. 1982.

ROBERT L. JOHNS

Brown, Arthur McKimmon (November 9, 1867–December 4, 1939), surgeon.

Arthur McKimmon Brown was born in Raleigh, North Carolina. His family emphasized education, and he attended both public and private (Shaw University) high schools. A scholarship to Lincoln University (Pennsylvania) resulted in his graduation in 1888. That same year he entered medical school at the University of Michigan, graduating in 1891.

Brown passed the Alabama Board of Medicine's difficult qualifying examination, reputedly with the highest score made at that point, and began practicing medicine in Bessemer, Alabama. After brief surgical practices in Chicago and Cleveland, he established himself in Birmingham in 1894. His civic and business activities included establishing the People's Drug Store; serving as chairman of the Alabama Prison Improvement Board and as a director of a savings bank; and serving as a staff surgeon at Andrew Memorial Hospital in Tuskegee.

In 1898, Brown began his army career with a commission as a first lieutenant, assigned as a surgeon with the all black U. S. 10th Cavalry in Santiago, Cuba. Serving under battlefield conditions, he was commander of the unit for three months. Brown was the first black soldier commissioned in the regular army and the only black surgeon serving in Cuba during the Spanish-American war. Discharged in 1899, he was later denied a pension on the grounds that he was a civilian employee of the army and not actually in the army.

Brown practiced briefly in Chicago after his army discharge but ended his career practicing in Birmingham. He served as president of the National Medical Association, an organization for black physicians and those serving primarily the black population, in 1914. He was also a member of the Tri-State Medical, Dental, and Pharmaceutical Association.

See also MEDICAL ASSOCIATIONS [3]; MEDICAL EDUCATION [3]; SPANISH-AMERICAN WAR [5];

REFERENCES

Krapp, Kristine, ed *Notable Black American Scientists*. 1999.

Logan, Rayford W., and Michael R. Winston, eds. *Dictionary of American Negro Biography*. 1982.

Sammons, Vivian Ovelton. *Blacks in Science and Medicine*. 1990.

CARRELL P. HORTON

Browne, Hugh M. (June 1851–October 30, 1923), educator, civil rights leader. Hugh Browne was born in Washington, D.C. and had a background of family prominence. Browne was educated in local schools, then received his bachelor's and master's degrees from Howard University in 1875 and 1878, respectively. He received a B.D. degree from Princeton Theological Seminary, also in 1878, and then was ordained in the Presbyterian church. He pastored Shiloh Presbyterian Church in New York, then for eighteen months was professor at Liberia College in Liberia. After other short-term appointments, he was principal of Philadelphia's Institute for Colored Youth from 1902 until his 1913 retirement.

While in Liberia, Browne began to reexamine educational systems, believing that black children should not be forced to fit into curricula designed for children of other heritages and environments. Browne contended that the main purpose of education was to enable black students to adapt general concepts to specific environments and thus solve the problems of that environment. Otherwise, he contended, blacks could not escape the political and economic control of whites. Browne also taught summer training sessions in educational methodology for teachers from all over the South.

From 1904 to 1913, Browne was secretary of the Committee of Twelve, an outgrowth of an early Carnegie Hall meeting of African American leaders that aimed to soften the effects of the division between Booker T. Washington and W. E. B. Du Bois. His own philosophy of correlating academic and industrial education helped to address the dispute between the two leaders.

REFERENCE

Logan, Rayford W., and Michael R. Winston, eds. *Dictionary of American Negro Biography*. 1982.

VALENCIA PRICE

Brown, Lee Patrick (October 4, 1937–), mayor. Lee Brown, the first African-American mayor of Houston, the nation's fourth largest city, was born in Wewoka, Oklahoma, and received a B.S. degree from

Lee Brown. (AP/Wide World Photos)

Fresno State University in 1960. That same year, he joined the San Jose, California, police force, where he remained for eight years. During that time he acquired two master's degrees. In 1970, he was awarded a doctorate in criminology by the University of California, Berkeley.

In 1975, after occupying teaching positions in criminology (at Portland State College in Oregon and Howard University), Brown was appointed sheriff of Multnomah County, Oregon, a largely white area. His success with community groups garnered widespread attention, and subsequently Brown accepted offers to become public safety commissioner of Atlanta, Georgia, in 1978, and police chief of Houston, Texas, in 1982.

In 1990, New York mayor David Dinkins appointed Brown as the city's police commissioner. During his two years as chief of the largest police force in the nation, Brown received credit for his advocacy of neighborhood patrols and increases in police officer personnel. However, he was widely criticized for his failure to crack down swiftly on African-American rioters during the Crown Heights riot in summer 1991.

In 1997, Brown, then a Rice University professor, announced his candidacy for mayor of Houston.

Despite his lack of name recognition, Brown forged an alliance of black and liberal white voters, who were also energized by a ballot referendum on city affirmative action policies, and he won a narrow victory.
See also CROWN HEIGHTS RIOT [2]; HOUSTON, TEXAS [3]; NEW YORK CITY [4].

REFERENCE

Brown, Lee, et al., eds. *Crime and Its Impact on the Black Community*. 1975.

GREG ROBINSON

Brown, Ronald H. (Update)

Brown, Ronald H. (Update) (August 1, 1941– April 3, 1996), politician. Brown was a close Clinton adviser, as well as a visible and controversial figure, during his years in the Commerce Department. Though dogged by Republican charges of corruption and income tax evasion, he also was celebrated for his economic diplomacy, by which he sought to obtain trade agreements and open markets for the United States in countries such as China. On April 3, 1996, while on a trip to Croatia, Brown and his party were killed in an airplane crash.

REFERENCE

"Brown, Ronald H." In *Notable Black American Men*. 1998.

GREG ROBINSON

Brown, Solomon G.

Brown, Solomon G. (February 14, 1829–1903), technician, legislator. Brown was born to free parents in Washington, D.C. His father's death in 1833 left the family in poverty, and he could not pursue a formal education. About 1844, Brown found a job at the Post Office, where he worked for Samuel F. B. Morse and Joseph Henry installing wires between Washington and Baltimore for the first long-distance trial of the electric telegraph. This effort formally succeeded on May 24, 1844.

Brown continued to work for Morse and Henry; in 1845 he became a battery tender for the Morse Telegraph Company. Brown later found work as a packer for the chemical manufacturers Gillman and Brothers. After Joseph Henry, Morse's associate, became secretary of the new Smithsonian Institute, Brown found employment there in 1852. Brown was a scientific technician at the Smithsonian Institute from 1852 to 1903. Brown had the official title of packer, but his responsibilities were wide. For example, he

prepared most of the illustrations for science lectures until 1887, and 1869 his duties included transportation, registry, and storage of animal specimens.

Brown was an active member of the community; he gave the first of many lectures on science in 1854. He served as a trustee of Wilberforce University as well as a local Presbyterian church. An active member of many organizations, Brown also served three consecutive terms as an elected member of the legislature of the District of Columbia beginning in 1871.
See also WILBERFORCE UNIVERSITY [5]; WASHINGTON, D.C. [5].

REFERENCES

Hayden, Robert C. "Solomon G. Brown." In *Dictionary of American Negro Biography*, edited by Rayford W. Logan and Michael R. Winston. 1982.

Simmons, William J. *Men of Mark*. 1887.

ROBERT L. JOHNS

Brown, Wesley A[nthony]

Brown, Wesley A[nthony] (April 3, 1927–), graduate Naval Academy, civil engineer. Wesley A. Brown was the first African American to graduate from the United States Naval Academy. He was born in Baltimore, Maryland, and grew up in Washington, D.C., where he graduated from Dunbar High School. Representative Adam Clayton Powell, Jr. appointed him to the Naval Academy in June 1945. Although racial harassment gave him a difficult first year, Brown graduated in 1949 with a B.S. in mechanical engineering. A *Saturday Evening Post* article (June 15, 1949) covered his experience. In 1950–1951 he studied at Rensselaer Polytechnic Institute in Troy, New York, where he earned a civil engineering master's degree.

Brown served for twenty years in the Navy's Civil Engineering Corps, beginning as a trainee in the Boston Naval Shipyard in 1949–50 and ending as Public Works Officer and Officer in Charge of Construction at the Naval Air Station in Brooklyn, New York. He continued his work as an engineer after his retirement from the Navy in 1969 as a lieutenant commander. Between 1969 and 1976, Brown worked in building construction for the New York State University system. In 1976 he went to Howard University where he was responsible for the Physical Facilities. He retired from this position in 1988. Brown was elected to an Alumni Trustee of the U.S. Naval Academy, serving from 1985 to 1988.
See also ENGINEERING [2]; MILITARY [4].

REFERENCES

Department of Defense. *Black Americans in Defense of Our Nation*. 1982.

District of Columbia Water and Sewer Authority Board of Directors Wesley A. Brown Confirmation Resolution of 1998. PR 12-955. http://www.dcwatch.com/council112/12-955.htm.

McCarthy, Kate. "Breaking Barriers at the Academy." *Inside Annapolis Magazine Online!* http://annapolismag.com/FM/issuefeature4.html.

Who's Who Among Black Americans, 9th ed. 1996.

ROBERT L. JOHNS

Brown, Willie Lewis, Jr. (Update)

Brown, Willie Lewis, Jr. (Update) (March 20, 1934–), politician. In the 1990 election, Brown's tenure was limited when the state's voters passed Proposition 140, limiting members of the Assembly to three two-year terms and state senators to two four-year terms. In November 1994, the Republicans gained a slim majority in the Assembly. However, through a parliamentary maneuver, Brown retained his post as speaker. In 1996, Brown resigned his post prior to making a successful run for Mayor of San Francisco.

During his tenure as mayor, Brown distinguished himself in San Francisco by construction of a new central library and by introducing plans for the conversion of the abandoned naval base at Treasure Island. Brown remains one of the most influential African-American leaders in California.

REFERENCES

Groodgame, Dan. "Jesse Jackson's Alter Ego." *Time* (June 13, 1988): 28.

Von Hoffman, Nicholas. "Willie Brown in Deep Doo-Doo." *Gentleman's Quarterly* (March 1990): 292- 295.

THADDEUS RUSSELL

Broyard, Anatole Paul

Broyard, Anatole Paul (July 16, 1920–October 11, 1990), critic. Anatole Broyard, who passed as white and was part of New York intellectual circles, was born in the French Quarter of New Orleans. In the mid-1920s, his family moved to Brooklyn, New York, where Broyard's father, a carpenter, passed as white in order to join a restricted union. Anatole Broyard attended Brooklyn College. Shortly after graduating in 1941, he was drafted into the Army and attended Officer's Candidate School. Ironically, though

he was listed by the military as white, Captain Broyard was assigned command of an all-black unit.

After the war, Broyard moved to New York's Greenwich Village and attended the New School for Social Research on the GI Bill. During the 1950s, he was active in Village bohemian and Beat circles, ran a bookstore, and taught at the New School. In 1963, he joined a New York advertising agency as a copywriter. While Broyard wrote essays for intellectual journals and a much-praised short story, "What the Cytoscope Says," he was unable to achieve his goal to write a novel.

In 1970, Broyard was hired by the *New York Times* as one of its two daily book reviewers. He occupied that position until 1984, then became a columnist for the Sunday *Times* Book Review. Broyard's columns were noted for their fluent form and for his eclectic knowledge and tastes. In his last years, he began a memoir (which was posthumously published as *When Kafka Was the Rage*). He also wrote *Intoxicated by My Illness* (1992), an account of his struggle with terminal cancer. In 1996, Henry Louis Gates, Jr., "outed" Broyard as black in an article in *The New Yorker*. *See also* CRITCISM, LITERARY [2]; JOURNALISM [3].

REFERENCE

Gates, Henry Louis, Jr. *Thirteen Ways of Looking at a Black Man*. 1997.

GREG ROBINSON

Brunson, Dorothy

Brunson, Dorothy (March 13, 1938–), broadcasting executive, entrepreneur. Dorothy Brunson was born in Glensville, Georgia and grew up in Harlem. After graduating from Empire State College with a degree in business and finance, she worked at WWRL-Radio in New York City. Three months after that, she was named controller and later, assistant general manager of the station. In 1969 she cofounded one of the first black advertising agencies in the nation, Howard Sanders Advertising. Inner City Broadcasting came to Brunson in 1973 to ask her to organize investors for the radio stations that it owned. Inner City directed the local black community-oriented station, WLIP-AM Radio. Brunson became general manager, turned the station around, and purchased the music counterpart WLIP-FM.

Successful management of these stations made her ready to start an empire of her own. In 1979 Brunson acquired Baltimore's WEBB-Radio. Since the station operated in the red when she began, she worked without salary but with confidence that she would overcome community protest and financial difficulties that surrounded the station. By 1986, she had transformed the station into a profitable enterprise. It also rose in ratings from the bottom of a thirty-five-station market to number ten. She then expanded her enterprise further by purchasing WIGO-AM in Atlanta and WMBS-AM in Wilmington, North Carolina. Through these stations, Brunson enlightened and informed the African American community; in Baltimore, WEBB became known as "the community voice." Keys to Brunson's success are the invention of the "urban contemporary" programming format and a superior ability to acquire advertising revenue.

See also ENTREPRENEURS [2]; RADIO [4].

REFERENCES

LaBlanc, Michael L., ed. *Contemporary Black Biography*, vol. 1. 1992.

Smikle, Ken. "Dorothy Brunson." *Black Enterprise* 17 (April 1987): 44-45.

VALENCIA PRICE

Bullard, Eugene (1894–October 13, 1961), World War I flying ace. Eugene Jacques Bullard was born in Columbus, Georgia, the grandson of a slave. As a child, he heard his father aver that segregation was unknown in France, and at the age of eight the young

Eugene Bullard. (Copyright by Jamie H. Cockield)

Bullard left home, determined to go there. After two years of wandering, he arrived in New York City, where at age ten he stowed away on a steamer bound for Scotland.

In Scotland, Bullard became a prizefighter, achieving some success as a welterweight in England, France, and North Africa. When World War I began in October 1914, the twenty-year-old Bullard joined the French Foreign Legion. He was wounded twice. In October 1916, he was selected for pilot training in the American Squadron (later renamed the Lafayette Escadrille), a branch of the French Flying Corps. created for the American pilots who had volunteered to fight with the French. On May 7, 1917, he became the first black fighter pilot in history.

Bullard, who the French nicknamed the Black Swallow of Death, claimed to have scored two kills, although only one, early in November 1917, was confirmed. A quarrel with a superior led to his discharge from the corps in January 1918, and he spent the rest of the war with the 170th French Infantry Regiment. For his service, he was awarded several medals, including the Croix de Guerre and France's highest honor, the Legion d'Honneur. After the war, in January 1918, the United States Army reorganized the Lafayette Escadrille as the 103rd Pursuit Squadron, but Bullard's application to join the squadron was denied. He had little interest in returning to the United States anyway.

Bullard remained in France, married a French woman, and worked as a bandleader, an athletic club director, and a nightclub operator in Paris. During World War II, he served with the French Army and was wounded. He also worked with the French resistance. Americans helped to smuggle him out of the country when the Germans took over, and he eventually made his way to New York City, where he took up residence in East Harlem and worked at various jobs, including operating an elevator in the RCA Building. In 1954, he was invited by the government of France to rekindle the everlasting flame at the Tomb of the Unknown Soldier under the Arc de Triomphe. He died in 1961 at age 67 and was buried in the French War Veterans Cemetery in Flushing, Queens, New York. Two daughters and two grandchildren survived him.

See also AEROSPACE [1]; WORLD WAR I [5].

REFERENCES

Bricktop, with James Haskins. *Bricktop*. 1983.

Carisella, P.J., and James Ryan. *The Black Swallow of Death*. 1972.

"Eugene Bullard, Ex-Pilot, Dead: American Flew for French." *The New York Times*, October 14, 1961.

Haskins, Jim. *Black Eagles: African Americans in Aviation.* New York, 1995.

JAMES HASKINS
KATHLEEN BENSON

Burch, Charles Eaton

Burch, Charles Eaton (July 14, 1891–March 23, 1948), educator, scholar. Eaton was a specialist in eighteenth-century literature, and an authority on Daniel Defoe. He had an extensive collection of works by and about Defoe. He was also one of the first educators in an American university to offer a course devoted to African American literature. Burch was born in Bermuda, where he received his elementary and secondary school education. He received his bachelor's degree in 1914 from Wilberforce University, a master's degree in 1918 from Columbia University, and the Ph.D. in 1933 from Ohio State University. He taught at Tuskegee Institute and Wilberforce University. He taught at Howard University from 1921 until his death in 1948, at which time he was head of the Department of English.

Burch was widely recognized as an authority on Daniel Defoe. He did research at Edinburgh University in 1927–1928 and returned to Scotland in 1938 for six months research which resulted in biographical and bibliographical discoveries. His findings were published over the ten-year period that followed. In the field of African American literature, Burch also made an important contribution through his course, Poetry and Prose of Negro Life, which he introduced at Howard in the early 1920s. Burch was married to Willa Carter Mayer, a local educator. His memory and scholarship are recognized in the Charles Eaton Burch Memorial Lectures established at Howard in 1949.
See also CRITICISM, LITERARY [2].

REFERENCES

Arvey, Verna. "Charles Eaton Burch, Who Treads an Unbeaten Path." *Opportunity* 20 (1942): 245-246.

Logan, Rayford W., and Michael R. Winston, eds. *Dictionary of American Negro Biography.* 1982.

Sinnette, Elinor Des Verney, and others. *Black Bibliophiles and Collectors.* 1990.

VALENCIA PRICE

Burrell Communications Group.

Burrell Communications Group. In 1996 Burrell Communications Group ranked sixteenth on the *Black Enterprise* list of the 100 top U.S. black businesses. As of 1998, the firm generated $168 million in annual billings, with offices in Chicago, Atlanta, and New York, providing advertising and marketing campaigns for major firms including Coca-Cola, Ford, McDonald's, Pillsbury, and Proctor & Gamble. Thomas J. Burrell, founder of the company, was one of the first to specialize in niche marketing, in this case targeting African American consumers. In so doing, he eschewed popular stereotypes. By successfully reaching the intended audiences, he earned several awards for successful marketing efforts.

Thomas J. Burrell attended Roosevelt College and pursue an advertising career. There were, however, virtually no black persons employed in this industry in Chicago at that time. Undaunted, in 1960, Burrell applied to work in the mailroom at Wade Advertising agency. He eventually proved himself as a copywriter, earning assignments on several major accounts.

Burrell attended a one-year Advanced Advertising Studies program at Northwestern University then went to work for Leo Burnett Advertising. Having acquired a wide variety of accounts, ranging from Betty Crocker to the British Overseas Airways Corporation, and confident of his talents, Burrell teamed with Emmett McBain in 1971, to form a new agency. The new firm, Burrell McBain Advertising, struggled at first, but major accounts were soon acquired, including McDonalds and Coca-Cola. McBain left the firm in 1974, and Burrell became sole owner, changing the firm's name to Burrell Advertising. The firm expanded rapidly in the 1980s, opening an Atlanta office and acquiring the Proctor and Gamble account in 1984. Burell's rise to prominence serves as a model in entrepreneurship and achievement in his field.
See also ENTREPRENEURS [2].

REFERENCES

Farris, King. *The Road Less Traveled By.* (http://www.utexas.edu/coc/admedium/Spring98_Practitioner/tcf.html).

Kirby, Joseph. "Casting a Wider Net." *Black Enterprise* 26 (March 199): 18.

Phelps, Shirelle, ed. *Contemporary Black Biography.* 2000.

DARIUS L. THIEME

Bush, George Washington

Bush, George Washington (1790?-April 5, 1863), pioneer. The origins and early years of George Washington Bush are clouded with obscurity. He is said to have fought in the War of 1812. A possible speculation is that he became acquainted with the Pacific Northwest as a worker for the Hudson Bay Company.

From some time in the 1820s Bush was a cattle trader in Missouri and became quite wealthy. He married a German woman in 1831, settled in Clay County, and had five sons. Seeking to escape racial prejudice, he joined the party of Michael T. Simmons in the spring of 1844 and headed towards Oregon Territory. There, Bush found that a meeting of settlers had voted to exclude blacks. After wintering at The Dalles, Bush and thirty-one others pushed on to the shore of Puget Sound.

Bush established a farm near present-day Olympia and prospered. But as a black he had no right to own land so his property was at risk. In 1853 when Washington Territory was separated from Oregon, his friends were able to pass a law in the new territorial legislature to exempt him from the provisions of the law. In 1855 Congress ratified this exemption. Bush, however, never had the right to vote because he was not legally a citizen of the United States. Nevertheless, his son William Owen Bush was elected to Washington's first state legislature in 1889.

See also OREGON [4]; WASHINGTON [5]; WEST, BLACKS IN THE [5].

REFERENCES

Green, Frank L. "George Washington Bush." In *American National Biography*, edited by John A. Garraty and Mark C. Carnes. 1999.

Greenlee, Marcia M. "George Washington Bush." In *Dictionary of American Negro Biography*, edited by Rayford W. Logan and Michael R. Winston. 1982.

Morgan, Murray. *Puget's Sound: A Narrative of Early Tacoma and the Southern Sound*. 1979.

ROBERT L. JOHNS

Bush, John Edward (November 15, 1856–December 11, 1916), politician and businessman. Born a slave in Moscow, Tennessee, Bush was sent to Arkansas at an early age, along with his mother and siblings. His mother died when he was seven, but he managed to complete high school in Little Rock's freedmen and public schools. He worked first as principal of two public high schools for African Americans, in Little Rock (1876) and in Hot Springs (1878). He returned to Little Rock in 1879.

Once back in Little Rock, Bush married and took a job as a clerk in the post office's railway service. He soon turned his attention to business and real estate and became increasingly influential in Republican politics and civil rights. In 1882, he was a co-founder of the Mosaic Templars of America, a fraternal organization that provided burial insurance, life insurance, and loans for its African American members. In 1889, he began publishing the *American Guide*, a newspaper for African Americans. He also assisted in establishing the Negro Capitol City Savings Bank. From 1898 until 1912 he served as receiver of the U.S. Land Office in Little Rock.

In 1884, Bush was a delegate to both county (Pulaski) and state (Arkansas) Republican Conventions. He was a delegate to the Republican National Convention from 1892 until 1912. Bush was vocal in his opposition to all segregationist practices and actively supported black boycotts of segregated bus lines in 1903. He combined his educational roots and his business acumen through active support of Booker T. Washington, serving for a time as vice president of the national executive committee of Washington's National Negro Business League. Bush continued his committed work until he suffered a stroke several months before his death.

See also ARKANSAS [1]; REPUBLICAN PARTY [4].

REFERENCES

Garraty, John A., and Mark C. Carnes, eds. *American National Biography*. 1999.

Logan, Rayford W., and Michael R. Winston, eds. *Dictionary of American Negro Biography*. 1982.

CARRELL P. HORTON

Butler, Thomas C. (1865–1905), soldier. Thomas Butler fought with distinction in the Indian and Spanish American Wars and in the pacification of the Philippines. Butler was born in Baltimore, Maryland. He studied to become a Roman Catholic priest but went to sea before finishing. After suffering shipwreck off Cape Hatteras in 1887, he decided to join the army. Butler enlisted in the 9th Cavalry and served in Wyoming and Nebraska and participated in the Sioux campaign of 1890–1891. He then transferred to the 25th Infantry at that time in Montana.

Butler served with the 25th Infantry during the Spanish American War. On July 1, 1898 he was with the unit of black infantrymen who took a key fort in the Spanish defenses of Santiago, Chile. One of the first to get into the fortification, Butler seized the Spanish flag. A white man dressed as an officer, perhaps a war correspondent, forced him to hand it over although Butler was able to conceal a corner of it. At the end of the war Butler was given a commission, but his unit was disbanded in 1899. He then joined as a first lieutenant a volunteer regiment formed to put down the insurgency in the Philippines. There he won on two occasions official recognition for his conduct and bravery from his regimental commander. Butler's regiment was mustered out in 1901, and he chose to remain in the Philippines where he died in June 1905. He was buried with military honors in Arlington National Cemetery.

See also INDIAN WARS [3]; SPANISH-AMERICAN WAR [5].

REFERENCES

Coston, W. Hilary. *The Spanish-American War Volunteer.* 1899.

Schubert, Frank N. *On the Trail of the Buffalo Soldier: Biographies of African Americans in the U.S. Army, 1866–1917.* 1995.

Schubert, Frank N. "Thomas C. Butler." In *Dictionary of American Negro Biography*, edited by Rayford W. Logan and Michael R. Winston. 1982.

ROBERT L. JOHNS

Butts, Calvin O. I., III (Update)

(July 22, 1949–), minister. During the 1970s and '80s, Butts earned a reputation as a community leader and activist. Butts attracted significant attention through his maverick political stance, particularly his support of independent presidential candidate Ross Perot in 1992. In 1998, Butts became the center of renewed controversy when he publicly accused New York Mayor Rudolph Giuliani of being a racist.

REFERENCE

Pooley, Eric. "The Education of Reverend Butts." *New York* (July 26, 1989): 42.

GREG ROBINSON

C

Caesar, John (? –January 18, 1837), insurrectionist, interpreter, partisan leader. Born to fugitive slave parents in Florida, Caesar grew up among the Seminoles and spoke English and Muskogee. He married a woman on one of the St. John's River plantations. Caesar's affiliation with plantation slaves facilitated his dialogue with leading slaves about supporting the Seminoles. An advisor to Emathca, the principal chief of the St. John's River Seminoles, Caesar persuaded blacks held in involuntary servitude to unite with the Seminoles against American forces. When the Second Seminole War (1835–1842) began, his clandestine agreement with the slaves proved successful.

As America's military moved to enforce the 1832 Treaty of Paynes Landing that called for the Seminole removal from Florida, the Seminoles were ready for war. In December 1835, slaves on several plantations rallied to the Seminole cause. They pillaged, burned, and ransacked the region. Caesar participated in the Battle of the Withlacoochee River. A master of the hit-and-run and surprise attack, he initiated guerrilla campaigns. On January 18, 1837, Captain Hanson's forces killed Caesar. Reported to have been of advanced age when the Second Seminole War took place, he served as interpreter, counselor, and commander of the black insurrectionists. The principal intermediary who brought the plantation slaves into the Seminole's armed conflict, Caesar not only urged them to revolt but he also organized partisan warfare as the war entered its second year and the Seminoles began experiencing difficulty.

See also INDIAN WARS [3].

REFERENCES

Porter, Kenneth Wiggins. "John Caesar: A Forgotten Hero of the Seminole War." *Journal of Negro History* 28 (January 1943): 53-65.

———. "John Caesar: Seminole Negro Partisan." *Journal of Negro History* 31 (April 1946): 190-207.

LINDA T. WYNN

Cailloux, André (1825–May 27, 1863), member Louisiana Native Guard. André Cailloux, a member of the Louisiana Native Guard, who died during the assault on the strategic Confederate strong point of Port Hudson, Louisiana, is the first black hero of the Civil War. Cailloux was born a slave in Plaquemines Parish, Louisiana, and was moved as a child to New Orleans. He learned how to roll cigars and was freed in 1836. An excellent horseman and athlete, Cailloux had also learned to read and write and became secretary of his mutual aid society. He boasted that he was the blackest man in a city where free blacks had their own caste system based on color.

When the Civil War broke out, the various mutual aid societies served as the centers for regiments of the Louisiana Native Guard. Cailloux was a captain in his. The regiments disbanded when Union forces took over New Orleans in April 1862 but were then re-formed when reinforcements did not materialize.

Federal officers were convinced that the black troops were unfit for use in combat, and the units were used mostly on work details. In May 1863 the troops demonstrated their quality in the Union efforts to take Port Hudson, a major Confederate strong point on the Mississippi. The Native Guard troops charged strong fortifications valiantly. Cailloux was slightly wounded during one charge and then killed leading his men during another. His body was not recovered until Port Hudson surrendered in July. In New Orleans Cailloux's courage was honored by an elaborate and well-attended funeral.

See also CIVIL WAR [2]; LOUISIANA [3].

REFERENCES

Mullener, Elizabeth. "Remembering Bravery." *New Orleans Times-Picayune*. 31 October 1998.

Ochs, Stephen J. *A Black Patriot and a White Priest: André Cailloux and Claude Paschal Maistre in Civil War New Orleans*. 2000.

Ripley, C. Peter. "André Callioux [sic]." In *Dictionary of American Negro Biography,* edited by Rayford W. Logan and Michael R. Winston. 1982.

ROBERT L. JOHNS

Caliver, Ambrose (February 25, 1894–January 29, 1962), educator, college administrator, public servant.

Caliver worked in academia and with the U.S. Office of Education addressing African American needs for adult literacy and academic training. Caliver was born in Saltsville, Virginia, the son of Ambrose and Cora Saunders Caliver. He graduated from Knoxville College in 1915 and received a degree in industrial arts from Tuskegee Institute (now University) in 1916. He received a degree in personnel management and administration from Harvard University in 1919. In 1920 Caliver received an M.A. degree from the University of Wisconsin and in 1930 the Ph.D. from Columbia University.

After serving as school principal in Tennessee and teacher and assistant principal in El Paso, Caliver took a teaching position at Fisk University where from 1918 to 1926 he taught manual and industrial arts. He also developed the manual arts program at Fisk and taught courses in education. He was named dean of the scholastic department in 1926 and in 1927 dean of the university, making him the first African American dean at the school.

In 1930 Caliver left Fisk and became a specialist in Negro education for the U.S. Office of Education. He held a number of positions in the office, including assistant to the U.S. Commission on Education in 1950 and chief of the Adult Education Section of the Office of Education in 1955. He made important contributions to literacy in this country, overseeing the preparation of instructional materials and training educators to work with adults. Caliver's numerous research projects in education resulted in important bulletins, pamphlets, circulars, and other items issued from his office between 1930 and 1938.

See also EDUCATION [2]; FISK UNIVERSITY [2].

REFERENCES

"Ambrose Caliver." *Ebony* 11 (1956): 40-42

Logan, Rayford W. and Michael R. Winston, eds. *Dictionary of American Negro Biography*. 1982.

Smith, Jessie Carney. *Notable Black American Men*. 1999.

JESSIE CARNEY SMITH

Cannon, Noah Calwell W. (c.1786–September 1850), author, preacher.

Cannon, an early pioneer in the A. M. E. Church, was born in Sussex County, Delaware, and died in Canonsburg, Canada. He was fourteen when a young girl in a religious class impressed upon him the necessity for conversion; when he was sixteen, he claimed to have been visited by an angel. This visitation in turn led to a vision in which he encountered both Heaven and Hell, met the Savior, and received the Call to preach. He never received a formal education, a fact he regretted.

After the death of his father, Cannon became a seaman; following this experience, he went to Philadelphia (c.1818) and became an active member of the A. M. E. Church. He also taught, became an exhorter, was licensed to preach, and traveled the A. M. E. Circuit. The New York Annual Conference appointed him missionary to New England in 1840 and later to the Toronto Circuit. In Ohio, he established an A.M.E. Church. In addition to his ministerial work, Cannon wrote *The Rock of Wisdom* (1833). It included several hymns and was designed to explain the Scriptures to readers.

See also AFRICAN AMERICAN METHODIST CHURCH [1].

REFERENCES

Berry, L. *A Century of Missions of the African Methodist Episcopal Church, 1840–1940*. 1942.

Sherman, Joan R. *Invisible Poets: Afro-Americans of the Nineteenth Century.* 1974.

HELEN R. HOUSTON

Cardozo, W[illiam] Warrick (April 6, 1905–August 11,1962), physician, pediatrician.

William Cardozo became known for his work as a pioneer investigator of sickle cell anemia. He was born in Washington, D.C., the son of prominent educator Francis L. Cardozo, Jr., and the grandson of noted South Carolina politician and educator Francis L. Cardozo. He received both his A.B. (1929) and M.D. degrees (1933) from Ohio State, followed by residencies at Cleveland's City Hospital and Chicago's Provident Hospital in 1934 and 1935. He held a General Education Board fellowship in pediatrics at Provident and at Children's Memorial Hospital. During this period, he began researching sickle cell anemia; the results of his pioneer study, "Immunologic Studies in Sickle Cell Anemia," were published in the *Archives of Internal Medicine* in October 1937.

That same year Cardozo returned to the District of Columbia, began a private practice, and became part-time instructor in pediatrics at Howard University's College of Medicine and Freedmen's Hospital. He later became an associate professor. In 1948 Cardozo was named a fellow of the American Academy of Pediatrics. For twenty years, he concentrated on gastrointestinal disorders in children. He retained his practice and for twenty-four years was school medical inspector for the District of Columbia Board of Health. His conclusions about sickle cell anemia are still valid: the disease is found almost exclusively in blacks and people of African descent, and it is inherited. Further, the presence of sickle cells in the blood does not mean that one is anemic or that the disease is fatal to all who carry it. Still, no cure has been found.

See also SCIENCE [5]; WASHINGTON, D.C. [5].

REFERENCES

Obituary. *Journal of the National Medical Association* 54 (November 1962): 730-31.

Logan, Rayford W., and Michael R. Winston, eds. *Dictionary of American Negro Biography.* 1982.

Sammons, Vivian Ovelton. *Blacks in Science and Medicine.* 1990.

JESSIE CARNEY SMITH

Carey, Mary Ann Shadd (1823–1893), abolitionist editor, educator, and attorney.

Carey was born in Wilmington, Delaware, to free parents who were active in the abolitionist movement. She became the first African American woman in North America to edit a newspaper and the first to practice law in the United States. Throughout her career she advocated that through education, thrift, and hard work black people could successfully achieve integration. Quaker-educated, Carey began a school for African Americans in Delaware and taught in neighboring states. She wrote for Frederick Douglas's *North Star* and published *Hints to Colored People of the North*, a pamphlet on black self-reliance. In 1851, while attending a lecture in Canada on the recently implemented Fugitive Slave Act, Carey met Henry Bibb, publisher of the abolitionist paper *Voice of the Fugitive*. Bibb convinced her to teach fugitive slaves in Canada West (Ontario) yet opposed her strong stance in favor of integration. She taught in Canada in the 1850s and edited her newspaper, *The Provincial Freeman*. With the outbreak of the Civil War, she returned to the United States and served as a recruitment officer for black volunteers in the Union Army. After the war she settled in Washington, D.C., where she worked as a teacher and principal. At the age of forty-one, she became the first woman to attend Howard University Law School. She completed her studies in 1871 but the university refused to grant her law degree until 1881, believing that a woman's graduation would attract negative publicity. Carey addressed the National Women's Suffrage Association in 1878 and spent her remaining years advancing the struggle for women's right to vote.

See also ABOLITION [1]; JOURNALISM [3].

REFERENCES

Hudson, Peter "Mary Ann Shadd Carey." In *Africana: The Encyclopedia of the African and African American Experience*, edited by Kwame Anthony Appiah and Henry Louis Gates, Jr. 1999.

Silverman, Jason H. "Mary Ann Shadd and the Search for Equality." In *Black Leaders of the Nineteenth Century*, edited by Leon F. Litwack and August Meier. 1991.

OMAR ALI

Carmichael, Stokely (Update) (July 29, 1941–November 15, 1998), activist.

Studies with Nkrumah of Ghana and Sé'kou Touré of Guinea confirmed his Pan-Africanism and, in 1978, moved

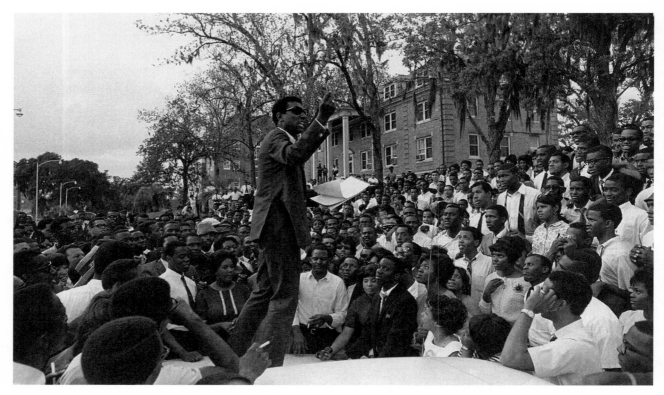

Stokely Carmichael speaking to a crowd about Black Power and the Vietnam War. (AP/Wide World Photos)

him to change his name to Kwame Toure. For the last thirty years of his life he made Conakry, Guinea, his home, and he continued his work in political education, condemning Western imperialism and promoting the goal of a unified socialist Africa. He died of prostate cancer in 1998.

REFERENCE

Smith, J.Y. "Kwame Ture, Civil Rights Activist, Dies At Age 57; As Stokely Carmichael, He Helped Lead Panthers." *The Washington Post*. November 16, 1998: C10.

GREG ROBINSON

Carter, Louis (February 20, 1876–July 16, 1941), army chaplain. Louis A. Carter was born in Auburn, Alabama, and was ordained a Baptist minister in 1899. He went on to earn a B.D. degree from Virginia Union University Divinity School in 1904 and became a pastor at First Baptist Church of Knoxville, Tennessee, the following year. In 1910 he became the eighth black chaplain in the army, serving its four black units.

Carter was a superb preacher who believed that personal contact was the key to success in his ministry. He supported sports and other recreational activities, such as vaudeville shows and debating clubs. He also worked to develop black pride both through programs about black history and through his efforts to make books about blacks available in libraries. He also saw to it that W. E. B. Du Bois's African American publication, *The Crisis*, was available, although he did on one occasion write Du Bois to protest the latter's pacifism.

Carter also dealt with the problems unique to African American troops. In 1915 in the Philippines, for example, there was no housing available for families of black soldiers below the rank of staff sergeant. Carter successfully helped the married enlisted men to secure a site on the base for housing, and was also instrumental in the financing and construction of the housing.

On April 29, 1936, Carter was the first black chaplain in the regular army to become a major. He took his retirement in February 1940 and died in Tucson, Arizona, the following year. A street at Fort Huachuca, Arizona, army base is named for him. *See also* MILITARY [4]; RELIGION [4].

REFERENCE

Stover, Earl P. "Louis A[ugustus] Carter." In *Dictionary of American Negro Biography*, edited by Rayford W. Logan and Michael R. Winston. 1982.

ROBERT L. JOHNS

Cassell, Albert Irvin (1895–1969), architect, entrepreneur, engineer, educator, planner.

For nearly fifty years Cassell was a prominent architect. He was born in Towson, Maryland, the third child of Truman and Charlotte Cassell. After graduating from high school in Baltimore, he worked his way through Cornell University and graduated in 1919 with the B.A. degree in architecture.

Cassell spent most of his professional years at Howard University, where be began in 1921 as a faculty member in the architecture department. The next year he became assistant professor and department head. He remained department head until 1928. During his administration, Cassell developed a strong School of Applied Science that ultimately developed into the College of Engineering and Architecture Cassell's career as architect began in 1919 when he and William A. Hazel designed five buildings at Tuskegee Institute (now University). While at Howard, Cassell designed eleven buildings, including three important landmarks: the Chemistry Building (1935); Frederick Douglass Memorial Hall (1935); and Founders Library (1938). Founders Library has been called the crown of his master plan for the campus. Subsequently Cassell supervised facilities on other historically black college campuses, including Virginia Union University and Morgan State College. He provided similar service to Provident Hospital and Free Dispensary, the Catholic Diocese of Washington, and the James Creek Alley Housing Development.

After Cassell's buildings at Howard, his most important contribution to the Washington, D.C., area was the Mayfair Mansion project, a seventeen-building garden-apartment complex located in the Northeast section which secured his position with middle-income African Americans for whom the complex was built.
See also ARCHITECTURE [1]; HOWARD UNIVERSITY [3]; INTELLECTUAL LIFE [3].

REFERENCES

"Built of Stern Stuff." *Washington Post*, November 25, 1995.

Logan, Rayford W., and Michael R. Winston, eds. *Dictionary of American Negro Biography*. 1991.

Robinson, Wilhelmina. *Historical Negro Biographies*. 1968.

FREDERICK D. SMITH, JR.

Chappell, Emma Carolyn Bayton (February 18, 1941–), bank founder, banking executive.

Emma Chappell has devoted her career to the banking industry, focusing on economic development of minorities. She was born in Philadelphia and educated at Berean Business Institute, Temple University, the American Institute of Banking, and Stonier Graduate School of Banking at Rutgers University.

After graduating from high school in 1959, Chappell moved into her first position in banking, as clerk-photographer at Philadelphia's Continental Bank. Next she worked as teller and loan review specialist and then completed an executive training program in 1971. On leave of absence from the bank in 1974, she developed and implemented the Model Cities Business and Commercial Project, later renamed the Philadelphia Commercial Development Project. Her bank assisted this project by helping minority entrepreneurs establish businesses in the city. In 1977 Chappell was promoted to vice-president of Continental Bank, becoming the first woman to hold the position.

Chappell took another leave from Continental in 1984 to head Jessie Jackson's Presidential campaign; she also was a founder of the Rainbow Coalition to promote racial equality. In 1990 Chappell was named chief executive officer of the United Bank of Philadelphia, an African American-owned enterprise. Under Chappell's leadership, the bank was aggressive in its capital development plan and received strong support from local business and financial leaders. Chappell saw the bank as a milestone in the local African American community. It continued to grow and in 1995 *Black Enterprise* named it Financial Company of the Year. Chappell has contributed to the economic development of Philadelphia's black community and concentrates on improving banking services in poor neighborhoods.
See also BANKING [1]; JACKSON, JESSE [3].

REFERENCES

Brown, Carolyn M. "A Bank Grows in Philly." *Black Enterprise* 25 (1995): 166-174.

Phelps, Shirelle, ed. *Contemporary Black Biography*, vol. 18. 1998.

Smith, Jessie Carney, ed *Notable Black American Women*, Book II. 1996.

JESSIE CARNEY SMITH

Chase, William Calvin (February 22, 1854–January 3, 1921), publisher. William Calvin Chase was the publisher and editor of the *Washington Bee*, published from 1882 to early 1922, a year after his death.

Chase was born in Washington, D.C. His father died when he was ten, and he took jobs selling newspapers and working around newspaper offices. His early education ended with completion of the preparatory department at Howard University. After he finished that, Chase worked at various government jobs; in addition, he worked for various newspapers serving the black community. In 1882 he founded his own paper, the *Washington Bee*. Chase was admitted to the bar in 1889, and he maintained a law practice in addition to his duties at his newspaper.

As editor of the *Washington Bee*, Chase attacked the growing racial discrimination of his era. Chase championed self-help and uplift, but he nonetheless argued against integrated education on the grounds that mixed schools would undermine racial pride.

Chase was noted for his erratic relations with other prominent blacks and often engaged in very personal attacks. For example, he labeled the National Association for the Advancement of Colored People at one point the National Association for the Advancement of Certain People. Until about 1905 he generally opposed Booker T. Washington, but when Washington began to subsidize the paper, he became a consistent and ardent defender. Between 1910 and 1920, he led a campaign against Roscoe Conkling Bruce, Washington's assistant superintendent for black schools, which resulted in Conkling's dismissal.

See also JOURNALISM [3]; WASHINGTON, D.C [5].

REFERENCES

Bruce, Dickson D., Jr. "William Calvin Chase." In *American National Biography*. edited by John A. Garraty and Mark C. Carnes. 1999.

Chase, Hal S. "W[illiam] Calvin Chase." In *Dictionary of American Negro Biography*. edited by Rayford W. Logan and Michael R. Winston. 1982.

Penn, I Garland. *The Afro-American Press and Its Editors*. 1891.

ROBERT L. JOHNS

Chase-Riboud, Barbara Dewayne (Update) (June 26, 1939–), sculptor, poet, and novelist. Chase-Riboud came to prominence as an author in 1979 with the publication of her first novel, *Sally*

Barbara Chase-Riboud. (© Jerry Bauer)

Hemings, a historical work based on Thomas Jefferson's relationship with his slave mistress. She won the Janet Heidinger Kafka Prize for fiction for that volume. Her claim that Jefferson had fathered seven children with Hemings proved extremely controversial, and she was both widely commended and criticized for her endeavor. However, she was vindicated in 1998, when DNA taken from Hemings's descendants confirmed that Jefferson had in fact fathered at least one of Hemings's children. In 1997, Chase-Riboud sued the makers of the film *Amistad*, including the director Steven Spielberg, for plagiarism, charging that the screenplay had been stolen from her work *Echo of Lions*, but in 1998 she withdrew her suit and strongly praised the film.

REFERENCE

"Chase-Riboud, Barbara." In *Contemporary Black Biography* 20. 1998.

PAMELA WILKINSON
UPDATED BY GREG ROBINSON

Chavis, Benjamin Franklin, Jr., (Muhammad) (Update) (January 22, 1948–), civil rights

Benjamin Franklin Chavis, Jr. (AP/Wide World Photos)

activist. Following his resignation from the NAACP, Chavis joined the Nation of Islam as an organizer and close adviser of Minister Louis Farrakhan. In 1995, Chavis was the principal organizer of the Million Man March. In February 1997, he announced his conversion to Islam, and he took the name Benjamin Chavis Muhammad. The United Church of Christ subsequently defrocked him. He was named by Farrakhan to lead Malcolm X's old mosque in Harlem.

REFERENCE

"Benjamin Franklin Chavis, Jr." *Religious Leaders of America*, 2nd ed. 1999.

GREG ROBINSON

Chenault, Kenneth Irvine (June 2, 1951–),

business executive, lawyer. As president of the network service provider American Express, Kenneth Chenault is in one of the most visible positions in corporate America. Born in Hempstead, New York, he is son of Hortenius Chenault, a dentist, and Ann Chenault, a dental hygienist. He graduated from Bowdoin College in 1973, then Harvard Law School in 1973.

First an associate with the corporate law firm Rogers & Wells in New York City in 1977–1979, Chenault moved to Bain & Company in 1979–1981, a consulting firm in Boston, where he was introduced to large corporations and their chief executives. He left and entered a fast track with American Express Company, first as director of strategic planning in 1981, then vice president of merchandise services in 1983, and senior vice president and general manager of the division in 1984. Between 1986 and 1995, Chenault held other top positions in the Platinum/ Gold Card Division, the Personal Card Division, the Consumer Card and Financial Services Group, and American Express Travel Related Services.

Chenault was named vice president of American Express in 1995. Two years later American Express announced that Chenault was heir apparent to the position of president and chief operating officer. The position would he his when Harvey Golub, now chair and CEO of American Express, retires in the year 2003. Throughout his career, Chenault's tenure in various positions was always brief; his change in position always came as a result of promotions and in recognition of his skilled ability to move the company forward.

See also BLACK BUSINESS COMMUNITY [1]; NEW YORK CITY [4].

REFERENCES

Bigelow, Barbara Carlisle. *Contemporary Black Biography*, vol. 4., 1993.

Smith, Jessie Carney, ed. *Notable Black American Men.* 1999.

Who's Who in America, 50th ed., 1996. 5.

JESSIE CARNEY SMITH

Chester, Thomas Morris (May 11, 1834–Sep-

tember 30, 1892), journalist, lawyer, civil rights activist, federal government official. Chester was born in Harrisburg, Pennsylvania, to George and Jane Maria Chester. He attended Allegheny Institute, later renamed Avery College; in 1856 he graduated from Thetford Academy in Vermont. Chester spent some time in Liberia where he founded and published the *Star of Liberia*.

In 1865, the *Philadelphia Press* hired Chester to report on the Civil War, thus making him one of the first black war correspondents and the first and only black war correspondent for a major daily. Writing under the name "Rollin," he was critical of white commanders of black troops and gave special attention to the bravery and dedication of these troops. He returned to Harrisburg in 1865, where he engaged in civil rights protests and became an officer in the Pennsylvania State Equal Rights League.

Chester spent some time in Liberia teaching "recaptive slaves" and emigrants. He also began to read law. Later, he traveled throughout Russia and England raising money for the Garnet Equal Rights League. When his mission ended in May of 1867, Chester enrolled in on of the four Inns of Court— London's Middle Temple—where he studied law. In 1870, he became the first black American called to the English bar. In 1873, now in New Orleans, he became the first black admitted to the Louisiana bar and he joined the state militia. The local press in 1879 attacked him for supporting the exodus of southern blacks to Kansas. Chester spent little time in New Orleans after that, and in 1881 he was the first black admitted to practice before the Pennsylvania Supreme Court. He continued to serve the legal needs of the black and poor in Louisiana, Washington, D.C., and Pennsylvania.

REFERENCES

Blackett, R. J. M., ed. *Thomas Morris Chester, Black Civil War Correspondent*. 1989.

Logan, Rayford W., and Michael R. Winston, eds. *Dictionary of American Negro Biography*. 1982.

Smith, Jessie Carney, editor. *Notable Black American Men*. 1999.

JESSIE CARNEY SMITH

Childress, Alvin (c. 1908–April, 19, 1986), actor. Born in Meridian, Mississippi, Alvin Childress was the performer who starred as Amos Jones on *The Amos n' Andy Show* (1951–1953), television's first program with an all black cast, and one of the most popular comedies in American history. The seventy-eight episode series occupied a prime time slot until CBS reluctantly pulled the show from its network line-up, bowing to pressure from the NAACP and other groups, who protested that the show was denigrating to African Americans. After the civil rights movement, nearly two decades later, African Americans began to tolerate diverse images of blackness and accepted a comedic TV series, *Sanford and Son*, that matched the caliber, flair, and popularity of *The Amos n' Andy Show*. Ironically, Childress made a guest appearance on one episode of *Sanford and Son* in 1972,

Alvin Childress, dressed as a cab driver from "The Amos 'n' Andy Show." (AP/Wide World Photos)

but prior to this role and after the cancellation of *Amos n' Andy*, the talented actor had trouble finding steady acting work. He had resorted to parking cars to earn a living before taking a job with the Los Angeles County Civil Service Commission.

Childress's TV appearances include *Perry Mason* (1964), *Banyon* (1971), *Good Times* (1974), *The Jeffersons* (1975), *Fish* (1977) and *Sister, Sister* (1982). Film credits include *Crimson Fog* (1932), *Harlem is Heaven* (1932), *Dixie Love* (1934), *Keep Punching* (1939), *Anna Lucasta* (1958), *Thunderbolt* and *Lightfoot* (1974), *The Day of the Locust* (1975), and *Bingo Long Traveling All-Stars and Motor Kings* (1976). Childress's career began on the stage with productions such as *Sweet Land* (1931), *Savage Rhythm* (1931), *Haiti* (1938), and *Natural Man* (1941).

See also AMOS 'N' ANDY [1]; TELEVISION [1].

REFERENCES

Bogle, Donald. *Blacks in American Films and TV: An Encyclopedia*. 1988.

Bogle, Donald. *Toms, Coons, Mulattoes, Mammies and Bucks: An Interpretive History of Blacks in American Film*. 1988.

Dawson, Cheryl. "An Inside Look at Alvin Childress." *Black Stars* (1975): 64-66.

Gray, John. *Blacks in Film and Television: A Pan-African Bibliography of Films, Filmmakers and Performers*. 1990.

Peterson, Bernard L. Jr. *African American Theater Directory, 1816–1960: A Comprehensive Guide to Early Black Theater Organizations, Companies, Theatres, and Performing Groups.* 1997.

Woll, Allen. *Dictionary of the Black Theater: Broadway, Off-Broadway, and Selected Harlem Theater.* 1983.

F. ZEAL HARRIS

Clark, Alexander G. (1826–May 31, 1891),

entrepreneur, religious and civil rights leader, lawyer, diplomat, politician. Clark fought for the cause of African Americans through his various affiliations; he also had a notable public career. Clark was born in Washington County, Pennsylvania, to John and Rebecca (Darnes) Clark. Although originally he had limited education, he learned the trade of barbering. He worked as bartender on a steamer then moved to Muscatine, Iowa, in 1842 and opened a barbershop. Later, he had business relationships with steamboat companies, became involved in real estate, invested his money wisely, and became a wealthy man.

In 1849 Clark cofounded the local African Methodist Episcopal Church. He devoted himself to his church and to the Prince Hall Masonry. For a while, he recruited for the Civil War, fought for soldiers' pensions, and supported such movements as women's suffrage. In 1869 he was a vice-president of the Republican State Convention of Iowa and later delegate or alternate to Republican conventions in Philadelphia and Cincinnati. Clark was owner (1884–1887) of the *Chicago Conservator* and used the paper for racial protest. He became a great orator who was referred to as the "Colored Orator of the West." In oratorical skills, some said that he was second only to his friend of forty years, Frederick Douglass.

Clark graduated from the University of Iowa Law School in 1884, then moved to Chicago where he opened a law practice. On August 8, 1890, he was appointed minister and consul-general to Liberia. Upon his death in Monrovia, his body was returned to Muscatine and given a state funeral.
See also AFRICAN METHODIST EPISCOPAL CHURCH [1]; AMBASSADORS AND DIPLOMATS [1]; DOUGLAS, FREDERICK [2].

REFERENCES

Logan, Rayford W., and Michael R. Winston, eds. *Dictionary of American Negro Biography.* 1882.

Simmons, William J. *Men of Mark.* 1887.

RAYMOND WINBUSH

Clark Atlanta University. Clark Atlanta Uni-

versity, a historically black college in Atlanta and the flagship college of the Atlanta University Consortium, was founded as Atlanta University in 1866 by officers of the American Missionary Association. Although classes were initially conducted on the elementary level, demand for secondary school facilities quickly expanded. In 1872, the University opened a college department and normal school, despite the opposition of Atlanta city officials who attempted to have a street driven through the school's campus. The University became further embattled during the Jim Crow era. In 1890, after college administrators refused to abandon integrated education, the Georgia legislature stripped Atlanta of the federal land-grant funds which had represented twenty percent of its budget, leading to a significant deficit. The campus was nearly overrun by hostile whites during the Atlanta Riot of 1906. Nevertheless, the University produced an estimated seventy-five percent of black Atlanta teachers and maintained higher admission standards than the University of Georgia. During this period, the University and its surrounding Sweet Auburn neighborhood also became home base for the black intellectuals of the "Talented Tenth," notably the renowned scholar/activist W. E. B. Du Bois, who joined Atlanta's faculty in 1897. In addition to teaching, DuBois organized the annual Atlanta University Conferences, a series of important sociological studies. After DuBois's departure in 1910, his disciple Augustus Dill continued the conferences.

During the 1920s, Atlanta's growing intellectual prominence led its trustees to dramatically reshape the University. In 1924, Atlanta began offering night and summer college courses and inaugurated a master's degree program. The following year, it eliminated all pre-college education. Finally, in 1929, Atlanta University joined Morehouse College and Spelman College, two other historically black institutions, to form the Atlanta University Center. Morehouse and Spelman took over all undergraduate curricula, and Atlanta University became devoted exclusively to graduate and professional education. The affiliates shared a common library and other resources. Morehouse president John Hope was selected to head the new center, becoming Atlanta University's first African American president. Soon after, Morris Brown College, the Atlanta School for

Social Work, and Gammon College (later the Inter-denominational Theological Center) also joined the center.

Following consolidation, Atlanta University remained a dominant force in African American higher education. In 1934, Du Bois returned to Atlanta, where he spent an additional ten years, and in 1940 he founded *Phylon*, a prestigious journal of race and culture. Other African American leaders, such as Whitney M. Young and Rev. Ralph Abernathy, also taught or were educated there. In 1960, Atlanta University students formed the shock troops for the demonstrations which desgregated Atlanta's restaurants and department stores.

Although the integration of the University of Georgia during the 1960s cut into Atlanta University Center's potential student pool, its educational prestige was unaffected, and it continued to attract important scholars to its faculty. However, the University suffered a severe budgetary crisis during the 1970s and 1980s. As a result, in 1988 it merged with Clark College, a historically black Atlanta institution, and was renamed Clark Atlanta University. In the late 1990s, Clark Atlanta University had 232 students and 317 full-time faculty.

See also ATLANTA UNIVERSITY CENTER [1]; ATLANTA, GEORGIA [1]; GEORGIA [2]; HOPE, JOHN [3]; WILKINS, J. ERNEST, JR [5].

REFERENCES

Adams, Myron W. *A History of Atlanta University*. 1930.

Bacote, Clarence Albert. *The Story of Atlanta University: A Century of Service, 1869–1969*. 1969.

GREG ROBINSON

Clarke, John Henrik (January 1, 1915–July 16, 1998), historian.

John Henrik Clarke, a founding father of Afrocentrism, was born in Union Springs, Alabama. He moved to Harlem in 1933. During the 1930s, he attempted, unsuccessfully, to publish plays and poems and began his intensive reading of African and world history under the guidance of the African-American bibliographer Arthur Schomburg. Clarke also became involved in the Young Communists League. Though he never actually joined the Communist Party, he was long active in left-wing African-American groups, such as the Harlem Writers Guild.

In 1941, Clarke entered the U.S. military, and he served throughout the war as a master sergeant in the Army Air Forces. During the postwar years, he taught African and Afro-American history at the New School for Social Research, worked as a columnist and writer, and began developing his thesis that black Americans were Africans who shared in Africa's advanced cultural and political legacy.

During the 1960s, Clarke was energized by the Civil Rights Movement. In 1962 he began a twenty-year assignment as assistant editor of the newspaper *Freedomways*. He also became a close associate of Malcolm X and in 1964 drew up the charter for Malcolm X's Organization of Afro-American Unity. Clarke also continued his historical/literary pursuits, eventually writing twenty-three books. In 1966 he edited an anthology, *American Negro Short Stories*, and two years later compiled the anthology *William Styron's Nat Turner: Ten Black Writers Respond*. In 1970, Clarke became a professor of Black Studies at Hunter College. Even after retiring in 1986, he continued to lecture and write on Africa's legacy.

See also ALABAMA [1]; HARLEM WRITERS GUILD [3]; JOURNALISM [3]; MALCOLM X [3].

REFERENCE

Bourne, St. Clair. *John Henrik Clarke: A Great and Mighty Walk* (film). 1995.

GREG ROBINSON

Clarke, Lewis G. (1815–1897), abolitionist.

Lewis G. Clarke was a fugitive slave who became an ardent abolitionist. He was born in Madison County, Kentucky, one of ten children. His grandfather and owner, Samuel Campbell, made unfulfilled promises to free the family. Clarke's father was white.

An aunt, who was notorious for her mistreatment of young slaves, claimed Clarke as part of her dowry when he was six, and he suffered the woman's cruelties for ten years. Then in 1831 Samuel Campbell died, and the family was broken up and sold at auction. Clarke became a field laborer. When he was inherited by a new owner, the man preferred to allow Clarke to hire out his time; that is, Clarke worked for wages but gave his owner most of his earnings beyond a sum to cover living expenses.

In Clarke's first attempt to escape in August 1841, he assumed the role of master to a darker-skinned companion, but they soon gave up the attempt because neither could read. Two weeks later Clarke set off alone and managed to reach Canada. He later returned to Oberlin, Ohio, in search of his brother Milton. From contact with the abolitionists there, he became an anti-slavery advocate, speaking widely and effectively. By 1861 he was living in Canada, but he returned with his children to Oberlin in 1871 after the death of his wife. Clarke died in Lexington, Kentucky, and his body was returned to Oberlin for burial. In *Uncle Tom's Cabin* Harriet Beecher Stowe based the character of George Harris on Clarke.

See also ABOLITION [1]; SLAVERY [5].

REFERENCES

Clarke, Lewis G. *Narrative of the Sufferings of Lewis Clarke, During a Captivity of more than Twenty-Five Years, Among the Algerines of Kentucky, One of the So Called Christian States of North America.* 1845.

Volk, Betty. "Lewis G. Clarke." In *Dictionary of American Negro Biography*, edited by Rayford W. Logan and Michael R. Winston. 1982.

ROBERT L. JOHNS

Clark, Joseph Samuel (1871–1944), university

president. Joseph Samuel Clark led the reestablishment of Southern University in Baton Rouge, Louisiana, in 1914 and served as president of the institution until his retirement in 1938. He saw the school grow from forty-seven students and nine teachers to fifteen hundred students and 139 teachers.

Clark was born near Sparta, Louisiana. He received a B.A. degree from Leland College, New Orleans, in 1901. In 1913 he received an M.A. from Selma University. He also did additional postgraduate study, but both of his doctorates were honorary. Clark had been a schoolteacher throughout Louisiana when he became president of Baton Rouge College, an institution supported by a local Baptist association.

Established in 1879, Southern University had a troubled existence in New Orleans. The state decided in 1912 to move the institution. On September 1, 1913, Clark was named president of the school, which began operations the following year. In 1924 the school began to offer a complete college curriculum.

Clark was a persuasive speaker who had no choice but to preach racial harmony as he built up the state financed institution. He was neat, punctual, and courteous, and he inculcated these traits in his students. He also felt that manual work built character, and until 1930 every student had to do nonacademic work for one hour daily. Beyond the bounds of the campus, Clark was active in many organizations. His son, Felton Grandison, followed him in the presidency of

Southern University and built on the legacy of his father.

See also LOUISIANA [3]; NEW ORLEANS, LOUISIANA [4].

REFERENCES

Cade, John Brother. *The Man Christened Josiah Clark, Who, As J. S. Clark Became President of a Louisiana State Land Grant College.* 1945.

"Joseph Samuel Clark." [Obituary.] *Journal of Negro History.* January 1945.

Perkins, Huel D. "J[oseph] S[amuel] Clark." In *Dictionary of American Negro Biography*, edited by Rayford W. Logan and Michael R. Winston. 1982.

ROBERT L. JOHNS

Clark, Mamie Phipps (October 18, 1917–Au-

gust 11, 1983), psychologist. Mamie Phipps Clark was born in Hot Springs, Arkansas. At the peak of the Depression, she won a merit scholarship to Howard University (Washington, D.C.) Having encountered gender discrimination in mathematics, Clark was persuaded by her future husband, Kenneth, to go into psychology.

Clark received a B.A. from Howard in 1938 and a M.A. in 1939, having conducted research in New York on self-identification in black children. In 1940, Clark and her husband, who was her research partner, were awarded a Rosenwald Fellowship to continue their work. She entered Columbia University, where she received a Ph.D. in psychology in 1943. She and her husband, who had received his Ph.D. a year earlier, were the first African Americans to receive doctorates in psychology from Columbia.

Prejudice confronted Clark at Columbia and during her job search. Although the Clarks published several articles related to school desegregation during the 1940s, Clark's early post-graduate jobs did not match her qualifications. While working as a research psychologist with the armed services from 1945 to 1946, Clark did psychological testing at a New York shelter for homeless girls. This work revealed the paucity of psychological services for minorities and led to the Clarks' founding Northside Center for Child Development in 1946, the first full-time child guidance center to be located in Harlem and the first to include educational services. The Clarks' "doll study," which investigated black children's racial preferences, was among the Clark studies cited in the 1954 *Brown v. Board of Education* decision to overturn segregation. Clark was given an Alumni Award by Columbia in 1972.

See also HOWARD UNIVERSITY [3]; PSYCHOLOGY AND PSYCHIATRY [4].

REFERENCES

Hine, Darlene Clark, ed. *Facts on File Encyclopedia of Black Women in America*, vol. 12. 1997.

Sammon, Vivian Ovelton. *Blacks in Science and Medicine*. 1990.

CARRELL P. HORTON

Clay, Cassius. *See* Ali, Muhammad.

Cleage, Albert B., Jr. [Jaramogi Abebe Agyeman]

(June 13, 1911–February 20, 2000), clergyman. Albert B. Cleage was born on June 13,1911, and graduated from Wayne State University in 1937 with a degree in sociology. He received a divinity degree from Oberlin in 1943, the year he married Doris Graham. (One of the two daughters of this union is Pearl Cleage, the noted author.) The couple divorced in 1955.

After service as a Congregational minister in Kentucky, California, and Massachusetts, Cleage became pastor of St. Mark's Community Church in Detroit, renamed Central United Church of Christ in 1953.

Albert Cleage. (AP/Wide World Photos)

There he became increasingly involved in political and community activism as he grew convinced that white resistance blocked black advancement and that blacks could depend only on their own efforts. In 1967 Cleage unveiled a twenty-foot portrait of a black Madonna with Jesus at his church, and changed its name to the Shrine of the Black Madonna.

This church became the mother church of the Black Christian Nationalist Movement, which called for economic self-sufficiency in the black community and presented the figure of Jesus as a black revolutionary. Other churches across the country came to espouse the same philosophy, and the movement soon numbered 50,000 members. Cleage expounded on his theology in *The Black Messiah* (1968) and *Black Christian Nationalism* (1972). In the early 1970s he adopted the name Jaramogi Abebe Agyeman. Cleage's political organization, Black Slate, Inc., was very influential in Detroit politics, particularly in the 1973 election of Coleman Young as Detroit's first African American mayor.

See also PAN AFRICAN ORTHODOX CHURCH [4].

REFERENCES

"Albert Cleage Is Dead at 88; Led Black Nationalist Church." *New York Times*, 27 February 2000.

Brennan, Carol. "Jaramogi Abebe Agyeman." In *Contemporary Black Biography*, vol. 10, edited by L. Mpho Mabunda. 1996.

"Rev. Albert B. Cleage, Jr., Founder of Black Liberation Theology, Dies." [Obituary at Shrine of the Black Madonna Bookstore and Cultural Center.] http://www.shrinebookstore.com/#Jaramogi Robert L. Johns.

ROBERT L. JOHNS

Cleage, Pearl

(Dec 7, 1948–), writer. Pearl Cleage, whose plays, essays, poetry, and fiction address issues relevant to African-American women, garnered attention in the early 1980s when she received an Audelco playwrighting award for *Hospice* (1983), a one-act play about a strained relationship between a daughter and her mother who is fighting cancer. Strong praise and criticism came for the militant stance against sexism of *Flyin West* (1992), a portrait of five African-American female homesteaders. This work established Cleage as a worthy yet controversial writer, and performances of her work quickly multiplied in theaters around the country.

Born in Springfield, Massachusetts and raised in Detroit, Michigan, Cleage studied playwriting at Howard University, Washington D.C. (1966–1969) and received her B.A. from Spelman in Atlanta, Georgia (1971). Later she pursued graduate-level creative writing in the West Indies and Afro-American studies at Atlanta University. She held positions as executive producer for WXIA Atlanta (1972–1973), press secretary to Atlanta's first black mayor, Maynard Jackson (1974–1976) and instructor at Emory University (1978).

Writing by Cleage has appeared in *Essence*, *Ms.*, and *Atlanta Gazette* and numerous play anthologies, many of which are collections of dramas written by women. She is the author of two books of poetry, *We Don't Need No Music* (1971), and *Dear Dark Faces* (1980), but she is most well known for the plays, *Flyin' West* and *Blues for an Alabama Sky* (1992), and two collections of her essays on sexism and racism; *Mad At Miles: A Black Woman's Guide to Truth*, and *Deals with the Devil and Other Reasons to Riot*.
See also DRAMA [2].

REFERENCES

American Theater 9, no. 8 (1992); 11.

LaBlanc, Michael L. ed. *Contemporary Black Biography: Profiles from the International Black Community*. 1992.

May, Hal and James G. Lesniak, eds. *Contemporary Authors, New Revision Series*, vol. 27. 1989.

Peterson, Jane T. and Suzanne Bennett. *Women Playwrights of Diversity: A Bio-Bibliographical Sourcebook*. 1997.

F. ZEAL HARRIS

Clem, Charles Douglass (July 10, 1876–1934),

poet and writer. He was born in Johnson City, Tennessee. He started his schooling in Kentucky and finished his elementary curriculum in Oklahoma. There is a claim that he graduated from Greenville College (now Tusculum), Greenville, Tennessee, in 1898, but there is no evidence that he ever attended the school.

Clem's career was varied: he worked in Kentucky coal mines, taught school in Oklahoma for two years, and edited the *Western World* (Oklahoma) in 1901–1902. He worked as an assistant steward in the Elks club of Chanute, Kansas and then became editor of the *Coffeyville* (Kansas) *Vindicator* in 1904. In 1907 he worked for the Santa Fe Railway before becoming in 1909 head of the linoleum and rug department of the Rosenthal Department Store in Chanute. Clem held this position until 1926. In 1929 he was doing janito-

rial work for the Rosenthal Mercantile Company. Clem enjoyed some standing in the local African American community, serving as president of the Chanute chapter of the NAACP and as an officer in the Prince Hall Masons.

Clem's publications include two volumes of poetry, *Rhymes of a Rhymster* (1901) and *A Little Souvenir* (1901). Prose and poetry were included in *The Upas Tree of Kansas* (1917). In non-fiction he published *Oklahoma, Her People and Professions* in 1892 and *Fourteen Years in Metaphysics* in 1913. These works have been little studies. At some point in his life he lectured extensively on "metaphysical science" and gave poetry recitals in Colorado, Kansas, and Oklahoma.
See also LITERATURE [3].

REFERENCES

Rush, Theressa Gunnels, and others. *Black American Writers Past and Present*. 1975.

Sherman, Joan R. "A Poet With a Purpose." *Negro History Bulletin*, November 1971.

ROBERT L. JOHNS

Cleveland, Ohio (Update).

Equality remained a distant dream for most black Clevelanders at the end of the century. In 1999, an urban affairs study found that Cleveland was, after Atlanta, the most racially segregated metropolis in the United States. Educational achievement among African Americans remained low. In 1996, Mayor Michael P. White implemented a popular "school-choice" voucher program, which provided $2,500 per year in public funding for poor parents, who were thus unable to send their children to private and religious schools. However, in May of 2000, a federal court ruled that the voucher program was unconstitutional.

REFERENCES

Davis, Russell H. *Black Americans in Cleveland*.

Kusmer, Kenneth. *A Ghetto Takes Shape: Black Cleveland, 1870–1930*. 1976.

Porter, Philip W. *Cleveland: Confused City on a Screw*. 1976.

Van Tassel, David D., and John J. Grabowski, eds. *The Encyclopedia of Cleveland History*. 1987.

GREG ROBINSON

Clough, Inez (c. 1870–November 24, 1933),

actress. Little is known of Inez Clough's life until she appeared on stage for the first time in the show

Oriental America in 1896. This production went to England the following year, and Clough remained there when it closed, working in music halls and also in pantomimes. She then returned to the United States in 1906 and found work in a succession of black musicals: *Shoo-Fly Regiment* (1906), *Abyssinia* (1907), *Bandana Land* (1908), and *Mr. Lode of Koal* (1909). This genre of theater declined after 1909, and Clough worked in vaudeville and gave concerts. In 1916 she joined the Lafayette Players, a stock company giving abridged versions of popular plays.

Clough had a part in the production of *Three Negro Plays*, by white author Ridgely Torrence, which opened on April 5, 1917. These one-act plays were the first serious dramas presented in a Broadway theater by a black cast. She was named one of the ten best actresses of the year for her role as Procula in "Simon the Cyrenian." She went on to appear in *Chocolate Dandies* (1924), *Earth* (1927), *Harlem, an Episode of Life in New York's Black Belt* (1929), and *Wade in the Water* (1929). Her distinguished acting career also included roles in three movies: *The Simp* (1921), *Ties of Blood* (1921), and *The Crimson Fog* (1932). One of her last projects was as a featured voice in a radio series about 'life among colored folk' which ran for more than a year beginning in late 1930. On November 24, 1933, Clough died after a long illness.

See also DRAMA [2].

REFERENCES

Johns, Robert L. "Inez Clough." In *Notable Black American Women, Book II*, edited by Jessie Carney Smith. 1996.

Johnson, James Weldon. *Black Manhattan*. 1940.

Kellner, Bruce. *The Harlem Renaissance*. 1982.

Tanner, Jo A. *Dusky Maidens*. 1992.

ROBERT L. JOHNS

Cochran, Johnnie L., Jr.

Cochran, Johnnie L., Jr. (October 2, 1937–), lawyer. Cochran gained national recognition as a primary defense lawyer for O. J. Simpson in the former football star's trial for the double murder of his ex-wife and her friend. Cochran was born in Shreveport, Louisiana. His family moved to Los Angeles, where he attended public schools, the University of California, Los Angeles (B.A., 1959), and Loyola Marymount University School of Law (J.D., 1962).

Cochran began his career as deputy city attorney for the City of Los Angeles (1963), entered private

Johnnie Cochran, 1995. (Archive Photos, Inc.)

practice (1965), became the first African-American assistant district attorney of Los Angeles County (1978), and in 1978, returned to private practice as head of The Cochran Firm, specializing in personal injury plaintiff's tort law. His career has been influenced by Martin Luther King, Jr.'s admonition, "If you don't stand for something, you'll fall for anything," and his own belief that one must question the "official" version of events.

As a result of this philosophy, he has represented and successfully defended many high profile personalities including: Elmer "Geronimo" Pratt, Michael Jackson, Snoop Doggy Dog, and Jim Brown. His outside work includes adjunct professor at the Los Angeles School of Law and Loyola University School of Law, and Chairman of the Rules Committee of the Democratic National Convention (1994). Cochran became the first lawyer to win both the Criminal Trial Lawyer of the Year Award and Los Angeles Civil Trial Lawyer of the Year Award (1990). Cochran's life story is detailed in his autobiography, *Journey to Justice* (1996).

See also LAWYERS [3]; O.J. SIMPSON TRIAL [S]; SIMPSON, O.J. [5].

REFERENCES

Mabunda, Mpho, and Shirelle Phelps, eds. *Contemporary Black Biography*, vol. 11. 1996.

Smith, Jessie Carney, ed. *Notable Black American Men*. 1999.

HELEN R. HOUSTON

Collins, Cardiss Robertson (September 24, 1931–), Congresswoman. Collins is the first African American woman to serve in the U. S. Congress. Born in St. Louis, Cardiss Robertson moved with her family to Detroit when she was ten years old. She studied accounting at Northwestern University and in 1958 married George Washington Collins, a local politician. Collins helped to organize campaigns for her husband. Her own career in politics began when she became Democratic committeewoman in Chicago's twenty-fourth ward.

After U.S. Congressman George Collins died in 1972, Cardiss Collins resigned her position with the Illinois Department of Revenue, ran for his seat, and won handily. She began her new position on June 5, 1973. In 1979 she became the first woman to chair the Congressional Black Caucus. Two years later she became the first African American and the first woman to be appointed Democratic whip-at-large. In the mid-1980s, she led inquiries into the employment practices of the airline industry. She also investigated college sports and pressed colleges and universities to meet the mandates of Title IX of the Educational Amendments of 1972 regarding women athletes. The NCAA yielded to her prodding and moved to bring about gender equity in sports. Collins introduced the Non-Discrimination in Advertising Act aimed to correct injustices against minority-owned media. In 1993 she coauthored the Child Safety Protection Act that set standards for bicycle helmets and required warning labels on potentially dangerous toys.

Throughout her political career, Collins has been a strong advocate of civil rights, the rights of women and the poor, and of universal health insurance. She wrote the resolution that designated October as National Breast Cancer Awareness Month.
See also CONGRESSIONAL BLACK CAUCUS [2]; DEMOCRATIC PARTY [2].

REFERENCES

Hine, Darlene Clark, ed. *Black Women in America*, vol. 1. 1993.

Mabunda, L. Mpho, ed. *Contemporary Black Biography*, vol. 10. 1996.

Smith, Jessie Carney, ed. *Notable Black American Women*. 1992.

JESSIE CARNEY SMITH

Colored Farmers' Alliance. Colored Farmers' Alliance, an agrarian organization founded in Houston County, Texas, in 1886, the Colored Farmers' Alliance became the largest organization of primarily black farmers and agricultural laborers in the late nineteenth century. It began by espousing self-help and economic cooperation but took a series of radical measures with lobbying efforts, boycotts, and calls for strikes as it met resistance from local authorities and the segregated Southern Farmers' Alliance.

Within five years the Colored Alliance spread to every southern state and maintained an estimated membership of 1,200,000, of whom 300,000 were women. African Americans who joined the Colored Alliance were previously active in the Grange, the Agricultural Wheel, and the Knights of Labor. Robert M. Humphrey, a white Baptist minister and former Confederate soldier, served as the organization's General Superintendent and national spokesperson. In 1891 the Colored Alliance launched a national cotton pickers' strike, demanding a minimum of one dollar per hundred pounds. The strike was broken by the Southern Alliance leadership and local planters. Frustrated members became active in independent electoral politics. The organization voted unanimously to endorse the failed Lodge Bill, for federal supervision of elections. The Colored Alliance served as the primary network for recruitment and development of black populists in the People's Party, the most successful third party in the 1890s. As the new party grew, the Colored Alliance began to dissolve, but its tradition of black agrarian radicalism was revived in the Southern Tenant Farmers' Union and the Alabama Sharecroppers Union in the 1930s.
See also LABOR AND LABOR UNIONS [3].

REFERENCES

Abromowitz, Jack. "Accommodation and Militancy in Negro Life 1876–1916." Ph.D. dissertation, Columbia University. 1950.

Gaither, Gerald H. *Blacks and the Populist Revolt: Ballots and Bigotry in the "New South."* 1977.

Goodwyn, Lawrence C. "The Populist Response to Black America." In *Democratic Promise: The Populist Moment in America.* 1976.

OMAR ALI

Combs, Sean "Puffy" (November 4, 1969–), rapper, producer, songwriter, entrepreneur. Sean "Puffy" Combs was born on November 4, 1969, the son of a well-known street hustler who was murdered when Combs was three. Nicknamed "Puffy" for his exaggerated 'huffing and puffing' displays of anger as a

Sean "Puffy" Combs, speaking at a pre-Grammy party. (AP/Wide World Photos)

child, Combs attended Howard University in Washington, D.C., where he became a successful party and concert promoter. He returned to New York after two years and convinced Andre Harrell-then president of Uptown Records-to give him an internship. Combs worked ardently, and within a year Harrell promoted him to vice president of promotion.

At Uptown, Combs established himself as a producer for Mary J. Blige and Jodeci. After an argument with Harrell in 1993, he formed his own label-Bad Boy Records. That year he negotiated a $15 million deal with Arista Records that granted him full creative control and distribution. His artists-Lil Kim, Notorious B.I.G., Total, and Mase-sold millions of albums, and his own 1997 album, *No Way Out*, sold over seven million copies. In 1997 he was responsible for nearly sixty percent of the year's hit pop songs.

While he is often criticized for his reliance on well-known samples, his musical and business accomplishments are undeniable. He owns two successful restaurants and a clothing line, and publishes *Notorious* magazine. His Daddy's House social program is a non-profit charity organization that services inner city children and the homeless. At the close of 1999,

however, Combs ran into legal trouble on weapons charges stemming from a nightclub shooting incident. *See also* MUSIC [4]; RAP [4]; RECORDING INDUSTRY [4].

REFERENCES

Manheim, James. "Sean 'Puffy' Combs." In *Contemporary Black Biography*, Vol. 17, edited by Shirelle Phelps. 1998.

Muhammed, Tariq K. "Hip-Hop Moguls: Beyond the Hype." *Black Enterprise*. December 1999: 79-85.

RACHEL ZELLARS

Commission on Interracial Cooperation.

In the wake of the racially motivated violence that swept across the United States in the Red Summer of 1919, The Commission on Interracial Cooperation (CIC) was organized to promote more harmonious relationships between the races, especially in the South. Based in Atlanta, and directed by Will Alexander, a white Southerner, the CIC encouraged more equitable treatment of African Americans through a variety of initiatives including leadership training for blacks and whites and by sponsoring research and education on issues of race in Southern life. The CIC also promoted its agenda through its monthly organ called the *Southern Frontier*.

Organized on state and local levels, the CIC brought together moderate and liberal whites with respected members of African-American communities to address racial issues. In contrast to more radical organizations such as the Southern Conference for Human Welfare, the CIC maintained a relatively cautious position, addressing, for instance, cases of discrimination, but failing to formally challenge segregation. The women's division launched a related group, The Association of Southern Women for the Prevention of Lynching, which played an important role in the battle against lynching.

Despite some successes, the CIC never appealed to a wide audience in either black or white communities. By the 1940s, interest in the organization stagnated while many of the whites involved with the CIC took on roles in New Deal initiatives. Despite some efforts to resurrect the CIC, the organization was dismantled in early 1944, when a new group, the Southern Regional Council, was created to take its place.
See also ATLANTA RIOT OF 1906 [1]; ASSOCIATION OF SOUTHERN WOMEN FOR THE PREVENTION OF LYNCHING [S]; SOUTHERN REGIONAL COUNCIL [5].

REFERENCES

Egerton, John. *Speak Now Against the Day: The Generation Before the Civil Rights Movement in the South*. 1994.

Franklin, John Hope. *From Slavery to Freedom: A History of African Americans*. Seventh Edition. 1994.

Sullivan, Patricia. *Days of Hope: Race and Democracy in the New Deal Era*. 1996.

PATRICK DICKSON

Connerly, Ward (June 15, 1939–), businessman, activist.

Connerly rose from virtual obscurity in 1996 when, as chairman of the of the California Civil Rights Initiative (CCRI), he led a successful fight to roll back affirmative action policies in the state. His contempt for racial and minority preferences, set-asides, and quotas has thrust him into the national spotlight and made him a controversial figure, especially within the black community.

Connerly was born to a poor family in Leesville, Louisiana. His father left home when he was a year old and his mother died when he was four. Subsequently, he was raised by relatives. He attended American

Ward Connerly. (AP/Wide World Photos)

River Junior College, then Sacramento State College, where he earned a B.A. degree in political science.

A member of the Republican Party in 1969, Connerly was appointed to the University of California Board of Regents, where in July 1995 he assisted in abolishing the university's race-based system of admissions preferences. Then as head of CCRI, Connerly took on the problematic passage of Proposition 209, designed to prevent the state from providing preferential treatment to minorities in the areas of public employment, public education, and public contracting. Connerly helped the CCRI collect nearly 700,000 of the one million signatures needed to get the initiative before voters. In November 1996, Proposition 209 passed, making Connerly a highly lauded and highly criticized figure.

Subsequently, Connerly acted as chairman of the American Civil Rights Institute, a national, not-for-profit organization whose aim is to educate the public about the long-term consequences inherent in granting racial and gender preferences.

See also AFFIRMATIVE ACTION [1]; CALIFORNIA [1]; REPUBLICAN PARTY [4].

REFERENCES

Mabunda, L. Mpho, and Shirelle Phelps, eds. *Contemporary Black Biography*, vol. 14. 1997.

"Ward Connerly Biography." http://www.yaf.org/speakers/connerly.html.

Wood, Daniel B. "Why a Man Who Knows Racism Fights Affirmative Action." *Christian Science Monitor*, March 1, 1996, p. 1.

KEVIN C. KRETSCHMER

Conyers, John, Jr. (Update) (May 16, 1929–), Congressman.

Conyers has served as chairman of the Government Operations Committee, and has also served on the House Small Business Committee and the Speaker's Task Force on Minority Set-Asides. In 1998, as the ranking Democrat on the Judiciary Committee, Conyers was an outstanding opponent of the impeachment of President Bill Clinton.

REFERENCE

"John Conyers." In *Notable Black American Men*. 1998.

GREG ROBINSON

Cook, George F. T. (June 18, 1835–1912), educator.

George F. T. Cook was born in Washington,

John Conyers. (AP/Wide World Photos)

D.C. A son of the Rev. John F. Cook, Sr., a prominent clergyman and educator who had been a slave, Cook received his early education at the school his father founded for black children. He entered Oberlin College in 1853 but returned to Washington after his father's death in 1855, to join with his brother, John, Jr., in continuing the family-run school.

The Cook school closed in 1867, and in 1868 Cook was appointed Superintendent of the Colored Public Schools of Washington and Georgetown. He held this position until 1900. During his years of service, the black public schools grew from a staff of fifty teachers to 352 and from an average student attendance of 2,532 to a total of 12,748 students.

Cook's achievements as superintendent occurred despite some problems. Governmental control of the African American system was transferred several times. In 1873 control passed from the U. S. Department of the Interior to the government of the District of Columbia. The territorial government of the District was abolished in 1874 in favor of a three-commissioner system. Cook was re-appointed superintendent after both of these changes. In 1900, however, black and white schools were placed under the control of a single white superintendent, with Cook assigned

to be one of the superintendent's two assistants. Cook resigned his position when this change was made. Under Cook's leadership, the Washington black school system was considered to have the highest quality of any Negro system in the United States.

See also EDUCATION [2]; WASHINGTON, D.C [5].

REFERENCE

Logan, Rayford W., and Michael R. Winston, eds. *Dictionary of American Negro Biography*. 1982.

CARRELL P. HORTON

Cook, John Francis, Jr.

Cook, John Francis, Jr. (September 21, 1833–January 20, 1910), public official. John Francis Cook, Jr., was born in Washington, D.C., a son of John F. Cook, Sr., a prominent African American educator and clergyman. He received his early schooling at Union Seminary, founded by his father, and attended Oberlin College from 1853 until the death of his father in 1855.

Cook and his brother George assumed control of Union Seminary when their father died. Cook, Jr., remained with the school until Washington opened black public schools in 1867. Subsequently, he took a clerkship in the District tax collection office. In 1874 he was appointed tax collector, a position he held for the next ten years. He also served as a justice of the peace for seven years (1869–1876).

Cook was active in Republican politics and in business. He was elected to the Washington board of aldermen the first year blacks were allowed to vote (1868) and served as a delegate to the Republican national convention three times. In business, he amassed considerable wealth by investing in real estate.

Cook did not desert education. He fought for public support for black schools and for school integration. He served on the District of Columbia Board of Education from 1906 until a few months before he died and was a trustee of predominantly black Howard University for thirty-five years.

The John F. Cook, Jr., family was part of Washington's black elite. Cook did not, however, forget the black community. He worked to promote advancement of this community in all areas. He served as a Grand Master of the Eureka Lodge, as president of the Coleridge-Taylor Choral Society, and as trustee of the Frederick Douglass Memorial and Historical Association.

See also EDUCATION [2]; WASHINGTON, D.C. [5].

REFERENCES

Garraty, John A., and Mark C. Carnes, eds. *American National Biography*, vol. 5. 1999.

Logan, Rayford W., and Michael R. Winston, eds. *Dictionary of American Negro Biography*. 1982.

CARRELL P. HORTON

Cook, John Francis, Sr.

Cook, John Francis, Sr. (1810–March 21, 1855), educator and clergyman. John Francis Cook, Sr., was born a slave in Washington, D.C. When he was sixteen, an aunt purchased his freedom, and he became a shoemaker's apprentice. In 1831 he began work in the U.S. Land Office. After studying on his own and attending school, he was able in 1834 to take charge of the school he had attended and renamed it Union Seminary. Cook headed Union Seminary for the rest of his life, leaving it only once, when an anti-Negro riot in 1835 caused him to leave Washington for a year in Columbia, Pennsylvania.

Cook began to study for the ministry in 1836, preaching in an A.M.E. church and helping to organize the Union Bethel Church before leaving to found a Presbyterian church in 1840. The First Colored Presbyterian Church of Washington was organized officially in 1841, with Cook as its pastor for thirteen years. He was ordained as a Presbyterian minister in 1843, after spending more than a year studying for the required theology examination. He is reputed to have been Washington's first African American Presbyterian minister.

Cook did not confine his activities to education and religion. He was active in the Negro Convention Movement, in which he held an office twice; was a charter member of the local chapter of the Grand United Order of Odd Fellows; and was a founder of a cemetery (Harmony) for blacks in Washington.

Cook was married twice. Sources disagree on the number of his children, citing either five or seven, but those who lived to adulthood followed in their father's footsteps and became community leaders.
See also EDUCATION [2]; RELIGION [4]; WASHINGTON, D.C [5].

REFERENCES

Garraty, John A., and Mark C. Carnes, eds. *American National Biography*, vol. 5. 1999.

Logan, Rayford W., and Michael R. Winston, eds. *Dictionary of American Negro Biography*. 1982.

CARRELL P. HORTON

Corrothers, James David

Corrothers, James David (July 2, 1869–February 12, 1917), writer, minister. Corrothers was born in Cass County, Michigan, of Scotch, Irish, and Indian descent and reared in South Haven, Michigan, by his paternal grandfather. He attended public school (1874–1883), followed that by working in a variety of jobs, and then attended Northwestern University (1890–1893), and Bennett College, in Greensboro, North Carolina. He married Fanny Clemens, who died, along with one of their two sons, of tuberculosis around 1898. He married again and divorced, and married his third wife, Rosina B. Harvey, in 1906, with whom he had another son.

Upon getting a job in the late 1880s with the *Chicago Tribune*, Corrothers' first article was rewritten and published under the name of a white writer. His disagreement toward this action led to his being fired. In 1894, he created the character Sandy Jenkins, around whom he built a number of sketches that were published in the *Chicago Evening Journal*. As a result of the racism he experienced, his lack of money, and his belief that the church could aid black people, he entered the ministry. He was ordained a Methodist minister (1894), later became a Baptist leader, and then became a Presbyterian minister (1914). His poems appeared in numerous publications. For the most part, his dialect poetry was printed in the white press and his Standard English poetry was printed in the black press. His publications include a 1902 collection of short fiction, *The Black Cat Club: Negro Humor & Folklore* (1902), *Selected Poems* (1907) and *The Dream and the Song* (1914). In the year before his death, he wrote his autobiography, *In Spite of the Handicap*.
See also DIALECTIC POETRY [2]; JOURNALISM [3]; LITERATURE [3]; RELIGION [4].

REFERENCES

Barton, Rebecca Chalmers. *Witnesses for Freedom: Negro Americans in Autobiography*. 1948.

Logan, Rayford W., and Michael R. Winston, eds. *Dictionary of American Negro Biography*. 1982.

Yarbrough, Richard. "James D. Corrothers." *DLB: Afro-American Writers Before the Harlem Renaissance*, ed. By Trudier Harris and Thadious M. Davis. 1986.

HELEN R. HOUSTON

Cosby, William Henry, Jr. "Bill" (Update)

Cosby, William Henry, Jr. "Bill" (Update) (July 12, 1937–), comedian and philanthropist. In 1995, Cosby produced another unsuccessful syndicated series, *The Cosby Mysteries*. In 1996, he

Bill Cosby. (AP/Wide World Photos)

began a new hit series, *Cosby*, in which he played a working-class man from Queens, New York.

In 1997, Cosby's life was shattered when his son Ennis was robbed and murdered in Los Angeles. (Mikail Markhasev, a Russian immigrant, was convicted of the murder in 1998.) In the fall of 1997, Cosby was the target of an extortion plot by Autumn Jackson, an African-American woman who threatened to reveal that Cosby was her father unless he paid her. At Jackson's extortion trial, Cosby was forced to admit to an extramarital affair with Jackson's mother, but he denied he was Jackson's father. After Cosby's assertion was confirmed by DNA testing, Jackson was convicted. In 1998, he began a new television series, *Kids Say the Darnedest Things*.

REFERENCE

"William Henry Cosby, Jr." In *Encyclopedia of World Biography*, 2nd ed. 1999.

GREG ROBINSON

Cotter, Joseph Seamon, Jr. (September 2, 1895–February 3, 1919), poet. Cotter, the son of Maria F. and Joseph Seamon Cotter, Sr., poet and educator, was born in Louisville, Kentucky. His early life was spent surrounded by poetry and books in his father's library. He learned to read at an early age, influenced by his older sister, Florence Olivia. Because of her, he entered Fisk University (Nashville,

Tennessee) where he spent a year and a half before being stricken by tuberculosis. His sister soon returned home and died of the same disease, an event that prompted him to turn to writing poetry.

His first poem was written upon her death, "To Florence." His poetry anticipates the Harlem Renaissance poetry in its use of traditional form, free verse, and experimentation. The themes are racial pride, identity, heritage, love, color, and freedom. Titles of poems which appear in his collection, *The Band of Gideon and Other Lyrics* (1918), are indicative of his themes: "The Mulatto to His Critics," "Is this the Price of Love?" "Is it Because I Am Black?" "Sonnet to Negro Soldiers" appears in the June 1918, "Soldiers' Number" of the *Crisis* and speaks of the black man's bravery in both the war and on the homefront, the death of prejudice through bloodshed, and ultimately freedom. His one act play, "On the Fields of France" in the *Crisis* (June 1920) and poems in the *A. M. E. Zion Quarterly Review* (1920, 1921) were published posthumously.

See also LITERATURE [3]; LOUISVILLE, KENTUCKY [3].

REFERENCES

Brawley, Benjamin. *The Negro Genius.* 1972..

Payne, James Robert. "Joseph Seamon Cotter, Jr." *DLB: Afro-American Writers Before the Harlem Renaissance,* ed. by Trudier Harris and Thadious M. Davis. 1986.

HELEN R. HOUSTON

Cotter, Joseph Seamon, Sr. (February 2, 1861–March 14, 1949), educator, writer, civic leader. Cotter, a poet, was a contemporary of Paul L. Dunbar, the author of nine publications, the father of a talented poet who died early, and a proponent of Booker T. Washington's philosophy. He published in newspapers and periodicals and has been frequently anthologized. Cotter was born in Nelson County, Kentucky, moved to Louisville with his mother and remained there to the end of his life. He could read at four, left school at eight, and worked as a manual laborer; at twenty-two, he entered night school and after ten months began teaching, but continued his educational pursuits.

Cotter served as both a model teacher and principal and promoted racial pride and uplift. He was a storyteller, initiated a storytelling contest, and maintained membership in the Louisville Colored Orphans Society, Kentucky Negro Educational Association, Association for the Study of Negro Life and History,

Storytellers League, and the National Association of Colored People (NAACP).

Cotter wrote in both dialect and standard English and was the author of such works as *A Rhyming* (1895); *Links of Friendship* (1898); *Caleb, the Degenerate, a Play in Four Acts; a Study of the Types Customs, and Needs of the American Negro* (1903); *A White Song and a Black Song* (1909); *A Negro Tale* (1912); *Collected Poems* (1938); *Sequel to the "Pied Piper of Hamlin"* (1939); and *Negroes and Others at Work and Play* (1947). His early work reflected traditional forms and addressed racial concerns, personalities, and religion.

See also DIALECTIC POETRY [2]; EDUCATION [2]; LITERATURE [3].

REFERENCES

Brooks, A. Russell. "Joseph Seamon Cotter, Sr." *Afro-American Writers before the Renaissance*, edited Trudier Harris and Thadius M. Davis. 1984.

Logan, Rayford W., and Michael R. Winston, eds. *Dictionary of American Negro Biography*. 1982.

Sherman, Joan R. *Invisible Poets: Afro-Americans of the Nineteenth Century*. 1974.

HELEN R. HOUSTON

Crockett, George William, Jr. (August 10, 1909–September 7, 1997), champion of civil rights. Born in Jacksonville, Florida, he took his B.A. degree at Morehouse College in 1931 and his law degree at the University of Michigan School of Law in 1934. In 1939 he became the first African American attorney at the United States Department of Labor in Washington, D. C. President Franklin D. Roosevelt appointed him hearings officer of the Fair Employment Practices Committee in 1943. In 1944 he became head of the United Auto Workers Fair Employment Practices Office, returning to private practice in Detroit in 1946.

In 1949 Crockett undertook the defense of eleven communists charged under the Smith Act; his vigorous defense to four months in jail for contempt of court and a narrow escape from disbarment. In 1964 Crockett again demonstrated his commitment to civil rights by becoming director of Project Mississippi for the National Lawyers Guild. He sought election to Detroit Recorder's Court in 1960. He won a six-year term then and a second in 1972.

As a judge Crockett attracted remark for his lenient treatment of first-time offenders ad his concern for

civil rights. In 1969 a policeman was killed outside a black church where a meeting of black separatists was underway. The police stormed the church and arrested 140 persons. Crockett went to the police station, declared court in session, and began freeing those he deemed held without probable cause. Almost all were released.

Crockett's popularity with blacks in Detroit was shown by his election to the House of Representative in 1980 with 98 percent of the vote. He served six terms.

See also MOREHOUSE COLLEGE [4].

REFERENCES

Brennan, Carol. "George Crockett, Jr." In *Contemporary Black Biography*. Vol. 10, edited by L. Mpho Mabunda. 1996.

Thomas, Robert McG., Jr. "George W. Crockett Dies at 88; Was a Civil Rights Crusader." *New York Times*, 15 September 1997.

Who's Who in Colored America. 7th ed. 1950.

ROBERT L. JOHNS

Crogman, William H. (May 5, 1841–October 16, 1931), college president. William H. Crogman was born on St Martin in the Leeward Islands. Befriended by a New England ship owner, B. L. Boomer, Crogman sailed the world from 1855 to 1866. Beginning his formal schooling then, he displayed keenness that led to his expedited graduation from Pierce Academy in Middleboro, Massachusetts, in 1868. That year he became the first black teacher at Claflin College in Orangeburg, South Carolina. In 1873, Crogman completed a four-year course in three to become a member of the first graduating class of Atlanta University. He immediately began to teach Latin and Greek at Clark College.

In 1880 Crogman became a professor of classics at Clark, a position he held until he ascended to the presidency of the college in 1903. His seven-year tenure was marked by the college's move away from vocational programs prominent at other black institutions of higher learning, such as the Tuskegee Institute, to a more liberal arts format. He returned to teaching in 1910, retired in 1921 and spent the last years of his life in Philadelphia. In addition to his activities with Clark, he was actively involved in the Methodist Church, and, as commissioner of the 1895 Cotton States Exhibition, was largely responsible for assembling the black exhibits.

Crogman was also an historian of black achievements. With J. L. Nichols he was co-author of *Progress of a Race, or the Remarkable Advancement of the American Negro* (1897). Revised and published as *The Colored American in 1901*, it appeared with further revisions under the original title in 1920.

See also AMERICAN NEGRO ACADEMY [1]; CLARK ATLANTA UNIVERSITY [S]; HISTORIANS/HISTORIOGRAPHY [3]; INTELLECTUAL LIFE [3].

REFERENCES

Crogman, William H. *Talks for the Times.* [Biographical sketch by Edward L. Parks.] 1896.

Culp, D. W. *Twentieth Century Negro Literature.* 1902.

Kennedy, Melvin D. "William H[enry] Crogman." In *Dictionary of American Negro Biography*, edited by Rayford W. Logan and Michael R. Winston. 1982.

ROBERT L. JOHNS

Cromwell, Oliver

Cromwell, Oliver (1752–1853), soldier. Cromwell was born free in Columbus near the city of Burlington, NJ, where he worked as a farmer before joining the war for American independence. At the outbreak of the war, he enlisted in a company attached to the Second New Jersey Regiment under the command of Colonel Israel Shreve. Though General George Washington had initially opposed the inclusion of black soldiers in the Continental Army, Cromwell was among the soldiers who accompanied him across the Delaware River.

Cromwell subsequently fought in the battles of Princeton and Brandywine in 1777, the battle of Monmouth in 1778, and reportedly witnessed the last man killed in the war at the battle of Yorktown in 1781. On June 5, 1783, General Washington personally signed Cromwell's honorable discharge papers and awarded him a medal as a private in the New Jersey Battalion. An endorsement of Cromwell stated that he was "honored with the Badge of Merit for six years faithful service." Following the war, he applied for a veteran's pension but was denied. Since he was unable to read or write, local lawyers, judges and politicians came to Cromwell's assistance. He was eventually granted a federal pension of ninety-six dollars a year. With his pension in hand, Cromwell purchased a one-hundred-acre farm in Burlington County. He spent his last years at his residence on Union Street in Burlington, where he lived to be just over one hundred years old. Cromwell is buried in the cemetery of the Broad Street Methodist Church near his home. At his death in January 1853, he was survived by several children, grandchildren, and great-grandchildren.

See also AMERICAN REVOLUTION [1]; MILITARY[4].

REFERENCES

Logan, Rayford, ed. "Oliver Cromwell." In *Dictionary of American Negro Biography*, edited by Rayford Logan and Michael Winston. 1982.

Biographical sketch, Oliver Cromwell Black History Society of Historic Burlington City, New Jersey.

Quarles, Benjamin. *The Negro in the American Revolution*. 1961.

OMAR ALI

Crothers, Scatman

Crothers, Scatman (May 23, 1910–November 22, 1986), actor and singer. Benjamin Sherman Crothers was born in Terre Haute, Indiana. He adopted the name "Scatman" when he was hired by radio station KSMK, Dayton, Ohio, in 1932. By this time he was a guitarist as well as a singer. His musical career flourished, and he was leading his own band when he came to Hollywood in 1943. Over the years he continued to appear with the band as he found work as a supporting actor in television and film.

Crothers began his film work in 1953 with *Walking My Baby Back Home* and had appeared as a supporting actor in some twenty-nine movies by 1985, not counting movies made for television like *The Harlem Globetrotters on Gilligan's Island* (1981) and *The Journey of Natty Gann* (1985). He is most often mentioned for his role as Orderly Turkle in *One Flew Over the Cuckoo's Nest* (1975). His television work was extensive although he had a continuing role in only one hit series. Between 1974 and 1978, Crothers was a regular as Louie the garbageman on *Chico and the Man*. Among his more noticeable limited appearances was the role of Mingo in *Roots* (January 1977).

Crothers also gave voice to many cartoon characters such as Penrod Pooch in *Hong Kong Phooey* (1974) and Scat Cat in *The Aristocats* (1970). Although Crothers never became a superstar, he was a well known and liked entertainer in a career that lasted more than a half-century from his beginnings as a ukulele-playing singer.

See also MUSIC [4]; TELEVISION [5].

REFERENCES

Brooks, Tim, and Earle Marsh. *The Complete Directory to Prime Time Network TV Shows, 1946–Present*. 5th edition. New York, 1992.

Mapp, Edward. *Directory of Blacks in the Performing Arts.* 2nd edition. 1990.

"Scatman Crothers." *Ebony*, July 1978.

"Scatman Crothers." [Filmography.] http://us.imdb.com/Name?Crothers,+Scatman Accessed 21 May 2000.

"Scatman Crothers." [Filmography.] http://www.oe-pages.com/ARTS/Ballet/miracle100/. Accessed 16 June 2000.

ROBERT L. JOHNS

Crouch, Stanley (December 14, 1945–), critic and essayist. Stanley Crouch was born in Los Angeles, where he was raised by his mother Emma Bea Crouch, a domestic. During his boyhood, he became fascinated by jazz music. In 1965, after attending school and junior college in Los Angeles, he was inspired by the Watts riot to become involved in the Black Power and Black Arts movements, and he joined the Watts Repertory Theatre Company as an actor and writer. In 1968, Crouch was hired by California's Claremont College as an instructor, and he later became the first full-time faculty member of the Black Studies Center.

By 1975, Crouch left Claremont and moved to New York. Disenchanted with Black Nationalism, he became a disciple of writers Ralph Ellison and Albert Murray, who celebrated the centrality of blacks in a pluralistic American culture. He joined the staff of the weekly *Village Voice* as a jazz and cultural critic, where he remained until 1989. At the *Voice*, Crouch became controversial for his forthright critiques of modern jazz, African-American literature, and other subjects. *Notes of a Hanging Judge* (1990), a collection of his *Voice* columns, was a finalist for the National Book Award.

During the 1990s, Crouch worked as a freelance scholar and essayist, and functioned as an advisor to the Lincoln Center Jazz Program. In 1994, the same year a second essay collection, *The All-American Skin Game*, appeared, Crouch won the prestigious Guggenheim "genius" award. In 1995, Crouch joined the *New York Daily News* as a columnist. *Always In Pursuit: Fresh American Perspectives*, a collection made up mostly of his *News* columns, was published in 1998. *See also* JAZZ [3]; JOURNALISM [3]; INTELLECTUAL LIFE [3].

REFERENCE

Crouch, Stanley. *Always in Pursuit: Fresh American Perspectives.* 1998.

GREG ROBINSON

Crown Heights Riot. On August 19, 1991, a speeding car carrying a group of Hasidic Jews through Brooklyn's Crown Heights neighborhood went out of control and struck two black children, including 7-year-old Gavin Cato, who died of his injuries. The incident was the climax to a long period of tension between Hasidic and African-American (especially West Indian) residents over race-related socioeconomic inequalities. When private ambulances arrived to aid the Hasidim, but ignored the injured blacks, African Americans rioted. Shouting "Kill the Jews!," some 500 blacks set fire to a yeshiva van, looted stores, and threw bottles at Hasidic homes and at the police. Three black youths set upon Yankel Rosenbaum, a yeshiva student from Australia, and fatally stabbed him. The rioting continued throughout the night. The next day, when New York's black mayor David Dinkins traveled to Crown Heights calling for calm, he was jeered by the crowds. When the rioting showed no signs of ending after the third day, Dinkins authorized police to crack down. Police restored order by the end of August 22.

In 1992, Lemrick Nelson, Jr., a 17-year-old African American, was indicted for the murder of Rosenbaum. Despite the evidence of his fingerprints on the murder weapon, Nelson was acquitted the following year. After Nelson's trial, New York Governor Mario Cuomo commissioned a report on the riot. The report, which appeared in 1993, sharply criticized Dinkins for not acting more diligently to quell the riot, and this helped to defeat him in that year's mayoral race. In 1997, Nelson was convicted of violating Rosenbaum's federal civil rights and was sentenced to 19 1/2 years in prison.
See also DINKINS, DAVID (UPDATE) [S]; NEW YORK CITY [4].

REFERENCES

Gourevitch, Philip. "The Crown Heights Riot and Its Aftermath." *Commentary.* January 1993: 29-35.

"2 Blacks Found Guilty In N.Y. Slaying Of Hasidic Jew/Violation of civil rights found in riot death in Crown Heights." *San Francisco Chronicle.* February 11, 1997.

GREG ROBINSON

Crumpler, Rebecca Davis Lee (February 8, 1831?-March 9, 1895), physician. Crumpler was the first African American woman to receive the M.D. degree in the United States. She was born about 1831 in Richmond, Virginia, or in Delaware, to Absolum Davis and Matilda Webber. But Rebecca Lee was raised in Pennsylvania by an aunt. She had moved to

Charlestown, Massachusetts, by 1852 and for eight years worked as a nurse. With recommendation from physicians whom she had served as nurse, in 1860 she was admitted to the four-year medical program at New England Female Medical College. On March 11, 1864, she received her Doctress of Medicine degree.

Around graduation, Rebecca Lee married Arthur Crumpler and practiced in Boston. When the Civil War ended, she moved to Richmond, Virginia, where the Freedmen's Bureau arranged for her to treat black patients, many of whom had left the plantation and had no medical provisions. She returned to Boston in 1869, and by 1883 she was no longer in active practice. In that year Crumpler published a book of medical advice for women and their children, *A Book of Medical Discourses*. She died in Fairview, Massachusetts, while a resident of Hyde Park. Crumpler's pioneering work led to the formation of the Rebecca Lee Society, the first medical society for African American women.

See also BOSTON, MASSACHUSETTS [1]; MEDICAL ASSOCIATIONS [3]; MEDICAL EDUCATION [3].

REFERENCES

Garraty, John A., and Mark C. Carnes, general eds. *American National Biography*. 1999.

Hine, Darlene Clarke, ed. *Black Women in America*. 1993.

Krapp. Kristine, ed. *Notable Black American Scientists*. 1999.

JESSIE CARNEY SMITH

Culp, Daniel Wallace

Culp, Daniel Wallace (1845?-?), educator, editor, minister, physician. Although biographical information on Culp is scanty, his enduring legacy appears to be the compilation of essays by African American writers published as *Twentieth Century Negro Literature*. Culp was born a slave in Union County, South Carolina. In 1876 he was the first student to graduate from Biddle University, the forerunner of Johnson C. Smith University in Charlotte, North Carolina. That same year, Culp enrolled in Princeton Theological Seminary, where racial prejudice was evident among the students. Although several white students left school when Culp enrolled, they soon returned. By the end of the year, however, he had won their respect and friendship.

When Culp graduated from the seminary in 1879, the Freedmen's Board of the Northern Presbyterian Church hired him, assigning him to pastorates in different states, including Florida. While in Jacksonville, he was also principal of Stanton School when the noted African American scholar James Weldon Johnson was a student there. Culp was such a poor teacher that many parents removed their children from the school and sent them elsewhere. Then the school board removed Culp from the institution.

Deciding to study medicine, Culp initially enrolled at the University of Michigan and in 1891 graduated with honors from the Ohio Medical University. His only known book, *Twentieth Century Negro Literature* (1902), covered a variety of topics relating to African Americans written by one hundred African Americans and included as many photo engravings. The work became an important source for information and images of blacks during that time.

See also LITERATURE [3]; RELIGION [4].

REFERENCES

Burkett, Randall K., and others. *Black Biography*, 1790–1950, vol. 1. 1991.

Culp, Daniel Wallace. *Twentieth Century Negro Literature*. 1902.

Johnson, James Weldon. *Along This Way*. 1933.

JESSIE CARNEY SMITH

D

Dallas, Texas. The city of Dallas began as a trading post on the Trinity River, established in 1841 in the northern part of the independent Republic of Texas. By 1860 the population numbered only 678, including ninety-seven African-American slaves. When a fire burned several businesses that year, the town's white residents blamed the slaves, three of whom were hanged. After the Civil War, emancipated black Texans moved to Dallas in search of jobs, education, and, not least, security, for they faced the threat of violence in rural areas. The Freedmen's Bureau helped to organize schools, but their resources and reach were severely limited by white hostility. By 1870, African Americans had formed communities on the outskirts of Dallas and had founded Baptist and Methodist churches. Segregated black public schools were established in the 1870s.

By the 1890s, there were stirrings of black self-sufficiency. The first black doctor and dentist arrived, a black high school was created, and the African-American branch of the Masonic Order founded a college. Black commercial activity expanded to include grocery stores, barbershops, and a newspaper, the *Express*. Some African-American voters abandoned their usual Republican leanings in the 1890s and joined labor leader Melvin Wade in supporting the Populist Party; white fears of this biracial alliance may have contributed to the repression that followed.

State and local laws of the early twentieth century reinforced separation of the races in a wide variety of public areas. Black electoral participation was curtailed through measures similar to those applied across the segregated South; Texas had a state poll tax and a whites-only primary that discouraged black voting. In the 1920s a resurgent Ku Klux Klan harassed blacks in Dallas, home to the organization's strongest chapter.

Despite these trials, a black middle class emerged. The Knights of Pythias completed an impressive temple in 1915. A chapter of the NAACP was formed in 1918, and the Dallas Negro Chamber of Commerce emerged in 1925. African-American cultural activities centered on Elm Street's ("Deep Ellum") commercial and entertainment-oriented area east of downtown. Community lobbying led to the opening of the Dunbar branch of the Dallas Public Library in 1929, and a building to house black exhibits was constructed for the Texas Centennial celebration in 1936.

While the Great Depression sharply increased unemployment among Dallas's nearly 40,000 African-American residents, some black leaders began to seek political solutions to the community's problems. Businessman A. Maceo Smith organized the Progressive Voters League with the aim of influencing Dallas city council elections. His efforts resulted in a second black high school and several new parks, followed in the 1940s by black public housing developments and the inclusion of blacks on the city's police force.

World War II brought the city out of its economic depression. By 1950, when its population had increased to 434,000, Dallas's almost 57,000 black residents found themselves with roughly two houses available for every three black families in their still strictly segregated neighborhoods. Moves into previously all-white areas met with bombings and harassment. In 1954 white business leaders moved to create a new middle- class black neighborhood, Hamilton Park, that provided homes for more than three thousand people.

Desegregation in Dallas followed national patterns. The city's professional baseball team signed its first black player in 1952, and for the rest of the century black and white Dallas residents would come together in enthusiastic support for the city's professional sports teams, especially the National Football League's Dallas Cowboys. Later came the integration of the State Fair, hospitals, and public transportation and accommodations. The school board held off on integration until federal court decisions in the 1960s required it, but African Americans won seats on the board in the late 1960s. Court-ordered school busing resulted in substantial white migration to the city's suburbs, and in the 1980s African-American educational reformers shifted their efforts toward the improvement of facilities and programs. Marvin Edwards became Dallas's first black superintendent of schools in 1988, and a federal judge certified the school system as desegregated in 1994.

Black participation in the political process increased from the 1960s onward. Democrats Joseph Lockridge and later Zan Holmes Jr. were elected to the Texas state legislature, and African Americans won seats on the Dallas city council, aided by a judge's ruling against citywide at-large elections in 1971. Minorities' share of city contracts increased, and blacks made up 20 percent of the police force by 1992. In May of 1995 Dallas elected its first black mayor when attorney Ron Kirk defeated one Hispanic and one white opponent with broad support across all three groups.

Economic mainstays of African-American Dallas in the late twentieth century included the Proline cosmetics corporation, which ranked eighteenth among black-owned companies in the United States by 1988. The more than one million residents of Dallas enjoyed the city's growing institutions of African-American culture in the 1990s. The Black Dance Theater drew regional attention, and the Museum of African American Life and Culture exposed visitors of all backgrounds to the sources of the black community's resilience.

See also MAYORS [3]; TEXAS [5].

REFERENCES

Barr, Alwyn. *Black Texans: A History of African Americans in Texas, 1528–1995*. 1996.

Govenar, Alan B., and Jay F. Brakefield. *Deep Ellum and Central Track: Where the Black and White Worlds of Dallas Converged*. 1998.

Hazel, Michael V. *Dallas: A History of "Big D."* 1997.

Linden, Glenn M. *Desegregating Schools in Dallas: Four Decades in the Federal Courts*. 1995.

Payne, Darwin. *Big D: Triumphs and Troubles of an American Supercity in the Twentieth Century*. 1994.

Schutze, Jim. *The Accommodation: The Politics of Race in an American City*. 1986.

Wilson, William H. *Hamilton Park: A Planned Black Community in Dallas*. 1998.

JAMES MANHEIM

Dancy, John Campbell, Jr.

(April 13, 1888– September 10, 1968), organization executive, community leader. Dancy worked through the Detroit Urban League for 42 years to promote human relations and to provide for Detroit's black community. Born in Salisbury, North Carolina, to John C. Dancy, a public official, and Laura Coleman Dancy, he attended grade school at Livingstone College in his hometown and then studied at Phillips-Exeter Academy from 1904 to 1906. He graduated from the University of Pennsylvania in 1910.

After serving as principal of Smallwood Institute in Claremont, Virginia, and secretary of the YMCA in Norfolk, he left in 1916 to become secretary of the Big Brother Program in New York City and to work with the Children's Court. There he met Eugene Kinckle Jones, executive secretary of the National Urban League, who influenced him to become active with the local league. In 1918 Dancy moved to Detroit and headed the Detroit Urban League. He helped to break the color barrier in employment of blacks in the private and public sectors.

In 1920 Dancy brought national attention to Detroit when he persuaded the United Community Services to hire a black stenographer. He supported the Brewster Homes, Detroit's first government-funded housing project for blacks, and introduced residents to art and music. He took special pride in the Green Pastures Camp that gave free summer camp experiences to hundreds of black youth. Dancy's life is chronicled in his autobiography, *Sand Against the Wind* (1966).

See also DETROIT, MICHIGAN [2]; NATIONAL URBAN LEAGUE [4].

REFERENCES

Garraty, John A., and Mark C. Carnes, eds. *American National Biography*. 1999.

Logan, Rayford W., and Michael R. Winston, eds. *Dictionary of American Negro Biography*. 1982.

RAYMOND WINBUSH

Daniels, William Boone "Billy"

(1915–October 24, 1988), singer. Billy Daniels was born in Jacksonville, Florida. As a boy he sang with street groups, in a church choir, and in school choral groups. His activities in music continued at Florida A & M University. On a visit to New York in 1934, some college friends took him to a Harlem nightclub, the Hot Cha Club, where they encouraged him to sing. He was well received, and an engagement followed at the club for $25 per week. More jobs followed, including one with the Erkine Hawkins orchestra in 1938, and others at a variety of Harlem and 52nd Street locales.

A break came in 1949, when he was booked at the Park Avenue Restaurant as a headliner. Business was good, the pay was much better, and several major engagements followed, including the Flamingo Club in Las Vegas and clubs in Reno, Hollywood, and Chicago. He also appeared in singing roles in films, and in the Broadway musicals *Golden Boy* (1964), *Hello Dolly* (1975), and *Bubbling Brown Sugar* (1977). He also had his own television show in 1951.

Daniels toured widely in the United States and Europe, playing major venues in principal cities and quickly acquiring a reputation for his talent, showmanship, and for his lyric tenor voice. A major artist of the day, he recorded frequently with Erkine Hawkins and others. He was noted particularly for his captivating renditions of romantic ballads, especially of his trademark song, "That Old Black Magic." He died in Los Angeles of cancer.

See also HARLEM, NEW YORK [3]; MUSIC [4]; TELEVISION [5].

REFERENCES

"Billy Daniels Hits the Top." *Ebony*. September 1950: 40.

"Famed Singer Billy Daniels Dies." *Jet*. October 24, 1988: 57.

Southern, Eileen. *Biographical Dictionary of Afro-American Composers and Musicians*. 1982.

DARIUS L. THIEME

Davis, Angela Yvonne (Update)

(January 26, 1944–), political activist. Davis left the Communist Party in 1991, but remained politically active. In 1995, she was a prominent feminist critic of the Million Man March. She is the author of several books, including *If They Come in the Morning* (1971), *Women, Race, and Class* (1983), and *Women, Culture, and Politics* (1989), and *Blues Legends and Black Feminism* (1998). Her autobiography, *Angela Davis: An Autobiography*, originally published in 1974, was reissued in 1988.

REFERENCES

Lanker, Brian. *I Dream a World: Portraits of Black Women Who Changed America*. 1989.

Cimons, Marlene. "'Unity' march exclusion divides women." *Los Angeles Times*. October 17, 1995: A14.

GREG ROBINSON

Davis, Arthur Paul

(November 21, 1904–April 21, 1996) was a scholar and educator. He was born in Hampton, Virginia. As a Phi Beta Kappa graduate of Columbia University in New York City (B.A., 1927; M.A. 1929; Ph.D. 1942), he became acquainted with

Angela Davis. (AP/Wide World Photos)

many persons of the Harlem Renaissance. He taught at North Carolina Central University in 1927–28, at Virginia Union University from 1929 to 1944, and at Howard University from 1944 until his retirement in 1980.

Davis was trained as a specialist in eighteenth-century English Literature, and he published *Isaac Watts: His Life and Works in 1943*. However, he turned the focus of his work to African American literature. He says that in 1929 he was the first person to teach a course in black literature. His teaching and publications over the years played an important role in the development of this field of study. He was a coeditor with Sterling A. Brown and Ulysses Lee of *The Negro Caravan: Writings by American Negroes* (1941); when this work of over a thousand pages was reprinted in 1969, it became a standard college text. Davis coedited *Cavalcade: Negro American Authors from 1760 to the Present* (1971) with Saunders Redding and helped update a two volume edition (1990) and a supplement (1992). A selection of Davis's academic work appears in *From the Dark Tower: Afro-American Writers from 1900 to 1960* (1974).

Davis also prepared materials for use in secondary schools. He was a columnist for the *Norfolk Journal and Guide from 1933 to 1950*. In 1972–1973 he gave twenty-six widely distributed radio talks; they give a conspectus of black writing.

See also EDUCATION [2]; HARLEM RENAISSANCE [3].

REFERENCES

Davis, Arthus P. "William Roscoe Davis (1812–1904), A Virginia Patriarch." *Negro History Bulletin*, January 1950.

Metzger, Linda, ed. *Black Writers*. 1989.

Rush, Theressa Gunnels, and others. *Black American Writers Past and Present*. 1975.

Saxon, Wolfgang. "Arthur P. Davis: Encouraged Generations of Black Writers." *New York Times,* 24 April 1996.

ROBERT L. JOHNS

Davis, Daniel Webster (March 25, 1862–October 25, 1913), educator, author, orator, businessman, leader. Davis was born in Caroline County, Virginia. He moved with his widowed mother shortly after the Civil War to Richmond, Virginia, where he received his education in the public schools and in 1880 began to teach in the Richmond public schools. He was ordained a Baptist minister in 1895. The following year, he became pastor of Second Baptist Church; the congregation grew from thirty-two to five hundred.

Davis conducted summer schools in Virginia, West Virginia, and the Carolinas; three schools in Virginia bear his name. Because of his popularity as a speaker, he was called upon to speak at commencements, participate in the Central Lyceum Bureau (1900, 1902), lecture at the Chatauqua Assembly at Laurel Park (1900), and to provide a lecture series at Hampton Institute on "Negro Ideals."

His publications include *The Industrial History of the Negro Race* (collaborated with Giles Jackson 1908; revised 1911), *The Life and Service of William Washington Brown* (1910); two poetry collections: *Idle Moments* (1895) and *'Weh Down Souf* (1897); and a weekly newspaper, *Social Drifts*. Like much nineteenth century poetry, his was didactic, utilized dialect, and focused on race and religion.

As a leader, Davis was president of the Virginia Building, Loan and Trust Company, of the Jonesboro Agricultural and Industrial Academy, and of the Dunbar Literary and Historical Society; he was also a member of the Society for Better Housing and Living in Richmond, Virginia, and prominent in masonic circles. *See also* DIALECTIC POETRY [2]; EDUCATION [2]; VIRGINIA [5].

REFERENCES

Culp, Daniel Wallace. *Twentieth Century Literature*. 1902.

Penn, I. Garland. *The Afro-American Press and Its Editors*. 1891.

Sherman, Joan R. *Invisible Poets: Afro-Americans of the Nineteenth Century*. 1974.

HELEN R. HOUSTON

Davis Harry E. (1882–1955), politician. Harry E. Davis was born and spent his entire life in Cleveland, Ohio. After a year at Hiram College (1904– 1905), he transferred to Western Reserve University and graduated from its school of law in 1908. In addition to the practice of law, he had a rich career in public service and was active in civic and fraternal organizations.

Davis, who was a Republican, was elected to the Ohio General Assembly in 1921 as a Cuyahoga County representative and served for three terms. From 1928– 1934 he served Cleveland as a city civil service commissioner. His public service career culminated with his election and service as a state senator on two occasions, 1947–1949 and 1953–1954.

In 1910 Davis joined a Masonic lodge and became interested in the organization's history. He researched Negro Masonry for more than twenty-five years and published several works on the topic, including a book (1944). He worked diligently to promote racial harmony within the Masonic fraternity. Davis' work with the Cleveland branch of the National Association for the Advancement of Colored People led to his being chosen as director for the national organization, a position he held from 1919 until he died. He also worked to promote racial harmony through his membership on the board of a settlement house. At the time of his death, Davis had just completed a manuscript on the history of blacks in Cleveland which was published in 1972 by his brother Russell.

See also CLEVELAND, OHIO [2]; FRATERNAL ORDERS AND MUTUAL AID ASSOCIATIONS [2]; NATIONAL ASSOCIATION FOR THE ADVANCEMENT OF COLORED PEOPLE (NAACP) [4]; REPUBLICAN PARTY [4].

REFERENCE

Logan, Rayford W., and Michael R. Winston, eds. *Dictionary of American Negro Biography*. 1982.

CARRELL P. HORTON

Davis, John Henry "Blind John" (December 7, 1913–October 12, 1985), blues musician. Davis was born in Hattiesbury, Mississippi. The family moved to Chicago in 1916. Davis lost his eyesight when he was nine. As a youth he taught himself to play the piano to earn money in the sporting houses run by his father. Davis built a local reputation and wide repertoire and also played in a number of white clubs. In 1933 he formed Johnny Lee's Music Masters and later the Johnny Davis Rhythm Boys, groups which performed in white speakeasies in and around Chicago.

An accomplished arranger, Davis became house pianist for Lester Melrose's Wabash Music Company. From 1937 to 1942 he played on over a hundred recordings. He played with many major blues figures like Memphis Minnie and Sonny Boy Williamson, and his collaboration with Tampa Red (Hudson Whittaker) led to a lasting friendship. Davis continued playing with his group, mostly in white clubs throughout the Midwest. A small group, the John Davis Trio, recorded for MGM records in 1949 and in 1951, but after this Davis did mostly solo work in the Chicago area. He went to Europe in 1952 with Big Bill Broonzy and recorded there. His house was burned in 1955 and his wife died a few days later.

Davis continued to play in clubs. During the 1970s he made many trips to Europe and played in festivals in the Midwest. There were a number of recording sessions scattered over these years. He died in Chicago. Davis had a major talent, but he never achieved the popularity of other blues pianists like Memphis Slim (Peter Chatman.)

See also BLUES, THE [1]; CHICAGO, ILLINOIS [1].

REFERENCES

Currier, Terry. "Blind John Davis." *Blues Notes*, January 1996.

Santelli, Robert. *The Big Book of Blues*. 1993.

ROBERT L. JOHNS

Davis, Ossie (Update) (December 18, 1917–), actor and playwright. Ossie Davis was born in Cogdell, Georgia, to Kince Charles Davis, a railroad construction worker, and Laura Cooper Davis. After finishing high school in Waycross, Georgia, he hitchhiked north and attended Howard University. In 1937, Davis left Howard and went to New York City, where he worked at odd jobs before joining Harlem's Rose McClendon Players in 1939.

Through the 1970s, '80s, and early '90s, Davis continued his performing career, notably in a radio series, *The Ossie Davis and Ruby Dee Hour* (1974–1976), in the public television series *With Ossie and*

Ossie Davis. (The Artists Agency)

Ruby (1981), in the role of Martin Luther King, Sr., in Abby Mann's television miniseries *King* (1977), and in the Spike Lee films *Do the Right Thing* (1989), *Jungle Fever* (1991), as well as the Eddie Murphy film *Doctor Dolittle* (1998). Throughout the early 1990s, he was a semi-regular on the television series *Evening Shade*. Davis also has written several children's books, which include plays based on the lives of Frederick Douglass and Langston Hughes, and a novel, *Just Like Martin* (1992), about a southern boy, inspired by the life of the Rev. Dr. Martin Luther King, Jr. In 1998 Davis celebrated his fiftieth wedding anniversary with Ruby Dee by publishing a joint memoir, *With Ossie and Ruby Dee: In This Life Together*.

REFERENCES

Davis, Ossie, and Ruby Dee. *With Ossie and Ruby Dee: In This Life Together*. 1998.

Landay, Eileen. *Black Film Stars*. 1973.

McMurray, Emily J., and Owen O'Donnell, eds. *Contemporary Theater, Film and Television*. 1992.

SUSAN MCINTOSH
UPDATED BY GREG ROBINSON

Davis, Richard L. (December 24, 1864–January 1900), coal miner, union organizer. Davis was a staunch defender of workers' rights. He was born in Roanoke, Virginia, and educated in the local schools at night. Beginning at age eight and continuing for nine years, he worked in a local tobacco factory. His disgust with work conditions led him to migrate to West Virginia in 1881, where he became a coal miner. Then he moved to Rendville, Ohio, married, and continued to work as a coal miner until he died.

Davis was elected to the executive board of the United Mine Workers of America (UMWA) for District Six, Ohio, in 1891. Both in 1896 and 1897, he was elected to the national executive board. Davis, who then held the highest position by an African American in that union, had local, regional, and national influence. He called for an end to segregation in housing and in the mines. He called on the labor press to support laborers of all races, and he criticized the unjust policies of the coal companies. Davis also urged African Americans to join the union, although many were reluctant to do so.

Throughout the 1890s Davis continued to defend workers' rights. He worked to build new local chapters and to strengthen existing ones. Although his life was threatened during his efforts to organize unions in West Virginia and Alabama and his organizing efforts caused him to lose his job, he persevered. By 1898 the UMWA refused to hire him as a paid organizer. Nonetheless, Davis remained committed to organized labor.

See also LABOR AND LABOR UNIONS [3]; OHIO [4].

REFERENCES

Foner, Philip. *Organized Labor and the Black Worker, 1619–1973*. 1974.

Garraty, John A., and Mark C. Carnes, general eds. *American National Biography*. 1999.

Trotter, Joe W., Jr. *Coal, Class, and Color: Blacks in Southern West Virginia, 1915–32*. 1990.

RAYMOND WINBUSH

Day, William Howard (October 16, 1825–December 2, 1900), abolitionist, editor, educator, minister. William Howard Day's mother, Eliza Dixon, a destitute widow, shaped his future by allowing J. P. Williston, a white reformer, to legally adopt her son. Williston raised Day in his home and church, oversaw his education, and apprenticed him to a printer at the city's leading newspaper. As the sole black, Day entered Oberlin College in 1843 with an enviable record as an orator and volunteer teacher to fugitive slaves. Following college, Day worked in the printing business, and tried, without success, to establish several abolitionist/black newspapers. The first of these, *The Aliened American*, lasted a year, from 1853 to 1854.

As a teacher and educational leader, Day was vital to countless numbers of black children and adults. In Harrisburg, Pennsylvania, he became the first black elected to the School Board and eventually was elected chairman. In Cleveland, he had earlier been hired as the first black librarian at the Cleveland Library Association. Day was also appointed superintendent of schools for the Maryland and Delaware Freedmen's Bureau.

Day's religion was inseparable from his secular work and life. When he returned to New York City, his birthplace, he affiliated with the American Freedmen's Friend Society and was lay editor of the *Zion Standard and Weekly Review*, the organ of the African Methodist Episcopal Zion Church (AMEZ). When he died, the Harrisburg newspaper printed a front-page obituary, a first for a black person.

See also CLEVELAND, OHIO [2]; JOURNALISM [3]; OHIO [4].

REFERENCES

Garraty, John A., and Mark C. Carnes, eds. *American National Biography*, vol. 6. 1999.

Ripley, C. Peter, ed. *The Black Abolitionist Papers*, vol. 4. 1991.

Smith, Jessie Carney, ed. *Notable Black American Men*. 1999.

DOLORES NICHOLSON

Dean, William H., Jr.

Dean, William H., Jr. (July 6, 1910–January 8, 1952), economist, United Nations official. William H. Dean, Jr. was born in Lynchburg, West Virginia, and attended Bowdoin College. Elected to Phi Beta Kappa in his junior year, he graduated in 1930 and went on to earn a Ph.D. in economics from Harvard in 1938. He ended his nine-year teaching post at Atlanta University in 1942 to work for the government as a price executive in the Office of Price Administration for the Virgin Islands.

Dean was director of the Community Relations Projects of the National Urban League from 1944 to 1946. He then began to work for the United Nations, heading the African Unit of the Division of Economic Stability. In 1949 Dean served on missions to Haiti and Libya, and wrote the report, *Mission to Haiti* (1949), an excellent analysis of the conditions in that country. He headed a six-man mission in late 1951 to Italian Somaliland (the coastal region of present-day Eritrea). The goal of the mission was to determine how the area could become self-supporting. Dean was very distressed by the living conditions there and by the attitudes of the Italian officials in charge.

On his return to New York, Dean committed suicide in the apartment of his father-in-law, Channing H. Tobias, then director of the Phelps-Stokes foundation. Dean's perfectionism and sensitivity to rebuffs due to his race, such as the refusal of the New York City university system hire him despite glowing recommendations, are also advanced as factors in his death.
See also ATLANTA UNIVERSITY [1]; ECONOMICS [2]; NATIONAL URBAN LEAGUE [4].

REFERENCES

Cobb, W. Montague. "In Memoriam." [Obituary.] *Journal of the National Medical Association*, November 1952.

Logan, Rayford W. "William H. Dean, Jr." In *Dictionary of American Negro Biography*, edited by Rayford W. Logan and Michael R. Winston. 1982.

ROBERT L. JOHNS

De Baptiste, Richard

De Baptiste, Richard (November 11, 1831– April 21, 1901), minister, organizer, editor. Richard De Baptiste was born free in Fredericksburg, Virginia, but moved with his family to Detroit when he was nine. Richard De Baptiste was licensed to preach in the Baptist Church in 1858, after which he taught school and pastored a church in Mount Pleasant, Ohio. In January of 1863, he moved to Chicago to pastor the Olivet Baptist Church, the platform from which he exerted most of his influence on black Baptist congregations, both in Chicago and nationwide.

De Baptiste's dynamic preaching and development of a church school caused the Olivet congregation to experience rapid growth, as the church attracted recent black immigrants from the rural South. Olivet became Chicago's largest black congregation by the end of the 1860s, and De Baptiste's advocacy of all-black religious associations was highly influential both in the city and at the national level. He was instrumental in uniting black Baptist churches across the United States to form the Consolidated American Baptist Convention in 1866, the first national black Baptist association. De Baptiste was the association's president from 1867 to 1873.

The years of his presidency proved to be the peak of De Baptiste's influence. His congregation declined in the late 1870s, and he began a second career as a journalist as editor of the *Chicago Conservator* in 1878. By 1881, De Baptiste's congregation had declined to the point that he resigned his position as head of the church. He continued his journalistic efforts with several newspapers in addition to serving small black churches in the Chicago vicinity until his death.
See also BAPTISTS [1]; CHICAGO, ILLINOIS [1]; RELIGION [4].

REFERENCES

Logan, Rayford W., and Michael R. Winston, eds *Dictionary of American Negro Biography*. 1982.

Penn, Irving Garland. *The Afro-American Press and Its Editors*. 1891.

Simmons, William J. *Men of Mark: Eminent, Progressive, Rising*. 1887.

JESSIE CARNEY SMITH

Deindustrialization

Deindustrialization. Until the early nineteenth century, the economy of the United States remained predominantly agricultural, with the bulk of the country's population living and working on small farms in the countryside. When entrepreneurs discovered ways to produce and distribute goods on a much larger scale, however, the prospect of massive profits fueled an economic revolution. The U.S. moved from a predominantly agricultural-based society to a primarily industrialized and urbanized one. Soon, American manufacturers were mass-producing steel, woolen goods, farm machinery, processed foods, and so on; and large, strategically located cities were providing them with access to labor, materials, ancillary services, and local, intercity and international markets.

After World War II, however, technological changes in transportation, communications, and automation made it possible for increasingly centralized and internationally dominant American-based manufacturing corporations to search the United States and abroad for more attractive industrial environments. However, they did not immediately take advantage of these opportunities, striking instead a truce with American labor unions and continuing to make sizable profits by virtue of their international position of superiority. As late as 1960, there was virtually no Third World production of manufactured goods for export.

Yet, faced with mounting international competition, from Japan and Western Europe in particular, the economic downturn of the mid-1970s seems to have set off a significant mobility of U.S. capital. Since that time, many U.S.-based multinationals have launched aggressive searches for locations that provide cheaper and more abundant resources, less expensive and more pliant labor, and a high degree of political stability. In the 1990s, the National Labor Relations Board (NLRB) and several federal court decisions removed some of the last remaining legal impediments to such mobility. A large scale "deindustrialization" of the United States resulted from these shifts in capital, with manufacturing development occurring primarily abroad and increasing numbers of U.S. jobs ending up in the less lucrative and less promising service sector, e.g. bagging groceries, waiting tables, or serving as a bank teller.

In terms of impact on individuals, Chicago's South Works provides an example. Of the thousands of workers laid off between 1978 and 1984, fully fifty percent found it impossible to obtain adequate alternative employment. For black workers, that figure was sixty percent. Combining the unemployed and the re-employed, average household income dropped from $22,000 to $12,500; eleven percent were evicted from their homes; one-quarter felt compelled to find cheaper residences; and an additional one-third were behind on their mortgage or rent payments.

Deindustrialization has been uniquely problematic for African Americans. During slavery, blacks were denied the right to own property; throughout that period, even free blacks faced a dual wage system and other forms of racial discrimination that made it difficult for them to accumulate wealth. After the emancipation promise of "forty acres and a mule" failed to materialize, black accumulation of wealth continued to be retarded by the nature of available employment. Little could be saved while working as a sharecropper, domestic servant, or leased convict, and employment and wage discrimination continued to plague blacks who attempted to work outside those situations. Many blacks moved to the increasingly industrialized North in a futile search for the economic opportunities white immigrants had enjoyed for decades. By the time legally sanctioned discrimination finally began to be struck down, it was essentially too late. The American economic system was undergoing fundamental changes that would seriously reduce the options for moving up the financial ladder. In particular, rapid growth in technology was allowing mechanization of much of the manual and semiskilled work in unionized industries that had been providing decent wages, benefits, and opportunities for skill development and advancement. In addition, many of the remaining manufacturing jobs were shifting to the Third World.

Despite some highly publicized instances to the contrary, e.g., college-educated black couples presently out-earning comparable white couples, the bulk of African Americans seem to have been left behind in an economic sense. For example, blacks find themselves significantly underrepresented in the managerial and professional ranks. Since World War II, the black unemployment rate has been roughly twice the white rate across virtually every major category of occupation and educational attainment. Estimates also indicate that as many as one-half of all black males are presently unemployed, no longer looking for work, or unaccounted for, and that number appears to be increasing. The situation is better for black women, but many remain locked in clerical and domestic positions that offer minimal wages and virtually no skill development, benefits, or advancement.

Black family income has remained at only slightly more than one-half of white family income during this same period; and, by the 1990s, the median white household possessed wealth worth $44,408; while the figure was only $24,604 for the median black household. Thus, although African Americans represented thirteen percent of the U. S. population, they held less than one-half percent of the nation's wealth. Meanwhile, approximately three out of every ten African Americans are still categorized as poor, and approximately one-half of all black children find themselves in families living below the poverty line. Compared to whites, blacks have remained three times more likely to be poor since World War II, and that is true for black children as well, while the median income of poor black families is also some twenty percent lower than for poor white families.

See also BLACK MIDDLE CLASS [S]; CLASS AND SOCIETY [2]; ECONOMICS [2]; INDUSTRIALIZATION [3].

REFERENCES

Carnoy, Martin. *Faded Dreams: The Politics and Economics of Race in America*. 1994.

Bluestone, Barry and Bennett Harrison, *The Deindustrialization of America*. 1982.

Harrison, Bennett and Barry Bluestone, *The Great U-Turn: Corporate Restructuring and the Polarizing of America*. 1988.

Pinkney, Alphonso. *The Myth of Black Progress*. 1984.

Pohlmann, Marcus. *Black Politics in Conservative America*. 1999.

Pohlmann, Marcus. *Governing the Postindustrial City*. 1993.

MARCUS D. POHLMANN

Delany, Hubert T. (1901–January 28, 1990), lawyer, educator, civil rights advocate. Hubert Delany was the fifth African-American jurist in New York City and an outspoken advocate for children. He was born in Raleigh, North Carolina, one of ten children of Henry Beard, a bishop in the Episcopal Church in America, and Nanny Logan Delany. His sisters, Bessie and Sadie Delany, gained popularity in the 1990s for their book *Having Our Say*.

Delany left Raleigh for New York City, where he worked as a baggage handler to earn money for college. He also was a farm worker in Connecticut and taught in Harlem's elementary schools. A 1923 graduate of City College in New York, Delany took a law degree at New York University in 1926 and then set up private practice. He became known as a civil rights advocate, which led to his appointment as assistant United States attorney in the criminal division in 1927. He remained there until 1933 and served eight years on New York City's Tax Commission.

New York mayor Fiorello H. LaGuardia appointed Delany to the New York City Domestic Relations Court in 1942, which allowed him the opportunity to act on his interest in race relations and in ensuring the rights of children. When a Democrat was elected to the mayoral office in 1955, the Republican Delany was replaced with a Democrat, Edward R. Dudley. Delany became chairman of the Intergroup Committee on New York Public Schools that year and worked with the committee to eradicate segregation in the system. He was also named to a committee to study low income housing in 1963, one of many such appointments in the years following his departure from the bench.

See also DELANY, CLARISSA SCOTT [2]; LAWYERS [3]; NEW YORK CITY [4].

REFERENCES

Delany, Sarah, and A. Elizabeth Delany. *Having Our Say*. 1993.

"Hubert T. Delany, 89, Ex-Judge and Civil Rights Advocate, Dies." *New York Times*, December 31, 1990.

Smith, Jessie Carney, ed. *Notable Black American Men*. 1999.

JESSIE CARNEY SMITH

Delany, Sarah Louise "Sadie" (Update) (September 19, 1889–January 25, 1999), teacher and writer and **Annie Elizabeth "Bessie"** (September 3, 1891–September 25, 1995), dentist and writer. Sadie Delany was born in Lynch's Station, Virginia, and her sister Bessie was born in Raleigh, North Carolina, where the two girls and their eight siblings grew up. Their father was Henry Beard Delany, a minister who later became the nation's first black Episcopal bishop. Their mother, Nanny Delany, was the matron of St. Augustine's School in Raleigh. After graduating from St. Augustine's in 1910 and 1911, respectively, Sadie and Bessie worked briefly as teachers in the South.

In 1916, Sadie moved to New York, where she attended Pratt Institute, then Columbia University Teachers College, where she received a bachelor's degree in domestic science in 1920 and a master's degree in 1925. In 1928, after deliberately missing an employment interview so that school officials could not exclude her on racial grounds, she obtained a position at Theodore Roosevelt High School, an all-white school, thus becoming the first black female domestic science teacher in New York City. She taught at Theodore Roosevelt until her retirement. Bessie moved to New York in 1919 and graduated from Columbia University Dental School in 1923, becoming only the second black woman dentist in

The Delany Sisters, Bessie and Sadie. (The New York Times Corporation)

New York. She set up a dental office in Harlem. She practiced until the 1950s, when she retired to care for her mother.

In 1991, Amy Hill Hearth, a journalist, interviewed the Delany sisters for a newspaper article. In 1993 Hill expanded the interviews into a bestselling book, *Having Our Say: The Delany Sisters' First 100 Years*, which was subsequently turned into a successful play. In 1994, a sequel, *The Delany Sisters' Book of Everyday Widsom*, was published.

REFERENCE

Delany, Sarah and A. Elizabeth, with Amy Hill Hearth. *Having Our Say: The Delany Sisters' First 100 Years*. 1993.

GREG ROBINSON

Dellums, C[ottrell] L[awrence] (1900– December 7, 1989), labor organizer and civil rights leader. Originally from Corsicana, Texas, Dellums spent most of his life in Oakland, California. He helped found the Brotherhood of Sleeping Car Porters in 1925 with black socialist A. Philip Randolph. The union, the first in the country established and led

by African Americans, won the first in a series of major contracts with the Pullman Company in 1937. After being fired in the early 1920s from his $2-a-day job with the Pullman Company, Dellums made a living running a billiard parlor. He helped organize the union at a time when railroad workers were approximately one-third of all documented African American wage earners. The union helped develop future civil rights leadership. Dellums was elected vice president of the union in 1929 and became its president in 1966, succeeding Randolph. Throughout the 1930s and 1940s, Dellums lent his support to black ministers and civil rights workers. In 1941, under pressure that Randolph and Dellums would organize a Negro March on Washington, President Franklin D. Roosevelt signed an executive order, mandating non-discriminatory employment practices in wartime industries. In 1948, Dellums became the first West Coast Regional Director of the National Association for the Advancement of Colored People (NAACP). In 1959, he was appointed by California Governor Edmund (Pat) Brown to the state's first Fair Employment Practices Commission (now the Fair Employment and Housing Commission). Dellums served on the commission for the next twenty-six years. During this time he also led the first black voter registration drive in Oakland. Known as a person of great warmth and gentleness, he died in his home of a heart attack at the age of eighty-nine. Dellums is the uncle of Representative Ronald V. Dellums of California.

See also BROTHERHOOD OF SLEEPING CAR PORTERS [1]; LABOR AND LABOR UNIONS [3]; SAN FRANCISCO AND OAKLAND, CALIFORNIA [5].

REFERENCES

"C. L. Dellums Helped Found Porters Union," *Los Angeles Times*, December 20, 1989.

Fitrakis, Bob ed. "Reflections on Black History," *The Free Press*. 1998.

OMAR ALI

Democratic Party (Update). The alliance between the African-American community and the Democratic party has been strained in recent years, as blacks resist having their votes taken for granted and white Democrats seeking conservative and moderate white votes distance themselves from black issues at times. Black leaders accused Bill Clinton, for example, of downplaying black interests in his successful bid for the presidency in 1992. Still, a larger propor-

tion of the black vote than that of any other large ethnic group continued to go to the Democrats. Clinton's own victory in the Democratic primaries was made possible partly by large-scale black electoral support, and in the general election, an estimated 82 percent of blacks that voted did so for the Democratic candidate. Clinton responded by appointing more blacks to his cabinet than any previous president. Despite their misgivings over welfare reform and other issues, black voters supported Clinton's reelection in 1996 in similar numbers, and African Americans represented Clinton's firmest base of public support during his impeachment crisis two years later. Whether the black-Democratic alliance will continue or dissolve depends on the new urban crisis and the response of new generation Democrats to the challenges that these issues present. To date, however, African-American Democrats have achieved much in and through their political party.

REFERENCES

Frye, Hardy. *Black Parties and Political Power: A Case Study*. 1980.

Walton, Hanes, Jr. "The Democrats and African Americans: The American Idea." In *Democrats and the American Idea: A Bicentennial Appraisal*. Peter B. Kovler, ed. 1992: 333-348.

HANES WALTON, JR.
MERVYN DYMALLY
UPDATED BY GREG ROBINSON

Denby, Charles

Denby, Charles (August 25, 1907–October 10, 1983), autoworker, newspaper editor. Charles Denby was the son of successful farmers in Lowndes County, Alabama. He attended Tuskegee Institute where he studied mechanics and took one class from noted scientist George Washington Carver. The foundation of Denby's militant activities was grounded in his Marxist beliefs as a staunch follower of Raya Dunayevskaya and his later alliance with the News and Letters Committees, a Marxist-Humanist organization he helped found with his wife.

Denby's autobiography, *Indignant Heart: A Black Worker's Journal*, chronicles the struggle of blacks and organized labor as well as the events of the Civil Rights Movement. His editorship of *News and Letters*, a movement newspaper, lasted nearly 30 years, and ended only with his death. In the 1940s Denby was a prime mover in strike actions and getting black workers to become more militant in organizing for their own benefit. He influenced black workers in resisting overtures by the Communist Party because of its refusal to support strikes organized by black workers.

Returning to the South in the late 1950s, Denby used his expertise to assist disenfranchised black farmers in becoming self-sufficient. He organized the Michigan-Lowndes County Christian Movement for Human Rights to help sharecroppers evicted when they tried to register to vote. He supported black women workers who leveled harsh criticism against the predominantly black male leadership during the Montgomery Bus Strike Movement. In 1966 he was a leading figure in organizing a rally to assist displaced farmers to solicit labor unions' financial support. He used his journalistic talents to express the need for international solidarity with the workers' freedom struggles in other countries.

See also LABOR AND LABOR UNIONS [3]; LOWNDES COUNTY FREEDOM ORGANIZATION [3].

REFERENCES

Smith, Jessie Carney, ed. *Notable Black American Men*. 1999.

DOLORES NICHOLSON

Derham, James, (also spelled Durham)

Derham, James, (also spelled Durham) (May 1, 1762–?), physician. Derham was the earliest known African American physician in the United States. He was born a slave in Philadelphia. Little is known about his ancestry, but it is known that his early masters taught him to read and write and saw that he had some religious instruction. While a child, Derham became the property of John Kearsley, Jr., a Philadelphia physician, who taught Derham to compound drugs and to provide simple assistance to patients.

After Kearsley died in 1777, Derham became the property of Gregory West, surgeon to the Sixteenth British Regiment. Later he became slave to Roberto Dow, a New Orleans physician. With his medical background, Derham was able to assist Dow with medical services. Derham purchased his freedom on April 2, 1783.

While in Philadelphia in 1788, Derham met prominent local physician Benjamin Rush. By now Derham had become fluent in Spanish and French. Rush was so impressed with Derham's medical and linguistic ability that he maintained contact with him after Derham returned to New Orleans and resumed his medical practice in 1789. Derham, who treated diphtheria patients, also was able to help contain the yellow fever epidemic in New Orleans in 1796.

Derham's business was threatened on August 14, 1801, when medical officials restricted unlicensed physicians from practicing without a medical degree. He appears to have practiced briefly after 1801. Benjamin Rush tried to persuade him to relocate to Philadelphia, but there is no evidence that he did. No further record of Derham's activities has been found after that time.

See also EDUCATION [2]; LOUISIANA [3]; NEW ORLEANS [4]; LOUISIANA [3].

REFERENCES

Logan, Rayford W., and Michael R. Winston, eds. *Dictionary of American Negro Biography*. 1982.

Morais, Herbert M. *The History of the Negro in Medicine*. 1967.

Woodson, Carter G. *Education of the Negro Prior to 1861*. 1919.

FREDERICK D. SMITH, JR.

Detroit, Michigan (Update). After several decades in which its name evoked urban decay, African-American Detroit experienced a modest revival of its fortunes at the end of the twentieth century. The revival went in tandem with a resurgence of the automobile industry that had first drawn Detroit's large African-American population northward. A federal "enterprise zone" established in the city in 1995 drew over $2 billion in investment from the automobile troika of General Motors, Ford, and Chrysler (now Daimler-Chrysler) in its first two years; those investments and the late 1990s opening of three large downtown gambling casinos resulted in thousands of new jobs. Crime fell, and the city's unemployment rate dropped out of its chronic double digits. Charged with jump-starting and nurturing the city's revitalization was African-American mayor Dennis Archer, viewed by some as possessing a more hands-on, technically oriented management style than his populist predecessor, Coleman Young (elected in 1973 as Detroit's first African-American mayor). An attorney and former Michigan Supreme Court justice, Archer was elected over a Young-backed opponent in 1993 and cruised to re-election four years later with 83 percent of the vote. The Detroit metropolitan area remained among the most racially segregated in the U.S., and community tensions ran high after several incidents, most notably the 1992 killing of a black man, Malice Green, during a traffic stop conducted by two white police officers. The city's cultural map was enriched by the 1997 reopening, after a $38 million transformation, of its Museum of African-American History; the largest museum of its type in the U.S., it featured a spectacular, African-inspired rotunda and won praise for its lifelike displays chronicling the trials enslaved Africans endured. Detroit's musical vitality was demonstrated anew in the 1990s as multiple generations of the Winans family, led by Perfecting Church pastor the Rev. Marvin Winans, inspired a host of other artists who came to dominate the black gospel genre.

REFERENCES

Ankeny, Robert. "Building Blocks." *Crain's Detroit Business*, November 24, 1997, p. 11.

"Archer, Dennis." *Current Biography Yearbook*. 1997.

Mitchell, Jacqueline. "On the Rebound." *Emerge* (October, 1997), 54-57.

Spratling, Cassandra, and Kelley Carter. "Sunday Proving Grounds: Gospel Singers and Musicians Showcase Their Talents in Metro Detroit Churches." *Detroit Free Press* (December 20, 1998): D1.

JAMES MANHEIM

Dickerson, Spencer C. (December 1, 1871–February 25, 1948), physician. Spencer C. Dickerson was an army officer and a physician who became the first African American pathologist at Provident Hospital, Chicago. Dickerson was born in Austin, Texas. He attended Tillotson (now Huston-Tillotson) College and taught in Nashville, Tennessee, before enrolling in the University of Chicago. Excelling in academics and athletics, he earned a B.S. degree there in 1897. He obtained a M.D. degree at Rush Medical College, Chicago, in 1901. Dickerson interned at Freedmen's Hospital, Washington, D.C., and established a practice in New Bedford, Massachusetts.

Dickerson returned to Chicago in 1907 and became the first black pathologist at Provident Hospital, holding the position until 1912. In the course of his long association with the hospital he held positions such as ophthalmologist and otolaryngologist (1920–1937), departmental chairman (1930–1937), and chair of the executive committee (1943–1946). Concurrent with this career was his participation in the Illinois National Guard during which he saw two periods of active duty.

Enlisting in the guard as a private in 1914, he was mustered into service with the rank of second lieutenant for Mexican border duty in 1916. When his unit was federalized in 1917 because of World War I,

Dickerson became a captain and saw service overseas in France. Remaining with the guard after the war, he received several promotions, became commanding officer of the Medical Department Detachment in 1929, and retired as a brigadier general in 1934. Dickerson died of a heart ailment in 1948.

See also BLACK HOSPITALS [1]; MEDICAL EDUCATION [3]; WORLD WAR I [5].

REFERENCES

Christian, Garna L. "Spencer C. Dickerson." In *Handbook of Texas Online*. http://www.tsha.utexas.edu/handbook/online/articles/view/DD/fdi35.html.

Johnson, Charles, Jr. "Spencer C. Dickerson." In *Dictionary of American Negro Biography*, edited by Rayford W. Logan and Michael R. Winston. 1982.

ROBERT L. JOHNS

Dillard University.

Dillard University, a historically black college located in New Orleans, Louisiana, grew out of two institutions, Straight College and New Orleans University. Straight College (originally Straight University) was founded by the American Missionary Association in 1869 in order to educate emancipated African Americans. Straight featured both secondary and undergraduate programs and briefly housed a Law Department. New Orleans University, created by the Methodist Episcopal Church, was originally called the Union Normal School. Following the end of Reconstruction, Union was transformed into an undergraduate institution, New Orleans University, while the Gilbert Academy was established under university auspices as a secondary school. Shortly thereafter, a medical department and nursing school were added, and the Sarah Goodridge Hospital and Nursing Training School (later Flint-Goodridge Hospital) was set up as a teaching institution. Although the medical school closed in 1911, Flint-Goodridge Hospital remained affiliated with the university until 1983.

In 1930, Straight College and New Orleans University merged. The new institution was named Dillard University in honor of James Hardy Dillard, a pioneering educator of African Americans in the South. Will W. Alexander, the director of the Commission on Interracial Cooperation and a leading Southern white liberal, was named acting president. Following Alexander's departure in 1937, the distinguished educator Albert Dent became Dillard's first African American president. During these years, a student theater group, the Dillard Players, became nationally known. By 2000, Dillard had 1697 students and 125 full-time faculty. In addition to its academic and athletic programs, it sponsors a notable yearly conference on Black-Jewish relations.

See also BOND, HORACE MANN [1]; BUGGS, CHARLES WESLEY [1]; CATLETT, ELIZABETH [1]; DAVIS, WILLIAM ALLISON [2]; GRANGER, LESTER BLACKWELL [2]; LOUISIANA [3]; NEW ORLEANS, LOUISIANA [4].

REFERENCE

Dent, Jessie Covington, *Reminiscences of Dillard University: The Early Years*. 1991.

GREG ROBINSON

Dinkins, David Norman (Update)

(July 10, 1927–), politician. In 1989, Dinkins ran for mayor against incumbent Edward I. Koch. Dinkins presented himself as a civil alternative to the acrimonious Koch and as someone who could better handle the city's racial problems, which he accused the three-term mayor of exacerbating. He defeated Koch in the Democratic primary and in the election defeated Republican Rudolph Giuliani by a slim margin, thereby becoming the first African-American mayor in New York City's history. His tenure as mayor had its share of budgetary and political problems. He earned the reputation of a cautious and careful administrator, proving reasonably adept in negotiating the treacherous complexities of New York City's racial and ethnic politics, but he was widely criticized as ineffective and biased in his handling of black boycotts of Korean-American shop owners in 1992 and in his response to the Crown Heights riot in 1993. Following his narrow defeat for reelection by Rudolph Giuliani in 1993, Dinkins hosted a radio show and taught at Columbia University. A longtime tennis fan, he remained active on the board of the United States Tennis Association.

REFERENCES

"David Dinkins." In *Encyclopedia of World Biography*, 2nd ed. 1999.

Moritz, Charles ed. *Current Biography Yearbook*. 1990.

JAMES BRADLEY
UPDATED BY GREG ROBINSON

Dixon, Julian

(August 8, 1934–), U.S. Congressman. He was born in Washington, D.C., but grew up in Los Angeles. He earned a bachelor's degree from

David Dinkins. (AP/Wide World Photos)

Los Angeles State College in 1962 and a law degree from Southwestern University, Los Angeles, in 1967. Between 1957 and 1960 Dixon served in the U.S. Army.

Dixon practiced law in Los Angeles, and in 1972 he won a seat in the California State Assembly, serving three terms. In 1978 he was elected to the House of Representatives, where his eleventh consecutive term ended in 2000. He revealed that he was an effective politician in a number of difficult situations. For example, as chairman of the National Democratic Convention's Rules Committee in 1984, he had to handle Jesse Jackson's challenge to the way the party selected delegates without producing a major televised confrontation. Later as chairman of the House Ethics Committee, he had to deal with the scandal which led to the resignation of Speaker Jim Wright in 1989. Dixon won appointment to the Permanent Select Committee on Intelligence, on which he is now the ranking minority member. He also became a member of the powerful Appropriations Committee. When the Democrats controlled the House, he served as chairman of the subcommittee on the District of Columbia.

Dixon has accrued much power in the House, and he is consistent in looking after the interests of his district. For example, he sought ways to diminish the effect of the cuts in defense spending on his district. At the same time, he has been a reliable liberal voice in Congress.

See also CALIFORNIA [1]; DEMOCRATIC PARTY [2]; LOS ANGELES, CALIFORNIA [3].

REFERENCES

Manheim, James M. "Julian C. Dixon." In *Contemporary Black Biography*, vol. 24, edited by Shirelle Phelps. 2000.

"Rep. Julian Dixon (D-CA-32nd)." http://legislators.com/cgi-bin/member.pl?dir=congressorg2&_member=ca32.

ROBERT L. JOHNS

Dorman, Isaiah (?–June 25, 1876), frontiersman and interpreter. Isaiah Dorman was a frontiersman and interpreter, who died at the Battle of the Little Big Horn. Nothing is known of his origins before his arrival among the Sioux about 1850. Dorman enters the written historical record in 1865 when he settled near Fort Rice, located near the present town of Bismarck, North Dakota. At that time he was married to a woman of the Santee Sioux. He earned his living

Julian C. Dixon talking to the media. (AP/Wide World Photos)

by cutting wood first for the fort and then for a trading firm. In November of that year he was hired to carry the mail between Fort Rice and Fort Wadsworth during a period when the trip was becoming too dangerous for a single soldier. Although he made only one trip, he confirmed a reputation for competence and dependability. From this time on, he worked in various capacities for the army. After serving as guide and interpreter for the 1871 survey for the Northern Pacific Railroad that November, he was hired by the army as post interpreter.

Dorman was a great success in this role. General Custer specifically requested his services for the Little Big Horn campaign in 1876. During the battle, Dorman was severely wounded. The dying Dorman had to be left behind when the troops moved to a new position. Descriptions vary, but his body was mutilated when found. At the time of his death, the army owed Dorman just over a hundred dollars for his services. This sum was never claimed.

See also INDIAN WARS [3]; WEST, BLACKS IN THE [5].

REFERENCES

Ege, Robert J. "Isaiah Dorman." In *Dictionary of American Negro Biography*, edited by Rayford W. Logan and Michael R. 1982.

Garraty, John A., and Mark C. Carnes, eds. *American National Biography*. 1999.

McConnell, Roland C. "Isaiah Dorman and the Custer Expedition." *Journal of Negro History*, July 1948.

ROBERT L. JOHNS

Downing, Henry F. (c. 1846–February 19, 1928), consul and writer. An early Pan-Africanist, Downing advocated self-reliance for African Americans and Africans and held leadership positions in America and Africa during the late nineteenth century. Born in Manhattan, New York, Downing enlisted with the Union Navy in August 1864. Following the Union's victory in the Civil War, Downing took up residency in Liberia and became a private secretary to the country's Secretary of State, before returning to America.

Downing's involvement with New York's Democratic Party in the 1880s led to his appointment by President Grover Cleveland as U.S. Consul to Loanda, Angola, and Portuguese West Africa. As a consul and as a manager of the Afro-American Advice Bureau, he promoted the natural resources of Africa and worked to widen trade between Africa and the U.S. In 1900, Downing began serving on the executive committee of the Pan-African Association. By 1913, Downing entered a more reflective and creative period, and the first of his plays and novels was serialized in *The African Times and The Orient*. His plays include *The Shuttlecock or Israel in Russia, The Exiles, The Sinews of War, Human Nature, The Arabian Lovers, Lord Eldred's Other Daughter, Melic Ric*, and *The Statute and The Wasp*. He co-wrote with his second wife *Placing Paul's Play*, and *Which Should She Have Saved?* A few of Downing's plays were published in London by F. Griffiths, and he also wrote a novel, *The American Calvarymen*, and two non-fiction books, *Liberia and Her People* and *A Short History of Liberia*

See also AMBASSADORS AND DIPLOMATS [1]; CIVIL WAR [2]; LITERATURE [3].

REFERENCES

Crisis 15, (1918); 186.

Journal of American Negro History 3 (1918); 444.

Logan, Rayford W. and Michael R. Winston. *Dictionary of American Negro Biography*. 1982.

Rush, Theresa, Carol Myers, and Ester Arata. *Black American Writers Past and Present: A Biographical and Bibliographical Dictionary*. 1975

F. ZEAL HARRIS

Dudley, Edward Richard (March 11, 1911–), lawyer, statesman, judge. Edward Dudley initially hoped to become a dentist as a 1932 graduate of Johnson C. Smith University. However, the Great Depression halted further studies at Howard University in 1934, and a move to New York City set Dudley on a different career path. He graduated from St. John's Law School in 1941 and also became involved with the city's Democratic Party.

Dudley's support of Democratic campaigns as a district captain paid off professionally when he was named assistant attorney general in 1942. After World War II, Dudley became a legal aide to the governor of the Virgin Islands, and the international experience prepared him for his appointment as minister to Liberia by President Truman in 1948. One year later, Dudley became the first African American ambassador. He distinguished himself by implementing the first Point Four Program in Africa—a foreign aid project.

After leaving the post in 1953, Dudley held a series of judgeships in New York, although he interrupted his legal career to become borough president of Manhattan from 1961 through the end of 1964. During this time he became the first African American to be nominated for state attorney general (he lost the election) and the first African American to be named the chairman of the New York County Democratic Committee. In 1965, he was elected to the State Supreme Court, First District, Manhattan. After other administrative designations, in 1971 Dudley became administrative judge for the New York State Supreme Court for Manhattan. He retired from the bench in 1985.

See also AMBASSADORS AND DIPLOMATS [1]; DEMOCRATIC PARTY [2]; LAWYERS [3]; NEW YORK CITY [4].

REFERENCES

Smith, Jessie Carney, ed. *Notable Black American Men.* 1999.

Who's Who Among African Americans, 1998–99, 10th ed. 1997.

Who's Who in American Politics, 1979–80, 7th ed. 1979.

RAYMOND WINBUSH

Dudley, Sherman H. (c. 1870–March 1, 1940), theatrical promoter and organizer. S. H. Dudley—he preferred to use the initials—was a notable theatrical promoter and organizer. He was born in Dallas, Texas, and he began his career in medicine shows. His name begins to appear in print with various minstrel shows in the 1890s. He joined the movement away from the minstrel tradition with his musical *The Smart Set* in 1896, which featured a chorus of beautiful women. For many years Dudley produced annual new versions of this show, and he also became a major producer of other people's shows.

Dudley became a star performer in his own right in the early 1900s. He introduced his most successful act when he appeared onstage talking to a mule that was dressed in overalls and seemed to understand the comedian. This act still convulsed audiences when Dudley retired from the stage in 1917.

In 1911 Dudley formed Dudley's Theatrical Enterprise, with four theaters, one in Washington and three in Virginia. Dudley himself owned two of the theaters. From this seed grew the Theater Owner's Booking Association (TOBA). By 1916 the circuit grew to over twenty-eight theaters throughout the country. Acts now could sign for an entire eight-month season on one circuit. Although TOBA could ensure steady work, its control over bookings meant that performers tended to dislike it. Dudley had to sell his theaters at the beginning of the Depression. He died on his Maryland farm, where he raised thoroughbred cattle and racehorses.

See also MUSICAL THEATER [4]; TEXAS [5].

REFERENCES

Fax, Elton C. "Sherman H. Dudley." In *Dictionary of Negro American Biography,* edited by Rayford W. Logan and Michael R. Winston. 1982.

Monsho, Kharen. "Sherman H. Dudley." In *The Handbook of Texas Online.* http://www.tsha.utexas.edu/handbook/online/articles/view/DD/fdumj.html.

ROBERT L. JOHNS

Durham, John Stephens (July 18, 1861–October 16, 1919), journalist, lawyer, diplomat. John Stephens Durham was born in Philadelphia, a descendant of two founders of the African Methodist Episcopal Church. Although he had worked as a teacher and had a degree in civil engineering from Towne Scientific College-a branch of the University of Pennsylvania-Durham took a job as assistant editor for the *Philadelphia Evening Bulletin,* reporting on international and African American affairs.

Heavily active in the Philadelphia African American community and a Republican, Durham won the support of community leaders in his bid for a diplomatic post. President Benjamin Harrison appointed

Mervyn Dymally. (AP/Wide World Photos)

him U.S. Consul in the Dominican Republic in 1890. In 1891 he replaced Frederick Douglass as minister-in-residence and consul-general to Haiti and charge d'affaires in the Dominican Republic. Durham handled serious diplomatic issues well, but resigned his position in 1893 after a change in administrations.

Thereafter, Durham split his time between Philadelphia, where he established a law practice, and the international scene. Shortly after resigning his diplomatic post, he became manager of a sugar refinery in the Dominican Republic, and, in 1902, combined his law career and his expertise in international affairs as an assistant attorney with the Spanish Treaty Claims Commission in Cuba. In the course of that three-year post, he reported on the damage done by an erupting volcano in Martinique, later published as *The Martinique Horror* and St. Vincent Calamity. Durham was a sought-after speaker; a collection of his speeches was published as *To Teach the Negro History* (1897). He died of stomach cancer in 1919.

See also AMBASSADORS AND DIPLOMATS [1]; PHILADELPHIA, PENNSYLVANIA [4]; REPUBLICAN PARTY [5].

REFERENCES

Christmas, Walter, ed. *Negroes in Public Affairs and Government*, vol. 1. 1966.

Logan, Rayford W., and Michael R. Winston, eds. *Dictionary of American Negro Biography*. 1982.

CARRELL P. HORTON

Dymally, Mervyn Malcolm (May 12, 1926–),
politician, educator, entrepreneur. Mervyn Dymally came to the United States from the West Indies in 1946 to study at Lincoln University in Jefferson City, Missouri. In 1954 he received his B.A. degree from California State University in Los Angeles, the M.A. degree from the Sacramento campus in 1969, and the Ph.D. degree from United States International University in San Diego in 1978. Dymally taught exceptional children in Los Angeles in 1956, and then entered the political arena.

A California state senator from 1963 to 1966, Dymally was elected lieutenant governor of California in 1974. His assignment included heading the State Commission for Economic Development and the Commission of the Californias. He lost reelection in 1978; in November 1980 he was elected to the U.S. Congress representing Californias 31st Congressional District, southern Los Angeles County. Until he retired in 1992, Dymally served on several committees and from 1987 to 1989 chaired the Congressional Black Caucus. Dymally sponsored legislation in support of human rights groups and was particularly concerned with U.S. policies toward African nations and Caribbean. He supported increased funding for minority students and senior citizens, and better opportunities for minority-owned and operated energy firms.

An expert in Caribbean affairs, science and technology, and educational opportunity, Dymally also authored the book *The Black Politician: His Struggle for Power* (1971). After retirement, he became president of Dymally International Group, Incorporated, a consulting and financial advisory firm.

See also CALIFORNIA [1]; CONGRESSIONAL BLACK CAUCUS [2]; LINCOLN UNIVERSITY [3].

REFERENCES

Henderson, Ashyia N., and Shirelle Phelps, eds. *Who's Who Among African Americans*, 12th ed. 1999.

"Mervyn Malcolm Dymally." http://www.vitrade.com/who_is_who/dymally/mervyn_malcolm_dymally.htm.

"Profile of Directors. Mervyn Dymally." http://www.vitrade.com/who_is_who/dymally/ifcl_profile_of_directors.htm.

RAYMOND WINBUSH

E

Eagleson, William Lewis (August 9, 1835–June 22, 1899), editor, political activist. Born in St. Louis, Eagleson was important in the development of the African American community in the West. While a young man, he learned the printing and barbering trades that he drew upon throughout his life. In 1865 he married Elizabeth McKinney, and they had nine children. The Eaglesons moved to Fort Scott, Kansas, in the 1870s where he began publishing the *Colored Citizen*, the first black-owned newspaper in the state. Later he moved the paper to Topeka, which had a much larger African American community. Eagleson and associate editor T. W. Henderson, a prominent local minister, used the paper to promote greater African American participation in the Republican Party and to promote themselves politically. After the paper ceased publication in 1880, Eagleson began to publish the *Kansas Herald*. By June that year, the newspaper closed, and Eagleson's career in journalism was over.

Eagleston left public life for a while and worked at various jobs. By the mid-1880s, he became disillusioned with the Republican Party and became a Democrat. In 1889 he was active in building the all-black town, Langston City, Oklahoma, and recruited settlers to the new land. He relocated to Langston City in 1891 but later returned to Topeka. He pursued other interests and made an unsuccessful attempt to publish another newspaper. His last effort to help the African American community was to create a home for the aged. Eagleson is remembered for establishing the first two black-owned newspapers in the frontier West. *See also* JOURNALISM [3]; WEST, BLACKS IN THE [5].

REFERENCES

Cox, Thomas C. *Blacks in Topeka, Kansas, 1865–1915*. 1982.

Garraty, John A., and Mark C. Carnes, general eds. *American National Biography*, vol. 7. 1999.

Logan, Rayford W., and Michael R. Winston, eds. *Dictionary of American Negro Biography*. 1982.

JESSIE CARNEY SMITH

Easton, Hosea (September 1, 1798–1837), abolitionist. In 1837 Hosea Easton published one of the earliest analyses of slavery by an African American. Although *A Treatise on the Intellectual Character, and Civil and Political Condition of the Colored People of the United States* addresses the issues facing African Americans in a comprehensive fashion, it attracted little enduring attention.

Easton came from a distinguished family of mixed African, white, and Native American heritage. His father, James (1854–1830), was a skilled ironworker in North Bridgewater (now Brockton), Massachusetts. James Easton instituted a manual training school for young black men; its failure after a nearly ten-year existence, coupled with that of his father's business, embittered Hosea.

The early years of Hosea Easton are obscure, but by 1828 he was active in Boston and taking his position among the elite. His first publication was a "Thanksgiving Day Address" to the black population of Providence, Rhode Island (1828). He was a delegate to the first National Colored Convention, held in Philadelphia in 1831, as well as to following conventions. In 1833 Easton became pastor of Talcott Street Congregational Church, Hartford, Connecticut. Racial tensions and violence in the city ran high, and in 1836, just after Easton became pastor of the Colored Methodist Episcopal Zion church, the building was burned out.

Easton clearly perceived the limitations of self-help and uplift within the black community to improve the situation. *A Treatise* addressed whites and called on them to realize the deleterious effects of racism and to take steps to repair the damages it caused. The work appeared shortly before his death.
See also INTELLECTUAL LIFE [3]; SLAVERY [5].

REFERENCES

"In Search of History." http://www.newhavenadvocate.com/articles/lblood2.html.

Price, George R. and James Brewer Stewart, eds. *To Heal the Scourge of Prejudice: The Life and Writings of Hosea Easton*. 1999.

ROBERT L. JOHNS

Edison, Harry "Sweets" (October 10, 1915–July 27, 1999), musician. Born in Columbus, Ohio, in his early childhood Edison stayed with an uncle in Kentucky, who introduced him to music. He returned to Columbus when he was twelve and began playing trumpet in a variety of groups. In 1937 he joined Lucky Millinder's band in New York, and it was here that Count Basic heard him, was impressed with his talent, and persuaded him to join his band in Kansas City. He became a fixture with the band almost immediately, bringing new improvisational talents and a bright sense of humor. His riff style often included riding long, sustained notes of non-resolution over the harmony, together with innovative muting and imaginative embellishments.

After the band briefly broke up in 1950, Edison continued with a variety of groups, playing and touring with Jazz at the Philharmonic, Buddy Rich, and Coleman Hawkins. He returned briefly to the reconstituted Basie band and toured Europe with the group in 1970. Singers he worked and recorded with over the years included Jimmy Rushing, Josephine

Harry "Sweets" Edison, playing trumpet. (Copyright by Jack Vartoogian)

Baker, and Frank Sinatra. Later, he was active on the West Coast, forming his own groups and working with Louis Bellson and Eddie "Lockjaw" Davis in the 1980s.

Initially inspired by jazz great Louis Armstrong, Edison favored a direct, full tone, with highly imaginative solo playing. He has left a plentiful recorded legacy, and may be seen in the pioneering jazz film, *Jammin' the Blues*. Edison died in Columbus.
See also BASIE, WILLIAM JAMES "COUNT" [1]; JAZZ [3].

REFERENCES

Chilton, John. *Who's Who of Jazz*. 1970.

Kernfeld, Barry, ed. *New Grove Dictionary of Jazz*. 1994.

Schuller, Gunther. *The Swing Era*. 1989.

DARIUS L. THIEME

Ellis, George Washington (May 4, 1875–November 26, 1919), lawyer. George Washington Ellis was born in Weston, Missouri. He received his elementary and secondary education in Weston and in

Atchison, Kansas, and went on to receive two degrees from the University of Kansas: L.L.B. (1893) and B.A. (1897). He did further work at the Gunton Institute of Economics and Sociology (New York) and at the Howard University (Washington, D.C.) School of Pedagogy.

Ellis' career involved him in the practice of law, sociological research, and government service as a diplomat. He practiced law in Kansas from 1893 to 1897, leaving to study in New York. In 1899 he was appointed to the Census Division of the U. S. Department of the Interior in Washington, followed in 1902 by his appointment as secretary of the U. S. legation in the Republic of Liberia.

For eight years, Ellis served in Liberia. There he used his sociological research skills to study various African tribes. He published several ethnological works on Africa and is credited by some as first to recognize the Vai language of Africa as a written language Ellis resigned his diplomatic post in 1910, came back to the United States, and opened a law practice in Chicago. He was elected the City of Chicago's assistant corporation counsel in 1917 and held this position until his death.

Ellis' many honors include being named knight commander of the Order of African Redemption by Liberia and elected as a fellow of the Royal Geographical Society of Great Britain. As a Republican, he was a frequent campaign speaker and an influential party member. He died in Chicago.

See also AFRICA [1]; CHICAGO, ILLINOIS [1]; LAWYERS [3].

REFERENCES

Johnson, Allen, and Dumas Malone, eds. *Dictionary of American Biography.* 1983.

Logan, Rayford W., and Michael R. Winston, eds. *Dictionary of American Negro Biography.* 1982.

CARRELL P. HORTON

Ellison, William (1790–December 5, 1861), artisan and planter.

He was born a slave near Winnsboro, South Carolina. In about 1802 he began an apprenticeship to a cotton-gin maker. The skills his acquired in this new technology were the foundations on which he built to become one of the richest free blacks in the South. Gaining his freedom in 1816, Ellison moved to Stateburg and set up a business building and repairing cotton gins. His prosperity enabled him to purchase and free the members of his family. By 1820 he owned a work force of two male slaves, and he soon began to acquire land. Ellison's marginal status in the community became visible in 1824 when the vestry of Holy Cross Episcopal Church allowed him and his family to move from the gallery reserved for slaves and free blacks to a bench at the rear of the main floor twenty years later; he was able to rent a pew at the very back of the church.

By 1840 the changing pattern of his slave ownership suggests that agriculture was becoming a major source of income in addition to his shop, which now included carpentry and blacksmith work. In 1860 Ellison owned 900 acres of land and 63 slaves. Unreliable tradition depicts him as a harsh master, and the ratio of male to female suggests that he systematically sold off the girl children. In addition to his shop, he owned two substantial houses where 16 members of the family were living in 1850. The children married into the elite of Charleston's free blacks. Ellison died just at the beginning of the Civil War.

See also ENTREPRENEURS [2]; SOUTH CAROLINA [5].

REFERENCES

Johns, Robert L. "William Ellison." In *Notable Black American Men*, edited by Jessie Carney Smith. 1999.

Johnson, Michael P., and James L. Roark. *Black Masters: A Free Family of Color in the Old South.* 1984.

ROBERT L. JOHNS

Emanuel, James A., Sr. (June 14, 1921–), poet, teacher, critic.

Emanuel was born in Alliance, Nebraska, and educated at Howard University (B.A. 1950), Northwestern University (M.A. 1953), and Columbia University (Ph. D. 1962). His work experience includes the Civilian Conservation Corps, the U. S. War Department, and academic positions at City College of the City University of New York; he has been a Fulbright Professor at the University of Grenoble, France (1968–1969), and the University of Warsaw, Poland (1975–1976), and at the University of Toulouse, France (1979–1981).

As a poet, Emanuel has given readings and lectures in numerous settings and locales, including Europe and Africa. He has provided poetry readings on both the BBC and "The Voice of America." His themes are broad and encompass the human experience. His titles reflect some of his focuses: "Emmett Till," "White Power Structure," "Black Poet on the Firing Line," and "Kickass". His published works include *The Treehouse and Other Poems* (1968), *At Bay* (1968), *Panther Man* (1970), *Black Man Abroad: The Toulouse Poems* (1978), *A Chisel in the Dark: Poems, Selected and*

New (1980), *The Broken Bowl: New and Uncollected Poems* (1983), *Deadly James and Other Poems* (1987), *A Poet's Mind* (1987), *Whole Grain* (1991), and *Jazz From the Haiku King* (1999).

Emanuel has co-edited *Dark Symphony: Negro Literature in America* (1968), published a collection of essays, *Langston Hughes* (1967), and has written numerous critical articles in which he addresses such subjects as blackness, literary theory, and the Black Aesthetic.

See also EXPATRIATES [2]; LITERATURE [3].

REFERENCES

Holdt, Marvin. "James A. Emanuel: Black Man Abroad." *Black American Literature Forum* 13 (1979): 79-85.

May, Hal, ed., *Black Writers*. 1989.

Rush, Theressa Gunnels, and others. *Black American Writers Past and Present*. 1975.

HELEN R. HOUSTON

Espy, Michael (November 30, 1953–), government official. Mike Espy, the first African-American Congressman from Mississippi since Reconstruction, and later U.S. Secretary of Agriculture, was born in Yazoo City, Mississippi. His father, Henry Espy, who had taken over the family's mortuary business, was also a former inspector for the U.S Department of Agriculture. Espy attended integrated Catholic schools, then in 1969 became the only black at Yazoo City High School. Espy attended Howard University, receiving his B.A. in 1975. In 1978, after he received a law degree from the University of Santa Clara in California, Espy returned to Mississippi and was appointed assistant secretary of state. In 1984, he was promoted to assistant state attorney general.

In 1986, Espy ran in the Democratic primary for the Congressional seat representing Mississippi's second district, which had been redrawn to give African-Americans a slight majority. His opponents included the grandson of a former and the cousin of a longtime U.S. Senator. Espy ran a vigorous campaign and won, with 50.1 percent of the vote, barely avoiding a runoff. In the general election, despite winning only 10 percent of the white vote, Espy unseated Republican incumbent Webb Franklin thanks to overwhelming black support. In his successful reelection campaigns in 1988, 1990, and 1992, Espy won significant white support. In Congress, Espy distinguished himself as a member of the Agriculture Committee. Politically he was a moderate who supported antipoverty programs

for Mississippi, opposed aid to the Nicaraguan contras, and upheld abortion rights; but he also supported school prayer and capital punishment, and served as the outstanding Congressional supporter of (and spokesperson for) the National Rifle Association.

In 1992, Espy was a prominent early supporter of Arkansas Governor Bill Clinton's successful Presidential candidacy. Clinton responded in 1993 by appointing Espy U.S. Secretary of Agriculture, making him not only the first African American, but the first Southerner to hold the post. As Secretary, Espy fought for aid to farmers after the catastrophic 1993 Mississippi River floods, and he overhauled the department's food inspection process. He also visited China in an effort to persuade Chinese leaders to import American wheat.

In October 1994, following rumors of bribery and corruption, Espy resigned as Secretary of Agriculture and opened a law office in Jackson, Mississippi. Donald Smaltz was engaged as a Special Prosecutor to investigate Espy, and in 1995, Espy was indicted on 30 counts of accepting gifts, of $34,000 in transportation and tickets to sporting events, from Tyson Foods and other companies regulated by Espy's department. Over the following years, Espy's trial was repeatedly delayed due to appeals by subordinates. Meanwhile, Smaltz was widely criticized for pursuing Espy, despite having a weak case against him. In 1998, Espy pleaded guilty to using campaign funds to pay legal bills, and was fined $50,000. However, that December, in a verdict that was widely seen as a reproof to the institution of the Special Prosecutor, a Mississippi jury acquitted Espy of all criminal charges.

See also MISSISSIPPI [4]; PRESIDENTS OF THE UNITED STATES [4].

REFERENCE

Smith, Jessie Carney, ed., "Mike Espy." *Notable Black American Men*. 1999.

GREG ROBINSON

Everett, Francine (Franceine Williamson) (April 13, 1917–May 27, 1999), actress. Francine Everett was born in Louisburg, North Carolina. Her family moved to Harlem, and she attended St. Mark's School but dropped out to work as a singer and dancer. A strikingly beautiful woman, she was in the chorus at Small's Paradise about 1933 and worked with the Four Black Cats, a night club act, in the same year. She married but her husband died in an accident after one year. In 1936 Everett joined the Federal

Theater Project in Harlem. There she met Rex Ingram, who became her second husband. The pair moved to California that year. Ingram played "De Lawd" in *Green Pastures*, but Everett turned down a role as an angel. Their marriage ended in divorce in 1939.

Everett pursued a career in independent black films. She acted with boxer Henry Armstrong in *Keep Punching* (1939) and appeared in the same year in *Paradise in Harlem*. In 1943 she began appearing as a vocalist in more that fifty short musical films. From 1945 to 1946 she made such "race" films as *Big Timers* (1945) and *Dirty Gerty from Harlem, U.S.A.* (1946). Two bit parts in Hollywood films (1949 and 1950) mark the end of her entertainment career. From the 1961 to her retirement in 1985, Everett held a clerical job at Harlem Hospital. After being mugged twice in her later years, she was fearful of leaving her apartment unless someone was with her, although she continued to receive invitations to participate in seminars and panels on black films.
See also FILM [2].

REFERENCES

Escamilla, Brian. "Francine Everett." In *Contemporary Black Biography*, vol. 23, edited by David G. Oblender. 2000.

Watkins, Mel. "Francine Everett, Striking Star of All-Black Movies, Is Dead." *New York Times*, 20 June 1999.

ROBERT L. JOHNS

Myrlie Evers-Williams. (AP/Wide World Press)

Evers-Williams, Myrlie Beasley

(March 17, 1933–), organization executive, civil rights activist. Evers-Williams, first known for her fight for racial justice and equality, rose to a highly visible position as chair of the NAACP's Board of Directors, the second African American women in that post. Born in Vicksburg, Mississippi, Evers-Williams attended Alcorn A & M College but dropped out after she met fellow student Medgar Evers and married him.

Medgar Evers was involved with the NAACP during and after college. He became field secretary of the NAACP in 1954 and then headed the NAACP's Mississippi State Office when it opened in 1955. Myrlie Evers was his secretary. Their work with the NAACP during the Civil Rights Movement brought them numerous death threats. After Medgar Evers organized a boycott in downtown Jackson, the threats peaked and their home was firebombed. Threats became reality in the family's driveway on June 12, 1963, when Evers was murdered. Byron de la Beckwith, a white salesman, an outspoken segregationist, and a

founding member of the White Citizen's Council, was indicted for the crime. Although he was set free, and retried but not convicted, Myrlie Evers continued to fight for justice ending with a third trial and conviction of de la Beckwith on February 5, 1994, and a life prison sentence.

Myrlie Evers started a new life in California. There she continued her studies at Pomona College and graduated in 1968. Later, in 1976, she married Walter Edward Williams, a civil rights worker and former longshoreman. She established a career of her own, working first as assistant director of planning and development for the Claremont College system. In 1973–1975 she was vice-president for advertising and publicity for the New York advertising firm, Seligman and Lapz, and traveled widely for the company. She continued her work in corporate America and in 1975 became consumer affairs director for Atlantic Richfield Company (ARCO). Her task was to oversee funding for community projects and approve funding for outreach programs. While with the company, she developed the concept for the first booklet in corporate America dealing with women in nontraditional roles, *Women at ARCO*. Now living in Los Angeles, Mayor Tom Bradley appointed Evers-Williams to the Board of Public Works, making her the first African American woman member.

Her association with the NAACP continued and was strengthened in 1995 when she was elected chair of its Board of Directors. She had been a member of the board for some time and served as vice-chair. Recognizing her leadership ability and knowledge of board operations, other board members encouraged her to seek its chairmanship. This followed the dismissal of executive director Benjamin F. Chavis and charges that executive director William G. Gibson had misused $1.4 million. Her campaign was brief, and she won by one vote. During her tenure, Evers-Williams strengthened the association, eliminated its debt, and restored national confidence in the organization. Evers-Williams stepped down from the board's chairmanship in 1998 and was succeeded by activist Julian Bond.

In addition to her career and her work in civil rights, Evers-Williams is a writer. Her book, *For Us the Living* (1967), tells the story of Medgar Evers' Mississippi's civil rights struggle, and her family's experiences through it all. Evers-Williams was contributing editor for *Ladies Home Journal* from the 1970s to 1984 and joined other editors in covering the Vietnam Peace Talks held in Paris.

See also EVERS, MEDGAR WYLIE [2]; NATIONAL ASSOCIATION FOR THE ADVANCEMENT OF COLORED PEOPLE (NAACP) [4].

REFERENCES

Hine, Darlene Clark, ed. *Black Women in America*. vol. 2. 1993.

Mabunda, L. Mpho, ed. *Contemporary Black Biography*. vol. 8. 1995.

Smith, Jessie Carney, ed. *Notable Black American Women*, Book II. 1996.

JESSIE CARNEY SMITH

Expatriates (Update). Athletes have long represented a special category of African-American expatriates. Beginning with Jack Johnson, black boxers have lived and/or fought in Europe and other parts of the world. Both during and after the Jim Crow era, many African-American baseball players spent large portions of their careers playing both winter and summer ball in Latin America, where they were untroubled by segregation or American racism. In more recent decades, African-American baseball players such as Roy White, Warren Cromartie, and Cecil Fielder have starred in Japanese leagues, while black basketball players have been lured to European teams.

In the 1980s and 1990s, changing racial and political tensions in the United States and throughout the world have had an impact on African-American expatriation. While many African Americans still prefer to live abroad, many have preferred to be "transatlantic commuters" rather than expatriates. Those for whom racism is a compelling reason to flee the United States in order to live and be buried elsewhere are now exceptions.

REFERENCES

Dunbar, Ernest. *The Black Expatriates*. 1968.

Fabre, Michel. *From Harlem to Paris: Black American Writers in France, 1840–1980*. 1991.

MICHEL FABRE
UPDATED BY GREG ROBINSON

F

Farley, James Conway (August 10, 1854–1910), photographer. James Conway Farley was born in Prince Edward County, Virginia. His parents had both been slaves. In 1861, following the death of his father, he and his mother moved to Richmond where Davis spent three years in public school.

Early on, Farley had jobs assisting in making candles at the hotel where his mother worked and working with a baker. His pathway to a career in photography had its roots in his employment in 1872 as a photo technician in the chemical department of C. R. Rees and Company, a photography firm in downtown Richmond. In 1875, he progressed to setting scenes and making pictures for the G. W. Davis Photo Gallery, another downtown firm. While working with the Photo Gallery, some white employees wanted Davis fired, but the Gallery owner fired them instead. At the time, Farley was one of few African Americans working as a photographer. He had a successful career for thirty-five years. He opened his own studio, the Jefferson Fine Arts Gallery, in 1895. He specialized in photographing individuals and groups and transferring the photos to greeting cards.

Farley's work is known to have received special recognition twice. He received first prize for his exhibit at the Richmond Colored Industrial Fair in 1884. A year later his work was rewarded with an honor at the New Orleans World Exposition. Only a few examples of his work exist, but one of his photographs was known to be on display at the Valentine Museum in Richmond as late as 1982.

See also PHOTOGRAPHY [4]; RICHMOND, VIRGINIA [4].

REFERENCES

Logan, Rayford W., and Michael R. Winston, eds. *Dictionary of American Negro Biography* 1982.

Simmons, William J., ed. *Men of Mark.* 1887.

Willis-Thomas, Deborah. *Black Photographers, 1840–1961.* 1985.

CARRELL P. HORTON

Farrakhan, Louis Abdul (Update) (May 17, 1933–). In the United States throughout the 1990s, Farrakhan remained an immensely controversial figure. In January 1995, newspapers revealed that Qubilah Shabazz, daughter of Malcolm X, had plotted with a gunman to assassinate Farrakhan. He responded by expressing sympathy for Shabazz, and he helped persuade federal officials to allow Shabazz to plea-bargain. Later that year, Farrakhan's plans for a Million Man March on Washington drew national attention. In October 1995, he delivered the keynote speech at the march, and he called for black men to repent for their treatment of their wives and to organize in their communities. In March 1996, Farrakhan drew widespread condemnation following a trip to

Louis Farrakhan. (AP/Wide World Photos).

Walter Fauntroy. (AP/Wide World Photos).

the Middle East that included stops in Iran, Libya, Syria and Nigeria, and for his announcement that Libyan dictator Mohamar Khadaffi had contributed $1 billion to the Nation of Islam.

Farrakhan returned to the public eye in 2000 after spending several months recovering from prostate cancer. Included in his activities were an admission on national television that his statements may have helped lead to Malcolm X's assassination, and an announcement of plans for a Million Family March, as a follow-up to the Million Man March of 1995.

REFERENCES

Clifford, Timothy. "Congress wants Farrakhan to explain Libyan ties." *Knight-Ridder/Tribune News* Service. Jan 30, 1996: p130K4589.

Hanchett, Doug. "Farrakhan regrets Malcolm X rhetoric." *Boston Herald*. May 11, 2000: 7.

Parish, Norm. "Farrakhan Visits Area, Beats Drum For Million Family March In Washington." *St Louis Post-Dispatch*. August 23, 2000: B3

GREG ROBINSON

Fauntroy, Walter E. (February 6, 1933–), minister, civil rights activist, politician. Walter Fauntroy was born in Washington, D.C., and graduated from Virginia Union University in 1955. Following his graduation from Yale Divinity School three years later, he became an ordained Baptist minister. Determined to eradicate segregation and racism, Fauntroy became a key strategist with the Southern Christian Leadership Conference (SCLC), working alongside Martin Luther King, Jr., on several important campaigns to increase public awareness of the injustice of racism. One of his most famous roles was as coordinator for the 1963 March on Washington.

Fauntroy's activities apart from SCLC likewise aimed to elevate the black community. He involved his Washington-based New Bethel Baptist Church congregation in civil rights agitation and formed the Model Inner City Community Organization to improve living conditions. His high-profile status in the Washington, D.C., community led to his 1967 appointment as vice chairman of the Washington City Council; he served for two years.

In 1970 the District of Columbia gained the right to elect a non-voting member to the House of Representatives. Fauntroy won the election and served in Congress for twenty years. In 1973 he was instrumental in procuring legislation that gave residents of Washington the right to directly elect a mayor and council members. Always concerned with the city's lack of power, he began to seek statehood for the district in the mid-1970s. Fauntroy left Congress to run for mayor in 1990 but was defeated by Sharon Pratt Kelly. After the loss in the election Fauntroy returned to his ministry and also established Walter E. Fauntroy and Associates, a consulting firm.

See also BAPTISTS [1]; CIVIL RIGHTS MOVEMENT [2]; KING, MARTIN LUTHER KING, JR. [3]; SOUTHERN CHRISTIAN LEADERSHIP CONFERENCE (SCLC) [5]; WASHINGTON, D.C. [5].

REFERENCES

Hardin, Blaine. "Chapter One: 1972–1975." [Series on the crises in Washington, D.C.] *Washington Post* June 18, 1995.

Johnson, Anne Janette. "Walter E. Fauntroy." In *Contemporary Black Biography.* Edited by L. Mpho Mabunda and Shirelle Phelps. 1996.

National Black Leadership Roundtable. "The Honorable Walter E. Fauntroy." http://www.nblr.org/faultroy.html.

ROBERT L. JOHNS

The Fellowship of Reconciliation.

The Fellowship of Reconciliation (FOR) was founded by English and German pacifists after the outbreak of World War I in 1914. FOR's American branch was founded one year later. Composed largely of the utopian left of American Protestantism, FOR has been at the cutting edge of social justice throughout its history, advocating nonviolent direct action to bring an end to war, racism, and economic injustice.

Much of the organization's early work involved keeping the United States out of the World War I and defending the rights of conscientious objectors. In 1916, the FOR helped to found the American Civil Liberties Union to defend the rights of pacifists. Prior to World War II, membership boomed, and the organization became a vocal critic of the internment of Japanese-Americans. Its commitment to pacifism has led the FOR to oppose all militarism, protesting every American war as well as nuclear arms proliferation.

In addition to its anti-war work, FOR has been a consistent advocate of racial equality and justice. In 1942, FOR created the Congress of Racial Equality (CORE), which was the first civil rights organization to use Gandhian techniques to achieve gains for African-Americans. In 1947, the organization spon-

sored the first "freedom rides" into the South to test the enforcement of Supreme Court anti-discrimination rulings. CORE became an important part of the civil rights movement, sponsoring freedom rides in 1961 and doing important voter registration work in Mississippi. Though FOR's membership has dwindled since the 1960s, it continues its work as the oldest peace organization in the United States and as a continued advocate non-violent protest.

See also CONGRESS OF RACIAL EQUALITY (CORE) [2]; FREEDOM RIDES [S]; LEWIS, JOHN [3].

REFERENCES

Chatfield, Charles, ed., *Peace Movements in America.* 1973.

Wittner, Lawrence S., *Rebels Against War: the American Peace Movement.* 1984.

MICHAEL WADE FUQUAY

Fishburne, Laurence (1961–), actor. Laurence Fishburne began his acting career with his stage debut at age ten and soon landed a three-year role on the television soap opera *One Life to Live*. Accepted into the prestigious High School of Performing Arts in New York City, Fishburne's fame was quick in coming. When he was fifteen, he landed a role in Francis Ford Coppola's *Apocalypse Now*, which led to work in other Coppola films *Rumble Fish* (1983), *The Cotton Club* (1984), and *Gardens of Stone* (1987).

Laurence Fishburne. (Archive Photos, Inc.)

Fishburne was careful in his choice of characters in order to avoid the typecasting which plagued so many of his fellow African American actors. He proved to be adept at choosing quality projects, taking roles in such highly acclaimed films as the *Color Purple* (1985), *Boyz N the Hood* (1991) and *Othello* (1995), the last of which was notable as the first time an African American played Othello in film. In 1993 Fishburne was nominated for an Academy Award for his role in *What's Love Got to Do with It*. Such was the power of his acting that Fishburne won roles not originally written for African American actors, such as his portrayal of a crazy gangster in *King of New York* (1990).

Even after achieving fame, Fishburne often lent his celebrity to lower-profile projects, including a series of acclaimed HBO movies with strong African American themes such as *The Tuskegee Airmen* (1995), *Miss Evers' Boys* (1997), and *Always Outnumbered* (1998). He also sporadically appeared in plays and on television, most notably in the television series *Tribeca*, for which he won an Emmy in 1993.
See also FILM [2].

REFERENCES

Current Biography Yearbook. 1996.

"Laurence Fishburne." In *Contemporary Black Biography*, vol. 22, edited by Shirelle Phelps. 1999.

FREDERICK D. SMITH, JR.

Fisher, Ada [Lois] Sipuel (February 8, 1924–October, 18, 1995), civil rights pioneer. Fisher was born in Chickashaw, Oklahoma. She married Warren W. Fisher in 1944 before her 1945 graduation from Langston University, the segregated state-supported institution of higher learning.

Fisher applied for admission to the University of Oklahoma School of Law in 1946. She was given a letter stating that the sole reason she was refused admission was her race, and she brought suit in state courts in April 1947. In January 1948 the United States Supreme Court ordered the state to provide her a legal education immediately. The State Board of Regents established a segregated law school in the state capital. Fisher then asked again for admission to the state law school on the grounds that the new school could not provide an equal education. She lost in August, but the case was not appealed as the NAACP concentrated on George W. McLaurin's application to the doctoral program in education.

In 1948 the state legislature voted to admit blacks to all graduate programs; in 1950 the Supreme Court outlawed all segregation at the graduate level. Fisher enrolled in law school in June 1949 after more than three years of effort. She graduated in 1951. Later she returned to the university, earning a master's degree in history in 1968.

After working in private practice in Chicashaw, Fisher joined the faculty at Langston University in 1957. She served from 1974 on as chair of the social sciences department and later as assistant to the president for academic affairs. In 1991 the University of Oklahoma awarded her an honorary doctorate of humane letters.
See also EDUCATION [2]; OKLAHOMA [4].

REFERENCES

Garraty, John A., and Mark C. Carnes, eds. *American National Biography*, 1999.

Johns, Robert L. "Ada Fisher." In *Notable Black American Women*, edited by Jessie Carney Smith, 1992.

ROBERT L. JOHNS

Flake, Floyd H., (January 30, 1945–), minister and former Congressman. Born in Los Angeles, he earned a B.A. degree at Wilberforce University in 1967 and a doctorate at United Theological Seminary in 1995. From 1970 to 1973 Flake was associate dean at Lincoln University, Pennsylvania, from 1970 to 1973. There he became alarmed by the failure of the recently integrated schools to educate young African Americans. Flake then went to Boston University as dean of students, university chaplain and director of the Martin Luther King Jr. Afro-American Center. In 1976 he took over Allen African Methodist Episcopal Church in Queens.

Flake built up the church and increased its membership. He also involved himself and the church in the community. For example, he is one of the major sources of new housing in the community through projects like the Allen A.M.E./Hall Estates, which in 1996 opened fifty new houses near the church-sponsored senior-citizens center. His philosophy is expressed in his book, *The Way of the Bootstrapper: Nine Action Ways for Achieving Your Dreams (1999)*.

In 1986 Flake was elected to the House of Representatives and held his seat until he resigned in the middle of 1997 just after he dedicated a twenty-three

Reverend Congressman, Floyd Harold Flake, during a sermon on August 3, 1997. (AP/Wide World Photos)

million dollar cathedral for his church. Floyd attracted national attention when he threw his support to the Republican-backed school voucher plan in early 1997. He also showed that he was comfortable with Republican stress on traditional family values by opening his pulpit to presidential candidate George Bush Jr. In May 2000 he announced that he was taking a position with Edison Schools, Inc., a large for-profit school management company.

See also AFRICAN METHODIST EPISCOPAL ZION CHURCH [1]; NEW YORK CITY [4].

REFERENCES

Brennan, Carol. "Floyd H. Flake" In *Contemporary Black Biography*, Vol. 18, edited by Shirelle Phelps. 1998.

Hicks, Jonathan P. "Rep Flake Breaks With Party to Back School Vouchers." *New York Times*, 12 March 1997.

Traub, James. "Hopefuls, Street Toughs; Power Brokers; Networkers; Strivers; Grande Dames; Mus-

clemen; Exiles; Reformers; Purists; Clones; Big Mouths; Outsiders; Air Kissers; Fanatics; Gossips; Nightclubbers; Floyd Flake's Middle America." *New York Sunday Times Magazine*, 19 October 1997.

Who's Who Among Black Americans, 9th ed. 1996.

Wyatt, Edward. "Floyd Flake to Take Post With Education Company." *New York Times*, 3 May, 2000.

ROBERT L. JOHNS

Fletcher, Alphonse, Jr.

Fletcher, Alphonse, Jr. (December 19, 1965–), stock broker, financial adviser, philanthropist. Alphonse Fletcher Jr. was born in New London, Connecticut, and graduated from Harvard University in 1987. Upon graduation Fletcher joined Bear, Stearns and Company, a Wall Street investment firm. There he developed stock trading strategies by using his mathematical and computer skills. In 1989 he moved to Kidder, Peabody and Company, one of the largest firms in the field of investment. Fletcher's incredible knack for playing the stock market brought an estimated $25 million in profit to the firm in 1990.

However, by 1991 relations between Fletcher and the firm were severed over a dispute about the exact terms of his financial package. Fletcher filed two suits and arbitrators ruled that Kidder, Peabody owed him $1.26 million in back compensation in 1992; after five years and a number of hearings, his claims of racial discrimination were judged to be without foundation.

Fletcher founded Fletcher Asset Management as soon as he broke with Kidder, Peabody. The firm's record was amazing even in a strong stock market. Average annual returns over the first five years were over 300%, giving him a fortune at that point estimated around $50 million. In 1995 he opened his firm to outside investors. He also left behind his income arbitrage strategy as profits declined in that area. Growth has been more modest since then. Fletcher serves on the boards of several nonprofit organizations and uses his wealth for philanthropic endeavors. Perhaps the most salient is the establishment of the Alphonse Fletcher Jr. University Professorship at Harvard in 1996.

See also INVESTMENT BANKING [3].

REFERENCES

"Alphonse Fletcher, Jr." *American Medical Association Foundation.* http://www.ama-assn.org/med-sci/erf/people/fletcher.htm.

Jacobson, Robert R. "Alphonso [sic] Fletcher, Jr." In *Contemporary Black Biography*, vol. 16, edited by Shirelle Phelps. 1998.

"University Professorship Named for Fletcher." *Harvard University Gazette*, 25 April 1996.

Whitford, David. "The Mysterious Manager with the Triple-Digit Returns: And He Endowed A Chair At Harvard In His 20s." *Fortune*, July 5, 1999.

ROBERT L. JOHNS

Fletcher, Benjamin Harrison

Fletcher, Benjamin Harrison (April 13, 1890–July 10, 1949), labor leader. Benjamin Harrison Fletcher was born in Philadelphia, but little is known about his personal life. However, his professional life was inextricably entwined with his relationship with the labor movement.

Fletcher's work on the Philadelphia waterfront as a teenager brought him into contact with labor agitators of the Industrial Workers of the World (IWW), who were considered radicals. The union's militancy and stance on interracial equality appealed to young Fletcher, and in 1911 he volunteered to become corresponding secretary for the local IWW chapter (Local 8). At some point, he joined the Socialist Party.

Fletcher became an important part of Local 8's organization of dockworkers, which combined sound organizational principles with egalitarian racial policies. He became a recognized spokesperson for the African American working class, organizing dockworkers in several cities, but most notably in Philadelphia.

Fletcher's activities led to his indictment by the Department of Justice in 1917, which charged him with wartime disloyalty and acts of subversion. He was convicted and sentenced to seven years in prison. A conditional pardon by President Harding in 1918 led to his release, and he returned promptly to working with Philadelphia longshoremen, ignoring an admonition to avoid trouble. In 1923, in the face of increasing dissension among longshoremen, Fletcher and his followers formed the integrated Independent Longshoremen's Union, but the group returned to Local 8 after a year. The IWW, however, lost its competitive battle with the International Longshoremen's Association, and a number of its leaders defected. Fletcher did not. As a consequence his influence suffered a decline, although he campaigned for worker unity until his death.

See also LABOR AND LABOR UNIONS [3]; PHILADELPHIA, PENNSYLVANIA [4].

REFERENCES

Garraty, John A., and Mark C. Carnes, eds. *American National Biography.* 1999.

Logan, Rayford W., and Michael R. Winston, eds. *Dictionary of American Negro Biography,* 1982.

CARRELL P. HORTON

Florida (Update)

Florida (Update). Although the state is not usually thought of as part of the Deep South, African Americans in Florida have historically suffered the effects of discrimination more pervasive, and often more violent, that that of almost any other southern state. One of several African Americans who broke the white stranglehold on the state's Congressional delegation in the 1990s, Carrie P. Meek of Miami looked back on a 1940s graduate-school career spent in Michigan—at Florida state expense—because of the thorough segregation of Florida's university system. In spite of the progress they made, black political figures encountered resistance when they entered the corridors of power. Willie Logan, a Florida state representative from the Miami suburb of Opa-Locka, was ousted from a slated slot as legislative party leader on the pretext that he lacked fund-raising skills; blacks responded by sitting out some elections in which they normally would have favored Democrats, and Republican Jeb Bush was elected governor. Federal judge Alcee Hastings was impeached and convicted by the U.S. House of Representatives in the late 1980s, but voters demonstrated their lack of faith in the legally murky impeachment proceedings by electing Hastings to the House from Florida's twenty-third district in 1992. Many political tensions were rooted in wider social strains that arose between Florida's African-American community and its large population of immigrants from the Caribbean countries of Cuba and Haiti. Those immigrants often seemed to find an easier process of assimilation into Floridian society than did native-born African Americans. Rarely mentioned in the legends recounting the exploits of millionaire developer Henry Flagler and his associates is the fact that African Americans played key roles in the establishment of Florida's tourism industry. That industry, however, came under pressure in the early 1990s from a boycott organized by a group of African-

American attorneys dismayed at the inequalities they perceived in industry employment patterns and in south Florida's treatment of blacks generally; the boycott enjoyed some success.

REFERENCES

Barone, Michael, and Grant Ujifusa. *The Almanac of American Politics 2000*. 1999.

Cain, Joy Duckett. "Miami: The City of Magic." *Essence* (April, 1997), 111.

Morin, Paula M. "Alcee L. Hastings." In *Contemporary Black Biography*, volume 16. 1997.

JAMES MANHEIM

Ford, Barney Launcelot (1822–December 14, 1902), civil rights activist, entrepreneur, political leader.

Barney Ford was the son of a plantation owner and his female slave. He gave himself middle and last names as an adult. Largely self-taught, he absorbed knowledge from each new plantation to which he was sold. When he finally escaped to Chicago, his skills at mimicry and disguises helped him avoid being captured. As a freedman, Ford became an underground conductor who helped fugitive slaves escape to Canada. After moving to Denver during the Civil War, he helped freed slaves find employment. Upon operation of a family-owned livery business, he continued to be an underground connection. From these efforts, Ford began to realize the need for blacks to use the political system to enact laws to enfranchise blacks.

While living in Colorado, Ford became a lobbyist to keep the territory from becoming a state until all males had equal rights; he also worked to pass a state public accommodations bill prohibiting discrimination. Ford worked to improve segregated schools and to organize adult education for blacks in Denver. As a staunch Republican, Ford served on the county committee and made an unsuccessful run for the state legislature. He was the first black to serve on a Colorado grand jury. As an entrepreneur, Ford operated hotels, livery stables, restaurants, and barbershops. When recovering from a series of financial setbacks, Ford prospected for gold, a venture that was chancy, at best. He succeeding in striking gold, and the hill upon which he found the gold was named Barney Ford Hill. He used his riches to build a house in Breckenridge, Colorado, which still stands today.

See also ENTREPRENEURS [2]; COLORADO [2].

REFERENCES

http://www.denvergov.org/AboutDenver/history_char_ford.htm.

Garraty, John A., and Mark C. Garraty, eds. *American National Biography*. vol. 8. 1999.

Logan, Rayford W., and Michael R. Winston, eds. *Dictionary of American Negro Biography*. 1982.

DOLORES NICHOLSON

Ford, Harold Eugene, Jr. (May 11, 1970–), U.S. Congressman.

Harold Ford, Jr., the first of a "second generation" of African Americans in Congress, was born in Memphis, Tenn., in 1970. Four years later, Harold Ford, Sr., an affluent mortician and political activist, became Tennessee's first African-American Congressman. Harold Ford, Jr., spent his boyhood shuttling between Memphis and Washington, D.C. In 1988, he entered the University of Pennsylvania, where he received a B.A. degree in 1992. He thereafter attended the University of Michigan Law School, receiving his J.D. in 1996.

In 1996, Ford, Sr., announced his retirement from Congress. The younger Ford, then still in law school, decided to run for his father's seat in the House of

Harold Ford Jr., Congressman. (AP/Wide World Photos).

Representatives. With help from his father's organization, he won easily. At 26, Ford was the youngest member of the 105th Congress. He spent most of his evenings during his first term studying for the bar examination, which he passed in 1998. Apart from his youthful appearance, Ford was notable for his advocacy of conservative policies, including budget cuts, anticrime legislation, and support for welfare reform, which his father had opposed. Critics derided Ford as a child of privilege who had been given a BMW car while in prep school. Nevertheless, Memphis voters reelected him in 1998 by a 4 to 1 margin over his Republican opponent. Ford also gained national attention in September 1998 when he was rebuked for breaking House rules by referring to President Bill Clinton as a "liar" on the House floor (although he voted against impeachment three months later).
See also MEMPHIS, TENNESSEE [3]; TENNESSEE [5].

REFERENCE

Milbank, Dana. "Harold Ford, Jr., Storms His Father's House." *New York Times*, Oct. 25, 1998.

GREG ROBINSON

Ford, Harold Eugene, Sr. (Update) (May 20, 1945–), politician. In 1970, Ford ran successfully for the Tennessee state legislature, holding the same Shelby County seat his great-grandfather had occupied in the 1890s. During his four years in the Tennessee House of Representatives, Ford was chosen to be Majority Whip. In 1974, he ran for the U.S. House of Representatives and won, becoming the first black Tennessean elected to Congress. Ford was subsequently reelected ten times.

Ford retired from Congress at the end of 1996. After leaving Congress, he worked as a lobbyist and political organizer in Memphis, and became a frequent adviser to his son and successor in Congress, Harold Ford, Jr.

REFERENCE

Bernsen, Charles. "The Fords of Memphis: A Family Saga." *Memphis Commercial Appeal*, July 1-4, 1990.

MARCUS D. POHLMANN
UPDATED BY GREG ROBINSON

Foreman, George Edward (Update) (January 22, 1948–), boxer. Foreman was stripped of his WBA crown in March of 1995 for failing to fight contender Tony Tucker, and he retained his IBC champion until June 1995. Following his defeat by Shannon Briggs on November 22, 1997, Foreman dropped out of competition for the heavyweight championship. His retirement from the ring came after a planned bout with former champion Larry Holmes fell through. Foreman moved on the realm of business, where he scored again, this time as the pitchman for a nonstick, fat-draining grill bearing his name. The company making the grill purchased from Foreman in January of 2000 all rights to Foreman's name and image for $137 million in cash and stock.

REFERENCES

Berger, Phil. "Body and Soul." *New York Times Magazine*, March 24, 1991, pp. 41-42, 62- 64.

Hoffman, Ken. "George Foreman grills competition." *The Houston Chronicle*. March 7, 2000: 1.

GREG ROBINSON

Francis, Milton A. (1882–1961), physician. Milton A. Francis was born in Washington, D. C., son of an obstetrician. He attended public school in Washington and went on to receive his M.D. from Howard University in 1906.

After interning, Francis joined the staff of Washington's Freedmen's Hospital's Genitourinary Department, where he went on to become the first black specialist in genitourinary diseases. Working at first under the department's head, but never with him, he became the virtual head when the senior staffer and his assistants went to serve in World War I in 1917. He served in this position until 1922, when he recruited a director of the Genito-Urinary Outpatient Clinic. In 1930, Francis decreased the time he devoted to urological surgery and increased the time he spent in private practice. He retired from practice in 1959.

Shortly after retirement, Francis established a trust fund at Howard University, with income to be used for loans and scholarships to medical students. At the time, the gift was the largest single contribution from a living alumnus. When he died, despite the fact that the initial proceeds of $200,000 were reduced to $100,000 after his will was contested by his widow, the gift still ranked as the largest to date.

George Foreman, weighing in, Atlantic City, NJ, 1997. (AP/Wide World Photos)

Francis and his first wife were patrons of the arts and presented both Marian Anderson and Roland Hayes in their first performances before theater audiences.

When his first wife died after a long illness, he remarried after an interval of years. His second wife, also, became chronically ill. Reputedly suffering from depression, Francis committed suicide in 1961.
See also HOWARD UNIVERSITY [3]; MEDICAL EDUCATION [3]; WASHINGTON, D.C. [3].

REFERENCES

Logan, Rayford W., and Michael R. Winston, eds. *Dictionary of American Negro Biography.* 1982.

Sammons, Vivian Ovelton. *Blacks in Science and Medicine.* 1990.

CARRELL P. HORTON

Frank, Free (Frank McWorter) (1777–1854),
slave, entrepreneur. Free Frank was a slave, entrepreneur, and pioneer who purchased the freedom of fourteen members of his family, including himself. He was born in 1777 in Union County, South Carolina, to an African-born mother and George McWorter, her white owner. In 1795 his owner moved to Pulaski County, Kentucky.

By 1810 Free Frank was hiring his own time—that is, paying his owner a fixed sum out of his earnings. The War of 1812 led him to mine for niter and from it make saltpeter, a ingredient of gunpowder. In 1817 he was able to buy his wife and two years later, himself. Free Frank's efforts to buy the freedom of members of his family stretched over nearly forty years and involved the expenditure of some fifteen thousand dollars.

In 1830 Free Frank moved to Pike County, Illinois. After establishing a farm and taking up stock raising, he turned to land speculation. In 1836, the Illinois legislature approved his establishment of the town of New Philadelphia. So far as is known, he was the first black to legally found a town. His hopes for the town included the establishment of a Free Will Baptist Seminary to serve both as educational establishment and church building.

Hampered by social and legal handicap for example, even in Illinois he lacked a legal surname

Free Frank exemplifies the entrepreneurial skills of antebellum blacks. In 1988 his grave was placed on the National Register of Historic Places, one of the three graves so recognized in Illinois.

See also BLACK TOWNS [1]; ENTREPRENEURS [2]; FREE BLACKS, 1619 1860 [2].

REFERENCES

Walker, Jeffrey E. Free Frank McWorter. In *Encyclopedia of African American Business History*, edited by Juliet E. K. Walker. 1999.

Walker, Juliet E. K. *Free Frank: A Black Pioneer on the Antebellum Frontier*. 1983.

ROBERT L.JOHNS

Franklin, John Hope (Update) (January 2, 1915–). John Hope Franklin retired in 1992. In 1995, he was awarded the Presidential Medal of Freedom, and also received the Spingarn Medal from the National Association for the Advancement of Colored People. In 1997, Franklin was called out of retirement to chair President Bill Clinton's Initiative on Race.

Conservative critics accused the panel of pro-black bias on racial issues, and Franklin was criticized for his statement that the period after emancipation was in many ways worse for black Americans than slavery. Despite the controversy, the Commission's final report, issued in September 1998, was almost completely ignored by Congress. Franklin co-wrote the book *Runaway Slaves*, published in 1999, which won the 2000 Lincoln Prize (for a work of history that popularizes Abraham Lincoln or his message).

REFERENCE

Franklin, John Hope. *Race and History: Selected Essays, 1938–1988*, especially "John Hope Franklin: A Life of Learning," Baton Rouge, La., 1989, pp. 277-291.

GREG ROBINSON

Franks, Gary (1954?-), politician, entrepreneur. Franks is the first African American congressman elected from Connecticut. His father, who had not completed the sixth grade in school, was successful in his determination that his six children would become college graduates. A native Connecticut native, Franks graduated from Yale University in 1975. In the late

John Hope Franklin. (Fisk University Library)

Gary Franks addressing supporters. (AP/Wide World Photos)

1970s, after working as an industrial and labor relations executive in Fairfield County, Connecticut, he opened his own real estate business and became highly successful.

Franks entered local politics as alderman in Waterbury, where he served three terms. But he was unsuccessful when he ran for state alderman in 1986. His earlier success, however, led him to run on the Republican ticket for the U.S. House of Representatives. He won the seat in November, 1990, a feat that came when African American representation in highly visible positions, such as mayors of major cities or in the U.S. Senate, was lacking. Franks' platform was attractive to the voters of Connecticut. He was an advocate for abortion rights for women. In his view, chief drug pushers should receive the death penalty. He advocated a constitutional amendment to prohibit burning the U.S. flag. Franks favored reductions in capital gains tax and an increase in federal income taxes.

His win, making him the top-ranking black Republican elected, was highly touted by Republicans. They saw the victory as attractive enough to encourage more minorities to join the Republican Party and participate in their programs. At the same time, African Americans saw Franks as the first of their race to be elected to Congress from the state of Connecticut. *See also* CONNECTICUT [2]; CONGRESSIONAL BLACK CAUCUS [2]; REPUBLICAN PARTY [4].

REFERENCES

Bigelow, Barbara Carlisle, ed. *Contemporary Black Biography*, Vol. 2. 1992.

"Connecticut Salon a Favorite among 3 Blacks Seeking GOP Seats in U.S. House." *Jet* Semptember 24, 1990:16.

McCoy, Frank. "Freshmen on the Hill." *Black Enterprise*. April 1991: 25.

RAYMOND WINBUSH

Freedom Rides. Initially organized by the Congress of Racial Equality (CORE) in 1961, the Freedom Rides were interracial groups riding throughout the South on buses. Freedom Rides attempted to galvanize the Justice Department into enforcing federal desegregation laws in interstate travel, and especially in bus and train terminals. White riders sat on the back of the bus, and black riders on the front, challenging long-standing southern racist transportation practices. Once at the terminal, white Freedom Riders proceeded to the "black" waiting room, while blacks attempted to use the facilities in the "white" waiting room.

Freedom Rides were a continuation of the student-led sit-in movement that was sparked in February 1, 1960 by four African-American college freshmen in Greensboro, North Carolina. When these students remained at a Woolworth's lunch counter after being refused service, they inspired hundreds of similar nonviolent student demonstrations. Essentially, Freedom Rides took the tradition of sit-ins on the road.

The idea for the 1961 Freedom Rides was conceived by Tom Gaither, a black man, and Gordon Carvey, a white man, who were field secretaries of CORE. In light of the 1960 *Boynton v. Virginia Supreme Court* judgment that banned segregation in bus and train terminals, Gaither and Carvey decided that compliance with the law should be gauged. The two activists were additionally inspired by the 1947 Journey of Reconciliation. Also motivated by a Supreme Court ruling, the Journey of Reconciliation was an interracial group of sixteen activists that traveled through the South to test *Morgan v. Virginia*, the 1946 federal case that resulted in the legal ban of segregation on interstate buses and trains. In the spirit of the Journey of Reconciliation, CORE began organizing and planning for the first Freedom Rides.

In early 1961, CORE, headed by its director and co-founder James Farmer, began carefully selecting the thirteen original Freedom Riders. The chosen group was seven blacks and six whites, from college students to civil rights veterans, including a Journey of Reconciliation participant, white activist James Peck. The journey for the riders began on May 4th from Washington D.C. to Atlanta, Georgia, on two buses. The plan was to continue through Alabama, Mississippi, and finally to New Orleans, Louisiana, on May 17th for a desegregation rally.

The first episode of violence occurred in Rock Hill, South Carolina, where twenty-one-year old John Lewis, future Student Nonviolent Coordinating Committee (SNCC) national chairman and Congressman, and Albert Bigelow, an elderly white pacifist, were knocked unconscious by young white men. On May 14, 1961, the Freedom Riders boarded a Greyhound and a Trailways bus in Atlanta and headed for Birmingham, Alabama. The Trailways bus met six Ku Klux Klansmen in Anniston, Alabama, who threw the African Americans into backseats, and hit two white riders on the head. In Birmingham, the bus encountered about twenty men with pipes who beat the riders when they disembarked.

In Anniston, the Greyhound bus faced two hundred angry whites. The bus retreated, but its tires were slashed. Once the tires blew out, a firebomb was tossed into the bus through the glass. The riders managed to escape before the bus went up in flames. The following day, another mob prevented the Freedom Riders from boarding a bus in Birmingham. With the help of John Seigenthaler, Attorney General Robert Kennedy's assistant, the riders took a plane to New Orleans instead. The bus journey was continued under the leadership of SNCC, with the coordination efforts of SNCC members Diane Nash and John Lewis.

Birmingham Police Commissioner "Bull" Connor used many tactics, including incarceration, to try to stop the students, but to no avail. Finally, the governor of Alabama, John Patterson, very reluctantly promised Robert Kennedy to protect the riders. As the new Freedom Riders left for Montgomery on May 20, 1961, it appeared that Governor Patterson had kept his word. However, by the time the bus arrived in Montgomery, all forms of police protection had disappeared. A mob of over one thousand whites viciously attacked the riders and John Seigenthaler.

On May 24th, twenty-seven determined Freedom Riders, with the protection of National Guardsmen, headed for Jackson, Mississippi. In Mississippi, they were arrested for sixty days. A new group of riders came to Jackson, and was also arrested. Eventually, 328 Freedom Riders had been incarcerated in Jackson. As per their philosophy, the riders chose jail over bail.

The Freedom Rides brought international attention to the southern struggle of desegregation, which put pressure on the authorities. Finally, on November 1, 1961, a huge victory for the Freedom Riders and all integrationists was won when the Interstate Commerce Commission (ICC) made segregated travel facilities illegal.

See also ALABAMA[1] ; BIRMINGHAM, ALABAMA [1]; CIVIL RIGHTS MOVEMENT [2]; CONGRESS OF RACIAL EQUALITY (CORE) [2]; MISSISSIPPI [4]; SIT-INS [5].

REFERENCES

Farmer, James. *Lay Bare the Heart: An Autobiography of the Civil Rights Movement.* 1985.

Hampton, Henry, and Steve Fayer. *Voices of Freedom: An Oral History of the Civil Rights Movement From the 1950s Through the 1980s.* 1990.

Meier, August, and Elliot Rudwick. *CORE: A Study in the Civil Rights Movement, 1942–1968.* 1973.

Peck, James. *Freedom Ride.* 1962.

Zinn, Howard. *SNCC: The New Abolitionists.* 1965.

JESSICA L. GRAHAM

Freeman, Elizabeth (Mum Bett, Mumbet)

Freeman, Elizabeth (Mum Bett, Mumbet), (c. 1744–December 28, 1829), servant. As plaintiff in a law suit, Mum Bett joined a black laborer named Bront in suing for their freedom in 1781. After she won her case, she adopted the name Elizabeth Freeman. The victory was a significant step in the abolition of slavery in Massachusetts although the final decision by the Massachusetts Supreme Court that the new state constitution prohibited slavery came in another case.

Freeman was born a slave in New York State and in 1758 seems to have passed into the possession of John Ashley of Sheffield, Massachusetts, a judge in the Court of Common Pleas from 1761 to 1781. Freeman never learned to read or write, but she heard discussion of the Bill of Rights and the Massachusetts constitution adopted in 1780. She considered that the language about all people being created free and equal might well apply to her.

In 1780 Mrs. Ashley became angry and struck at Freeman's sister with a heated shovel; Freeman was burned on the arm when she interposed. Leaving the house, she brought suit for her freedom in a case heard on August 21, 1781. She won. Her lawyer was Theodore Sedgwick, father of Theodore Sedgwick Jr., a noted abolitionist. Freeman became a servant in the Sedgwick family and followed them to Stockbridge in 1785. When Freeman retired, she had accumulated enough money to buy a small house. She mentions great-grandchildren in the will she signed with a cross on October 18, 1829. She was buried in the Sedgwick family plot in Stockbridge Cemetery.

See also FREE BLACKS, 1619 1860 [2]; SLAVERY [5].

REFERENCES

Johns, Robert L. "Elizabeth Freeman, 'Mum Bett', 'Mumbet.'" In *Notable Black American Women*, edited by Jessie Carney Smith. 1992.

Logan, Rayford W. "Elizabeth [Mumbet, Mum Bett] Freeman." In *Dictionary of American Negro Biography*, edited by Rayford W. Logan and Michael R. Winston. 1982.

ROBERT L. JOHNS

Fudge, Ann (1951?-), corporate executive. Ann Fudge was born in Washington, D.C., and, after witnessing riots in the city that followed the assassination of Martin Luther King, Jr., became determined to become a pioneer for her race. She graduated from Simmons College in 1973 and became a personnel executive for General Electric. In 1977 Fudge received an M.B.A. degree from Harvard Business School and went to work at the Minneapolis-based General Mills company.

Fudge's rise up the corporate ladder at General Mills was swift. In 1978 she became assistant product manager, in 1980 she was product manager, and in 1983 she became director of marketing. The last position put her in charge of four brands. A new breakfast cereal, Honey Nut Cheerios, was developed under her watch and became one of the top performers for the division.

Although General Mills offered her another promotion, Fudge chose to leave the company in 1986 for Kraft General Foods in White Plains, New York, in order to be closer to her ailing mother. There she revived old brands such as Shake 'N Bake and Stove Top Stuffing, which both saw an immediate jump in sales. During her tenure with Kraft, Fudge held various posts until she became executive vice-president in 1993, a position she retained when she became president of Maxwell House Coffee division in 1994. Her incredible success made Fudge the target of speculation that she would be the first African American woman to head a major company.

See also BLACK BUSINESS COMMUNITY [1].

REFERENCES

"Fudge, Anne." In *Contemporary Black Biography*, vol. 11, edited by L. Mpho Mabunda, and Shirelle Phelps. 1996.

Johnson, Pamela. "Wonder Women." *Essence* 26 (May 1995): 112-150.

Reynolds, Rhonda. "Ann M. Fudge: Brewing Success." *Black Enterprise* 25 (August 1994): 68-70.

JESSIE CARNEY SMITH

Fulani, Lenora Branch (April 25, 1950–), developmental psychologist and independent political leader. Fulani twice ran for President of the United

Lenora Fulani. (AP/Wide World Photos)

States as an independent, making history in 1988 when she became the first woman and the first African American to get on the ballot in all fifty states. She is a pioneer of left/center/right coalitions, a founder of the Reform Party, and chair of the Committee for a Unified Independent Party, Inc., a strategy center for political independents. Fulani was raised in Chester, Pennsylvania, the daughter of a nurse and a baggage carrier on the Pennsylvania Railroad. A youth leader in church and school, she won a scholarship to Hofstra University. The mother of two children, Ainka and Amani, Fulani went on to study at Columbia University's Teachers College and the City University of New York, where she received her Ph.D. in developmental psychology. While working as a researcher at Rockefeller University specializing in the interplay of social environment and learning, she decided that the social crisis in the black community required her to leave academia for activism.

With Dr. Fred Newman, the major theoretical influence in her work, she co-founded the All-Stars Talent Show Network and the Development School for Youth, which now reach over twenty-thousand inner-city youths. In 1993, with activists who supported Ross Perot for President in 1992, Fulani launched a nation-wide effort to create a new pro-reform populist party that could provide black Americans with an electoral alternative. She has spearheaded numerous legislative and legal reform initiatives including ballot access reform, term limits, and same day voter registration. Fulani writes a nationally syndicated column and hosts a weekly public affairs television show.

See also PRESIDENTS OF THE UNITED STATES [4]; PSYCHOLOGY AND PSYCHIATRY [4].

REFERENCES

Ali, Omar "Perot." In *History in Dispute: American Social and Political Movements, 1945–2000*, edited by Robert J. Allison. 2000.

Bigelow, Barbara C., ed. *Contemporary Black Biography: Profiles from the International Black Community.* 1996.

Fulani, Lenora B. *The Making of a Fringe Candidate.* 1992.

OMAR ALI

Fuller, Samuel B. (1905–1988), entrepreneur, publisher. Samuel Fuller, widely known as S. B. Fuller, became one of the most successful African American entrepreneurs in mid-twentieth-century America. Born in Monroe, Louisiana, to parents who were sharecroppers, Fuller moved to Memphis and then in 1938 to Chicago where he worked as a coal hiker. After working with a Commonwealth Burial Association for four years, he invested twenty-five dollars in soap that he peddled door-to-door. His company, known as Fuller Products, was incorporated in 1929. He carried a lone of thirty products that his staff of salespeople marketed from door-to-door chiefly on Chicago's South Side where African Americans were concentrated. Ten years later he had expanded into a factory and had become one of Chicago's leading black entrepreneurs.

Fuller Products manufactured health and beauty aids and cleaning products. His enterprises consisted of real estate-including the Regal Theater, Fuller Department Store and Office Building, a New York Real Estate Trust, the *Pittsburgh Courier*, the Fuller Guaranty Corporation, and the Fuller Philco Appliance Center. He became known as a master salesman and a motivational genius who trained others to promote his business and to engage in business for themselves. His employees called themselves Fullerites; his administrative staff consisted of people who were college graduates.

By the 1960s, however, Fuller's business investments began to decline until Fuller Products Com-

pany declared bankruptcy in 1969. He partially revived his business in the 1970s and established centers in at least eight cities. He left his mark on many African Americans who in the latter twentieth century became leading entrepreneurs.

See also ENTREPRENEURS [2]; JOURNALISM [3].

REFERENCES

Ingham, John N., and Lynne B. Feldman. *African-American Business Leaders.* 1994.

Smith, Jessie Carney, ed. *Notable Black American Men.* 1999.

Walker, Juliet E. K. *Encyclopedia of African American Business History.* 1999.

JESSIE CARNEY SMITH

Futrell, Mary Hatwood (May 24, 1940–), educator, organization leader, political activist, reformer. Futrell served an unprecedented third term as president of the National Education Association and as especially influential in the national education area. Futrell was born in Alta Vista, Virginia, and graduated from Virginia State University with a B.A. degree in business education. She completed her M.A. and Ed.D. degrees at George Washington University.

After twenty years as a classroom teacher, the tireless educator moved up the ranks at NEA to become its president. During her administration she held a passionate belief that education is the primary force that shapes people. She was concerned about a number of contemporary issues that affect schools including the student dropout rate, child care for young families, Head Start programs, drug programs in schools, expanded use of computers in teaching, and more college loans. Futrell called for changes, including improved salaries and improved working conditions, to make the teaching profession lucrative and attractive to new teachers. She deplored autocratic decision-making processes in education that leave the teacher's voice unheard.

Futrell's administration saw a phenomenal increase in membership in the NEA; she also built the organization into America's largest union. Most of all, Futrell wanted to see reform in education and called on politicians, educators, and others to restructure America's schools. On August 31, 1989, after serving her third term, Futrell left NEA but continued to work for education reform, this time through the Center for the Study of Education and National Development. Subsequently, Futrell served as dean of the

Graduate School of Education and Human Development at George Washington University.
See also EDUCATION [2].

REFERENCES

Howard, Michael E. "A Conversation with Mary Hatwood Futrell." *Black Enterprise 20* (October 1989): 30.

Smith, Jessie Carney, ed. *Notable Black American Women*. 1992.

Who's Who Among African Americans, 12th ed. 1999.

JESSIE CARNEY SMITH

G

Gandy, John Manuel (October 31, 1870–1947), educator. John Manuel Gandy was born near Starkville, Mississippi, in Oktibbeha County. His grandparents were mixed racially, but both his parents had been slaves. As tenant farmers, the family moved often, resulting in frequent school changes for John. The Gandys moved to Sallislaw, Oklahoma, while Gandy was attending Jackson College (1886–1888).

Gandy had an unceasing desire to learn. At age eighteen, he had completed his Jackson College work, but he left Oberlin Academy after two years because of insufficient funds. After an unsuccessful attempt to enter Colgate University, Colgate students gave him financial help, and he entered Fisk University. Gandy received his bachelor's and master's degrees from Fisk (in 1898 and 1901, respectively). He studied later at Columbia, Illinois Wesleyan, and, at age sixty-four, at Cornell.

Gandy began his teaching career at age fifteen. He taught in Mississippi during the summers while he was a student at Fisk. After receiving his bachelor's degree, he was hired to teach at Virginia Normal and Collegiate Institute in Petersburg. In 1914 he was appointed acting president of that institution. Later that same year he was elected president and served in that position until he became president emeritus in 1943.

Virginia Normal, which was to become Virginia State College, prospered under Gandy's leadership. He placed strong emphasis on academic quality and recruited his faculty from quality institutions. The institution moved from a non-accredited school to an A-rated, fully accredited 4-year college during Gandy's administration and enlarged its physical plant. Gandy's achievements were recognized by honorary degrees and an award from the Harmon Foundation.

See also EDUCATION [2]; VIRGINIA [5].

REFERENCE

Logan, Rayford W., and Michael R. Winston, eds. *Dictionary of American Negro Biography*. 1982.

CARRELL P. HORTON

Gardiner, Leon (November 25, 1892–March 5, 1945), bibliophile. Leon Gardiner was born in Atlantic City, New Jersey. In 1902, the Gardiner family moved to Philadelphia. His parents encouraged Leon's early interest in reading, which he maintained while also becoming interested in music and photography. Racial discrimination, however, prevented his attendance at an established photography school in Philadelphia.

As a young man, Gardiner began to collect articles related to African-American history and attended meetings of the Afro-American Historical Society. These activities brought him in contact with others of like interests and led to his participation in the establishment of a nucleus of black bibliophiles.

Gardiner worked nights at a Philadelphia post office and pursued his research activities strenuously by day. His reputation as a researcher was well known. His work was published in Philadelphia newspapers during the 1930s and 1940s, and he offered assistance freely to other researchers.

With membership in the Association for the Study of Negro Life and History and the Philadelphia Society for Negro Records and Research, Gardiner was instrumental in maintaining valuable collections intact. He is credited with having done more than anyone else to salvage early black collections. His own collections were given to the Historical Society of Pennsylvania and the Berean Institute in 1933, which helped fulfill Gardiner's dream of establishing a national repository of black materials in Philadelphia. Gardiner's pace took its toll on his health, but he refused to slow down. He continued his work until his sudden death from a heart attack.

See also BOOK COLLECTORS AND COLLECTIONS [1]; HISTORIANS/HISTORIOGRAPHY [3]; PHILADELPHIA, PENNSYLVANIA [4].

REFERENCES

Garraty, John A., and Mark C. Carnes, eds. *American National Biography*. 1999.

Logan, Rayford W., and Michael R. Winston, eds. *Dictionary of American Negro Biography*. 1982.

Sinnette, Elinor Des Zerney and others. *Black Bibliophiles and Collectors*. 1990.

CARRELL P. HORTON

Gardner, Newport (Occramer Marycoo)

(1746?-1826), singing master and a community leader. He was born in Africa and became the slave of Caleb Gardner of Newport, Rhode Island, in 1760. Gardner became a fervent Christian and joined the Congregational Church, of which he was a long-time sexton. Gardner was a slave until 1791 but allowed to use his free time and any money he earned as he wished.

Gardner had a strong clear voice and was able to take lessons from an itinerant singing master. Gardner became a singing master himself and taught music to mostly white students. He also began to compose music, but most is lost. There is one song that may be his and the text of a choral work.

Gardner was a organizer of the African Union Society founded on November 10, 1780, and became its first secretary. This society is the earliest attested African American mutual aid society in the United States. In 1807 Gardner was an organizer of the African Benevolent Society, and he became the principal teacher of the school it established. It was from this society that the first black church in Newport, the Colored Union Church, grew. It was founded on June 23, 1825.

Gardner had not renounced his desire to return to Africa; he had tried to maintain the command of his original language. Nostalgia was backed by missionary fervor. An attempt to go in the 1770s fell through, but on January 4, 1826, the eighty-year-old Gardner set sail for African. He arrived in Monrovia on February 6, where he died within six months.

See also CONCERT MUSIC [2].

REFERENCES

Johns, Robert L. "Newport Gardner." In *Notable Black American Men*, edited by Jessie Carney Smith. 1999.

Smith, Eileen, ed. *Readings in Black American Music*. 1971.

Wright, Josephine, and Eileen Southern, eds. "Newport Gardner." *The Black Perspective in Music*, July 1976.

ROBERT L. JOHNS

Gaston, Arthur George

(July 4, 1892–January 19, 1996), entrepreneur. Arthur Gaston was born in a log cabin in Demopolis, Alabama, the grandson of former slaves. He studied at Carrie Tuggle Institute through the tenth grade and joined the U.S. Army in 1910. Discharged in 1918, he worked for the Tennessee Coal and Iron Company in Westfield, Alabama, before beginning his own business in 1923. Eventually named the Booker T. Washington Burial Society in honor of Washington's influence on Gaston, the business was incorporated as the Booker T. Washington Insurance Company in 1932. Gaston's enterprises grew to include the Booker T. Washington Business School (1929), Brown Belle Bottling Company (1939), A. G. Gaston Motel (1954), Vulcan Realty and Investment Corporation (1955), the A. G. Gaston Home for senior citizens (1963), two radio stations (1975), and the A. G. Gaston Construction Company (1986). He was once called the richest African American in the country.

A behind-the-scenes figure in Alabama's civil rights movement, in 1957 Gaston advanced loans to blacks after whites pressured boycotters, paid bail for arrested demonstrators, and, through the Gaston Motel, provided lodging to protestors, including Martin Luther King, Jr. His failure to play a public role in the movement caused some to mistakenly label Gaston an

"Uncle Tom." Ever the disciple of Booker T. Washington's work ethic, Gaston continued working in his various enterprises even after turning 100. He died in 1996 at age 103.

REFERENCES

Gaston A. G. *Green Power: The Successful Way of A. G. Gaston*. 1968.

Smith, Jessie Carney. *Notable Black American Men*. 1999.

Walker, Juliet E. K. *Encyclopedia of African American Business History*. 1999.

JESSIE CARNEY SMITH

Gates, Henry Louis, Jr. (September 16, 1950–), teacher, scholar, writer. Henry Louis Gates Jr. was born in Keyser, West Virginia. He attended Yale and Clare College, Cambridge, where he received a doctorate in literature in 1979. He taught at Yale, Cornell, and Duke before going to Harvard in 1991. Gates came to public attention in 1981 when he received one of the first MacArthur Foundation "genius" grants, and again in 1983, when he published a rediscovered 1859 novel by an African-American woman, *Our Nig*, the first such work of its kind to found. His major scholarly work is *The Signifying Monkey: A Theory of African American Literary Criticism* (1988) which links literary analysis with black vernacular expression. Critic Ismael Reed called it "the Rosetta Stone of the American multicultural Renaissance."

Gates emerged in the 1990's as a popularizer of black scholarship and a spokesperson on racial issues. His work in establishing and chairing Harvard University's Department of African-American Studies helped give the field legitimacy. He has also successfully championed the inclusion of black writers in the American literary canon, serving as co-editor of *The Norton Anthology of African American Literature* (1996). He is co-editor, too, of *Africana 2000*, a massive CD-ROM encyclopedia of the African Diaspora, as well as its print version, *Africana: The Encyclopedia of the African and African American Experience* (1999).

Gates has distinguished himself as an effective fundraiser; a prolific writer and editor of books and articles; a spokesperson for cultural diversity, reparations, and affirmative action; and as the host of a six-part BBC/PBS film series, "Wonders of the African World."
See also BLACK STUDIES [1]; BOSTON, MASSACHUSETTS [1]; CRITICISM, LITERARY; [2]; INTELLECTUAL LIFE [3].

REFERENCES

Bigelow, Barbara Carlisle, ed., *Contemporary Black Biography*, vol. 3. 1993.

Time, April 22, 1991; February 3, 1992.

RICHARD NEWMAN

Henry Louis Gates, Jr. (Copyright by Jerry Bauer)

Gay Men (Update). In 1993, when the subject of admitting gays and lesbians into the military was being nationally debated, the contributions and the important legal precedent of Sgt. Perry Watkins, an African American who had successfully litigated his discharge on grounds of sexual orientation, were largely ignored by activists and the media. Similarly, the media and public all but ignored the life and tragic death of Glenn Burke, a former outfielder for the Los Angeles Dodgers and Oakland Athletics, and openly gay major league baseball player.

Black gay artists and intellectuals have established inroads into areas of expression outside of literature. Jazzman Billy Strayhorn collaborated with Duke Ellington to produce immortal songs. Harvard theologian Peter Gomes has elucidated biblical teachings on sexuality. Actor Howard Rollins, start of such films as A Soldier's Story and the television series *In the Heat of the Night*, was a major sex symbol before disease cut short his career. Producer/director/playwright George C. Wolfe has made major contributions to American theater, including direction of the landmark drama *Angels in America*.

REFERENCES

Hemphill, Essex, ed. *Brother to Brother: New Writings by Black Gay Men*. 1991.

Reid-Pharr, Robert. "The Spectacle of Blackness." *Radical America* 24, no. 4 (Winter 1992).

ROBERT REID-PHARR
UPDATED BY GREG ROBINSON

Gaynor, Florence S. (October 29, 1920–September 16, 1993), hospital administrator.

Florence S. Gaynor graduated from the nursing school at Lincoln Hospital in the Bronx in 1946 and started her career in New York City hospitals. She continued her studies at New York University, earning a B.S. degree in 1964 and an M.A. degree in 1966, and further studies, most notably at the University of Oslo in Norway, prepared her for an impressive career in health care administration.

Gaynor returned to Lincoln Hospital in 1965 and worked her way up through the administrative ranks until she became assistant administrator in 1970. The following year she became the first African American woman to head a major teaching hospital in the United States when she was chosen to be the new executive director of Harlem's Sydenham Hospital. Taking control in a time of financial crisis, Gaynor managed to keep the hospital afloat while also commanding a major expansion program. Her developments included a brand new Neighborhood Family Care Center (NFCC), located in Central Harlem near Sydenham, which also included a sickle cell anemia clinic.

Eighteen months later, Gaynor took the opportunity to head New Jersey's largest hospital, Martland Hospital. She left in 1976 for Meharry Medical College, a historically black institution in Nashville, where she stayed for four years. She ended her administrative career at the West Philadelphia Community and Mental Health Consortium in 1984. Among her affiliations, in 1973 she was president of the National Association of Health Care Executives.

See also MEDICAL EDUCATION [3]; NURSING [4].

REFERENCES

Bailey, Peter. "The Lady Takes Charge." In *Ebony* 7 (November 1971): 157-66.

Editors of Ebony. *The Ebony Success Library* vol. 1. 1973.

VALENCIA PRICE

Gilbert, John Wesley (July 6, 1864–November 18, 1923), educator, religious worker, journalist, archaeologist.

Gilbert was born in Hephzibah, Georgia, attended public schools in Augusta, and studied one year at Atlanta Baptist Seminary. He continued his studies at Paine College and graduated in June 1886. Gilbert enrolled as a junior at Brown University, excelled in Greek, and graduated with honors in June 1888. He won a competitive scholarship from Brown to study at the American School in Athens, Greece, in the 1890–1891 school year, becoming the first African American admitted there. He also worked there as a guide for tourists to support himself.

Gilbert traveled throughout Greece and engaged in excavations both in Greece and on the Mediterranean Islands, becoming one of the first known African American archaeologists while publishing accounts of his experiences in the *New York Independent* and other journals. He found and traced the Eretria's ancient walls, located the towers of the structure, and helped to make a map of ancient Eretria. He wrote his thesis on the demes (villages) of Attica. He visited Europe's largest and most important cities, where he examined the political systems and studied local customs. For his work, Brown University awarded him the Master of Arts degree in 1891.

In 1895 Gilbert entered the ministry in the Colored Methodist Episcopal Church and was superintendent of African missions for many years. He took a trip to the Belgian Congo, where he joined Bishop W. R. Lambuth in founding the mission at Wembo, Nyama. During this period, Gilbert also returned to teach at Paine College. He was subsequently named dean of theology and full professor of Greek.

See also AFRICAN METHODIST EPISCOPAL CHURCH [1]; ANTHROPOLOGISTS [1]; ARCHEOLOGY, HISTORICAL [1].

REFERENCES

Afro-American Encyclopedia, vol. 4. 1974.

Culp, Daniel Wallace. *Twentieth Century Negro Literature*. 1902.

Gibson, John William. *Progress of a Race*. 1902.

JESSIE CARNEY SMITH

Gillespie, Marcia Ann (July 10, 1944–), author, editor.

Marcia Ann Gillespie is an author, editor, and, most importantly, a trailblazer in the magazine industry. She was born in Rockville Centre, New York, and received her B.A. in American Studies in 1966 from Lake Forest College. Upon graduation from college, she began working in the New York division of Time-Life Books. In 1971, she was hired as editor-in-chief of the newly formed *Essence* magazine. As editor from 1971–1980, she is credited with creating a readership of over two million, thus transforming the publication into one of the fastest growing women's magazines in the United States. During her tenure, advertising increased ten-fold, and *Essence* won the National Magazine Award—the magazine industry's most prestigious honor. She was also honored as "One of the Fifty Faces for America's Future" by *Time* magazine in 1979.

In 1980, Gillespie became a contributing editor at *Ms.* magazine. In 1987, she began writing a regular column for *Ms.* and was named its executive editor in 1988. Four years later she became editor-in-chief. She has been responsible for transforming *Ms.* into an accessible, wide-ranging feminist monthly-attracting younger, multi-racial readers. She served as president of Liberty Media for Women, LLC, a powerful and influential media company owned by women, and she was among a group of women investors who purchased *Ms.* in 1998. Gillespie also served as a member of the National Council of Negro Women.
See also JOURNALISM [3].

REFERENCES

"Gillespie, Marcia A." *Who's Who Among African Americans*, 1998–1999, edited by Shirelle Phelps. 1997.

Houston, Gary. "Gillespie, Marcia Ann." *Black Women in America: Business and Professions*, edited by Darlene Clark Hine. 1997.

RACHEL ZELLARS

Glover, Savion (November 19, 1973–), dancer.

Tap veteran Gregory Hines has called Savion Glover "the best tap dancer that ever lived." Born in Newark, New Jersey, Glover grew up in a housing project with his mother. From age two, he illustrated an affinity for rhythm, beating out sounds on pots and pans at will. Yvette Glover enrolled Savion in tap dance at age seven at New York City's Broadway Dance Center. Savion recalls tapping in cowboy boots-the only hard-soled shoes his mother could afford-for seven months before receiving his first pair of tap shoes.

At twelve, he secured the lead role in Broadway's *The Tap Dance Kid*. In 1989, he was nominated for his first Tony award for his performance in *Black and Blue*. In the same year, he starred with Gregory Hines and Sammy Davis Jr. in the movie *Tap*. In 1992, he became the youngest recipient of a National Endowment for the Arts (NEA) grant for choreography. From 1991–1994, he starred in the Broadway production, *Jelly's Last Jam*, and taught children's tap classes wherever he traveled. From 1991–1995, he was a regular guest on *Sesame Street*.

His greatest accomplishment has been his involvement in the original *Bring in 'da Noise, Bring in 'da Funk* which began late in 1995. The show, a dramatic display of Black musical styles including hip-hop and new styles of tap dance, garnered nine Tony nominations in 1996. Serving as the Broadway show's choreographer and star, Glover won one of the show's four awards for "Best Choreographer."

Marcia Ann Gillespie. (AP/Wide World Photos)

Savion Glover (wearing white pants) with other cast members, performing a number from "Bring in 'Da Noise, Bring in 'Da Funk." (AP/Wide World Photos)

See also MUSICAL THEATER [4]; TAP DANCE [5]; THEATRICAL DANCE [5].

REFERENCES

"Rat-A-Tat-Tap: Dance Phenom Savion Glover's Furious Feet Raise an Exhilarating Racket on Broadway." www.people. aol.com. 1997.

Whitney, Barbara. "Savion Glover, Year in Review." www.britannica.com. 1996.

RACHEL ZELLARS

Deep End of the Ocean (1999), *Girl, Interrupted* (1999), and *The Adventures of Rocky and Bullwinkle* (2000).

REFERENCES

Hine, Darlene Clark. *Black Women in America*, 1993, pp. 491-493.

Moritz, Charles. *Current Biography Yearbook,* 1993.

"Whoopi Goldberg." In *Contemporary Theatre, Film and Television*, Volume 23. 1999.

GREG ROBINSON

Goldberg, Whoopi (Update) (November 13, 1950–), actress, comedienne. In 1994, Goldberg hosted the Academy Awards. Her subsequent film appearances include *The Player* (1995), *Boys on the Side* (1996), *How Stella Got Her Groove Back* (1998), and *The Ghosts of Mississippi* (1998). In 1997, following a short-lived late-night talk show, *The Whoopi Goldberg Show*, she returned to Broadway in *A Funny Thing Happened on the Way to the Forum*. In 1998, she revived the television quiz show *"Hollywood Squares"* as a starring vehicle. Film work after that included *The*

Golf (Update). Through the early 1990s, the most successful black golfer by far was Calvin Peete. In 1982 Peete became the first black multiple winner, capturing the Greater Milwaukee Open for the second time, the Anheuser-Busch Classic, the BC Open, and the Pensacola Open and had his best finish in a grand slam event, placing third in the PGA championship. In April 1997, Eldred "Tiger" Woods, a twenty-one-year-old African American, astounded the golf world by shooting a record low score to win the Masters Tournament. Woods' feat rocketed him to instant national stardom and revolutionized the role and visibility of blacks in golf. Woods continued to heighten his popularity in 2000 with a victory in the British Open, making him the youngest player ever to win all of golf's major tournaments.

REFERENCES

Barkow, Al. *The History of the PGA Tour*. 1989.

http://espn.go.com/golfonline/britishopen00/s/2000/ 0723/648236.html (article on Woods' British Open victory and legacy)

McRae, Finley F. "Hidden Traps Beneath the Placid Greens." American Visions (April 1991): 26-29.

GREG ROBINSON

Gomes, Peter John

Gomes, Peter John (May 22, 1942–), theologian. Peter Gomes, whom Time magazine called "one of America's great preachers," was born in Boston and grew up in Plymouth, Massachusetts. Gomes' father was a Cape Verdean immigrant who labored in the local cranberry bogs, while his mother was a fourth-generation African-American Bostonian, from an affluent family, who had studied music at the New England Conservatory before becoming the first African American to work in Cambridge's City Hall. Gomes attended Bates College in Lewiston, Maine, where he received his B.A. in 1965, then attended Harvard University Divinity School. After Gomes earned an STB degree from Harvard in 1968, he was ordained a minister in the American Baptist Church.

Peter Gomes. (Copyright by Jerry Bauer)

He subsequently took a position as Professor of History and Director of Freshman Studies at the Tuskegee Institute.

In 1970, Gomes accepted the post of assistant minister at Harvard's prestigious Memorial Church, and was named Professor of Christian Morals. Over the following two decades, Gomes was a notable figure at Harvard, for his dynamic preaching and thoughtful biblical exegesis, and for his conservative Republican politics. In 1984 and 1988, Gomes was selected to deliver sermons at the inaugurations of Presidents Ronald Reagan and George Bush.

In 1991, at a rally held in protest of an antigay piece in the conservative Harvard magazine Peninsula, Gomes came out as "a Christian who happens as well to be gay." He thereafter became an important figure in the gay rights movement. In 1998, two years after he published a best-selling Bible analysis, *The Good Book*, Gomes announced that Memorial Church would solemnize same-sex unions.
See also RELIGION [4]; GAY MEN [2].

REFERENCE

Gomes, Peter J. *The Good Book: Reading the Bible with Mind and Heart*. 1996.

GREG ROBINSON

Gordone, Charles

Gordone, Charles (October 12, 1925– November 17, 1995), playwright and educator. Born in Cleveland, Ohio, raised in Elkhart, Indiana, and trained in drama at Los Angeles State College (1952), Gordone became the first African-American dramatist to receive a Pulitzer Prize for his play *No Place to Be Somebody* (1969). The play was Gordone's first, and it premiered at the Joseph Papp Public Theater on May 4, 1969 before winning the Pulitzer in 1970 and moving to Broadway in 1971. The play tells the story of an African-American petty hustler who owns a saloon and attempts to evade the local white Mafia.

Although Gordone wrote other plays, including *Gordone is a Mutha* (1973) and *The Last Chord* (1976), none were received as favorably as *No Place to be Somebody* and his national visibility dropped. After using theater in 1975 as rehabilitation therapy at a Youth Correctional Institution in Bordentown, New Jersey, Gordone, disenchanted by urban living, relocated to teach English and theater at Texas A&M University in 1986. He had served as chair and cofounder of the Congress of Racial Equality's Committee for the Employment of Negro Performers in

Charles Gordone. (AP/Wide World Photos)

the 1962, and through the 1980s and early 1990s, he remained a theater reformer, passionately advocating interracial and multicultural casting for people of color. More than a mere lecturer, Gordone directed plays for school and community theater, often using mixed race casts or non-traditional casting to broaden American's tolerance for a multi-ethnic society.
See also CONGRESS OF RACIAL EQUALITY (CORE) [2]; DRAMA [2].

REFERENCES

Pogrebin, Robin. "Charles Gordone is Dead at 70; Won a Pulitzer Prize for His First Play." *The New York Times*, 19 November 1995, sec. 1, p. 51.

Turner, Allan. "Playwright's Real Life Was in the West; Quest to find America Brought Him to A&M." *The Houston Chronicle*, 21 November 1995, sec. A, p.11.

Woll, Allen. *Dictionary of the Black Theater: Broadway, Off-Broadway, and selected Harlem Theater*. 1983.

F. ZEAL HARRIS

Gourdin, Edward Orval (August 10, 1897–1966), athlete, soldier, judge. Edward Gourdin was an

outstanding college athlete, an army officer in World War II, and was the third African American to serve on the Massachusetts bench. Gourdin was born in Jacksonville, Florida. His demonstrated athletic and scholarly abilities prompted his family to take him to Massachusetts, where in 1921 he graduated from Harvard College. In 1924 he received his LL.B. degree from Harvard Law School.

He was one of the few African Americans of that era to be recognized in athletics. At Harvard, Gourdin was a member of the track, baseball, and basketball teams. He was National Amateur Athletic Union junior 100-yard dash champion in 1920. In 1924, he also won the broad jump at the Olympic games in Paris. Also, while at Harvard, Gourdin was a member of the National Championship Rifle Team.

In addition to a successful law practice in Boston, Gourdin accepted President Franklin D. Roosevelt's appointment as assistant district attorney and then became chief of the legal division. He had been a member of the Harvard Student Army Training Corps and commissioned a second lieutenant. In 1941, when World War II began, Gourdin, then a colonel, became commanding officer of the Third Battalion of the 372nd. He continued to rise in rank until he retired in 1959 as brigadier-general in the Massachusetts National Guard. During this period, Gourdin resumed work as assistant U.S. district attorney, a position he held until 1952, when he became a special justice of the Roxbury District Court-the third of his race to hold the post. In 1958 the governor appointed Gourdin to the Massachusetts Superior Court.
See also OLYMPIC MOVEMENT, THE [4]; TRACK AND FIELD [5]; WORLD WAR II [5].

REFERENCES

Chalk, Ocania. *Black College Sport*. 1976.

Henderson, Edwin B. *Negro in Sports*. 1939.

Logan, Rayford W., and Michael R. Winston, eds. *Dictionary of American Negro Biography*. 1982.

FREDERICK D. SMITH, JR.

Grandmaster Flash (Joseph Saddler) (January 1, 1957–), music artist. Born Joseph Saddler in Barbados, Grandmaster Flash got his start in the vibrant street party scene of the Bronx in 1970s New York. A prominent DJ, Flash pioneered a number of record mixing innovations, including "scratching,"

"break mixing," "punch phasing," and the "beat box." Flash's mastery of these techniques placed him at the forefront of the rap music scene which exploded into national popularity in the early 1980s.

Flash's innovations centered around the use of multiple turntables to combine the best parts of good songs to create an exciting new combination of beats and melodies. In addition to creating new sounds, Flash added an element of showmanship to his performances, mixing records behind his back and including friends who "shouted out" to hype the audience. These shout outs evolved into complex rhyming lyrics and became a permanent part of Flash's act when he formed Grandmaster Flash and the Furious Five. The group's 1981 single, "The Adventures of Grandmaster Flash on the Wheels of Steel," introduced a national audience to the exciting rhythmic montage of sound made possible by Flash's technological innovations. Their 1982 hit, "The Message," won critical acclaim and demonstrated that rap music could tackle the pressing issues of urban poverty and violence. Although the group broke up in 1982, their work remained influential to rap and hip hop music. Flash remained active in the hip-hop scene and is known for his role as music director on the *Chris Rock Show*.

See also MUSIC [4]; RAP [4]; RECORDING INDUSTRY [4].

REFERENCES

George, Nelson. *Hip Hop America*. 1988.

Toop, David. *Rap Attack 3*. 1999.

Rose, Tricia. *Black Noise: Rap Music and Black Culture in Contemporary America*. 1994.

MICHAEL WADE FUQUAY

Gravely, Samuel L., Jr. (June 4, 1922–), U.S.
Navy admiral. Gravely was born in Richmond, Virginia. He interrupted his education at Virginia Union University in 1942 in order to join the naval reserve. By end of this period of his service, Gravely was the first black to reach the rank of captain. In 1946 Gravely left the navy, returned to Virginia Union, and earned his bachelor's degree in 1948. He then took a job in the Post Office. Following President Harry S Truman's 1948 order ending segregation in the military, the armed forces increased their efforts at the recruitment of blacks, and Gravely returned to active service in 1952.

Admiral Samuel L. Gravely, in uniform. (Copyright by Admiral Samuel L. Gravely)

In 1961 Gravely became the first black officer to command a ship when he was temporarily placed in command of the USS *Theodore E. Chandler*, and the following year as a lieutenant commander he became the first black to command a fighting ship, the USS *Falgout*. In 1966 he was the first black commander to lead a ship, the USS *Taussig*, into direct offensive action. Gravely became the first African American admiral in 1971; he retired as a three-star admiral. He eventually rose to command the third fleet, based in Hawaii, from 1976 to 1978. Gravely spent the following two years before his retirement in 1980 as director of the Defense Communications Agency.

In retirement Gravely continued to be active as a consultant and speaker. Between 1984 and 1987 he worked with the Educational Foundation of the Armed Forces Communications and Electronics Association, serving as executive director of education and training. *See also* MILITARY [4].

REFERENCES

Armstrong, Robin. "Samuel L. Gravely, Jr." In *Contemporary Black Biography*, Vol. 5, edited by Barbara Carlisle Bigelow. 1994.

Irvin, Donna L. Samuel L. Gravely Jr. In *Notable Black American Men*, edited by Jessie Carney Smith. 1999.

ROBERT L. JOHNS

Greene, Maurice (July 23, 1974–), athlete.

Maurice Greene's record at sprint events is so impressive that he has the nickname, "The Kansas Cannonball." Greene holds both the 60 meter (indoor) and the 100 meter World Records. On June 16, 1999, in Athens, he moved ahead of the previous 100 meter record by 0.05 of a second.

Born in Kansas City, Kansas, Greene got his start in running when he was in the fourth grade, in an eraser shuttle race for fifth graders that he won easily. While at F. L. Schlagle High School in Kansas City, he developed speed on the track and the football field. He won his third straight Kansas high school state meet in 1993, in the 100- and 200-meter sprint double.

Greene took second place in the 100 meter U.S.A. National Championships and first place in the same 1997 contest, when he was ranked number one in the U.S. and number two in the world in the 100 meter.

In 1998 he set a world record in the indoor 60 meter at 6.39 in Madrid and was ranked number one in the world and in the U.S. in the 100 meter. In 1999 Greene took first place in the World Championships, won first place in the 200 meter, and first place in the 4 x 100 meter relay, all held in Seville. He was number one again in the U.S., both in the 100 meter and 200 meter. Greene won two gold medals at the Sydney Olympics in 2000: in the 100 meters and as a member of the 4x100 meter relay team. His charming personality and impressive performances enabled Greene to win the hearts of people worldwide.

See also OLYMPIC MOVEMENT, THE [4]; TRACK AND FIELD [5].

REFERENCES

Burgess, Zack. "Greene Goes for the Gold." *Insight on the News* 15 (August 2, 1999): 39.

Layden, Tim. "Youth Movement." *Sports Illustrated* 86 (June 23, 1997): 58.

"Maurice Greene." http://www/his/net/bio_greene.html.

FREDERICK D. SMITH, JR.

Maurice Greene, celebrates his victory in the 100 meter dash. (Corbis Corporation)

Gregg, John Andrew (February 18, 1877–February 1953), bishop, educator.

John Gregg was committed to the intellectual and spiritual development of African Americans. Gregg was born in Eureka, Kansas, the son of Alexander Gregg and Eliza Frances Allen. He joined the Twenty-third Kansas Volunteers during the Spanish American War. He became a minister in the African Methodist Episcopal Church in 1898 then entered the University of Kansas that same year. He graduated in 1902 and taught school briefly. In 1903 he was ordained a deacon and became minister to Mount Olive Church in Emporia.

After serving as teacher and administrator of the A.M.E. mission station in Cape Colony, South Africa, he returned to the United States in 1906 and pastored other churches for over five years. From 1913 to 1920, Gregg was president of Edward Waters College and of Wilberforce University from 1920 to 1924. In May 1924, Gregg was elected bishop, and for the next four years he was assigned to South Africa. Howard University appointed Gregg its first African American president in 1926, a position that he refused in order to remain with the church. He returned to the United States in 1928 and held a succession of assignments in Kansas, Virginia, and Florida.

During World War II, Gregg toured with U.S. troops in the European and Pacific theaters and worked to boost morale of the African American soldiers and to promote racial harmony. He published several pieces about the church and its philosophy. He also wrote *Christian Brotherhood* (1930) and *Of Men and Of Arms* (1945).

See also AFRICAN [1]; AFRICAN METHODIST EPISCOPAL CHURCH; [1]; SPANISH-AMERICAN WAR [5]; WILBERFORCE UNIVERSITY [5]; WORLD WAR II [5].

REFERENCES

Garraty, John A., and Mark C. Carnes, general eds. *American Negro Biography*. 1999.

Logan, Rayford W., and Michael R. Winston, eds. *Dictionary of American Negro Biography*. 1982.

Wright, Richard R., Jr. *The Bishops of the African Methodist Episcopal Church*. 1963.

VALENCIA PRICE

Gregory, Dick. *See* Gregory, Richard Claxton.

Gregory, Richard Claxton "Dick" (Update), comedian, activist, and rights advocate. In 1995, Gregory staged a hunger strike to protest the Republican "welfare reform" bills, and in 1998 he joined conservative Republicans to demand an investigation of the "murder" of Commerce Secretary Ron Brown. During the mid-1990s, he also returned to performing, notably in a limited run off-Broadway show, "Dick Gregory Live," in October 1995.

After Gregory achieved the pinnacle of success in the world of stand-up comedy, he made a decision to place his celebrity status in the service of his fierce and uncompromising commitment to human rights. Throughout the various shifts and turns of his career for more than three decades, he has kept faith with those commitments.

REFERENCES

Gregory, Dick, with Martin Lipsyte. *Nigger: An Autobiography*. 1964.

Gregory, Dick, with James R. McGraw. *Up from Nigger*. 1976.

Watkins, Mel. *On the Real Side: Laughing, Lying and Signifying—The Underground Tradition of African-American Humor That Transformed American Culture from Slavery to Richard Pryor*. 1994.

JAMES A. MILLER
GREG ROBINSON

Gregory, Thomas Montgomery (August 31, 1887–November 21, 1971), educator. Gregory was born in Washington D.C., and with Alaine Locke, founded the Howard University Players, the only black university drama organization, and one of the only two college-level theater groups existing in the United States in 1921. Professional training in dramatic arts spread from campuses to secondary schools and communities across the nation as drama troupes were established for the purpose of enacting African-American life. This trend is sometimes referred to as the "Little Theater Movement" (1919–1945). An early initiator of the movement for national black theater, Gregory also founded the Atlantic City Neighborhood Theater. During his thirty-two year residency in New Jersey (1924–1956), he served as principal of the New Jersey Avenue School and as the city's supervisor of public schools.

In addition to his zealous work as a theater practitioner and educator, Gregory fought for the admission of Blacks to the Officer Candidate Schools of the United States Army, pressing the Department of War to provide black leadership for black troops. Gregory was commissioned a 1st Lieutenant, Infantry at Fort Des Moines, Iowa in October, 1917. In an historical review "of the Negro in Chicago" (1927), Gregory was highlighted as one of the "Nations Foremost Characters" who had visited the city. Gregory co-edited and selected *Plays of Negro Life: A Sourcebook of Native American Drama* (1927) with Alaine Locke and contributed an essay to *The New Negro* (1925) edited by Alaine Locke. Other writings by Gregory were published in *Crisis, Opportunity and New Republic*.

See also DRAMA [2]; MILITARY [4].

REFERENCES

Boris, Joseph J. *Who's Who in Colored America: A Biographical Dictionary of Notable Persons of African Descent in America*. 1927.

Couch, William Jr. *New Black Playwrights*. 1968.

"T. Montgomery Gregory, 84, Retired Howard Professor" Obituary. *The Washington Afro-American*, 27 November 1971, sec 1, p. 1.

The Washington Intercollegiate Club of Chicago. "1779–The Negro in Chicago-1927." In *Intercollegian Wonder Book*. 1927.

F. ZEAL HARRIS

Grier, Pamela Suzette "Pam" (May 26, 1949–), actress.

Pam Grier gained fame as the queen of blaxploitation films in the 1970s. She became a pinup for African American college students and a strong, independent image for white women in the women's liberation movement. Grier was born in Winston-Salem, North Carolina, and grew up on the bases where her father was stationed in the military. She studied at Denver's Metropolitan State College, working for a while as a cheerleader for the Denver Broncos. She was also the only African American contestant in the Miss Colorado Universe contest of 1967. Grier left college in 1968 and moved to Los Angeles to work part-time, study acting, and begin an acting career.

In 1969 Grier landed her first film role, *The Big Bird Cage*, a grade B movie. Her career progressed as she had lead roles in several films, including *Beyond the Valley of the Dolls* (1969) and the lead role in *Coffy* (1973), her first big break. The film was a commercial success, catapulted Grier to stardom, and set precedents for other African American actresses. She has appeared in numerous films since then, including *Black Mama, White Mama* (1972), *Foxy Brown (1974)*, *Friday Foster* (1975), *Greased Lightning* (1977), *Stand Alone* (1985), *Serial Killer* (1995), *Jackie Brown* (1997), and *In Too Deep* (1999). Grier fan Quentin Tarantino helped bring Grier back into the spotlight with his film *Jackie Brown*, giving Grier a role similar to those in her early films, that of a strong woman with the ability to fend for herself.

See also BLAXPLOITATION FILMS (UPDATE) [S]; FILM [2].

REFERENCES

Mabunda, L. Mpho, ed. *Contemporary Black Biography*, vol. 9. 1995.

Smith, Jessie Carney, ed. *Notable Black American Women*, Book II. 1996.

"The Ultimate Pam Grier Shrine: Filmography." http://members.xoom.com/tupgs2/Filmog.htm.

JESSIE CARNEY SMITH

Pam Grier. (Corbis Corporation)

Griffey, Ken, Jr. (November 21, 1969–), baseball player.

Ken Griffey, Jr. was born to play baseball. Son of major league star Ken Griffey, Junior grew up around big league clubhouses and learned the game from the best. At age eight, he hit eleven home runs in his first six Little League games. He starred at Cincinnati's Moeller High School where he was twice player of the year. In 1987 as a high school senior, the Seattle Mariners picked him first overall in the Major League draft. He earned a spot on the Mariners in 1989, at the age of 19. From then on he has been a super-star.

Among his many accomplishments are 10 straight gold glove awards, 10 straight starts in the All-Star game and seven Silver Slugger Awards. In 1997 he hit 56 home runs and drove in 146 RBIs en route to a unanimous selection as the American League's Most Valuable Player. In 1999, he was the youngest player selected to Major League Baseball's All Century Team. In spring 2000, Griffey was traded to the Cincinnati Reds, where his father was a coach. Although still too young to have set any career records, his performance over his first ten seasons indicates that he has an excellent chance to break a number of important records, including Henry Aaron's "unbreakable" career home run mark. He was the youngest player in history to reach the 350 and 400 home run plateaus. Griffey's on the field success has been complemented by his off the field life. He has won numerous awards for community service and his All-American persona has made him one of the most important star icons in contemporary sports marketing.

See also BASEBALL [1].

REFERENCES

Horton, C. Jemal. "Can't Miss Kid is Now the Main Man." *Washington Post.* July 23, 1998.

Christopher, Matt. *At the Plate with Ken Griffey, Jr.* 1997.

Gutman, Bill. *Ken Griffey, Jr.: A Biography.* 1998.

Loverro, Thom. "Junior's HOME RUN: Griffey got his wish to play in his hometown, but his strong-armed tactics have sent shock waves through the major leagues." *The Washington Times.* March 26, 2000: 1.

MICHAEL WADE FUQUAY

Griffith-Joyner, Florence Delorez (Update)

(December 21, 1959–September 21, 1998), athlete. In 1995, Griffith-Joyner was elected to the Track and Field Hall of Fame. On September 21, 1998, Griffith-Joyner died suddenly of an apparent seizure, leading to charges that she had been improperly medicated by doctors. In August 2000, the family of Griffith-Joyner filed a wrongful death lawsuit against Barnes-Jewish Hospital in St. Louis, where Griffith-Joyner had been treated two years earlier after a previous seizure, for failure to properly diagnose her condition.

REFERENCES

Davis, Michael D. *Black American Women in Olympic Track and Field.* 1992.

Hine, Darlene Clark. *Black Women in America.* 1993.

Pfeifer, Stuart, and Daniel Yi. "Track Star Joyner's Family Sues Hospital in Her Death." *Los Angeles Times.* August 8, 2000: B-1.

GREG ROBINSON

Guillaume, Robert

(November 30, 1927–), actor. Robert Guillaume was born Robert Peter Williams in St. Louis, Missouri. His grandmother raised him and his siblings during the Depression. After a bumpy childhood, Guillaume served in the U.S. Army before moving on to work at a number of jobs

Tony Gwynn, in San Diego Padres uniform. (San Diego Padres)

and take night classes. Blessed with vocal talent, he transferred to the music school of Washington University, St. Louis. After spending the summer of 1957 at the Aspen Music Festival on scholarship, he took an apprenticeship at the Karamu Theater in Cleveland, Ohio. He soon found work in musicals and in 1972 landed the lead role in *Purlie*. He received a Tony nomination for his 1976 role in an all-black revival of *Guys and Dolls*.

Guillaume landed the role of Benson in the ABC series *Soap* in 1977. His performances on *Soap* won him an Emmy for best supporting actor in 1979 and the lead in a spin-off series, *Benson*, which ran from 1979 to 1986. While on *Benson*, Guillaume won his second Emmy in 1985. Although his follow-up series, *The Robert Guillaume Show* (1989), was quickly canceled, Guillaume continued to work in theater and film. He played in the movie *Lean on Me* in 1989 and took over the lead in the musical *Phantom of the Opera* in 1990. He also sang in clubs and did voice roles for animated works like *The Lion King* (1994).

From 1998 to 2000, Guillaume had a major supporting role on the series *Sports Night*. The show won critical approval but few viewers. Guillaume suffered a slight stoke on January 14, 1999, but soon returned to the show.

See also TELEVISION [5].

REFERENCES

"Robert Guillaume." Internet Movie Database. [Filmography] http://us.imdb.org/M/person-exact?+Guillaume,+Robert.

"Robert Guillaume." Sports Night biographies. http://abc.go.com/primetime/sports_night/bios/sn_guillaume.html.

Sipal, Iva. "Robert Guillaume." In *Contemporary Black Biography*, vol. 3, edited by Barbara Carlisle Bigelow. 1993.

ROBERT L. JOHNS

Gwynn, Anthony Keith "Tony" (May 9, 1960–), baseball player. Gwynn was born in Los Angeles and grew up in Long Beach, California, where he attended Polytechnic High School. He attended college at San Diego State University, where he was all-conference in both baseball and basketball. Drafted for basketball by the San Diego Clippers and for baseball by the San Diego Padres on the same day in 1981, he chose the Padres, for whom he would play his entire professional career.

In the 1980s and 1990s, Tony Gwynn built a reputation as the most consistent hitter in Major League baseball. He batted over .300 in seventeen consecutive seasons (1983–1999), won the National League batting title eight times (1984, 1987–1989, 1994–1997) and made the All-Star team fourteen times. In 1999, he surpassed 3,000 career hits, a mark that virtually assures him a place in the Baseball Hall of Fame.

Gwynn quickly became a star in San Diego, where he led the Padres to the franchise's first World Series in 1984, the year he won his first batting title. In 1994 Gwynn captured the imagination of baseball fans by bidding to become the first player since Ted Williams in 1953 to bat over .400, finishing with an average of .394. In 1997, at the age of 37, Gwynn won his eighth batting title, a tribute to both his skills and remarkable longevity. Gwynn maintained his dominance at the plate by becoming a consummate student of the game-spending hours watching tapes, memorizing the tendencies of pitchers, and discussing the theory of hitting with legendary batsmen like Ted Williams.

See also BASEBALL [1].

REFERENCES

Goldenbach, Alan. "Tony Gwynn: an Aztec's Conquest." *The Press-Enterprise*. August 3, 1999.

Bloom, Barry. *Tony Gwynn: Mr. Padre*. 1999.

MICHAEL WADE FUQUAY

H

Hamid, Sufi Abdul (January 6, 1903–July 30, 1938), social activist, religious and labor leader. Hamid was born Eugene Brown in Philadelphia, Pennsylvania. Various sources give differing accounts of his personal life, including name changes, associations, and schooling prior to 1928. Active in Chicago at that time, he changed his name to Bishop Conshankin and formed the Illinois Civic Association, leading boycotts urging white-owned business to hire African Americans, using the slogan "Don't Buy Where You Can't Work."

In 1930 Hamid moved to New York City and founded the International Islamic Industrial Alliance. Continuing activities urging black employment, the organization changed its name to the Negro Industrial and Clerical Alliance and targeted small businesses as well as Woolworth's and Blumstein's department stores. Hamid spoke regularly to crowds; his speeches, however, began to take on an abrasive anti-semitic overtone, and this led to legal challenges, particularly after a major protest rally in 1934 at Blumstein's.

Hamid was accused by the Communist Party of being a "Black Hitler" and denounced by mainline ministers and black newspapers. Hamid was arrested and charged with spreading anti-semitism, and in 1935 the Lerner Corporation won an injunction against his activities. Hamid dropped from public view to reflect in a study of eastern religion. In 1938 he erected an imposing temple of worship; the Universal Holy Temple of Tranquility, a religious organization and economic cooperative, and became His Holiness, Bishop Amiru Al-Mu-Minin Sufi A. Hamid. His new life was short, however, as he died in an airplane accident.

See also HARLEM BOYCOTTS [3]; NEW YORK STATE [4]; PHILADELPHIA [4].

REFERENCES

Garraty, John A., and Mark C. Carnes, eds. *American National Biography*. 1999.

McKay, Claude. *Harlem: Negro Metropolis*. 1940.

Ottley, Roi. *New World A-Coming*. 1943.

DARIUS L. THIEME

Hamilton, Thomas (April 26, 1823–May 29, 1865), journalist, anti-slavery activist. Hamilton used the press to promote the work of African Americans, to stimulate racial pride, and to agitate for civil rights. Born in New York City, he was educated in the African Free Schools and the African Methodist Episcopal Church. He learned about abolitionism and the reform press at home and apparently never departed from what he was taught. In 1836 Hamilton began work as a carrier for the *Colored American*, then he became bookkeeper and clerk for the *New York Evangelist* and the *National Anti-Slavery Standard*.

In 1841 Hamilton founded the *People's Press*, a militant weekly he published for two years. Hamilton return to the *New York Evangelist* and the *National Anti-Slavery Standard*, and at the same time he began to work for the *New York Independent*. He supplemented his income by working as a bookseller. Working out of the American Anti-Slavery Society's offices in New York, he distributed books and tracts on such themes as temperance and anti-slavery.

An important African American journalist of the Civil War period, Hamilton began in 1857 to publish two periodicals, the *Anglo-American Magazine* and the *Weekly Anglo-African*, each designed to enhance the black image. The *Anglo-American* published works of black writers and activists such as Frederick Douglass and Frances E. W. Harper. The *Anglo-African*, which published editorials, became the most influential black journal of that period. Around the mid-1860s, Hamilton began to publish books and pamphlets by and about African Americans, including William Wells Brown's *The Black Man: His Antecedents, His Genius, and His Achievements* (1863).

See also ANGLO-AFRICAN, THE [1]; DEMOCRATIC PARTY [2]; INTELLECTUAL LIFE [3]; JOURNALISM [3].

REFERENCES

Garraty, John A., and Mark C. Carnes, general editors. *American National Biography*. 1999.

Penn, I. Garland. *The Afro-American Press and Its Editors*. 1891.

Ripley, C. Peter, and others. *The Black Abolitionist Papers*. 1992.

JESSIE CARNEY SMITH

Hampton, Henry (January 8, 1940–November 21, 1998), filmmaker. Henry Hampton, producer and director of *Eyes on the Prize* (1987), received six Emmy Awards and the Charles Frankel Prize, awarded by President George Bush in 1990 for being one of five Americans who made outstanding contributions to the humanities. *Eyes on the Prize*, a six-part film series, documented the civil rights movement from 1954–1984.

Hampton is noted for his artistic blend of archival news footage with interviews, sound effects, and a balanced historical point of view in more than 60 films ranging from industrial or training films commissioned by companies to highly innovative independent documentaries, created by Blackside Inc., Hampton's film production company. He founded Blackside in Boston, Massachusetts in 1968 for the purpose of creating entertainment of historical significance. *The Great Depression (1993), Malcolm X: Make It Plain (1994), and I'll Make Me a World: A Century of African-American Arts (1999)*, explore the meaning of democracy, culture, and society while confronting racism.

Born in St. Louis, Missouri, and struck by polio at age fifteen, Hampton, partially crippled by the disease, earned a B.A. in both English and Premedical Studies from Washington University in Missouri in 1961. In addition to leading a career as an established producer and filmmaker, Hampton served as Chairperson of the Board of Directors for the Museum of Afro-American History (1965–1990). Before his death in 1998, Hampton had received fourteen honorary degrees from institutions of higher learning across the nation and developed a reputation for training filmmakers of color.

See also ST. LOUIS [5]; MISSOURI [4].

REFERENCES

American Visions, 9 (1994): 46.

Jet v. 95, 1998, p. 59.

LaBlanc, Michael L. ed. *Contemporary Black Biography: Profiles from the International Black Community*. 1989.

McKinley, Jesse. "Henry Hampton Dies at 58; Produced 'Eyes on the Prize'" *The New York Times*, 24 November 1998, sec. B, 10.

F. ZEAL HARRIS

Hannah, Marc (October 13, 1956–), engineer, computer expert, entrepreneur. Hannah has distinguished himself as a special effects expert for movies and television productions. Hannah was born in Chicago and received his B.S. degree from Illinois Institute of Technology and both his M.S. and Ph.D. degrees from Stanford University. He was one of the founders of Silicon Graphics Incorporated (SGI), a principal scientist with and vice president of the company. SGI is strategically located in Silicon Valley, with an additional research and development center in England. Hannah designs computers that create special effects as seen in the movies that contracted with the firm: *Terminator 2, Jurassic Park, The Hunt for Red October, Beauty and the Beast, and Field of Dreams.* SGI also created special effects for two Michael Jackson films.

Hannah focuses is on graphics; he determines the capability of the computers to produce special effects. SGI's equipment may be purchased by movie studios or other companies that use their own artists to create the desired designs. For example, in the making of *Terminator 2*, George Lucas's company purchased SGI's expensive equipment. Less costly models of SGI computers are now available to individual artists and small firms.

SGI has diversified and, thus, reaches other markets; it works with companies like Nintendo to develop new products. It also has spin-off companies, such as Silicon Studios. Hannah conceptualizes new products, and teams of developers are used to complete them. His commitment to SGI continues, however, as he searches out other consumer interests and determines how to respond to them.
See also CHICAGO [1]; ENGINEERING [2].

REFERENCES

Ebony, February 1993, pp. 55-58.

Mabunda, L. Mpho, ed. *Contemporary Black Biography*. 1996.

FREDERICK D. SMITH, JR.

Harris, E. Lynn (1955–), novelist. E. Lynn Harris, born in Flint, Michigan, and raised in Little Rock, Arkansas, is a novelist who has used his writing to overcome his depression from years of living in denial about his homosexuality. In 1977, he graduated from the University of Arkansas at Fayetteville with a B.A. in journalism. After studying business at Southern Methodist University, he worked as a salesman for IBM, Hewlett-Packard, and AT&T for thirteen years before committing his life to writing.

In 1990, he decided to become a professional writer although he had no formal training. In 1992, he self-published his first novel, *Invisible Life*—a story of a young man coming to terms with his own homosexuality. He sold his books to black-owned bookstores and beauty salons throughout Atlanta before attracting Anchor Books. *Invisible Life* spent eleven months as number one on the Blackboard Bestseller List of African-American Titles. In 1992, *Essence* magazine named the book one of the year's ten best. In 1994, he released his second novel, *Just As I Am*.

His 1996 *And This Too Shall Pass* remained on *The New York Times* bestseller list for nine weeks. His other works include *If This World Were Mine* (1997) and *Abide with Me* (1999). His writing has appeared in *Essence* and the award-winning anthology *Brotherman: The Odyssey of Black Men in America*, and *Go the Way*

Your Blood Beats. He is also a frequent contributor to the gay periodical, *The Advocate*. He lives in both New York City and Chicago.
See also GAY MEN [2]; LITERATURE [3].

REFERENCES

"Harris, E. Lynn." *Contemporary Authors*. Edited by Scot Peacock. 1998.

Weaver, Kimberly. "Harris, E. Lynn." *Oxford Companion to African American Literature*. Edited by William Andrews and F. Foster, et al. 1997.

RACHEL ZELLARS

Harrison, Samuel (April 15, 1818–August 11, 1900), army chaplain, clergyman, civil rights advocate. Born in Philadelphia, Harrison and his slave parents, Jennie and William, were owned by the Bolton family of Savannah, Georgia. The Harrisons were manumitted and, after William's death, moved to New York City, where Jennie stayed on as a servant to the Boltons. She remarried, to a man whose intemperance forced her to send nine-year-old Samuel to live with a minister uncle in Philadelphia, where he became apprenticed as a shoemaker. Before long Jennie left her alcoholic husband and joined her son in the Quaker City.

While attending a black Presbyterian church service, Harrison had a religious conversion experience and vowed to devote his life to the ministry. In 1836 he enrolled briefly in an industrial arts school in Peterboro, New York, then at Western Reserve College in Hudson, Ohio, which he attended until financial difficulties forced him to return to Philadelphia in 1839. After working for a short time as a bookseller, Harrison began his own shoemaking business. He married his childhood friend, Ellen Rhodes, and the couple eventually had thirteen children. In 1847 Harrison and his family moved to Newark, New Jersey, where he helped minister to a black Presbyterian congregation. Two years later a vacancy at the Second Congregational Church in Pittsfield, Massachusetts, afforded Harrison the opportunity to become pastor of his own congregation and, since Congregationalists were dogmatically aligned with Presbyterians, he began ministering to the oldest established church of African Americans in Berkshire County in January 1850.

Harrison was an anti-colonizationist and an outspoken critic of the Fugitive Slave Law. Books from his library included an annotated copy of Hinton Rowan Helper's contentious *The Impending Crisis of the South* (1857). In 1862 he lectured to a Williamstown, Massachusetts, congregation on "The Cause and Cure for the War," a fiery oration in which he trumpeted support for the enlistment of black troops. For undisclosed reasons, Harrison retired from his Pittsfield pulpit in July 1862 and began working with the National Freedmen's Relief Association to solicit aid for former slaves living on the then militarily occupied Sea Islands of South Carolina. In July of the following year, Harrison journeyed to Boston and met with John A. Andrew, the abolitionist Massachusetts governor, who requested that he travel to South Carolina to "express the sympathy of the Commonwealth" to surviving members of the Fifty-Fourth Massachusetts Regiment, the first black unit mustered in the North, which had fought valiantly at Fort Wagner. Harrison set off in August 1863. He preached to soldiers and freedmen for six weeks before returning North, only to be officially appointed chaplain of the Fifty-fourth by Andrew. He reported for duty at Morris Island, S.C., on November 12, 1863. Immediately, the issue of discriminatory pay practices drew protest from Harrison, who demanded that he receive the same wages as white chaplains. Letters on Harrison's behalf were penned by Andrew and Attorney General Edward Bates to President Lincoln. Taken ill in March 1864, Harrison was honorably discharged from the army. After rejoining the National Freedmen's Relief Association and attending, along with Frederick Douglass, the Syracuse, N.Y. National Convention of Colored Men in October 1864, Harrison served as minister to black congregations in Newport R.I. (1865), Springfield, Mass. (1866–1870), and Portland, Maine (1870–1872), before resuming the pastorship of the Second Congregational Church in Pittsfield. He served as chaplain of the W.W. Rockwell Post 125 (1882, 1883, 1885–1894).

An impassioned orator and writer, Harrison published a variety of tracts on racial equality, enfranchisement, Reconstruction, and "historical perspectives," including: *Pittsfield Twenty-five Years Ago* (1874), *A Centennial Sermon* (1876), *An Appeal of a Colored Man to his Fellow-Citizens of a Fairer Hue in the United States* (1877), and *Pittsfield Then and Now* (1886). Harrison's first wife, Ellen, passed away in 1883. Two years later he married Springfield resident Sarah J. Croom. His autobiography, *Rev. Samuel Harrison: His Life Story*, appeared in 1899. Harrison died in 1900. Two years later a tablet commemorating his forty years of ministry on behalf of Pittsfield African Americans was placed at the Second Congregational Church, with the inscription: "A Wise Leader, an Honored Citizen, an Ardent Patriot, a beloved Messenger of the Lord, he wrought well for his People, his Country and his God."

See also FUGITIVE SLAVE LAW [2]; FREDERICK DOUGLASS [2]; RECONSTRUCTION [4].

REFERENCES

Berkshire Evangel. September 1900.

Blassingame, John W. "Negro Chaplains in the Civil War." *Negro History Bulletin*. October 1963.

Harrison, Samuel. *Rev. Samuel Harrison: His Life Story*. 1899.

Pittsfield Sun. December 11, 1902.

Wills, Davis W., and Richard Newman, eds. *Black Apostles at Home and Abroad*. 1982.

RANDY F. WEINSTEIN

Hart, William Henry Harrison

Hart, William Henry Harrison (October 31, 1857–January 6, 1934), lawyer, educator, civil rights leader. William Hart was born in Eufaula, Alabama, the son of Henry Clay Hart and Jennie Dunn Hart. From 1867 to 1874 he attended the American Missionary school in Eufaula. During his last year there he was a poll worker on election day and distributed tickets to illiterate voters. This infuriated those in the community who sought to overthrow current officials, forcing Hart to leave town. He walked from Eufaula to Washington, D.C., where, in 1880, he entered Howard University's Preparatory Department and in 1885 received his B.A. from the university. In 1887 he received his LL.B. degree, in 1899 his M.A. degree, and in 1891 an LL.M. degree, all from Howard.

From 1888 to 1891 Hart was private secretary to Senator William M. Evarts of New York. He became special assistant to the U.S. district attorney for Washington in 1889. A member of the bar of all courts in Washington as well as the U.S. Supreme Court, he joined the law faculty at Howard in 1890 and remained until 1922. Hart also served as assistant librarian of Congress in 1893–1897 and then was appointed dean of Howard's Department of Agriculture.

A humanitarian, in 1897 he founded the Hart Farm School for Colored Boys and Junior Republic for Dependent Children, where over two hundred wards were taught basic education and farming. He had a cultural side as well; in the mid-1880s he produced theatrical plays in the Washington area. Hart was also known for his work as an activist in early civil rights. Hart had been convicted in Maryland for refusing to occupy a segregated railroad car, appealed the decision, and in *Hart v. the State of Maryland* won the case. *See also* LAWYERS [3]; SUFFRAGE, NINETEENTH-CENTURY [5].

REFERENCES

Hershaw, L. M. "William H. H. Hart." *Journal of Negro History* 19 (April 1934): 211-13.

Logan, Rayford W. *Howard University: The First Hundred Years, 1867–1967.* 1969.

Logan, Rayford W., and Michael R. Winston, eds. *Dictionary of American Negro Biography.* 1982.

RAYMOND WINBUSH

Harvard, Beverly (December 22, 1950–), police chief. Harvard was born in Macon, Georgia, one of seven children. She earned a bachelor's degree in sociology from Morris Brown College in 1972 and a master's degree in urban government from Georgia State University in 1980. She graduated from the Federal Bureau of Investigation's National Academy in Quantico, Virginia, in 1983.

The five-feet-four-inch Harvard prepared to become a police officer in Atlanta to win a bet with her husband who claimed that her size and strength would deter her. She passed the test for police recruits in 1973 and joined the Atlanta police force. At that time, the Atlanta environment was hostile to African American and women officers, but Harvard persevered, working her way up from street patrols to a 1982 appointment to deputy chief. Harvard became the youngest, the first African American, and the first woman to hold the post in Atlanta.

On October 26, 1994, Atlanta Mayor Bill Campbell appointed Harvard acting police chief. Six months later, she was named chief in her own right, making her the only African American woman to head a law enforcement department in a major city, a post she still held as of July 2000. Harvard promptly investigated corruption within the department, leading to the arrest of six officers. Among other changes, she set goals to lower the city's crime rate, to curb violence among youth, and to establish a close relationship between the community and the police force. *See also* ATLANTA, GEORGIA [1].

REFERENCES

Current Biography Yearbook, 1997. 1997.

Eddings, Jerelyn. "Atlanta's Top Cop Makes Her Mark." *U.S. News & World Report* 117 (December 26, 1994): 82.

Mabunda, L. Mpho, and Shirelle Phelps, eds. *Contemporary Black Biography*, vol. 11. 1996.

JESSIE CARNEY SMITH

Hayes, Isaac (August 20, 1942–), singer, musician, composer, record producer. Hayes was born in Covington, Tennessee and attended Memphis public schools. He played saxophone in his high school band, sang in church choirs, and began playing saxophone and piano in local clubs as early as the 1950s, completing his first solo recording in 1962. From 1962 to 1965, he played in the Memphis area R & B club circuit, including Sir Isaac and the Doo-Dads. He soon formed a songwriting and producing partnership with his friend, David Porter. The team worked together for several years at Stax Records in Memphis, establishing the Memphis Sound.

Hayes and Porter together wrote and produced numerous recordings, and Hayes personally worked

Isaac Hayes at the piano. (AP/Wide World Photos)

as arranger, pianist, organist, and producer, with major Stax artists such as Otis Redding and Carla Thomas. Their hit songs of the period 1965–1968 included "Soul Man" and "Hold On, I'm Coming," followed by the *Hot Buttered Soul* album, which went platinum in 1969. Perhaps the crowning achievement of this period was Hayes' 1971 score for the film, *Shaft*, an instant hit for both the film and the subsequent record releases. *Shaft*, earned Hayes an Academy Award, two Grammys, and a Golden Globe award. Next came *Black Moses*, another Grammy winner, in 1972.

Hayes' style blends rhythm and blues with jazz elements, including sampling and a liberal use of synthesizers and overdubbing. He fits his music to his artists (including himself), and the result often crosses over various performing styles (blues, jazz, gospel, etc.). The movie *Shaft 2000*, follows in this vein, and Hayes' artistic efforts continue.

See also BLAXPLOITATION FILMS [S]; RAP [4]; RECORDING INDUSTRY [4]; RHYTHM AND BLUES [4]; SAM AND DAVE [5].

REFERENCES

Floyd, Samuel, ed.. *International Dictionary of Black Composers*. 2000.

Hardy, Phil, and Dave Laing. *Encyclopedia of Rock*. 1987.

Hitchcock, H. Wiley, and Stanley Sadie, eds. *The New Grove Dictionary of American Music*. 1986.

DARIUS L. THIEME

Height, Dorothy (Update)

Height, Dorothy (Update) (March 24, 1912–), organization executive and activist. In 1993, Height was awarded the Spingarn Medal by the National Association for the Advancement of Colored People. In 1996, in a break with moderate colleagues, she addressed the Million Man March. In December 1997, Height resigned from the National Council of Negro Women.

REFERENCES

Giddings, Paula. *In Search of Sisterhood*. 1988.

Hill, Ruth Edmonds, and Patricia Miller King, eds. *The Black Women Oral History Project*. 1991.

GREG ROBINSON

Hemings, Sally (Update)

Hemings, Sally (Update) (1773–1836), slave. Sally Hemings is supposedly the mistress of Thomas Jefferson. Although Jeffersonians such as Virgimius Dabney and Dumas Malone long denied the story of Jefferson's affair with Hemings, in 1998 researchers announced that a comparative DNA study of Hemings's descendants and Jefferson's white descendants conclusively demonstrated that Jefferson was indeed the father of at least one of Hemings's children. A year later, The Thomas Jefferson Memorial Foundation, which owns Monticello, Jefferson's home, announced that after extensive analysis, they had come to the conclusion that Jefferson had certainly sired one and probably all of Hemings's children.

REFERENCES

Brodie, Fawn F. *Jefferson: An Intimate Biography*. 1974.

Chase-Riboud, Barbara. *Sally Hemings: A Novel*. 1979.

GREG ROBINSON

Hemphill, Essex

Hemphill, Essex (April 16, 1957–November 4, 1995), author, poet, activist. Essex Hemphill was an author, poet, performance artist, and black gay activist who challenged silence, exclusion, and homophobia within black communities and institutions. As the eldest of five children, he was born in Chicago and grew up in Washington D.C. Hemphill fought to create an accessible African American gay history. In 1978, Hemphill founded *The Nethula Journal of Contemporary Literature*. He ran the journal for several years before becoming increasingly involved in performance poetry. He performed at the Kennedy Center for Performing Arts, the Folger Shakespeare Library, the 1994 National Black Arts Festival, and the Whitney Museum. Hemphill self-published three books: *Diamonds in the Kitty* (1982), *Plums* (1983), *Earth Life* (1985)— and a larger collection, *Conditions* (1986).

His work may be seen in the film, *Looking for Langston* and two docudramas by Marlon Riggs: *Tongues Untied* and *Black Is, Black Ain't*. Hemphill won the National Library Association's "New Authors in Poetry" Award for *Ceremonies*, published by Penguin in 1992. His radical poems, prose, and expository writing in *Ceremonies* explored African American urban and black gay realities. He also won a Lambda Award for editing the 1991 anthology *Brother to Brother: New Writings by Black Gay Men*—his best-known work. In 1986, he received a fellowship for poetry from the National Endowment for the Arts (NEA). Hemphill died from AIDS complications on November 5, 1995. *See also* GAY MEN [2]; WASHINGTON, D.C. [5].

REFERENCES

Price, Deb. *"Discovering the Voice of Black Gay Men."* www.qrd.org. 2000.

Walsh, Sheila. "Essex Hemphill Dies." *The Washington Blade*. 10 Nov. 1995.

RACHEL ZELLARS

Hendricks, Barbara, (November 20, 1948–), lyric soprano. Hendricks was born in Stephens, Arkansas. While she was studying science at the University of Nebraska, a trustee of the Aspen Institute for Humanistic Studies heard her sing at a community gathering and invited her to study at the Aspen Music Festival. There in the summer of 1968 the famed mezzo-soprano Jennie Tourel, who took her on as a student. Hendricks finished her degree at Nebraska in 1969. She then sent two years at the Juilliard School of Music in New York City, where she benefited from the continued tutelage of Tourel.

Hendricks soon filled in the large gaps in her musical training and soon after ending her studies at Juilliard she was winning competitions and gaining recognition as a singer. She began performing opera in Europe, but her debut in a staged opera in the United States came only in 1975 in San Francisco. Appearances with major orchestras in the United States marked further growth in her reputation. In 1977 following her marriage to her Swedish-born European manager, Martin Engstrom, she moved to Paris. She continued a major career as a recitalist and opera singer and even appeared as Mimi in a filmed version of *La Bohéme* in 1988. Hendricks made her Metropolitan Opera debut in 1986. She deliberately limits her appearances in opera, however, finding that recitals make fewer demands on her voice and time.

Hendricks now lives in Switzerland. In addition to pursuing her highly successful musical career, she devotes much effort to relief work, serving as a goodwill ambassador for the United Nations High Commissioner For Refugees.

See also CONCERT MUSIC [2]; EXPATRIATES [2]; OPERA [4].

REFERENCES

"Barbara Hendricks." *Current Biography Yearbook*. 1989.

"Barbara Hendricks: A Passion For Opera and Human Rights; Arkansas Native Is One of Increasing Number of Major Black Divas." *Ebony*, May 1990.

"Nichols, Jomel. Barbara Hendricks." *In Contemporary Black Biography*. Vol. 3, edited by Barbara Carlisle Bigelow. 1993.

"Olson, Elizabeth. ARTS ABROAD; Living Normally," for Opera, Refugees, and 2 Children. *New York Times*, 24 March 1998.

ROBERT L. JOHNS

Henry, Aaron "Doc" (1922–1997), civil rights and political activist. Aaron Henry was a stalwart warrior and a bulwark for African Americans in the Delta area of Mississippi where he sought their civil rights. "Doc" Henry, as he was known, was born in Tallahatchie County, Mississippi, and raised in Clarksdale, where he completed secondary education. He served in the U.S. Army (1943–1946) and began the fight for equality on a Hawaiian army base where segregated housing was practiced. After being discharged, Henry attended Xavier University in New Orleans, graduating with a degree in pharmacy. After that, he practiced pharmacy and was co-owner of two Clarksdale drugstores.

Henry joined the National Association for the Advancement of Colored People (NAACP) in 1954 and was state president from 1960 to 1993. He was also state chairman of the Council of Federated Organizations and was a pivotal force in attempts to form a biracial committee with the National Council of Churches' Commission on Religion and Race. Highly regarded as a speaker, Henry influenced Andrew Goodman to become a voter registration volunteer in Mississippi where he, James Chaney, and Michael Schwerner became martyrs after their murders in Philadelphia, Mississippi.

When the Mississippi Freedom Democratic Party held its inaugural statewide convention at Jackson's Masonic Temple, Henry ran, albeit unsuccessfully, for governor as a Freedom candidate. He was also active in the Mississippi Summer Project of 1964. His continuing efforts also paved the way for reapportionment, a legislative action that led to the election of black representatives inclusive of Henry who served until 1996.

See also COUNCIL OF FEDERATED ORGANIZATIONS [2]; MISSISSIPPI [4].

REFERENCES

Branch, Taylor. *Pillar of Fire: America in the King Years 1963–65*. 1998.

Kasher, Steven. *The Civil Rights Movement: A Photographic History, 1954–68.* 1996.

The New York Public Library African American Reference. 1999.

DOLORES NICHOLSON

Herman, Alexis Margaret (July 16, 1947–),

U.S. Secretary of Labor. Alexis Herman was born in Mobile, Alabama, the daughter of Alex Herman, a mortician and community activist, and Gloria Caponis, a teacher. She attended Catholic schools in Alabama and Wisconsin, then enrolled at Xavier University, an African-American Catholic college, where she received her B.A. in 1970. During the early 1970s, Herman worked briefly as a social worker, for Interfaith, Inc., and Catholic Charities in Mobile, and as an employment counselor for the Southern Regional Council's Black Women's Program. In 1974 she became national director of the Minority Women's

Employment Recruitment and Training Program (RTP). Based on her success with RTP, Herman was chosen in 1977 to head the U.S. Labor Department's Women's Bureau. In 1981, Herman left the federal government to found the consulting firm Green-Herman & Associates (later A.M. Herman & Associates), which advises businesses on minority hiring issues. She became closely involved with a number of political leaders, most notably Ron Brown. In 1989 Brown, then Chair of the Democratic National Committee, named Herman his deputy.

In December 1996, after Herman had spent three years heading the White House Public Liaison Office, Clinton nominated Herman as U.S. Secretary of Labor. Despite opposition from both conservatives and labor groups, she was confirmed on April 29, 1997. Herman was much praised for her settlement of a strike by UPS workers in Summer 1997, but she was unable to achieve desired progress vis-a-vis her main goals of intensifying job training and proposing better daycare and welfare-to-work programs.

See also PRESIDENTS OF THE UNITED STATES [4]; PUBLIC RELATIONS [4].

REFERENCES

"Alexis M. Herman." in *Contemporary Black Biography.* Vol. 15. 1997.

"Alexis Herman praised for role in UPS strike settlement." *Jet 92* (September 8, 1997): 4.

GREG ROBINSON

Higginbotham, A. Leon, Jr. (February 25,

1928–December 14, 1998), judge. A. Leon Higginbotham, Jr., one of the nation's most prominent African-American judges, was born in Trenton, New Jersey. In 1944, he enrolled at Purdue University, but left after the college's president informed him that the college would not provide heated dormitories to black students. Higginbotham graduated from Antioch College in 1949. He then attended Yale Law School, graduating with honors in 1952. In 1954, after serving briefly as assistant district attorney in Philadelphia, he helped to found Norris, Green, Harris and Higginbotham, a Philadelphia law firm. Higginbotham also became active in the local chapter of the NAACP, which he served as president starting in 1960.

In 1962, Higginbotham was named Commissioner of the Federal Trade Commission. Two years later, he was appointed to the U.S. District Court by President Lyndon Johnson. He soon became an outstanding member of the court and he distinguished himself by

Alexis Herman. (AP/Wide World Photos).

A. Leon Higginbotham Jr. (Copyright by A. Leon Higginbotham Jr.)

his liberal opinions on abortion and prisoner's rights. In 1977, Higginbotham was elevated to the U.S. Court of Appeals for the Third Circuit by President Jimmy Carter. In 1989, the year after he published *In the Matter of Color*, a study of race and the legal process, he became Chief Judge (of the U.S. Court of Appeals), only the third African American to hold such a position. After retiring from the bench in 1993, Higginbotham was named law professor at Harvard University. He also served as counsel to the elite New York law firm of Paul, Weiss, Rifkind, Wharton and Garrison. In 1995, he was awarded the Presidential Medal of Freedom and the NAACP's Spingarn Medal. In 1996, he published a second study of race and law, *Shades of Freedom*.

See also SPINGARN MEDAL [5].

REFERENCES

"A(loysius) Leon Higgenbotham, Jr." in *Notable Black American Men*. 1999.

GREG ROBINSON

Hightower, Dennis F. (October 28, 1941–), corporate executive. Dennis F. Hightower was born in Washington, D.C. A high school graduate at sixteen, he earned a B. S. from Washington's Howard University in 1962 and went on to earn an M. B. A. from Harvard Business School in 1974.

Hightower rose to become a major in the Army during service in Vietnam from 1962–1970, earning the Purple Heart and two Bronze Stars in the process. When he left the service (1970), he took his first corporate job with Xerox's research and engineering group. He left Xerox in 1972 to attend Harvard.

Jobs with several corporations followed Hightower's graduation from Harvard. He worked with an international management consulting firm (McKinney & Co.) for four years. He then took a position with General Electric as manager of its Business Lighting Group until 1981 when Mattel recruited him, and he became vice president of corporate planning. A three-year stint in executive management positions with Russell Reynolds Associates, Inc., began in 1984 and preceded his employment by the Walt Disney Company in 1987.

Since 1987, Hightower has held several positions with Disney. He was president of the Consumer Products Division for Europe, Asia, and Africa from 1987–1995, president of the Television and Telecommunications Division during 1995–1996, after which he worked as a consultant.

Hightower's success in the corporate world is considered to have broadened the horizons for African Americans who aspire to corporate careers. In fact, he has spent part of his time helping to train future entrepreneurs. Hightower has received an Alumni Achievement Award from both Howard (1984) and Harvard (1992).

See also WASHINGTON, D.C. [5].

REFERENCES

Black Enterprise, 25 (June 1995): 30.

Black Enterprise, 26 (December 1995): 58-62.

Phelps, Shirelle, ed. *Contemporary Black Biography*. 1997.

CARRELL P. HORTON

Hill, Andrew (June 30, 1937–), avant-garde jazz pianist, composer. Born in Chicago, Andrew Hill developed an early interest in music, playing with other musicians in his early teens, and performing with Paul Williams's rhythm & blues group as early as 1950. He came in contact with many prominent jazz musicians of the day, including Charlie Parker, Miles Davis and Dinah Washington. Early influences included Barry Harris, Bud Powell, Art Tatum, and Thelonius Monk. In 1961 he left Chicago for New York, as Dinah Washington's accompanist.

Hill moved to Los Angeles in 1962, playing at The Lighthouse and with Rahsaan Roland Kirk, and returned to New York in 1963, where he played with numerous major artists, including Eric Dolphy, Jackie McLean, and with LeRoi Jones' Black Arts Repertory Theatre in 1965. Hill's recordings from this period remain highly acclaimed by fans and critics, and his 1964 release *Point of Departure* is thought to be among the finest albums of the 1960s.

From 1970 to 1971 Hill served as composer in residence at Colgate University, and following his time there, toured with the Smithsonian Heritage Program in the early 1970s, receiving a Smithsonian Fellowship in 1975. Hill held further academic and teaching posts during the late 1970s, as he took an extended sabbatical from the jazz world. In the mid 1990s, he returned to New York and began recording again. His music is dense, highly original, taking steps of creativity and improvisation beyond those of Ornette Coleman and Cecil Taylor. Harmonically and melodically at times abstract, at times mellow, he shows African influences as well as those of his jazz predecessors.

See also CHICAGO, ILLINOIS [1]; ILLINOIS [3].

REFERENCES

Feather, Leonard, and Ira Gitler. *The Biographical Dictionary of Jazz*. 1988.

The New Grove Dictionary of Jazz, vol.1., edited by Barry Kernfeld.1988.

Southern. Eileen. *Biographical Dictionary of Afro-American and African Musicians*. 1982

DARIUS L. THIEME

Hilliard, Earl Frederick (April 9, 1942–), U.S. Congressman, lawyer, civil rights activist. Earl Hilliard, activist in the modern civil rights movement in Alabama, is the first African American elected as representative to the U.S. Congress since Reconstruction. Born in Birmingham to William and Iola Frazier Hilliard, he was educated at Morehouse College (B.A., 1964), Howard University School of Law (J.D., 1967), and Atlanta University School of Business (M.B.A., 1970). Hilliard began his career as a teacher at Miles College (1967–1968) and then was assistant to the president of Alabama State University (1968–1970).

Earl Hilliard, viewing civil rights statue in Birmingham, Alabama. (AP/Wide world Photos)

Hilliard's work with the voter-registration drives and participation protest marches during the civil rights era of the 1960s gave him access to many blacks in the area. Elected to the Alabama House of Representatives in 1974, he chaired the first Alabama Black Legislative Caucus. Hilliard ran for office again in 1980, winning election to the state senate. Redistricting in Alabama after the 1990 census made possible the new Seventh Congressional District, which encompassed black neighborhoods around Birmingham and Montgomery. In a runoff election in 1992, Hilliard narrowly won a seat in the U.S. Congress.

In Congress, Hilliard has served on the House Agriculture Committee and the Committee on International Relations. He was first vice chair of the Congressional Black Caucus and later vice chair of the Progressive Caucus. He has aggressively represented the interests of his home state, as was demonstrated in the federal transportation grant that he obtained to restore ferry service in the predominantly black town of Gees Bend. He also enabled Alabama to receive three of the federal government's "enterprise zones," providing tax incentives to promote business in depressed areas.

See also ALABAMA [1].

REFERENCES

"Congressman Earl F. Hilliard." http://www.house.gov/hilliard/bio.htm.

Phelps, Shirelle, ed. *Contemporary Black Biography*, vol. 24. 2000.

Who's Who Among African Americans, 12th ed. 1999.

RAYMOND WINBUSH

Hilyer, Amanda Gray (March 24, 1870–June 29, 1957), entrepreneur, pharmacist, civic worker, civil rights leader. Amanda Hilyer worked for over sixty years to improve the life for African Americans in Washington, D.C. Hilyer was born in Atchison, Kansas, educated in the local public schools, and around 1897 moved to Washington, D.C., with her husband, Arthur S. Gray. In Washington, Hilyer continued her education, graduating from Howard University in 1903 with the pharmaceutical graduate degree. The Grays opened a pharmacy at 12th and U Streets, NW, the center of commerce for African Americans.

Hilyer closed the pharmacy in 1917, when her husband died, and became involved in supporting the efforts of African American men in the military during World War I. Her war work took her to Camp Sherman in Chillicothe, Ohio. When the war ended, she may have lived in St. Louis, where she was president of the Phyllis Wheatley YWCA.

In 1923 she married Andrew F. Hilyer. After he died, she remained involved in local civic activities, including the Iona Whipper Home for Unwed Mothers which she served as president and board member. She and other African American women and their organizations restored the Frederick Douglass home in the Anacostia section of Washington. She was a member of the Citizens' Committee for Freedmen's Hospital Nurses, the Board of Trustees of Berean Baptist Church, and the Association for the Study of Negro Life and History, as the organization was known then. After she died, her commitment to the uplift of African Americans was demonstrated in her will that gave financial support to her church, the Whipper home, Howard University, the local YWCA, and other groups.
See also ENTREPRENEURS [2]; KANSAS [3].

REFERENCES

Afro-American (July 16, 1957).

Logan, Rayford W., and Michael R. Winston, eds. *Dictionary of American Negro Biography*. 1982.

Smith, Jessie Carney, ed. *Notable Black American Women*. 1992.

JESSIE CARNEY SMITH

Holland, William H. (1841–May 27, 1907), educator, politician, soldier. William Holland helped found a public black college in Texas and was perhaps the first African American to direct a public institution for the hearing and visually impaired. Born a slave in Marshall, Texas, he was the son of Captain Byrd (Bird) Holland, later secretary of state of Texas. His father bought William Holland's freedom and that of his two brothers in the 1850s and sent them to Ohio for an education. Holland joined the 16th U.S. Colored Troops on October 22, 1864, a regiment of historic significance for its participation in the battles of Nashville and Overton Hill in Tennessee.

From 1867 to 1869, Holland was a student in Oberlin College's preparatory department, then he returned to Texas where he taught in Austin and vicinity. A Republican, he was elected to represent Waller County in the Fifteenth Texas Legislature. Holland's political astuteness led to the creation of Prairie View Normal School, a state school for blacks. He and fellow African American state politician, Norris Wright Cuney, were instrumental in the passage on April 5, 1887, of a bill creating the Texas Institute for Deaf, Dumb, and Blind Colored Youth. The institute opened on August 15, 1887, with Holland as founding superintendent—a position he held for eleven years, left in 1898, and was reappointed on April 21, 1904. He remained in the post until he died. Holland founded the "Friend in Need" organization that provided financial aid to African American students. He died at home in Wells, Texas.
See also TEXAS [5].

REFERENCES

Brewer, J. Mason. *Negro Legislators of Texas*. 1970.

Levstik, Frank R. "William Holland: Black Soldier, Politician and Educator. *Negro History Bulletin* (May 1973): 110-111.

Logan, Rayford W., and Michael R. Winston, eds. *Dictionary of American Negro Biography*. 1982.

VALENCIA PRICE

Holmes, Dwight Oliver Wendell (November 5, 1877–September 7, 1963), teacher, university administrator, author, scholar, college president. Holmes was born in Lewisburg, West Virginia, to the Rev. John Alexander and Sarah (Bollin) Holmes on November 15, 1877. Following completion of the preparatory and college courses at Howard University, he received the Bachelor of Arts degree in 1901. Holmes began his educational career in St. Louis, Missouri, the following year. Subsequently, he held teaching and administrative positions in Baltimore, Maryland, and Washington, D.C. Holmes did graduate study at Howard University, the Johns Hopkins University, and Teachers College, Columbia University, where he received the M.A. (1915) and the Ph.D (1934).

Holmes served as teacher, department head, and professor of education and administration. While at Howard University, he served as registrar (1919–1921); dean of the College of Education (1921–1931); acting president (1931); and dean of the graduate school (1934–1937). Holmes published articles in a number of academic journals and authored a book, *The Evolution of the Negro College* (1934). Additionally, Holmes penned a number of book reviews in the *Journal of Negro Education*.

In 1937, Holmes became Morgan College's first president of African descent. Two years later, it became Morgan State College, then Morgan State University in 1975. He directed the academy's transfer from the authority of the Methodist Church to the State of Maryland. Holmes retired from Morgan State College in 1948 and died on September 7, 1963. His second wife and granddaughter survived him.
See also WEST VIRGINIA [5].

REFERENCES

"Dr. D. O. Holmes Rites Wednesday." *Washington Post*, September 9, 1963.

Logan, Rayford W. and Michael R. Winston, eds. *Dictionary of American Negro Biography*. 1982.

Ohles, Frederick, Shirley M. Ohles, and John G. Ramsay. *Biographical Dictionary of Modern American Educators*. 1997.

Who's Who in America, vol. 24. 1947.

LINDA T. WYNN

Holstein, Caspar A.

(December 6, 1876–April 5, 1944), entrepreneur, racketeer, philanthropist. Born in Christiansted, a town in St. Croix, Caspar Holstein and his mother moved to New York City in 1894, where he completed his high school education. Among his first jobs was as a bellhop in a local hotel. After serving in the U.S. Navy, he returned to this job and is believed to have crafted a new betting method for policy numbers, an accomplishment that played prominently in making his fortune.

Within a year, his numbers system took hold, and he demonstrated his wealth through expensive purchases such as real estate ventures. Holstein distributed his wealth across a range of interests, among them the Turf Club, where he sponsored affairs for people of diverse social and economic backgrounds. He gave generously to the Harlem community, to two black colleges, and elsewhere. Prominent among his charities was *Opportunity* magazine's annual literary banquets held during the height of the Harlem Renaissance artistic movement. During the banquets, the Casper Holstein Award was given to African American artists for their poetry, plays, music, and other expressions of creativity.

With his numbers business flourishing-earning him as much as five thousand dollars per day-he became rich and well known. On September 23, 1928, white gangsters kidnapped Holstein and demanded fifty thousand dollars for his safe return. Some suspected that gangster Dutch Schultz wanted to move in on Holstein's business, and the kidnapping was just a ruse to force him out. After the incident, Holstein did leave the numbers business. He worked at his legitimate businesses but eventually died penniless.
See also HARLEM RENAISSANCE [3].

REFERENCES

Hansen, Axel. *From These Shores*. 1996.

Schoen, Allon. *Harlem on My Mind: Cultural Capital of Black America*, 1900–1968. 1969.

Smith, Jessie Carney, ed. *Notable Black American Men*. 1999.

JESSIE CARNEY SMITH

Holyfield, Evander (Update)

(October 19, 1962–), professional boxer. Holyfield returned to the ring in 1996, and he defeated Mike Tyson to win the WBA Heavyweight title. In June 1997, he won a rematch from Tyson (who was suspended for biting Holyfield's ear). He successfully defended his title in September 1998.

In March 1999, Holyfield retained his title following a controversial draw against Lennox Lewis, in a fight that many felt Lewis won easily. In the Novem-

Evander Holyfield. (Corbis Corporation)

ber 1999 rematch, Lewis won a unanimous decision to take the title. Holyfield regained a portion of the heavyweight title in August 2000, with a unanimous decision win over John Ruiz.

Holyfield made further headlines during 2000 when he announced the formation of his own record label, titled Real Deal (also his boxing nickname), and with his divorce from his second wife, Dr. Janice Itson Holyfield.

REFERENCES

Current Biography Yearbook 1993. 1993.

"Holyfield: Split Decision Is Final." *The Atlanta Journal-Constitution*. June 17, 2000: C2.

Tierney, Mike. "Last Round Won Crown for Holyfield." *The Atlanta Journal-Constitution*. August 14, 2000: C1.

GREG ROBINSON

Houston, Whitney (August 9, 1963–), singer, actress, model. Whitney Houston was born in Newark and grew up in East Orange, New Jersey. She comes from a family of performers: her mother, Cissy Houston, is a long-time gospel performer, and her husband, Bobby Brown, is also a singer. As a child, Houston sang in the choir of her church, New Hope Baptist Church, and sang her first solo at the age of twelve. After briefly working as a teen model, Houston returned to music following her graduation from high school. She performed in minor capacities such as backup singing and advertising, but she did not sign a record contract until 1985. Her first album, *Whitney Houston* (1985), became the best-selling debut album for any solo artist, selling thirteen million copies and winning a Grammy Award and two National Music awards. Her follow-up albums, *Whitney* (1987) and *I'm Your Baby Tonight* (1990), succeeded in similar fashion.

Houston's fourth album accompanied her acting debut in *The Bodyguard* (1992). Houston performed the Dolly Parton song "I Will Always Love You" in the film, and it became the longest running number-one single in history. The film grossed $390 million, the soundtrack sold twenty-four million copies, and Houston's fame was at its peak.

Houston's career slowed down somewhat after that, as she continued to appear in occasional acting roles and released only one album, *My Love is Your Love* (1998), in addition to several singles. Beginning in late 1999, Houston became the subject of rampant drug abuse rumors, due to erratic public behavior. Houston has adamantly denied the rumors.
See also ADVERTISING [1]; NEWARK, NEW JERSEY [4]; RECORDING INDUSTRY [4]; RHYTHM AND BLUES [4].

REFERENCES

Bigelow, Barbara Carlisle, ed. *Contemporary Black Biography*, vol. 7. 1994.

Current Biography Yearbook. 1986.

Smith, Jessie Carney, ed. *Notable Black American Women*, Book II. 1996.

JESSIE CARNEY SMITH

Hughes, Albert and Allen (1972–), filmmakers.

Albert and Allen Hughes are biracial, black and Armenian fraternal twins, who at age 22, co-produced and co-directed a compelling coming of age movie debut, *Menace II Society* (1993), winning Best Picture Honors for the film at the 1994 MTV Music Awards. Considered progenitors of a promising new school of young black filmmakers of the early 1990s, they were characterized as filmmakers who, using brutal honesty and experimental cinematography, portrayed the harsh realities of black working-class inner-city life.

Praised for their talent, the Hughes brothers did not escape criticism. Their incorporation of graphic displays of violence in their films brought accusations that they glamorized anti-social behavior. However, after the commercial success of *Menace II Society*, the brothers created another "ghetto" or "hood" film, *Dead Presidents* (1995) whose title is a metaphor for dollar bills. *Menace II Society* is set in the early 1990s, in the Watts area of South Central Los Angeles, while *Dead Presidents* is set in the Bronx in the late 1960s. Both depict how a lack of opportunities and access to socially approved occupations can force an individual into a life of crime, and both explore the meaning of black manhood.

Prior to their two feature films, the twins, born in Detroit, Michigan, but raised in Pomono, California, directed an episode of the television series, *America's Most Wanted*. They directed music videos, many of which while still in their teens, for classic R & B singer, Marvin Gaye (posthumously), and popular hip-hop artists including Tone-Loc, KRS-One, Too-Short, Yo-Yo, and Tupac Shakur.
See also DETROIT [2].

REFERENCES

Billboard, 108; n16 (1996): 8.

Ethnic NewsWatch Contempora Magazine 38; No. 27; (1995): 18.

Nazarian, Eric. "The Underworld: The Cinema of Allen and Albert Hughes." *AIM: Armenian International Magazine*, 10; No. 3 (1999): 52.

Quendrith, Johnson. "Born II Direct: The Hughes Brothers Interview" 3 April 2000. http://www.dga.org.magazine/v20-3/hughes.html.

F. ZEAL HARRIS

Huston-Tillotson College. Huston-Tillotson

College, a historically black institution in Austin, Texas, descends from two separate institutions. Samuel Huston College was founded in Dallas in 1876 by Rev. George Warren Richardson, a Methodist minister from Minnesota, as a school for colored boys. In 1878, the school moved to Austin, where it was absorbed by the Freedman's Aid Society of the Methodist Episcopal Church. In 1887, Samuel Huston, an Iowa farmer, donated approximately $10,000 in property to the school, which was renamed in his honor. Samuel Huston College was chartered by the state of Texas in 1910, and approved as a senior college in 1926. In 1945, Huston offered Jackie Robinson his first job, as basketball coach, but he elected to pursue a career in professional baseball instead.

Tillotson College was founded as a secondary school in 1875 by the American Missionary Association, and was named for Rev. George Jeffrey Tillotson, a Connecticut Congregational minister who raised $16,000 for the school. In 1887, six years after the opening of Allen Hall, the first African American college building west of the Mississippi River, Tillotson Collegiate and Normal Institute was chartered. It featured outstanding Education and Music Departments. In 1909, the school became Tillotson College. During the 1930s Tillotson gained renown in educational circles for its President, Mary Elizabeth Branch, who was only the second African American woman college president.

Although the two crosstown colleges had were longtime academic and athletic rivals, they merged in 1952. Today, Huston-Tillotson College boasts 605 students and 39 full-time faculty. It is associated with the United Methodist Church and the UNCF.
See also AMERICAN MISSIONARY ASSOCIATION [1]; EDUCATION [2]; UNITED CHURCH OF CHRIST [5].

REFERENCE

Jones, William Henry, *Tillotson College From 1930–1940: A Study of the Total Institution*. 1940.

GREG ROBINSON

college, the handsome, distinguished Jackman worked part-time as a model. He had a close relationship with poet Countee Cullen that brought him in contact with the leading artists and patrons of the Harlem Renaissance era, the 1920s. He established lasting friendships with some of them, especially Arna Bontemps.

In 1919 Jackman helped to found the Harlem Experimental Theatre Company-the forerunner of Harlem's little theater movement-and directed its first production, Georgia Douglas Johnson's *Plumes*. The theater brought together a number of African American actors and playwrights. Jackman was a talented journalist who from 1935 to 1937 was associate editor of *Challenge* magazine and contributing editor and advisory editor of *Phylon* from 1944 until he died.

Jackman valued works by and about African Americans and saw a need to collect and preserve them. After Cullen died in 1947, Jackman established the Cullen Memorial Collection at Atlanta University and enriched it with materials from his collection as well as items he solicited from friends. A recognized authority on black arts and letters, he aided Carl Van Vechten in gathering important works for the James Weldon Johnson Memorial Collection at Yale University; he also helped to develop the collections at Fisk University and the Schomburg Collection in New York City.

See also BOOK COLLECTORS AND COLLECTIONS [1]; CULLEN, COUNTEE [2].

Harold Jackman. (Archives/Special Collections Atlanta University Center, Woodruff Library)

Jackman, Harold (1901–July 8, 1961), educator, model, editor, bibliophile. Jackman helped to nurture the major artistic movements in Harlem and in greater New York known as the Harlem Renaissance. Born in London, Jackman grew up in Harlem and graduated from New York University. He received his master's degree from Columbia University and later became a junior high school history teacher. During and after

REFERENCES

Bontemps, Arna. *The Harlem Renaissance Remembered.* 1972.

Lewis, David Levering. *When Harlem was in Vogue.* 1981.

Smith, Jessie Carney, ed. *Notable Black American Men.* 1999.

JESSIE CARNEY SMITH

Jackson, Alexine Clement (June 10, 1936–), organization executive. Alexine Clement Jackson was born in Sumter, South Carolina. Her mother died when she was four, and her father and stepmother raised her from age five. The Jackson family emphasized education and public commitment, instilling values that helped steer Jackson's course. She graduated *magna cum laude* with a bachelor's degree from Spelman College.

After her marriage, Jackson and her physician husband lived at Camp Pendleton, California, during his service in the Navy. During the height of the civil rights struggle, they moved to Greenwood, Mississippi in 1963, where Jackson became actively involved with community service. In 1968 the family moved Iowa City, Iowa, where Jackson earned a master's degree in speech pathology and audiology from the University of Iowa.

When the Jacksons moved to Washington, D.C., in 1973, Jackson began volunteer work with the YWCA, leading first to her position as president of the YWCA National Capital Area and then to the position of national president, a post she started in 1996. Her work with the YWCA has enabled her to continue the fight against racism in addition to focusing on other issues important to women. She has also served as a leader or board member on several other organizations related to the arts and to social problems.

Jackson was named Woman of the Year by *Washington Woman* magazine in 1985 and was named Washingtonian of the Year by *Washingtonian* magazine in 1994. She has also received awards from the Cultural Alliance, the Arlington Chapter of Links, Inc., and Junior Citizens Corps, Inc. Spelman College gave her an honorary doctorate in 1998.
See also SOUTH CAROLINA [5].

REFERENCES

http://www.ywca.org.

Phelps, Shirelle, ed. *Contemporary Black Biography.* vol. 22, 1999.

"A Salute to the Diversity of Today's Black Woman." *Ebony,* March 1999, pp. 100-108.

CARRELL P. HORTON

Jackson, Janet (May 16, 1966–), singer, actress. Janet Jackson is arguably the most successful female African-American pop star of the twentieth century. She grew up as the youngest of nine children in her famous family, and began her performing career at age five, opening up for the Jackson 5 in Las Vegas. She was well-known for her role as "Penny" on the seventies sitcom *Good Times,* and also starred in the programs *Diff'rent Strokes* and *Fame.* She began her singing career in earnest at age sixteen at the prompting of her father. Her first two albums, released in 1982 and 1984 respectively, sold poorly. In 1985 she was introduced to producers Jimmy Jam and Terry Lewis. Their collaboration on *Control* (1986) and the image of a slimmer, more choreographed Jackson helped make the album a huge success. The album sold over ten million copies worldwide and reached number one on Billboard pop and r & b charts. Her fourth album, *Rhythm Nation 1814,* (1989) achieved identical successes.

Jackson left A & M in 1991 and signed with Virgin Records, receiving the largest recording contract to that date at thirty-two million dollars. Her 1993 appearance in the film *Poetic Justice* received tepid reviews, but her subsequent album *janet* spawned five

Janet Jackson, 1995. (AP/Wide World Photos)

number one hits. A 1995 compilation, *Design of a Decade 1986–1996*, provided her 13th number one hit, "Runaway." Her 1997 album, *The Velvet Rope*, received a lukewarm reception but soon gained recognition with the single "Together Again," a joyful tribute song to friends who have perished from AIDS, that was the album's first number one single. Jackson made another film appearance in *The Nutty Professor II: The Klumps*, which premiered in July 2000.

See also JACKSON, MICHAEL, AND THE JACKSON FAMILY [3, S]; LEE, SHELTON JACKSON "SPIKE" [3].

REFERENCES

"Janet Jackson." www.wallofsound.go.com/artists/janetjackson/home.html.

"Janet Jackson." www.rollingstone.tunes.com/sections.

"Janet Jackson." www.top40countdown.com/biography/janetjackson.htm.

RACHEL ZELLARS

Jackson, Jesse Louis (Update) (October 8, 1941–), minister, politician, civil rights activist. During the early 1990s, Jackson remained largely outside the national spotlight. He was disappointed by the

Jesse Jackson, writing. (AP/Wide World Photos)

failure of his bid to assume leadership of the National Association for the Advancement of Colored People following the resignation of Rev. Benjamin Chavis. Jackson returned to widespread public prominence in the mid-1990s. In 1996, he was a supporter of the successful congressional campaign of his son, Jesse Jackson, Jr. In 1998, he became a close adviser to President Bill Clinton following reports of Clinton's extramarital affair. Later that year, he announced that he was considering another presidential run in 2000.

Jackson has been the most prominent civil rights leader and African-American national figure since the death of Martin Luther King, Jr. The history of national black politics in the 1970s and 1980s was largely his story. He has shown a great ability for making alliances, as well as a talent for defining issues and generating controversy. The essential dilemma of Jackson's career, as with many of his peers, has been the search for a way to advance and further the agenda of the civil rights movement as a national movement at a time when the political temper of the country has been increasingly conservative.

REFERENCES

Gibbons, Arnold. *Race, Politics, and the White Media: The Jesse Jackson Campaigns*. 1993.

Hatch, Roger D., and Frank E. Watkins, eds. *Reverend Jesse L. Jackson: Straight From the Heart*. 1987.

"Jesse Jackson." *Notable Black American Men*. 1999.

MICHAEL ERIC DYSON
UPDATED BY GREG ROBINSON

Jackson, Jesse Louis, Jr. (March 11, 1965–), U.S. Congressman, civil rights activist, organization executive, author. A native of Greeneville, South Carolina, Jackson is the son of the Reverend Jesse and Jacqueline Davis Jackson. He attended Le Mans Academy and St. Albans Episcopal Prep School. After completing his secondary education, Jackson entered North Carolina Agricultural and Technical University in Greensboro, graduating *magna cum laude* in 1987 with a B.S. in business management. In 1990, he earned the Master of Arts degree in theology from Chicago Theological Seminary and in 1993 a law degree from the University of Illinois. After law school, Jackson became the national field director for the Rainbow Coalition, a political action group inau-

Jesse Jackson Jr. (AP/Wide World Photos)

gurated by his father. In 1991 Jackson married Sandra Lee Stevens.

Jackson resigned from the Rainbow Coalition to enter politics as a Democratic candidate for Chicago's Second Congressional District. He became a member of the U. S. House of Representatives on December 12, 1995. While in office, Jackson co-wrote the book *Legal Lynching* with his father in 1996. Representative Jackson was appointed to serve on the House Appropriations Committee, the Subcommittee on Labor, Health and Human Services, and Education, and the Subcommittee on Foreign Operations, Export Financing and Related Programs. Jackson made a point of campaigning to those of his own age group, encouraging voter registration and heightened political activism from young people.

See also JACKSON, JESSE LOUIS [3].

REFERENCES

Mabunda, L. Mpho, and Shirelle Phelps, eds. *Contemporary Black Biography*, vol. 14. 1997.

Smith, Jessie Carney and Joseph M. Palmisano, eds. *The African American Almanac*. 8th ed. 2000.

Trandahl, Jeff. Clerk of the House of Representatives. *List of Standing Committees and Select Committee and their Subcommittees of the House of Representatives of the United States Together with Joint Committees of the Congress, One Hundred Sixth Congress*.

LINDA T. WYNN

Jackson Lee, Sheila (July 12, 1950–), U.S. Congresswoman. Jackson Lee was born in New York City. Her J.D. degree from the University of Virginia in 1975 followed a B.A. from Yale in 1972. She established a law practice in Houston, Texas, and then served as staff counsel to the U.S. House Select Committee on Assassinations from 1977 to 1978. From 1980 to 1987 she worked as an attorney for United Energy Resources.

Jackson Lee became an associate municipal judge in Houston in 1987. In 1990 she was elected an at-large member of the Houston City Council. She was reelected handily in 1992, but a term-limit initiative resulted in her ineligibility to stand for a third term. In 1994 she challenged incumbent Congressman Craig Washington in the Democratic primary for the Eighteenth Congressional District of Texas. She won the primary after a vicious campaign. She then won the election easily with seventy-seven percent of the vote, in a 1996 special election following a Supreme Court decision mandated redistricting.

In Congress Jackson Lee served on the Judiciary and Science committees. On the Science Committee she was a member of the subcommittee on Space and Aeronautics. On the Judiciary Committee, she was the ranking member on the Immigration and Claims Subcommittee and served also on the Subcommittee on Crime. Jackson Lee participated in the impeachment hearings for President Clinton in 1998. Although she opposed impeachment, she drafted an unsuccessful resolution to censure Clinton for his actions. In addition to serving as a whip for the Congressional Black Caucus, she was founder and chairperson of the Congressional Children's Caucus. *See also* NEW YORK CITY [4].

REFERENCES

"A Salute to the Diversity of Today's Black Woman: Sheila Jackson Lee." *Ebony*, March 1999.

Manheim, James M. "Sheila Jackson Lee." In *Contemporary Black Biography*, edited by Shirelle Phelps. 1999.

"Representative Sheila Jackson Lee." http://www.house. gov/jackson lee/bio.htm Accessed 13 July 2000.

ROBERT L. JOHNS

Jackson, Michael, and the Jackson Family (Update), pop singers and performers. A dominant influence on American popular music since the 1960s, the Jackson family consists of the nine children of Joseph and Katherine Jackson. The couple's first five sons, Sigmund "Jackie" (May 4, 1951–), Toriano "Tito" (October 15, 1953–), Jermaine (December 11, 1954–), Marlon (March 12, 1957–) and Michael (August 29, 1958–), began singing in 1962. Their other children, Maureen "Rebbie" (May 29, 1950–), LaToya (May 29, 1956–), Steven "Randy" (October 29, 1962–), and Janet (May 16, 1966–) In 1995 Janet joined her brother Michael on the hit single "Scream", and her 1996 hit single "Runaway" became her sixteenth gold-certified single, placing her among an exclusive league of female artists. She released *The Velvet Rope* album in 1997 and promoted it with a world tour throughout 1998.

In January of 1996, Jackson and wife Lisa Marie Presley announced plans for a divorce. That November, Jackson married Debbie Rowe, who gave birth to Jackson's son in February 1997. They had a daughter in April of 1998. Rowe filed for divorce in October of 1999. Despite internal family conflicts, the Jacksons remain, collectively and individually, the most prominent and productive family in African-American popular music.

REFERENCES

Bradberry, Grace. "Jackson to divorce." *The Times (London, England)*. Oct 9, 1999, p. 16.

Jackson, Michael. "Michael Jackson Speaks." *Jet*, January 10, 1994, p. 60.

Orth, Maureen. "Nightmare in Neverland." *Vanity Fair*, January 1994, p. 70.

Taraborrelli, Randy. *Michael Jackson: The Magic and the Madness*. 1991.

HARRIS FRIEDBERG
UPDATED BY GREG ROBINSON

Jackson, Samuel Leroy (December 21, 1948–),

actor. Born in Washington, D.C. and raised in Chattanooga, Tennessee, Jackson overcame childhood stuttering, received a degree in theater from Morehouse College in Atlanta, Georgia in 1972, and became an actor noted for a distinctive style of diction and an electrifying presence in more than 60 films and numerous theater productions. Although he was the first actor ever to be awarded a Best Performance award at the 1991 Cannes Film Festival, for his performance in Spike Lee's *Jungle Fever* (1991), Jackson did not achieve mainstream fame until he was nominated for an Academy Award as Best Supporting actor in Quentin Tarantino's *Pulp Fiction* (1994). Before becoming one of Hollywood's most popular actors of the 1990s,

Samuel L. Jackson. (Archive Photos, Inc.)

Jackson lived in New York City and had a strong working relationship with the Negro Ensemble Company, leading a substantial career in theater, interrupted occasionally by film and TV work from the 1970s to mid 1980s.

Jackson's prolific work includes an array of diverse major films with roles spanning from highly serious to highly comedic characters: *Ragtime* (1981) *Eddie Murphy Raw* (1987), *School Daze* (1988), *Coming To America* (1988), *Do the Right Thing* (1989), *The Return of Superfly* (1990), *Mo' Better Blues* (1990), *Goodfellas* (1990), *Exorcist III: The Legion* (1990), *Strictly Business* (1991), *Jungle Fever* (1991), *Juice* (1992), *Menace to Society* (1993), *Jurassic Park* (1993), *Fresh* (1994), *Losing Isaiah* (1995), *Eve's Bayou* (1997), *The Negotiator* (1988), and *Star Wars: Episode 1-The Phantom Menace* (1999), and *Shaft* (2000). Jackson also co-founded the Just US Theater Company in Atlanta, Georgia in 1976.
See also FILM [2]; WASHINGTON, D.C. [5].

REFERENCES

Jet 96 (1999): 54.

LaBlanc, Michael L., ed. *Contemporary Black Biography: Profiles from the International Black Community*. 1989.

Stevens, Tracy, editorial director. *International Television & Video Almanac, 44th edition*. 1999.

Unterburger, Amy L., ed. *International Dictionary of Films and Filmmakers: Actors and Actresses*. 1997.

F. ZEAL HARRIS

Shirley Ann Jackson. (AP/Wide World Photos)

Jackson, Shirley Ann (August 5, 1946–), physicist. Shirley Ann Jackson was born in Washington, D.C. She received a B.S. from the Massachusetts Institute of Technology (MIT) in 1968 and in 1973 became the first African-American female to receive a Ph.D. in physics from MIT. During the 1970s, Dr. Jackson spent several years working for physics laboratories in the United States and abroad. From 1976 until 1991, she taught physics at Rutgers University in New Jersey.

In 1991, Dr. Jackson was appointed a commissioner of the Nuclear Regulatory Commission and in 1995 she became chair of the commission. She resigned this position in 1998 to become president of the Rensselaer Polytechnic Institute in Troy, New York. *See also* PHYSICS [4]; SCIENCE [5].

REFERENCES

"Shirley Ann Jackson," in *Notable Black American Scientists*. 1999.

ELLY DICKASON

Jacksonville, Florida. Jacksonville, Florida traces its origins to 1564 when French Hugenots settled what they called Wacca Pilatka, "cows crossing." The English called the area Cowford when they controlled it (1763–1983). In 1816 the first American settlers arrived in the area. In 1821 a farmer from southern Georgia moved into the Jacksonville area with his slaves. He immediately noticed the good ground and the close proximity to rivers and the coastal areas. Jacksonville grew slowly but steadily. Jacksonville, a bustling seaport divided by the St Johns River, joined Pensacola and Tallahassee as Florida's significant centers for economic, political, and social development.

Much produce grown in the hinterland was shipped through the city for transport to other areas. Most of Florida's development occurred along the path from Jacksonville to Pensacola. Jacksonville's mild climate and coastal location made it a good place for agricultural production. During the 1825–1860 period white settlers flooded into the area, many bringing their slaves. There were also eighty-seven free blacks that lived in a section of the city referred to as Negro Hill. These residents literally lived in a different world, cut off from all social and intellectual outlets of the city. Most free blacks were poor, landless, unskilled or semiskilled workers who performed the undesirable tasks whites avoided.

By 1860, of Duval County's 5,074 residents, 2,170 were African American. Jacksonville, which was Florida's third largest city, had 1,132 whites, 908 slaves, and 87 free blacks. Like most urban areas, Jacksonville had a ring of working class neighborhoods which developed in and around the commercial district. The African American community was located in one of these rings.

After the Civil War, African Americans flooded into Jacksonville to take advantage of cheap land and economic opportunities. These new arrivals built a thriving community filled with all of the social and economic institutions for advancement. African Americans found a home in the predominately black areas of the city. LaVilla, an overwhelmingly black community founded in 1869, became the center of African-American life in Jacksonville during the post-war period. The community was the result of the largesse of Francis F. L'Engle, a prominent lawyer who owned land in the Jacksonville area. He sold this land in quarter-acre lots to black settlers offering some 99 year leases. Thus, L'Engle played an essential role in developing LaVilla.

L'Engle was the first mayor and served as the local liaison to the city officials in Jacksonville. LaVilla's independent political status gave African American an opportunity to learn the importance of voting and political activity. It also gave potential political leaders a forum from which they could launch their political careers. L'Engle's example helped to create a political tie between the black and white communities. In

LaVilla, the small white minority lived was forced to work with African Americans who dominated the local government and police forces. Thus, LaVilla served a vital role as the incubator for future African American leadership that controlled the city during the two decades after freedom.

As in all regions, most African Americans in Jacksonville believed that education was the key to making their freedom real. In 1866 the AME Church established Edward Waters College which was supplemented by Cookman Institute, First Baptist Academy, and Boylan Home Industrial Training School. A group of local African American citizens organized the Colored Educational that worked closely with the American Missionary Association (AMA) to provide educational venues. The AMA donated $16,000 and their organization's expertise to help the Colored Educational Association in founding Stanton Normal School, one of the oldest and most successful African American schools in Jacksonville. The school started with six teachers and 348 students. In 1876 when the public school board took control of education, they adopted Stanton as the first African American public school.

Just as important was the development of economic institutions. The Afro-American life Insurance Company produced the economic foundation of Jacksonville's black community. This company was supplemented by hundreds of small enterprises run by blacks. Segregation forced blacks to provide all of the services required for survival. Therefore, hundreds of caterers, barbers, druggists, and mercantile establishments were available.

During the 1930–1960 period Jacksonville's African American community grew steadily but not as rapidly as the white community. However, it was able to have a comfortable niche in the segregated city that provided blacks with the necessary tools to struggle for full equality. In 1967, the city and county consolidated government creating a permanent place for African Americans within the political structure. Today, making up an important part of the city, over twenty-five percent of Jacksonville's more than one millions residents are black.

See also BASEBALL [1]; BETHUNE-COOKMAN COLLEGE [1]; FLORIDA [2]; FORTUNE, TIMOTHY THOMAS [2]; NEGRO NATIONAL ANTHEM [4]; PAINTING AND SCULPTURE.

REFERENCES

Bartley, Abel A. *Keeping the Faith: Race, Politics and Social Development in Jacksonville, Florida 1940–1970.* 2000.

Crooks, James B. *Jacksonville After the Fire, 1901–1919: A New South City.* 1991.

Kenney, Patricia L. "LaVilla, Florida, 1866–1887 Reconstruction Dreams and the Formation of a Black Community", in *The African American Heritage of Florida.* Edited by David Colburn and Jane Landers. 1995.

Walch, Barbara Hunter. *New Black Voices: The Growth and Contributions of Sallye Mathis and Mary Singleton in Florida Government.* 1990.

ABEL BARTLEY

Jefferson, William Jennings

Jefferson, William Jennings (March 14, 1947–), U.S. Congressman, lawyer. Jefferson was born in Lake Providence, Louisiana. He received a B.A. degree from Southern University, Baton Rouge, Louisiana, in 1969 and a doctorate of law at Howard University in 1972. He worked as law clerk to a federal judge from 1972 to 1973 and as legislative assistant to Senator J. Bennett Johnson from 1973 to 1975, after which he established a successful law firm.

Jefferson was elected to the Louisiana state senate in 1979 and was twice reelected. During his terms, he became chairman of the Senate and Governmental Affairs Committee. Jefferson also twice tried to become mayor of New Orleans, but lost both elections. In 1990 he won the U.S. House seat vacated by long-time Congresswoman Lindy Boggs; he was the first black representative from Louisiana since Reconstruction.

In Congress, Jefferson has served on the Committee on Ways and Means and its Subcommittees on Trade and Human Resources. In the House he also has served on the Democratic Party's steering committee and is a deputy whip at-large. He is also active in Democratic politics outside the House, serving, for example, as state co-chair of the Clinton-Gore campaign in 1992 and 1996. He is a member of the Democratic National Committee. In 1999, he ran an unsuccessful campaign to unseat incumbent Mike Foster as governor of Lousiana.

See also LOUISIANA [3].

REFERENCES

Ayres, R. Drummond, Jr. "Louisiana Governor Defeats 11 Foes to Win Second Term." *New York Times*, 24 October 1999.

Manheim, James M. "William J. Jefferson." In *Contemporary Black Biography*, vol. 25. 2000.

"Resume of William J. Jefferson." http://www.house.gov/jefferson/biography.htm Accessed 20 June 2000.

Who's Who Among Black Americans. 12th ed. 1999.

ROBERT L. JOHNS

Johnson, Earvin, Jr. "Magic" (Update)

(August 14, 1959–), basketball player. Johnson led the Los Angeles Lakers to the National Basketball Association (NBA) Championship in 1980, 1982, 1985, 1987, and 1988. Johnson was named the league's MVP three times (1987, 1989, 1990), Playoff MVP three times (1980, 1982, 1987), and All-Star Game MVP twice (1990, 1992), his desire to win translated into an unselfish style of play that elevated passing to an art form (his 10,141 career assists ranks him second in NBA history) and stressed teamwork over individual accolades.

In mid-season 1995–1996, Johnson rejoined the badly faltering Lakers as a player-coach. He once again retired at the end of the season. During his retirement, Johnson continued his AIDS education efforts, and he encouraged business to enter inner-city neighborhoods, notably through his successful Magic Johnson Cineplex movie theater in South Central Los Angeles, opened in 1995. In 1997, he starred in a short-lived late-night talk show.

In 1998, Johnson teamed with Starbucks to open franchises in urban sites where the chain had not yet expanded. This joint venture proved to be a quick success, and Johnson and Starbucks opened seven further locations, with plans for more than fifty. Johnson followed that up by teaming again, this time with the T.G.I. Friday's restaurant chain, to open restaurants in similar locations, with the first in Atlanta.

REFERENCES

Bernstein, Elizabeth. "Magic's Kingdom." *Restaurant Business*. Nov. 15, 1999, p36.

Johnson, Earvin "Magic," and Roy S. Johnson. *Magic's Touch*. 1989.

Pascarelli, Peter F. *The Courage of Magic Johnson: From Boyhood Dreams to Superstar to His Toughest Challenge*. 1992.

JILL DUPONT
UPDATED BY GREG ROBINSON

Johnson, Edward Austin

(November 23, 1860–July 24, 1944), teacher, lawyer, and politician. Edward Johnson was born a slave in Raleigh, North Carolina. After schooling in Raleigh, he spent a year at Atlanta University (1882–1883). He then taught school in Atlanta. In 1885 he returned to Raleigh to become principal of Washington School. At this time he wrote *A School History of the Negro Race in America from 1619 to 1890* (1891), which was widely used in North Carolina and Virginia.

In 1891 Johnson earned a law degree at Shaw University. He joined the university's department as a teacher in 1893, serving also as dean from 1895. A devoted Republican and delegate to three national nominating conventions, he was an elected alderman in Raleigh in 1897–1899. His political activity earned him a position as federal government clerk from 1897 to 1907.

Chase pursued many lines of business and was a founder of the North Carolina Mutual and Provident Association. With Booker T. Washington, he was a co-founder of the National Negro Business League in 1900. He wrote a popular work, *History of the Negro Soldiers in the Spanish-American War and Other Items of Interest* (1899) and a utopian novel, *Light Ahead for the Negro* (1904). *Adam vs. Ape-Man in Ethiopia* (1931) was his last published work.

Chase left the South in 1907 and opened a law practice in Harlem. He served one term as the first black elected to the New York State legislature (1917–1918). He became legally blind in 1925 but continued to be active. His final attempt at electoral politics was a failed effort to secure the Republican nomination for the twenty-first Congressional district in 1928. *See also* NORTH CAROLINA [4].

REFERENCES

Contee, Clarence G., Jr. "Edward A[ustin] Johnson." In *Dictionary of American Negro Biography*, edited by Rayford W. Logan and Michael R. Winston. 1982.

Lawson, Edwin R. "Edward Austin Johnson." In *Dictionary of North Carolina Biography*, edited by William S. Powell. 1988.

Vicary, Elizabeth Zoe. "Edward Austin Johnson." In *American National Biography*, John A. Garraty and Mark C. Carnes, general editors. 1999.

ROBERT L. JOHNS

Johnson, Hazel Winifred

(1927–), military officer, nurse, educator. Johnson was born in Malvern, Pennsylvania, and grew up on a farm in Chester. She enrolled in New York's Harlem Hospital in 1950 where she completed basic nursing education. In 1955 she enlisted in the U.S. Army Nurse Corps and rose in rank to become first lieutenant in May 1960. In

1979, when Johnson was 52 years old, she became the first African American female general in the U.S. military and the first African American chief of the Army Nurse Corps. She oversaw the work of 7,000 men and women who were in the Army, Army National Guard, and Army Reserves; she also set policy and oversaw operations of medical centers and clinics in the U.S. and abroad. While in the army, Johnson completed additional study in nursing, earning a bachelor's degree from Villanova University, a master's degree from Columbia University, and a Ph.D. from Catholic University.

Johnson's varied experiences during and after military service included surgical directorate at the U.S. Army Medical Research and Development Command in Washington, D.C.; dean of Walter Reed Army Institute of Nursing; chief nurse of the U.S. Army Medical Command in Korea; assistant dean of the School or Nursing at the University of Maryland; and professor of nursing at George Mason University. Not until two years after Johnson retired in 1983 did any branch of the military have another African American female general, Sheridan Grace Cadoria. Johnson has been well decorated for her service in the military, receiving among other recognitions the Distinguished Service Medal, the Legion of Merit, the Meritorious Service Medal, an Army Commendation Medal.
See also NURSING [4].

REFERENCES

Hine, Darlene Clark, ed. *Facts on File Encyclopedia of Black Women in America*. 1997.

Phelps, Shirelle, ed. *Contemporary Black Biography*. 1999.

Sammons, Vivian Ovelton. *Blacks in Science and Medicine*. 1990.

JESSIE CARNEY SMITH

Johnson, Michael Duane

Johnson, Michael Duane (September 13, 1967–), athlete. Johnson became a star in the 1996 summer Olympics in Atlanta when he won double victories, the 200 and 400-yard meter. Johnson was born in Dallas and graduated from Baylor University in 1990 with a B.A. degree. While at Baylor, he broke the college's record in track and later won the National Collegiate Athletic Association's indoor championship. In his senior year, he was the top-ranked runner in the 200 and 400 meter sprints the first male athlete to hold the dual rank.

Johnson became a professional runner in 1990; while running in European and Asian competitions (where track is far more popular than in the United States), he was practically unbeatable. In 1991 he won the world championship in the 200 meter. The schedule of the 1992 Summer Olympics, held in Barcelona, would not permit him to run his favorite 200 and 400 meters. He chose the 200 meter, but food poisoning slowed him and he finished; however, he was a part of the 4x400 relay team days later and won a gold medal.

His winnings continued. In 1993 Johnson won the world championship in the 200 and 400 meter sprints. In Sweden in 1995, he won world championships again in the 200 and 400 meter sprints. This was a history-making feat, since no other man had met this record. In the 1996 Summer Olympics held in Atlanta, Johnson won the 400 meter relay in record-setting time, and he broke his own world record in the 200 meter when he finished in 19.32 seconds.
See also DALLAS [S].

REFERENCES

Phelps, Shirelle, ed. *Contemporary Black Biography*, vol. 13. 1997.

USA Today, August 4, 1992. E4.

Washington Post, February 23, 1996, F1

FREDERICK D. SMITH, JR.

Johnson, Mordecai Wyatt

Johnson, Mordecai Wyatt (January 12, 1890–September 10, 1976), university president. Mordecai

Mordecai Johnson. (Temple University)

Johnson served as Howard University's first African-American president from 1926 until his 1960 retirement. Born in Paris, Tennessee, Johnson entered Morehouse College in Atlanta in 1905. He graduated in 1911 with a B.A. and began teaching English at the college. He earned a second B.A. in social sciences in 1913 from the University of Chicago. With a desire to become a minister, he enrolled in Rochester Theological Seminary and graduated in 1916. In 1923, he earned the Master of Sacred Theology from Harvard University. He held Doctor of Divinity degrees from Howard University and Gammon Theology Seminary, as well. He pastored at the First Baptist Church in Charleston, West Virginia, for nine years and founded a local branch of the National Association for the Advancement of Colored People (NAACP) there. In 1926, the board of trustees at Howard University unanimously recommended Johnson as the school's first African-American president. In 1929, he was honored with the prestigious NAACP Spingarn Medal for the advancement of African Americans in 1928.

Johnson is also remembered for promoting a policy of academic freedom at Howard University. He was known to quote Gandhi in his speeches to the student body and was an outspoken proponent of independence in Africa during the 1940's. He rallied to secure annual federal financial support for Howard, and is credited with establishing Howard's academic prominence. By the time of his retirement, the University was producing fifty-percent of the nation's African American physicians, and its law school was a vanguard in the burgeoning Civil Rights Movement. Johnson retired as president of Howard University on June 30, 1960.

See also ADAMS, NUMA POMPILIUS GARFIELD [1]; COUNCIL ON AFRICAN AFFAIRS [2]; HOWARD UNIVERSITY [3]; SPINGARN MEDAL [5].

REFERENCES

"Johnson, Modecai Wyatt." Encyclopedia of Black America, edited by W. Augustus Low and Virgil Clift. 1981.

"Johnson, Modecai Wyatt." African-American Encyclopedia, edited by. Michael W. Williams. 1993.

"Johnson, Modecai Wyatt." Encyclopedia of African American Culture and History, edited by Jack Salzman, David Smith, and Cornel West. 1996.

RACHEL ZELLARS

Johnson, William (1809–June 17, 1851), businessman.

William Johnson was a pre-Civil War businessman who achieved remarkable success in Natchez, Mississippi. His diary, covering the years 1835 to 1851, provides a unique window into the life of a free African American.

Born a slave, Johnson was emancipated in 1820. He was apprenticed to his brother-in-law, James Miller, a barber. Johnson took over the shop in 1830. Johnson's clientele at his barbershop were white—in this era it was customary for black barbers to cut white patrons' hair. Johnson's success as a barber served as a foundation for his varied business endeavors. Eventually, he had three barber shops and ran a bathhouse. He also acquired real estate, lent money, and sold wallpaper and toys for a period. By his death Johnson owned 350 acres of land and fifteen slaves. Among the buildings constructed by Johnson was a substantial home for his family. This building is now part of a National Historic Park.

Johnson appears to have been able to conduct business on equal terms with whites. but he was nonetheless limited by the segregation of his era. For example, he had access to the courts but could not serve on juries. The ambiguity of his social status is exemplified by the fact that he and two members of his family were the only blacks buried in the white section of the Natchez Cemetery. Johnson was shot to death as the result of a quarrel over land. The racial status of his murderer, Baylor Winn, was ambiguous, and Winn was acquitted after two trials.

See also BANKING [1]; ENTREPRENEURS[2]; HAIR AND BEAUTY CULTURE [3].

REFERENCES

Davis, Edwin Adams. "William Johnson." In Dictionary of American Negro Autobiography, edited by Rayford W. Logan and Michael R. Winston. 1982.

Hogan, William Ransom, and Edward Adams Davis, eds. William Johnson's Natchez: The Ante-Bellum Diary of a Free Negro. 1951.

Lissek, Devorah. "William Johnson." In American National Biography, edited by John A Garraty and Mark C. Carnes. 1999.

ROBERT L. JOHNS

Jones, Caroline Robinson (February 15, 1942–), entrepreneur.

Caroline Jones was born in Benton Harbor, Michigan, and attended the University of Michigan, from which she graduated with a B.A. degree in 1963.

That year Jones became a secretary with the advertising firm J. Walter Thompson Company. The firm accepted Jones into its copywriters' program, making her the first African American woman ever trained as a copywriter in the history of the company's 100 years of advertising. From 1968 to 1977 she divided her time between general market and African American agencies. During this period she helped to establish Zebra Associates, a pioneering African American advertising agency.

In mid-1977, Jones teamed with advertising legend Frank Mingo to found Mingo-Jones Advertising; she was named executive vice president and creative director. Among the advertising clients were Miller High Life beer, Kentucky Fried Chicken, Westinghouse Electric (added in 1982), and a number of blue-chip customers.

Jones left the company in 1986 and opened her own agency, Caroline Jones Incorporated, becoming the second African American woman to head a national advertising agency. Her company conducted business for international and domestic clients who needed to outsource advertising, public relations, and special events. Her clients included Anheuser-Busch Companies, Ryder Systems, Inc., Prudential, Western Union, the United States Postal Service, and Toys R Us. Jones also helped organize a January 1999 advertiser's summit, aimed at improving the image of minorities that advertisers put forth as well as demonstrating how advertisers can tap into the minority market, one traditionally left under-developed.
See also ADVERTISING [1]; PUBLIC RELATION [4].

REFERENCES

"Caroline Jones." http://www.adcenter.vcu.edu/people/board/jones.html.

Farris, King. "The Road Less Traveled By." http://www.utexas.edu/coc/admedium/Spring98_Practitioner/tcf/html.

Henderson, Ashiya, and Shirelle Phelps, eds. *Who's Who among African Americans*, 12th ed. 1999.

Teinowitz, Ira. "Ad Groups Host January Media Summit: Quick Reaction Surprises Sharpton." *Advertising Age*. December 14, 1998. p3.

JESSIE CARNEY SMITH

Jones, Elaine R. (March 2, 1944–), organization executive, lawyer, civil rights activist. Elaine Jones has spent her life working for civil rights causes. Born in Norfolk, Virginia, the daughter of a Pullman porter and a teacher, Jones received her bachelor's degree in 1965 from Howard University. The first African American woman enrolled in the University of Virginia School of Law, she graduated in 1970. Then, she joined the NAACP Legal Defense Fund (LDF), founded in 1940 as an arm of the NAACP but separated in 1957 for tax purposes. Jones argued in the South until 1973 against racially-motivated death penalties, then she became managing attorney of LDF's New York Office.

Jones was special assistant to U.S. Secretary of Transportation William T. Coleman from 1975 to 1977, then she helped to establish and run the Washington, D.C. LDF office. She was named deputy director-counsel in 1988, second in command behind Julius Chambers. She wrote scores of briefs to support or protest nominations that either Presidents Reagan or Bush made. One of these was against the nominations to the U.S. Supreme Court of Robert H. Bork in 1987 and Clarence Thomas in 1991.

In 1993 Jones was named director-counsel of LDF, following the three men who had held the post earlier: Thurgood Marshall (its founder), Jack Greenberg (Jones's law school dean at Virginia), and Julius Chambers. She also had powerful connections with the Clinton administration and particularly with Hiliary Rodham Clinton; the two had worked together on the American Bar Association's commission on women in law. Jones is known as a "political mastermind" and in 2000 continued to lead LDF in its various legal efforts.
See also NAACP LEGAL DEFENSE AND EDUCATION FUND [4]; VIRGINIA [5].

REFERENCES

Bigelow, Barbara Carlisle, ed. *Contemporary Black Biography*, vol. 17. 1994.

Norment, Lynn. "Introducing: Elaine R. Jones, Nation's Top Civil Rights Lawyer." *Ebony* 48 (June 1993): 66-67.

Smith, Jessie Carney, ed. *Notable Black American Women*. 1996.

JESSIE CARNEY SMITH

Jones, Frederick M. (May 17, 1892–February 21, 1961), inventor. Frederick M. Jones revolutionized refrigeration technology by his invention of portable cooling units. He was born in Cincinnati, Ohio.

controlled temperature. After the war Jones continued to secure patents in the area of refrigeration as the corporation's business boomed. Jones was able to witness a great technological revolution produced by his inventions before he died of lung cancer in 1961. *See also* CINCINNATI, OHIO [1]; INVENTORS AND INVENTIONS [3].

REFERENCES

"Frederick M. Jones (1893–1961) *Inventor of the Week*. http://web.mit.edu/invent/www/jones.html.

"Frederick McKinley Jones, Inventor." *Faces of Science: African American in the Sciences*. http://www.lib.lsu.edu/lib/chem/display/jones.htlml.

Hayden, Robert C. "Frederick McKinley Jones." In *Dictionary of American Negro Biography*, edited by Rayford W. Logan and Michael R. Winston. 1982.

ROBERT L. JOHNS

Frederick McKinley Jones, holding model of train car. (Corbis Corporation)

An orphan at the age of nine, he went to live with a Catholic priest in Kentucky, where he did odd jobs around the church and completed the sixth grade.

Jones worked as a mechanic throughout the midwest. He was in Hallock, Minnesota when the war broke out, repairing farm machinery. He served in the army, then he returned to his job in Hallock. During the twenties he studied electronics on his own. He developed a local reputation for his inventions, including a means of combining sound with motion-picture film. This reputation led to a job with Cinema Supplies, a manufacturer of sound equipment for movie houses. He received his first patent, for a movie ticket-dispensing device, in 1939.

In the late 1930s Jones worked quietly on a portable air-cooling device for trucks. The owner of Cinema Supplies, Joseph A. Navaro, sold out to RCA, and he and Jones founded U.S. Thermo Control (now Thermo King). Jones secured his patent on his refrigerating unit on July 12, 1940. This invention revolutionized the long-distance transportation of perishable foods and led to further innovations. For example, during World War II Jones designed a portable cooling unit which allowed the army to keep blood at

Jones, Grace (1952–), performer. The daughter of a minister, Jones was born Grace Mendoza in Spanishtown, Jamaica, in 1952, but moved to Syracuse, New York, with her family when she was twelve. She began modeling as a teen in New York City, and found great success when she moved to Paris and found work for a number of European designers. Island Records founder Chris Blackwell became a friend, and Jones released her first album on his reggae label in 1977. It included her first hit singles, "I Need a Man" and "La Vie en Rose." Her fourth release, 1980's *Warm Leatherette*, did well on the British charts. In North America, Jones developed somewhat of a cult following because of her racy live act.

Jones' unusual looks piqued the interest of the film industry in the 1980s, and she appeared in films alongside such co-stars as Arnold Schwarzegger and Eddie Murphy. She earned positive reviews for her performance in the 1984 action film *Conan the Destroyer* opposite Schwarzegger. She also appeared in the 1985 James Bond move *A View to a Kill*. Her last major Hollywood film was *Boomerang* (1992), with Eddie Murphy. Jones's recording career has continued into the 1990s with songs produced by Tricky, Puff Daddy, and Roni Size. Jones, who has an adult son, Paolo, still performs in nightclubs and models.
See also FAGAN, GARTH [2].

REFERENCES

Larkin, Colin, compiler and editor, *The Encyclopedia of Popular Music*, third edition, Muze. 1998.

Romanowski, Patricia, and Holly George-Warren, *The New Encyclopedia of Rock & Roll*. 1995.

Shelley, Jim, "Eye of the Hurricane," *Telegraph* (London), April 26, 1999.

CAROL BRENNAN

Jones, Laurence Clifton (November 21, 1884–c.1975), school founder.

Jones made it possible for many African Americans in the deep woods of Mississippi to receive an education through the school that he founded there. Born in St. Joseph, Missouri, Jones graduated from Iowa State University in 1907. Influenced by the work and philosophy of Booker T. Washington, who founded Tuskegee Institute, Jones nonetheless turned down a position at Tuskegee to work in Hinds County from 1907 to 1909. Then he set out for Piney Woods, between Jackson and Gulfport, Mississippi.

There Jones saw first hand the need for education. He invested his earnings in land on which to build a school. To garner community support, he talked to rural people about the importance of education. By 1910, he had founded a school, though classes had to be held outside. On May 17, 1913, Piney Woods Industrial School officially opened.

Piney Woods offered students traditional book learning along with industrial and religious instruction; the students were active in literary societies as well. The first class graduated from the Normal Department in 1918. Jones organized several vocal groups called the Cotton Blossom Singers who traveled widely and became musical messengers for Piney Woods. In the late 1930s his International Sweethearts of Rhythm, a group of young women singers, also raised money for the school.

Jones's work was nationally recognized in December 1954, when "The Little Professor of Piney Woods" was celebrated on the television program, *This Is Your Life*. In 2000, the school continued to operate in Mississippi's Black Belt, with students from many states.

REFERENCES

Day, Beth. *The Little Professor of Piney Woods*. 1955.

Jones, Laurence. *Piney Woods and Its Story*. 1922.

Smith, Jessie Carney. *Notable Black American Men*. 1999.

JESSIE CARNEY SMITH

Jones, Marion (October 12, 1975–), track and field athlete.

Born in Los Angeles, California, Marion Jones exhibited an early interest in sports, beginning to participate in organized track at age seven and in basketball by the sixth grade. In high school in Oxnard, California, Jones starred in both track and basketball. When she graduated (1993), she had set the national high school record in the 200-meter sprint, won state titles in the 100- and 200-meter events, and received two high school Athlete of the Year awards. Her basketball team's star shooting guard, with an average 24.6 points per game, Jones was named in her senior year the California Division I Player of the Year.

Entering the University of North Carolina-Chapel Hill with a basketball scholarship, Jones pursued both track and basketball, but her track achievements did not match her basketball record. She was the basketball team's starting point guard as a freshman and led the team to the 1994 National Collegiate Athletic Association Women's Championship title.

After graduation from college (1997), Jones decided to focus on track. Her success led to her being named Woman of the Year (1997) and Female Athlete of the Year (1998) by *Track & Field News* and receipt of an Owens Award as Outstanding U. S. Track and Field Athlete (1998), and the International Amateur Athletic Federation Athlete of the Year award (1997 and 1998). In 1998, she became the first woman since 1948 to win all three events (100-meter, 200-meter, and long jump) at the USA Outdoor Championships. Her streak of thirty-seven consecutive first-place finishes in sprint and long jump established her dominance in the sport. At the 2000 Olympics, she won three gold and two bronze medals.
See also OLYMPIC MOVEMENT, THE [4].

REFERENCES

Phelps, Shirelle, ed. *Contemporary Black Biography*. 1999.

Sport, 91 (May 2000): 72.

Sports Illustrated, 91 (August 30, 1999): 54-55.

CARRELL P. HORTON

Jones, Roy, Jr. (January 16, 1969–), professional boxer.

Roy Jones, Jr., was born in Pensacola, Florida, where he attended Pensacola Junior College. His father, an ex-boxer, coached his son along with other

Roy Jones Jr., giving his opponent an uppercut. (AP/Wide World Photos)

aspiring boxers in the boxing gym he operated. He also managed his son for a time, and some though the senior Jones treated him harshly.

Jones amassed an amateur record of 121-13, won the National Junior Olympics title at fourteen, Golden Gloves championships (1986 and 1987), and the Silver Medal at the 1988 Olympic Games. He won his first professional title, IBF middleweight, in 1993. The IBF super middleweight title followed in 1994; the WBC and WBA light heavyweight in 1997 and 1998; and in 1999, he won the IBF light heavyweight title, making him the first undisputed light heavyweight champion since 1985.

Jones was voted Outstanding Boxer of the 1988 Olympic Games, but a scoring error cost him the Gold Medal. He first lost and then regained the WBC light heavyweight title because of a disputed foul in 1997. Jones changed managers in the mid-1990s, and after that only the lack of qualified challengers hampered his worldwide acclaim.

Boxing did not consume all of Jones' energy. His charitable and community service activities include running a youth program in Pensacola. He also plays basketball as a hobby and raises birds for cock-fighting. In addition to numerous boxing awards (1993–

1996), he received the Outstanding Achievement Award (1996) from the Congress of Racial Equality, the Harlem Globetrotters' Honorary Ambassador of Goodwill award (1997) and the Escambia-Pensacola Human Relations Commission 1997 Olive Branch Award for humanitarianism.

See also BOXING [1, S]; FLORIDA [2].

REFERENCES

1997 Information Please, *Sports Almanac.* 1997

Phelps, Shirelle, ed., *Contemporary Black Biography,* v. 22, 1999.

CARRELL P. HORTON

Jones, Scipio Africanus

Jones, Scipio Africanus (c. 1863–March 28, 1943), lawyer, civil rights activist. Jones grew up in Tulip, Arkansas, and moved to Little Rock by 1881. He graduated from Shorter College in 1885. Jones was forced to read law under white lawyers, since the University of Arkansas law school did not admit blacks. After being admitted to the state bar in 1889, he began to serve the black community. He was national attorney general for the Mosaic Templars of America and active in the Republican Party, despite

Scipio A. Jones. (Fisk University Library)

the constant display of exclusionary tactics by white party members. Jones encouraged qualified blacks to run as candidates for political office.

Jones's fame as a trial lawyer was the result of a 1919 race riot in Elaine, Arkansas. The killing of a white lawman after breaking up a meeting of black farmers provoked a riot that officially left five whites and twenty-five blacks (although believed to be nearer two hundred) dead. Despite the killings on both sides, twelve black men were convicted for the death of one of the white victims, and no white perpetrators were arrested. The NAACP retained a white lawyer, George W. Murphy, to appeal the sentences, and the local Citizen's Defense Fund Commission retained Jones to assist him. After the state Supreme Court granted a new trial for six of the defendants, Murphy died during the proceedings. Then Jones worked alone on an appeal that was later denied. He worked relentlessly until circumstances forced him to appeal to the U.S. Supreme Court. In 1923, a landmark decision was handed down that resulted in the release of the six blacks not covered in the appeal, and a gubernatorial conditional pardon for the other six defendants.

See also ARKANSAS [1]; INTELLECTUAL LIFE [3].

REFERENCES

The New York Public Library African American Reference Desk. 1999.

Nichols, Cheryl. "Roots." *Arkansas Times*, February 12, 1999.

Smith, Jessie Carney, ed. *Black Firsts*. 1994.

Smith. Jessie Carney, ed. *Notable Black American Men*. 1999.

DOLORES NICHOLSON

Jordan, Barbara Charline (Update) (February 21, 1936–January 17, 1996), U.S. Congresswoman and professor.

In January 1996, two years after she received the Presidential Medal of Freedom, Barbara Jordan died. Her obituaries explained much that she had kept private during her lifetime, confirming that she had suffered from multiple sclerosis. Reports also discussed her lesbianism and named her "longtime companion."

REFERENCES

Aynesworth, Hugh. "Barbara Jordan, respected former lawmaker, dies: 3-term congresswoman was 59." *The Washington Times*. January 18, 1996: 4.

Dahir, Mubarak S. "Barbara Jordan's silence causes sense of disappointment, abandonment." *Knight-Ridder/Tribune News Service*. February 28, 1996:228K7514.

Haskins, James. *Barbara Jordan*. 1977.

GREG ROBINSON

Jordan, Michael Jeffrey (Update) (February 17, 1963–), basketball player, basketball team administrator.

In the spring of 1995, Jordan resumed his basketball career, ending his retirement by returning to the Bulls. He quickly proved that he had lost none of his skill. The Bulls finished the season in 1996 with a new NBA won-lost record of 72-10, and went on to win the NBA championship. Jordan won the NBA Most Valuable Payer Award.

The same year, Jordan starred in a popular semi-animated movie *Space Jam*, playing opposite Bugs Bunny. Jordan led the Bulls to NBA championships in each of the two following two years, and in 1998 won his fifth MVP award. By this time, he was a worldwide celebrity, whose name was known even in countries where basketball is not played. By the end of 1998, Jordan had scored 29,277 points, third on the all-time NBA list, and was first in scoring average with 31.5 points per game. He spoke several times of retiring, but he had not made a definite statement before a player's strike postponed the resumption of NBA play.

On January 13, 1999, Michael Jordan announced his second and final retirement from basketball. He said that he no longer had the desire to play. "Men-

Barbara Jordan. (AP/Wide World Photos)

tally, I'm exhausted," Jordan said. "I know from a career standpoint I've accomplished everything I could as an individual. Right now, I just don't have the mental challenges that I've had in the past to proceed as a basketball player."

His retirement came after leading the Bulls to their sixth championship in eight seasons in June 1998. Jordan leaves with the highest career scoring average in the NBA's history. He planned to devote more time to his three children, family and to perfect his golf game.

His departure from playing basketball, though, was not the end of his involvement with the sport. In January 2000, Jordan became a minority owner and president of basketball operations for the Washington Wizards franchise. Jordan immediately took over the day to day decision making involving the team's roster and coaches. Jordan also took the position of CEO for his brand of Nike shoes, which Nike spun off from the regular Nike line to become its own standalone brand.

REFERENCES

Naughton, Jim. *Talking to the Air: The Rise of Michael Jordan*. 1992.

Wyche, Steve. "Jordan Brings His Game to the Wizards; NBA Legend Joins Front Office, Becomes Part Owner of Franchise." *The Washington Post* January 20, 2000: A01.

JIM NAUGHTON
UPDATED BY GREG ROBINSON

Jordan, Vernon Eulion, Jr. (Update) (August 8, 1935–), lawyer, civil rights leader. Over the following years, Jordan was a visible "first friend" of the Clintons, golfing and vacationing with the president and functioning as a behind-the-scenes adviser. In March 1998, Jordan testified before a grand jury investigating Clinton's sexual relationship with Monica Lewinsky that he had helped find Lewinsky a job and a lawyer.

REFERENCES

Henry, John C. "House team puts Jordan in the hot seat; No startling evidence appears to emerge during 3-hour grilling." *Houston Chronicle*. February 3, 1999: 1.

"Jordan, Vernon." *Current Biography*, August 1993, pp. 25-29.

Michael Jordan and Coach Phil Jackson hold their MVP and NBA Championship trophies in Salt Lake City, UT. (Archive Photos, Inc.)

Pertman, Adam. "Vernon Jordan: No. 1 FOB on Martha's Vineyard." *The Boston Globe*, August 25, 1993, p. 53.

Williams, Marjorie. "Clinton's Mr. Inside." *Vanity Fair*, March 1993), pp. 172-175.

GREG ROBINSON

Joyner, Marjorie Stewart (October 24, 1896–December 27, 1994), entrepreneur, inventor, philanthropist, educator, pioneer. Joyner contributed in diverse ways to Chicago culture. She was a nationally known, influential leader in black cosmetology. Born near Monterey, Virginia, Stewart was the daughter of George Emmanuel and Annie Dougherty Stewart. After her parents divorced, Joyner moved to Chicago in 1912 to continue her studies. She married Robert S. Joyner in 1916, and they had two daughters.

In 1916 Joyner graduated from A. B. Molar Beauty School, and a few weeks later she opened her own shop in a racially mixed neighborhood. Initially, her customers were white. That same year she met Madam C. J. Walker, her mentor, and completed Walker's training course. She became certified as a "Walker agent," establishing a relationship that would con-

Vernon Jordan, civil rights leader. (The Library of Congress)

tinue until Walker died in 1919. In 1919 Joyner also became national supervisor for over 200 Walker beauty colleges. Later she was named a vice president and chief instructor.

Joyner invented and received a patent for a permanent wave machine in 1928. She and her close associates used the machine in their work. In 1987 the Smithsonian Institution included the item and other examples of Joyner's career in its exhibit on black migration. For twenty-five years Joyner continued to develop new products for the Walker Company. To help promote the black beauty culture industry, in 1945 Joyner founded the United Beauty School Owners and Teachers Association and the Alpha Chi Omega sorority and fraternity.

At age 73, Joyner received her bachelor's degree from Bethune Cookman College. Until she was nearly 100 years old, Joyner was active in philanthropic work and each day spent some time reading the *Chicago Defender*, with which she had been affiliated since 1929. *See also* CHICAGO [1]; HAIR AND BEAUTY CULTURE [3].

REFERENCES

Ortiz, Lou. "Black Cosmetology Pioneer Is a Role Model for Success." *Chicago Sun-Times*, November 18, 1991.

Smith, Jessie Carney, ed. *Notable Black American Women*, 1996.

Walker, Juliet E. K., ed. *Encyclopedia of African American Business History*. 1999.

JESSIE CARNEY SMITH

Julius Rosenwald Fund. Founded in Chicago in 1917, the Julius Rosenwald Fund was a charitable organization that provided massive funding for African American education and social services. Julius Rosenwald, Chairman of the Board of the Sears Roebuck mail-order business, created the Fund originally as a mechanism for his personal charitable activities. In 1927 Rosenwald ended his active involvement in the Fund, hired a professional staff led by Edwin Embree, and established a twenty million-dollar endowment with the stipulation that the entire amount be disbursed within twenty-five years after his death.

Rosenwald had met African American leader Booker T. Washington in 1911 and had been intrigued by Washington's philosophy of racial self-help through education. He directed a large proportion of the assets of the Rosenwald Fund, once created, to supporting the construction of African American schools by providing funds to match government aid or black community subscriptions. By the time of Rosenwald's death in 1932, when the building program ended, the Fund had provided $4.4 million and assisted in building 5,357 black schools in the South. The Fund provided additional sums to provide schools with libraries, transportation, and equipment.

The Rosenwald Fund provided grants to African Americans in many areas in addition to education. For example, it established YMCA and YWCA branches in black neighborhoods of cities such as Chicago, provided fellowships to black artists, scientists and scholars, organized race relations conferences, and funded public health activities (including preliminary funding for the notorious Tuskegee syphilis experiment of the 1930s). The Fund exhausted itself and closed in 1947, fifteen years after Rosenwald's death. *See also* BOND, HORACE MANN [1]; BUGGS, CHARLES WESLEY [1]; CLAYTOR, WILLIAM WALDRON SCHIEFFELIN [2]; DOUGLAS, AARON [2]; EDUCATION [2]; JUST, ERNEST EVERETT [3]; MURALISTS [4]; NURSING [4]; PUBLIC HEALTH [4].

REFERENCE

Edwin R. Embree and Julia Waxman, *Investment in People*. 1952.

GREG ROBINSON

Jumping. Jumping refers to a vibrant form of music, called jump blues, which involves swinging rhythms and lively dancing. Its early popularity peaked in the post-World War II years of the late 1940s, but influenced various music traditions for years to come.

Louis Thomas Jordan (1908–1975), the creator of jump blues and son of a bandleader and music teacher, absorbed the black musical traditions of the American South while growing up in Arkansas. After playing in various bands through the 1930s, Jordan formed his own group, the Tympany Five. Appealing to both white and black audiences, Jordan developed a unique shuffle boogie rhythm. Having its roots in boogie-woogie music, jump was a jazzier form of blues, emphasizing horns and de-emphasizing the guitar. Key characteristics were lively saxophone solos, two-four drum patterns, walking boogie bass lines, and a theatrical stage performance. At first largely instrumental, singers later added a smooth gospel-influenced vocal style. Clever, humorous lyrics describing everyday life were set to the upbeat rhythms.

Veterans returning from World War II found this new blues style played by small combos exciting. Jump blues became the dominant black music form and Jordan's Tympany Five was a popular bands through the 1940s. Jordan produced a string of popular hits, some becoming million seller recordings. These included "Is You Is or Is You Ain't (My Baby)," "Choo Choo Ch'Boogie," "Ain't Nobody Here But Us Chickens," "Saturday Night Fish Fry," and "Caledonia." He worked with renown musical artists including Bing Crosby, Louis Armstrong, and Ella Fitzgerald. Jordan and his jump music also appeared in several short films including *Shout Sister Shout* (1949).

Other leading jump blues artists included Amos Milburn, Roy Milton, Jimmy Liggins, Joe Liggins, Wynonie Harris, Floyd Dixon, Charles Brown, T-Bone Walker, Big Joe Turner, and Eddie "Cleanhead" Vinson. Several black radio disc jockeys gained notoriety promoting this popular lively music and speaking colorful street language on the air. Two noted jockeys, Vernon Winslow and Al Benson, set a future trend for modern pop radio.

Jump blues posed a profound effect on the emergence of rhythm and blues. By 1949 the popularity of jump blues led *Billboard Magazine* to change its music chart titles from black pop to rhythm and blues, a new name for this new music. Jump blues had its direct influences on the emergence of rock and roll as well. In 1954 Chuck Berry, a young guitarist from St. Louis, blended jump blues with white hillbilly sounds to create such famous songs as "Maybelleine" and "Johnny B. Goode." He also borrowed from Jordan's theatrical jumping blues stage presence. Jump blues music enjoyed a revival in the 1990s spurred by the New York and London musical *Five Guys Named Moe*. *See also* BROWN, JAMES JOE, JR. [1]; JORDAN, LOUIS [3]; LITTLE RICHARD, RICHARD (RICHARD PENNIMAN) [3]; RHYTHM AND BLUES [4]; TURNER, JOSEPH VERNON "BIG JOE" [5].

REFERENCES

Chilton, John. *Let the Good Times Roll: The Story of Louis Jordan and His Music.* 1994.

Jordan, Louis. *The Best of Louis Jordan* (sound recording). 1989.

National Public Radio. *From Jumpstreet (sound recording): A Story of Black Music.* 1982.

Stewart, Earl L. *African American Music: An Introduction.* 1998.

Ward, Brian. *Just My Soul Responding: Rhythm and Blues, Black Consciousness, and Race Relations.* 1998.

RICHARD C. HANES

K

Kemp, Maida Springer (May 12, 1910–), labor leader, women's and civil rights activist. Born in the Republic of Panama, Maida Kemp migrated with her mother to the Harlem section of New York City at age seven. Kemp's mother, Adina Stewart, was a member of Marcus Garvey's Universal Negro Improvement Association, held stock in one of Garvey's self-help agencies, and was a Black Cross nurse for the Garvey movement. Kemp studied at the Malone School of Beauty Culture and became a licensed beautician.

Displeased with work conditions in a nonunion garment shop in 1932, Kemp joined the International Ladies Garment Workers' Union (ILGWU) and worked with the Strike Committee. The union sent her to its own educational facility for training, and she became a member of its executive committee. As education director for Local 132 in 1942, she designed a program that forged common bonds among workers. She continued her work with Local 22 and by 1947, she became the first African American to serve as its business agent.

Further studies in worker education in Sweden and Denmark, and at Oxford University in 1951, established ties between Kemp and African students also studying abroad. As a result of these relationships, Kemp began working with several African nations on worker issues, and by the 1970s she was a recognized international expert in labor education. Her alliances with important African leaders prompted her appointment to the ILGWU international staff in the 1980s and led to her being named a consultant for the African Labor History Center.

REFERENCES

Hine, Darlene Clark, ed. *Black Women in America*, vol. 1. 1993.

Salem, Dorothy, ed. *African American Women: A Biographical Dictionary*. 1993.

Smith, Jessie Carney, ed. *Notable Black American Women, Book II*. 1996.

JESSIE CARNEY SMITH

Kentucky (Update). African Americans in Kentucky attained increasingly visible positions in the state's government and society as the twentieth century drew to a close. In government, Arnold Simpson was elected in 1994 from a predominately-white northern Kentucky House of Representatives district. Roy P. Peterson served as secretary of the state's Education, Arts and Humanities Cabinet from 1995 until his death in 1998, when Marlene M. Helm took over the post. Other state officials appointed in the late 1990s were Laura M. Douglas, Secretary of Cabinet for Public Protection, and Robert Peters, Kentucky Personnel Cabinet Secretary.

Prominent African Americans outside of public office in Kentucky include Cornelius Martin, CEO of Bowling Green's Martin Automotive Group, considered by *Black Enterprise* magazine in 1995 to be one of the leading automobile dealerships in the country. Orlando "Tubby" Smith was named as the head basketball coach at the University of Kentucky in 1997 and guided the team to a national championship in 1998.

The significance of African Americans in Kentucky history is being documented through several museums still in the planning stages. The City of Louisville made plans to create the African American Heritage Center and the Muhammad Ali Museum, while more modest facilities include the Underground Railroad Museum in Maysville. Yet, despite these individual advancements and institutional developments, there is concern that segregation in Kentucky schools still exists. Legal struggles over the progress of desegregation in Jefferson and Fayette County public schools remain unresolved, and efforts to end de-facto segregation in Louisville and Lexington have stirred up controversy. Both Louisville and Lexington have also experienced a public outcry over recent deaths of African American suspects at the hands of the police, raising allegations of racism and police brutality.

REFERENCES

Black Enterprise, June 25, 1995, p. 111.

Lexington Herald-Leader, June 17, 1997, p. 1.

Office of Communications of Kentucky Governor Paul Patton.

JOHN A. HARDIN

Keyes, Alan (August 7, 1950–), presidential candidate.He has drawn attention as a conservative African American Republican, making the run in 1996 and 2000. Keyes was born in New York City. He holds two degrees in government affairs from Harvard University, a B.A. (1972) and a Ph.D. (1979).

Keyes was at the State Department from 1978 to 1988. He served in Bombay, India in 1979–1980. After two year in Washington, D.C., he became U.S. Ambassador to the United Nations Economic and Social Council (1983–1985). His final position at State was Assistant Secretary of State for International Organization Affairs from 1985 to 1988. Keyes became increasingly involved in politics For example, from 1989 to 1992 he was president of Citizens Against Government Waste. He furthered his conservative political agenda as a syndicated columnist for Scripps Howard in 1991–1992 and in 1994–1999 as host of the syndicated radio talk show, *The Alan Keyes Show; America's Wake-Up Call*. He has also published two books: *Masters of the Dream: The Strength and Betrayal of Black*

Alan Keyes. (AP/Wide World Photos)

America (1995) and *Our Character, Our Future: Reclaiming America's Moral Destiny* (1996).

In 1988 and again in 1992 Keyes was the Republican nominee for U.S. Senator from Maryland. In 1996 and 2000 Keyes campaigned vigorously for the Republican nomination for the presidency. In 2000 he attracted much attention in the early primaries as he proved attractive to conservative voters. For example, Floyd Flake, a former Democratic Congressman, found much to admire in Keyes's positions. On principle Keyes continued to campaign even after George Bush Jr. locked in the nomination.

See also MARYLAND [3]; REPUBLICAN PARTY [4].

REFERENCES

Alan Keyes For President. http://www.keyes2000.org/

Dao, James. "Keyes Draws the Few, but Devoted: A Republican Candidate Lifts His Voice on Issues of Morality." *New York Times*, 1 September 1999.

Flake, Floyd. "Keyes: The Candidate We Can't Forget." *New York Post.* Posted at http://www.keyes2000.org/ news/articles/cant_forget.shtml Accessed 30 May 2000.

"Keyes Continues Run for President." *Associated Press.*

ROBERT L. JOHNS

Koontz, Elizabeth Duncan (June 3, 1919– January 6, 1989), educator, administrator. Elizabeth Duncan Koontz was born in Salisbury, North Carolina, and received her bachelor's degree in 1938 from Livingstone College. In 1941 she received a master's degree from Atlanta University, followed by graduate study at Columbia University, Indiana University, and North Carolina College. Koontz held several teaching positions in North Carolina, as she participated in numerous educational organizations and rose in rank through each of them.

In 1952 Koontz became active in the National Education Association immediately upon their acceptance of African American memberships. She had previously belonged to the North Carolina Negro Teachers Association. Koontz moved to the national level in NEA by 1965, becoming the first African American president of NEA's Department of Classroom Teachers. Koontz was installed as president of NEA on June 6, 1968–the first African American to hold that post. She brought to the office firsthand experiences from the classroom as well as a change from conservative ideas to liberal activism.

Koontz was active in women's rights as well. In January 1969, President Richard M. Nixon appointed her director of the U.S. Department of Labor's Women's Bureau. Again, she was the first African American to hold the post, and subsequently, she became deputy assistant secretary for Labor Employment Standards. Koontz resigned from the bureau in March 1973 and held several positions in her native state. She retired in April 1982 to return to Salisbury and pursue her interests in education and the status of women.

See also NORTH CAROLINA [4].

REFERENCES

Current Biography Yearbook 1969. 1969.

Obituary. *New York Times*, January 8, 1989.

Smith, Jessie Carney, ed. *Notable Black American Women*. 1992.

VALENCIA PRICE

L

L L Cool J (Smith, James Todd) (January 14, 1968–), musician, actor, writer. L(adies)L(ove) Cool J(ames) is the largest selling rap musician to date, with more than twenty million albums sold worldwide. Born in St. Albans, Queens, New York, and raised by his grandparents, he began rapping at age nine. On his thirteenth birthday, he received DJ equipment as a gift from his grandfather. LL Cool J arrived on the music scene in 1985 with his first hit record, "I Can't Live Without My Radio." "Rock the Bells" soon followed, and in 1986, he achieved his first million selling album, *Radio*.

In 1987, his second album, Bigger and Deffer, contained the first rap ballad, "I Need Love." *Walking With A Panther* (1989) met with negative critical response, but still sold more than five hundred thousand copies. The follow-up, *Mama Said Knock You Out* (1990), won a Grammy Award for "Best Rap Solo Performance," remaining on the Billboard charts for over a year, and selling more than one million units. *14 Shots to the Dome* (1993) became another platinum album for the artist, and he won his second Grammy award for "Best Rap Solo Performance" for his single, "Hey Lover."

He has released three more successful albums to date (*Mr. Smith*, 1995; *All World*, 1996; *Phenomenon*, 1997). LL Cool J's accomplishments include 15 New York Music Awards, 10 Soul Train Awards, and a Billboard Music Award. In 1998, he published an autobiography, *I Make My Own Rules*. He has also acted in television and films, including *Toys* (1992), *Halloween: H20* (1998), and *Any Given Sunday* (1999). *See also* FILM [2]; HUDLIN, WARRINGTON [3]; NEW YORK CITY [4]; RAP [4].

REFERENCES

George, Nelson. *Hip-Hop America*. 1998.

Rose, Tricia. *Black Noise: Rap Muisic and Black Culture in Contemporary America*. 1994.

RACHEL ZELLARS

Lafayette Players. The Lafayette Players was the first enduring African American stock theater company, and it offered the first opportunity for black actors to appear in non-musical presentations. The group was formed in 1915 as the Anita Bush Players and presented its first play, *The Girl at the Fort*, on November 19, 1915, at the Lincoln Theater in Harlem. The group was successful, but a dispute with the Lincoln management led it to transfer to the Lafayette Theater, where it began to present plays on December 27, 1915. By March of the following year Bush transferred ownership of the players to the Lafayette Theater management, and the group became known as the Lafayette Players.

At the height of the Lafayette Player's success from 1919 to 1921, four traveling companies used the name

L L Cool J. (Corbis Corporation)

and were booked on the circuit controlled by the corporate owner. The Lafayette Players was continuously active until 1923 when film undercut live entertainment. The name of Lafayette Players was used by various successor groups on an intermittent basis until 1928; a group was also active under the name in Los Angeles from 1928 to 1932.

The Lafayette Players presented over 250 productions, mostly of abbreviated Broadway plays or classics; only a handful were "race plays." The early production schedule called for a new play every week. The presentations almost always shared the bill with vaudeville acts and movies. The most famous among the early players are Charles Gilpin (1878–1930), who played the lead in Eugene O'Neill's *The Emperor Jones* on Broadway in 1920, and Clarence Muse (1889–1979), who had a long career in Hollywood.
See also BUSH, ANITA [1]; GILPIN, CHARLES SIDNEY [2]; MICHEAUX, OSCAR [4].

REFERENCE

Johns, Robert L. "Anita Bush." In *Notable Black American Women*, edited by Jessie Carney Smith. 1992.

Peterson, Bernard L., Jr. *The African American Theatre Directory, 1816–1960*. 1997.

ROBERT L. JOHNS

Lafon, Thomy (December 28, 1810–December 22, 1893), entrepreneur, philanthropist. Lafon was a highly successful real estate investor who, through his own frugality, became wealthy then donated much of his fortune to individuals, educational, religious, and charitable groups in New Orleans. Lafon was born free in New Orleans to Pierre Laralde and Modest Foucher. He may have been partially educated in Europe.

Lafon taught school for a while but appears to have been more involved in business than in other occupations. By some accounts, in 1842, before the Civil War, he was already a merchant; other accounts identify Lafon as an operator of a small dry goods store about 1850. He was a broker as well, becoming the second leading black broker up to 1870.

In the 1860s, Lafon centered his attention on real estate, buying and selling property for a sizeable profit. His real estate worth by 1860 was $10,000, and by 1870 his worth had increased to $55,000.

Lafon was active in the community and agitated for the rights of African Americans, particularly their right to vote and to attend white schools in racially segregated New Orleans. So concerned was Lafon with the needy that he gave his wealth freely to the deserving poor. He supported charities of the Roman Catholic Church as well, much out of his own concern for the church's mission. Among the other groups that benefited from his wealth were the American Anti-Slavery Society, the Underground Railroad, the Lafon Orphan Boys' Asylum, and the Home for Aged Colored Men and Women. After his death, his will further provided support for a number of charities, including Straight and New Orleans universities. *See also* COUVENT INSTITUTE [2].

REFERENCES

Ingham, John N., and Lynne B. Feldman. *African-American Business Leaders*. 1994.

Malone, Dumas, ed. *Dictionary of American Biography*. 1943.

Smith, Jessie Carney, ed. *Notable Black American Men*. 1999.

JESSIE CARNEY SMITH

Latimer, Lewis Howard (September 4, 1848–December 11, 1928), engineer and inventor.

A pioneer in the development of electric lighting, Latimer was born in Chelsea, Massachusetts, the son of a runaway. In his youth, Latimer sold copies of abolitionist William Lloyd Garrison's *Liberator*. In 1863 Latimer enlisted in the Union Navy and saw action on the James River aboard the U.S.S. *Massoit*. Honorably discharged in 1865, he became an office boy for patent solicitors Crosby and Gould.

With secondhand drafting tools and available books, Latimer trained himself as a mechanical draftsman. In 1876 Latimer prepared drawings for Alexander Graham Bell's telephone. Four years later, he joined United States Electric Lighting Co., a competitor of Thomas A. Edison, who had patented the incandescent light in 1879. Latimer shared a patent for an electric lamp in 1881 and the following year made his most important invention: a carbon filament that increased the brightness and longevity of light bulbs. The filament's lower cost made electric lighting more accessible.

Latimer supervised the installation of electric-light systems in New York City, Philadelphia, Montreal, and London. In 1884 Edison Electric Light Co. hired him to conduct research on electrical lighting. Latimer published *Incandescent Electric Lighting* in 1896, a technical book for lighting engineers, and served as an expert witness for Edison against patent infringements by rival companies.

Latimer circulated a petition presented in 1902 to New York City Mayor Seth Low, regarding lack of African American representation on the school board and taught mechanical drawing to immigrants at the Henry Street Settlement in Manhattan. Latimer's *Poems of Love and Life* was privately published in 1925, three years before he died in Flushing, NY, at the age of eighty.

See also PATENTS AND INVENTIONS [3].

REFERENCES

Clarke, John. "Henrick and Lewis H. Latimer." In *Dictionary of American Negro Biography*, edited by Rayford Logan and Michael Winston. 1982.

Hayden, Robert C. *Eight Black American Inventors*. 1972.

Klein, Aaron E. *The Hidden Contributors: Black Scientists and Inventors in America*. 1971.

OMAR ALI

Lewis Latimer. (Schomberg Center)

Layton, John Turner (1849–February 14, 1916), educator, composer.

John Turner Layton was a music educator and a hymn composer who had a major role in the musical life of Washington, D.C. Of his early life, little is known. He was born in New Jersey. He is supposed to have served in the Civil War despite his youth. There are no known dates for his studies at various schools like the New England Conservatory in Boston, but he became a thoroughly competent musician.

In 1873 Layton became choir director of the Metropolitan African Methodist Episcopal Church in Washington and held the post for forty-three years. He began to teach music in the public schools in 1883, eventually becoming the first male director of music for the colored schools.

Layton had a significant impact on the preparation of the 1897 hymnal of the AME Church, the first to include music. In 1895 he proposed the new hymnal to the Bishops' Council, which accepted his idea and named him to a three man committee to carry it out. As the only musician on the committee, he was totally responsible for the music printed. The hymnal included over a dozen of Layton's own hymns.

Layton was much involved in the musical life of Washington, influencing many young musicians like the noted composer and violinist Clarence Cameron White. An organizer of the Coleridge-Taylor Choral Society in 1902 and its director until his death, he was a leader in bringing Samuel Coleridge-Taylor, the Afro-English composer, to this country in 1903 and again in 1906.

See also AFRICAN METHODIST EPISCOPAL CHURCH [1]; NEW JERSEY [4].

REFERENCE

Southern, Eileen. "John Turner Layton." In *Dictionary of American Negro Biography*, edited by Rayford W. Logan and Michael R. Winston. 1982.

ROBERT L. JOHNS

Lee, Shelton Jackson "Spike" (Update)

(March 20, 1957–), filmmaker. In the late 1990s, Lee continued to produce idiosyncratic and well-crafted films about the black experience. *Get on the Bus* (1996) celebrated the diversity and ideals of the Million Man March. *Four Girls and a Church* (1997) was a touching documentary about four girls murdered in a church bombing in Birmingham in 1963. *He Got Game* (1998)

explored the relationship between a teenage basketball star and his estranged father. His film *Summer of Sam* (1999), about the daily lives of New Yorkers during the 1977 rampage of the serial killer Son of Sam, received mixed reviews from critics and did poorly at the box office.

REFERENCES

Lee, Spike. *Spike Lee's Gotta Have It: Inside Guerilla Filmmaking*. 1987.

Lee, Spike, with Lisa Jones. *Do the Right Thing: A Spike Lee Joint*. 1989.

GREG ROBINSON

Leland, George Thomas "Mickey" (November 27, 1944–1989), politician, social activist. Leland was born in Lubbock, Texas, and grew up in the poor section of Houston, the Fifth Ward. Leland received his bachelor's degree from Texas Southern University in 1970. He worked at his alma mater before leaving to become director of special development projects at Hermann Hospital. During this period he decided that the best way to bring about change was through the Texas State Legislature. In

Spike Lee. (AP/Wide World Photos)

Mickey Leland, 1989. (AP/Wide World Photos)

1973, he gained a seat in the Texas House of Representatives, a post he held until 1978.

In 1978 Leland won the Congressional seat that Barbara Jordan had vacated. He became a strong supporter of minority business and pushed legislation for opening the entertainment industry to minorities. Moreover, Leland had an abiding interest in worldwide hunger and supported legislation to address the problem at home and abroad. He traveled to Appalachia, Indian reservations, migrant camps, refugee camps, Africa, and elsewhere to gain firsthand knowledge of the hunger problem. He established dialogue foreign heads of state because he believed that a political dialogue is imperative in order to address hunger problems.

While on a hunger trip to Africa on August 7, 1989, Leland and a contingency of Congressional aides and other Americans left Addis Ababa headed for refugee camps near the Sudan border. The plane flew nose first into a mountain and all aboard were killed. This tragic event left the world with the memory of one who died in support of programs to address world hunger.

See also HOUSTON, TEXAS [3].

REFERENCES

Bigelow. Barbara Carlisle, ed. *Contemporary Black Biography*, Vol. 2. 1992.

Graver, Earl G. "A Tribute to Mickey." *Black Enterprise*. October 1989.

Leland, Mickey. "What African Americans Can Do About Starvation in Africa." *Ebony*. October 1989: 80-84.

RAYMOND WINBUSH

LeMoyne-Owen College.

LeMoyne-Owen College, located in Memphis, Tennessee, is an independent liberal arts institution related to the United Church of Christ, through its United Church Board of Homeland Ministries, and the Tennessee Baptist Missionary and Education Convention.

The institution takes it names from two schools that are a part of its history: LeMoyne College and Owen Junior College. The roots of LeMoyne College date back to 1862, when Lucinda Humphrey, a hospital nurse at Camp Shiloh, Tennessee, began to teach the alphabet by candlelight to a group of African Americans who left slavery for Union camps. The school moved to Memphis in 1863, expanded, and in 1866 was renamed Lincoln School. Lincoln Chapel, destroyed by fire in 1866, was rebuilt and the school reopened in 1867. In need of financial assistance, Francis Julian LeMoyne, a prominent Washington, D.C., physician and member of the American Missionary Association, made a gift of $20,000 to the school. In 1871 the institution was renamed LeMoyne Normal and Commercial School. LeMoyne College moved to the site of the present institution in 1914; it became a junior college in 1924 and was certified as a four-year college by the State of Tennessee in 1934.

The Tennessee Baptist Missionary and Educational Convention set about in 1946 to build a Baptist junior college. It organized a Board of Trustees in 1953, and opened the school in 1954 as S. A. Owen Junior College to honor S. A. Owen, a prominent minister and civic leader. The name was soon changed to Owen College; its first class graduated in 1956. In 1958 the school became an accredited institution. The colleges merged in 1968 to become LeMoyne-Owen College.

See also AMERICAN MISSIONARY ASSOCIATION [1]; DANNER, MARGARET ESSIE [2]; TENNESSEE [5]; UNITED CHURCH OF CHRIST [5].

REFERENCES

"History of the College." http://www.mecca.org/LOC/page/history.html.

"LeMoyne-Owen College, Mission Statement." http://www.mecca.org/LOC/pagee/mission1.html.

JESSIE CARNEY SMITH

Lemus, Rienzi B[rock] (January 8, 1881–1945), labor leader. Rienzi B. Lemus was a labor leader who led the Brotherhood of Dining Car Employees from 1919 to 1941. He was born in Richmond, Virginia. At eighteen he enlisted in the army. The major part of his service was with the 25th Infantry during the Philippine insurrection. He was honorably discharged in March 1902.

During his service Lemus wrote about thirty letters to the *Richmond Planet* about what was going on in the Philippines, and he also supplied three articles for the *Colored American Magazine*, in March and May 1902 and in March 1903. These valuable eye-witness accounts tell about Philippine reaction to black soldiers.

After his discharge Lemus went to work for the railroads, first as a porter and then as a dining car employee. In 1919 Lemus organized the Brotherhood of Dining Care Employees, based mostly on New England lines. The Urban League helped to unite Lemus's organization with a similar one centered on eastern Pennsylvania railroads in 1920. Lemus became president of the new union.

Early successes included the eight-hour day and overtime in 1919 followed by a first agreement with one line about employment rules in 1921. By the end of the twenties the union had enrolled about half of the dining car employees east of the Mississippi. In the middle 1930s the union faced the challenge of the American Federation of Labor's Hotel and Restaurant Workers. The union declined, and Lemus was voted out of office in 1941. His union was absorbed by the Hotel and Restaurant Workers.

See also RICHMOND, VIRGINIA [4].

REFERENCES

Schubert, Frank N. "Rienzi Brock Lemus." In *Dictionary of American Negro Biography*, edited by Rayford W. Logan and Michael R. Winston. 1982.

Yenser, Thomas, ed. *Who's Who in Colored America, 1941–1944*. 1942.

ROBERT L. JOHNS

Leonard, Ray Charles "Sugar Ray" (Update) (May 17, 1956–), boxer. After a three-year retirement due to an eye injury sustained in 1984, Leonard returned to the ring in 1987 as a middleweight, dethroning Marvin Hagler as WBC champion in a controversial twelve-round split decision in

Sugar Ray Leonard. (AP/Wide World Photos)

Las Vegas. The victory over Hagler increased his career earnings to $53 million. In 1988, Leonard knocked out Canadian Don Lalonde, the WBC light heavyweight champion, which earned him both the WBC light heavyweight and super middleweight titles, making him the first boxer ever to win at least a share of titles in five different weight classes. His 37 professional bouts over fourteen years included 35 wins, 25 by knockout. Since his retirement in 1991, Leonard has worked as a commentator on boxing broadcasts and has appeared in several television commercials. Leonard returned to the ring at the age of forty-one in March 1997. He was pounded by Hector Camacho and retired again following the loss.

REFERENCES

Perrone, Vinnie. "Leonard Hit With Reality; Camacho Retains Title With Knockout In 5th." *Washington Post*, March 2, 1997: D1.

Porter, David L., ed. *Biographical Dictionary of American Sports: Basketball and Other Indoor Sports*, 1989.

NANCY YOUSEF
THADDEUS RUSSELL
UPDATED BY GREG ROBINSON

Lewis, Carl (Update) (July 1, 1961–), track and field athlete. Interestingly, Carl Lewis began to receive the appreciation and recognition merited by his

Carl Lewis, during the long jump event in Barcelona, 1992. (AP/Wide World Photos)

Delano Lewis, president and chief executive officer, National Public Radio. (AP/Wide World Photos)

lengthy, remarkable career only when he no longer appeared unbeatable. For while Lewis sustained his overall level of performance into the 1990s, his competition grew stronger and sometimes overtook him. The most dramatic example of this came at the United States Olympic Trials in 1992, when he failed to qualify in the event he had dominated perennially: the 100-meter dash. In defeat, Lewis became a more "human" figure—occasionally vulnerable to younger, talented challengers—and his achievements appeared all the more extraordinary. In the 1996 Olympics, Lewis won the long jump, thus tying an Olympic record with nine gold medals. He retired from active competition in September 1997.

REFERENCES

"Carl Lewis." In *Encyclopedia of World Biography* 2nd ed., 1998.

Lewis, Carl, and Jeffrey Marx. *Inside Track: My Professional Life in Amateur Track and Field*, 1992.

Smith, Gary. "'The Best Ever.' "*Sports Illustrated*, August 17, 1992, pp. 40-43.

JILL DUPONT
UPDATED BY GREG ROBINSON

Lewis, Delano Eugene (November 12, 1938–), business and broadcasting executive. Lewis was born in Arkansas City, Kansas and grew up in Kansas City. He received his B.A. degree from the University of Kansas in 1960 and the J.D. degree from Washburn School of Law in 1963. He was an attorney with the U.S. Department of Justice in 1963–1965 then became an attorney with the Equal Employment Opportunity Commission (EEOC) until he became a Peace Corps volunteer in Nigeria and Uganda in 1966.

Returning to Washington, D.C., in 1969, Lewis became legislative assistant for Senator Edward Brooke and for Congressman Walter Fauntroy. In 1973 Lewis moved to private enterprise, as public affairs manager of Chesapeake and Potomac Telephone Company. As he moved up in rank, he continued to address internal issues such as hiring and promotion and explored the expansion and service needs of the company. He was named president of the company in 1983 and chief executive officer in 1988. In his commitment to community service, Lewis became president of Greater Washington Board of Trade, used his fund raising expertise to promote a number of local charities, and became a patron of the arts.

Lewis left his successful position and from 1994 to 1998, he was president of National Public Radio in Washington, D.C. On June 7, 1999, he was named U.S. Ambassador to the Republic of South Africa. *See also* AMBASSADORS AND DIPLOMATS [1]; KANSAS [3].

REFERENCES

Bigelow, Barbara Carlisle, ed. *Contemporary Black Biography*, 1994.

Conciatore, Jacqueline. "Delano Lewis Will Retire From Running NPR." *Current* April 1998.

"Delano Lewis." NPR Online. http://www.npr.org/inside/bios/diewis.html.

Johnson, Anne Janette. "Delano Lewis." In *Contemporary Black Biography*, Edited by Barbara Carlisle Bigelow. 1994.

ROBERT L. JOHNS

Lewis, Elma (September 15, 1921–), educator, school founder. Elma Lewis has contributed widely to the cultural development of African Americans through the school and center for artists she founded. Lewis was born in Roxbury, Massachusetts, to Barbados emigrants Clairmont and Edwardine Lewis, who followed Marcus Garvey and his Universal Improvement Association that espoused black empowerment. At age thirteen, Jones enrolled in the Doris Jones School of Dance, studying there through her sophomore year at Boston's Emerson College. She graduated from Emerson in 1943 with a degree in literature interpretation. The next year she received her master's degree from Boston University.

In the late 1940s, Lewis was an elementary school teacher and social worker/speech therapist at ten schools

Elma Lewis during an interview. (AP/Wide World Photos)

and organizations. Using second-handed furniture and a piano, she founded the Elma Lewis School of Fine Arts on January 30, 1950, to teach music, drama, and dance to young people and adults. Roxbury's black community supported the school for over 18 years. When it soon outgrew its quarters, Lewis moved the school to a larger facility; later on she moved again to better quarters. Many of her students went on to successful careers as dancers, musicians, and film stars. Lewis's series of free summer concerts held in Roxbury's Franklin Park, called Playhouse in the Park, brought capacity crowds and stars such as Duke Ellington, Odetta, and Arthur Fielder's Boston Pops.

In 1969, Lewis became founder/director of the National Center of Afro-American Artists, with her school as its teaching arm. The center promoted and showcased the works of black Americans in the arts. Lewis and her school also became involved in civil rights activities and helped to quell racial disturbances.

Lewis has been widely recognized for her work, as seen, for example, in 1981 when she became one of the first individuals to receive a McArthur Foundation genius award. Altogether, she has received over 400 awards.

See also ART COLLECTIONS [1]; BEATTY, TALLEY [1]; BENJAMIN, FRED [1].

REFERENCES

Bailey, Suzanne. "The Undeferred Dream of Elma Lewis." *Essence* 4 (July 1973): 40-41.

Editors of *Ebony*. *Ebony Success Library*, vol. 1. 1973.

Russell, Dick. *Black Genius and the American Experience*. 1998.

JESSIE CARNEY SMITH

Lewis, Henry, Jr. (October 16, 1932–January 26, 1996), conductor. Henry Lewis, the first African American to lead a major symphony orchestra, was born in Los Angeles, the son of an auto dealer and a nurse. During his childhood, he attended Catholic schools. He studied piano, clarinet, and double bass, and soon began to conduct. Despite parental opposition to a musical career, in 1950 Lewis joined the Los Angeles Philharmonic as a double bassist. Meanwhile, he attended the University of Southern California on a music scholarship, though he left without earning a degree.

In 1955 Lewis joined the U.S. Army, where he gained his first experience as a conductor by leading the Seventh Army Symphony Orchestra. After his discharge in 1958, Lewis returned to the Los Angeles Philharmonic as a bassist; he also began accepting guest conductor jobs. In 1960, Lewis married the rising opera star Marilyn Horne, who helped to build his career. The following year, after the illness of guest conductor Igor Markevitch, Lewis first conducted the Los Angeles Philharmonic. His success led to his appointment as associate conductor.

In 1968, after three years of touring as a conductor, Lewis was selected to lead the New Jersey Symphony Orchestra in Newark, where he remained until his death. Lewis built the orchestra from a semiprofessional group into an orchestra of national stature, and introduced a year-round performance schedule. He was notable for conducting the orchestra in concerts in Newark's African-American ghettoes. He also toured as a guest conductor at the Metropolitan Opera (where he was its first black conductor), at the New York Philharmonic, and in Europe.

See also BLACK ACADEMY OF ARTS AND LETTERS [1]; CONCERT MUSIC [2].

REFERENCE

Baker's Biographical Dictionary of Musicians. Eighth edition. Revised by Nicolas Slonimsky. 1992.

GREG ROBINSON

Lewis, Theophilus (March 4, 1891–September 3, 1974), drama critic, writer.

Lewis was born in Baltimore, Maryland. His high school education took place in night classes at Dewitt Clinton High School in New York City. He had a varied experience as a worker, and he served overseas in the Army during World War I. In 1922 he secured a job in the post office, which he held until retirement. Lewis lived in the Bronx at the time of his death.

From September 1923 to July 1927 Lewis was drama critic for the monthly magazine *The Messenger*, run by A. Philip Randolph and Chandler Owen. The magazine could not pay Lewis for his work but did purchase his theater tickets. Lewis provided the only sustained drama criticism in an African-American periodical during the height of the Harlem Renaissance. Lewis criticized what he saw as a lack of ambition and wasted talent in African-American theater of the time. He felt that black actors were performing unchallenging works, and that black writers were not providing those works, nor were black audiences demanding them. He also reviewed books for the magazine and published four of his own stories in it.

Though he was unable to live off of his writing, Lewis did not cease his activity with the end of the Renaissance. For several years beginning in April 1936, he had a column, *Plays and a Point of View*, in *Interracial Review*. He also published articles in other magazines, and especially in *America*, after he converted to Catholicism in 1939.

See also DRAMA [2]; HARLEM RENAISSANCE [3]; INTELLECTUAL LIFE [3]; LITERARY MAGAZINES [3]; THURMAN, WALLACE [5].

REFERENCES

Grimes-Williams, Joanna L. "Theophilus Lewis." *The Oxford Companion to African American Literature.* William L. Andrews, Frances Foster Smith, Trudier Harris, eds. 1997.

Kellner, Bruce, ed. *The Harlem Renaissance: A Historical Dictionary for the Era.* 1984.

Kornweibel, Theodore, Jr. "Theophilus Lewis and the Theater of the Harlem Renaissance." In *The Harlem Renaissance Remembered*, edited by Arna Bontemps. 1972.

May, Hal, and Susan Trosky. *Contemporary Authors.* Volume 125, 1989.

Scally, Mary Anthony. *Negro Catholic Writers, 1900–1943*, 1943.

ROBERT L. JOHNS

Lindsay, Inabel Burns (February 13, 1900–September 10, 1983), social worker, educator.

Born in St. Joseph, Missouri, Lindsay graduated from Howard University in 1920. She began graduate study at New York School of Social Work, but it was not until 1937 that she completed her master's degree at the University of Chicago School of Social Service Administration. In 1952 she completed her doctoral degree at the University of Pittsburgh.

Between 1921 and 1936, Lindsay held various positions. She was research assistant for a survey in Springfield, Illinois, that sociologist Charles S. Johnson directed. From this position she also wrote for *Opportunity*, the National Urban League's official organ. After that, she was employed with several social work agencies in St. Louis and was a caseworker for the Provident Association, a child and family welfare agency. About 1934, after Provident had expanded the number of districts it maintained, Lindsay was named a district superintendent. Later on, Provident and other private agencies of this nature became public welfare agencies.

In the late 1930s, Lindsay began work for Howard University as director of the social work program, a division of the graduate school. In 1944 Lindsay was appointed acting dean of the later autonomous School of Social Work while the university searched for a man to head the school. In the meantime, Lindsay, whose acting status was removed, became the first dean of the school.

After retiring in 1967, Lindsay was consultant to the U.S. Department of Health, Education, and Welfare, and visiting lecturer at the University of Maryland. She published a number of articles in social work journals.

See also MISSOURI [4].

REFERENCES

Black Women Oral History Project Interview with Inabel Burns Lindsay. 1980.

Smith, Jessie Carney, ed. *Notable Black American Women.* 1992.

RAYMOND WINBUSH

Los Angeles, California (Update).

Los Angeles became a sharply balkanized locality in the minds of many of its African-American residents in the 1990s. The divide between African Americans and other residents of the Los Angeles area had already been indelibly underscored by the 1991 beating of black motorist Rodney King and by the riots that followed a partial acquittal of the four white police officers involved. On June 12, 1994, Nicole Brown Simpson, the estranged wife of former professional football star O. J. Simpson, was murdered in the city together with a male companion, Ronald Goldman. Considerable circumstantial evidence linked Simpson with the crime, but his defense team argued that Simpson had been framed by Los Angeles police officers. The racial divide opened once again when a predominantly black jury acquitted Simpson in 1995, but a predominantly white panel in the suburb of Santa Monica found him responsible for the murders two years later in a wrongful-death lawsuit brought by Brown's family. A *Los Angeles Times* opinion poll conducted before the second trial found that 71 percent of white residents believed that Simpson was guilty, but only 10 percent of blacks agreed. Part of the alienation blacks experienced came from what many perceived as a reduction in the opportunities available to them: attacks on affirmative action policies at the state government level were coupled with a decline in black political power in the Los Angeles basin itself.

The percentage of blacks in the population of Los Angeles County dropped from seventeen percent in the 1970s to about ten percent at the century's end as the area's Hispanic and Asian populations exploded. Latino groups challenged blacks' hard-won share of political patronage jobs, and relations between blacks and Koreans, whose retail establishments bore the brunt of the 1991 riots, remained poor. The bleak social conditions of southern California's inner cities found expression in the new "gangsta rap" music genre, whose texts reproduced the violence endemic to those communities.

REFERENCES

Aubry, Erin J. "The L.A. Reality." *Black Enterprise*, November 1995: 143.

"The Fading of Black Power: Los Angeles Politics." *The Economist* (US). May 16, 1998: 26.

"If At First You Don't Succeed. . . The Simpson Verdict." *The Economist* (US). February 8, 1997: 29.

Streisand, Betsy. "And Justice for All." *U.S. News and World Report.* October 9, 1995: 47.

JAMES MANHEIM

Louisville, Kentucky (Update).

In the late 1990s, African Americans continued their drive to occupy a position of economic equality in Louisville as several blacks made impressive showings as entrepreneurs. Charlie W. Johnson's Active Transportation Inc. employed 300 persons and achieved over $50 million in annual sales in the automobile transport business. Juanita Farley Burks operated three businesses in construction, health care, and personnel recruiting. Among her first clients were Ford Motor Company, McDonnell Douglas, and General Electric.

The corporate sector also lent its support to the Louisville Black Achievers Program. Modeled on the first Black Achievers Program in 1971 at the New York Harlem YMCA, Louisville's Chestnut Street YMCA obtained support from local corporate sponsors to create a similar mentoring and scholarship program. By 1995, the program annually donated over $1 million in scholarships to academically-promising African-American students.

At the same time, Louisville African Americans expressed continuing displeasure with the local police department. Many blacks complained about excessive force used in apprehending blacks, and in several cases, African Americans died at the hands of police officers. In all instances, the police officers involved were absolved.

In April 1996, *Time Magazine* cited Jefferson County (and Louisville) as one of the most desegregated school districts in the nation. Yet, African Americans lamented a trend toward re-segregation of schools and challenged the school system to prevent exclusion of black students from attending prestigious "magnet" schools that were, ironically, formerly black schools.

Coincidentally, Louisville African Americans lent their support to the formation of two organizations focusing on local African American culture and history. In 1999, plans were announced for the creation of the Muhammad Ali Museum to honor Louisville's most notable African American son. Also, the African American Heritage Foundation announced plans to convert the National Landmark-designated Old Trolley Barn in the Russell District into a Kentucky African American Heritage Center. Both facilities are expected to expand national awareness of African Americans' impressive contributions to Louisville, the state, and the nation.

REFERENCES

Louisville Courier-Journal, January 6, 2000, p. B-4.

Louisville Courier-Journal, February 19, 1995, p. B-8.

Black Enterprise, June 25, 1995, p. 100.

JOHN A. HARDIN

Loury, Glenn Cartman (September 3, 1948–), economist. Born in Chicago, Glenn Loury attended Chicago schools and Northwestern University, earning his Ph. D. in economics in 1976. One of the nation's outstanding economists and an expert on black enterprise and equal opportunity, his teaching career includes appointments as Assistant Professor of Economics at Northwestern, 1976–79; Associate Professor and Professor of Economics at the University of Michigan, 1979–82; and Professor at the John F. Kennedy School of Government, Harvard University from 1982 to 1991. In 1991 he moved to Boston University, becoming a Professor in 1994 and director of the Institute on Race and Social Division in 1997.

Loury's many publications in the field of economics have earned him the American Book Award, and the Christianity Today Award (1996). His honors include the Templeton Award for Education in a Free Society in 1997–1998 and the Leavey Award for Excellence in Free Enterprise Education, in 1986. Loury was selected and participated in the February 1983 national meeting of the Board of Economists, convened by *Black Enterprise* magazine.

Loury's many recent publications relating to the study of modern market economics include a wide ranging discussion of entrepreneurship issues: affirmative action, race and responsibility, whether affirmative action policies will eliminate negative stereotypes, and the intergenerational distribution of earnings. In 1995, Loury published *One by One from the Inside Out: Essays and Reviews on Race and Responsibility in America*, in which he puts forth his opinions on topics like the civil rights movement, black-Jewish relations, and political correctness.

See also CLASS AND SOCIETY [2]; CONSERVATISM [2].

REFERENCES

"Black Enterprise Report: Outlook for Black Economic Development." *Black Enterprise*. June 13, 1983: 247–258.

Who's Who Among African Americans, 12th ed. 2000.

DARIUS L. THIEME

Lowndes County Freedom Organization.

In the early spring of 1965 in Lowndes County, Alabama, black activist Stokely Carmichael and other members of the civil rights organization called the Student Nonviolent Coordinating Committee (SNCC) created the Lowndes County Freedom Organization (LCFO). Lowndes County, a rural farming area just south of Montgomery, at that time had a population of fifteen thousand of which over seventy percent were black. However, white supremacy was the cornerstone of law and society, historically enforced by violence and open intimidation. The black population was poor and politically voiceless. As a result of the violent intimidation, none of the blacks in the county was registered to vote in elections thus maintaining the white dominance.

SNCC had devoted considerable energy to registering blacks to vote in the Deep South from 1961 to 1965. In 1964 SNCC created the Mississippi Freedom Democratic Party (MFDP) to represent black voters in the Democratic Party. However, the MFDP failed to gain acceptance at the 1964 Democratic National Convention held in Atlantic City, New Jersey. In reaction to the racism dominant in the Alabama Democratic Party, Carmichael decided the time was right to counter the political domination and create an independent black political party. He believed the drive for racial integration was just another form of white supremacy. Carmichael argued that blacks should speak for themselves, using their own words and ideas, and gain independence in their own communities.

An unusual Alabama state law provided that any group of citizens who nominated candidates for county offices and won at least twenty percent of the vote could be formally recognized as a county political party. Carmichael and SNCC began organizing in several counties, including the mostly black Lowndes County. On May 3, 1965, five new county freedom organizations met to nominate candidates to the offices of sheriff, tax assessor, and school boards.

The LCFO adopted the image of a black panther in contrast to the Alabama Democratic Party's white rooster symbol. The panther symbolized power, dignity, and determination. The determination was soon evident at a May 8 local election when nine hundred of almost two thousand registered black voters in Lowndes County voted despite risking their personal safety. In recognition of the risk involved, the LCFO's saying at the time was "Vote the panther, then go home." The LCFO was successful in electing some black officials.

The LCFO was a landmark organization not only for transforming the goals of civil rights advocates from integration to liberation, but also for introducing the black panther image later adopted by the militant Black Panther organization in Oakland, California. The LCFO represented the growing differences within the civil rights movement over desired goals and how to achieve them. The peaceful civil disobedience tactics of Dr. Martin Luther King, Jr. and the Southern Christian Leadership Conference (SCLC) were increasingly challenged by the more confrontational strategies of SNCC. The SCLC urged blacks in Lowndes County to remain in the Democratic Party and fight for change within the organization. Instead, independent black political activity developed.
See also ALABAMA [1]; CARMICHAEL, STOKELY [1]; STUDENT NONVIOLENT COORDINATING COMMITTEE [5].

REFERENCES

Carmichael, Stokely. "Power and racism: What we want." *Black Scholar* 27 (1997): 52-57. (Reprint of 1966 essay)

Carmichael, Stokely, and Charles V. Hamilton. *Black Power: Politics of Liberation in America*. 1967.

Cone, James H. *Risks of Faith: The Emergence of a Black Theology of Liberation, 1968–1998*. 1999.

Hall, Raymond L. *Black Separatism in the United States*. 1978.

Stanton, Mary. *From Selma to Sorrow: The Life and Death of Viola Liuzzo*. 1998.

RICHARD C. HANES

Lucas, Sam (August 7, 1840–January 10, 1916), entertainer. Sam Lucas was born in Washington, Ohio. His long career as an entertainer runs from minstrel shows to motion pictures. Before the Civil War, he was a barber. He served in the U.S. Army during the war and then became an entertainer. Beginning as a singer and guitar player on passenger steamboats, he soon joined the minstrel shows formed by blacks to compete with those presented by white companies. By 1875 Lucas was enough of a star to publish *Sam Lucas' Plantation Songster*. He was also touring with the very popular Hyers Sisters' company and premiered with them "Grandfather's Clock (Was Too Tall For the Shelf)," a major hit.

Lucas became the first black to play the role of Uncle Tom in a white production in 1878; he repeated this first in 1914 when he was the first black to play the role in a full length motion picture. During the 1880s Lucas formed an act with his wife, the former Carrie Melvin, and seems to have worked mostly out of Boston. Lucas continued to play in vaudeville during the rest of his life, but he also appeared in a series of landmark shows. From late 1899 to early 1901 he appeared in Robert Cole's and Billy Johnson's *A Trip to Coontown*, the first full-length black musical comedy and the first to draw white spectators in large numbers. Ernest Hogan's *Rufus Rastus* (1901), along with Cole and Johnson's *Shoo Fly Regiment* (1906) and *Red Moon* (1909), followed. *See also* MINSTRELS/MINSTRELSY [4]; MUSICAL THEATER [4].

REFERENCES

Johns, Robert L. "Sam Lucas." In *Notable Black American Men*, edited by Jessie Carney Smith. 1999.

Sampson, Henry T. *The Ghost Walks*. 1988.

Southern, Eileen. *Biographical Dictionary of Afro-American and African Musicians*. 1982.

ROBERT L. JOHNS

M

Macarty, Victor-Eugéne (1821–c. 1890), entertainer, politician. Victor-Eugéne Macarty was an amateur actor, singer, pianist and composer, and he also played a prominent role in Reconstruction politics in Louisiana. Macarty was born in New Orleans. His mother was a placée, that is, the recognized mistress of a white man, who at his death in 1840 willed her a substantial amount of property which she was able to build into a small fortune. Her son could pass for white.

Macarty's abilities as a pianist were early recognized, and he was able to study at the Imperial Conservatory in Paris. Returning to New Orleans, he found his talents as a society entertainer in great demand. He had the leads in dramatic productions of the free people of color. In addition to his skills on the piano, he had a fine baritone voice and talent as a comedian. Only a few of his musical compositions survive; among them are the two pieces of *Fleurs de Salon* (1854).

During Reconstruction Macarty played a role both in civil rights and in politics. He brought suit against the St. Charles Theater in 1869 for being denied a seat in the white section of the audience. The manager continued to insist on segregation, and the theater was boycotted until 1875, when a national civil rights law was passed. Beginning with an appointment as administrator of assessments for New Orleans in 1869, Macarty held various other positions under the spon-

sorship of the radical wing of the Republicans. In addition, he was a prosperous businessman.
See also NEW ORLEANS [4].

REFERENCES

Christian, Marcus B. "Victor-Eugéne Macarty." In *Dictionary of American Negro Biography*, edited by Rayford W. Logan and Michael R. Winston. 1982.

Southern, Eileen. *Biographical Dictionary of Afro-American and African Musicians*. 1982.

Trotter, James Monroe. *Music and Some Highly Musical People*. 1878.

ROBERT L. JOHNS

Mahoney, Mary Eliza (May 7, 1845–January 4, 1936), nurse, civil rights activist, suffragist. Mahoney was born in the Dorchester section of Boston and grew up in Roxbury. Interested in nursing as a career, she sought employment at the New England Hospital for Women and Children. She cooked and cleaned the facility until she was accepted as a student nurse in 1878.

The hospital took pride in its integrated patient population, as did the training component, the School of Nursing. Mahoney completed her training on August 1, 1879, and became the first African American professional nurse in the United States. She registered with the Nurses Directory at the Massachusetts Medical Library in search of private duty

Mary E.P. Mahoney. (Fisk University Library)

Wynton Marsalis. (AP/Wide World Photos)

work. Although she was identified as "colored," families who wanted to employ her constantly sought her out.

When the Nurses Associated Alumni of the United States and Canada was organized in 1896, Mahoney was one of its few African American members. The organization later became the American Nurses Association. In 1908 Mahoney supported Martha Franklin to organize the National Association of Colored Graduate Nurses (NACGN). That same year she moved to New York to head the Howard Orphan Asylum for Black Children located in Kings Park.

Mahoney's concern for the plight of women transcended the nursing profession; she was known also for her work as a suffragist. When she was seventy-six years old, in 1921, she was among the first women in her city to register to vote. In 1936, the NACGN gave her a lasting tribute by establishing an award in her name to recognize distinguished African American nurses. Although the ANA and the NACGN merged in 1951, the award has been preserved.
See also NURSING [4].

REFERENCES

Carnegie, M. E. *The Path We Tread*. 1986.

Hine, Darlene Clark. *Black Women in America*. 1993.

Smith, Jessie Carney, ed. *Notable Black American Women*, 1992.

JESSIE CARNEY SMITH

Marsalis, Wynton (Update) (October 18, 1961–), jazz trumpeter and composer. During the 1990s, Wynton Marsalis built the Lincoln Center jazz program into the most prestigious center for jazz in the United States, although he faced frequent complaints that he concentrated on playing the music of a small canon of jazz greats and ignored the contributions of white jazz musicians. Marsalis also composed several pieces, including *In My Father's House* (1995) and *Blood on the Fields* (1996), for which he was awarded the Pulitzer Prize in 1997, as well as several adaptations of the music of his hero Duke Ellington, including *Harlem* (1999).

In March 2000, Marsalis was a recipient of a Black History Makers Award from the Associated Black Charities of New York. He also continued his prodigious release schedule, with six new titles in 1999, including a seven-disc set of live performances from the famed Village Vanguard club in New York.

REFERENCES

Crouch, Stanley. "Wynton Marsalis: 1987." *Downbeat* 54, no. 11 (1987): 17-19.

Giddins, Gary. "Wynton Marsalis and Other Neoclassical Lions." In *Rhythm-a-ning*. 1985: 156-161.

"Wynton Marsalis." In *Notable Black American Men*. 1998.

EDDIE S. MEADOWS
UPDATED BY GREG ROBINSON

Marshall, Thurgood (Update) (July 2, 1908–January 24, 1993), civil rights lawyer, associate justice of U. S. Supreme Court.

Marshall died on January 24, 1993. His extraordinary contributions to American life were memorialized in an outpouring of popular grief and adulation greater than that expressed for any previous justice. Marshall has been the object of some controversy since his death. Immediately after Marshall's death, a public debate opened over Marshall's instructions regarding his confidential Supreme Court papers. Ultimately, the Library of Congress opened them to public access without restriction. In 1996, newly uncovered documents demonstrated that Marshall had passed secret information to FBI Director J. Edgar Hoover during his years at the National Association for the Advancement of Colored People. These developments have not detracted from Marshall's heroic position in American history, in tribute to which he was honored by the erection of a statue in his native Baltimore in 1995.

REFERENCES

Bland, Randall W. *Private Pressure on Public Law: The Legal Career of Justice Thurgood Marshall*. 1973.

Thurgood Marshall. (Corbis Corporation)

Kluger, Richard. *Simple Justice: The History of Brown v. Board of Education and Black America's Struggle for Equality*. 1977.

Rowan, Carl. *Dream Makers, Dream Breakers: The World of Justice Thurgood Marshall*. 1993.

Williams, Juan. *Thurgood Marshall*. 1998.

RANDALL KENNEDY
UPDATED BY GREG ROBINSON

Martin, Louis Emanuel (November 18, 1912–January 27, 1997), journalist, politician.

Though unknown to Americans at large, Louis E. Martin was known in Washington corridors of power as "the godfather of black politics." He also left a considerable legacy in the world of print journalism, having served as editor at large black newspapers, the *Chicago Defender* and the *Michigan Chronicle*.

Martin was born in Shelbyville, Tennessee, the son of a Cuban doctor and his American wife, who moved the family to Savannah, Georgia. In Savannah Martin met Gertrude Scott, the woman who would later become his wife (they married in 1937) of 60 years. Martin got his B.A. in journalism from the University of Michigan in 1934. In 1936 he landed a job as a reporter at the *Chicago Defender*. A year later he moved to Detroit to become the first editor and publisher of the *Michigan Chronicle*, where he spent the next 11 years. During that time, Martin became a Democrat and began using the newspaper to urge its black readership to vote Democratic. In 1942 he was elected to the Wayne County Board of Supervisors, and in 1944 he served as assistant publicity director for the Democratic National Committee. He was also a founding member of the National Newspaper Publishers Association, a group comprised of black publishers. In 1947 he returned to the *Chicago Defender*, this time as editor-in-chief. He stayed in that position for the next 12 years.

Martin's political career began in earnest when he was recruited by R. Sargent Shriver to work in the 1960 presidential campaign of Shriver's brother-in-law, John F. Kennedy. Martin played a role in convincing Kennedy to place a sympathy call to Coretta Scott King after her husband, the Reverend Martin Luther King, Jr., was arrested in Atlanta on a traffic violation. The phone call received national press attention and was considered a key to the large black voter turnout that tipped the scales in Kennedy's favor. Kennedy showed his appreciation the next year by naming Martin deputy chairman of the Democratic National Committee, a post he held until 1969. Martin became a trusted political advisor to both Kennedy and his White House successor, Lyndon B. Johnson. He also used his position to push for the appointment of more blacks to high-level posts. Chiefly, he was instrumental in Johnson's naming Robert Weaver as secretary of the newly-created Department of Housing and Urban Development in 1966, the first black cabinet official in U.S. history.

In 1969 Martin returned to publishing as a vice president and editorial director of Sengstacke Newspapers, the parent group of the *Chicago Defender*. In 1978, when President Jimmy Carter called, Martin left publishing once gain to serve in the nation's capital. Following the end of the Carter administration in 1981, Martin stayed in the D.C. area to become the assistant vice president for communications at Howard University, where he remained until 1987. Also beginning in 1981, Martin became chairman of the board of Calmar Communications, a public relations firm founded by his wife and her sister. After a stroke in 1988, Martin and his wife moved to the sunnier climate of Diamond Bar, California, in 1990. In addition to continuing his Calmar duties, Martin contributed weekly columns to the *Chicago Defender* from 1987 until his death in 1997.
See also TENNESSEE [5].

REFERENCES

Lewis, Niel A. "Louis E. Martin, 84, Aide to 3 Democratic Presidents." *New York Times*, January 30, 1997. D21.

Phelps, Shirelle, ed. *Contemporary Black Biography*. 1997.

Who's Who in America. 1980.

KEVIN C. KRETSCHMER

Mayors (Update).

Mayors (Update). By 1993, white mayors had succeeded blacks in the nation's four largest cities — New York City, Los Angeles, Chicago, and Philadelphia. That year, following a shift of fewer than 100,000 votes, New York Mayor DAVID DINKINS lost a close mayoral race, becoming the firstbig-city black mayor to fail to be reelected. The negative trend continued in the mid-1990s. Although in 1995 Lee Brown became the first black mayor of Houston, and Ron Kirk became Dallas's first African-American mayor, the heavily black city of Gary, Indiana, elected a white mayor that year, and white mayors took power following the departure of black mayors in Seattle in

1998 and Oakland in 1999. Despite the setbacks, the office of mayor continues to be a main focus of black political aspiration, and African Americans have established themselves as solid, responsible chief executives in cities in every part of the country.

REFERENCES

Browning, Rufus, ed. *Racial Politics in American Cities*. 1990.

Moss, Larry Edward. *Black Political Ascendancy in Urban Centers, and Black Control of the Local Police*. 1977.

GREG ROBINSON

McAfee, Charles

McAfee, Charles (December 25, 1932–), architect. Charles McAfee was born in Los Angeles and grew up in Wichita, Kansas. He was a corporal in the U.S. Army in 1953–55, and then graduated from the University of Nebraska with a bachelor's degree in architecture in 1958.

After college, Charles McAfee turned down an offer to work in Los Angeles with his mentor, black architect Paul Revere Williams. Instead, he opened his own business in downtown Wichita, now known as Charles F. McAfee, Architecture, Engineering, Planning and Interiors. Among his designs are the *Wichita Eagle-Beacon* building (annex) in 1969, and the multiple award-winning McKnight Art Center on the campus of Wichita State University.

Expanding his business, McAfee opened an Atlanta office in 1974. His first assignment there was to plan a $35 million rapid-rail station. McAfee's daughter Cheryl worked with her father's firm in Wichita for eleven years before moving to Atlanta in 1992 to become president of the branch office. She also had responsibility to oversee the planning, design and construction of over thirty-two sports projects for the Olympic construction project. The Atlanta office manages the conversion of thirty-three sites to post-game use.

Another daughter, Charyl, manages McAfee offices in Dallas and Oklahoma City. McAfee's firm, under contract with the Federal Aviation Administration, has designed seventy buildings across the country. McAfee projects are found in all fifty states. The company expanded again in 1994 to include McAfee Manufacturing Company, maker of modular, affordable, factory-built housing. It is said to be the only company that builds modular homes designed for urban use.
See also KANSAS [3]; LOS ANGELES [3].

REFERENCES

"Top Women Architects" *Ebony 50* (August 1995): pp. 54-58.

Russell, Dick. *Black Genius and the American Experience*. 1998.

Who's Who Among African Americans, 12th ed. 1999.

JESSIE CARNEY SMITH

McCall, H. Carl

McCall, H. Carl (c. 1935–), government official. H. Carl McCall, the first black statewide-elected official in New York, was born in Boston. He was educated at Dartmouth College and attended classes at the University of Edinburgh in Scotland. In 1961, after receiving a Master of Divinity degree from Andover-Newton Theological Seminary, McCall was ordained a minister in the United Church of Christ and was named to head the Blue Hill Protestant Center in New York. During the 1960s and early 1970s, McCall worked as a minister and community activist with the Taconic Foundation and the New York City Council Against Poverty. In 1974, McCall was elected to the New York State Senate, where he served for five years. In 1979, President Jimmy Carter appointed McCall ambassador for special political affairs to the United Nations. Following his resignation in 1981, McCall was briefly a vice president at WNET-TV. In 1982, he ran unsuccessfully as the Liberal candidate for Lieutenant Governor. He there-

after served for three years as chair of the New York City board of education, and also served on the boards of the Port Authority and the New York City Human Rights Administration.

In 1985, McCall left public service and joined Citicorp/ Citibank as a vice president. There he combined fiscal expertise with social reform. In 1993, New York State Comptroller Edward Regan resigned, and Governor Mario Cuomo appointed McCall to the post. He subsequently won election in his own right in 1994 and 1998. As Comptroller, McCall has joined with African-American institutions such as Carver Bank to invest New York's funds in ways likely to promote economic development in minority communities.
See also BOSTON [1]; NEW YORK [4].

REFERENCE

Who's Who Among African Americans, 12th ed. 1999.

GREG ROBINSON

McClellan, George Marion

McClellan, George Marion (September 29, 1860–May 17, 1934), poet, short story writer. He was born in Belfast, Tennessee, and graduated from Fisk University in 1885. After three years of study at Hartford Theological Seminary, he became a Congregational minister in Louisville, Kentucky. He earned an M.A. from Fisk in 1890 and finished his B.D. degree at Hartford in 1891. After serving as a fiscal agent for Fisk in 1892–1894, as teacher and chaplain at State Normal School in Normal, Alabama, in 1894–1896, and as minister in Memphis in 1897–1899, McClellan became a teacher and later principal in the Louisville public schools. He visited Los Angles in search of treatment for his son, who died of tuberculosis in 1917. McClellan himself moved to Los Angeles in 1924 and later died there.

McClellan published *Poems* in 1895–the work also included five prose pieces. A critic has labeled the work "genteel sentimentalism." McClellan had a chance to present his views on African American literature in an essay, "The Negro As Writer," published in *Twentieth Century Negro Literature* in 1902. He extended his range somewhat beyond the genteel, assimilationist tradition in *Old Greenbottom Inn*, a collection of five short stories which appeared in 1906. The title story deals with an interracial love affair with tragic consequences. In his final verse collection, *The Path of Dreams* (1916), only ten of the forty-six poems

H. Carl McCall. (AP/Wide World Photos)

are new. Five short stories are also included, but only one is new. In spite of demonstrations of increased technical skill in the new work, McClellan remains interesting more as a representative author than as an original one.

See also LITERATURE [3]; TENNESSEE [5].

REFERENCES

Bruce, Dickson D., Jr. "George Marion McClellan." In *Afro-American Writers Before the Harlem Renaissance*, edited by Trudier Harris. 1986.

Culp, D. W. *Twentieth Century Negro Literature*. 1902.

Rush, Theressa Gunnels, Carol Fairbanks Myers, and Esther Spring Arata. *Black American Writers Past and Present*. 1975.

ROBERT L. JOHNS

McFerren, Viola Harris (October 31,1931–), civil rights and social activist.

The eleventh of twelve children, Viola H. McFerren was born to Joseph T. and Rose Webb Harris in Michigan City, Mississippi. She received her education in the Benton County, Mississippi, and Fayette County, Tennessee, school systems. Formerly married to John McFerren (married 1950; divorced 1980) and the mother of five children, McFerren later attended Jackson State Community College and Memphis State University.

An unrelenting champion of the right of blacks to exercise their freedom to vote, in 1960 McFerren was one of the organizers of Fayette County's "Tent City," a makeshift community that was formed when hundreds of black tenant farmers who registered to vote were thrown off the land by white property owners. Tent City attracted national attention. By the end of 1960 the U. S. Department of Justice stepped in to ensure that the civil rights of blacks in the West Tennessee county were not violated. A plaintiff in the 1965 school desegregation case, McFerren also intervened in the federal case initiated by black teachers dismissed by the Fayette County Board of Education.

Due to diehard racist attitudes and behaviors directed toward blacks, ranging from police brutality to malevolent treatment from white businesses, in the 1960s McFerren organized a refusal-to-purchase campaign against white merchants. In 1966, President Lyndon Johnson appointed McFerren to the National Advisory Committee, U. S. Office of Economic Opportunity. For her role as a "fearless leader of voter registration, desegregation and equal housing in Fay-

ette County," McFerren was given the Woman of Achievement Award for Heroism in 1992.

See also CIVIL RIGHTS MOVEMENT [2]; MISSISSIPPI [4].

REFERENCES

Hamburger, Robert. *Our Portion of Hell, Fayette County, Tennessee: An Oral Struggle for Civil Rights*. 1973.

Wynn, Linda T. "Toward a Perfect Democracy: The Struggle of African Americans in Fayette County, Tennessee to Fulfill the Unfulfilled Right of the Franchise." *Tennessee Historical Quarterly*. 1996.

Smith, Jessie Carney, ed. *Notable Black American Women*, Book II. 1996.

LINDA T. WYNN

McGhee, Frederick Lamar (1861–September 9, 1912), lawyer, activist.

Frederick Lamar McGhee, a lawyer and activist, was a cofounder of the Niagara Movement, a precursor of the National Association for the Advancement of Colored People. McGhee was born in Aberdeen, Mississippi, to slave parents. He grew up in Knoxville, Tennessee, where his parents moved after the Civil War. His father was a Baptist minister, but McGhee was Roman Catholic as an adult. Orphaned in 1873, he studied at Presbyterian Knoxville College but did not take a degree. Instead, he moved to Chicago and studied law in the office of Edward H. Morris, a prominent African American lawyer. McGee was admitted to the Illinois bar in 1885.

After practicing in Chicago, McGhee moved to St. Paul, Minnesota, in 1889. There he became the first black admitted to the Minnesota Bar and also the first admitted to practice before the state Supreme Court. He established a very successful practice as a trial lawyer, serving an interracial group of clients.

In 1898 McGhee helped revive the Afro-American League, soon renamed the Afro-American Council. For some time he worked in cooperation with Booker T. Washington. McGhee headed the legal department of the council and became financial secretary in 1903, but eventually he found Washington too conciliatory towards whites. In reaction, McGhee joined with W. E. B. Du Bois in founding the Niagara Movement in 1905. Du Bois attributed the initial idea of the movement to McGhee. McGhee was also prominent in the early days of the NAACP and established the first chapter in Minnesota in 1912, shortly before his death from pleurisy.

See also LAWYERS [3]; MINNESOTA [4].

REFERENCES

Contee, Clarence C., Sr. "Frederick L[amar] McGhee." In *Dictionary of American Negro Biography*, edited by Rayford W. Logan and Michael R. Winston. 1982.

Parker, Donna Grear. "Frederick Lamar McGhee." In *American National Biography*, edited by John A. Garraty and Mark C. Carnes. 1999.

ROBERT L. JOHNS

McGirt, James Ephriam (1874–June 12, 1930), poet.

James McGirt, born in Robeson County near Lumberton, North Carolina, felt driven to write. He was educated at a Lumberton private school and became infatuated with three young female schoolmates. However, it was to be an unrequited love, and each became the subject of a love poem.

Later, the family moved to Greensboro, North Carolina, where he resumed his education in the public schools, then enrolled in Bennett College (1892–1895). Upon graduation, McGirt worked as a manual laborer and pursued publication of his poetry; he published his first volume of poetry in 1899, *Avenging the Maine and Other Poems* and the second, *Some Simple Songs and a Few More Ambitious Attempts* in 1901, a re-working of the first volume.

When he failed to achieve success as a poet, he moved to Philadelphia and began to edit and publish *McGirt's Magazine* (monthly September 1903–August 1908; quarterly 1909), an illustrated magazine devoted to art, science, literature, and topics of general interest to a black audience. The magazine also allowed him space for his own work. As the magazine grew, McGirt relocated and merged the magazine and all its properties into McGirt Publishing, and sold stock in the new venture. In 1905 he published another volume of poetry, *For Your Sweet Sake*, which was followed in 1907 by a volume of short stories, *The Triumphs of Ephriam*. The publishing company failed in 1909, and McGirt returned to Greensboro, where he took over a family business (Star Hair Grower Manufacturing Company, a cosmetics business) which, like the enterprise in Philadelphia, was the source of employment for many black workers. During the period following his publishing company's collapse, he also worked as a realtor.

See also NORTH CAROLINA [4].

REFERENCES

Logan, Rayford W., and Michael R. Winston, eds. *Dictionary of American Negro Biography*. 1982.

Packer, John W. "James Ephraim McGirt: Poet of Hope Deferred." *North Carolina Historical Review* 31 (July 1954): 320-35.

Sherman, John R. *Invisible Poets: Afro-Americans of the Nineteenth Century*. 1974.

HELEN R. HOUSTON

McHenry, Donald F. (October 13, 1936–), United Nations ambassador.

Born in St. Louis, McHenry grew up in an impoverished neighborhood in East St. Louis, Illinois, and graduated from Illinois State University in 1957. He received his master's degree from Southern Illinois University in 1959 and then became English instructor at Howard University. He studied international relations at Georgetown University. McHenry joined the Department of State as foreign affairs officer in the Dependent Areas Section, Office of U.N. Political Affairs (1963–1966). He briefly served as assistant to the Secretary of State, then in 1968–1969 he acted as special assistant to the counselor of the Department of State.

The Brookings Institute invited McHenry to be guest scholar (1971–1973), during which time he also was a lecturer at Georgetown University. Then he was director of humanitarian policy studies at the Carnegie Endowment for International Peace (1973–1977) and lectured at American University in 1975.

President Carter named McHenry deputy representative in the U.N. Security Council. He and his friend, U.N. Ambassador Andrew Young, established a good relationship and complemented each other at the U.N. From 1978 to 1979, McHenry worked with Angola to strengthen its relationship with the United States and brought an end to negotiations on a U.N. plan for Namibia independence. McHenry was chief U.S. negotiator for other U.N. plans involving South Africa.

After Young resigned under pressure on August 15, 1979, McHenry was sworn in the following month as permanent representative to the U.N. and representative in the Security Council. He left in 1981, after which he was a Distinguished Professor at Georgetown and president of the IRC Group.

See also AMBASSADORS AND DIPLOMATS [1]; ST. LOUIS, MISSOURI [5].

REFERENCES

Current Biography Yearbook. 1980.

Who's Who Among African Americans, 12th ed. 1999.

JESSIE CARNEY SMITH

McJunkin, George (1851–1922), cowboy. He made a significant paleontological discovery by finding the partially fossilized bones of an extinct species of bison. McJunkin was born a slave on a ranch near Midway, Texas. George McJunkin is said to have acquired about four years of schooling, but he had a sharp mind and keen sense of observation. At seventeen he joined a cattle drive and then worked for a number of outfits before he ended up in the Cimarron valley in northeastern New Mexico. There he won a place for himself in the community where he spent the rrest of his life.

McJunkin earned the reputation of being one of the top cowboys in the county and became foreman of the Crowfoot Ranch, near Folsom, New Mexico. His interest, however, was caught by science, and he kept a small library of books in his room. Thus, he was prepared to recognize the bones he found about 1906 as being significantly different from normal cow or bison bones. Although he talked often of the bones and tried to get an expert to examine them, no one looked at them while he was living. McJunkin had no family, and his cabin burned down after being struck by lightning. He died in the Folsom Hotel nursed by friends who read the Bible to him and saw that he was supplied with bootleg whiskey.

In 1926 the bones were finally examined; more importantly arrowheads associated with the finds proved the presence of human populations in North America several thousand years earlier than previous believed.
See also NEW MEXICO [4]; WEST, BLACK IN THE [5].

REFERENCES

Germond, Mary F. "George McJunkin." In *Dictionary of American Negro Biography*, edited by Rayford W. Logan and Michael R. Winston. 1982.

Preston, Douglas. "Journal: Fossils and the Folsom Cowboy." *Natural History*, February 1997.

ROBERT L. JOHNS

McKinney, Cynthia Ann (March 15, 1955–), U.S. Congresswoman. McKinney was born in Atlanta and educated at the University of Southern California, where she earned a bachelor's degree in 1978, and at Fletcher School of Law and Diplomacy of Tufts University.

Following graduation from college, McKinney was exposed to the painful sting of racism. On a trip with her father to Alabama to protest the conviction of

Cynthia McKinney. (Public domain, source unknown)

Tommy Lee Hines, a retarded black man accused of a sexual attack on a white woman, Ku Klux Klan members threatened her. The National Guard settled the disturbance at the event. She decided then that she would enter politics.

McKinney was a diplomatic fellow at Spelman College in 1984. From 1988 to 1992, she taught at Clark Atlanta University and Agnes Scott College. Her career in politics began in 1988, when she was elected as an at-large member to the Georgia State House of Representatives. Her father, Billy McKinney, was already a member of the legislature and the two became the only father-daughter team in a state legislature. McKinney was elected to Congress in 1992, where she quickly made a reputation as an outspoken, liberal crusader for the poor and rural citizens of her state. She gained notoriety with vehement arguments against Republicans on such issues as abortion.

McKinney's Congressional district was redrawn prior to the 1996 election after being ruled unconstitutional, eliminating the black voter majority McKinney had enjoyed in her previous election wins. An overwhelmingly negative campaign between McKinney and her white Republican opponent followed, but McKinney won re-election for a third term, proving that a black liberal candidate could win in a white majority district.

See also ATLANTA, GEORGIA [1].

REFERENCES

"Cynthia A. McKinney." http://clerkweb.house.gov/womenbio/BIO/mckinney.htm

Mabunda, L. Mpho, and Shirelle Phelps, eds. *Contemporary Black Biography*, vol. 11. 1996.

Who's Who Among African Americans, 12th ed. 1999.

RAYMOND WINBUSH

McMillan, Terry (Update)

McMillan, Terry (Update) (October 18, 1951–), novelist and short story writer. McMillan's third novel, *Waiting to Exhale* (1992), became a bestseller within the first week of its release. Though this novel deals with many African-American themes, McMillan's treatment of male-female relationships in a gripping narrative ensures a wide readership. The novel centers on the friendships among four African-American women in Phoenix, Ariz., and how each of them looks for and hides from love. McMillan's tough, sexy style clearly has a wide appeal; the paperback rights for *Waiting to Exhale* were auctioned in the sixth week of its hardcover publication for $2.64 million. McMillan's next book, *How Stella Got Her Groove Back* (1996) also quickly became a bestseller. The work deals with the revitalization of a black woman through her affair with a young West Indian

man she meets while on vacation. During the 1990s, both *Waiting to Exhale* and *How Stella Got Her Groove Back* were turned into hit movies, whose success at the box office demonstrated both strong appeal to black (especially female) viewers and a sizable crossover to white audiences. The acclaim received by these film adaptations not only fueled McMillan's sales and popularity but also provided vital employment opportunity for African-American casts and directors.

Nevertheless, the commercial success of *Waiting to Exhale* and *How Stella Got Her Groove Back* has confirmed for some critics the belief that McMillan is more a writer of potboilers than she is a serious novelist. But McMillan, who lives in the San Francisco Bay area, hopes her success will open doors for other African-American writers. To this end, in 1991 McMillan edited *Breaking Ice: An Anthology of Contemporary African-American Fiction*, which includes short stories and book excerpts by fifty-seven African-American writers, ranging from well-known to new voices.

REFERENCES

Awkward, Michael. "Chronicling Everyday Travails and Triumphs." *Callaloo* 2, no. 3 (Summer 1988): 649–650.

Edwards, Audrey. "Terry McMillan: Waiting to Inhale." *Essence* (October 1992): 77-78, 82, 118.

AMRITJIT SINGH
UPDATED BY GREG ROBINSON

McWorter, Frank

McWorter, Frank. *See* Frank, Free.

Terry McMillan. (Corbis Corporation)

Meek, Carrie P.

Meek, Carrie P. (April 29, 1926–), educator, U.S. Congresswoman. The granddaughter of a slave and the daughter of a sharecropper and a domestic, Carrie Meek was born in Tallahassee, Florida. She graduated from Florida A & M University with a B.S. degree in 1956. In 1948 Meek received her M.S. degree from the University of Michigan and later studied at Florida Atlantic University.

Meek began a teaching career at Bethune-Cookman College from 1949 to 1958. She moved to Florida A & M University for the next three years (1958–1961). She was women's basketball coach at both institutions. After teaching at Miami-Dade Community College from 1961 to 1968, Meek moved into administrative posts, as associate dean for community services and assistant to the president (1968–1979) and as special assistant to the vice president beginning 1982.

Carrie Meek. (The Gamma Liaison Network)

In the 1960s and 1970s, Meek became acquainted with the inequity in federally funded programs for blacks in Dade County and concluded that only the government could correct the problems. In 1979, with encouragement, she ran for a seat in the Florida House of Representatives and won; she was reelected in 1980. Meek was so popular in her senatorial district that she decided to run for Congress in 1992, representing the 17th District. Meek won by a staggering margin. A 67-year-old grandmother, she became the first African American woman since Reconstruction to be elected to Congress from Florida. Her record in Congress is impressive: she served on the House Appropriations Committee, drafted a bill to ease restrictions on Haitian refugees, and advised President Clinton as he worked to reduce the budget deficit without cutting social welfare programs.
See also FLORIDA [2].

REFERENCES

Bigelow, Barbara Carlisle, ed. *Contemporary Black Biography*. 1992.

Smith, Jessie Carney, ed. *Notable Black American Women*. 1996.

RAYMOND WINBUSH

Memphis, Tennessee (Update). Memphis, Tennessee, located on a bluff overlooking the Mississippi River, received its first African-American settler shortly after its founding in 1819. Its early black population was largely free, and Shelby County's state representatives opposed slavery. African Americans worked as domestics, stevedores, draymen, blacksmiths, and artisans.

Following the 1987 election, black union leader James Smith called for a leadership summit before the next mayoral election. In the Spring of 1991, two "unity conferences" were held, one at the grassroots level led by City Councilman Shep Wilbun and one at the leadership level led by congressman Harold Ford. The result was a consensus black candidate, W. W. Herenton, and the Herenton campaign succeeded in uniting the various black elite and mass groups under the banner of an uncompromising black political crusade. For the Memphis African-American community, Herenton's election as the city's first African-American mayor marked a high point in a political struggle that had spanned generations. Soon, blacks would regularly hold a majority of the seats on the city's school board and city council.

Yet, despite political victories, the city's commerce and service-oriented economy has offered African Americans far more low-wage positions than higher paying ones. This has left Memphis with arguably the poorest black underclass of any large U.S. city. As the 20th century drew to a close, despite the federal "War on Poverty," more than a third of that population was still impoverished; and as for the intensity of the poverty, six census tracts had a median household income below $5,500, while three zip codes had median household incomes below $6,500. Consequently, a sizable number of black Memphian have ended up disproportionately poor, disillusioned and militant, as well as suspicious of political leaders, including many of their own black leaders.

Lastly, the emphasis on electoral politics should not obscure the amount of "direct action" that has occurred in the streets of Memphis. Educator Ida B. Wells led protests against segregation and lynchings, and even proceeded to take her message worldwide. Businessman Bert Roddy headed the first Memphis branch of the NAACP; and subsequently led by the likes of Kesse Turner and Maxine Smith, they would be at the forefront of much of this resistance. In 1960, for example, a sizable number of student sit-ins appeared and a boycott was launched against downtown retailers. A major sanitation workers' strike occurred in 1968, while the police, firefighters and teachers would walk the picket lines tens years later. Meanwhile, public protests against police brutality began in the 19ty century and continue to this day.

REFERENCES

Biles, Roger. *Memphis in the Great Depression.* 1986.

Capers, Gerald. *The Biography of a River Town.* 1966.

Crawford, Charles. *Yesterday's Memphis.* 1976.

Jalenak, James. *Beale Street Politics.* 1961.

Lamon, Lester. *Blacks in Tennessee, 1791–1970.* 1981.

Lee, George. *Beale Street, Where the Blues Began.* 1969.

McKee, Margaret. *Beale Black and Blue.* 1961.

Miller, William. *Marcus D. Pohlmann Mr. Crump of Memphis.* 1964.

Pohlmann, Marcus and Michael Kirby. *Marcus D. Pohlmann Racial Politics at the Cossroads.* 1996.

Sigafoos, Robert. *Cotton Row to Beale Street.* 1979.

Tucker, David. *Memphis Since Crump.* 1980.

Wright, William. *Memphis Politics.* 1962.

MARCUS D. POHLMANN

Métoyer, Louis

Métoyer, Louis (c. 1770–March 11, 1832), plantation owner. Louis Métoyer was the second son of Marie-Thérèse, aka "Coincoin," and Claude Thomas Pierre Métoyer. Louis received his freedom on May 28, 1802, although the community seems to have considered him free long before this date. Tradition says he received the grant of land that became the foundation of the Melrose plantation in 1796. The grant of 912 acres may have been to his mother, but by 1813 Louis Métoyer is recorded as the owner.

Much of the interest in the Melrose rises from the fact that the preservation of the original buildings and gardens makes it a unique example of the life of a group of rich rural free people of color. Six more houses of the same grandeur survived into the twentieth century before being destroyed.

Yucca, the original main residence and later a slave hospital, is dated 1796–1800. The design of this building and that of the African House (c.1800), slave fort and provision house, are variously attributed to Marie-Thérèse and Louis Métoyer. The construction of the big house belongs to Louis; it was built by Serafin Llorens. Métoyer was also a generous contributor to the construction of the Chapel of Saint Augustine (1829).

Métoyer married a woman of Native American heritage in 1801. He built up his estate by frugality and hard work. By 1810 he owned fifteen slaves, and his prosperity continued to increase. Melrose passed to Louis Métoyer son, Thélophile Lewis, but Thélophile lost ownership in 1846. Melrose is now a National Historic Site.

See also ARCHITECTURE [1]; BANKING [1]; ENTREPRENEURS [2]; INTELLECTUAL LIFE [3]; METOYER, MARIE THERESE [3].

REFERENCES

Mills, Gary B. *The Forgotten People: Cane River's Creoles of Color.* 1976.

Spivey, Christine. "Early Success of the Métoyer Gens de Coleur [sic] Libre." *The Student Historical Journal 1995–1996.* [Loyola University New Orleans.] http://www.loyno.edu/~history/journal/1995–6/spivey.htm Accessed May 17, 2000.

ROBERT L. JOHNS

Métoyer, Marie-Thérèse [Coincoin]

Métoyer, Marie-Thérése [Coincoin] (1742–1816), freed slave, landowner. Marie-Thérése Métoyer was a freed slave, who established a wealthy and cohesive family group of free people of color. (In Louisiana, the *gens de couleur libres* were often considered a separate group-neither black nor white.) The woman baptized as Marie-Thérése at her birth at Natchitoches, Louisiana, is now perhaps better known by the name given by her African-born parents, Coincoin (Second Daughter).

Coincoin had already borne five children when she was rented as a housekeeper to Claude Thomas Pierre Métoyer. To Métoyer she bore ten children. In 1778, under pressure to end the alliance, Métoyer finally purchased Coincoin and the child at her breast, giving them their freedom. Nonetheless, the liaison continued. When Métoyer took a legal wife in 1786, he gave Coincoin a small plot of land and an annuity. She then displayed great determination and acumen in building up a fortune of her own. She used her money over the years to buy her children's freedom.

In 1794 she qualified for a 640 acre land grant from the Spanish government, the first major step in building up her landholdings. By her death in 1816, Coincoin had added even more land to her original grant. She also owned sixteen slaves.

Coincoin's children followed their mother's example of hard work and good management to build the family's wealth. Some of her descendants still live on family land, and Melrose Plantation, the major surviving estate grounds, is a National Historical Monument.

See also ENTREPRENEURS [2].

REFERENCES

Mills, Gary B. "Coincoin." In *Black Women in America: An Historical Encyclopedia*, edited by Darlene Clark Hine. 1993.

Mills, Gary B. *The Forgotten People: Cane River's Creoles of Color.* 1976.

Spivey, Christine. "Early Success of the Métoyer Gens de Coleur [sic] Libre." *The Student Historical Journal 1995–1996*. http://www.loyno.edu/~history/journal/1995–6/spivey.htm

ROBERT L. JOHNS

Mexico (Update).

During the early colonial period New Spain, or Mexico, played a significant role in defining the African-American experience. For about a century beginning in 1521 more black slaves disembarked at the colony's port of Veracruz than at any place else on the American mainland. Once in Mexico the African-American population was dispersed throughout the viceroyalty instead of being confined to coastal regions. In an environmentally varied area like Mexico with correspondingly parochial living conditions and lifestyles, this dispersion resulted in multiple African-American experiences.

Moreover, because of New Spain's material and human resources, all Europe considered it the model colony, especially during the sixteenth and early seventeenth centuries. When Old World settlers moved into other mainland American areas they often tried to emulate precedents set in Mexico or set in the Caribbean and maintained in Mexico. Antecedents involving Afro-Mexicans proved no exception to this general rule. And Mexico's multiple regional experiences provided viable sets of precedents for many settings in the Americas. Thus Mexico served as an important early colonial proving ground for the varied and broader black economic, social, and political experiences that sprang up throughout the post-1521 Western Hemisphere.

Sweeping impersonal structural conditions dictated Mexico's heavy involvement in the Atlantic slave trade. Silver production exploded within the northern zones of the colony after 1546 with the discovery of rich veins of ore from Zacatecas to Parral and the implementation of European mining techniques. This came on the heels of a dramatic decline in the native Indian populations due to the introduction of such European diseases as smallpox, bubonic plague, measles, and a host of respiratory maladies for which the indigenous population had little natural defense.

Many scholars estimate that the viceroyalty lost over 70 percent of its Indian population between 1543 and 1610 alone. Faced with a demographic crisis at a time when the area's colonial economy had just begun rapidly to expand, Spaniards opted to import large numbers of African slaves. Iberians had resorted to this strategy during the depopulation of their Caribbean island possessions about a half century earlier. Black slaves would ensure against a potential labor shortage at this critical stage in New Spain's colonial economic growth.

Over 100,000 Africans contributed their labor to the material development of Mexico. The period of heaviest importation lasted from about 1570 to 1620. Growth in Mexico's silver and sugar industries, as well as the rise of Spanish-American cities, created demand for slave workers and the capital to pay for them as well.

Concurrent events in Europe and Africa made it easier to meet Mexico's demand for slaves. Between 1580 and 1640 Portugal came under Spanish rule. This gave Spaniards access to the machinery of the Portuguese slave trade that had grown up along the west coast of Africa during the two previous centuries. At the same time this Spanish control created friction among both Europeans and their respective African allies.

Eventually this friction erupted into violence in the form of the so-called Angolan wars, which raged from 1595 to 1624 in the Luanda region of west-central Africa. Resident Portuguese traders on the island of Sao Tome and the Mbundan allies on the adjacent African mainland bristled at heightened Iberian economic and political involvement in the Luanda region and decided to resist militarily. European-based Portuguese and Spaniards, along with their Angolan allies, successfully wore down the malcontents by force of their greater human and material resources. Given the rising need for slaves in the Americas, principally Mexico, the cost of defeat for the Mbundans was enslavement and an Atlantic passage to Veracruz. Indeed, over 80 percent of the African slaves who landed on Mexican shores between 1595 and 1630 came from the war-torn Luanda region of Africa.

Once in Mexico, however, local conditions dominated in shaping the bond persons' experiences.

Spaniards clustered in urban settings. There they employed African slaves as domestic servants. Slave labor contributed to public works projects. Owners rented Africans for day labor. And blacks toiled in ubiquitous *obrajes,* small urban-based textile shops that produced cheap cloth for local consumption by the colony's poor. Craftsmen made apprentices of slaves and assigned native Mexicans less skilled tasks. Professionals such as architects and engineers favored black slaves to execute skilled menial tasks; these Spaniards expected Indians to complete less skilled assignments.

In the countryside black slaves took up positions as skilled workers and livestock husbandmen on the plantations and haciendas that sprang up in many parts of the viceroyalty. They served as blacksmiths, carpenters, and field labor bosses. Some Indians also lived on Spanish estates, but the majority of native workers continued to reside in their own villages. On sugar plantations blacks worked in the oppressively hot and demanding refining houses where temperatures normally topped 100 degrees Fahrenheit, and a mistake could cause loss of product, limb, and life. After 1550 Indians could not legally engage in refining tasks. Whites feared that the harsh working conditions would raise Indian death rates. Finally, black slaves significantly contributed to the skilled labor force within the Mexican mining industry, especially in the refining process.

Africans toiled at occupations that linked the urban and rural dimensions of the Hispanic colonial economy. Slaves disproportionately served in the ranks of the legendary muleteers and itinerant merchants who urged animals along the roads and pathways that linked locales with one another throughout the viceroyalty.

In all these urban and rural occupations African slaves worked alongside Indians, supplementing rather than replacing them as black slaves had on the Caribbean islands during the generation after initial European contact with the islands. Slaves also assumed more skilled and even supervisory positions over Indians because slave laborers proved more fixed and reliable. In response to high native mortality rates Spaniards abolished Indian slavery in 1542. That left only Indian tribute and wage laborers, and the former rotated service to Spanish overlords among individual villagers, while the latter group frequently came and went.

Just as important, Indians died in alarming numbers during the first century of Spanish settlement in Mexico. African slaves provided a much more dependable labor force in both these respects. They generally stayed wherever their masters wanted them to stay, and, previously exposed to Old World diseases, they died no more frequently than Europeans in epidemics that ravaged the colony's indigenous population.

Afro-Mexicans' social experience proved both negative and positive in nature from the perspective of the colony's development. Whites had to control vast numbers of blacks and Indians in a setting thousands of miles removed from Spain at a time when such distances translated into months of travel. For this reason the Europeans required local mechanisms to order subordinate peoples. To meet this need whites developed the *sistema de las castas,* where caste identification was equated with physical racial identification. By primarily dividing blacks, whites, and Indians on the basis of their skin color, and then using these divisions to rank groups within the society, white Spaniards effectively controlled Indians and blacks. This ordering had an inherent logic since whites had conquered Indians and enslaved Africans.

This logic, backed at times by force, eventually compelled both subordinate groups to accept Spaniards' elevated positions of power as the natural order of things. This important social development was then transferred throughout the Americas by colonizers from all over Europe. This concept of social ordering by race made possible the sole association of blacks with slavery in the Americas, an innovation that represented the most negative social heritage that racial pluralism in areas like Mexico left to the modern American societies. Blacks, by their mere presence in New Spain, unwillingly contributed to this precedent.

By 1630 whites realized that Mexico's Indian population decline had ceased. Spaniards no longer saw the need to import expensive African slaves. And from that point onward Mexico steadily withdrew from participation in the Atlantic slave trade. The absence of new African arrivals forced blacks to interact socially with other racial groups within the society. This interaction represented the most positive social contribution that African Americans made to Mexico's social growth. From at least 1630 onward an average of 25 to 35 percent of all Afro-Mexicans crossed racial lines in establishing social ties like marriage, godparenting, and marriage witnessing, three to four times the percentage of whites and five to six times the percentage of Indians.

In this sense Afro-Mexicans worked harder to break down the caste system and slowly create the more ethnically and class-based system that came to dominate Mexican social life from the late nineteenth century to the present. Blacks' association with whites in the initial conquest of the region and, more important, their position within the colonial labor force facilitated racially outgoing social activity.

As expensive skilled slave laborers, Africans and their descendants came into contact with large numbers of Indians in the work place. Under such labor market conditions blacks enjoyed status over more transient Indian workers. This afforded blacks the opportunity to interact not only with the dominant white population but with the Indian population, which was subordinate to blacks, as well. Black males especially took advantage of the social opportunities their labor status afforded them. A high level of miscegenation, or race mixture, occurred as blacks mixed not only with whites but more frequently with Indians. The fact that children from the latter unions followed the station of their Indian mothers and enjoyed freedom from slavery under Spanish law gave black males added incentive to seek these matches.

Extraordinary consequences arose from Afro-Mexicans' somewhat intermediate social position between whites and Indians. With one foot chained in the Spanish world as slaves, and the other striding into the Indian world as co-workers, blacks inevitably provided a link between the Iberian and native communities. In this capacity they played an important role in the racial and cultural amalgamation of Mexican society; they helped lay the foundations for what later scholars labeled *mestizaje.* This racial and cultural amalgamation eventually blurred color and ethnic lines. By 1900, after nearly four centuries of racial miscegenation with whites, Indians, and the racial hybrids that resulted, and after nearly 300 years of cultural isolation from Africa, Afro- Mexicans became physically and culturally nearly indistinguishable from the rest of the Mexican population. By this time they had ceased being Afro-Mexicans and became Mexicans.

Blacks' political life proved perhaps the most uneven dimension of their experience in the Mexican context. Throughout the colonial period whites politically disfranchised their slave and free black counterparts. Laws denied Afro-Mexicans the right to vote or hold political office. Blacks did, however, exert some measure of political influence. As members of local militia companies, many of which were segregated, they often wrested political concessions from whites. Mainly in rural villages along the eastern and western coastal regions, blacks secured relief from onerous tribute payments. These were special taxes that only blacks and Indians were held responsible for paying. As early as the 1630s, and into the early 18th century, black militiamen routinely negotiated release from these fees because they were able to demonstrate their value as soldiers. For example, they repelled minor pirate attacks that were made along the shores of southern and eastern settlement. They participated in quelling Indian uprisings in frontier zones and even protected urban properties amidst periodic tumultuous protests, such as the 1692 grain riots in Mexico City. During all of these episode, colonial officials were struck by the reliability of black militia forces, as opposed to other colonists who frequently shied away from combat situations. But it was a bold pirate raid upon the port of Veracruz in 1680 that truly increased black political capital. The punishing attack, which was one of the worst in Mexican colonial history, exposed the full weaknesses of the defense scheme, revealing that the government could not wholly depend upon white forces to serve as an effective military deterrent. Realizing this, both the number of blacks involved in the military ranks, and their political influence, increased markedly.

By the 1760s, black militia soldiers had garnered not only tribute relief, but had secured selected court immunities, protecting them from prosecution under normal civilian procedure. Over the course of the 18thcentury, the militiamen had also illegally arranged to transfer many of their privileges to civilian family members, including distant aunts and cousins. Consequently, by the 1770s, it was not uncommon to find the black population of entire regions and provinces claiming tribute exemption on the score of a few black militiamen. Meanwhile, their political influence extended into other arenas. Afro-Mexican militiamen, especially those living in rural townships where few whites resided, found themselves recruited as bailiffs, couriers and policemen. As the provincial authorities increasingly came to rely upon these soldiers to run the minute affairs of government, the militiamen utilized their new positions to appeal for land titles, fishing rights, and special farming privileges. When their requests were rebuffed, some threatened to ignite a black rebellion. Others plotted to withhold their military services or stage labor stoppages on provincial plantations and estates.

Black soldiers occasionally forged alliances with rural clergyman to augment their political authority.

The town of Acayucan, located along Mexico's eastern coast, witnessed frequent corroboration between the local priest and the militia in the 1760s, resulting in bitter feuds that divided the town's black population. Successive armed groups of black militiamen raised multiple plots to replace key political figures with men of their own liking. Although the countryside served as home to some of the most visibly active Afro-Mexican political interactions, larger urban centers, such as Merida, Guadalajara, Mexico City and Puebla, did not remain untouched from black political jockeying. The militiamen in these cities played pivotal roles as night patrolmen. Walking beats on the streets yielded numerous opportunities to acquire political influence. However, because of the greater concentration of powerful government officials in these settings, as well as the increased number of whites, the overall political power the militiamen possessed was muted in comparison to the lesser towns and villages of the coastal zones.

A series of military reform efforts initiated by the crown after 1762 slowly eradicated the scope of black privileges and political power in much of the colony. Yet, the constant threat of attack kept a window of political power open for blacks in selected areas even into the early 19th century. For example, in 1768 members of the Afro-Mexican militia company of San Lorenzo de los Negros, Veracruz, won crown approval for the legal incorporation of their village in return for the blacks' services in defending the port of Veracruz from a threatened English attack that never materialized. In the Yucatan, a colony of relatively autonomous black soldiers was founded at the site of San Fernando Ake in the late 1790s. Designed to protect the zone from possible invasion, and comprised of settlers from places as disparate as Santo Domingo, New York, and Senegal, the settlement persisted as a black township into the 1820s.

The political power acquired by blacks through the military helped generate a sense of racial identity. Despite extensive race mixture and cultural contact with whites and Indians. Afro-Mexicans often found the space and time to express themselves as a group. The militia was one arena fro such exchange, but uniquely powerful in that it also offered the support of strong government patrons. Militia interactions were frequently solidified by participation in guilds and all-black religious brotherhoods *(cofradias)*. Therefore, although blacks were key components in fostering Mexican *mestizaje*, they were not neutrally absorbed in the process. They actively shaped the society they were assimilating into, even though the distinctive aspects of their African cultural heritage were becoming more distant.

While the military was one important route for acquiring political power, other Afro-Mexicans exerted political power through illegal action, such as slave rebellion or the foundation of runaway slave communities (palenques) such as Yanga and Coolillo in the present state of Veracruz, Mandinga in eastern Oaxaca, and Cuijla on the Pacific shores of modern Guerrero. In these strongholds they set up their own rival political orders, some with heavy west-African influences. From palenques they exercised political influence over surrounding Indian populations; this political influence competed with the Spanish political order. Blacks threatened Spanish political authority even more directly through revolt. Slave uprisings occurred throughout the colonial period, but they represented the greatest danger in the sixteenth century when black slaves outnumbered white settlers in New Spain. The incidence of revolt remained high throughout the entire three centuries of Spanish rule. For example, the district of Córdoba, Veracruz, experienced five major slave revolts between 1725 and 1768 involving over two thousand bondsmen on each occasion. As Bishop Alonso de la Mota y Escobar put it, "Bad to have them (blacks), but much worse not to have them."

Afro-Mexicans did not receive the right to participate legally in Mexico's political life until after independence. The caste system was outlawed in 1822 and slavery abolished seven years later. Afro-Mexicans bought these concessions with their blood in the struggle to break from Spain. Slaves and free *Afrocastas* (persons of mixed African ancestry) served in disproportionately high numbers among the insurgent ranks in the struggle for independence. Afro-Mexicans were prominently represented in the rebel forces that operated all along the eastern and western coastal regions. José María Morelos and Vicente Guerrero both reportedly had African ancestry. After independence "El negro Guerrero" went on to become the third president of Mexico. During his administration Mexico outlawed slavery. Indeed, he and his Afro-Mexican constituents made up one of the most important factions in the populist Yorkino political upsurge between 1827 and 1829 within the new republic.

By the end of the nineteenth century the African presence in Mexico had all but slipped from the popular mind. Three centuries of extensive miscegenation with Indians and racially mixed individuals had so blurred the groups' physical distinctiveness that they were indistinguishable from the country's "mestizo" majority. And the same chronological separation from west-African cultural influences had all but obliterated the group's cultural identity. Yet this largely forgotten people had made significant contributions to the historical growth of the Mexican nation and by extension the development of the Americas in general.

Mexican slaves during the late sixteenth and early seventeenth centuries provided critical incentive for the institutionalization of the Atlantic slave trade. Successful implementation of African slave labor in New Spain encouraged its use elsewhere. The Caribbean precedent of identifying slavery with the black race alone received critical legitimization within the exemplary Mexican setting.

Afro-Mexicans provided political input during the colonial period through institutions such as the militia, and extralegally through flight and rebellion. They contributed heavily, for their numbers, to the independence struggle with Spain. And they played an important role in increasing popular participation in politics during the first decade after the break with the mother country.

Economically, Africans provided essential labor input into the colonial Mexican economy just as it boomed. Wealth produced in New Spain attracted European settlement in other parts of the Americas. This, in turn, greatly accelerated New World development. The social resistance of blacks to racist and cultural barriers created hybrid racial and ethnic ties between Spaniards and Indians. The resulting racial and cultural mix laid the foundations for modern Mexican society. Other areas of Spanish America like Peru, Bolivia, Colombia, and Ecuador built on this Mexican precedent and forged their national societies in the same manner.

Mexico was the first setting where whites, blacks, and Indians came together in large numbers. Blacks in this setting helped to provide much of the blueprint for the building of modern Latin America and to a lesser degree non-Ibero North America. Columbus may have discovered the New World in 1492, but African Americans in places like Mexico helped to shape it in the centuries that followed.

REFERENCES

Aguirre Beltràn, Gonzalo. *Población negra de México.* 2nd ed. 1972.

Carroll, Patrick J. *Blacks in Colonial Veracruz: Race, Ethnicity, and Regional Development.* 1991.

Chance, John. *Race and Class in Colonial Oaxaca.* 1978.

Curtin, Philip. *The Atlantic Slave Trade.* 1969.

Kilson, Martin, and Robert Rotberg, eds. *The African Diaspora.* 1976.

Miller, Joseph. *Way of Death.* 1988.

Palmer, Colin. *Slave of the White God, 1570–1650.* 1976.

Rout, Leslie B., Jr. *The African Experience in Spanish America, 1502 to the Present.* 1976.

Vinson, III, Ben. *Bearing Arms for His Majesty: The Free-Colored Militia in Colonial Mexico,* 2001.

PATRICK J. CARROLL
UPDATED BY BEN VINSON III

Mfume, Kweisi (October 24, 1948–), U.S. Congressman, civil rights leader, and president of the National Association for the Advancement of Colored People (NAACP). Born Frizzell Gray in Turners Station, Maryland, the eldest of four children, Mfume grew up in a poor community just outside of Baltimore. His mother Mary Willis worked on an assembly line at an airplane parts manufacturer. His abusive stepfather, Clifton Gray, abandoned the family when Mfume was twelve years old. Four years later his mother was diagnosed with cancer and literally died in Mfume's arms. Devastated by his mother's death, Mfume dropped out of high school and began working odd jobs to make ends meet while he and his three sisters lived with relatives. Mfume found that he could make much more money hustling on the streets than shining shoes or pushing bread through a slicer.

By the age of twenty-two his life seemed to have completely spun out of control; he had already fathered five children from four different women, gang life on the streets had became deadly, and a number of his closest friends had been sent back in body bags from Vietnam. Despite these troubles, Mfume resolved to turn his life around. He began taking night GED courses for his high school equivalency degree and then enrolled at Baltimore Community College.

Mfume developed a keen interest in politics in the early 1970s while working as a disc jockey on local radio stations. During this time he changed his name from Frizzell Gray to Kweisi Mfume (a name brought to him by his great aunt, roughly translating from the West African Igbo language as "conquering son of kings").

Kweisi Mfume (second from right) meets with Bill Clinton, Al Gore Jr., and Carol Moseley-Braun, 1993. (AP/Wide World Photos)

In 1976 Mfume graduated magna cum laude with a degree in urban planning from Morgan State University. Two years later he parlayed his growing fame as a talk radio provocateur to win a seat as a maverick Democratic Party member of the Baltimore City Council. Mfume served two terms in the City Council and then went on to graduate school at Johns Hopkins University. He received an M.A. in political science and briefly taught political science and communications at Morgan State University. In 1986 he won the seat of the Seventh Congressional District vacated by his political mentor, the legendary black politician Parren J. Mitchell. Mfume went on to serve five terms in the United States Congress, rising to the position of Chairman of the Congressional Black Caucus (CBC).

By the early 1990s Mfume's relentless campaign to end apartheid earned him the respect and friendship of Nelson Mandela. While having co-sponsored legislation favorable to the development of independent parties in the early 1990s, Mfume remained committed to the Democratic Party as the electoral vehicle for the advancement of African Americans. In 1996 he left Congress to accept the position of president and chief executive officer of the National Association for the Advancement of Colored People (NAACP). As president of the NAACP, Mfume has pursued corporate donations to retire the organization's debt and has worked to recruit younger African Americans to the nation's oldest civil rights organization. The targets he has selected to revitalize the group's civil rights agenda include: the dearth of African Americans in television programming, the Confederate battle flag's 38-year perch on the South Carolina Statehouse, the hotel industry's treatment of black guests, and the costs of gun violence. His autobiography, *No Free Ride: From The Mean Streets To The Mainstream*, details his rich life. *See also* BALTIMORE, MARYLAND [1]; CONGRESSIONAL BLACK CAUCUS [2]; MARYLAND [3]; NATIONAL ASSOCIATION FOR THE ADVANCEMENT OF COLORED PEOPLE (NAACP) [4].

REFERENCES

Mfume, Kweisi. *No Free Ride: From The Mean Streets To The Mainstream*. 1996.

Robinson, Alonford James, Jr. *Africana: The Encyclopedia of the African and African American Experience*. Edited by Kwame Anthony Appiah and Henry Louis Gates, Jr. 1999.

OMAR ALI

Miami, Florida. Blacks have comprised a significant portion of Miami's population from its inception. After the Civil War, black settlements sprang up in Lemon City, a few miles north of what became Miami and in Coconut Grove to the south. Agricultural and railroad expansion brought thousands of blacks to the area in the 1890s.

On July 28, 1896, black men accounted for 162 of the 367 votes to establish Miami. Colored Town arose as a direct outcome of the city's incorporation when land deeds to property within the city limits restricted sales to blacks. A black business and professional community evolved to meet the needs of the residents despite pockets of destitution and a dearth of municipal services.

In 1944, Miami announced its first multiracial group organized to address the problems between blacks and whites. Composed of six blacks and six whites, the Dade County Interracial Committee looked at problems relating to housing, health, and recreation. In the same year, Miami hired its first black police officers. Two years later, they obtained civil service classification. Beginning in 1965, black political activism bore fruit. Blacks were elected to city and county commissions, the county school board, the Florida State House of Representatives and Senate, and as mayors of various cities.

Relations between blacks and Miami's police were rarely friendly. From 1968 to 1980, there were many racial confrontations-almost all involving clashes with city police. Black anger over the inequities and bigotry of the criminal justice system led to a series of racial disturbances. Between July 1970 and January 1979, Dade County met with thirteen eruptions of violence between the races. In May 1980, Dade County experienced its worst riot when an all-white Tampa jury acquitted five white police officers in the beating death of a black motorist. When the rioting ceased, eighteen people (eight whites and ten blacks) were dead, hundreds were arrested, and property damage totaled more than one hundred million dollars. In 1982 and 1989, the city of Miami was rocked again by two major race riots involving the killing of young blacks by Hispanic police officers.

Since 1960, immigrants from Cuba, Haiti, and the Caribbean Basin have affected blacks in the area. American-born blacks' perception of being replaced by these newcomers in the work force led to tensions between the two groups. As Black Miamians move forward in the 21st century, they are more ethnically diverse. They have progressed along the economic, educational, political, and social continuum. *See also* FLORIDA [2]; MIAMI RIOT OF 1980 [4].

REFERENCES

Dunn, Marvin. *Black Miami in the Twentieth Century*. 1997.

Elliott, Joan C. "Carrie Meek," in *Notable Black American Women, Book II*. Smith, Jessie Carney, ed. 1996.

Porter, Bruce and Marvin Dunn. *The Miami Riot of 1980: Crossing the Bounds*, 1984.

LINDA T. WYNN

Military (Update). In the 1990s, African-Americans in the military experienced new visibility, both positive and negative. General Colin Powell, the first African-American to chair the Joint Chiefs of Staff, became a national hero, best-selling author, and widely touted presidential candidate. However, in 1998, Sergeant Gene McKinney, the Army's highest-ranking enlisted man, was court-martialed for sexual harassment. Though acquitted of sexual misconduct, McKinney was convicted of obstructing justice, and he was forced to retire. The same year, following sensational reports of rape and sexual harassment of mostly white female recruits by black drill instructors at the mixed-gender Aberdeen Training Grounds in Maryland, Sergeant Delmar Simpson and Captain Derreck Robertson were among those convicted of crimes.

REFERENCES

MacGregor, Morris J., and Bernard C. Nalty, eds. *Blacks in the United States Armed Forces: Basic Documents*. 13 vols. 1977.

Nalty, Bernard C. *Strength for the Fight: A History of Black Americans in the Military*. 1989.

GREG ROBINSON

Million Man March. In early 1995, Minister Louis Farrakhan (*See also* FARRAKHAN, LOUIS) of the Nation of Islam proposed a Million Man March on Washington for that fall. The organizers described the March as an opportunity for black men to take responsibility for their lives and communities, and to demonstrate their repentance for their mistreatment of black women. In addition, the March was designed to unite blacks and to point up the lack of national action against racial inequality.

Overview of the Million Man March. (Archive Photos)

Even as March organizers, most notably ousted NAACP head Rev. Benjamin F. Chavis Muhammad, began an extensive publicity campaign, many whites and African Americans spoke out against the proposed March. Feminist scholar Angela Davis and Black leader Amiri Baraka led the criticism of the exclusion of black women, while journalist Carl Rowan and scholar Roger Wilkins denounced the whole idea as racially discriminatory. Many blacks whom supported the idealistic goals of the March refused to participate because of its association with Farrakhan and his nationalist, anti-Semitic message, although many blacks who dissented with Farrakhan's views nonetheless decided to participate in the gathering.

On October 16, 1995, the March gathered at the Lincoln Memorial, site of the 1963 March on Washington. Organizers claimed a million blacks participated, although the Park Service counted 400,000. Numerous speakers, including Dorothy Height and the Rev. Jesse Jackson, addressed the crowd. Farrakhan

delivered the climactic address, reminding the marchers, "We are in progress toward a more perfect union." The March stimulated black voter registration and political activism, but its long-term impact is unclear.

See also CHAVIS, BENJAMIN FRANKLIN, JR. "MUHAMMAD" [1]; FARRAKHAN, LOUIS ABDUL [2]; HEIGHT, DOROTHY [3]; LEE, SHELTON JACKSON "SPIKE" [6]; NATION OF ISLAM [4]; PARKS, ROSA LOUISE MCCAULEY [4]; ROWAN, CARL THOMAS [4].

REFERENCE

Davidson, Joe. "March for black men draws thousands to U.S. Capitol; rally's speakers emphasize need for males to take control of own lives." *Wall Street Journal.* October 17, 1995: p. A22.

GREG ROBINSON

Mingo-Jones Advertising Agency. Following his university preparation (B.S., University of Illinois, 1961; M.S. Northwestern University), the majority of Frank Mingo's career was spent in advertising, where he moved swiftly through the ranks with vice presidencies at major advertising agencies. Among his assignments was supervising the $100 million Miller's beer account at McCann Erickson before transferring to the J. Walter Thompson agency. Caroline Jones followed a similar path of apprenticeship. Following her graduation from the University of Michigan, she took a job as a secretary at the J. Walter Thompson agency in 1963. She then entered the firm's copywriters' program, and had successful experiences with both African-American and general market accounts, helping to found a pioneering black advertising agency, Zebra. At this point in time Frank Mingo and Caroline Jones joined forces, founding their own firm in New York City in 1977: The Mingo-Jones Advertising Agency.

The new firm grew rapidly, due to the enterprising talent of its founders, and their commitment to showing African Americans in positive roles as a constituency of the buying public. By 1984, the Mingo-Jones agency had among their clients Hueblein's, Seagrams, the Miller Brewing Company, Goodyear Tire and Rubber, Liggett & Myers, and Westinghouse Electric, as well as the New York regional account for Kentucky Fried Chicken, introducing the award-winning motto "We Do Chicken Right."

The firm's billing grew to more than $60 million, ranking it high on the list of black owned agencies and corporations. In 1987 Caroline Jones left, to establish her own company, Caroline Jones Advertising. In 1989, following the sudden death of Frank Mingo, vice president Sam Chisholm took over the original firm. Frank Mingo was subsequently elected posthumously to the American Advertising Foundation's Hall of Fame.

See also ADVERTISING [1].

REFERENCES

Who's Who Among African Americans, 6th ed., 1990–91. 1990.

Farris, King. The Road Less Traveled By. http://www.utexas.edu/coc/admedium/Spring98_Practitioner/tcf.html

Salzman, Jack, et al, eds. *Encyclopedia of African-American Culture and History*. 1996.

DARIUS L. THIEME

Missouri (Update).

In the 1990's African American Missourians attempt to fully secure the promise of the American dream, like that of African-Americans nationally has its ups and downs. Unemployment and poverty are at an all time low. The number of African Americans finishing high school has climbed over the past decade, and the number of African Americans, who have completed at least four years of college has increased in 1990's. The gap, however, between whites and African-America income persist. The percent of African Americans in poverty is twice that of whites, and the same is true of the unemployment rate. The median income for a Black household is $15,000 less than for a white household. In 1998 in education the percentage of African-Americans and whites twenty-five years and older who completed high school is seventy-six percent and eighty-four percent respectively. Also in 1998 only fifteen per cent of African Americans and twenty-five of whites twenty-five years and older have completed four years of college. In the area of economics, nationally the annual median income in 1997 was $25,000 for African Americans and $37,900 for white Americans. In St. Louis, Missouri the number of households with less than $5,000 annually was twice as high for African Americans then for the white population. In 1997 thirty-seven percent of the African Americans and sixteen percent of the white children were living below the federal poverty line. Among working adults twenty-one percent of African Americans nine percent of white Americans were living below the federal poverty line in 1997. Nationally unemployment rates in 1998 were nine percent for African Americans and four percent for white Americans. In Missouri the situation was more grim. In the St. Louis region in 1998 unemployment rates for African Americans were eleven percent and three percent for white Americans.

Both nationally and locally incarceration rates are eroding the Black community. Nationally almost thirty percent of young African Americans are under some kind of correctional control, incarceration, probation or parole. A 1998 Sentencing Project found that 1.4 million African-American men—thirteen percent of the population—cannot vote because felony convictions. Given this rate of incarceration, three in ten of the next generation of African-American men can be expected to lose the right to vote.

Over the past decade, St. Louis or Kansas City or statewide politics was almost always about race. The November 2000 United States Senate campaign between Republican incumbent John Ashcroft and his Democratic challenger Governor Mel Carnahan quickly turned to race. For leading the successful opposition to Judge Ronnie White, the first and only African-American State Supreme Court member, nominated for a federal court seat, Ashcroft was labeled a racist. State Republicans responded by releasing a 1960 picture of Carnahan appearing in black face for a minstrel show sponsored by his college fraternity at what is now the University of Missouri-Rolla. Race and politics has also been a recurring theme in the battle to end court order desegregation in Kansas City and St. Louis Schools. With court ordered desegregation at an end in October of 1999, the State Board of Education, on the recommendation of the State Commissioner of Education, revoked the Kansas City Public School system's accreditation. St. Louis Public Schools were given a two-year stay of execution on a similar recommendation that they, too, lose their accreditation. Many experts agree that this state action will result in the total resegregation of the public schools in Kansas City and St. Louis. Many people say we are still fighting the Civil War in Missouri.

REFERENCE

Green, Lorenzo J., Kremer, Gary R., Holland, Antonio F. *Missouri's Black Heritage*. Revised Edition. 1993.

ANTONIO F. HOLLAND

Mitchell, Parren J.

(April 29, 1922–), U.S. Congressman. Mitchell was born in Baltimore, Maryland. He served as an infantry officer in the U.S. Army from 1942 to 1946. In 1950 he earned a bachelor's degree from Morgan State College. Then after suing for

Parren Mitchell, 1971. (Corbis Corporation)

admission, he became the first black student at the University of Maryland, where he took a degree in sociology in 1952. After teaching two years at Morgan State, he worked for local government and community programs in such positions as probation officer, executive secretary to a commission overseeing enforcement of the new state law on public accommodations, and executive secretary of an anti-poverty program. In 1968, he returned to teach at Morgan State.

Mitchell ran unsuccessfully in the Democratic primary for the Seventh Congressional District seat in 1968, but in 1970 he was successful in securing the nomination and winning the election. He thus became Maryland's first African American congressman and the first elected since 1895 south of the Mason-Dixon line. He served in Congress until he retired in 1987.

In Congress Mitchell was chairman of the Small Business Committee among other committee assignments, whip-at-large, and chair of the Congressional Black Caucus. He was much concerned about empowering minority business. In 1976, for example, he secured a ten percent set aside in federal grants to local governing bodies for minority firms as contractors. He also won an increase in the budget of the Small Business Administration in 1978. This interest in the support of minority economic development led him to found the Minority Business Enterprise Legal Defense and Education Fund after he left Congress.

See also BALTIMORE, MARYLAND [1].

REFERENCES

"Our Founder: Biographical Sketch of Parren J. Mitchell." http://www.mbeldef.org/founder.htm.

Clay, William L. *Just Permanent Interests: Black Americans in Congress, 1870–1991.* 1992.

Gross, Delphine Ava. "Parren J. Mitchell." In *Notable Black American Men*, edited by Jessie Carney Smith. 1999.

ROBERT L. JOHNS

Moravian Church. The Moravian Church was one of the first churches in America to admit African Americans — both slave and free — to membership. Originally part of the Protestant Reformation, the church became increasingly active as a missionary church among non-Christians outside Europe, and its members arrived among West Indian slaves early in the 1730s. Moravians came to America in 1735 to escape persecution and to work among Native Americans and African American slaves. After settling briefly in Georgia, they moved to Pennsylvania, establishing the community of Bethlehem in 1741. In 1753, they settled in central North Carolina, near what later became Salem and then Winston-Salem. Bethlehem and Winston-Salem still contain the largest Moravian communities in the United States, though nineteenth-century congregations emerged in the Ohio Valley, the upper Midwest, and the Southeast.

Eighteenth-century Moravians counted all races among "the Children of God," but they also practiced chattel slavery. Moravian missionaries welcomed slaves as potential converts while reminding them to accept their divinely-ordained servitude. The church also bought slaves, to profit from their labor while bringing them the Gospel. Conversion was difficult for blacks, though, because they had to adopt the same dress, behavior, music, and family patterns as whites. A handful of slaves living in or near Bethlehem or Salem did join the church, however, in the decades before the American Revolution. These early converts still suffered some cruelties of slavery, fear of sale and the absence of surnames, for example, but they also enjoyed some aspects of racial equality. Black Moravians often worked and lived in the same quarters and conditions as white Moravians. Blacks sat with whites in the meeting house, participated in church synods, were buried in racially integrated cemeteries, and even participated in ceremonies such as foot-washing and the kiss of peace that involved direct physical contact with white members.

After the American Revolution, Pennsylvania enacted a gradual emancipation law in 1780, and the black population of Bethlehem decreased. In North Carolina, at the same time, slavery continued to expand, and in and around Salem the number of black Moravians continued to rise. But white Moravians in North Carolina grew more restrictive toward slaves and free blacks. Also, younger Moravians began to demand that the church separate black and white members, excluding blacks from foot-washing, from the kiss of peace, from the cemetery, and finally from the meeting house itself. In 1822 a segregated Moravian Church established a separate congregation, with a white minister, for its black members.

In the years between their expulsion from white services and their emancipation from slavery, black Moravians maintained their own religious community around Salem. They had a separate meeting house, cemetery, and, briefly, a school. It was hardly an independent community, though; the minister and teachers were white, and both services and lessons followed white models and emphasized white values. As a result, many slaves and free blacks around Salem ignored it, preferring instead to attend Methodist services or sermons preached by non-denominational black preachers. This trend continued after Emancipation.

But the black Moravian community survived. Early in the twentieth century it finally gained a formal designation, Saint Philip's Moravian Church, and in 1966 it received its first black minister. In 2000 Saint Philip's was one of the South's oldest black churches in continuous operation and served a small but proud congregation.

See also BOOK COLLECTORS AND COLLECTIONS [1]; MCGUIRE, GEORGE ALEXANDER [3].

REFERENCES

Sensbach, Jon. F. *A Separate Canan: The Making of an Afro-Moravian World in North Carolina, 1763–1840.* 1998.

Thorp, Daniel B. "Chattel with a Soul: The Autobiography of a Moravian Slave." *Pennsylvania Magazine of History and Biography,* CXII (1988): 433-451.

Thorp, Daniel B. "New Wine in Old Bottles: Cultural Persistence Among Non-White Converts to the Moravian Church." *Transactions of the Moravian Historical Society,* 30 (1998): 1-8.

DANIEL B. THORP

Morgan, Clement Garnett

Morgan, Clement Garnett (1859–June 1, 1929), lawyer. Morgan was born to slave parents in Stafford County, Virginia. After Emancipation, the family moved to Washington, D.C., where Clement graduated from high school. He worked as a barber in Washington and taught school in St. Louis before traveling to Boston, where he graduated from Boston Latin School, Harvard College, and in 1893 from Harvard Law School. He was a brilliant student and orator and a strong supporter of Harvard schoolmate, W. E. B. Du Bois.

Morgan practiced law in Cambridge and was active in local Republican politics. He was the first African American elected to the Common Council of Cambridge from a predominantly white district and ran successfully for alderman after serving his Council term.

Morgan allied himself with Du Bois in opposition to Booker T. Washington's accommodationist philosophy. In an attempt to reconcile differences between the Du Bois and Washington supporters, Morgan helped organize in 1904 the Committee of Twelve for the Advancement of the Negro Race, comprised of supporters of both sides. The attempt failed, and the next year Morgan joined the Du Bois-founded Niagara Movement and headed its Massachusetts branch. Morgan and William Trotter, whom he had defended when Trotter was charged with inciting a riot in 1903 after disrupting a Washington speech, had serious differences that threatened Morgan's leadership. Du Bois interceded on Morgan's behalf, but a later feud between Du Bois and Trotter contributed to the 1909 collapse of the Niagara Movement. Morgan joined the National Association for the Advancement of Colored People in 1910 and served on the Boston branch executive committee (1912–1914).
See also VIRGINIA [5].

REFERENCES

Garraty, John A., and Mark C. Carnes, eds. *American National Biography.* 1999.

Logan, Rayford W., and Michael R. Winston, eds. *Dictionary of American Negro Biography.* 1982.

CARRELL P. HORTON

Morgan, Rose Meta

Morgan, Rose Meta (1913–), entrepreneur. Rose Morgan was cofounder of the Rose Meta House of Beauty, a leading black hair care and cosmetic manufacturing company in the post-World War II period. Morgan was born in Shelby, Mississippi, the daughter of Winnie and Chappel Morgan. The family of thirteen moved to Chicago when Rose was six years old. After high school, Morgan attended Morris Beauty Academy. Her second husband was heavyweight boxing champion Joe Louis, to whom she was married from 1955 to 1958.

When she was fourteen, Morgan opened her first business, a small beauty shop in her neighborhood. Her first big break came in 1938 when she styled Ethel Waters' hair prior to a Chicago performance. So impressed with her craft was Waters that she invited Morgan to go with her to New York City. In 1944, Morgan and Olivia Clark invested $10,000 in cash and secured credit for $40,000 to purchase a five-story mansion in the Harlem section of New York City to be used for their joint business, Rose Meta House of Beauty, that opened in 1947. The business was an immediate success, bringing in 70,000 customers and $180,000 in earnings, with a net profit of $45,000. In addition to operators, the staff included a registered nurse and licensed masseurs. It had become the largest black beauty shop in the world. By 1950 the business had expanded to three shops in New York City and a staff of 300. It's receipts grossed $3 million.

Morgan in 1965 became a founder and major shareholder in the Freedom National Bank in New York City. Morgan's business acumen led her to found in 1972 one of the first black physical fitness centers, Trim-Away Figure Contouring.
See also ENTREPRENEURS [2].

REFERENCES

Mabunda, L. Mpho, and Shirelle Phelps, ed. *Contemporary Black Biography*. 1996.

Smith, Jessie Carney, ed. *Notable Black American Women*. 1992.

Walker, Juliet W. K., ed. *Encyclopedia of African American Business History*. 1999.

JESSIE CARNEY SMITH

Morial, Ernest Nathan "Dutch" (October 9, 1929–December 24, 1989), mayor, politician, lawyer, judge. Morial was born into a Creole Catholic family from New Orleans' Seventh Ward. He attended local parochial schools and graduated from Xavier University in New Orleans in 1951. Morial had an enviable record for accomplishing judicial and political firsts in Louisiana. He was the first black to

Ernest "Dutch" Nathan Morial. (Amistad Research Center)

graduate from the Louisiana State University School of Law (J.D., 1954), the first black lawyer hired in the U.S. Attorney's office in Louisiana (1965), the first black Democrat to serve in the state legislature since Reconstruction (1967), and later to be a delegate at the Democratic National Convention. He was also the first black judge on the New Orleans Parish Juvenile Court (1970), the first black elected to the Louisiana Fourth Circuit Court of Appeals, and the first black elected as mayor of New Orleans (1977).

As the city's highest ranking official, Morial was credited with creating the first Office of Economic Development and Office of Minority Business Development, developing the Almonaster industrial tract, overcoming severe budget problems, and solving a serious police strike that threatened to paralyze the city. Morial and his partner, A. P. Turead, filed successful lawsuits to integrate public schools, recreational facilities, taxicabs, and the city's airport and municipal auditorium. Morial was denied a successive third term as mayor when his bid to change the city charter was rejected at the polls. In 1994, his son, Marc, was elected mayor of New Orleans.
See also FRATERNITIES AND SORORITIES [2]; MAYORS [3]; NEW ORLEANS, LOUISIANA [4].

REFERENCES

Marcus, France Frank. "Ernest Morial, Former Mayor of New Orleans." *New York Times*, December 25, 1989, p. 54.

"Phantom of Mayor's Race is Talk of New Orleans." *New York Times*, November 23, 1989, p. 20.

Smith, Jessie Carney, ed. *Notable Black American Men*. 1999.

DOLORES NICHOLSON

Morrison, Toni (Update)

Morrison, Toni (Update) (February 18, 1931–) writer. By the 1980s, Toni Morrison was considered by the literary world to be one of the major American novelists. In 1992 — five years after she received the Pulitzer Prize for *Beloved* and the year of publication both for her sixth novel, *Jazz*, and for a series of lectures on American literature, *Playing in the Dark* — Morrison was being referred to internationally as one of the greatest American writers of all time. In 1993 she became the first black woman in history to be awarded the Nobel Prize for literature.

Morrison's ability to cross boundaries as a cultural commentator is reflected in *Race-ing Justice and Engendering Power: Essays on Anita Hill, Clarence Thomas, and the Construction of Social Reality*, a collection of essays about the nomination of Supreme Court Justice Clarence Thomas and the accusations of sexual harassment brought against him by law professor Anita Hill. The essays in the collection were written by scholars from various fields, then edited and introduced by Morrison. At the same time, she wrote poetry and lyrics for the song cycles "Dare Degga" and "Honey and Rue".

Morrison's reputation was confirmed in 1998 by the critical success of her novel *Paradise*. That year, with aid from entertainer Oprah Winfrey, her work also reached a new, wider public. After an endorsement from Winfrey's "Oprah Book Club," sales of *Paradise* climbed into bestseller range. The same year, Winfrey produced and starred in a film adaptation of Morrison's novel *Beloved*.

REFERENCES

http://www.luminarium.org/contemporary/tonimorrison/toni.htm (website of Morrison related materials)

Lubiano, Wahneema. "Toni Morrison." In Lea Baechler and A. Walton Litz, eds. *African American Writers*. New York, 1991, pp. 321-334.

Middleton, David L. *Toni Morrison: An Annotated Bibliography*. 1987.

Morrison, Toni. "Memory, Creation, and Writing." *Thought* 59 (December 1984): 385-390.

WAHNEEMA LUBIANO
UPDATED BY GREG ROBINSON

Toni Morrison. (AP/Wide World Photos)

Morton, Ferdinand Quintin

Morton, Ferdinand Quintin (September 9, 1881–?), lawyer, political figure, government worker, baseball official. Morton was a leader in New York City's political machine (known as Tammany Hall), and in his position as public servant, his charge was to help increase the number of black employees. He was born in Macon, Mississippi, the son of Edward James Morton and Mattie Shelton Morton, former slaves. The family moved to Washington, D.C., in 1890, when Edward Morton became a clerk in the Treasury Department. Ferdinand Morton graduated from Phillips Exeter Academy in New Hampshire in 1902 and then entered Harvard University and in 1905 Boston University Law School. He apparently left both schools due to financial difficulties.

In New York City in 1908, he worked on the Democratic campaign for the unsuccessful presidential candidate William Jennings Bryan. After that, Morton worked as a law clerk for two years and in 1910 passed the New York State Bar examination. In 1915 Morton was elected chairman of Tammany Hall's United Colored Democracy (UCD), whose

Carol Moseley-Braun. (AP/Wide World Photos)

purpose was to persuade black Republicans in New York to join the Democratic Party.

In 1916, Morton was appointed assistant district attorney, for New York County. He supervised the office's Indictment Bureau (1921–1922), then in 1923 he became the first African American member of the New York Municipal Civil Service Commission and one of the city's highest paid blacks.

Beginning 1935 Morton was baseball commissioner for the Negro National League, serving the final two years that the NNL was the lone black league and the first two after the rival Negro American League was formed. Still with the Civil Service Commission, he served as its president (1946–1948), until health problems forced him to retire. *See also* HARLEM RENAISSANCE [3]; HARLEM, NEW YORK [3]; UNITED COLORED DEMOCRACY [5].

REFERENCES

Dodson, Howard, and others. *The Black New Yorkers*. 2000.

Garraty, John A., and Mark C. Carnes, general editors. *American National Biography*. 1999. *Who's Who in Colored America, 1941–1944*. 6th ed.

FREDERICK D. SMITH, JR.

Moseley-Braun, Carol (Update) (August 16, 1947–) politician. During her first year in the Senate, Carol Moseley-Braun sponsored several pieces of civil rights legislation, including the Gender Equity in Education Act and the 1993 Violence Against Women Act, and reintroduced the Equal Rights Amendment. Moseley-Braun became unpopular following revelations of her personal use of campaign funds and as a result of her public support for Sami Abocha's dictatorial regime in Nigeria, where she visited in 1996. Following an acrimonious campaign, she was narrowly defeated for reelection in 1998.

REFERENCE

"Carol Moseley-Braun." In *Encyclopedia of World Biography*." 2nd Ed. 1999.

GREG ROBINSON

Mosley, Walter (Update) (January 12, 1952–), novelist. The son of an African-American janitor and a Jewish clerk, Walter Mosley was born in Los Angeles, Calif., and raised in the South Central section of that city. Mosley was unable to find a publisher for his

Walter Mosley. (Copyright by Jerry Bauer)

first novel, *Gone Fishing*, and shortly thereafter, he completed *Devil in a Blue Dress*, the first of his "Easy Rawlins" detective novels. Within a week of submitting the manuscript, Mosley signed a publishing contract with the publishing company Norton, quit his job, and began writing full time.

Mosley's hero, Ezekiel "Easy" Rawlins, is an African-American detective working the South Central section of Los Angeles with his sidekick "Mouse." *Devil in a Blue Dress* (1990) finds him in his late thirties, struggling to make his way in the often violent and racist, yet colorful and endearing, working-class world of South Central just after World War II. Mosley's subsequent novels—*A Red Death* (1991), *A White Butterfly* (1992), and *Black Betty* (1994)—see Rawlins through the McCarthy era and into the early 1960s. From the outset, the series was praised by critics and sold relatively well, but it became exceptionally popular after President Bill Clinton mentioned Mosley as one of his favorite authors during his 1992 campaign. Three of the books were nominated for Gold Dagger Awards by the British Crime Writers Association; *A White Butterfly* was nominated for the Edgar Award by the Mystery Writers of America. The film version of *Devil in a Blue Dress*—starring Denzel Washington—was released in September 1995. Mosley published a novel about the blues, *R. L.'s Dream*, in 1995.

Mosley departed from the Easy Rawlins series after *The Little Yellow Dog* (1997). In 1998 he published another mystery, *Always Outnumbered, Always Outgunned*, and he published a science fiction novel, *Blue Light*.

REFERENCES

Lyall, Sarah. "Heroes in Black, Not White." *New York Times*, June 15, 1994, p. C1, 8.

McCullough, Bob. "Walter Mosley: Interview." *Publisher's Weekly* (May 23, 1994): 67-68.

PAMELA WILKINSON
UPDATED BY GREG ROBINSON

Moten, Lucy Ellen (1851– August 24, 1933), educator. Lucy Moten was born in Fauquier County, Virginia, near White Sulphur Springs, to free black parents. In search of better educational opportunities for their daughter, the family moved to the District of Columbia. Moten attended the District's tuition schools for free blacks until 1862, when she switched to the black public schools just established. Moten attended Howard University's preparatory and normal departments, where she studied for two years. In 1870–1873, she taught at a local grammar school and then moved to Salem, Massachusetts, where she resumed her education at Salem Normal School. She graduated in 1875 and returned to teaching. Later, she attended Spencerian Business College, graduating in 1883.

That same year, on recommendation of board member Frederick Douglass, Moten became princi-

Eddie Murphy, 1987. (AP/Wide World Photos)

pal of Minor Normal School in the District. She set high standards for education and personal behavior and urged students to continue to educate themselves. The school had high admission requirements and small classes. So concerned with the students' health was Moten that she studied medicine at Howard University Medical School, graduating 1897 with an M.D. degree. She used her new knowledge to begin a series of lectures on health and hygiene that she and later other physicians taught.

Moten initiated a one-year teacher training course for college graduates. As result, she prepared most of the primary teachers for the local public schools. Her graduates were also sought out elsewhere in the country. In 1896, Moten expanded the curriculum from one to two years. At the end of her 37 years at the school, she had set a foundation for it to become a four-year institution. In time, the school became a part of the University of the District of Columbia. *See also* VIRGINIA [5].

REFERENCES

Garraty, John A., and Mark C. Carnes, general eds. *American National Biography*. vol. 16. 1999.

Logan, Rayford W., and Michael R. Winston, eds. *Dictionary of American Negro Biography*. 1982.

Smith, Jessie Carney, ed. *Notable Black American Women*. 1992.

JESSIE CARNEY SMITH

Murphy, Eddie (Update) (April 3, 1961–), actor and comedian. Eddie Murphy was born in Brooklyn, N.Y. His father was a New York policeman and amateur comedian, and his mother a phone operator. Murphy's father was killed on duty when his son was three years old; his mother remarried, and the family moved from Brooklyn, when Murphy was nine, to the Long Island, N.Y., town of Roosevelt.

Following a stream of largely unsuccessful films, including *Beverly Hills Cop III* (1994) and *Vampire in Brooklyn* (1995), Murphy's career was revitalized in 1996 by *The Nutty Professor*, a remake of the Jerry Lewis classic. In 1997, Murphy, long known for his homophobic humor and comments, was arrested for picking up a transvestite prostitute in his car, although Murphy contended he had merely done so as a kindness. Despite the unfavorable publicity, Murphy's career continued unabated.

In 1998 Murphy starred in a popular remake of *Dr. Dolittle*, and in the same year his voice was featured in the animated film *Mulan*. Murphy's success continued the next year with the television series *The P.J.'s* and the box office success of *Bowfinger*. In 2000, Murphy returned with a sequel to his biggest success of the late 1990s with *The Nutty Professor 2: The Klumps*, in which he again played the entire family of the title character. The film received little praise from critics, but did very well with audiences.

REFERENCE

"Eddie Murphy." In *Contemporary Black Biography*, vol. 20. 1999.

SUSAN MCINTOSH
UPDATED BY GREG ROBINSON

N

NAACP. *See* National Association for the Advancement of Colored People.

Nabrit, Samuel Milton (February 21, 1905–), biologist, college president. Nabrit was born in Macon, Georgia. He received his B.S. degree from Morehouse College in 1925. He then went to Brown University, where he received an M.S. in 1928, and a Ph.D. in 1932. He was the first African American to receive a Ph.D. in biology from the school. From 1925 to 1931, Nabrit taught biology at Morehouse while working on his graduate degrees. He also conducted research each summer at the Marine Biological Laboratory, Woods Hole, Massachusetts. His work on biological regeneration was published in the *Biological Bulletin* and was still cited as late as the 1980s.

From 1932 to 1947, Nabrit chaired Atlanta University's biology department. His research focused on the ability of fish to re-grow their tail fins. Several journals published the results of this work, including the *Journal of Parasitology* and the *Journal of Experimental Zoology*. In 1943, he helped to organize the National Institute of Science and was its third president.

Nabrit was promoted to dean of Atlanta University's School of Arts and Sciences in 1947. He then left to become the second president of Texas Southern University in Houston, serving from 1947 to 1966. During his years there, he helped to found Upward Bound, a program designed to increase student reten-

tion. He was also president of the Association of Colleges and Secondary Schools and beginning in 1956 served a six-year term on the National Science Board. In 1966 President Lyndon Johnson appointed Nabrit to a term on the Atomic Energy Commission. From 1967 until his 1981 retirement, Nabrit was director of the Southern Fellowships Fund.

See also SCIENCE EDUCATION [5]; SCIENTIFIC INSTITUTIONS [5].

REFERENCES

Current Biography Yearbook, 1963. 1963.

Krapp, Kristine, ed. *Notable Black American Scientists.* 1999.

Sammons, Vivian Ovelton. *Blacks in Science and Medicine.* 1990.

JESSIE CARNEY SMITH

Nail, John E. "Jack" (August 22, 1883–March 6, 1947), entrepreneur, realtor. John Nail was born in New London, Connecticut, and grew up in New York City. In the 1900s, he worked in his father's real estate business. Then he set up his own business and became a real estate agent in the Bronx. Soon he accepted employment with the Afro-American Realty Company, one of New York's most successful black real estate businesses.

In 1908, Nail and colleague, Henry C. Parker, left sales and established the firm Nail & Parker, Inc., with Nail as president and Parker as secretary-treasurer.

Realizing the need for blacks to own property in Harlem to secure the community, Nail urged them to invest. Soon the firm dismantled the segregated unwritten housing laws in the community, and the company prospered. Nail & Parker became agents for St. Philip's Episcopal Church in 1911 and negotiated a million-dollar deal for the church. The firm bought and sold other large-scale properties; its most well-known client was hair-care magnate Madame C. J. Walker, for whom they purchased her famous $200,000 Irvington-on-the Hudson property.

The Depression took its toll on businesses in Harlem, and in 1933 the company closed. Nail organized a new business, John E. Nail Company, Inc., that was involved in several large transactions. Beyond the real estate business, Nail, an advocate of racial solidarity, was active in other ventures, such as Harlem's Colored Merchant Association. CMA was developed in at least twenty-five other cities, and the Harlem chapter became a demonstration project for the national black community.
See also CONNECTICUT[2].

REFERENCES

Garraty, John A. and Mark C. Carnes, general eds. *American National Biography*. 1999.

Ingham, John N., and Lynne B. Feldmann. *African American Business Leaders*. 1994.

Logan, Rayford W., and Michael R. Winston, eds. *Dictionary of American Negro Biography*. 1982.

JESSIE CARNEY SMITH

Napier, James Carroll (June 9, 1845–April 21, 1940), attorney, businessperson, civil rights leader, educator, politician. Napier was one of four children born to William Carroll and Jane Elizabeth Watkins Napier near Nashville, Tennessee. He was the grandson of Elias Napier, a wealthy white physician and iron producer from Dickson County, Tennessee.

In 1870, he entered Howard University's Law School, receiving his degree with the nation's first class of black law graduates in 1872. He was admitted to the Bar of the Supreme Court of the District of Columbia and to the bar in Nashville. In 1878, Napier married Nettie Langston. Later, they adopted a daughter, Carrie Langston Napier.

The first black to preside over the Nashville City Council, Napier used racial segregation to his advantage. During his tenure on the council (1878–1889),

James C. Napier. (Fisk University Library)

Napier insisted on the employment of black teachers and administrators to staff black schools. He was also instrumental in the appointment of the first black firefighters.

In 1902, Napier organized Tennessee's first branch of the National Negro Business League. A founder of the One-Cent Savings Bank and Trust Company (1904), Napier served as the bank's cashier (known today as Citizens Savings Bank and Trust Company, it is the oldest continuously operating black bank).

From 1908 to 1930, Napier lectured at Meharry Medical College in medical jurisprudence. In 1911, President Taft appointed Napier as Register of the U. S. Treasury. After the 1912 election of President Woodrow Wilson, Napier left the position in July 1913. He returned to Nashville and served on the boards of trust at Fisk and Howard universities, Meharry Medical College, and the official board of Howard Congregational Church.
See also TENNESSEE [5].

REFERENCES

Lovett, Bobby L., and Linda T. Wynn, eds. *Profiles of African Americans in Tennessee History*. 1996.

Lovett, Bobby L. *The African-American History of Nashville, Tennessee, 1780–1930*. 1999.

Wynn, Linda T. "James C. Napier." in *Notable Black American Men*. Jessie Carney Smith, ed. 1999.

LINDA T. WYNN

Nash, Charles Edmund (May 23, 1844–July 21, 1913), U.S. Congressman.

Charles Edmund Nash was the only black elected to Congress from Louisiana who was actually allowed to take his seat. (J. Willis Menard and P. B. S. Pinchbeck were also elected but not allowed to do so.) Nash was born in Opelousas, Louisiana, to free parents. As a young man he became a bricklayer in New Orleans.

Nash enlisted in the Union forces in 1863 and later became a sergeant. During the closing days of the war, he lost the lower third of his right leg in an attack on Fort Blakely, Alabama. A field promotion to first lieutenant made shortly before his discharge did not win approval.

In 1869 Nash was appointed night inspector at the New Orleans Custom House, a political bastion of radical Republicans. From this base he won nomination and election in 1874 as congressman from the 6th Congressional District. In Washington Nash not only suffered from his lack of influence as freshman member, he also faced a Democratic house. His only bill died in committee, and he was allowed to speak on the floor only once, on June 7, 1876. He spoke on the political situation in Louisiana.

Opposition of the Democrats and disunity among Republicans ensured that Nash lost his bid for reelection by more than five thousand votes. He returned to brick-laying except for three-and-a-half months as postmaster in Washington, Louisiana, in 1882. When he could no longer lay bricks because of the disabilities of age, he found work as a cigar maker.

See also LOUISIANA [3].

REFERENCES

Foner, Eric. *Freedom's Lawmakers.* 1993.

Holt, Thomas. "Charles Edmund Nash." In *Dictionary of American Negro Biography*, edited by Rayford W. Logan and Michael R. Winston. 1982.

ROBERT L. JOHNS

National Association for the Advancement of Colored People (NAACP)(Update).

The National Association for the Advancement of Colored People (NAACP) spent most of the late 1990s attempting to assess its role. In February of 1995, NAACP Board Chairman William Gibson was forced to resign, and Myrlie Evers-Williams, widow of slain civil rights leader Medgar Evers, was named to the position. Under Evers-Williams supervision, the organization restructured its finances and reaffirmed its intergrationist mission. In December 1995, Representative Kweisi Mfume announced that he would leave Congress to take over the daily operation of the NAACP. Under Mfume's leadership, the organization erased its fiscal deficit and renewed its activism on many fronts, including human rights, environmental racism,and justice for African-Americans. In February of 1998, Evers-Williams resigned and civil rights veteran Julian Bond became chair of the board. Bond spoke forcefully of the need for the NAACP to renew its focus on encouraging blacks to gain power through voting, and the NAACP took credit for the increase in the black vote in the 1998 congressional elections.

REFERENCE

Walker, Adrian. "Bond succeeds Evers-Williams as chairman of the NAACP." *Raleigh News & Observer.* Feb 22, 1998: A5.

GREG ROBINSON

National Black Network.

Sensing a readiness in the market in 1971, Eugene D. Jackson and Sidney L. Small raised $1,000,000 of venture capital and founded the Unity Broadcasting Network, parent company of the National Black Network (NBN).

Jackson served as industrial engineer for Colgate Palmolive (1967–1968), and held management appointments at the Black Economic Union and the Interracial Council for Business Opportunity. For four years, Jackson was business manager for ABC radio. His partner and half-owner, Sidney L. Small, was experienced in marketing and advertising, having worked with Time Inc. (1969–1971). Thus, with expertise in finance and in management, the two were able to put together a financial package to support the new venture. In 1973 NBN went on the airwaves and became black America's most effective forum in the nation. From coast to coast, NBN broadcast news shows, commentaries, and other programs. The programs could also be heard in the Gulf of Mexico and the Canadian border. Early programs included "Black Issues and the Black Press," "One Black Man's Opinion," and a one-hour weekly series, the "Ossie Davis and Ruby Dee Show." Mal Goode, veteran journalist on ABC News in New York, was a member of NBN's highly regarded broadcast team.

NBN grossed $2,650,000 in 1976; its support came from such advertisers as Armour-Dial, AT&T, and Campbell Soup Company. In 1998 NBN ranked #87 on the *Black Enterprise* list of the top 100 industrial/

service companies. NBN Broadcasting Inc. is located in New York City.

See also ADVERTISING [1]; CLASS AND SOCIETY [2]; RADIO [4].

REFERENCES

Bennett, Hal, and Lew Roberts. "National Black Network: Black Radio's Big Brother." *Black Enterprise* 8 (June 1977): 141-47.

Dodson, Howard, ed.. *The Black New Yorkers*. 2000.

Who's Who Among African Americans, 13th ed. 2000.

DARIUS L. THIEME

National Medical Association.

The National Medical Association (NMA) is a historically black national organization of physicians. Headquartered in Washington, D.C., it has some 22,000 members and publishes the monthly *Journal of the National Medical Association*. The organization was a response to the refusal of local and national medical associations to accept African American members. It was not until 1968 that the American Medical Association ended racial discrimination in all constituent organizations.

The NMA was founded as The National Association of Colored Physicians, Dentists, and Pharmacists on September 18, 1895, at a meeting held during the Cotton States and International Exhibition in Atlanta, Georgia. I. Garland Penn presided at this critical first meeting, and Robert H. Boyd became the first president. Although it had humble beginnings, the membership grew from fewer than fifty in 1904 to more than 500 by 1912. It became the National Medical Association in 1903, and six years later began publishing the *Journal of the National Medical Association*. The association served as a way to increase the visibility of black doctors, and frequently addressed issues of racial discrimination and health problems of particular concern to the black community.

Still making its presence felt nearly a century later, the NMA works to improve the status of black doctors, to address issues of black health care, and to improve the overall practice of medicine. It also serves as a networking apparatus for African American doctors and maintains a nationwide referral service.

See also BOYD, ROBERT FULTON [1]; CANNON, GEORGE EPPS [1]; COBB, WILLIAM MONTAGUE [2]; DAILEY, ULYSSES GRANT [2]; DISEASES AND EPIDEMICS [2]; FULLER, SOLOMON CARTER [2]; GILES, ROSCOE CONKLING [2]; HEALTH PROFESSIONS [3]; HEALTH AND HEALTH CARE PROVIDERS [3]; KENNEY, JOHN ANDREW [3]; LYNK, MILES VANDAHURST [3]; MCCARROLL, ERNEST MAE [3]; MEDICAL ASSOCIATIONS [3]; NATIONAL HOSPITAL ASSOCIATION [4]; PHARMACY [4]; POINDEXTER, HILDRUS A. [4]; PROFESSIONAL ORGANIZATIONS [4]; PUBLIC HEALTH [4]; SCIENTIFIC ASSOCIATIONS [5]; SURGERY [5]; TROPICAL DISEASES [5].

REFERENCES

Low, W. Augustus, and Virgil A. Clift, eds. *Encyclopedia of Black America*. 1981.

Morais, Herbert M. *The History of the Negro in Medicine*. 1968.

National Medical Association OnLine: http://www.natmed.org/home.as

ROBERT L. JOHNS

Nation of Islam (Update).

During the mid-1990s, Minister Farrakhan sought to broaden the appeal of the Nation of Islam and improve the organization's shaky finances. In 1995, Farrakhan organized the Million Man March. Farrakhan's leadership and his keynote address at the March brought him new legitimacy as a black leader. Shortly afterward, he was forced to discipline and later dismiss a chief assistant, Minister Khallid Muhammad, after Muhammad gave a series of excessive nationalist and anti-Semitic speeches at Howard University. In 1996, Farrakhan announced that the Nation of Islam would receive a $1 billion contribution from Libyan dictator Moammar Khaddafi. During this period, the Nation of Islam gained some notable new members, including boxer Mike Tyson and ousted NAACP leader Rev. Benjamin Chavis (who officially converted to Islam in 1997). However, despite the Nation of Islam's nationwide visibility and the continuing popularity of its nationalist message in inner-city communities, its membership remained small.

REFERENCES

"Ex-Head of NAACP Joins Nation of Islam." *Los Angeles Times*, Feb 25, 1997:1.

Mannies, Jo. "Libyan Gift is "Family Business,' Chavis Says: U.S. Has No Right To Block $1 Billion Donation, He Says." *St. Louis Post-Dispatch*, September 28, 1996:1A.

GREG ROBINSON

Nevada (Update).

Although African Americans arrived in large numbers only during World War II, they have been present at every stage of Nevada's development. In the nineteenth century mountain man James P. Beckwourth went through the area; there is a pass named after him just north of Reno. African-American men accompanied Jedediah Smith, John C. Fremont and other fur traders or explorers. Rancher Ben Palmer, who arrived in Carson Valley in the early 1850s, was one of the wealthiest men in Douglas County for several decades during the nineteenth century. One of his sister's children was the first non-Native-American child born in the territory.

Most nineteenth-century African Americans lived on the Comstock, the chief silver-producing area, and in Carson City. Almost entirely barred from mining, black men and women alike did menial labor. However, some owned and operated businesses, from barbershops to cafes and hotels. W. H. C. Stephenson practiced medicine in Virginia City in the 1860s and the '70s. The small black population supported two lodges of Prince Hall Masons, churches in Virginia City and Carson City, and other organizations. William M. Bird, a barber, Thomas Detter, published a book, *Nellie Brown*, in 1871 while he lived in Elko. Poet James Whitfied was also a resident of Elko.

Nevada law was openly racist at its beginning; no nonwhites could vote, hold office, serve on juries, marry whites, testify against whites, or send their children to public schools, unless separate schools were established. Protests from the African-American community plus national developments eliminated much governmental discrimination by the mid 1870s. Parents in Carson City raised money, built a schoolhouse, and then sued when the school board refused to hire a teacher. In 1872, in a suit they brought, the discriminatory school law was invalidated by the state Supreme Court. Although complete data are lacking, it is probable that private discrimination lessened in the 1870s and then increased at the end of the century.

The African-American population declined even more rapidly than the overall population in the 1880s, when the Comstock mines ceased producing heavily, and did not recover until the 1940s. From 1900 to about 1940, the largest community was in Reno (in northern Nevada). Reno's Bethel African Methodist Episcopal Church is the oldest African-American church in the state.

Substantial numbers of African-American workers were hired during World War II at a war plant, Basic Magnesium, in Henderson, in southern Nevada's Clark County. Before this, the chief employer of black workers in the small African-American population of Las Vegas (the principal city in Clark County) was the Union Pacific Railroad, but there were also several black-owned businesses. However, with the coming of the new workers from the South (principally Arkansas and Louisiana) the black community found itself largely confined to the Westside, across the railroad tracks from downtown Las Vegas.

The Westside continues to be the core of the black community in southern Nevada, but it has spilled over into North Las Vegas and other surrounding areas. The Westside for several decades was almost entirely black, with few African Americans living elsewhere, but higher proportions have moved out to other parts of the southern metropolitan area in the last two decades.

For the last forty years the largest African-American population in the state has lived in Clark County, with smaller concentrations in Reno-Sparks and Mineral County. African Americans are scarce in the small counties (together comprising less than 15 percent of the state's population), except Mineral.

Rising private discrimination in the late 1930s earned Nevada the reputation of "the Mississippi of the West." Branches of the National Association for the Advancement of Colored People operated in Reno from 1919 to 1924 and Las Vegas from 1927 to the late 1930s. There was also branches in Hawthorne (for about 20 years) and Elko and Henderson for briefer times. The most important present branches—in Las Vegas and Reno-Sparks—both date to 1945. The Las Vegas branch began efforts to secure civil rights laws in 1939, but significant advances did not occur until 1959–1960, when a state district court judge invalidated the antimiscegenation law and the legislature, at the urging of Gov. Grant Sawyer, repealed various discriminatory laws left over from the nineteenth century and prohibited discrimination in apprenticeship programs. A threatened public march organized by the NAACP against southern Nevada casinos, the largest employers in the state, ended public accommodations discrimination in southern but not northern Nevada.

Not until 1965 was a law passed forbidding discrimination in public accommodations and employment; only then did northern Nevada casinos admit black customers (except for a brief episode during the 1960 Winter Olympics). Not until 1971 was a fair housing act passed, and the Equal Rights Commission has been weakened since it was created in 1961. Nevada retains some of its reluctance to abandon racial discrimination.

Court action—initiated largely by Nevada's first African-American attorney, Charles Kellar, in cooperation with the NAACP and the League of Women Voters—brought about desegregation of elementary schools in Clark County. Other suits, some brought by federal agencies, ended discriminatory practices at the state prison, opened up employment in southern Nevada's casino industry, and stopped discriminatory practices by a labor union. Litigation in Reno led in the 1980s to the hiring of the first African- American fire fighters in the area.

Nevada's first black legislator was Woodrow Wilson, elected in 1966. The Rev. Willie Wynn became the first African-American cabinet officer in Nevada history under Gov. Paul Laxalt in the late 1960s. In the 1990s there have been several prominent black public officials, including the city manager of Reno, the Sparks postmaster, local elected officials in both southern and northern Nevada, and a member of the board of regents of the university system. For two decades the southern black community has been represented by legislators elected from predominantly black districts. In 1999 Joe Neal was in his 20th year as a State Senator and Assemblymen Morse Arberry and Wendell Williams had also served several terms. In the 1990s Senators Bernice Mathews and Maurice Washington were elected from nonblack northern districts.

Dr. Charles I. West was the first African-American physician since Dr. Stephenson in the previous century. Dr. James B. McMillan was the state's first black dentist; both arrived in the 1950s. Today there are many black health professionals in the state at all levels. The first laparoscopic operation in southern Nevada was performed by Dr. Harriston Lee Bass, Jr.

Attorney Kellar had to sue to get the right to practiced law in Nevada, but there are now prominent African-American attorneys in both Las Vegas and Reno. Several have been elected to judgeships. Addeliar D. Guy, Earle White, Jr., and Lee A. Gates have been district court judges in Clark County.

There are many black educators in the state. Dr. Paul Meacham was president of Southern Nevada Community College for several years in the 1980s and Michael Coray in 1999 was Vice President of the University of Nevada, Reno. Claude G. Perkins was superintendent of Clark County schools from 1978 to 1981.

Churches, among which Baptist and Church of God in Christ congregations are most common, are strong in Nevada's African-American community. Civil rights organizations other than the NAACP are scarce, but the Northern Nevada Black Cultural Awareness Society developed vigorous programs in the 1990s. In Clark County, the Fordyce Club maintains social ties with Fordyce, Ark., one of the major sources of wartime immigration to Clark County.

Economic development within the black community has been slow, but during the 1990s there have been growing numbers of successful business people. In northern Nevada, Luther Mack owned several fast-food stores and, for several years, a TV station. In southern Nevada during the 1990s John J. Edmond owned a shopping center, Donald Givens was a casino executive, and a large local bus company had black owners.

In the arts, Laverne Ligon's Simba dance group has been critically acclaimed. Young artists Wayne Horne, Jr. and Tony Trigg and poets Nancy Ellen-Webb Williams and Jimi S. Bufkin received recognition.

The rise of a successful middle class should not obscure the fact that poverty rates are high in African-American areas. The ratio of African-American to white household incomes in Nevada in 1992 was 70.8 percent, higher than the national average of 62.9 percent but close to that for Western states.

The first black newspaper in the south was *The Missile*, published by the NAACP. Dr. West started publishing the *Las Vegas Voice* in the 1950s; it survives as the *Las Vegas Sentinel-Voice*. The Rev. Vincent L. Thompson published the *Reno Observer* in Reno during the 1970s. There are prominent black employees in all the media of mass communication in the state, although not in large numbers.

Black Nevadans have made significant contributions to the state in spite of pervasive discrimination. Today there are prominent and successful black men and women in all occupational fields, although a legacy of past discrimination survives.

REFERENCES

McMillan, James B., *Fighting Back: A Life in the Struggle for Civil Rights*. 1997.

ELMER R. RUSCO

The Neville Brothers. (Arthur "Art" [December 17, 1937–], Charles [1939–], Aaron [January 24, 1941–], Cyril [October 10, 1948–]), music artists. Since joining forces in 1975, the Neville Brothers have fused the eclectic sounds of New Orleans into a distinctive style that has propelled them to the forefront of that city's music scene. The Neville style, described as a "harmony based, funk-groove," draws on a rich array of African American musical traditions, including jazz, reggae, gospel, rythmn and blues, rock, and zydeco. The success of their music has earned them critical acclaim and a national following.

The Nevilles first appeared on the music scene when Art recorded festival favorite "Mardi Gras Mambo" in 1954. In the 1960s, Aaron gained notice with a series of hits, including "Tell It Like It Is," which climbed to #1 on the R&B charts and #2 on the pop charts in 1966. Art and Aaron briefly worked together as the Neville Sounds in the mid 1960s. After their mother's death in 1975, all four brothers united to fulfill her wish that they work together. They recorded "The Wild Tchoupitoulas" in 1976, earning critical praise and a major record deal. Since then, the Nevilles have recorded dozens of albums, with their greatest success coming in 1989 when *Yellow Moon* earned a Grammy Award. But more than their recordings, it is the Neville Brothers' dynamic live shows, particularly at the New Orleans club Tipitina's, which have earned them a popular following and acclaim as the essence of the New Orleans sound.

See also NEW ORLEANS, LOUISIANA [4]; RHYTHM AND BLUES [4].

REFERENCE

Neville, Art, Aaron Neville, Charles Neville, Cyril Neville, and David Ritz. *The Brothers*. 2000.

MICHAEL WADE FUQUAY

New Jersey (Update).

It is not clear when persons of African descent first arrived on New Jersey soil, although it is likely the Dutch introduced them. Fort Nassau, erected by the Dutch West India Company in 1623 near present-day Gloucester City and occupied intermittently until 1651, seemingly had slaves by 1637, possibly earlier. Evidence also points to a black presence by 1639 in the Dutch settlement of Pavonia (in or near present-day Jersey City). Certainly it was the Dutch who, after the English seized New Jersey from them in 1664, brought African slaves into New Jersey in significant numbers. They were encouraged by the colony's 1664 Concessions and Agreement that offered settlers additional land for every slave imported before 1667. Eventually most slaves were brought in by the English. They were acquired from the West Indies, especially Barbados, until the mid-eighteenth century when they began to be imported directly from Africa.

After World War II African Americans continued to arrive from the South on an even larger scale until the end of the 1960s. The more than twofold increase in the black population from 318,565 in 1950 to 770,292 in 1970 coincided with the abandonment by many whites of the state's cities and led to the enlargement of the state's black ghettos. Their myriad social and economic ills caused many to erupt in violence during the 1960s. The violence that occurred in 1967 in Newark, the state's largest city, involved twenty-six fatalities and was by far the most serious.

Black protest in the 1960s was also directed towards discriminatory treatment in housing, employment and, especially in South Jersey, public accommodations (e.g., hotels, restaurants, theatres, parks, and beaches). Perhaps the most important symbol of the success of the protest in the political arena was the election in 1970 of Kenneth Gibson as Newark's first African-American mayor.

By 1980 virtually all black life in New Jersey, the nation's most urbanized and densely populated state, had an urban essence and texture. Over 95 percent of the state's African Americans were urban dwellers in 1980. In 1990, when blacks numbered 1,036,825 and constituted 13.4 percent of the overall population, they comprised majorities in nine major New Jersey communities: Newark, East Orange, Camden, Irvington, Plainfield, Orange, Willingboro, Atlantic City, and Asbury Park. By 1999, the black population had increased to an estimated 1,188,236, constituting 14.6 percent of the state's population, the highest percentage ever.

New Jersey in 1996, with a figure of $46,803, ranked first among states in terms of median household income and had only 8.9 percent of its residents living in poverty-the fifth lowest percent among states. By this year substantial progress for the black community could be counted on several fronts as well. Still, some of the state's predominantly black municipalities were among the nation's poorest, a reality suggesting that a disproportionate number of black New Jerseyans have benefited less from the general economic well-being the state has experienced in recent years.

REFERENCES

Cooley, Henry Scofield. *A Study of Slavery in New Jersey*. 1896.

Greene, Larry A. "A History of Afro-Americans in New Jersey." *The Journal of the Rutgers University Libraries*, Vol. LVI, No.1., 1994.

Hagan, Lee, Larry A. Greene, Leonard Harris, and Clement A. Price. "New Jersey Afro-Americans: From Colonial times to the Present." In *The New Jersey Ethnic Experience*, Barbara Cunningham, ed., pp. 64-87. 1977.

Price, Clement Alexander. *Freedom Not Far Distant: A Documentary History of Afro-Americans in New Jersey.* 1980.

Wright, Giles R. *Afro-Americans in New Jersey: A Short History.* 1988.

Wright, Marion M. Thompson. *The Education of Negroes in New Jersey.* 1941.

GILES R. WRIGHT

New York Age. *See* Fortune, T. Thomas, Washington, Booker T., Barnett, B. Wells.

New York City (Update). Despite the city's long history of progessive social policy and massive anti-poverty spending, New York's citizens of African ancestry endured rising difficulties in the last years of the twentieth century. Among the underlying causes was the erosion of the city's base of manufacturing jobs; New York's economic problems were masked by the glittering midtown prosperity generated during the 1990s stock market boom, but the explosion in Wall Street profits held few benefits for ordinary African Americans. The defeat of Democratic African-American mayor David Dinkins at the hands of law-and-order Republican Rudolph Giuliani in 1993 inaugurated a long reign of aggressive police tactics that engendered mistrust of the police in parts of the African-American community even as crime dropped sharply. Two incidents in particular received national publicity. In 1997, Haitian immigrant Abner Louima was tortured and sexually brutalized by a group of New York police officers, some of whom were later convicted of criminal offenses in connection with the incident. In 1999 an unarmed African immigrant, Amadou Diallo, was shot to death by police; the officers claimed that they had mistaken Diallo's wallet for a weapon, and were acquitted in February of 2000.

Among the leaders of the protests that materialized in the wake of the Diallo incident was the Rev. Al Sharpton, a fiery activist who had first come to prominence with the alleged abduction of upstate teenager Tawana Brawley in the 1980s. Sharpton was one of several clergymen who commanded community-wide followings; another was the Rev. Floyd Flake, pastor of the Allen African Methodist Episcopal Church, who served several terms in the U.S. Congress.

African-American New Yorkers connected with the entertainment industry continued to play a dominant role in the 1990s. Brooklyn-based filmmaker Spike Lee forged a distinctive quasi-improvisational style that captured the rhythms of New York life in such films as *Crooklyn* and *Summer of Sam.* Lee was noted for incorporating hip-hop music into the soundtracks of his films, and New York hip-hop musicians, despite a well-publicized and sometimes violent rivalry with their West Coast counterparts, continued to advance the frontiers of the genre.

REFERENCES

George, Nelson. *Hip Hop America.* 1998.

Lippert, Barbara. "He's Gotta Have It (All)." *New York* (May 11, 1998), 20.

Moore, Acel. "For Citizens and Police, Diallo Case Hard to Swallow." *Knight- Ridder/Tribune News Service* (February 29, 2000).

Scherer, Ron. "For New York's Minorities, Healing Begins Slowly." *Christian Science Monitor* (June 10, 1999), 2.

Sharpton, Al, with Anthony Walton. *Go and Tell Pharoah: The Autobiography of the Reverend Al Sharpton.* 1996.

JAMES MANHEIM

Nichols, Nichelle (Grace Nichols) (c. December 1936–), actress, singer. Best known as Lieutenant Uhura, the lead female member of the "classic" cast of the original *Star Trek,* one of the most popular science-fiction television series (1966–69) in the history of broadcasting in America. Television's first interracial kiss was performed by Nichols and the series' lead, William Shatner, in the episode "Plato's Stepchildren." Despite playing a revolutionary role as an intelligent, articulate, and dignified woman and African-American during the 1960s, Nichols felt that her character's potential was minimized and considered leaving the show. Martin Luther King Jr. convinced her to continue her critical work as the then sole-representative of an African-American "of the future," and the only space African-American space traveler on television.

Nichols was born in Robbin, Illinois and began her performing career in the 1940s and 50s, singing and

Nichelle Nichols. (The Gamma Liaison Network)

dancing for Duke Ellington and Lionel Hampton. She was trained in ballet and Afro-Cuban dance and later toured the U.S. and Canada and as a nightclub entertainer before landing her role on *Star Trek*. Nichols appears in six *Star Trek* motion pictures as well as *Porgy and Bess* (1959), *Doctor You've Got to be Kidding* (1967), *Truck Turner* (1974), *The Supernatural* (1987), *Gargoyles* (1994) and *The Adventures of Captain Zoom* (1995). Never abandoning her love of singing and dancing for live audiences, she made a return to the stage, performing the one-woman theatrical show, *Reflections* (1992), a musical tribute to great African-American female performers.

Nichols, endorsed by the National Aeronautics Space Administration (NASA), also worked to recruit women and people of color as astronauts in the late 1970s.

See also JEMISON, MAE CAROL [3]; TELEVISION [5].

REFERENCES

Jet Vol. 87; n2 (1994); 62.

LaBlanc, Michael L. ed. *Contemporary Black Biography: Profiles from the International Black Community*, vol. 11, 1989.

Nichols, Nichelle. *Beyond Uhura: Star Trek and Other Memories*. c1994.

Stevens, Tracy, ed. *International Television & Video Almanac*, 44th edition. 1999.

F. ZEAL HARRIS

North Carolina (Update). Since 1968 blacks have returned to the North Carolina General Assembly as representatives and senators; won election as mayors of such major cities as Raleigh, Durham, and Chapel Hill; served in cabinet, Council of State, and judicial posts, including the chief justice of the state supreme court. In 1992 blacks were elected as representatives to Congress after almost a century's absence. Despite repeated legal challenges to the boundaries of the first and twelfth congressional districts, the two representatives—Eva Clayton and Mel Watt respectively—won reelection in 1994, 1996, and 1998. Between 1970 and 1997 voters chose 506 black elected officials in North Carolina. Sixty-five served in the U.S. Congress and state legislature; 354 in city and county offices; twenty-nine in law enforcement; and ninety-six in education.

In 1990 blacks constituted 22 percent (1,461,562) of the state's population. By 1998 the black population had increased almost 14 percent to 1,665,273. Significantly, the 1980 census revealed that more blacks moved into the state (92,991) than those who left it (72,475).

With congressional redistricting again scheduled after the 2000 census, the boundaries of the two congressional seats held by blacks certainly will be subject to revision. Legal challenges to the Swann busing decision also may test the state and nation's commitment to integrated schools. Advocates of neighborhood schools, both white and black, have become disillusioned with the long bus trips endured by their children. Yet economic disparities and residential patterns remain diverse. Black per capita income in 1990 ($7,926) was only 55 percent of white per capita income ($14,450).

REFERENCES

Anderson, Eric. *Race and Politics in North Carolina*. 1981.

Crow, Jeffrey J., Paul D. Escott, and Flora J. Hatley. *A History of African Americans in North Carolina*. 1992.

JEFFREY J. CROW

North Star. Frederick Douglass began publication of *North Star*, a four-page weekly newspaper, in Rochester, New York, on December 3, 1847. This was the third anti-slavery paper at the time; the others were William Lloyd Garrison's *The Liberator* (Boston) and the *National Anti-Slavery Standard* (New York City). Douglass' paper differed from the others in that it was aimed not only at abolitionist causes, but also promoted women's rights and suffrage. Martin Delany was listed as co-editor until July of the following year and remained a regular contributor; other black correspondents for the paper include James McCune Smith, William J. Wilson, Samuel Ringgold Ward, and William Wells Brown. William C. Nell worked as printer for the paper, and his name was listed on the masthead until June 23, 1848.

By the middle of 1849 *North Star* had four thousand subscribers, but finances remained a problem and depended on contributions and fund-raising projects. By 1851 Douglass had aligned himself with the Liberty Party and became an advocate of political action as the means of abolishing slavery. This led to a break with Garrison and Nell, who were steadfast in advocating moral suasion as the only proper course of action. In 1851 Douglass merged *North Star* with *Liberty Party Paper* as *Frederick Douglass' Paper*, subsidized by Gerrit Smith, a wealthy white abolitionist. *Frederick Douglass' Paper* ceased publication in July 1860.

North Star not only furnished an outlet for the views of Frederick Douglass and other abolitionists, its headquarters in Rochester were an important way station on the Underground Railroad, offering assistance to more than four hundred individuals.

See also BEMAN, AMOS GERRY [1]; CLARK, PETER HUMPHRIES [2]; DELANY, MARTIN ROBISON [2]; DOUGLASS, FREDERICK [2]; FREDERICK DOUGLASS'S PAPER [2]; JACOBS, HARRIET ANN [3]; JOURNALISM [3]; NELL, WILLIAM COOPER [4]; NEW YORK STATE [4]; WHITFIELD, JAMES MONROE [5].

REFERENCES

Danky, James P., and Maureen E. Hady, eds. *African-American Newspapers and Periodicals: A National Bibliography*. 1998.

Ripley, C. Peter, and others, eds. *The Black Abolitionist Papers*, vol. 4. 1991.

Smith, Jessie Carney, ed. *Notable Black American Men*. [Martin Delaney, Frederick Douglass, and William C. Nell] 1999.

ROBERT L. JOHNS

O

O.J. Simpson Trial. On June 12, 1994, Nicole Brown Simpson and her friend Ronald Goldman were murdered in Los Angeles. Evidence implicated football star O.J. Simpson, Nicole's former husband. On June 17, when authorities scheduled Simpson for questioning, he tried to flee the country. After a nationally televised freeway auto chase, Simpson was captured and jailed. At a preliminary hearing in July, police reported finding blood in Simpson's house and car and on a glove that matched one in Simpson's house.

Simpson's murder trial opened before Judge Lance Ito in January of 1995 and lasted over eight months, during which time it was the object of intense media scrutiny and provoked a national debate over issues of race and domestic violence. The "dream team" of highly-paid defense counsel, led by Johnnie Cochran, an African American (*See also* COCHRAN, JOHNNIE), and assisted by Robert Shapiro and F. Lee Bailey, charged that police investigator Mark Fuhrman had framed Simpson out of racial prejudice. Prosecutors Marcia Clark and Christopher Darden, an African American, pointed to Simpson's history of wife battering and accused the defense of irresponsibly playing the "race card." However, the defense was able to show that Fuhrman had lied about his past utterances of racial slurs, and the prosecution's case was further weakened when the bloodstained glove found in Simpson's house was shown not to fit his hand. In October of 1995, the largely black jury acquitted Simpson. However, in February 1997, fol-

lowing a civil trial, Simpson lost an $8.5 million wrongful death suit brought by the victims' families.

REFERENCE

Toobin, Jeffrey. *The Run of His Life*. 1997.

GREG ROBINSON

O'Leary, Hazel Rollins (Update) (May 17, 1937–) corporate executive. The policy of Northern States Power regarding the storage of nuclear waste earned her some criticism from environmental groups. In 1990 Northern States sought to build nuclear storage facilities at Prairie Island, Minnesota, next to the Mdewakanton Sioux Indian Reservation. After the Sioux protested, a judge prohibited an expansion of the nuclear waste site. O'Leary then drafted a compromise with regulators that permitted Northern States to open the storage facility on a reduced scale. Her background in energy regulation and her commitment to conservation attracted the attention of President Bill Clinton, who in 1993 offered O'Leary the post of secretary of energy. When confirmed, O'Leary became the first woman ever to hold that post.

O'Leary's tenure as energy secretary was troubled. Critics charged that she had sold access to her office by forcing companies to contribute to her favorite charity. Following her resignation on January 20, 1997, a special prosecutor was appointed to investigate the allegations. Shortly afterward, O'Leary again made

Hazel O'Leary. (AP/Wide World Photos)

headlines when she admitted in a deposition that watchdogs who made complaints in nuclear facilities were routinely harassed.

REFERENCES

New York Times, January 19, 1992.

Nixon, Will. "Bill and Al's Green Adventure." *Environmental Magazine* (May 1993).

Washington Post, January 19, 1993.

JAMES BRADLEY

Owens, Major Robert (June 28, 1936–), politician, librarian, writer. Born and raised in Memphis, Owens graduated from Morehouse College in 1956. One year later he received his master's degree in library science from Atlanta University (now Clark Atlanta). He joined the Brooklyn public library staff in 1958. From 1954 to 1966, as chairman of the Brooklyn Congress of Racial Equality(CORE) he was in direct contact with civil rights activities and local political movements.

Owens accepted Mayor John Lindsay's appointment as Commissioner of Community Development for New York City, with responsibility for antipoverty and self-help programs. Continuing his interest in political life, Owens was elected in 1974 to the New York State Senate. Since 1983, he has been a member of the U.S. House of Representatives representing New York's 12th district and later the 11th district when redistricting occurred.

In Congress, Owens performed well. He was appointed chair of the House Subcommittee on Select Education in 1987, a post he held six years. He also chaired the Congressional Black Caucus. After that, Owens was a member of the Education and Workforce Committee where he helped to guide federal involvement in education, job training, programs for the aging, and other areas. In 2000, he was ranking Democrat on the Subcommittee for Workforce Protections. Although Owens is a politician and no longer a practicing librarian, he remains an outspoken advocate for libraries as well as for education in general. He consistently proposes or supports legislation for funding to strengthen both areas.
See also MEMPHIS [3].

REFERENCES

ALA Yearbook of Library and Information Services. 1988.

Bigelow, Barbara Carlisle, ed. *Contemporary Black Biography*, vol. 6. 1994.

"Congressman Major Owens, United States Representative." http://www.house.gov/owens/info.htm June 1, 2000.

JESSIE CARNEY SMITH

Owens, Dana Elaine. *See* Queen Latifah.

P

Page, Clarence (June 2, 1947–), journalist. Clarence Page was born in Dayton, Ohio, and became interested in journalism in high school, taking the Southeast Ohio High School Newspaper Association award for best feature article. He continued newspaper work at Ohio University in Athens and graduated with a bachelor's degree in journalism in 1969.

Page's tenure with the Chicago *Tribune* immediately after graduation was briefly interrupted by his draft induction into the military in 1970. However, he returned to the paper the next year as reporter and assistant editor and quickly made his mark as a member of the paper's task force series on vote fraud that won a Pulitzer Prize in 1972. Other recognitions were quick to come his way; he won the 1976 Edward Scott Beck Award for his reporting on the changing politics of Southern Africa, and the 1980 Illinois United Press International award for his investigative series on "The Black Tax."

A freelance writer, Page has been published in a number of sources, including the *Chicago Reader*, *New Republic*, the *Wall Street Journal*, and *Emerge*. His nationally syndicated columns appear on Sundays and Wednesdays on the Chicago *Tribune*'s op-ed page. Page made history in 1989 when he became the first black columnist to win a Pulitzer Prize. In 1996 he wrote his first book, *Showing My Color: Impolite Essays on Race and Identity*. Also breaking into the medium of television, Page became a regular news analyst for ABC News, an occasional panelist on *The McLaughlin Group*, a regular contributor to *NewsHour with Jim Lehrer*, and a host of several Public Broadcasting System documentaries.

See also JOURNALISM [3].

REFERENCES

"About Clarence Page." http://chicagotribune.com/neews/columnists/page/feature/0,1438,2734,00/html

"Clarence Page." In *Contemporary Black Biography*, vol. 4, edited by Barbara Carlisle Bigelow. 1993.

RAYMOND WINBUSH

Parks, Henry Green (September 29, 1916– April 24, 1989), entrepreneur, business executive, civic leader. Six months after he was born in Atlanta, Parks and his family moved to Dayton, Ohio, where they sought a better life. He was greatly influence by his father, who taught him to take risks and make hard choices; these attributes helped him to become successful later on. While studying at Ohio State University, he roomed with Jesse Owens, later an Olympic gold medallist. He worked his way through college and graduated in 1939. While in college, educator Mary McLeod Bethune became his mentor and later helped him find employment with the Resident War Productive Training Center in Wilberforce, Ohio. There he met boxer Joe Louis, who became his partner in several enterprises. Parks became road manager for the boxer's wife, Marva

Louis, and also headed a beverage company that produced Joe Louis Punch.

Parks was sales representative for Pabst Brewing Company in 1940–1942 . Co-worker W. B. Graham and Parks founded a public relations and advertising business in 1942. In 1949 Parks became part owner and salesman of Crayton Southern Sausage in Cleveland. The business escalated, causing his partners some concern and a desire to curb progress; Parks objected, however, and decided to sell his interest in the firm.

After relocating to Baltimore and working in several capacities, Parks, with the backing of William "Little Willie" Adams, started a new business in 1951 with the opening of Parks Sausage Company. He was a pioneer in giving demonstrations and taste tests in supermarkets. He also aimed a marketing campaign in white and black communities and gave gifts to children. The company symbol, Parky the Pig, became widely recognized. Though the company struggled at first, in time it prospered and had a positive, national reputation. From 1969 to 1977, the company traded shares on NASDAQ stock exchange until it was taken over privately. In the mid-1970s Parks, now suffering from Parkinson's disease, and Adams sold their interest in the company.
See also ATLANTA [1].

REFERENCES

Garraty, John A., and Mark C. Carnes, general editors. *American National Biography*. 1999.

Editors of *Ebony*. *Ebony Success Library*, vols. 1-2. 1973

Smith, Jessie Carney, and Joseph M. Palmisano, eds. *The African American Almanac*, 8th ed. 2000.

FREDERICK D. SMITH, JR.

Parks, Rosa Louise McCauley (Update)

(February 4, 1913–), civil rights leader. During the 1990s, Parks took an increasingly visible role as African-American elder statesperson. She wrote three books, including an autobiography and a book of children's letters to her, *Dear Mrs. Parks*. She also was the recipient of nationwide sympathy after her house in Detroit was robbed in 1994. In 1996, though confined to a wheelchair, she spoke at the Million Man March.

REFERENCE

"Rosa Parks." In *Encyclopedia of World Biography*, 2nd ed. 1998.

GREG ROBINSON

Parsons, Richard Dean

(April 4, 1948–), lawyer, political advisor, corporate executive. Richard D. Parsons grew up in Queens, New York. Graduating from high school at age 16, he completed his undergraduate studies at the University of Hawaii in 1968, and graduated first in his class from Union University's Albany Law School.

Parsons began his career as assistant counsel for New York Governor Nelson Rockefeller in 1971, and followed Rockefeller to Washington, D.C., when he became Gerald Ford's vice president in 1974. Parsons acted as general counsel and associate director of the White House Domestic Council until the end of the Ford Administration.

In 1977 Parsons joined the law firm of Patterson, Belknap, Webb & Tyler. He attained partner status in just two years, but left the firm in 1988 to become the chief operating officer of the Dime Savings Bank of New York. Despite his lack of background in banking, Parsons initiated a massive turnaround at the finan-

Richard Dean Parsons. (Time-Warner Inc.)

Rosa Parks, age 43, riding in the front of a bus. (Corbis Corporation)

cially troubled banking giant. By 1990, Parsons was CEO and chairman of the board. As such he engineered the merger of Dime Savings with Anchor Savings Bank to create Dime Bancorp in early 1995, resulting in what was then the fourth-largest thrift institution in the country.

On October 1, 1994, Parsons was named president of Time Warner Inc., becoming one of the highest-ranking black officers in corporate America. Once again entering an industry in which he had no background, Parsons' sharp business acumen guided Time Warner into healthy growth, positioning the company for the largest merger ever as plans to combine with America Online went forward in the year 2000.

See also NEW YORK CITY [4].

REFERENCES

"Parsons, Richard: Files-NarrativeSummary." http://www. ford.utexas.edu/library/faintro/parsons1.htm

"Richard Parsons." In *Contemporary Black Biography*, vol. 11, edited by L. Mpho Mabunda and Shirelle Phelps. 1996.

"Time Warner About Time Warner Inc.," http://www. pathfinder.com/corp/about/timewarnerinc/ corporate/exec-parsons.html

KEVIN C. KRETSCHMER

Payne, Donald Milford (July 16, 1934–), politician. Payne, in 2000 in his sixth term as U.S. Representative from Newark, New Jersey, was born in Newark. He received his B.A. degree from Seton Hall in 1957 and from 1957 to 1963 he did graduate studies there. He taught in the Newark public school system from 1957 to 1964 then left to join Prudential Life Insurance Company as a manager. He was also a volunteer with the local YMCA and gradually he rose in rank to become national president in 1970, the first African American ever to hold that position. In 1973 he was elected chair of the Y's World Refugee and Rehabilitation Committee, a position that required him to travel to over eighty countries.

Payne entered the political arena in 1960s and early 1970s. His political career included election to the Newark City Council in 1982 and election to the U.S. Congress in 1988, representing the 10th Congressional District. He won by an overwhelming majority and became the state's first African American Congressman.

In 2000 as a member of the House Committee on Education and Workforce, Payne serves on the Subcommittee on Early Childhood, Youth and Families and Employer-Employee Relations. He is a ranking member of the International Relations Committee and its Subcommittee on Africa. Payne is past chair of the Congressional Black Caucus. In addition to his work on other committees, he is a leading advocate of education and has been involved in passing key legislation such as that relating to student loans, work opportunities, and support of students in high poverty school districts.
See also NEWARK, NEW JERSEY [4].

REFERENCES

Bigelow, Barbara Carlisle, ed. *Contemporary Black Biography*, 1992.

"Biography of Donald M. Payne." http://www.house.gov/payne/bio-engl.htm

Cheers, D. Michael. "Donald Payne: New Jersey's First Black Congressman." *Ebony* 44 (May 1989): 92-94.

RAYMOND WINBUSH

Pelham, Benjamin B. (1862–October 7, 1948), editor, politician, municipal official. Pelham was born in Detroit into a family of free, prosperous blacks who had relocated there from Virginia in 1862. Pelham became a newsboy for the *Detroit Post*, later renamed the *Post Tribune*, Michigan's leading Republican daily.

He completed high school, became an apprentice typesetter for the paper, and enrolled in an accounting course in a local business college.

In 1879, Pelham's older brother Robert Jr., had joined Benjamin as an apprentice typesetter. Robert began publishing his own eight-page newspaper, the *Venture*, from the small printing firm that the two had established. The brothers and two associates founded the *Plaindealer*, a weekly and the successor to the *Venture*. To sustain themselves, the brothers continued their work for the *Post Tribune*.

The paper covered African American affairs comprehensively. Important black figures of that period, including Frederick Douglass, John R. Lynch, and Ida B. Wells Barnett, wrote articles, helping to make the *Plaindealer* one of the nation's leading African American newspapers, particularly in Michigan and in the Midwest. Because the paper was the political voice for African Americans in the Midwest, by 1884 it had helped Pelham to gain national political influence and led to his election as delegate-at-large to the Republican National Convention.

In 1893 the *Plaindealer* stopped publication. Pelham became clerk in the local Internal Revenue Office and then held a position in Office of the Treasurer in Detroit (1900–1906). Known as a shrewd politician, the long- time Republican had by 1906 formed his own black political machine. He continued to work in local government after the Democrats were in power until he retired in 1942.
See also DETROIT [2].

REFERENCES

Garraty, John A., and Mark C. Carnes, general eds. *American Negro Biography*. 1999.

Logan, Rayford W., and Michael R. Winston, eds. *Dictionary of American Negro Biography*. 1982.

Robinson, Wilhelmena. *Historical Negro Biographies*. 1968.

JESSIE CARNEY SMITH

Pennsylvania (Update). In the later decades of the twentieth century, the position of blacks in Pennsylvania remained uncertain. Although 80 percent of the state's African-American community was concentrated in Allegheny, Delaware, Dauphin, and Philadelphia counties, black communities continued to grow. Growth was particularly impressive in the north of the state, in cities such as Williamsport and Erie.

Meanwhile, African Americans developed considerable political clout. On the local level, Philadelphia elected W. Wilson Goode as its first African-American mayor in 1983. On the state level, by 1993, there were fifteen black state representatives and three senators, and in 1994, state Rep. Dwight Evans finished a strong second in the Democratic gubernatorial primary. On the national level, U.S. Rep. William Grey III attained the position of House Majority Whip before his resignation from office in 1990. The fight for economic empowerment has been more difficult. Beginning in the 1970s and increasing in the 1980s, industrial downsizing in factory communities such as Chester and Johnstown led to high levels of black unemployment and poverty.

African-American Pennsylvanians have made significant contributions in diverse fields. Some notable figures are writer David Bradley, born in Altoona; composer/musicologist Harry T. Burleigh, born in Erie; Hall of Fame catcher Roy Campanella, born in Philadelphia; basketball legend Wilt Chamberlain, born in Philadelphia; performer/educator Bill Cosby, born in Philadelphia; jazz musician John Coltrane raised in Philadelphia; educator-critic Alain Locke, born in Philadelphia; civil rights and gay activist Bayard Rustin, born in West Chester; painter Henry Ossawa Tanner, born in Pittsburgh; singer/actress Ethel Waters, born in Chester; open-heart-surgery pioneer Dr. Daniel Hale Williams, born in Hollidayburg; and playwright August Wilson, born in Pittsburgh.

REFERENCES

Adelman, Debra. *Waiting for the Lord: Nineteenth Century Black Communities in Susquehanna County. Pennsylvania.* 1997.

Blockson, Charles L. *African Americans in Pennsylvania: A History and Guide.* 1994.

Carter, Alice Roston. *Can I Get a Witness? Growing Up in the Black Middle Class in Erie, Pennsylvania.* 1991.

Dickerson, Dennis C. *Out of the Crucible: Black Steelworkers in Western Pennsylvania, 1875–1980.* 1986.

Downey, Dennis, and Raymond M. Hyster. *No Crooked Death: Coatesville, Pennsylvania and the Lynching of Zachariah Walker.* 1991.

Gottlieb, Peter. *Making Their Own Way: Southern Blacks' Migration to Pittsburgh, 1916–1930.* 1987.

Gregg, Robert S. *Sparks From the Anvil of Oppression: Philadelphia's African Methodists and Southern Migrants, 1890–1940.* 1993.

Harris, Richard E. *Politics and Prejudice: A History of Chester, Pennsylvania Negroes.* 1991.

Hopkins, Leroy, and Eric Ledell Smith. *The African Americans in Pennsylvania.* 1994.

McBride, David, ed. *Blacks in Pennsylvania History: Research and Educational Perspectives.* 1983.

Moss, Emerson I. *African Americans in the Wyoming Valley, 1778–1990.* 1992.

Nash, Garry B. *Forging Freedom: The Formation of Philadelphia's Black Community, 1720–1840.* 1991.

Slaughter, Thomas P. *Bloody Dawn: The Christiana Riot and Racial Violence in the Antebellum North.* 1991.

Smith, Eric Ledell and Trotter Jr., Joe Williams. Eds. *African Americans in Pennsylvanis: Shifting Historical Perspectives.*

Thompson, Sarah S. *Journey from Jerusalem: An Illustrated Introduction to Erie's African American History. 1795–1995.* 1996.

ERIC LEDELL SMITH

Perkins, Edward Joseph (June 8, 1928–), diplomat, ambassador. Perkins was born in Sterlington, Louisiana. He attended a two-room segregated school and waited nearly 40 years before continuing his education. From 1958 to 1966 he was in the U.S. Army and Air Force Exchange Service. Later he attended Lewis and Clark College and then transferred to the University of Maryland, graduating in 1968. He continued his education at the University of Southern California, graduating in 1972 with a master's degree and in 1978 with a doctoral degree.

While in college, Perkins worked for the U.S. Foreign Service's Agency for International Development. He left in 1970 to become assistant director management on the U.S. Mission to Thailand. Next he was staff assistant in the Office of the Director General of the Foreign Service, in 1972 and then personnel officer (1972–1974). Perkins advanced his career by serving as management analysis officer (1975–1978) and later director of the Office of West African Affairs (1983–1985) for the U.S. Department of State. He was counselor for political affairs for Accra, Ghana (1978–1981) and deputy chief of mission in Monrovia, Liberia (1981–1983). In 1983 he studied French at the Foreign Service Institute.

In 1985 President Ronald Reagan appointed Perkins ambassador to Liberia and one year later ambassador to South Africa. Until he left the position in 1989,

Perkins worked to improve conditions in South Africa and helped to reduce racist policies there. He was named director general of Foreign Service. Perkins was appointed as U.S. ambassador to the United Nations in 1992 for a brief period; then, until he retired in 1996, he was ambassador to Australia.

REFERENCES

Bigelow, Barbara Carlisle, ed. *Contemporary Black Biography*, vol. 5. 1994.

Smith, Jessie Carney, ed. *Notable Black American Men*. 1999.

Who's Who Among African Americans, 12th ed. 1999.

RAYMOND WINBUSH

Perry, Heman Edward (March 5, 1873–January 3, 1929), businessman. Heman Edward Perry was an entrepreneur who made a profound impression on African American business in Atlanta, Georgia. Born in Houston, Texas, Perry acquired only a few years of formal education. He received extensive practical business experience as he helped out in his father's different business activities. Beginning sometime in the 1890s, he spent twelve years in New York City. There he worked for several insurance companies and speculated in stocks.

Perry arrived in Atlanta in 1908, with the aim of establishing a soundly-financed insurance company to serve the African American market. His first effort to raise capital fell short of the necessary sum, and he returned the money to his investors. A second effort was successful, however, and Standard Life Insurance Company was launched in 1913. By 1924 the company operated in twelve states and the District of Columbia.

In 1917 Perry organized Service Enterprises with money borrowed from Standard Life. Service Enterprises came to comprise eleven organizations, including a realty company, a construction company, a laundry, and a printing company. Perry's companies built five hundred homes and sold the land for Booker T. Washington High School to the city of Atlanta. In 1921 Perry opened the Citizens Trust Bank.

Perry ran into trouble in 1924 due to overexpansion and mismanagement. His problems led to Standard Life passing into white ownership; the other businesses, including the bank, were reorganized. Perry moved to Kansas City, Missouri, where he tried to reestablish himself but soon died of a heart attack.

See also ATLANTA, GEORGIA [1]; GEORGIA [2].

REFERENCES

Henderson, Alexa B. "Heman Edward Perry." In *American National Biography*, edited by John A. Garraty and Mark C. Carnes. 1999.

Ingam, John N. and Lynne B. Feldman. *African-American Business Leaders: A Biographical Dictionary*. 1994.

ROBERT L. JOHNS

Philadelphia, Pennsylvania (Update). Racial polarization defined Philadelphia's civic life during and after the 1970s reign of Republican mayor Frank Rizzo; at the century's end that polarization was more muted, even if no less entwined into the fabric of the city. The mayoralty returned to white hands in 1991 after the eight years in office of Democrat W. Wilson Goode, the city's first African-American mayor. Philadelphia thus became the first large American city to elect a white mayor after a period of African-American control, but the sucessor, Ed Rendell, was considered a less divisive figure than Rizzo; he worked closely with African-American city council president John Street, and endorsed Street when the latter ran for mayor in 1999. Street, the son of a Pennsylvania tenant farmer, participated in Philadelphia's civil-rights struggles as a young man but later earned a reputation as a hard-working pragmatist; his farm-based habit of rising every morning at 4 a.m. served him well when he was faced with the stressful demands of city government. In the 1999 election Street faced moderate white Republican Sam Katz, and the campaign was notably free of racial appeals. When Street emerged victorious, however, it was with an estimated 95 percent of the black vote, while Katz notched margins nearly that large in the city's white ethnic wards. Another rising star in the ranks of Philadelphia's African-American politicians was U.S. Representative Chaka Fattah, elected in 1994 in Pennsylvania's Second District. Fattah emerged as a leader in an effort to persuade the U.S. federal government to issue an apology for its former encouragement of slavery. The U.S. national Republican Party held its convention in Philadelphia in 2000, and attempted to create a more diverse image than it had in the past through the inclusion of numerous African Americans and other minorities in its daily programs. Outside the political realm, Dr. Emma B. Chappell was among the black Philadelphians who gained national attention; through an impressive effort to gather funding from individual small investors, Chappell established and led as president the United Bank of Phila-delphia, the city's first black-owned bank in nearly four decades.

REFERENCES

Brown, Carolyn M. "A Bank Grows in Philly." *Black Enterprise* (June, 1995), 166.

Dionne, E. J., Jr. "Philadelphia's Classy Campaigners." *Nation's Cities Weekly* (November 8, 1999), 4.

Siegel, Fred. "Why Race Matters Less—Fair Philly." *New Republic* (November 1, 1999), 13.

"Street Smart: Philadelphia Activist-Turned-Mayor John Street Now Presides over the City Government He Once Battled." *People Weekly* (January 17, 2000), 105.

JAMES MANHEIM

Phylon.

Phylon was a quarterly journal founded by W. E. B. DuBois, edited by him from 1940 to1944, and published under the auspices of Atlanta Univer-sity. The journal was designed to replace the school's earlier publications, which had initiated a more scien-tific approach to the study of race. Even though this approach had been used by other institutions and some scholars were adapting their works to this, it was still necessary to revisit and revise what had and was taking place relative to race in academia. The focus was to be cultural and historical rather than biological and psychological. The original editorial board and contributing editors included Ira DeAugustine Reid, William Stanley Braithwaite, Mercer Cook, Horace M. Bond, and Rayford W. Logan. While the articles were to be devoted to the social sciences, there were works by and about individuals and topics germane to the humanities. Literary issues were addressed by such critics as Arthur P. Davis, Nick Aaron Ford, and Hugh Gloster, and original poetry and fiction also were published, including work by authors such as Langston Hughes and Countee Cullen. The journal ceased publication in 1988.

Freedom's Odyssey: African American History Essays from Phylon (1999), edited by Alexa B. Henderson and Janis S. Edmond, contains 29 scholarly essays on African American history that appeared in the journal. The topics include slave revolts, abolitionism, deseg-regation and the Civil Rights Movement.
See also JOURNALISM [3]; LITERARY MAGAZINES [3]; QUARLES, BENJAMIN [4].

REFERENCES

"Apology." *Phylon* 1 (1940): 3–5.

DeSantis, Christopher C. "Phylon." In *Oxford Compan-ion to African American Literature*, edited by William L. Andrews and others. 1997.

HELEN R. HOUSTON

Pickens, William

(January 15, 1881–April 6, 1954), educator, civil rights leader. William Pickens was an educator and a major civil rights leader. Born in Anderson County, South Carolina, to tenant farm-ers, he managed to secure an education. After three years at Talladega College, he transferred to Yale where he earned a degree in 1904, becoming the second black elected to the school's chapter of Phi Beta Kappa. Pickens taught at Talladega from 1904 to 1914, at Wiley University in Marshall, Texas, from 1914 to 1915, and at Morgan College in Baltimore, from 1915 to 1920, where he became the school's first African American dean.

Pickens, who had long been active in civil rights, became field secretary of the National Association for the Advancement of Colored People in 1920. Work-ing as liaison between branches and the national office, he was very popular with the membership but often at odds with national staff members, especially Walter White. Pickens's visibility was furthered by his oratorical skills and by his writing. For example, he was a syndicated columnist for the Associated Negro Press. He took a year's leave in 1937 to lecture for the Federal Forum Project, an adult education effort. In

William Pickens. (Fisk University Library)

May 1941 another leave allowed him to take a position selling war bonds for the Treasury Department.

Pickens's criticism of NAACP policy led to his being fired from the organization in 1942. Although he came under attack from a congressional committee as a communist in 1943, he remained with the Treasury Department until 1950, when he retired. It is estimated that Pickens's office sold over a billion dollars of bond to blacks by war's end.

See also AUTOBIOGRAPHY [1]; NATIONAL ASSOCIATION FOR THE ADVANCEMENT OF COLORED PEOPLE (NAACP) [4]; NEW NEGRO [4].

REFERENCES

Avery, Sheldon. "William Pickens." In *Dictionary of American Negro Biography*, edited by Rayford W. Logan and Michael R. Winston. 1982.

Carter, Linda M. "William Pickens." In *Notable Black American Men*, edited by Jessie Carney Smith. 1999.

Pickens, William. *The Heir of Slaves*. 1911.

ROBERT L. JOHNS

Pittsburgh, Pennsylvania (Update).

With well over a quarter of the city's total population, African Americans in Pittsburgh continued to play important roles in the city's political, social, and cultural life during the 1990s. They also experienced the decade's growing pains, especially in the areas of economic development, employment, and relationships with the police. The 1990s saw increasing debate over affirmative action, police brutality, and public housing policies.

With 30.9 percent of black males and 34.7 percent of black females not in the labor force in Pittsburgh in the mid-1990s, changes in guidelines for affirmative action initiatives for minority contractors raised serious concerns in the black community. Politicians and community leaders lamented the increasing poverty among blacks and the relatively few number of blacks in professional occupations.

Several incidences of alleged police brutality also rocked the black community during the 1990s. Three cases of alleged excessive force by white officers against blacks and the subsequent acquittals of the officers by all-white juries in two of the cases angered blacks. Also, controversy erupted over plans to demolish public housing structures and replace them with private housing for which tenants would be granted vouchers. While the Pittsburgh Housing Authority argued that there was too much unoccupied

public housing, advocates of the poor asserted that proposed privately funded space would be unaffordable even with federal grants.

On the plus side, The *Pittsburgh Courier* was revived as the *New Pittsburgh Courier*. In 1997, the first national convention of the NAACP to be held in Pittsburgh brought both money and media attention to the black community. African American businessmen were also becoming more involved in Pittsburgh's development efforts. In addition, black-oriented music, art, and theatrical groups, such as the Kuntu Repertory Theatre, continued to contribute substantially to cultural life.

REFERENCES

Fitzpatrick. Dan. "Public Housing, Private Struggles." *Pittsburgh Business Times and Journal*, September 5, 1997.

Hayes, John. "Black Theater Group Boasts Rich History." *Pittsburgh Post-Gazette Magazine*, January 20, 2000.

Heuck, Douglas. "The Roundtable: Black Business in Pittsburgh." *Post-Gazette.com* (www. post-gazette.com/newslinks/19990502roundtable.asp), July 15, 2000.

"Horror and Healing" (editorial). *Pittsburgh Post-Gazette*, April 30, 2000.

"Pushed to the Margins." *Pittsburgh Business Times and Journal*, April 12, 1996.

Steinman, Larry. "Police Brutality." *New Pittsburgh Courier*, March 6, 1999.

Toler, Sonya M. "Third Renaissance Inclusion." *New Pittsburgh Courier*, January 27, 1999.

"Trust the Public" (editorial). *Pittsburgh Post-Gazette*, June 2, 2000.

Wade, Treshea N. "Blacks Suffer 'Unusually Severe Economic Conditions.'" *New Pittsburgh Courier*, September 25, 1999.

SALLY A. MYERS

Pledger, William Anderson

(1852–January 8, 1904), lawyer, journalist. William Pledger was a politician and journalist. He was born near Jonesboro, Georgia. Little is known of his personal life. His formal education was scanty. He studied at Atlanta University as an adult and through private study gained a knowledge of the law. He was admitted to the bar in 1894.

Pledger moved to Atlanta after the Civil War. Some time after 1870 he moved to Athens, Georgia, where he taught school for five years and began to publish the Athens Blade. He became a delegate to the Republican national convention in 1876. A leader in the black-and-tan faction of the party, he became the first black chair of the Republican state committee in 1880 but was ousted by the white faction two year later. By the time he was reelected party chair in 1902, the Republicans had little power left in state politics. In 1888 Pledger ran for a seat in the state legislature but was defeated.

Pledger was active in the pursuit of civil rights.In 1882, for example, he led a group of armed blacks and succeeded in preventing a lynching in Athens. On the national scene he was an organizer of the Afro-American League in 1890. When the league was reorganized as the Afro-American Council in 1898, he served as a vice president. An active journalist, he founded the *Atlanta Weekly Defiance* and the *Atlanta Age* and served for a considerable period as vice president of the National Afro-American Press Association. *See also* GEORGIA [2].

REFERENCES

Adams, Cyrus Fields. "Col. William A. Pledger." *The Colored American Magazine*. June 1902.

Brattain, Michelle. "William Anderson Pledger." In *American National Biography*, edited by John A. Garraty and Mark C. Carnes. 1999.

Grant, Donald L. *The Way It Was in the South: The Black Experience in Georgia*. 1993.

ROBERT L. JOHNS

Poston, Ted (July 4, 1906–January 11, 1974), journalist, civil rights activist, writer. Theodore Roosevelt Augustus Major Poston, known as "Ted," was born in Hopkinsville, Kentucky, and got his start as a copy clerk for his father's newspaper, the *Contender*. After high school, he attended Tennessee Agricultural and Industrial State College (later Tennessee State University), graduating in 1928.

Poston resumed his newspaper work as a part-time columnist for the *Pittsburgh Courier* until 1929, when he joined the *New York Amsterdam News*. Around 1934, he became city editor of the paper, although he was fired in 1936 for leading a strike to unionize workers. In the late 1930s, Poston became the first African American to write full-time for a New York daily and one of the first full-time staffers with a big-city paper owned by whites when he signed on as a space writer for the *New York Post*. Poston was on leave from the newspaper from 1940 to 1945 while working as a publicist in Washington, D.C.; he also

Ted Poston, 1958. (AP/Wide World Photos)

headed the Negro News Desk in the Office of War Information. He covered assignments in the South that were potentially life-threatening for a black journalist, including the Scottsboro trial in Alabama and the Montgomery Bus Boycott. He retired in 1972.

In addition to his work as journalist, Poston wrote a number of short stories, including several based on his experiences in Hopkinsville. "Revolt of the Evil Fairies," which appeared in *New Republic* and a number of anthologies, illustrates racial barriers in the South by depicting a school play in which roles are assigned on the basis of skin color.
See also JOURNALISM [3].

REFERENCES

Hauk, Kathleen A. *Ted Poston: Pioneer American Journalist*. 1998.

Malinowski, Sharon, ed. *Black Writers*, 2nd ed. 1994.

Smith, Jessie Carney, ed. *Notable Black American Men*. 1999.

JESSIE CARNEY SMITH

Powell, Colin Luther (Update) (April 5, 1937–), Army officer. After leaving the government,

General Colin Powell. (L. Rogers Vando Jr.)

Powell, by now one of the most admired Americans continued his public activities. In October 1994, he traveled to Haiti as part of an American diplomatic mission, and he succeeded in brokering a deal with members of the ruling junta that enabled the country to return to constitutional rule without bloodshed.

Powell's reputation for honesty and moderation led to a widespread Powell-for-President boom. By mid-1995, national polls showed Powell leading all candidates in a presidential campaign, although he had not expressed views on domestic issues or even identified which political party he favored. His celebrity increased following publication of Powell's best-selling memoir, *My American Journey* (1995). For several months, Powell weighed a presidential run; he announced publicly that he was a Republican, but that he favored affirmative action. However, in December 1995 he stated that he did not have the "fire in his belly" to become president, and he withdrew from consideration. He remained in touch with Republican leaders, and he made a popular speech at the Republican convention. In later years, he toured the country as a much sought-after inspirational speaker and adviser. In April 1997, Powell founded America's Promise, a private foundation to aid disadvantaged youth.

REFERENCE

"Colin L(uther) Powell." In *Notable Black American Men.* 1999.

Powell, Colin, with Joseph E. Persico. *My American Journey*. 1995.

GREG ROBINSON

Pratt, Awadagin (March 6, 1966–), concert pianist, conductor. Pratt was born in Pittsburgh, Pennsylvania, and began studying piano at the age of six. In 1975, his family moved to Normal, Illinois, where his parents were university professors. He and his sister, Menah, were treated to a strict regimen of piano, violin and tennis lessons by their parents, firm believers in exposure to a variety of quality experiences.

Following high school graduation, Awadagin enrolled at the University of Illinois, studying piano, violin and conducting. In 1986, Pratt transferred to the Peabody Conservatory of Music in Baltimore, earning performance diplomas in piano and violin in 1989, and a graduate diploma in conducting in 1992, the first student to earn diplomas in these three performance areas.

Awadagin Pratt. (AP/Wide World Photos)

Beginning in 1992, Pratt rapidly earned a place among the country's leading performing artists by winning the Naumburg International Piano competition in 1992 and the Avery Fisher Career Grant in 1994. His touring schedule took him to concert stages throughout the United States as well as in Tokyo, Osaka, Zurich, Capetown, Amsterdam, and elsewhere. As a recording artist, Pratt's releases on EMI Records include *Live From South Africa* and *A Long Way from Normal*.

In the progression of his career, Pratt has developed a reputation for taking on a challenging repertoire of works by a variety of composers. An iconoclast in the tradition-bound world of classical music, he faced criticisms of his appearance (dreadlocks, casual concert attire) and his use of a low bench at the piano. Pratt has rejoined that he sought freedom to express his inner self and the introspective nature of the music and its message.

See also CONCERT MUSIC [2]; PITTSBURGH, PENNSYLVANIA [4].

REFERENCES

Chang, Yahlin, "The Piano Man's Not With a Band; In Every Way Awadagin Pratt Defies Stereotype." *Newsweek* 128. 25 November, 1996, 79c.

Salibury, Wilma, "Pianist Lights a Fire With Music, Audience." *Cleveland Plain Dealer*, January 25, 2000.

Smith, Scott McBride. "An American Original." *Piano & Keyboard*, May/June 1999: 25-29.

DARIUS L. THIEME

Presidents of the United States (Update).

Thomas Jefferson (Democratic-Republican, 1801–1809). The question of Thomas Jefferson and slavery was further complicated in 1998 when DNA tests conclusively proved the oft-told story that Jefferson had had an affair with his mulatto slave Sally Hemings that had produced at least one child. The fact that Jefferson never freed Hemings, his longtime mistress — who returned with him from France, where she was free, to live and die in slavery in the United States — and did not free his son(s) during his lifetime eloquently testifies to Jefferson's inner conflict and weaknesses regarding slavery.

Bill Clinton (Democrat, 1993–) Later Clinton appointments included Labor Secretary Alexis Herman (1994–) and Dr. David Satcher to succeed Dr. Joycelyn Elders as Surgeon General in 1997. Clinton also impressed many African Americans by his anti-

establishment background and demeanor, his defense of affirmative action, his employment of Betty Currie, an African American, as his personal secretary, and his evident closeness with African American friends such as Vernon Jordan. Nevertheless, if African Americans greeted Clinton as a change for the better (and supported him strongly following revelation of his affair with Monica S. Lewinsky), there was concern among members of the Congressional Black Caucus over his policies on some specific issues, notably welfare reform. Further, Clinton appointed white conservatives such as David Gergen, a former aide to Ronald Reagan, to important White House posts; and in 1993 he abandoned his support of Lani Guinier, a black legal scholar he had appointed chief civil rights officer in the Justice Department, after her nomination was attacked by conservatives.

REFERENCES

Butters, Patrick. "Jefferson Linked to Slave's Children." *The Washington Times*, Jan 27, 2000: 1.

"William Jefferson Clinton." In *Encyclopedia of World Biography*, 2nd ed. 1998.

GREG ROBINSON

Price, Hugh Bernard

(November 22, 1941–), organization executive. Hugh B. Price's ancestors include Nero Hawley (circa 1741–1817), a slave who was manumitted after serving in a Connecticut regi-

Hugh Price. (AP/Wide World Photos)

Barbara Proctor. (AP/Wide World Photos)

ment during the American Revolution; Augustus Hawley (1839–1908), Nero's great-grandson and a Civil War veteran; and Lewis Howard Latimer (1848–1928), noted inventor and Thomas Edison's colleague. Price's mother, Charlotte, an archivist, trained under Howard University bibliographer Dorothy Porter Wesley. His father, Kline, taught urology at Howard University Medical School. The couple was married in 1935. Hugh Price was born in Washington D.C., and educated in D.C. public schools. He married Marilyn Lloyd, a Mt. Holyoke College alumna, in 1963, and they have three daughters. That same year, Price graduated from Amherst College, and from Yale Law School in 1966.

After working with the New Haven Legal Assistance Association (1966–1968) and being appointed executive director of the Black Coalition of New Haven (1968–1970), Price became senior associate, then partner, of the urban affairs consulting firm, Cogen, Holt & Associates (1970–1975). A member of the editorial board of the *New York Times* (1978–1982), Price wrote passionately about education, urban policy, telecommunications, welfare, and criminal justice. As a senior vice president of the nation's largest public television station, WNET/Thirteen

(1982–1988), he headed the national production division, which aired such PBS series as *Great Performances* and *Nature*.

While vice president of the Rockefeller Foundation, a philanthropic organization (1988–1994), Price conceived of what later became the National Guard Youth Challenge Corps and the National Commission on Teaching and America's Future. Assuming the helm of the eighty-three-year-old National Urban League on July 1, 1994, Price revitalized the nonprofit, nonpartisan, community-based organization by launching, in conjunction with the Congress of National Black Churches and other dedicated groups, the Campaign for African-American Achievement. During this period he initiated the "achievement matters" campaign of public service with State Farm Life Insurance Company; revived *Opportunity Journal*, the League's official publication, whose predecessor appeared from 1923 to 1949; and implemented effective strategies to "assist African Americans in the achievement of social and economic equality."

A prolific writer who has published articles in the *New York Times*, the *Wall Street Journal*, and the *Los Angeles Times*, Price writes a weekly "To Be Equal" column for African-American papers across the nation. Serving on numerous boards, including the Metropolitan Life Insurance Company, Bell Atlantic, Sears Roebuck & Company, the Educational Testing Service, and the Urban Institute, Price was the recipient of the Medal of Honor from Yale Law School. He has received many honorary degrees from educational institutions, including Amherst College, Connecticut College, and George Washington University, and was appointed by President Bill Clinton to serve on the National Skills Standards Board.

See also NATIONAL URBAN LEAGUE [4].

REFERENCES

Price, Hugh B., and Charlotte S. Price. Correspondence/interview with Randy F. Weinstein. January 1999.

Who's Who in America. 1998.

RANDY F. WEINSTEIN

Proctor, Barbara Gardner (November 30, 1933–), entrepreneur. The first African American woman to head a national advertising agency, Barbara Proctor was born in Black Mountain, North Carolina, and earned two bachelor's degrees from Talladega

Members of Public Enemy. (Left to right) Terminator X, Flavor Flav (wearing clock), and Chuck D. (Corbis Corporation)

College in 1954. After college, Proctor worked as a music critic and contributing editor to *Downbeat* magazine, and also wrote descriptive comments for jazz record album covers for Vee-Jay Records International.

Proctor moved into advertising in the mid-1960s, gaining experience with three Chicago agencies: Post-Keys-Gardner Advertising (1965–68), Gene Taylor Associates (1968–69), and North Advertising Agency (1969–70). In 1971 Proctor became founder-president and creative director of Proctor & Gardner Advertising with the intention of tapping into the as-yet unnoticed African American market. Although she experienced a slow start, with only one client in her first six months, Proctor managed to build her

business into one of the largest African-American owned agencies with $12 million in billing by 1983. The firm had a staff of 25 and its clients were national companies such as Kraft Foods and Sears that sought business from the African American community.

However, this growth slowed significantly in the mid-1990s; Proctor & Gardner went into Chapter 11 bankruptcy in 1995, and Proctor officially dissolved the agency a year later. Never one to go down in defeat, Proctor moved her advertising business to the Internet, starting Proctor Communications Network to market Internet marketing expertise and web site design. She later renamed it Proctor Information Network, Inc.

See also ADVERTISING [1].

REFERENCES

Morton, Carol A. "Black Women in Corporate America." *Ebony* 32 (November 1975): 107.

Smith, Jessie Carney, ed. *Notable Black American Women.* 1992. *Who's Who in Finance and Industry,* 20th-22nd ed. 1977–81.

JESSIE CARNEY SMITH

Public Enemy. Drayton, William "Flavor Flav" (March16, 1959–), Ridenhour, Carlton "Chuck D" (August 1, 1960–), Rogers, Norman Lee "Terminator X" (August 25, 1966–). Public Enemy started with Chuck D and producer Hank Shocklee in 1982. With the addition of Flavor Flav in 1983, and DJ Terminator X and "Minister of Information" Professor Griff after signing with Def Jam Records in 1987, Public Enemy stormed the 1980s rap scene. The group also added an entourage of dance and martial arts performers, who at one time numbered fifty—the "S1W's."

Chuck D's distinct and heavy voice, Flavor Flav's jesterly disposition, and Terminator X's grinding, siren-ridden tracks made Public Enemy visually and audibly distinct from other rap sounds. Their 1987 album *Yo, Bum Rush the Show* introduced radical black political images and messages to rap music. The following year *It Takes a Nation of Millions to Hold Us Back* was acclaimed as a hip-hop classic and spawned numerous, frequently sampled songs and adages. *Fear of a Black Planet*, their controversial 1990 album, best articulates the group's political vantage and birthed the group's most well-known and influential song, AFight the Power."

The group's popularity waned after its 1991 album, *Apocalypse 91: The Enemy Strikes Black*, due to the changing trends of hip-hop and public conflicts within the group. While *Muse Sick N Hour Mess Age* (1994) and Chuck D's solo effort, *Autobiography of Mista Chuck* (1996) received harsh reviews, Chuck D continues to work as an outspoken grassroots activist, public speaker, writer, producer, and spokesperson for Rock the Vote.

See also FARRAKHAN, LOUIS ABDUL [2]; MUSIC [4]; NATION OF ISLAM [4]; NEW YORK CITY [4]; RAP [4]; RECORDING INDUSTRY [4].

REFERENCES

George, Nelson. *Hip-Hop America.* 1998.

A Public Enemy Biography." www.musicfinder. yahoo.com.

Rose, Tricia. *Black Noise: Rap Music and Black Culture in Contemporary America.* 1994.

Tate, Greg. "Public Enemy." www.brittanica.com.

RACHEL ZELLARS

Q

Queen Latifah. (Michael Ochs Archives)

Queen Latifah (Owens, Dana Elaine)
(March 18, 1970–), singer, actor. Born in East Or-

ange, New Jersey, Queen Latifah may be the most influential female MC to date. She chose her name at age eight-the Arabic word meaning "sensitive and delicate." As a teenager, she beatboxed as part of the female group Ladies Fresh. In 1988, she released "Wrath of my Madness," a song touting her strength and ability as an able MC. Her first album, *All Hail the Queen*, was released in 1989. Her second single, "Ladies First," received national attention for its assertive, woman-centered verses, and her Afrocentric image-filled video exposed her to MTV's wide-range of viewers. In 1991, she released *Nature of a Sista* and left Tommy Boy Records to join Motown. In 1993, she found her greatest success to date with *Black Reign* and won a Grammy for Best Rap Solo for "U.N.I.T.Y." The album, dedicated to her late brother, murdered during a car-jacking, achieved gold status and helped secure her acting career. In the same year, she began her role as the straightforward, yet humorous "Kadijah" on the FOX sitcom "Living Single." In 1997, she received the "Entertainer of the Year" Soul Train Lady of Soul award. In 1998, she co-starred in the movies *Sphere*, alongside Dustin Hoffman and Samuel Jackson, *Living Out Loud*, and *The Bone Collector* with Denzel Washington. She also released her fourth album, *Order in the Court*. In 1999—with the prompting of Rosie O'Donnell—she began hosting her own talk show. She also released her autobiography, *Ladies First: Revelations of a Strong Woman* (William & Morrow, Co.).

See also MUSIC [4]; RAP [4]; RECORDING INDUSTRY [4].

REFERENCE

Rose, Tricia. *Black Noise: Rap Music and Black Culture in Contemporary America*, 1994.

"Queen Latifah." www.rockonthenet.com. 2000.

RACHEL ZELLARS

R

Franklin Raines, 1996. (AP/Wide World Photos)

Raines, Franklin D. (January 14, 1949–), public official, investment banker. One of seven children, Raines grew up in Seattle, Washington. His working class family had been recipient of Aid to Families with Dependent Children, or welfare. He received his B.A. degree from Harvard College in 1971 and his J.D. degree from Harvard University Law School in 1976. He also attended Magdalen College at Oxford University as a Rhodes Scholar.

In 1977–79, Raines was named an associate director for economics and government with the Office of Management and Budget (OMB) and assistant director of the White House Domestic Policy Staff, handling such issues as welfare reform, food stamps, and social security. Raines was a general partner with the international investment banking firm, Lazard Freres & Company from 1979 to 1991.

From 1991 to 1996, Raines was vice chair of the Federal National Mortgage Association, better known as Fannie Mae. It provides financial assistance for lower-income Americans who are in the market for a home. It is also the world's largest non-bank financial service and the largest financier of home mortgages in the country. Then Raines joined President Bill Clinton's Cabinet from April 1996 to May 1998, where he was director of the Office of Management and Budget. He was the first director in a generation to balance the federal budget. He resigned to join the private sector and took office as chairman and chief executive officer of the Washington, D.C.-based Fannie Mae Corporation on January 1, 1999, becoming the first African American CEO of a major Fortune 500 company.

Raines's memberships have included the board of directors of Pfizer Inc., America Online, Inc., the

Boeing Company, and chair of the Visiting Committee of the Harvard Kennedy School of Government. He has served also as president of the Board of Overseers of Harvard.

See also SEATTLE, WASHINGTON [5].

REFERENCES

Farmer, Paula. "The First African American to Head a Fortune 500 Company, Franklin D. Raines Takes Over Fannie Mae." http://www.black-collegian.com/issues/1999–08/fdraines.shtml

"Franklin D. Raines: A Brilliant Career." http://www.diversityinc.com/Workforce/ceoprofiles/raines.cfm

Franklin D. Raines, Director of the Office of Management and Budget." http://www.usis.usemb.se/cabbio/raines.htm June 1, 2000

RAYMOND WINBUSH

Ranger, Joseph (c. 1760–?), seaman. Ranger, a free man of color, is thought to have been born in Northumberland County, Virginia, and later moved to Elizabeth City, Virginia. He enlisted in Virginia's navy (one of nine separate state navies independent of the continental navy) during the American Revolution and fought along with seventy-five other black men side by side with white men, and had the distinction of serving the longest term of any black man from Virginia. He served on four navy ships. Ranger was discharged six years after the war ended.

Ranger's first assignment was on the Hero; this was followed by a stint on the Dragon, a ship carrying 104 crewman. Later, he served on the Jefferson, which exploded during combat with the British on the James River. Finally, Ranger was transferred to the Patriot. This term of service ended when the entire crew was taken prisoner by the British until after the surrender at Yorktown. At the end of the conflict, he continued to serve on the Patriot and later the Liberty to defend Virginia's shores until 1787 and the last of the ships was retired.

Upon retirement, Ranger received a land grant of 100 acres. Later, following the 1832 Act of Congress and a declaration under oath before a court of record about his service (October 25, 1832), he was granted an annual pension of $96.

See also VIRGINIA [5].

REFERENCES

Jackson, Luther P. *Virginia Negro Soldiers and Seamen in the Revolutionary War*. 1944.

Logan, Rayford W., and Michael R. Winston, eds. *Dictionary of American Negro Biography*. 1982.

HELEN R. HOUSTON

Reason, Charles [Lewis] (July 21, 1818–August 16, 1893), educator and abolitionist. Charles Reason was born in New York. Like his older brother, Patrick, Charles Reason was educated at the African Free School in New York. Reason tried to become an Episcopal priest but was barred from the seminary because of his race. In the fall of 1849 he became professor of belles lettres—Greek, Latin, and French—at the abolitionist institution, Central College in McGrawville (now McGraw), New York. He is the first African American to hold a college professorship.

From 1852 to 1855 Reason headed the Institute for Colored Youth in Philadelphia. He put the struggling school on a firm foundation before he returned to New York City. He spent the rest of his life there, working until 1890 in the city's black schools as a teacher and principal. He had the reputation of being a master teacher.

In the 1830s, Reason worked closely with his classmates from the African Free School, Henry Highland Garnet and George Downing, in such endeavors as challenging New York's restrictive suffrage for African Americans. On another issue, Reason was steadfast in his opposition to the colonization movement; this later led to a split with Garnet. In Philadelphia Reason worked with the Underground Railroad. On his return to New York, he continued to speak out and supported his views with articles in the newspapers. One of his principal concerns was expanding educational opportunities for blacks, including manual labor and adult education. Reason also was a poet of some accomplishment.

See also HODGES, WILLIS AUGUSTUS [3].

REFERENCES

Johns, Robert L. "Charles Lewis Reason." In *Notable Black American Men*, edited by Jessie Carney Smith. 1999.

Ripley, C. Peter, and others, eds. *The Black Abolitionist Papers*. 1991.

Sherman, Joan R. "Charles [Lewis] Reason." In *Dictionary of American Negro Biography*, edited by Rayford W. Logan and Michael R. Winston. 1982.

ROBERT L. JOHNS

Reason, Patrick Henry (April 17, 1816–August 12, 1898), artist, abolistionist. Patrick Henry Reason was a noted graphic artist, an abolitionist, and a fraternal organization leader. Reason was born in New York City, the older brother of Charles Lewis Reason, a long-time and influential teacher in the city. The Reasons were educated at the New York African Free School. Patrick Reason's engraving of the school, made when he was thirteen, served as frontispiece to an 1830 history of the institution. He was apprenticed to an engraver and by 1846 was regularly producing plates for abolitionist literature. He produced portraits of both blacks and whites, sometimes producing the original drawing himself.

Reason also worked on such items as membership certificates, maps for books, and plates for bank notes, but he sometimes lost work opportunities since white engravers refused to work with him. In 1869 Reason moved to Cleveland, Ohio, where he continued to work as an engraver, most notably for a jewelry company. He died there of rectal cancer.

In the 1840s, Reason was instrumental in the formation of the New York lodge of Odd Fellows, a fraternal mutual aid society, working with Peter Ogden to gain authorization. Reason was much involved in the development of ritual and served as grand master. He was also very active in the Freemasons, serving as city and state grand master during the 1860s. Other community activities include working with organizations such as the Albany Convention of Colored Citizens (1840) and the New York Society for the Promotion of Education Among Colored Children (1847).

See also GRAPHIC ARTS [2].

REFERENCES

Porter, Dorothy B. "Patrick Henry Reason." In *Dictionary of American Negro Biography*, edited by Rayford W. Logan, and Michael R. Winston. 1982.

Porter, James R. *Modern Negro Art*. 1945.

ROBERT L. JOHNS

Redman, Joshua (February 1, 1969–), musician. Acclaimed by jazz authorities as the premier tenor saxophonist of his generation, Joshua Redman combines the influences of such swing masters as Dexter Gordon, John Coltrane and Stanley Turrentine with an appreciation for the modern to create his own distinctive sound. In addition, he has proven himself

Joshua Redman. (AP/Wide World Photos)

to be one of the top young composers in jazz with his bold, risky compositions that borrow heavily from popular music.

The son of renowned jazz saxophonist Dewey Redman, Joshua was born in Berkeley, California. Joshua's father, however, left for New York City by the time of his birth and he was raised by his mother, dancer Renee Shedroff. His mother nurtured Joshua's creativity and fostered his musical education. By five, Joshua was receiving music lessons and, by 10, he had taken up the saxophone. Despite a growing facility with several instruments, Joshua poured most of his energies into his schooling, graduating as valedictorian of his Berkeley high school class in 1986. Accepted to Harvard, Redman graduated *summa cum laude* in 1991 and was voted to Phi Beta Kappa. Though he was accepted to Yale Law School, Redman decided to make a go of jazz and moved to Brooklyn.

In November 1991, Redman won the prestigious Thelonious Monk International Jazz Saxophone Competition and became an immediate sensation on the international jazz scene. He has toured and recorded extensively over the last decade. Among his albums are *Joshua Redman*, 1992; *Wish*, 1993; *Mood Swing*, 1994; *Freedom in the Groove*, 1996; and *Timeless Tales (for Changing Times)*, 1999. Redman also regularly tours and records as a sideman for other artists, among them: Elvin Jones, Charlie Haden, Pat Metheny, Paul Motian, and his father, Dewey.

See also JAZZ [3].

REFERENCES

"Vandoren Performing Artist: Joshua Redman." http://www.vandoren.com/VVANDOREN_PLAYERS/jredman.htm.

Joshua Redman." http://jazzradio.org/joshua.htm.

"Artist Profile Joshua Redman." http://staff.twave.net/jazzzman/redman.htm.

KEVIN C. KRETSCHMER

Republican Party (Update).

During the 1990s, several high-profile black Republicans became active on the national stage, including television personality Tony Brown and conservative activist Alan Keyes, two members of Congress, Gary Franks of Connecticut and J.C. Watts of Oklahoma, a half-dozen state legislators, and such mayors as civil rights leader Charles Evers. In addition, General Colin Powell, one of the most admired men in America and a frequently touted presidential candidate, announced in 1995 that he was a Republican, and made a keynote speech at the GOP's 1996 convention. However, Republicans still represent only about one percent of black elected officials in the country, and many of them represent largely white constituencies. Alan Keyes made an unsuccessful bid for the Republican presidential in nomination in 2000, but fell behind early on to eventual nominee George W. Bush.

REFERENCES

Fulwood III, Sam. "Republicans Cast Watts as Leader, Healer." Los Angeles Times, Feb 22, 1999: A-1.

Gallman Vanessa. "Black GOP disappointed by lack of party support." *Knight-Ridder/Tribune News Service*, April 1, 1996: 401K2888.

GREG ROBINSON

Rice, Jerry

(October 13, 1962–), football player. Jerry Rice was born in Starkville, Mississippi and raised in the neighboring rural community of Craw-

ford. During the summers as a child, Rice helped his father, a bricklayer, an activity that developed his hands and his work ethic. Rice began playing football at B. L. Moor High School. He attended college at Mississippi Valley State University, where he was named a consensus All American at wide receiver, setting 18 Division 1AA records.

Rice was selected by the San Francisco 49ers in the first round of the 1985 National Football League (NFL) draft and went on to become the greatest wide receiver in football history, setting every important career record for receivers. At the end of the 1999 season, Rice held 14 NFL records, including career marks for receptions (1200), receiving yards (18,299), total touchdowns (180), receiving touchdowns (169), most consecutive games with a reception (193), most seasons with over 100 catches (4), and most seasons with over 1,000 yards (12). In 1995, at the age of 33, Rice set a single season record with 1,848 receiving yards. With the 49ers, Rice won three Super Bowl Championships (1988,1989,1994). He was named Super Bowl M.V.P. in 1988 and set ten Super Bowl records, including career and single game records for receptions (28, 11), receiving yards (512, 215), and touchdowns (7, 3). Rice's honors and awards are legion. He was named to the Pro Bowl 12 times, was the NFL Player of the Year twice (1987, 1990), and NFL Offensive Player of the Year in 1993. In 1999, ESPN's Sports Century named him the 27th greatest athlete of the twentieth century.

See also FOOTBALL [2].

REFERENCES

Minutaglio, Bill. *The Sporting News*. (September 13, 1999): 22.

Frei, Terry. "Mississippi Yearning." *The Sporting News*. (July 31, 1995).

Stewart, Mark. *Jerry Rice*. 1997.

Owens, Tom. *Jerry Rice: Speedy Wide Receiver*. 1998.

MICHAEL WADE FUQUAY

Rice, Norman Blann

(May 4, 1943–), mayor, banking executive. Born in Denver, Colorado, Rice received the B.A. degree in 1972 and the M.P.A. degree in 1974 from the University of Washington.

Rice's career began in 1971–1972 when he was news assistant editor for Seattle's KOMO TV News.

Jerry Rice. (AP/Wide World Photos)

In 1972–1974, he worked with the Seattle Urban League as assistant director of the media action project monitor. The next year Rice was executive assistant director of government service for the Puget Sound Council of Governments. From there he became involved in financial institutions, as manager of corporate contributions and social policy coordinator for Rainier National Bank.

Rice entered the political arena, serving three terms on Seattle's city council from 1978 to 1983, including the years 1983–1990 when he was the council's president. While on the council, Rice promoted assistance programs for senior citizens and for low income families. He sponsored anti-crime teams to aid communities and called for additional officers on the city's police force. Among the committees that he chaired were those on education, finance, public safety and transportation.

In 1990 Rice was elected mayor of Seattle, the first African American to hold that post. The popular politician ran for reelection in 1993 and won with 67 percent of the vote in a city with a small minority population. The ethnic composition at the time was 10 percent African American and 12 percent Asian American. In his second campaign, Rice advocated gun control, crackdown on drug trafficking, and enhanced safety for residents.

After leaving office in 1997, Rice was named executive vice president of the Federal Home Loan Bank of Seattle.

See also MAYORS [3]; SEATTLE, WASHINGTON [5]; WASHINGTON [5]; WEST, BLACKS IN THE [5].

REFERENCES

Shaefer, David. "Seattle Mayor Norman Rice." Interview. *Europe* 333 (February 1994): 25.

"The Parade of Cities." *Ebony* 45 (February 1990): 30-32.

Who's Who Among African Americans, 12th ed. 1999.

FREDERICK D. SMITH, JR.

Richards, Fannie Moore (October 1, 1840?-February 13, 1922), educator, school founder, social reformer, civil rights activist. Moore was born in Fredericksburg, Virginia, some time between 1840 and 1842. Laws in Virginia, made it difficult for African American children to receive an education. Some, however, including the Richards children,

Norman Rice. (The Gamma Liaison Network)

were educated in the homes of free blacks. Since the Richards family moved to Detroit sometime after 1851, Fannie Richards' early education was in the Detroit school system. At some time early on, the family lived in Toronto, where Richards attended a normal school. After that, she studied in Germany where she learned the concept of the kindergarten.

Richards opened a private school in Detroit to educate African American children. For forty years or more beginning in 1868, she taught in the public schools of Detroit and was the city's first African American professional teacher. During this time she successfully petitioned the school board to desegregate its schools, arguing that blacks deserved equal rights to whites in the public education sector. Once integration came, she was retained and became the city's first kindergarten teacher.

The plight of elderly African American women caught Richards' heart as well. Determined to help them, she founded the Phillis Wheatley Home to care for the needs of aging black women, becoming its founding president and chair of the board of trustees in 1901. To support the home, she contributed funds from her salary as a teacher and solicited support from other donors.

Richards retired from teaching on June 6, 1915. Since her death, the public school system, the public library system, and other groups have honored Richards widely for her work. The mayor of Detroit declared October 1, 1975, Fannie Richards' Day.
See also VIRGINIA [5].

REFERENCES

Logan, Rayford W., and Michael R. Winston, eds. *Dictionary of American Negro Biography*. 1982.

Robinson, Wilhelmina. *Historical Negro Biographies*. 1978.

Smith, Jessie Carney, ed. *Notable Black American Women*. 1992.

JESSIE CARNEY SMITH

Richardson, Willis (November 5, 1899–November 8, 1977), playwright. Occasionally referred to as the "father of black drama," Richardson wrote *The Chip Woman's Fortune* (1923), one of the first plays by an African American to receive a Broadway production. Performed by the Ethiopian Art Players, the one-act comedy opened to positive criticism on May 7, 1923. It tells the story of a woman who financially helps her son and her landlord after saving money she earns from collecting bits of coal from the streets.

Richardson's canon of 46 plays stresses the need for dignified ethical behavior in spite of adversity, social class, or race, and his characters often make deliberate displays of courage, nobility, and virtue, countering negative stereotypical depictions of blacks. During the height of his career from the Harlem Renaissance until the fold of the Federal Theater Project in the late 1930s, Richardson was encouraged by Alaine Locke, W. E. B. Du Bois, Mary Burrill, and Zora Neal Hurston. His plays were aggressively sought by university, professional, and community theater troups, many of them newly formed during what is referred to as "The Little Theater Movement" (1919–1945), who were in need of dramatic material written by and about blacks. After World War II, his work began to lose its commercial appeal and Richardson's name and plays virtually slipped into obscurity until his death in 1977. He was born in Wilmington, North Carolina and raised in Washington, D.C.
See also KARAMU HOUSE [3].

REFERENCES

Barksdale, Richard. *Black Writers of America*. 1972.

Hatch, James V., and Ted Shine, eds. *Black Theatre USA*. 1974,

Smith, Jessie Carney, ed. *Notable Black American Men*. 1999.

F. ZEAL HARRIS

Robinson, Jack Roosevelt "Jackie" (Update) (January 31, 1919–October 24, 1972), In 1997, major league baseball commemorated the fiftieth anniversary of Robinson's breaking of the baseball color line by retiring his number 42 from every team.

REFERENCE

Washington, Robin. "Tribute to Jackie; Baseball retires pioneer's No. 42." *Boston Herald*. April 16, 1997: 94.

GREG ROBINSON

Rodney King Riot. On March 3, 1991, following a high-speed chase, black motorist Rodney King was subdued with extreme force and arrested by officers of the Los Angeles Police Department for allegedly resisting arrest and threatening police officers. The broadcast of a videotape by a local citizen

Jackie Robinson. (AP/Wide World Photos)

that depicted King being beaten by white police officers made King a global symbol of American racism and police brutality. As a result of the beating, King suffered multiple injuries, spending two days in the hospital before being booked. The Los Angeles County District Attorney dismissed all charges against King on March 7. A week later, a grand jury indicted the police officers Sgt. Stacy Koon and officers Theodore J. Briseno, Laurence M. Powell, and Timothy Wind on charges of assault with a deadly weapon and unnecessary assault. Los Angeles Mayor Tom Bradley responded by establishing the Christopher Commission to investigate the LAPD. Releasing its findings in July 1991, the commission documented the LAPD's systematic use of excessive force and racial harassment.

In the officers' court trial, a jury of eleven whites and one Hispanic brought back a verdict of not guilty on April 29, 1992. The verdict ignited one of the worst riots in the nation's history. Los Angeles erupted into widespread racial violence. Blacks brutally beat and robbed non-black motorists, and burned and looted stores and other businesses for three days. President George Bush dispatched federal troops to the city.

In 1993, the four officers were tried in federal court for violating King's civil rights. The jury convicted Koon and Powell and acquitted Briseno and Wind. No violent response resulted from the verdicts.
See also BRADLEY, THOMAS "TOM" [1]; CALIFORNIA [1]; LOS ANGELES, CALIFORNIA [3]; URBAN RIOTS AND REBELLIONS [5]; WATERS, MAXINE MOORE [5].

REFERENCES

Hornsby, Alton, Jr. *Milestones in 20th Century African-American History*. 1993.

Wynn, Linda T. "Civil Rights," in Smith, Jessie Carney and Joseph M. Palmisano, eds. *The African American Almanac*, 8th ed. 2000.

LINDA T. WYNN

Roman, Charles Victor

Roman, Charles Victor (July 4, 1864–August 25, 1934), physician, educator, historian. Charles Roman was born in Williamsport, Pennsylvania, and graduated from Hamilton Collegiate Institute in Ontario. After teaching in Kentucky and Tennessee, he did additional study at Fisk University and in 1890 received his M.D. degree from Meharry Medical College.

For a brief period Roman practiced in nearby Clarksville, Tennessee, then in Dallas, Texas, where he remained from 1890 to 1904. He did post-graduate study at Chicago Medical College, and traveled to London for further study at the Royal Opthalmic Hospital and Central Nose and Throat, and Ear Hospital. He returned to Nashville to teach at Meharry Medical College from 1904 to 1933. He served nearby Fisk University as director of health and taught part time at Tennessee A. and I. State College, as it was known then. During World War I, Roman was medical lecturer in the U.S. Army.

Roman was the fifth president of the historically black National Medical Association (1904–05) and for ten years (1909–19) edited the *Journal of the National Medical Association*. He wrote several important books, including *A Knowledge of History Conducive to Racial Solidarity* (1911); other writings included "History of Meharry Medical College" published ten years after he died. In his works and speeches, which he was called often to give, he advocated support of African American institutions. He cited a need for African American history and the importance of teaching black children the deeds of their race.
See also PENNSYLVANIA [4].

REFERENCES

Cobb, W. Montague. "Medical History." *Journal of the National Medical Association* 45 (July 1953): 301-04.

Journal of Negro History. 20 (1935) 116-17.

Logan, Rayford W., and Michael R. Winston, eds. *Dictionary of American Negro Biography*. 1982.

JESSIE CARNEY SMITH

Roper, Moses

Roper, Moses (1815–?), fugitive slave, abolitionist. Moses Roper was a fugitive slave and abolitionist. He was born in Caswell County, North Carolina. Roper was told that his father's wife was so furious at his birth that she nearly killed the young infant; the intervention of his maternal grandmother saved his life. Roper was very light-skinned; he was also six feet five inches tall. When Roper was about six, the family slaves were separated. Roper passed through the hands of several owners, and eventually he ended up in the hands of a particularly vicious master, who made him a field worker.

Beginning about 1832, Roper engaged in a series of attempts to escape. Increasingly severe punishments when he was recaptured did not alter his determination. Towards the end of 1833 he was owned by a disreputable and alcoholic Floridian. During his final attempt at escape, Roper made a long and difficult flight from Florida to Savannah, Georgia. Along the way, he was able to secure a pass saying he was free. Thus he was able to find work on a ship bound for New York. After some time in Vermont, Roper found work in Boston, where he came in contact with Abolitionist circles.

Fearful of recapture, Roper made his way to England in late 1835 where in 1838 he published his *Narrative* and began to speak to anti-slavery groups. He claimed over two thousand addresses during his English stay. The following year he married a white Englishwoman, and the family moved to the Canadian West in 1844. Roper returned to England in 1846 and in 1854.
See also LITERATURE [3].

REFERENCES

Ripley, C. Peter, ed. *The Black Abolitionist Papers*. 1985.

Roper, Moses. *Narrative of the Adventure and Escape of Moses Roper*. 1838.

ROBERT L. JOHNS

Rowe, George Clinton

Rowe, George Clinton (May 1, 1853–October 3, 1903), poet, minister, editor. George Clinton Rowe was born in Litchfield, Connecticut, where he received his education, served an apprenticeship on the *Litchfield Enquirer*, earned a certificate of trade, and

Run D.M.C. (Corbis Corporation)

studied theology privately. In 1876, he moved to Hampton, Virginia, and worked in the Normal School Printing Office on such publications as *American Missionary*, *Southern Workman*, *Alumni Journal*, and *African Repository*.

Rowe established the Ocean Cottage Mission in Little England near Hampton Institute; published a pamphlet, *Sunbeam* (not extant); and built a chapel at the Institute. An ordained Congregational minister, he pastored Cypris Slash Congregational Church at McIntosh, Georgia, (1881–1885) and Plymouth Congregational Church in Charleston, South Carolina.

While at Plymouth, Rowe began to write. He published *Thoughts in Verse* (1887), a very successful and widely read book, and *Our Heroes* (1891). Other publications include *Decorations* (poem, 1891), *A Noble Life* (poem in memory of Joseph C. Price, first president of Livingstone College in North Carolina), and *The Aim of Life* (an address, 1892). Additionally, he edited and published the *Charleston Enquirer* (1893–1896).

His missionary efforts and writings were acknowledged at the 1896 centennial of the AME Zion Church, the Paris Exhibition (1900), and an interstate exposition (1901). Rowe's affiliations included the Georgia Congregational Association (c1888–1896), Preacher's Union in Charlotte (interdenominational, c1891–1896), and Literary Congress for the Atlanta Exposition.

See also CONNECTICUT [2].

REFERENCE

Sherman, Joan R. *Invisible Poets: Afro-Americans of the Nineteenth Century*. 1974.

HELEN R. HOUSTON

Run D.M.C. Simmons, Joseph "Run" (November 14, 1964–); McDaniel, Darryl "DMC" (May 31, 1964–); Mizell, Jason "Jam Master Jay" (January 21, 1965–). Flaunting untied Adidas sneakers, pricey Kangol hats, sweatsuits, and thick rope gold chains, Run D.M.C.'s ostentatious image and electric guitar-ridden sound captivated America's white youth culture in the 1980s. Joseph Simmons and Darryl McDaniels began rapping together and convinced Jason Mizell to join them as their deejay. Thanks to the fusion of hard-core rock and rap in songs like "Rock Box," Run D.M.C.'s self-titled debut album struck a chord with white, male, suburban rock fans, and the album sold over 500,000 copies to merit gold status. Their punchy, simple rhyme style and sparse tracks also appealed to rap and rock audiences.

In 1985, the group starred in the classic hip-hop film, *Krush Groove*, and released the platinum-selling *King of Rock*. A year later, the group released *Raising Hell*, the phenomenal success of which was propelled by the group's duet with the rock band, Aerosmith, on "Walk This Way" and MTV's heavy rotation of the cross-over video. The album sold over three million copies. The year 1988 saw the release of *Tougher Than Leather*, and while the album was platinum-selling, it was a commercial disappointment.

Audiences were gravitating away from hip-hop towards the more violent gangsta rap genre by the dawn of the 1990s, and the disappointing sales for Run D.M.C.'s album of that year, *Back From Hell*, indicated that trend. *Down with the King* found a hit single and went gold in 1993. However, the group disappeared from sight for the remainder of the decade, although Run D.M.C. planned a comeback in 2000 with their LP *Crown Royal*.
See also NEW YORK CITY [4]; RAP [4].

REFERENCES

George, Nelson. *Hip-Hop America*. 1998.

Rose, Tricia. *Black Noise: Rap Music and Black Culture in Contemporary America*. 1994.

"Run-D.M.C." www.rockonthenet.com.

RACHEL ZELLARS

Bayard Rustin. (The Library of Congress)

Rustin, Bayard (Update) (March 17, 1910–August 24, 1987), activist. After the mid-1960s, Rustin's calls for blacks to work within the political system and his close ties with Jewish groups and labor unions made him the target of attacks by younger radicals, while his support for American investment and educational efforts in South Africa during the 1970s and 1980s outraged opponents of the Apartheid regime. Toward the end of his life, he also became increasingly open about his homosexuality and spoke out in favor of equal rights for gays and lesbians. Following his death, the Bayard Rustin High School for the Humanities in New York City was named in his honor.

REFERENCES

Anderson, Jervis. *Bayard Rustin: The Troubles I've Seen*. 1996.

Rustin, Bayard. *Down the Line: The Collected Writings of Bayard Rustin*. 1971.

GREG ROBINSON

S

Saddler, Joseph. *See* Grandmaster Flash.

Sampson, Edith Spurlock (October 13, 1901–October 8, 1979), lawyer, judge. Born in Pittsburgh, Sampson grew up in a poor family of seven siblings. She attended the New York School of Social Work, and from 1922 to 1925, studied at the John Marshall

Edith Sampson. (AP/Wide World Photos)

Law School in Chicago. She continued studies at the Graduate Law School of Loyola University and became the first woman to earn a master of law degree from the school. That same year, she was admitted to the Illinois bar. Sampson took additional courses at the University of Chicago School of Social Service Administration.

For most of her life, Sampson maintained dual careers in social work and law. While in law school, she worked at the YWCA and the Illinois Children's Home and Aid Society. She became a probation officer and eventually a referee for the Juvenile Court of Cook County, Illinois. From 1927 to 1962 she also practiced law, with a specialty in criminal law and domestic relations. The U.S. Supreme Court admitted Sampson to practice before it in 1934, making her one of the first African American women so approved.

President Harry Truman named Sampson an alternate delegate to the fifth regular session of the United Nations General Assembly in 1950; in 1952 she was reappointed alternate delegate and later a member-at-large of the U.S. Commission for UNESCO. Following her United Nations work, she received a 1962 appointment as associate judge for the Municipal Court of Chicago, the first African American woman so chosen, and she held that post until her retirement in 1978.

See also PITTSBURGH [4].

REFERENCES

Current Biography Yearbook, 1975. 1975.

Garraty, John A., and Mark C. Carnes, general eds. *American National Biography*. 1999.

Smith, Jessie Carney, ed. *Notable Black American Women*. 1992.

VALENCIA PRICE

Sampson, John Patterson

Sampson, John Patterson (August 13, 1837–?) lawyer, clergyman, and author. Born to free black parents, Fannie and James, in Wilmington, N.C., Sampson was educated in Cambridge and Boston, Mass., graduating from Comer's Commercial College in 1856. After teaching in a Jamaica, Long Island, public school (1858–1860), he assumed the editorship of the *Colored Citizen*, a Cincinnati, Ohio, weekly devoted to the "interests of colored soldiers."

At the close of the Civil War, Sampson returned to Wilmington to run a school for freedmen. After failing to win an 1867 Republican seat in Congress, he served as a treasury department clerk in Washington, D.C. Studying both the law and theology, Sampson attended the National University Law School (1868) and the Western Theological Seminary in Allegheny, Pa. (1868–69). Admitted to the D.C. bar in 1873, Sampson was appointed a justice of the peace by President Rutheford B. Hayes and spent the next five years as a civil court judge, the first African-American lawyer to serve as a magistrate in the District of Columbia.

In 1881 Sampson permanently retired from the law and entered the African Methodist Episcopal ministry. That same year, he published *Mixed Races: Their Environment, Temperament, Heredity, and Phrenology*, the first comprehensive study of phrenology by an African-American, which black leaders such as Frederick Douglass, Henry McNeal Turner, and Edward Wilmot Blyden praised as a "scholarly blend of history, psychology, personal observation, and experimentation". Sampson ministered to black congregations in New Jersey throughout the 1880s, earning a doctorate from Wilberforce University, Ohio, in 1888. He married Marianna Cole of Bordentown, N.J., in September 1889, and the couple had one son, John P., Jr. Sampson organized the Ironside Industrial School, in New Jersey, and was president of the Frederick Douglass Hospital, Philadelphia.

Until his retirement in 1917, Sampson was pastor to AME congregations in Pennsylvania, Western Massachussetts, where he presided over the New England Conference, and New Jersey. Samson authored several other works and lectured widely on a variety of subjects—scientific, religious, and social. *See also* NORTH CAROLINA [4].

REFERENCES

Mather, Franklin, ed. *Who's Who of the Colored Race*. 1915.

Ripley, C. Peter, et al., eds. *The Black Abolitionist Papers. Vol. 5, The United States, 1859–1865*. 1992.

Sampson, John P. *Mixed Races: Their Environment, Temperament, Heredity, and Phrenology*. 1881.

Smith, J. Clay, Jr. *Emancipation: The Making of the Black Lawyer, 1844–1944*. 1993.

Weinstein, Randy F. *Against the Tide: Commentaries on a Collection of African Americana, 1711–1987*. 1996.

RANDY F. WEINSTEIN

Sanders, Barry

Sanders, Barry (1968–), athlete. Barry Sanders retired from professional football in 1999 as the National Football League's second all-time leading rusher. Heralded as one of the best running backs in the history of the game, Sanders achieved a career record of 15,269 rushing yards over ten seasons with the Detroit Lions.

Barry Sanders. (AP/Wide World Photos)

Sanders, the son of a roofer, was a star athlete in his hometown of Wichita, Kansas, but his slight build caused scouts from many of the more prestigious college teams to bypass him. At Oklahoma State University, he emerged as one of the most talented players in the United States. He set thirteen National Collegiate Athletic Association rushing records in his junior year alone, and took the coveted Heisman Trophy for that season. Forsaking a final year of school, Sanders was drafted by the Detroit Lions. After his first season, he was named NFL Rookie of the Year for 1989 and became a Pro Bowl athlete for every year of his professional career.

Over ten seasons with the Lions, Sanders' talents as a running back were so legendary that other teams designed their defensive strategies to outmaneuver him. His decision to leave the game in the summer of 1999 stirred a major controversy in Detroit, and Lions management even sued him for breach of contract. The suit was ruled in favor of the Lions, with Sanders ordered to pay back bonus money for each year left on his contract. In August of 2000, Sanders spoke publicly for the first time in over a year, and told a Detroit newspaper that he was quite contented in his retirement.

See also FOOTBALL [2].

REFERENCES

Sharp, Drew. "Sanders: 'I Like Retirement,'" *Detroit Free Press*, August14, 2000.

LaBlanc, Michael L. *Contemporary Black Biography*, vol. 1. 1992.

U★*X*★*L Sports Stars*, Series 1-4. 1994–98.

CAROL BRENNAN

San Francisco and Oakland, California (Update).

As the new millenium dawned, blacks retained a strong measure of political power. Although in 1999 former California Governor Edmund G. Brown became the first white mayor of Oakland in a generation, in San Francisco incumbent mayor Willie Brown, though forced into a runoff following a primary election, was easily re-elected. Education, meanwhile, remained an outstanding concern of Bay area African Americans. In Oakland's public schools, only 29 black males, less than 10 percent of the graduating class of 1999, had academic credentials sufficient for admission into the state university system. Meanwhile, in February of 1999, in response to a lawsuit filed by the parents of Chinese-American students, the San Francisco school board abandoned its 16 year-old desegregation plan, according to which race and ethnicity had been a main factor in pupil placement. Despite vociferous objections by African American parents who feared that their children would be ghettoized, in January of 2000 the board implemented a race-neutral plan which gave priority to neighborhood schools in admissions.

REFERENCES

Crouchett, Lawrence P., Lonnie G. Bunch, III and Martha Kendall Winnacker. *Visions Toward Tomorrow: The History of the East Bay Afro-American Community*. 1989.

Daniels, Douglas Henry. *Pioneer Urbanites: A Social and Cultural History of Black San Francisco*. 1980.

Wheeler, B. Gordon. *Black California: A History of African Americans in the Golden State*. 1993.

GREG ROBINSON

Satcher, David (March 2, 1941–), U.S. Surgeon General. David Satcher was born in Anniston, Alabama, one of nine children born to Wilmer Satcher, a foundry worker, and Anna Satcher. Satcher attended school in Anniston (helping out after school at his

David Satcher. (The Meharry Medical College Archives)

father's foundry), then attended Morehouse College in Atlanta on scholarship. After receiving his B.S. in 1963, Satcher attended medical school at Case Western Reserve University, and obtained an M.D. and a Ph.D. in cytogenetics. Following a residency in Rochester, New York, Satcher took a position at the hypertension clinic at the Martin Luther King, Jr. Hospital in the Watts neighborhood of Los Angeles, and taught epidemiology at the University of California, Los Angeles (UCLA) Medical Center.

In 1982, three years after he returned to Morehouse, Satcher became the president of Meharry Medical College in Nashville, Tennessee. During his ten years at Meharry, Satcher improved the curriculum of the school, which had almost lost its accreditation, and he saved Meharry-Hubbard Hospital from bankruptcy by engineering a merger with Nashville's Metropolitan Hospital.

In 1993, Satcher was appointed director of the federal Centers for Disease Control. During his tenure, the CDC broadened its focus on AIDS prevention and experimented with strategies for preventing violent crime. On September 12, 1997 (following Senate rejection of another African-American candidate), President Bill Clinton named Satcher U.S. Surgeon General, and the Senate confirmed him that year. As Surgeon General, Satcher has focused on educating Americans about physical fitness and smoking.

See also DISEASES AND EPIDEMICS [2]; PRESIDENTS OF THE UNITED STATES [4].

REFERENCE

"David Satcher." In *Notable Black American Men*. 1998.

GREG ROBINSON

Scarborough, William Sanders (1852–September 9, 1926), professor. William Scarborough was born in Macon, Georgia; his father was free and his mother was a quasi-free slave who lived in her own home with her husband. William Scarborough entered Atlanta University in 1869 but eventually graduated from Oberlin in 1875. He received an M.A. from the same institution in 1878.

In 1876 Scarborough accepted an appointment as professor of Latin and Greek at Wilberforce University. An active scholar in his field, he published a textbook, *First Lessons in Greek*, in 1881 and *The Birds of Aristophanes* in 1886. He was the third African American member of the American Philological Society. He contributed articles to national magazines, delivered many speeches to various organizations and gatherings, and was a committed leader of the African Methodist Episcopal Church.

Scarborough's years at Wilberforce were not always tranquil. In 1892 he was fired from the university but given a position in Payne Seminary, where he was responsible for raising the funds for his own salary. The ostensible reason for the dismissal was a desire to increase the emphasis on utilitarian subjects. In 1896 Scarborough was reappointed professor and became president of the institution in 1897. The university faced severe financial problems during his presidency, but it has been suggested tensions were aggravated by resentment concerning his 1881 marriage to a white woman. He held the presidency until 1920.

Scarborough's activities in Republican politics secured him a minor appointment in the Department of Agriculture, which he gave up in 1924 after the death of his patron President Warren G. Harding. Scarborough died at his home in Ohio.

See also AMERICAN NEGRO ACADEMY (ANA) [1]; BOOK COLLECTORS AND COLLECTIONS [1]; WILBERFORCE UNIVERSITY [5].

REFERENCES

Weisenburger, Francis P. "William Sanders Scarborough." In *Dictionary of American Negro Autobiography*, edited by Rayford W. Logan and Michael R. Winston. 1982.

Culp, D. W. *Twentieth Century Negro Literature*. 1902.

ROBERT L. JOHNS

Schmoke, Kurt (December 1, 1949–), mayor. Schmoke was born in Baltimore, Maryland. After attending Baltimore's public schools, Schmoke graduated from Yale in 1971. He then studied for two years at Oxford University as a Rhodes Scholar. He earned a J.D. from Harvard Law School in 1976.

Following a brief period at a prestigious Baltimore law firm, Schmoke joined the Carter administration in Washington, D.C., serving on the White House Domestic Policy Staff and in the Department of Transportation. In 1978 Schmoke returned to Baltimore as assistant United States attorney. On September 16, 1982, he won the Democratic primary and then the election for the office of Baltimore's state attorney, the chief prosecuting officer for the city. This office gave him the visibility to run for mayor.

Kurt Schmoke. (AP/Wide World Photos)

Schmoke's opponent was Clarence "Du" Burns, the first black mayor of Baltimore. Burns had succeeded William Donald Schaefer, who had been elected governor. Schmoke's margin of victory in the 1987 September primary was narrower than expected. He won two more races for the mayoralty, in 1991 and in 1995, before announcing his decision not to seek another term in 1999.

When Schmoke took office in 1988, his supporters had high hopes because he represented a break from the past. He made earnest efforts to improve education, reform public housing, revitalize neighborhoods, reduce crime, and foster economic development, but many of the city's problems, such as substance abuse, remained intractable. While some voters had questions about his effectiveness, almost all respected his personal integrity.

See also BALTIMORE, MARYLAND [1].

REFERENCES

Anft, Michael, and Molly Rath. "The End: What Kurt Schmoke Did Right, and How He Went Wrong." *Baltimore City Paper*, 1-7 December 1999.

"Kurt L. Schmoke." http://www.ihv.org/ihv%20htmls/schmoke.html.

Kram, Mark. "Kurt Schmoke." In *Contemporary Black Biography*, vol. 1, edited by Michael L. LaBlanc. 1992.

ROBERT L. JOHNS

Scott, Robert Cortez "Bobby" (April 30, 1947–), U.S. Congressman. Robert Scott is the first black member of the U.S. Congress from Virginia since Reconstruction. Born in Washington, D.C., he attended Harvard College and Boston College, receiving his law degree from the latter institution. After serving in the Massachusetts National Guard and the Army Reserve, Scott began practicing law upon graduation. In 1978, he won election to Virginia's House of Delegates and in 1983, to the Virginia State Senate, where he remained until his election in 1992 to the U.S. House of Representatives.

Scott's House sub-committee assignments reflect his legislative interests in education, job creation, health care, and crime prevention. As a member of the Education and Workplace Committee and the Judiciary Committee, Scott's first successful endeavor was the exemption of 33 predominantly black colleges and universities being penalized due to high student default rates. Subsequently, legislative efforts were directed against government voucher programs, a Constitutional amendment guaranteeing the right to religious expression in public schools, a crime bill increasing the use of the death penalty, and the impeachment of President Bill Clinton.

Scott has sponsored legislation giving recognition to black Civil War soldiers at the Battle of New Market Heights and awarding 14 of that number the Medal of Honor. He also pushes legislation for defense spending, since his district includes a military base, defense industries, and voters who are active and retired military personnel. In 2000, Scott sponsored H.R.4333–the Fairness and Accuracy in Student Testing Act. This will, if enacted, require school districts to use multiple measurements for promotion and graduation of secondary students.

See also WASHINGTON, D.C.[5].

REFERENCES

Oblender, David G., ed. *Contemporary Black Biography*, vol. 23. 2000.

"Robert C. Scott." www.house.gov/scott.

Who's Who Among African Americans. 12th ed. 1999.

DOLORES NICHOLSON

Shabazz, Betty (May 28, 1936–June 23, 1997), educator, activist. Betty Shabazz, the widow of Malcolm X who subsequently built a career of her own, was born Betty Sanders in Detroit, Michigan, and was adopted by the Malloy's, a neighborhood family. After

Betty Shabazz. (AP/Wide World Photos)

attending Tuskegee Institute, she moved to New York and transferred to Jersey City State College, where she received a B.A. degree. Sanders then began training at the Brooklyn State Hospital School of Nursing, where she received her R.N. in 1958. During this period, she joined the Nation of Islam and changed her name to Betty X (she became Betty Shabazz in 1964). She also met the charismatic leader Malcolm X, with whom she struck up a friendship. The couple married in 1958.

During the following seven years, as Malcolm X grew into a national figure, Shabazz rarely saw him, although they remained on good terms. Shabazz gave birth to their six daughters during this period. In 1965, Shabazz and four of the girls were listening to Malcolm X speak at New York's Audubon Ballroom as he was assassinated. Following the death of her husband, Shabazz cut her ties with the Nation of Islam and became an orthodox Muslim.

Following her husband's death, Shabazz earned a Ph.D. in education administration from the University of Massachusetts. She worked for two decades as Director of Public Relations for Medgar Evers College in New York. During these years, she also served as the guardian of Malcolm X's legacy. In 1995,

Shabazz began a weekly radio program on New York's WLIB. Two years later, she was badly burned in a fire set by her 12-year-old grandson Malcolm to protest his mother's absence. Despite many community blood donations, she died three weeks later.
See also MALCOLM X [3].

REFERENCE

Brown, Jamie Foster, ed. *Betty Shabazz: A Sisterfriends' Tribute in Words and Pictures*. 1998.

GREG ROBINSON

Sharecropper/Sharecropping Union. Prior to the American Civil War (1861–1865) most black Americans worked as slaves primarily in cotton fields on plantations in the South. Following emancipation in 1865, blacks were free but had no money or land. The war-torn South was going through traumatic social and economic change. White landowners sought a stable, low cost work force. Newly freed slaves sought to solidify family ties and refused to accept plantation discipline. New farming systems emerged including sharecropping in which white landowners divided up their estates and assigned each unit to a family. The owner often furnished sharecroppers with shelter, fuel, implements, feed for stock, seed, and one half of the needed fertilizers. The sharecroppers provided their own labor and the remainder of the fertilizer. The sharecropper would pay rent with up to half of his harvest. Food, clothing, and some supplies had to be purchased from local merchants on credit.

Under the sharecropping system, blacks were at the mercy of both landlords and merchants. Often semi-literate at best, they were frequently charged excessive rates of interest on their credit, and deceitful landowners shortchanged them in assessing the value of their harvests each year. The system basically guaranteed the families would remain in debt for many years. This type of recurring debt is known as debt peonage, a form of involuntary slavery in which blacks were legally bound to continue working for landlords as long as their debt persisted. Sharecroppers attempting to flee debt were frequently caught and returned by law authorities and faced severe whippings. Though the U.S. Supreme Court held such forms of servitude unconstitutional in 1911, sharecropping and its associated chronic indebtedness continued for decades.

Poverty and discrimination permeated the sharecroppers' world. Typically, sharecroppers lived in crowded, flimsy shacks, had worn clothes, and ate poor diets of corn bread, molasses, potatoes, and fatback. They suffered from white social and political dominance. Black families commonly operated forty-acre parcels whereas white tenant farmers averaged over ninety acres.

In 1931 mostly black sharecroppers in Alabama organized the Sharecropping Union to improve their general living conditions. Union members demanded the right to have their own gardens to raise their own food, sell their own crops, shorten the workday, institute wage labor for farm work, and receive advances of food until money was available from their crop sales. In reaction, white landowners organized in opposition. Violent confrontations ensued. However, the union survived, growing to 5,500 members by 1933 and remaining active until 1939.

In 1930 over 776,000 black sharecroppers worked the soil, but by 1959 only 121,000 remained. Boll weevil infestations, increased mechanization of farms, erosion and exhaustion of the land, and diversification of the South's agricultural economy took their toll. Sharecroppers' plots had become too small to be profitable, and sharecropping largely disappeared by the 1970s. Through the decades thousands had left for wage labor in the industrialized cities. Many blacks who remained in farming became migratory workers involved in seasonal day labor.

See also BIRMINGHAM, ALABAMA [1]; ODELL WALLER CASE [4].

REFERENCES

Conrad, David E. *The Forgotten Farmers: The Story of Sharecroppers in the New Deal*. 1982.

Daniel, Pete. *The Shadow of Slavery: Peonage in the South, 1901–1969*. 1990.

Jaynes, Gerald D. *Branches Without Roots: Genesis of the Black Working Class in the American South, 1862–1882*. 1986.

Kester, Howard. *Revolt Among the Sharecroppers*. 1997.

Tindall, George B. *The Emergence of the New South, 1913–1945*. 1967.

Wright, Gavin. *Old South, New South: Revolutions in the Southern Economy Since the Civil War*. 1996.

RICHARD C. HANES

Sharpton, Alfred, Jr. "Al" (Update)

(October 3, 1954–), political activist. In 1997, on the

Rev. Al Sharpton, attending the kickoff event of "A Season for Nonviolence," at the United Nations. (AP/Wide World Photos)

strength of a heavy black vote, Sharpton finished second in the Democratic primary race for Mayor of New York City, and narrowly missed qualifying for a runoff with the leading candidate, Ruth Messinger. However, Sharpton's attempt to moderate his image and reach out beyond blacks was set back in 1990s. In 1996, Sharpton was blamed for inciting a gunman to burn down a Harlem store, operated by a Jewish immigrant, where Sharpton had led an angry protest campaign. In 1998, Sharpton was drawn back into the Tawana Brawley controversy when Officer Steven Pagones won a judgment for libel against Sharpton and his partners, who had repeatedly accused him of participation in the alleged rape. In 1999, Sharpton led a mass protest against police brutality with the February 1999 shooting death of Amadou Diallo, an African immigrant, mistakenly shot by four policemen when he reached for his wallet.

REFERENCES

Finnegan, Michael, and Michael O. Allen. "Sharpton launches series of rallies against police brutality." *Knight-Ridder/Tribune News Service.* April 5, 1999: K4760.

Goldman, John J. "Sharpton found guilty of defaming ex-DA in alleged rape case." *Houston Chronicle.* July 14, 1998: 2.

GREG ROBINSON

Shaw, Alan (January 23, 1963–), computer network programmer. Shaw was born in Hanover, New Hampshire, to Earl and Harriet Shaw. After his parents divorced, Shaw and his two older brothers were raised by their mother. His father went on to earn a Ph.D. in physics at the University of California at Berkeley, while his mother later earned a Ph.D. in Psychology. Shaw went to Harvard University on a Bell Laboratories Engineering Scholarship. He applied for the scholarship at the urging of his father, who by then had become an eminent laser researcher at Bell Laboratories.

At Harvard, where he earned a bachelor's degree in applied mathematics, Shaw became interested in finding ways to solve inner city blight. After his master's degree in computer science at the Massachusetts Institute of Technology and during his Ph.D. in Media Technologies, Shaw hit on an idea which he explored in his doctoral dissertation. His idea was to use a network to link neighborhood people who might otherwise never speak to one another. He named the software Multi-User Sessions in Community, or MU-

SIC. In Dorchester in 1993 with help from a local church and an $8,000 Wood Foundation grant, Shaw's project soon spawned a food cooperative, a neighborhood crime watch and a jobs bulletin board. Then, with two years of federal funding totaling $206,000, Shaw helped an impoverished Newark, New Jersey, neighborhood, by placing several dozen computers in private homes and public buildings. Again, MUSIC was a success. MUSIC software was implemented in urban areas across the country. Shaw has also founded an Internet company, Imani Information Systems, whose mission is to discover ways that for-profit corporations can help non-profits organizations. *See also* NEW HAMPSHIRE [4].

REFERENCES

Hogan, Kevin. "Mojo's October Hellraiser!" *Mother Jones* (September/October 1995): 18.

Roach, Ronald. "Making Sweet 'Music'." *American Visions* (February/March 1996):38.

Russell, Dick. *Black Genius and the American Experience.* 1998.

KEVIN C. KRETSCHMER

Shaw, Earl D. (November 26, 1937–), physicist. Shaw was born in Clarksdale, Mississippi. He graduated at the age of sixteen from a gang-dominated vocational high school in Chicago. After almost dropping out, he received his B.A. in 1960 from the

Earl D. Shaw. (Copyright by Earl D. Shaw)

University of Illinois. Shaw then married and took a job, but a night class at Darmouth led to his taking an M.A. from that institution in 1964. At the the University of California, where he took his Ph.D. in 1969, he became involved in student protest and served as president of the Black Students' Union. He then became the first black hired by Bell Laboratories.

At Bell Laboratories Shaw became involved in laser research and was a co-inventor of the spin-flip Raman laser, which allows the wavelength of the light to be tuned. In 1971 Shaw left Bell and taught at the University of Rochester for three years. Bell enticed him back to recruit black physicists. Not only did Shaw have an appreciable impact on the development of the black scientific community, he continued his work on expanding the range of color of laser emissions, particularly free electron laser technology. This device offers the potential to study molecular activity important for biological functions, chemical reactions, and the electronic properties of semiconductors.

Shaw went to Rutgers University as professor of physics in 1991. There he continued to work on free electron laser. He became chair of the physics department in 1996. In addition to his scientific work, Shaw supported increasing numbers of African Americans in science.

See also MISSISSIPPI [4].

REFERENCES

Milite, George A. "Earl D. Shaw." In *Notable Black American Scientists*, edited by Kristine Krappe. 1999.

"Prof. Earl D. Shaw's Homepage." http://www.andromeda.rutgers.edu/earlshaw

Russell, Dick. *Black Genius and the American Experience*. 1998.

ROBERT L. JOHNS

Shepard, James Edward (November 3, 1875–October 6, 1947), educator, college founder. Shepard, one of the most respected African American educators in North Carolina, founded North Carolina College to prepare African American youth to become leaders. Born in Raleigh, he graduated from Shaw University in 1894 with a degree in pharmacy (Ph.G.), then worked as a pharmacist in Damill, Virginia. He joined other prominent African Americans in founding what became the North Carolina Mutual Insurance Company. Later, he founded and was a trustee of Durham's Mechanics and Farmers Bank. In 1899–1900, he was a clerk in the office of the recorder of deeds, Washing-

ton, D.C. Shepard held various other positions between 1899 and 1905 and was an early leader in North Carolina's Republican Party.

Shepard is primarily remembered as the founder, in 1910, of the National Religious Training School, which evolved into North Carolina College for Negroes, then North Carolina College, located in Durham. At first a private school, in 1923 the state of North Carolina took control of the National Training School and renamed it the Durham State Normal School. Two years later the school was renamed again and operated as a liberal arts school that prepared teachers and principals for the education profession. It was the first state-supported college in North Carolina for African Americans.

Though highly regarded as an educator, several African American leaders denounced him as one who capitulated to whites. He was known also for urging blacks everywhere to master the English language. *See also* NORTH CAROLINA [4].

REFERENCES

Garraty, John A., and Edward T. James, eds. *Dictionary of American Biography*. 1974.

Logan, Rayford W., and Michael R. Winston, eds. *Dictionary of American Negro Biography*. 1982.

Negro History Bulletin, November/December 1978: 900-02.

JESSIE CARNEY SMITH

Simmons, Ruth J. (July 3, 1945–), educator, college president. Simmons was born in Grapevine, Texas, one of twelve children born to Isaac Stubblefield, a farmer and factory worker, and Fannie Stubblefield, a homemaker. After graduating from Dillard University with a B.A. degree in 1967, she studied for a year in France on a Fulbright grant. She returned to earn a master's degree (1970) and doctorate in Romance languages (1973) from Radcliffe College, now a part of Harvard University.

From 1970 to 1990, Simmons held a number of positions at such colleges as Radcliffe and the University of New Orleans, and as assistant or associate dean of the University of Southern California at Los Angeles and Princeton University. From 1990 to 1992, she was provost at Spelman College and then left for Princeton University where she was vice-provost in 1992.

Although she was a candidate for many college president vacancies, Simmons was the unanimous choice among 350 candidates on the Smith College

Ruth Simmons. (Smith College)

list. In 1995, she was appointed the ninth president of Smith and when inaugurated on September 30 became the first African American woman president of a top-ranked college or university in the United States. Her tasks were to lead the institution into the 21st century, serve as a scholarly role model for students, develop the faculty, engage in financial planning, and become involved in all aspects of leadership of Smith. Soon after her tenure began, applications for admission poured into the college. Simmons is highly regarded in academic circles and elsewhere as a capable, vibrant, and dedicated leader.
See also TEXAS [5].

REFERENCES

Clarke, Caroline. "A New Face in the Ivory Tower." *Black Enterprise* 26 (October 1995): 120-28.

O'Reilly, David. "A Conversation with Ruth Simmons." *Philadelphia Inquirer*, March 2, 1995.

Phelps, Shirelle, ed. *Contemporary Black Biography*, vol. 13. 1997.

JESSIE CARNEY SMITH

Simpson, Joshua McCarter (c. 1820–1876),

poet. Joshua Simpson, known for his antebellum songs, was freeborn in Morgan County, Ohio; at the age of three, he was apprenticed to an English farmer, Isaac Kay. Seven years later, Kay died and Simpson was bound to another farmer. Here he remained until he was twenty-five. With little schooling, but a desire to learn and to help others, he embarked on a regimen of self education which included taking all of his worldly goods and walking from Windsor, Ohio, to Oberlin College, where he enrolled in 1844. However, he never became a teacher as he desired.

Once he learned to write, Simpson felt compelled to disclose the plight of his race through poetry. He believed poetry allowed him the freedom to voice his truths without fear of repercussion. His first poem was performed in public in 1842. His work later appeared in the *North Star* and the *Liberator*. William L. Garrison makes note of Simpson's having published a pamphlet, *Original Anti-Slavery Songs* (1852, not extant). His main publication, *The Emancipation Car* (1874) contains both prose, poetry, autobiographical information, and an essay against emigration schemes and arguments used by the supporters of slavery.

Simpson's poetry, sung to the tune of popular hymns and folk songs, addresses the conditions of slavery, the thirst/thrust for freedom, and generally refutes Thomas Nelson Page's plantation school of thought-that of the happy, contented slave. The songs of freedom printed in this collection represent the largest single collection by a black man up to his time. *See also* OHIO [4].

REFERENCE

Sherman, Joan R. *Invisible Poets: Afro-Americans of the Nineteenth Century*. 1974.

HELEN R. HOUSTON

Singleton, John Daniel (January 6, 1968–),

film director, writer, producer, actor. Born in South Central Los Angeles, John Singleton's interest in film began when he enrolled in Pasadena City College in 1986. Shortly after, he began studies at University of Southern California in Los Angeles, California. While studying film at USC he won three writing awards from the university and was signed by the Creative Artists Agency. He made his debut with the 1991 Columbia Picture *Boyz N the Hood*, whose widespread acclaim at the Cannes Film Festival that year popularized the film nationally. The film garnered two Oscar nominations—for Best Original Screenplay and Best Director, making Singleton the first African American and the youngest person to be nominated for the latter honor. Singleton's next two efforts were *Poetic Justice* (1993), which was nominated for an Academy Award for Best Original Song, and *Higher Learning* (1995). He received critical acclaim with his next film—the

John Singleton. (Corbis Corportation)

Norma Skalrek. (Copyright by Norma Sklarek)

1997 Warner Bros. release, *Rosewood*, the historically-based tale of an African American town destroyed by a lynch mob. Singleton's next feature, *Shaft*, debuted in June 2000, meeting with mixed reactions from critics and initial popularity with audiences.

In addition to his own movies, he has developed other projects through his production company, New Deal Productions. His awards include the 1991 Los Angeles Film Critics Association Award and the New York Film Critics Circle Best New Director Award for *Boyz N the Hood*. In 1992, he won the MTV Movie Award for Best New Filmmaker for *Boyz N the Hood*, as well.

See also FILM [2]; HUDLIN, WARRINGTON [3]; LOS ANGELES, CALIFORNIA [3]; STEREOTYPES [5].

REFERENCES

"Singleton, John." www.altculture.come/aentries/s/singletonx.html

www.singleton.homepage.com/bio.html

RACHEL ZELLARS

Sklarek, Norma Merrick (April 15, 1928–),

architect. Born in New York City, Sklarek became the first African American woman to be licensed as an architect in New York and in California. She received her bachelor's degree in architecture from Barnard in 1951. She passed a rigorous four-day examination in 1954 to become licensed in the state of New York.

The architectural firm Skidmore, Owens, Merrill hired Sklarek in 1955. During this same time she was a member of the architecture faculty at City College of New York. Her expertise in design led her to a new position in Los Angeles in 1960, when she joined the firm Gruen and Associates and taught architecture at the University of California, Los Angeles. She passed the state examination in 1962 certifying her to practice in California. Six years later, Skylark became the first woman to hold the position of director of architecture with Gruen, where she managed a large staff of architects.

In 1966, still at Gruen, Sklarek achieved another first. The American Institute of Architecture honored her with a fellowship, making her the first woman to achieve the award. After twenty years with the firm, in 1980 Sklarek left to become vice president of Weldon Becket Associates in Santa Monica. She left in 1985 to enter a partnership with two women to form Siegel, Sklarek, Diamond. In 1989 she became a principal in the Jerde Partnership in Venice, California.

Among the principal buildings credited to Sklarek are the American Embassy in Tokyo, the Pacific Design Center in Los Angeles, Terminal One at Los Angeles International Airport, and the Fox Plaza in San Francisco.

See also ARCHITECTURE [1].

REFERENCES

Hine, Darlene Clark, ed. *Black Women in America*. 1993.

Lanker, Brian. *I Dream a World.* 1989.

Smith, Jessie Carney, ed. *Notable Black American Women.* 1992.

VALENCIA PRICE

Smith, Anna Deavere (September 18, 1950–), playwright, performance artist, actress. Born in Baltimore, Maryland, Anna Deavere Smith, a 1996 recipient of the McArthur Foundation "Genius" Fellowship, is noted for developing a unique style of performance art that blends traditional theatrical elements with meticulous journalism to provide social commentary from multiple points-of-view about controversial events. *Fires in The Mirror: Crown Heights Brooklyn and Other Identities* (1991) and *Twilight: Los Angeles, 1992* (1993), both one-woman shows that Smith premiered to rave reviews and toured around the world, were written as responses to American urban insurrections. The two plays explore themes of racial conflict and racial identity. For *Fires in the Mirror*, Smith received an Obie and a Pulitzer Prize nomination.

Smith's characteristic writing technique involves interviewing people, seeking the "moment when most people say something that nobody else can say." Smith then selects portions of these interviews, arranging them into monologues and dialogues to tell a story, ending by memorizing and imitating her interviewees' speech and behavior for performance before

Anna Deavere Smith. (Archive Photos, Inc.)

a live audience. In juxtaposing the thoughts and attitudes of distinctly different people, Smith's plays present a documentary-style cross-section of Americans from the 1980s-90s. Her technique evolved while teaching theater at Carnegie Mellon University (1978–79). She also taught theater in several of America's top dramatic arts programs, including the University of Southern California (1982), New York University (1983–1984), Actors Conservatory Theater (1986), and Stanford University, where she has been the Ann O'Day Maples Professor of the Arts since 1992. In 1993, Smith was labeled by *Newsweek* magazine as the most exciting individual in American Theater." Smith's play *House Arrest* premiered in 1997.

See also DRAMA [2]; WOLFE, GEORGE C. [5].

REFERENCES

Hine, Darlene Clark, ed. *Facts on File Encyclopedia of Black Women in America: Theater Arts and Entertainment.* 1997.

Peterson, Jane T. and Suzanee Bennett. *Women Playwrights of Diversity: A Bio-Bibliographical Sourcebook.* 1997.

Performing Arts Journal. May-Sept, 50-51 (1995); 77.

Stepanek, Marcia. "Creative Reality: Anna Deavere-Smith" Interview of Anna Deavere Smith for the Association for Women in Communications, Washington. DC. 22 February 2000. http://www.awic-dc.org/text/womennews_Deveare-Smith.shtml.

F. ZEAL HARRIS

Smith, Barbara (November 16, 1946–), writer, educator. Barbara Smith is a lesbian writer, publisher, educator, and activist who was born in Cleveland, Ohio. She received her B.A. from Mount Holyoke College in 1969 and received her M.A. from the University of Pittsburgh in 1971. In 1974, she co-founded the Combahee River Collective, an early black feminist organization that challenged racism in the gay movement and homophobia in the black community.

She was the first to openly address the subject of black lesbian eroticism in the canon of African American literature. Her well-known 1977 essay, "Toward a Black Feminist Criticism," offered one of the first critical looks at matters of feminism, race, and literature together. Smith is co-founder and publisher of the now defunct, Kitchen Table: Women of Color Press. The Press was the first to focus on the realities and politics of women and lesbians of color.

Her publications include: *This Bridge Called My Back: Writings By Radical Women of Color* (1981), *All the*

Blacks Are Men, But Some of Us Are Brave: Black Women's Studies (1982), *Home Girls: A Black Feminist Anthology* (1983), *Yours in the Struggle: Three Feminist Perspectives on Anti-Semitism and Racism* (1984), and *The Truth That Never Hurts: Writings on Race, Gender, and Freedom* (1998). Additionally Smith has lectured and served as writer in residence at numerous colleges and universities, including Radcliffe College, Emerson College, University of Massachusetts, Boston University, Barnard College, and Mt. Holyoke College. She has remained an outspoken critic of the absence of a discussion of lesbianism within the African American literary canon.

See also BLACK STUDIES [1]; CRITICISM, FEMINIST [2]; INTELLECTUAL LIFE [3]; LESBIANS [3].

REFERENCES

Farajaje-Jones, Elias. Personal Interview. 13 April 2000.

"Smith, Barbara." *Who's Who in Black America*, Sixth edition, edited by Iris Loyd. 1990.

"Smith, Barbara." *Contemporary Authors*, edited by Donna Olendorf. 1994.

RACHEL ZELLARS

Barbara Smith. (Unknown source)

Smith, Barbara (August 24, 1949–), entrepreneur, model, author. Barbara Smith was born in western Pennsylvania and grew up in Everson, a working-class town near Pittsburgh. After developing an interest in modeling, she took weekend classes at John Robert Powers modeling school in Pittsburgh and graduated just before her high school commencement. When she was 19 years old, the slender and attractive Smith was selected to serve as a model for the Ebony Fashion Fair's traveling show. She moved to New York to participate in the fair and begin her modeling career.

Smith's beauty, grace, and intelligence won top spots for her. She appeared on five covers for *Essence*, the first model so honored. In 1976, she became the first African American to appear on the cover of *Mademoiselle*. Since then, Smith has appeared in over fifty print advertisements and television commercials, the most well known of which was a 1990s ad for Oil of Olay.

In the mid-1980s, Smith scaled back her modeling to concentrate on the restaurant business, an interest she acquired as a youth watching and assisting her mother and grandmother prepare for family get-togethers. Entering a partnership with Ark Restaurant

Corporation, she has opened three B. Smith restaurants, two in New York and one in Washington, D.C.

B. Smith, as she prefers to be known, published *B. Smith's Entertaining and Cooking for Friends* in 1995. In 1997 she began hosting "Smith with Style," a half-hour television show. In late 1999, Smith launched *B. Smith Style*, a magazine dedicated to her interests of food, fashion, and beauty.

See also PENNSYLVANIA [4].

REFERENCES

Current Biography Yearbook 1998. 1998.

Mabubda, L. Mpho, and Shirelle Phelps, eds. *Contemporary Black Biography.* vol. 11. 1996.

Reed, Julia. "Can B. Smith Be Martha?" *New York Times Magazine*, August 22, 1999.

JESSIE CARNEY SMITH

Smith, James Todd. *See* L L Cool J.

Smith, Joshua Bowen (1813–July 5, 1879), abolitionist. Joshua Bowen Smith was a prominent abolitionist leader. He was born in Coatesville, Pennsylvania, and educated in the local public school. Beginning in 1836 Smith worked as a headwaiter at the Mount Washington House in Boston. There he became acquainted with many white abolitionists. Smith opened his own very successful catering establishment in 1849.

From early on Smith gave much of his time to helping fugitive slaves. In reaction to the arrest in 1842 of fugitive George Latimer, father of the noted inventor Lewis H. Latimer, Smith became a founder and vice-president of the New England Freedom Association, an all black organization. This group not only defied the law but sometimes used violence to attain its ends. When the interracial Boston Committee of Vigilance came into being in 1846, Smith was a member of the executive committee. After the passage of the Fugitive Slave Act of 1850, Smith urged fugitives to arm themselves to resist recapture. Smith personally helped several fugitives to reach the safety of Canada and gave temporary employment to others. His catering business gave him good opportunity to follow the activities of slave hunters.

At the outbreak of the Civil War, Smith catered for the Twelfth Massachusetts Regiment. This proved his financial undoing since he had great difficulty in eventually collecting $23,760.80 on his expenditure of $40,378. His debts were thirty times the value of his estate when his will was proved. His community standing was not injured, however, and he was the first black member of St. Andrew's Lodge of Freemasons in 1867. Smith also represented Cambridge in the Massachusetts Senate in 1873 and 1874.
See also BOSTON, MASSACHUSETTS [1].

REFERENCES

Finkenbine, Roy E. "Joshua Bowen Smith." In *American National Biography*, edited by John A. Garraty and Mark C. Carnes. 1999.

Horton, James Oliver, and Lois E. Horton. *Black Bostonians: Family Life and Community Struggle in the Antebellum North*. 1979.

Porter, Dorothy B. AJoshua Bowen Smith." In *Dictionary of American Negro Biography*, edited by Rayford W. Logan and Michael R. Winston. 1982.

ROBERT L. JOHNS

Smith, Stephen. (c. 1795–November 14, 1873), businessman, minister. Stephen Smith was a businessman and minister. He was born near Harrisburg, Pennsylvania. In 1801 he was indentured to Thomas Boude, an officer during the Revolutionary War and timber dealer in Columbia, Pennsylvania. Smith was placed in charge of the business while a very young man. He purchased his freedom in 1816.

Smith soon became a prosperous lumberman. His success drew envy and spite. During the race riots of 1834–1835 in Columbia, his office was attacked. With his life in danger, he offered to sell out but found no takers and withdrew the offer. He and his long-time business partner William Whipper were able to withstand the panic of 1837. In 1842 Smith moved to Philadelphia, where he continued to prosper.

Smith was much involved in the Underground Railroad and other activities aimed at racial betterment, such as the national conventions of free people of color from 1834 to 1855. He was a member of numerous organizations like the Odd Fellows. John Brown was his guest for a week in 1858. The African Methodist Episcopal Church ordained him a local preacher in 1838, and he often preached in churches in Philadelphia and vicinity. In 1857 he built Zion AME Church and served as its pastor for a year or so during the Civil War.

Smith's philanthropy extended beyond his church. For example, he helped purchase the building formerly occupied by the Institute for Colored Youth and convert it into a meeting hall and stores for black businesses. In 1864 he helped found the Philadelphia Home for the Aged and Infirm, and he left it $250,000 in his will.
See also BANKING [1]; ENTREPRENEURS [2]; PENNSYLVANIA [4]; PHILADELPHIA, PENNSYLVANIA [4]; WHIPPER, WILLIAM [5].

REFERENCES

Fishel, Leslie H. "Stephen Smith." In *American National Biography*, edited by John A. Garraty and Mark C. Carnes. 1999.

McCormick, Richard P. "Stephen Smith." In *Dictionary of American Negro Biography*, edited by Rayford W. Logan and Michael. R. Smith. 1982.

ROBERT L. JOHNS

Smythe-Haithe, Mabel Murphy (April 3, 1918–), educator, government official. Smythe-Haithe was born in Montgomery, Alabama, and graduated from Mount Holyoke College in 1937. She received both her master's and doctoral degrees in economics from the University of Wisconsin.

She taught for a while at Lincoln University in Missouri and in 1945–1946 taught economics at Tennessee Agricultural and Industrial College, as it was known then. After teaching assignments in Japan for the U.S. Department of State, in 1953 Smythe-Haith became deputy director for the NAACP Legal Defense Fund. From 1954 to 1962, she held various positions, such as coordinating principal at New Lincoln School in New York and adjunct professor at Queens College and at City University of New York. After joining the Phelps Stokes Fund in 1970, Smythe-Haithe was promoted to vice-president of the fund, a position she held from 1972 to 1977.

For one year, 1973–1974, Smythe-Haithe was scholar in residence for the U.S. Commission on Civil Rights. President Carter named her ambassador to the United Republic of Cameroon in Yaounde from 1977 to 1980, then U.S. ambassador to the Republic of Equatorial Guinea in 1979–1980. For the next five years, she continued to serve her country well, both in assignments at home and abroad. She also became Melville J. Herskovits Professor of African Studies at Northwestern University and associate director of the university's African Studies Program.

A prolific writer, Smythe-Haithe has produced numerous articles and several books, among them *Intensive English Conversation* (1953), *The New Nigerian Elite* (1960), and *Curriculum for Understanding* (1965). She edited *Black American Reference Book* (1976) and the *American Negro Reference Book* (1974).
See also ALABAMA [1].

REFERENCES

Evory. Ann, ed. *Contemporary Authors*. 1973.

Smith, Jessie Carney, ed. *Notable Black American Women*. 1992.

Who's Who of American Women, 14th ed. 1985–86.

VALENCIA PRICE

Sowell, Thomas

Sowell, Thomas (June 30, 1930–), economist, social policy writer. A prolific author, columnist, essayist and speaker, Thomas Sowell is one of the best-known conservative voices in America. A libertarian, Sowell consistently attacks big government programs, though well-intentioned, as constantly enlarging the scope and nature of the problems suffered

Thomas Sowell. (AP/Wide World Photos)

by minorities. He manages to back up his claims with thoroughly researched and cogently reasoned arguments provided by anyone in the political right wing.

Born in Gastonia, North Carolina, Sowell was raised in Harlem, where he left home early and dropped out of high school. He later enlisted in the U.S. Marine Corps and worked as a photographer during the Korean War. After his military service he entered Harvard University, where he earned his bachelor's degree in economics and graduated magna cum laude in 1958. The following year he received a master's degree in economics from Columbia University. Following jobs as an economist with the Department of Labor and with AT & T, he earned a doctorate degree in economics from the University of Chicago in 1968.

Sowell has been on the faculty of many of the nation's top institutions, including Cornell University, Brandeis University, and the University of California, Los Angeles. Since 1980, he has been a senior fellow at the Hoover Institution, Stanford University. His many books advocating free-market economics and libertarian social policy have gained him wide attention from advocates and critics alike. Among Sowell's most popular works are those of his cultural trilogy: *Conquests and Cultures: An International History*, 1998; *Migrations and Cultures: A World View*, 1996; and *Race and Culture: A World View*, 1994. He is a nationally syndicated columnist for Creators Syndicate.

See also AFFIRMATIVE ACTION [1]; CLASS AND SOCIETY [2]; CONSERVATISM [2]; INTELLECTUAL LIFE[3]; THOMAS, CLARENCE [5].

REFERENCES

Brimelow, Peter. "Human Capital—Thomas Sowell, in a New Book, Takes on a Taboo: Why Nations Fail or Succeed." *Forbes* (July 6, 1998): 52.

Sowell, Thomas. "Curriculum Vita." http://www.tsowell.com/cv.html.

"Thomas Sowell—Libertarian." http://www.self-gov.org/celebs/Sowell.html.

KEVIN C. KRETSCHMER

St. Louis, Missouri (Update).

The problem of racial discrimination in St. Louis gained national attention as a result of the protest campaign against the Adam's Mark hotel chain that took place during the Spring of 2000. African American guests had previously filed suit against the St. Louis area-based chain, which they claimed had overcharged them for rooms and compelled them to wear special identifying wristbands. In March of 2000, Adam's Mark signed an $8 million settlement with the Justice Department, although it continued to deny any wrongdoing. In response, several individuals and organizations withdrew their business from Adam's Mark. The Organization of American Historians (OAH), which had planned to hold its annual convention at the St. Louis Adam's Mark, moved its events elsewhere. In cooperation with the OAH, the St. Louis NAACP and other groups organized a March Against Racism, which drew 300 people, as well as speeches and educational events.

REFERENCES

Greene, Lorenzo J., Gary R. Kremer, and Antonio F. Holland. *Missouri's Black Heritage*. Rev. ed. 1992.

Primm, James Neal. *St. Louis: Lion of the Valley*. 1981.

GREG ROBINSON

Straker, David Augustus

(July 11, 1842–February 14, 1908), educator, lawyer, reformer. Born in Bridgetown, Barbados, Straker was planning on pursuing a law degree at Middle Temple, England, when he was induced to come to the United States to help educate former slaves.

In 1871, he received his law degree with honors from Howard University. Also in 1871, Straker married Annie M. Carey, of Detroit, and was appointed clerk in the U. S. Treasury Department in Washington, D.C. After being inspector of customs at Charleston, South Carolina, for a year (1875), he entered private practice as a lawyer in South Carolina, and in 1876, he ran as the Republican candidate for state representative. He won the election, but the results were disputed by the Democrats, who assumed power themselves. Straker was elected to that same house seat in 1878 and 1880, but the Democrats refused to seat him each time. In 1880, Straker became special inspector of customs again in Charleston, serving in that capacity for two years.

In Detroit in 1887, Straker practiced law, in 1890 gaining renown for his handling of *Ferguson vs. Gies,* a civil rights case concerning equality of treatment in public facilities. Though Straker lost the jury trial, he successfully appealed the case to the Michigan Supreme Court, providing a precedent for other civil rights actions. Straker lectured throughout the United States, edited the *Detroit Advocate*, and wrote several books. He was a two-time Wayne county circuit court commissioner (the first black to be so elected, 1893) and the first president of the National Federation of Colored Men, a precursor to the NAACP. Straker died of pneumonia in 1908 and was buried in Detroit's Woodmere Cemetery.

See also DETROIT, MICHIGAN [2]; STEWART, THOMAS MCCANTS [5].

REFERENCES

Logan, Rayford W. and Michael R. Winston, eds. *Dictionary of American Negro Biography*. 1982.

Richings, G. F. *Evidences of Progress among Colored People*. 1896.

Simmons, William J. *Men of Mark*. 1887.

KEVIN C. KRETSCHMER

Sumner, Francis Cecil

(December 7, 1895–January 12, 1954), psychologist, educator. Francis Cecil Sumner was a psychologist who had a major impact on the development of black psychologists and the development of the discipline in black institutions. Sumner was born in Pine Bluff, Arkansas. Admitted to Lincoln University (Pennsylvania) in 1911, he graduated with honors in 1915. In 1918 and

1919 his graduate studies were interrupted by service with the army; nonetheless, he received his doctorate in psychology at Clark University on June 14, 1920, a first among African Americans. Sumner taught at Wilberforce University in 1920 and 1921 and at West Virginia State College from 1921 to 1928 before going to Howard University, where he became chair of the department in 1928. Under Sumner, this department became the foremost among black universities. A 1975 study showed that of the 300 African Americans with a psychology Ph.D, 60 received their bachelor or master's degrees from Howard, testament to the stature that the department shaped by Sumner held in this field.

While a proficient but unspectacular teacher, Sumner still influenced many students deeply. Committed to scholarship, he published over forty-five articles. His doctoral dissertation on Freud and Adler received high praise, and his research covered a variety of topics such as color perception, the legibility and coloring of lettering, and the psychology of religion. He contributed over two thousand abstracts to *Psychological Abstracts*, beginning in 1946. This was an impressive achievement, as they not only drew on his language skills (most of the source articles were in French and German), but were written in addition to his own research and heavy teaching load.

See also INTELLECTUAL LIFE [3].

REFERENCES

Logan, Rayford W. and Michael R. Winston, eds. *Dictionary of American Negro Biography*. 1982.

Garraty, John A. and Mark C. Carnes, eds. *American National Biography*. 1999.

ROBERT L. JOHNS

T

Tatum, Wilbert Arnold (January 23, 1933–), editor, publisher. Tatum was born in Durham, North Carolina, the son of Eugene Malcolm and Mittie Novesta Tatum-Smith. Tatum earned his B.S. degree from Lincoln University, his M.A. from Occidental College in 1972, and was named an honorary Doctor of Humane Letters by Yale University in 1988. He is widely known as both a publisher and public servant, having served in several capacities in various governmental offices, including as deputy president of the Borough of Manhattan (1973–1974), and vice president of the Health Insurance Plan of Greater New York (1978–1986).

Tatum is best known for his association with the *Amsterdam News*, which he served as the major stockholder, editor, publisher, and chief executive officer after purchasing it in 1983. The newspaper serves a unique, multicultural community from its offices in the center of Harlem, the hub of the black intellectual community in New York City. The *Amsterdam News* is well known for crusading, liberal journalism, having pioneered since its founding in 1909 coverage of civil rights issues, including discrimination, persecution, lynching, the Scottsboro trials, the labor unrest and subsequent riots at the Ford plant in Detroit, and the protest marches in the 1960s. In December 1997, Tatum handed over the day to day running of the *Amsterdam News* to his daughter, Elinor.

Tatum's roles in public organizations include his service as an executor of board member of several major entities, including the Inner City Broadcasting Corporation and the Sloan House YMCA. Honors he has received include the B'Nai B'rith Citation of Merit (1976) and the Man of the Year (1977), awarded by the American Jewish Congress.

See also AMSTERDAM NEWS [1].

REFERENCES

Danky, S. P. *African-American Newspapers and Periodicals*. 1998.

Who's Who Among African Americans, 1998–99. 10th ed. 1999.

Who's Who in America, 2000 Millennium Edition, vol. 2. 2000.

DARIUS L. THIEME

Taylor, Susan (January 23, 1946–), publishing company executive. Susan Taylor is a publishing company executive, columnist, and inspirational speaker best known for her position as longtime editor-in-chief of *Essence* magazine. Born in Harlem, she began her career as a licensed cosmetologist and actress with the Negro Ensemble Company. In her early twenties, she founded Nequai Cosmetics, working to develop beauty products for black women. In 1970, she began working at the new magazine, *Essence*, as a freelance beauty writer. In 1971, she was promoted to beauty editor, and in 1972, to fashion and beauty editor. In 1981, she became editor-in chief.

Susan Taylor, 1986. (AP/Wide World Photos)

During the eighties, she also served as executive producer and host for *Essence*'s spin-off television program. In 1991, she received her B.A. from Fordham University in social science and economics. She also holds honorary doctorates from Lincoln University, Delaware State University, and Spelman College, as well. She serves as senior vice president of Essence Communications, Inc.

During her tenure at *Essence*, the magazine grew to a circulation of over one million and a readership of seven and a half million-twenty nine percent of which is male. Her popular, spiritually-guided monthly column, "In the Spirit", spawned her first book by the same title in 1993. The book sold over 400,000 copies and became a national best-seller. In 1995, she published *Lessons in Living*. Taylor devotes her time to causes that support and affirm the lives of poor women, women in prison, and teenage mothers.
See also HARLEM [3].

REFERENCES

Patti, Nicholas. "Susan L. Taylor." *Contemporary Black Biography*, edited by L. Mpho Mabunda, 1996.

Marshall, Dianne. "Susan L. Taylor." *Notable Black American Women*, edited by. Jessie C. Smith. 1992.

"Taylor, Susan L." *Who's Who Among African Americans, 1998/1999*, edited by Shirelle Phelps. 1997.

RACHEL ZELLARS

Teague, Robert (October 26, 1929–), newscaster and writer. Bob Teague was born in Milwaukee, Wisconsin, and raised by his Aunt Letty, who taught him to be limited by neither color nor locale. He demonstrated a thirst for knowledge in high school, also becoming a star football player. Upon graduation (1946), he entered the University of Wisconsin on an athletic scholarship and became an All Big Ten halfback (1949). In his junior year, he began to focus on his academic career and graduated with a B.A. in journalism (1950).

He was hired as a sports writer for the *Milwaukee Journal* where he stayed until 1956. He was then offered a position at the *New York Times* as a sports writer, where he worked for six and a half years. He entered broadcasting in 1963 when he joined WNBC-TV as a reporter. He was the first reporter to write an entire news story in rhyme. In 1982, he was feted as the journalist with the longest continuous service to one television station in New York City.

In addition to his broadcast and print journalism, Teague has published *The Climate of Candor* (1962), a science fiction novel; *Letters to a Black Boy* (1968), a legacy for his son (Adam), providing him life lessons; *Adam in Blunderland*; (1971), *K-13 Super Spy* (1974), and *K-13 Super Spy in Outer Space* (1978), a nonviolent science fiction children's series; *Live and Off-Color* (1982), a candid look at broadcasting; and *The Flip Side of Soul: Letters to My Son* (1989).
See also WISCONSIN [5].

REFERENCES

Flynn, James J. *Negroes of Achievement in Modern America*. 1970.

"Teague Celebrates Twentieth Year with WNBC-TV." *Norfolk Journal and Guide*, April 7, 1982, NSC 4.

HELEN R. HOUSTON

Tennessee (Update). The National Civil Rights Museum opened in Memphis in 1991. The museum concentrates on the struggles of the 1950s and 1960s through its exhibits on the civil rights movement and supports worldwide human rights movements through its collections, educational programs, concerts, and a performing arts series.

The Carpetbag Theatre, the Knoxville-based collaboration of writers, artists, musicians, and dancers, is one of the oldest black touring groups in the United States. During the 1990s, the Theatre reached incarcerated women and others who suffer from poverty, undereducation, and low self-esteem. Black feminism, the death penalty and the black community, and environmental racism are central themes of Carpetbag productions. The nonprofit group performs worldwide and has received grants from a variety of arts groups, including the National Endowment for the Arts.

Tennessee paid tribute to Alex Haley (1921–1992) with a thirteen-foot bronze statue of the author—seated, book-in-hand, which was erected in Haley Heritage Square in Knoxville in 1998. It is the largest statue dedicated to a black man in the United States. Haley, who lived on his farm near Norris, also maintained a home in Knoxville.

Black women athletes took Tennessee to new heights during the 1990s. The University of Tennessee's Lady Volunteers won their third consecutive and fifth NCAA national championship in 1998, led by Chamique Holdsclaw, Tamika Catchings, and Semeka Randall, the trio referred to as "the Meeks." Holdsclaw went on to win medals and championships for the United States and was the number one draft pick for the Women's National Basketball Association Washington Mystics.

Appropriately, Knoxville is home to the Women's Basketball Hall of Fame that opened in 1999. Inductees for the year 2000 included Patricia (Trish) Roberts, the black University of Tennessee All-American who played on the 1976 Olympic team. Black women athletes in Tennessee have been instrumental in increasing the participation of women in sports in the United States.

According to the United States Census Bureau, black Tennesseans represented between sixteen and seventeen percent of the 1998 population.

REFERENCES

Carpetbag Theatre. www.korrnet.org/carpetbg.

National Civil Rights Museum. www.midsouth.rr.com/civilrights/museum.html.

University of Tennessee Lady Volunteers Basketball. www.utladyvols.com/bko/bkw.

Women's Basketball Hall of Fame. www.wbhof.com.

SHEILA VELAZQUEZ

Texas (Update). At the end of the twentieth century, a stark and horrifying image defined the situation of African Americans in Texas for many outside observers: a black man, James Byrd Jr., died near the east Texas town of Jasper after being chained to the back of a pickup truck and dragged for three miles on June 7, 1998. Two of the three white perpetrators of the crime had Ku Klux Klan ties. At the trial, a prosecutor compared the event to the lynchings of blacks carried out by the Klan in the nineteenth century. The case focused international attention on rural Texas and on the resurgence of hate groups across the U.S. Notwithstanding the horrific nature of the crime, however, Texans of African descent marked some progress in the 1990s, many of whom benefited from the state's resurgent economy as an economic boom revivified the state's oil industry. The state's two largest cities—Dallas and Houston, neither of which numbered blacks in the majority of its population—each elected African-American mayors in the 1990s. Dallas mayor Ron Kirk, elected in May of 1995, even won a majority of the white vote in his election bid, and easily won re-election. Houstonians in 1998 elected Lee P. Brown, a former police chief in Atlanta and New York City who had risen from a childhood as a migrant grape picker in California; he was joined in Houston's administration by an African-American school superintendent, city attorney, parks director, health director and communications deputy. Another black Texan who made headlines in the 1990s was Dr. Mae C. Jemison, who in 1992 became the first African-American female astronaut when she served on the crew of the space shuttle *Endeavor*. A reminder of progress still to be made came four years later: Jemison filed a lawsuit against police in her home town of Nassau Bay after being thrown to the ground during a routine traffic stop.

REFERENCES

Chappell, Kevin. "Houston's Lee P. Brown: A Can-Do Mayor for a Can-Do City." *Ebony* (January, 1999), 96.

"Former Astronaut Mae Jemison Arrested in Texas, Files Complaint Against White Police Officer." *Jet* (March 18, 1996), 8.

"Inferior No More: The Dallas Mayor's Race." *The Economist (US)* (May 13, 1995), A27.

Shlachter, Barry. "Second Defendant Gets Death Penalty in Texas Dragging Death." *Knight-Ridder/Tribune News Service* (September 24, 1999).

Shlachter, Barry. "White Supremacist Found Guilty in East Texas Dragging Death." *Knight-Ridder/Tribune News Service* (February 24, 1999).

JAMES MANHEIM

Thompson, Aaron Belford (August 5, 1883–January 26, 1929), poet.

Thompson was a successful poet, reciter, and humorist. He was born in Rossmoyne, Ohio, to John Henry and Clara Jane Thompson and educated in the public schools. His sisters, Priscilla Jane and Clara Ann, were also poets. Between the three siblings, seven volumes of poetry were produced. Even though there was a familial estrangement, he remembered his siblings in the dedication to his books.

Thompson's poetry was not well received by book publishers. Consequently, he bought a small press, set up, and began publishing his own work. In 1902, he married and moved to Indianapolis where he bought a home at 2109 Howard Street, with a well-equipped printing shop in the rear. He remained there and continued to self publish until his death.

His fame came as a result of his first volumes of poetry, *Morning Song*, dedicated to his sisters (1899) and *Echoes of Spring* (1901), dedicated to his brother, Garland. The second edition of the latter book contains an introduction by James Whitcomb Riley; it appears again in his 1907 collection, *Harvest of Thoughts*.

These volumes contain over 100 poems addressing such subjects as religion, love, nature, race, childhood, morality, and other conventional topics of the nineteenth century. Although contemporary critics have either ignored his work or reacted to it negatively, Thompson was well received in his day.
See also OHIO [4].

REFERENCES

Dabney, Wendell P. *Cincinnati's Colored Citizens: Historical, Sociological and Biographical*. 1926.

Sherman, Joan R. *Invisible Poets: Afro-Americans of the Nineteenth Century*. 1974.

White, Newman Ivey, and Walter Clinton Jackson, eds. *Anthology of American Negro Verse.*, 1924.

HELEN R. HOUSTON

Thompson, Eloise [Alberta Veronic] Bibb (June 28, 1880–January 8, 1928), writer.

Eloise Bibb was born in New Orleans. She published her first volume of poetry, *Poems* in 1895. Between 1899 and 1901 Bibb attended Oberlin College Preparatory School, where she completed five semesters. After teaching in New Orleans for two years, she entered Howard University's Teachers College, graduating in 1908. She then worked at Howard's Social Settlement until her 1911 marriage to Noah Davis Thompson.

The Thompsons moved to Los Angeles, where Eloise Thompson won recognition as a journalist. A fervent Catholic, she published an important article, "The Church and The Negro," in the official organ of the diocese of Monterey and Los Angeles. About 1915 she began to write plays. An early effort, *Reply to the Clansman*, was considered as a basis for a film, but the project fell through. (*The Clansman* refers to Thomas Dixon's novel, which D. W. Griffith filmed as *The Birth of a Nation*.)

In 1920 there was a production of Thompson's play *Caught*, and in 1922 one of *Africannus* (sometimes called *Africans*) in Los Angeles. A reviewer said that *Africannus* was the first play on an African country written by a black author and performed by blacks for a black audience presented in the city. *Cooped Up*, her third play of the decade, was performed in New York in 1924. Two short stories, "Mademoiselle Tasie" (1925) and "Masks" (1927) appeared in *Opportunity*.

Thompson moved to New York City a year before her death from cancer.
See also NEW ORLEANS, LOUISIANA [4].

REFERENCES

Etheridge, Sharynn Owens. "Eloise Bibb Thompson." In *Notable Black American Women*, edited by Jessie Carney Smith. 1992.

Jones, Sharon Lynette. "Eloise Alberta Veronica Thompson." In *American National Biography*, edited by John A. Garraty and Mark C. Carnes. 1999.

ROBERT L. JOHNS

Thompson, John W. (1950–), company executive.

John W. Thompson is president and chief executive officer of Symantec Corporation, a major computer software company best known for its anti-virus products. Thompson grew up in West Palm Beach, Florida, and attended Florida A amp; M University, where he majored in music before switching to business administration. He also holds a master's degree in management science from Sloan School of Management at Massachusetts Institute of Technology. After graduating from Florida A&M, he went to work for IBM in 1971, where he spent twenty-eight years before going to Symantec.

By the early 1990s IBM was struggling to maintain its position in computers. Thompson planned to leave in 1993 but was persuaded to stay on. In 1994 he became general manager of the Personal Software Products division of IBM, which was responsible for OS/2, IBM's operating system for personal computers. OS/2 faced severe competition from Microsoft's Windows 95, but Thompson managed to reposition it, generating an estimated billion dollars of annual sales. After a company restructuring in 1996, Thompson headed IBM Americas, an organization with 30,000 employees, which had responsibility for sales and support of technology products and support. This division generated $37 billion dollars of revenue.

In April 1999 Thompson moved to Symantec for a compensation package valued at around $64 million at the current stock prices. (Investors reacted very favorably to the news, raising the price of the stock five times.) Thompson planned to focus on the corporation market, as he strove to guarantee Symantec's continued profitability.
See also FLORIDA [2].

REFERENCES

Chang, Greg. "Symantec Surges Fivefold as Ex-IBM Exec Leads Revival." http://quote.bloomberg.com

Haney, Clare. "Thompson's Take." [Interview.] *InfoWorld*, 3 May 1999.

Karp, Hal. "Running to Win: John W. Thompson Leads the Pack at IBM." *Black Enterprise*, June 1997.

Symantec Corporation. Biographical information on John W. Thompson. http://www.symantec.com/corporate/ceo.htlm

ROBERT L. JOHNS

Tillman, Nathaniel Patrick "Tic," Sr.

(January 17, 1898–October 17, 1965), educator, philologist. Born in Birmingham, Tillman graduated from Morehouse College in 1920 and earned both his M.A. (1927) and Ph.D. (1940) from the University of Wisconsin. Tillman also studied at Cambridge University and at the University of Chicago. To support his studies, Tillman received a number of fellowships. He taught at Alcorn College in Mississippi for two years and then returned to Morehouse to remain throughout his career.

Tillman was registrar at Morehouse from 1924 to 1932. Beginning 1927, he was also professor of English and chair of the English Department. He was named acting academic dean of the school from 1932 to 1934; from then until 1957 he was chair and teacher in the English department. Concurrently, Tillman taught at nearby Atlanta University, serving from 1942 to 1962 as both a professor and chair of their English Department. Between 1955 and 1961, Tillman was acting dean, then dean of Atlanta's Graduate School of Arts and Sciences until health problems forced him to relinquish his administrative responsibilities and return to teaching.

Tillman's most enduring contribution was as an educator; he was regarded as one of the South's best teachers. He was known also as a skilled administrator and scholar. He contributed articles to scholarly journals such as *Phylon* and *Quarterly Journal of Higher Education Among Negroes*. His most well received scholarly work was on medieval English poet John Lydgate, called *Lydgate's Rhyme as Evidence of His Pronunciation*. In the 1940s and 1950s, Tillman was co-author of the style manual Atlanta University required its students to follow when writing theses.
See also BIRMINGHAM, ALABAMA [1].

REFERENCES

Bacote, Clarence A. *The Story of Atlanta University*. 1969.

Logan, Rayford W., and Michael R. Winston, eds. *Dictionary of American Negro Biography*. 1982.

VALENCIA PRICE

Toure, Kwame. *See* Carmichael, Stokely.

Towns, Edolphus

(1934–), U.S. Congressman. Edolphus Towns was born in Chadbourn, North Carolina. He attended North Carolina A & T State University, receiving his B.S. degree in 1956. He also earned a master's degree in social work in 1973. He taught in the New York City public schools and in Brooklyn's Medgar Evers College. In 1965, he became deputy administrator of Beth Israel Hospital. In 1976, he was the first African American to serve as Brooklyn's deputy borough president, holding office until 1982 when he was elected to the U.S. House of Representatives. He was elected to his eighth consecutive Congressional term in 1998.

As a Congressman, Towns has been a member of the House Commerce Committee and the Government Reform and Oversight Committee. He has served on subcommittees considering such issues as healthcare reform and universal access. He has sought to bring wider attention to the healthcare needs of women, senior citizens, and the economically disadvantaged. Towns has also been a strong advocate for improving training opportunities for minority physicians and for equalizing medical services in urban and rural communities. Additionally, he has sought greater protection for the nation's nutritional health and chaired important subcommittee hearings on the USDA's food inspection programs.

In the area of telecommunications, Towns has actively promoted family oriented television programming and guaranteed consumer access to the information super highway through his membership on the Telecommunications and Finance subcommittees. He has been an advocate of universal access to capital by minority entrepreneurs.

Towns' civic responsibilities include service on the Board of Trustees of Shaw University, the Advisory Board of Medgar Evers College and the Brookdale Hospital board. He is also an ordained Baptist minister. *See also* CONGRESSIONAL BLACK CAUCUS [2].

REFERENCES

Biography of Congressman Towns. Washington, D.C., U.S. House of Representatives, URL:http://house./gov/towns/

Phelps, Shirelle, ed. *Contemporary Black Biography*, vol. 19. 1999.

DARIUS L. THIEME

Tyler, Ralph Waldo (March 18, 1859–June 2, 1921), editor, journalist, government official. Born in Columbus, Ohio, in a family of eight children, Tyler held various jobs until 1888, when he joined the staff of the *Columbus Dispatch*. He worked up the ranks from janitor to manager's assistant and became secretary to the publisher. He joined the Republican Party in 1893 at the same time that he established what was to become a long-time correspondence with George

Ralph W. Tyler. (Fisk University Library)

A. Meyers, a Republic leader in Ohio. He covered the Republican National Convention in St. Louis and published accounts in the *Dispatch*.

In 1905, Tyler worked for a while for the *Ohio State Journal* of Columbus. Then he held a federal appointment for six years as auditor for the U.S. Navy Department. Tyler left the position in 1913, when black office holders were being removed from their

Mike Tyson. (AP/Wide World Photos)

posts. He became national organizer for the National Negro Business League. He also wrote syndicated accounts of his travels and conditions of blacks for the American Press Association.

During World War I, Tyler was National Colored Soldiers' Comfort Committee secretary in Washington, D.C. and government-backed war correspondent for the black press, making him the first and only African American war correspondent. He was sent to France to report on activities and conditions for black soldiers. After the war, Tyler returned to Ohio, lectured widely on black soldiers, and in April 1919 became editor of the *Cleveland Advocate* and associate editor of the *Columbus Ohio State Monitor*.
See also OHIO [4].

REFERENCES

Garraty, John A., and Mark C. Carnes, general eds. *American National Biography*. 1999.

Logan, Rayford W. and Michael R. Winston, eds. *Dictionary of American Negro Biography*. 1982.

Smith, Jessie Carney, ed. *Notable Black American Men*. 1999.

JESSIE CARNEY SMITH

Tyson, Michael Gerald "Mike" (Update)

(June 30, 1966–), professional boxer. Tyson easily won his first fight following his return and regained the heavyweight championship in 1996 after beating Bruce Seldon. However, in October of 1996, Tyson lost a ten-round TKO decision to Holyfield in a major upset. In May of 1997, Holyfield defended his title in a rematch with Tyson, who proceeded to bite Holyfield's ears. During the subsequent suspension, Tyson repeatedly applied for reinstatement. In late 1998 his suspension was lifted, and he fought again in January of 1999. However Tyson was jailed again on February 5 and sentenced to twelve months imprisonment for attacking two motorists after a minor automobile collision in August of 1998.

Tyson continued to have problems acquiring a license to fight in the United States, but in January of 2000, he fought the little regarded Julius Francis in London, knocking Francis out in the second round. Another European fight followed in June, as Tyson fought another unknown, Lou Savarese, winning this time in only 38 seconds. Tyson's behavior turned erratic at fight's end when he disregarded the referee's stoppage of the fight and continued hitting Savarese. After the fight, Tyson made threatening post-fight comments about heavyweight champion Lennox Lewis, prompting a fine and further criticism from media and boxing officials.

REFERENCE

"Tyson fined $187,500 for post-fight actions." *Milwaukee Journal Sentinel*. August 23, 2000: 02.

GREG ROBINSON

V

George B. Vashon. (Fisk University Library)

Vashon, George Boyer (July 25, 1824–October 5, 1878), lawyer, educator, and writer. Vashon was born in Carlisle, Pennsylvania. The family moved to Pittsburgh in 1829. There Vashon followed in his father's footsteps as an ardent abolitionist by becoming at the age of fourteen secretary of the Juvenile Anti-Slavery Society. He was the first black to graduate from Oberlin College in 1844.

Vashon then read law in Pittsburgh. After he was refused admission to the Pennsylvania bar in 1847, he determined to go to Haiti. On his way there, he stopped in New York, where he tested for admittance to the bar and was admitted on January 11, 1848. Vashon proceeded to Haiti, returning in 1850, and settled in Syracuse, New York, where he practiced law. In 1853, he published the first of his three known poems, "Vincent Ogé," a work that draws on his Haitian experiences.

The following year, Vashon became the third African-American professor at Central College, an abolitionist school in McGrawville, New York. After three years he found employment as a teacher in the Pittsburgh public schools and then as principal of Avery College, in Pennsylvania. Moving to Washington, D.C., in 1867, he worked as a solicitor at the Freedman's Bureau. When he took a position in a short-lived night school at Howard University in 1867, he became the first black appointed to the university's faculty. From 1869 to 1870 he was involved closely with the National Convention of Colored Men of America. He was also a frequent contributor to the *New Era*, an unsuccessful attempt to establish a national black newspaper. From 1874 to 1878 Vashon taught at Alcorn Agricultural and Mechanical College (now University) in Mississippi. He died there of yellow fever.

See also HOWARD UNIVERSITY [3]; INTELLECTUAL LIFE [3].

REFERENCES

Johns, Robert L. "George Boyer Vashon." In *Notable Black American Men*, edited by Jessie Carney Smith. 1999.

Sherman, Joan R. "George Boyer Vashon." In *Dictionary of American Negro Biography*, edited by Rayford W. Logan and Michael R. Winston. 1982.

Sherman, Joan R. *Invisible Poets*. 1974.

ROBERT L. JOHNS

Virgin Islands. The United States Virgin Islands, located about 40 miles east of Puerto Rico, consist of three main islands—St. Thomas, St. John, and St. Croix—an area of only 132 square miles. They are inhabited by approximately one hundred thousand people most of whom are descendants of African slaves. The history of the islands is a story of woe, exploitation, and a prolonged freedom struggle. Encountered by Columbus in 1493, successful colonization began in 1668 by the Danes who over the years imported many thousands of slaves from the West African coast.

The experience with plantation slavery in the Danish West Indies was marked by severe brutality, dehumanization, and rebellion. Slavery was ended in 1848 only to be replaced by a stringent system of contract labor. Ex-slaves were no better off than serfs who struggled against serious odds to overcome the legacy of their former enslavement.

Negotiations concerning U.S. purchase of the Islands commenced during the American Civil War and continued intermittently until the onset of World War I. The opening of the Panama Canal in 1914 and the possibility that the United States might be drawn into the war against Germany heightened America's security interests in acquiring the Islands. Finally, the U.S. forced Denmark to sell the islands for $25 million in gold. The transfer took place on March 31, 1917, one week prior to the U.S. entry into the war, and the renamed United States Virgin Islands were placed under the absolute rule of the all- white U.S. Navy.

The naval officers who administered the islands at first allowed the insular economy to deteriorate so badly that, by the time navy rule was ended in 1931, the islands had become an "effective poorhouse," as President Herbert Hoover described them, that required a massive infusion of federal assistance to alleviate starvation and poverty.

Human rights experienced a corresponding plunge, as racially motivated naval officers imprisoned or banished native dissidents and freedom fighters. As an "unincorporated territory" of the United States, the islands occupied the lowest rung of America's colonial ladder to which the Constitution and its Bill of Rights did not extend without specific Congressional authorization. Only gradually did Congress grant citizenship, civil liberties, and self-rule to the islanders.

After World War II, the development of tourism and refining industries (oil and bauxite) propelled the economy to unprecedented heights. Those benefiting the most, however, were not local but outside— mainly white continental American— interests, at the expense of human rights of black Virgin Islanders and British West Indians imported to work in service occupations associated with tourism and industry.

The employment of these bonded "aliens" from other West Indian islands was reminiscent of the "free colored" labor contracts during slavery and of the notorious labor law of 1849 which evoked a widespread labor revolt of 1878 in St. Croix. The grievous problems of British West Indian laborers in the Virgin Islands prompted efforts to generate a measure of hope and aspiration in place of despair among them.

Meanwhile, the position of native Virgin Islanders was not much better—their alienation from the society at large resulted in much trauma, including bloodshed exemplified by the 1972 "Fountain Valley massacre" in St. Croix of several white continental Americans by a few blacks. White entrepreneurs have been able to exercise disproportionate power and influence in the Virgin Islands by giving preference to British West Indians in tourist and business related employment, thus leaving the government bureaucracy to be staffed by native Virgin Islanders. Such "divide and rule" practices have given white continentals much political leverage to influence the constitutional and political future of the Islands.

Recent major problems troubling life in the Islands have been declines in tourism, mounting local government deficits, damage from hurricanes, and rampant crime fueled by illegal drugs. Assurance of civil liberties of the people of the U.S. Virgin Islands is no longer a key issue. All civil liberties in the U.S. Constitution, except indictment by grand jury, likewise protect residents of the Islands.

Two current issues are territorial control over territorial affairs and participation in the national political system. The territory of the Virgin Islands does not participate as an entity in Congress because it has only a single nonvoting representative in Congress. Citizens of the Virgin Islands are still not granted the right to vote for the President and Vice President, and therefore are not represented in the national political system in any meaningful capacity. Accordingly, they lack political power in Washington to achieve a greater measure of control over territorial affairs.

See also SLAVE TRADE [5].

REFERENCES

Boyer, William W. *America's Virgin Islands: A History of Human Rights and Wrongs.* 1983.

Boyer, William W. *Civil Liberties in the U.S. Virgin Islands, 1917–1949.* 1982.

Dookhan, Isaac. *A History of the Virgin Islands of the United States.* 1974.

Lewis, Gordon K. *The Virgin Islands: A Caribbean Lilliput.* 1972.

WILLIAM W. BOYER

Vroman, Mary Elizabeth (c. 1924–April 29, 1967), writer, teacher. Vroman, the first African-American woman in the Screen Writer's Guild, was born in Buffalo, New York, grew up in the West Indies, graduated from Alabama State Teachers College with a B. A. degree, and taught for twenty years in Alabama, Chicago, and New York.

Her first published story, "See How They Run," a Christopher Award winner, appeared in the *Ladies Home Journal* (June 1951); it is the story of a young, idealistic, third grade teacher in a segregated rural Alabama school. She also wrote the screenplay and served as an adviser for its film adaptation, *Bright Road* (1953). Her first novel, *Esther* (1963), is set in a small Southern town and reflects the dreams and aspirations of a grandmother for her grandchild, the struggles she encounters, and her refusal to be thwarted. The second novel, *Harlem Summer* (1967), is a young adult book that presents the response of a young southerner to racial conditions of various strata of the African-American community in the North. In her works, Vroman presents the realities of African-American life with optimism.

In 1965, Vroman wrote *Shaped With a Purpose: Delta Sigma Theta, The First Fifty Years*, a history of the service organization to which she belonged. She died of post-surgical complications.

See also NEW YORK [4].

REFERENCES

Blicksilver, Edith. "Mary Elizabeth Vroman." *DLB: Afro-American Fiction Writers After 1955*, edited by Thadious Davis and Trudier Harris. 1984.

Black Writers, edited by Hal May and others. 1989.

HELEN R. HOUSTON

Waddy, Harriet M. (June 20, 1904–February 21, 1999), military officer. Waddy was born in Jefferson City, Missouri, and died in Las Vegas, where she had moved in 1998. After graduating from Kansas State University, she worked during the Great Depression as an aid to educator and school founder Mary McLeod Bethune. In 1942 Waddy entered the Women's Army Auxiliary Corps officer candidate school at Fort Des Moines. WAAC became a part of the regular army later in 1942 and was renamed the Women's Army Corps. She became a recruiter for the army and in April 1943 made a radio announcement urging African American women to join the service. Although the military was racially segregated by official policy, she urged African American women not to retreat from fighting but to make a contribution to the war effort. Many of the women, however, were used as servants to clean officers' clubs. After Waddy was promoted to major and became an aide to WAC director Oveta Culp Hobby, she worked to ease their distress.

As one of only two African American women attaining the rank of major in the WAC, Waddy continued to oppose the military's racially insulting decrees. On a visit to WACs at Fort Des Moines, she called for the removal of references to "white" and "colored" from all official memoranda on information boards.

Waddy became a lieutenant colonel in 1948, retired from active service in 1952, and remained in the reserves until 1969. While still serving in the military, she began working for the Federal Aviation Administration, retiring from that position in 1969.
See also MISSOURI [4].

REFERENCES

Goldstein, Richard. "Harriet M. Waddy, WAC Officer, Dies at 94." *New York Times*, March 8, 1999.

Obituary. *New York Times*, March 1, 1999.

JESSIE CARNEY SMITH

Walden, Austin T. (April 12, 1885–July 2, 1965), attorney. Austin Walden was born in Fort Valley, Georgia, the son of former slaves. He became one of the country's leading civil rights attorneys. He attended Fort Valley Industrial School, earning his B.A. in 1902. He earned his M.A. from Atlanta University in 1907, and went on to study law, earning his LL.B. in 1911 from the University of Michigan. He entered U.S. Army service in 1912, commanding an infantry company in World War I and serving also as a trial judge advocate. Returning to the United States following the war, he practiced law for many years in Atlanta.

Walden was noted particularly for his advocacy in civil rights cases. In the 1930s he came to the defense of John Downer, convicted of rape. Walden participated in his rescue from a lynch mob. With his associate, Elbert Tuttle, he took Downer's case through the courts, insisting on the man's constitutional right to a jury trial. Unfortunately, the case was lost on appeal. Walden later supported African American schoolteachers in their efforts to win pay equity. He also brought suit in 1948 on behalf of Horace Ward's attempt to gain admission to the University of Georgia Law School.

Walden was active in politics, becoming a Democrat in 1940, founding the Atlanta Negro Voters League in 1949, and forming coalitions to achieve civil rights objectives in local political issues. He actively supported the presidential candidacies of Harry Truman, Adlai Stevenson, and John F. Kennedy. In 1964, Mayor Ivan Allen appointed him an alternate judge in Atlanta's municipal court, the first African American since reconstruction. Walden died in Atlanta.
See also GEORGIA [3].

REFERENCES

Garraty, John A., and Mark C. Carnes, eds. *American National Biography*. 1999.

Logan, Rayford W., and Michael R. Winston, eds. *Dictionary of American Negro Biography*. 1992.

DARIUS L. THIEME

Wallace, Phyllis Ann (1923–January 1993), economist. Born in Baltimore to John and Stevella Wallace, Phyllis Wallace graduated magna cum laude and Phi Beta Kappa from New York University in 1943. She received her M.A. (1944) and Ph.D. (1948) from Yale University. After graduating from Yale, Wallace taught at City College of New York and did research at the National Bureau of Economic Research where she specialized in trade and productivity issues. She taught economics at Atlanta University in 1953–1957 and in 1957–1965 was an economic analyst for the Central Intelligence Agency. From 1965 to 1968, Wallace was chief of technical studies for the Equal Employment Opportunity Commission (EEOC).

Wallace left EEOC in 1968 to conduct research on urban and youth in labor markets for the Metropolitan Applied Research Center. She joined the faculty at the Massachusetts Institute of Technology (MIT) in 1972, becoming the school's first black tenured faculty member in 1975. At MIT she directed a number of conferences and workshops and published a series of works on minorities and women in the work force. Her publications include *Pathways to Work: Unemployment among Black Teenage Females* (1974), *Black Women in the Labor Force* (1980), and *MBAs on the Fast Track* (1989).

While research and publication were important aspects of her life and work, Wallace was determined that neither race, gender, nor occupation would define her. She mentored a number of young people in business, economics, science, and the arts, encouraging them to follow nontraditional paths to careers as well.

Wallace retired from active teaching in 1986 and then concentrated on research, service on boards, and writing. In 1988 she became the first black and first woman president of the Industrial Relations Research Association.
See also BALTIMORE, MARYLAND [1].

REFERENCES

Obituary, *Boston Globe*, January 13, 1993.

Smith, Jessie Carney, ed. *Notable Black American Women*. 1992.

Walker, Juliet E. K., ed. *Encyclopedia of African American Business History*. 1999.

VALENCIA PRICE

Waller, John L. (January 12, 1850–October 13, 1907), political figure, journalist. An important political figure, John Waller was born a slave in New Madrid County, Missouri. He and his family were relocated to Inca, Iowa, in 1862 by Union troops during the Civil War. Waller studied law independently, and gained admission to the Iowa bar in 1877. He subsequently moved to Leavenworth, was admitted to the Kansas bar, and became the first black American to practice law in Leavenworth.

Moving to Lawrence, Kansas, Waller published a weekly newspaper, *The Western Recorder*, supporting Republican candidates and advocating for civil rights. Moving to Topeka in 1888, he founded *The American Citizen*, subsequently selling the paper in 1890 and moving to Kansas City. He was appointed Consul at Tamatave, Madagascar, in 1891 and served until 1894.

Soon after taking office as Consul, Waller established close ties with the Malagasy government and received a sizeable land grant in an area rich in natural resources. He planned to offer the land for colonization through a leasing program. The concept was opposed by the French government, which claimed a protectorate over the island. France subsequently invaded in 1894, establishing permanent control. In the process, Waller was charged with postal violations and transmitting military information. He was imprisoned in France. The U.S. State Department opened negotiations, arranged for his release in 1896, and he returned to Kansas.

In 1898 he led a volunteer regiment in the Spanish-American War in Cuba. Due to lack of recognition for black troops to the war effort and recalling his poor treatment in the Madagascar affair, Waller switched political allegiances, supporting the candidacy for president of William Jennings Bryan in 1900.
See also MISSOURI [4].

REFERENCES

"The John L. Waller Affair, 1895–1896." *Negro History Bulletin* 37 (February-March, 1974): 216-18.

Logan, Rayford W., and Michael R. Winston, eds. *Dictionary of American Negro Biography*. 1992.

DARIUS L. THIEME

Walton, Lester A. (April 20, 1882–October 16, 1965), diplomat, journalist, theater practitioner. Walton, born in St. Louis, Missouri, had a multifaceted career that included numerous accomplishments, such as gaining the support of the Associated Press in capitalizing "Negro" while a staff writer and columnist for the *New York World* (1922–c1932), negotiating treaties between the United States and Liberia (1937–1939), and helping to usher in the Harlem Renaissance by promoting grand-scale theater written by and marketed to African Americans in the first quarter of the twentieth century.

After leaving his hometown, Walton moved to New York, where from 1908–1924 he shifted between theater and journalism, working as manager and dramatic editor of *The New York Age*, producing and directing musicals such as *Darktown Follies* (1914), *Darkydom* (1915), and managing The Lafayette Players' Quality Amusement Corporation (1915–16 and 1919–1921). He was one of eleven black men who founded The Frogs (1908), an organization whose mission was to raise money in support of black entertainers and to establish an archive on African Americans in the field of entertainment.

In his mid-life, Walton wrote for the *New York Herald Tribune*, and became publicity director for the National Negro Business League before being appointed Envoy and Plenipotentiary to Liberia in July 1935 by President Franklin D. Roosevelt. In Liberia he earned distinction as a diplomat, and was appointed advisor to the country's United Nation's delegation

(1948). After two decades of political involvement, Walton returned to the U.S., and in 1953, with Sidney Poiter, Ruby Dee, Pearl Primus and other celebrities, founded the Coordinating Council for Negro Performers, an organization committed to increasing the employment of African-Americans in television.
See also AMBASSADORS AND DIPLOMATS [1]; FILM [2]; JOURNALISM [4]; MISSOURI [4].

REFERENCES

Garraty, John A. ed. *Dictionary of American Biography*. 1981.

Gray, Christopher. "Streetscapes: Harlem's Lafayette Theater; Jackhammering the Past" *The New York Times*, 11 November 1990, sec. 10, p. 6.

Peterson, Bernard L. Jr. *African American Theater Directory, 1816–1960: A Comprehensive Guide to Early Black Theater Organizations, Companies, Theatres, and Performing Groups*. 1997.

Southern Eileen. *The Greenwood Encyclopedia of Black Music, Biographical Dictionary of Afro-American and African Musicians*. 1982.

Young, Artee Felicita. "Lester Walton, Black Theatre Critic." Ph.D. thesis, University of Michigan, 1980.

F. ZEAL HARRIS

Warfield, William (Caesar) (January 22, 1920–), singer. Warfield was born in West Helena, Arkansas. Service in the U.S. Army followed his 1942

William Warfield. (Unknown source)

bachelor of music degree from Eastman School of Music. Warfield returned to Eastman for graduate study in 1946 and in 1947 joined the touring company of the musical, *Call Me Mister*. Further experience in the musical theater and further private voice lessons preceded his well-received Town Hall debut on March 19, 1950. In 1952 Warren joined the cast of a production of *Porgy and Bess*, where he met Leontyne Price, who became his wife. By 1958 career pressures drove the couple apart although they remained friends and did not divorce until 1972.

Warfield's career continued to flourish as he went on recital tours and sang with orchestras. His dramatic talents added luster to his career. For example, he played "De Lawd" in television productions of *Green Pastures* in 1957 and 1959. From 1961 on he appeared in several revivals of *Porgy and Bess* in the United States and abroad. He used his rich speaking voice in performances of works like Aaron Copland's *A Lincoln Portrait* and Jonathan Brace Brown's 1997 *Legacy of Vision*, which features words from Martin Luther King, Jr.'s "I Have a Dream" speech.. A recording of the Copland won Warfield a 1984 Grammy in the spoken word category.

In 1974 Warfield became professor of music at the University of Illinois School of Music in Urbana. He retired as chairman of the voice faculty in 1990 but took several other teaching positions after that. Warfield served a president of the National Association of Negro Musicians in 1984.

See also CONCERT MUSIC [2]; MUSIC [4]; MUSIC COLLECTIONS, BLACK [4]; PRICE, MARY VIOLET LEONTYNE [4]; SYMPHONY OF THE NEW WORLD [5].

REFERENCES

Thieme, Darius L. "William Warfield." In *Notable Black American Men*, edited by Jessie Carney Smith. 1999.

Warfield, William. *My Music and My Life*. 1991.

ROBERT L. JOHNS

Washington, Augustus

Washington, Augustus (c. 1820–1875), photographer, entrepreneur. August Washington was born free in New York City (some sources say Trenton, New Jersey), to a former slave father and a South Asian mother. He enrolled in Dartmouth College in 1843 but due to financial problems he left in fall 1844 for Hartford, Connecticut, to head North African School, one of the city's two schools for African American students. Although he received only a small salary, he eventually paid his college debts and planned to return to Dartmouth. Meanwhile, to sustain himself, he began to practice daguerreotypy in late 1846.

Washington promoted his business in the *Charter Oak*, an antislavery newspaper. He became highly successful as a daguerreotypist, actively seeking clients from all levels of society. Washington offered competitive prices and a wide array of cases, lockets, rings, and frames that would contain his miniatures, usually no larger than four by three inches.

Among his subjects were abolitionists William Lloyd Garrison and John Brown, and abolitionist writer Lydia Sigourney. Despite his success, Washington announced by public notice in the *Hartford Daily Courier* for March 29, 1853, that he planned to close his gallery in a few months for the purpose of foreign travel and other activities.

Persuaded that the 1850 Fugitive Slave Act would cause him to be enslaved, Washington and his family emigrated to Monrovia, Liberia, in 1853. Washington opened another successful gallery there and served prominent residents, including the president. By 1858 Washington left his work in photography to purchase a sugar plantation. Eventually, he was elected to the Liberian House and Senate.
See also PHOTOGRAPHY [4].

REFERENCES

"A Durable Memento." http://www.npg.si.edu/exh/awash/awintro.htm

Michaels, Barbara L. "Augustus Washington at the National Portrait Gallery." *Art in America* 88 162.

Sullivan, George. *Black Artists in Photography, 1840–1940*. 1996.

JESSIE CARNEY SMITH

Washington, Denzel (Update)

Washington, Denzel (Update) (December 28, 1954–), actor. His starring roles since the mid 1990s have included *Devil in a Blue Dress* (1995), an adaptation for Walter Mosley's novel; *Courage Under Fire* (1996); *The Preacher's Wife* (1997); *Love Jones* (1997); *Fallen* (1998); *He Got Game* (1998); and *The Siege* (1998).

Washington gained some of the best critical notices of his career with his performance in *The Hurricane* (2000), a film biography of boxer Rubin "Hurricane" Carter, who was incarcerated for murders he did not commit. Washington's accolades for the role included an Academy Award nomination for Best Actor, and winner of the Golden Globe for the same category.

REFERENCES

"Denzel Washington." In *Notable Black American Men*. 1999.

                                    GREG ROBINSON

Washington, D.C. (Update).

Washington, D.C. spent much of the 1990s mired in civic chaos, and its African-American residents, the majority there 1960, paid a heavy price as city services deteriorated. At the century's end it was reported that in some of Washington's poorer neighborhoods infant mortality rates compared unfavorably with those in Third World countries such as Sri Lanka and Jamaica. In 1997 Washingtonians suffered the highest rates in the U.S. of tuberculosis and new AIDS infections. Basic city government tasks such as crime control and street repair were hampered by mismanagement even as city employment rose to a per capita level higher than that of any other U.S. city. Some observers laid blame for the problems at the feet of Mayor Marion Berry, elected to a fourth term in office in 1994 despite having previously left office and served six months in prison on a cocaine possession conviction. Barry's confrontational style played well with parts of Washington's black electorate, but as the city careened toward insolvency in 1996 and 1997, the U.S. Congress, holder of the city's purse strings, stripped him of much of his power and placed the administration of several city departments in the hands of a financial oversight board. Barry vehemently protested these actions, but declined to run for a fifth term in 1998. The board's chief financial officer, Anthony Williams, another African American, was elected mayor. As technocratic as Barry was flamboyant, Williams even before his election had slashed the city's bloated payrolls, and by the year 2000 Washington was well on the way toward achieving the four consecutive balanced budgets that Congress had set as a condition for the re-establishment of home rule by the city government. Complicating the task of the budget balancing was the much-noted exodus of black professionals from the city to its suburbs, particularly those of Prince Georges County, Maryland.

REFERENCES

Barone, Michael, and Grant Ujifusa. *The Almanac of American Politics 2000*. 1999.

Clines, Francis X. "Washington Mayor Gets Things Done Quietly." *New York Times* (May 21, 2000), 20.

"Life After Barry: The Washington Mayor's Race." *The Economist (US)* (September 19, 1998), 37.

                                    JAMES MANHEIM

Washington, Kenneth "Kenny" William

(August 31, 1918–June 4, 1971), athlete, actor. Washington, a Los Angeles native, was a star high school athlete. He then played baseball and football for three seasons, 1936 to 1939, at UCLA, where he combined brilliant running with outstanding passing, made All-American honors, and became one of the West Coast's greatest collegiate football players. Jackie Robinson was among his teammates. Washington set numerous athletic records during his time at UCLA. He played defense as well as offense, playing 580 out of a possible 600 minutes during his last collegiate season. In 1999 UCLA remembered Washington's impressive record, naming him to the first team of its all-century football squad.

Upon leaving UCLA, Washington was unable to play in the NFL due to its policy against black players, so he instead played semi-professional football, during which he was named All-Pacific Coast halfback four times. Eventually, the Rams' move from Cleveland to Los Angeles paved the way for Washington's belated debut in pro football. Previous knee injuries limited his pro career to two seasons, but he still set a number of Rams' records. He retired at the end of the 1949 season.

Washington had ambition for a career in the movies and, beginning 1940, he landed roles in a number of films. His films included *While Thousands Cheer* (1940), *The Little Foxes* (1941), *The Foxes of Harrow* (1947), *Pinky* (1949), *The Jackie Robinson Story* (1950), and *Tarzan's Dead Silence* (1970).
See also FOOTBALL [2]; SPORTS [5].

REFERENCES

"Kenny Washington." http://us.imbd.com/Name?Washington,+Kenny

"Negroes Come Back to Pro Football." *Ebony* 1 (October 1946): 12-16.

"Kenny Washington Dead at 52; Was West Coast Football Star." *New York Times*, July 26, 1971, p. 32.

                                    FREDERICK D. SMITH, JR.

Washington, Sarah (Sara) Spencer

(June 6, 1889–1953), entrepreneur and philanthropist. Sarah

(Sara) Spencer Washington was born to Joshua and Ellen Douglass Phillips on June 6, 1889, in Berkley, Virginia. She attended the public schools of Berkley, the Lincoln Preparatory School in Philadelphia, Pennsylvania, and Norfolk Mission College in Norfolk, Virginia. Washington also studied beauty culture in York, Pennsylvania, and chemistry at Columbia University. From 1905 to 1913, she worked as a dressmaker. In 1913, Washington changed directions and pursued a career as a coiffeuse. As a beauty specialist, she established a hairdressing concern and instructed others in her system. On "a proverbial shoestring," Washington founded the Apex Hair and News Company six years after opening her business. As the lone proprietor and chief executive, she directed the Apex Beauty College in Atlantic City, New Jersey. Washington opened Apex beauty branches in nine other cities and several foreign countries. She survived the economic crisis of the 1930s and sustained her success through the Second World War. In 1937, Washington opened laboratories in Atlantic City and produced 75 different hair and beauty aids, which also sold in the West Indies and Africa. She employed hundreds of persons and reportedly had 45,000 global agents. Because of her entrepreneurial attainments and her leadership in the worldwide business community, Washington was awarded a medallion at the 1939 New York World's Fair. In the 1930s and 1940s, she was the leading exporter of black hair products. Washington established the Apex Community Drug Store, the Apex Rest and Tourist Home, and the Apex Publishing Company. She owned extensive business properties including, the Brigantine Hotel. Denied entrance to Atlantic City's golf courses because of her race, she converted her farmland into a nine-hole golf course and country club.

Washington not only possessed business acumen but she also had a philanthropic spirit. She established the Ellen P. Hunter Home for Girls; contributed yearly to the Betty Bacharach Home for Children which served youth of various races; gave land to the National Youth Administration to serve as a campsite for youth of African descent; and during the winter months gave coal to poor families. She awarded annual scholarships to students and financially contributed to deserving institutions.

America's leading African-American businesswoman at the time of her death in 1953, Madame Washington's enterprise was worth more than a million dollars. Avoiding credit, she was among industry giants such as Madame C. J. Walker and Annie M. Turnbo

Malone, founder of the Poro System and Poro Beauty College.

See also VIRGINIA [5].

REFERENCES

Smith, Jessie Carney, ed., *Notable Black American Women*. 1992.

Walker, Juliet E. K. *Encyclopedia of African American Business History*. 1999.

LINDA T. WYNN

Omar Wasow (December 22, 1970–), entrepreneur, media consultant. Omar Wasow, an entrepreneur and media consultant, is founder of New York Online (NYO), executive direct of BlackPlanet.com, and internet analyst for MSNBC and WNBC. He was born in Nairobi, Kenya to a Jewish father and African American mother. After growing up in New York City, he graduated from Stanford University in 1992 with a self-designed major in race and ethnic relations. He spent the following summer working with a voter registration project, and he later worked in a non-profit program for former drug dealers.

In 1993 he became cofounder of Diaspora, Inc., which the following year launched New York Online, a well-received local online community. With the success of New York Online, corporate clients like The College Board, United Artists, and Samsung sought out his help in launching their own sites. BlackPlanet.com, one of his recent projects, aims to build an online community for blacks in the United States and throughout the world. In addition to his company responsibilities, Wasow appears regularly on MSNBC and WNBC, is a member of the Board of Contributors of *USA Today*, writes an internet business column for FeedMag.com, and is in great demand as a speaker.

Wasow is active in politics. His interest in school reform led him to be a major player in the coalition which secured passage of charter school legislation in New York state. In recognition of his civic efforts, the Rockefeller Foundation named him a fellow in the Next Generation Leadership program.

See also NEW YORK CITY [4].

REFERENCES

The Advanced Marketing and Technology Symposium Series. "Omar Wasow Biography." Publicity release for MOBE XVI, 15, May 2000.

Brennan, Carol. "Omar Wasow." In *Contemporary Black Biography*, vol. 15, edited by Shirelle Phelps. 1997.

Friend, Tad. "It's, You Know, About Opinions and Stuff." *New York Times Sunday Magazine*, 15 June 1997.

"Omar Wasow's Media Kit." [Updated 1 March 1999.] http://www.nyo.com/omar/

ROBERT L. JOHNS

Waters, Maxine Moore (Update)

Waters, Maxine Moore (Update) (August 15, 1938–), U.S. Congresswoman. Following the outbreak of riots in her Los Angeles district after the acquittal of the police officers charged in the Rodney King case in April 1992, Waters received national attention for her statements about the root social causes of the riots. In 1993 Waters proposed legislation for the Youth Fair Chance Program, an inner-city job training program, and supported passage of AIDS and abortion-rights legislation. Over the course of her first two terms, Waters rapidly emerged as a major spokesperson for the black community and one of the most prominent women in Congress. In 1998, Waters distinguished herself as a defender of President Bill Clinton, and she voted against impeachment as a member of the House Judiciary Committee.

Maxine Waters. (AP/Wide World Photos)

REFERENCE

"Maxine Waters." In *Encyclopedia of World Biography*, 2nd ed. 1999.

LOUISE P. MAXWELL
UPDATED BY GREG ROBINSON

Watson, Barbara Mae

Watson, Barbara Mae (November 5, 1918–February 17, 1983), ambassador, state department official, lawyer, entrepreneur. Watson was born in New York City and graduated from Barnard College in 1943. From there she entered law school at St. John's University, but she soon withdrew, feeling it lacked challenge. After college, she held various positions in New York, including a three-year stint with the United Seaman's Service of New York. In 1946 Watson opened a charm school and modeling agency for African American women, known respectively as Barbara Watson Models and Barbara Watson Charm and Model School. She closed the agencies in 1956.

Watson worked at Hampton University for a brief period beginning in 1958, until she decided to re-enter law school, completing her degree at New York Law School. Upon graduation, Watson moved into city politics as an attorney for New York City, then executive director of the New York City Commission to the United Nations, where she coordinated relations between foreign dignitaries and the city.

Her career in the U.S. State Department began in 1966. Watson rose from special assistant to a deputy undersecretary of state to become director of the Bureau of Security and Consular Affairs, where she remained from 1968 to 1974. President Jimmy Carter named her assistant secretary for consular affairs and assistant secretary of state in 1977, making her the first African American and first woman with this diplomatic rank. She was named ambassador to Malaysia in 1980, with responsibility for all U.S. mission operations. After she retired in 1981, Watson worked as a consultant for the State Department and advised on international law for two Washington, D.C., legal firms. *See also* NEW YORK CITY [4].

REFERENCES

Editors of Ebony. *Ebony Success Library*. vols 1-2. 1973.

Smith, Jessie Carney, ed. *Notable Black American Women*, Book II. 1996.

Who's Who Among Black Americans, 1975–76. vol. 1, 1976.

JESSIE CARNEY SMITH

Watson, Robert Jose (April 10, 1946–), baseball player, general manager. Watson, the first African-American general manager of a major league baseball club, was born in Los Angeles and attended Harbor College. He served as a sergeant in the U.S. Marine Corps. Signed by the Houston Astros as a catcher, Watson made his debut with the team in 1966. He remained with the Astros, first in the outfield and then at first base, for thirteen years. After playing briefly for Boston, he played for the New York Yankees, from 1980–1982, then finished his career in 1984 with the Atlanta Braves. Watson was a solid though not outstanding player, and he was named to the National League (NL) All-Star team three times. He was the first player to hit for the "cycle" in both the National and American Leagues, and he was also credited in 1975 with scoring the NL's 1,000,000th run.

After his playing days ended, Watson served for several years as batting coach for the Oakland Athletics. In 1988, Watson was named general manager by the Houston Astros. In 1995, he was hired as general manager by the New York Yankees. Watson quickly built the club into a winner, not the least of which was his signing of manager Joe Torre and free agent outfielder Bernie Williams. Watson was also influential in bringing star rookie shortstop Derek Jeter to the Yankees. The Yankees won the World Championship in 1996 and reached the playoffs in 1997. In February 1998, just before the Yankees embarked on a record-breaking season, Watson resigned, reportedly due to his difficult relationship with Yankees owner George Steinbrenner, to join his son's financial management firm.

See also BASEBALL [1].

REFERENCES

"Bob Watson, baseball's only Black GM, leaves the Yankees." *Jet.* 93: February 23, 1998: 47.

Falkner, David. "Yankee pride." *The Sporting News* 222 (February 9, 1998): 50.

GREG ROBINSON

Watts, Julius Caesar, Jr. "J.C." (November 18, 1957–), U.S. Congressman, football player. J.C. Watts, a leading Congressional Republican, was born in Eufaula, Oklahoma, the son of a policeman. He later emphasized his childhood poverty, noting that he had only two pairs of pants, both patched. Watts

J.C. Watts. (AP/Wide World Photos)

attended the University of Oklahoma in Norman on a football scholarship, and he received a B.A. degree in journalism in 1981.

As quarterback, Watts led the University of Oklahoma to victories in the Orange Bowl in 1980 and 1981 and was named Most Valuable Player of both bowls. After graduation, Watts joined the Ottawa Roughriders of the Canadian Football League. In his rookie year, he led the Roughriders to the Grey Cup, and was named Most Valuable Player of the Cup game. He retired after four years with Ottawa and a year with Toronto.

Following his retirement from football, Watts returned to Norman, where he formed the Watts Energy Corporation. An ordained minister, Watts also became the youth director of Sunnylane Baptist Church in nearby Del City.

In 1994, relying on his football celebrity and conservative Republican politics, Watts campaigned for Congress. That fall, he was elected to the U.S. House of Representatives from Oklahoma's largely white fourth district, and he was easily reelected in 1996 and 1998. As the sole black Republican in Congress during the late 1990s, Watts has cultivated a color-blind image, declining to join the Congressional Black Caucus and calling for an end to affirmative action and welfare programs. In 1997, Watts was selected by House Republicans to respond to the President's State of the Union Address, and in November 1998 he was named chair of the congressional Republican Conference.

See also CONSERVATISM [2]; OKLAHOMA [4]; REPUBLICAN PARTY [4].

REFERENCES

De Capua, Sarah. *J. C. Watts, Jr.: Character Counts (Community Builders)*. 1999.

Lutz, Norma Jean. *J. C. Watts (Black Americans of Achievement)*. 1999.

Schmitt, Eric. "A Rising Republican Star, and Very Much His Own Man," *The New York Times*, Feb. 21, 2000: A10.

GREG ROBINSON

Webb, Wellington (Edward)

Webb, Wellington (Edward) (February 17, 1941–), mayor . Wellington Webb was born in Chicago, Illinois. As a child he was sent to live with his grandmother in Denver in order to help his asthma. Webb graduated from Colorado State College with a degree in education. Finding discrimination in his search for a teaching and coaching job, he took a series of social service jobs in Denver. In 1972 he won election to the Colorado State legislature, serving from 1973 to 1977. He headed the Colorado campaign to elect Jimmy Carter in 1976, and Carter appointed him regional director of the U.S. Department of Health. In 1980 when Carter lost his bid for reelection, Colorado governor Richard Lamm appointed Webb executive director of the State Department of Regulatory Agencies; Webb held that position until he was elected Denver city auditor in 1987.

Webb made his first, losing bid to become mayor of Denver in 1983. In 1991 he faced a well-financed opponent, Norm Early, a popular district attorney, who was also African American. Webb prevailed and became the first African-American mayor of Denver, a city where blacks make up only twelve percent of the population.

In his first term, Webb faced repeated charges of cronyism and incompetence. His chances for reelection against a woman with strong media backing appeared slim. He missed first place in the election by six votes and was an underdog for the runoff. His opponent miscalculated, and Webb was able to win. He was more fortunate in his election to a third term–he won handily, the first mayor elected without a runoff since 1979.

See also COLORADO [2]; WEST, BLACKS IN THE [5].

REFERENCES

Beil, David. "Oh, What a Tangled Webb Reprieve." *Campaigns and Elections*, July 1995.

Kram, Mark. Wellington Webb. In *Contemporary Black Biography*, vol. 3, edited by Barbara Carlisle Bigelow. 1992.

"Webb Elected To Third Term As Denver Mayor." *Jet*, 24 May 1999.

ROBERT L. JOHNS

Wellington Webb. (AP/Wide World Photos)

Webster, Milton Price

Webster, Milton Price (1887–1925), union organizer, union officer. Milton Price Webster was born in Clarksville, Tennessee. While still a young man, he relocated to Chicago to work as a porter for the Pullman Company that operated sleeping cars on the nation's railroads. Pullman porters were required to minister to the needs of passengers on the Pullman cars in many ways, including stowing luggage or shining their shoes if necessary. Some African Americans, particularly Asa Philip Randolph, held that the company hired porters to extend the master-slave relationship that existed during slavery.

In protest of the Pullman Company's discriminatory practices, on April 25, 1925, Randolph led in organizing the Brotherhood of Sleeping Car Porters (BSCP). Randolph and other BSCP leaders sought highly competent men to serve as district organizers; one of these was Milton Webster, a highly respected porter from Chicago where the most important division of the Pullman network existed. Company headquarters were there, as was a concentration of porters. Webster was also an influential Republican, a ward leader among the party's black members, and a bailiff in Cook County Court.

Next to Randolph, Webster became the second most important man in BSCP as well as first vice-president and chair of the Brotherhood's International Executive Board. The unpretentious, direct Webster was easy to know and handled the day-to-day union operations while the charismatic Randolph carried the porter's messages to the public. Webster's primary concern was for the workers and how to improve conditions at Pullman; he was also influential in determining union policy. Webster and Randolph worked hard to sustain the organization, particularly when members refused to strike in 1928. The two men then led the BSCP into the American Federation of Labor. Union organizers, including such leaders as Webster, Ashley L. Totten, Benjamin Smith, and C. L. Dellums, were indispensable to BSCP's success, but they paid a price to achieve their ends. They lost their homes and worked under severe privations, while hundreds of men lost their jobs due to Pullman backlash. Still, the union was revitalized and finally recognized in summer 1935 as the legal bargaining agent for Pullman porters.

See also BROTHERHOOD OF SLEEPING CAR PORTERS [1]; FAIR EMPLOYMENT PRACTICES COMMITTEE (FEPC) [2].

REFERENCES

Brazeal, Brailsford R. *The Brotherhood of Sleeping Car Porters*. 1946.

Harris, William H. *Keeping the Faith: A. Philip Randolph, Milton P. Webster, and the Brotherhood of Sleeping Car Porters, 1925–37*. 1977.

Smith, Jessie Carney, ed. *Notable Black American Men*. 1999.

JESSIE CARNEY SMITH

Weems, Renita (1954–), theologian, educator, writer, public speaker. After growing up in Atlanta, Renita Weems attended Wellesley College and graduated in 1976. She studied at Princeton Theological Seminary and earned the Master of Divinity degree and the Doctor of Philosophical degree in Old Testament and Hebrew languages, the first black woman to attain this honor. After working as a Wall Street stockbroker, economist, and accountant, in 1987 Weems became professor of Old Testament at Vanderbilt University Divinity School in 1987.

Weems gained visibility as a member of Bill Moyers' team of scholars, poets, and authors of the 1996 PBS show "Genesis," as one of two black members of a group that participated in a series of conversations about the Bible. Although she calls herself a writer and scholar who happens to preach, in 1997 *Ebony* magazine cited Weems as one of the fifteen greatest black women preachers in America. She is an ordained elder in the African Methodist Episcopal Church and also a well-known and nationally-recognized seminar leader and inspirational motivator who often addresses issues dealing with the empowerment of women.

Weems is author of a number of books on women's spirituality and wholeness. Her works include *Intimacy: Stories of Blessings, Betrayals and Birthings* (1993), *Just a Sister Away (A Womanist Vision of Women's Relationships in the Bible)* (1998), and *Listening for God: A Minister's Journey Through Silence and Doubt* (1999). She has also written scholarly works on Hebrew, including *Battered Love: Marriage, Sex and Violence in the Hebrew Prophets* (1995). She is co-author of Cece Winans' 1999 autobiography, *On a Positive Note; Her Joyous Faith, Her Life in Music, and Her Everyday Blessings. See also* ATLANTA [1].

REFERENCES

Kinnon, Joy Bennett. "15 Greatest Black Women Preachers in America." *Ebony* 27 (July 1996): 54–56.

Waddle, Ray. "Minister Juggles Diverse Roles." *Nashville Tennessean*, November 24, 1997, 1B–2B.

"Weems Lauded for Preaching Expertise." *Vanderbilt Today*, May 1998, 1.

DOLORES NICHOLSON

West, Cornel Ronald (June 2, 1953–), educator. Cornel West was born in Tulsa, Oklahoma. He graduated magna cum laude from Harvard, and received an M.A. and Ph.D. from Princeton. He taught at Union Seminary, Yale, University of Paris, and Princeton, where he was Director of the Afro-Ameri-

Cornel West. (Copyright Jerry Bauer.)

Cornel West Reader (1999). With Jack Salzman and David Lionel Smith, he is the coeditor of the *Encyclopedia of African American Culture and History.* He has also edited two books dealing with black-Jewish relations: *Jews and Blacks: A Dialogue on Race, Religion and Culture in America* (with Michael Lerner), and *Struggles in the Promised Land: Toward a History of Black-Jewish Relations* (with Jack Salzman), 1997. West made his first major foray into national politics during the 2000 presidential primaries, when he worked for Democrat Bill Bradley as an advisor and as cochairman of Bradley's Massachusetts' campaign.

See also INTELLECTUAL LIFE [3]; UNITARIAN UNIVERSALIST ASSOCIATION [5].

REFERENCES

"Cornel West." In *Contemporary Authors Online. 2000.*

Emerge, March 1993.

"hooks, bell and Cornel West," *Breaking Bread: Insurgent Black Intellectual Life.* 1991.

West, Cornel *The American Evasion of Philosophy: A Genealogy of Pragmatism.* 1989.

RICHARD NEWMAN

can Studies Program, before he moved to Harvard in 1994, when he took a position as Alphonse Fletcher Jr. University Professor.

Cornel West is one of the leading contemporary African-American intellectuals and activists at the beginning of the twenty-first century. The author or editor of more than 15 books, he is also a popular public speaker. West's work ranges over the fields of philosophy, literature, religion, music, and black history, and focuses on social thought, cultural and political criticism, modern philosophy, and issues of social justice. West has deep roots in the Baptist church, the source of his preaching style. His intellectual foundation combines democratic socialism, Christian compassion, the modernity of Franz Kafka, and black music. His intellectual heroes include Anton Chekhov and John Coltrane.

His books begin with professional works of scholarship, such as *The American Evasion of Philosophy: A Generation of Pragmatism* (1989) and *The Ethical Dimensions of Marxist Thought* (1991). West became a national figure with *Race Matters* (1993), a collection of essays that made the best seller list. His later books, *Keeping Faith* (1993) and *Restoring Hope* (1997), have been followed by a large compendium of his work, *The*

Wheat, Alan (October 16, 1951–), politician. Alan Wheat was born in Kansas City, Missouri. He graduated from Grinnell College (Iowa) with a degree in economics in 1972. From 1972 to 1975 he worked as an economist with the Kansas City Department of Housing and Urban Development and the Mid-America Regional Council of Kansas City.

Wheat began his Democratic political career with election to the Missouri House of Representatives in 1977, serving three terms. In 1982, a Missouri congressional seat became vacant which Wheat won. He was the only African American among the seven candidates. He retained his congressional seat until 1994, although he faced stiff competition in some campaigns. In 1994, Wheat sought and won the Democratic nomination for the Senate seat vacated by Senator John Danforth's retirement, but he lost in the general election.

While in Congress, Wheat served on the House Rules Committee in his first year and on the House Select Committee on Hunger in 1990. He became president of the Congressional Black Caucus (1990) and co-chaired the Credentials Committee during the 1992 Democratic National Convention. He worked to secure Federal funds for his district and was considered a liberal on bills that came before the House.

Alan Wheat. (AP/Wide World Photos)

Several "best legislator" awards were given to him by Missouri newspapers.

After leaving Congress, Wheat held executive management positions with CARE (1995) and Smith Kline Beecham (1996), a Washington-based drug company. He continued to be active in politics, serving as director of public liaison to the Clinton-Gore campaign chairman in 1996.

See also KANSAS CITY [3]; MISSOURI [4].

REFERENCES

Black Enterprise, 25 (November 1994): 32.

Mabunda, L. Mpho, and Shirelle Phelps, eds., *Contemporary Black Biography*. 1997.

Ploski, Harry A., and James Williams, eds. *The Negro Almanac*, 5th ed. 1989.

CARRELL P. HORTON

Whitaker, Forest

Whitaker, Forest (July 15, 1961–), actor, director. Forest Whitaker is a large, soft-voiced, intense actor possessing a wide acting range with numerous roles in independent, Hollywood, and foreign films. He received the distinguished Cannes Best Actor Trophy twice, first for playing jazz saxophonist Char-

lie Parker in *Bird* (1988), and the second time for a sensitive portrayal in *The Crying Game* (1993), as a captured British soldier who asks his executioner, a New Republic Army captain, to deliver his final words to his transgendered lover. Following the second award, Whitaker made his debut as a TV director in the feature *Strapped* (1993), and his film directing debut with *Waiting To Exhale* (1995).

Born in Longview Texas, but raised in Compton, California, Whitaker was a high school football star with a proclivity for performance. After deciding to train in fine arts, he studied voice, drama, and classical music at the University of Southern California. During the early 1980s, Whitaker performed and directed plays in American and British theaters while concurrently making appearances on popular television programs. In 1982, Whitaker landed a role in the film, *Fast Times At Ridgemont High* and performed with Nicholas Cage, Sean Penn, and Jennifer Jason Leigh. By the late 1980s, Whitaker was performing for top directors such as Martin Scorsese and Oliver Stone. Films and television movies include *Platoon* (1986), *The Color of Money* (1986) *Rage In Harlem* (1991), *Jason's Lyric* (1994), *Lush Life* (1993), *North and South* parts I and II (1993), *Species* (1994), *Phenomenon* (1996) and *Ghost Dog* (2000).

See also FILM [3]; TEXAS [5].

REFERENCES

Katz, Ephraim. *The Film Encyclopedia*, 3rd edition. 1998.

Mr. Showbiz Celebrities. Disney Enterprises. 1 March 2000. http://mrshowbiz.go.com/people/forestwhitaker/content/bio.html.

Stevens, Tracy, editorial director. *International Television & Video Almanac*, 44th edition. 1999.

Unterburger, Amy L., ed. *International Dictionary of Films and Filmmakers: Actors and Actresses*. 1997.

F. ZEAL HARRIS

Whitman, Albery

Whitman, Albery (May 30, 1851–June 29, 1901), minister, poet. Albery Whitman was born a slave in Hart County, Kentucky. Both parents were light skinned, and it is claimed that their son could pass. Little is known of Whitman's education. He seems to have attended Wilberforce University for six months and been in school for seven months in Troy, Ohio, around 1870. Family tradition says he could read at the age of three, and he published his first poetry at the age of twenty. (This poetry is lost.) He taught school

Forest Whitaker (third from right) on the set. (The Gamma Liaison Network)

for two years in Ohio and for six months at Wilberforce-not all classes at the school were of college level. Whitman was at Wilberforce long enough to become thoroughly impressed with African Methodist Episcopal bishop and university president Daniel Alexander Payne.

Whitman became an AME minister in the early 1870s. In Zanesville, Ohio, he oversaw the completion of a new church in 1876 and another in Springfield, Ohio, eighteen months later. The itinerant life of an AME minister led him to Kentucky, Arkansas, Kansas, Texas, and Georgia. He was pastor of Allen Temple in Atlanta when he died. His daughters, billed as the Whitman Sisters, became successful vaudeville performers and noted producers.

Whitman wrote long, technically proficient narrative poems. He published *Not a Man and Yet a Man* (1877), *The Rape of Florida* (1884—revised as *Twasinta's Seminoles* in 1885), and *An Idyll of the South* (1901), as well a collection of shorter pieces, *The World's Fair Poem* (1893). He rivals Frances Ellen Harper as the most important African American poet between Phillis Wheatley and Paul Laurence Dunbar.

See also BOOK COLLECTORS AND COLLECTIONS [1]; LITERATURE [3].

REFERENCES

Harris, Trudier, ed. *Afro-American Writers Before the Harlem Renaissance.* 1986.

Lucas, Ernestine G. *Wider Windows to the Past.* 1995.

Simmons, William J. *Men of Mark.* 1877.

ROBERT L. JOHNS

Williams, Avon N., Jr. (December 22, 1921–August 29, 1994), attorney, civil rights leader, politician. Born in Knoxville, Tennessee on December 22, 1921, Williams was the fourth of five children born to Avon and Carrie Belle Williams. He obtained an A. B. degree in 1940. A veteran of World War II, he earned the LL. B. (1947) and the LL. M. (1948) degrees from Boston University.

In 1949, Williams began his law practice in Knoxville as a cooperating attorney for the National Association for the Advancement of Colored People (NAACP) Legal Defense Fund. In 1950, he served as co-counsel in the *McSwain v. Board of Anderson County, Tennessee,* the state's first public school desegregation suit. The following year, Williams successfully litigated the *Gray v. University of Tennessee* case that opened the University of Tennessee's graduate school to four African American students. In 1953, he moved to Nashville and with partner attorney Z. Alexander Looby, in consultation with the NAACP Legal Defense Fund and Thurgood Marshall-Williams's cousin-filed the 1955 *Kelley v. Nashville Board of Education* case. Williams involved himself without payment in more than 24 major civil rights suits.

In 1962, Williams helped found Davidson County Independent Political Council, and later the Tennessee Voters Council, which he chaired from 1966 to 1985. From 1968 to 1991, he served in the state senate. In 1972, Senator Williams became the attorney of record in the *Geier v. Tennessee* case, which resulted in the predominately white University of Tennessee in Nashville merging with the predominately black Tennessee State University. Williams was a prevailing influence in the passage of Tennessee's civil rights law. *See also* TENNESSEE[5].

REFERENCES

Laska, Lewis L. "Avon N. Williams, Jr." in *Tennessee Encyclopedia of History and Culture*. Editor-in-chief, Carroll. Van West. 1998.

Lovett, Bobby L., and Linda T. Wynn. *Profiles of African Americans in Tennessee History*. 1996.

Smith, Jessie Carney, ed. *Notable Black American Men*. 1999.

LINDA T. WYNN

Williams, Juan (March 10, 1954–), journalist. Williams was born in Colon, Panama, and was three when the family moved to New York City. He grew up in the Bedford-Stuyvesant and Crown Heights neighborhoods of Brooklyn. He credits his mother, a garment worker who always picked up and brought home newspapers left on the subway, with inspiring his interest in journalism. Starting out in the New York public school system, he attended Oakwood School, Poughkeepsie, on a scholarship. After graduating from Haverford College in 1976 with a B.A. in philosophy, he became an intern at the Washington Post, beginning a twenty-three association with the paper.

At the *Post* Williams filled a number of positions, including White House reporter, op-ed columnist, and editorial writer. Winning recognition for his skills as a newspaper reporter, Williams also became visible on television from about 1988 on. He is a contributing

political analyst for the Fox New Channel and a regular panelist on Fox News Sunday. He has appeared on such other television programs as *Washington Week in Review*, *Nightline*, and *Crossfire* (CNN).

Williams has published numerous magazine articles and written documentaries for television, including *Politics-the New Black Power*, *Marion Anderson*, and *A. Philip Randolph-For Jobs and Freedom*. He is the author of *Eyes on the Prize: America's Civil Rights Years, 1954–1965* (1987), a best-selling book based on the television documentary series. His biography, *Thurgood Marshall: American Revolutionary*, appeared to great critical acclaim in 1998. In 2000 Williams became host of National Public Radio's *Talk of the Nation*, an afternoon call-in program.
See also JOURNALISM [3].

REFERENCES

Booknotes Transcript, 11 October 1998. [Juan Williams on Thurgood Marshall: American Revolutionary.] http://www.booknotes.org/transcripts/50484.htm.

De Leon, Ferdinand M. "Juan Williams in the New Voice of NPR's 'Talk of the Nation.'" *Seattle Times*, 10 February 2000.

"Juan Williams." *NPR Online*. http://www.npr.org/inside/bios/jwilliams.html.

ROBERT L. JOHNS

Williams, Paul Revere (February 18, 1894–January 23, 1980), architect, entrepreneur. One of the nation's first African American architects, Williams designed or co-designed over 3,000 homes ranging from modest to lavish. Born in Los Angeles, he attended the Los Angeles School of Art and took evening classes at the Beaux Arts Institute of Design. He worked his way through school by assisting local architects. He worked as a draftsman between 1913 and 1914, then with a planner and landscape architect between 1914 and 1916. Williams enrolled in engineering school at the University of Southern California where he remained until 1919, but never graduated. While there, however, he designed fraternity and sorority houses.

From 1916 to 1919, Williams worked with a residential architect who designed fine homes. He joined a larger firm, John C. Austin, where he remained from 1919 to 1921 gaining experience on large-scale projects. He became a registered architect in 1915, was licensed in 1921, and opened his own architectural firm, Paul R. Williams and Associates in 1922.

With a flourishing architectural business, Williams became popular for his design of posh hotels and other well-known structures. Williams helped to design the Los Angles International Airport, the Los Angeles County Court House, and the Federal Customs Building. He also built homes for such luminaries as E. L. Cord, Bud Abbott, William "Bojangles" Robinson, and Frank Sinatra. He worked in traditional, revival, or modern architectural style and incorporated features of English Tudor, Georgian, Spanish Colonial, Regency, and other periods. He left a rich legacy in the wide range of structures that he built. *See also* ARCHITECTURE [1].

REFERENCES

Current Biography Yearbook. 1941.

Mabunda, L. Mpho, ed. *Contemporary Black Biography*, vol. 9. 1994.

Smith, Jessie Carney, ed. *Notable Black American Men.* 1999.

Wilson, Flip (Clerow Wilson) (December 8, 1933–November 25, 1998), comedian. Wilson was born in Jersey City, New Jersey. Abandoned by his mother in 1940, he was placed in foster homes from which he ran away so often that he was sent to reform school. Wilson quit school at the age of sixteen, lied

Flip Wilson. (AP/Wide World Photos)

about his age, and joined the U.S. Air Force. He served until 1954.

Wilson then worked as a comic in small clubs and by 1960 was working in New York. An appearance in 1966 on the *Tonight Show* was followed by many others and led appearances on *Ed Sullivan Show* and *Rowan and Martin's Laugh-In*, and to his own special in 1968. NBC starred him in the *Flip Wilson Show*, which began on September 17, 1970, and ran until June 27, 1974. The program ranked among the top ten.

Wilson was the first black entertainer to host a successful weekly variety show on network television. He was noted for his story telling and his flamboyant impersonations of characters like the sassy waitress Geraldine.

After Wilson left the show in 1974, he went into semi-retirement, appearing in specials and in movies like *Uptown Saturday Night* (1974) and *The Fish That Saved Pittsburgh* (1979). He also starred in a daytime game show and a situation comedy that were failures. In the last decade of his life, Wilson limited his performances to occasional guest appearances on situation comedies. He died of liver cancer.

See also COMEDIANS [2]; MABLEY, JACKIE "MOMS" [3]; PRYOR, RICHARD FRANKLIN LENOX THOMAS [4]; TELEVISION [5].

REFERENCES

Ingram, Billy. "Flip Wilson: The Odd Disappearance of the Flip Wilson Show." TV Party. http://www.tvparty.com/flip.html.

Manheim, James M. "Flip Wilson." In *Contemporary Black Biography*, edited by Shirelle Phelps. 1999.

Watkins, Mel. "Flip Wilson, 64, Over-the-top Comic and TV Host, Dies." *New York Times*, 26 November 1998.

ROBERT L. JOHNS

Wilson, Clerow. *See* Wilson, Flip.

Wilson, William Julius (December 20, 1935–), sociologist, educator. Born in Derry Township, Pennsylvania, to Esco and Pauline Bracy Wilson, William Wilson received degrees in sociology from Wilberforce University (B.A., 1958), Bowling Green State Uni-

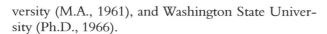

William Julius Wilson. (William Wilson)

Oprah Winfrey. (AP/Wide World Photos)

versity (M.A., 1961), and Washington State University (Ph.D., 1966).

He taught at the University of Massachusetts at Amherst (1965–71), then the University of Chicago (1971–96). While at Chicago he was appointed a full professor in 1975, named chair of the sociology department in 1978, and in 1994 he was named distinguished professor. The next year he received a rare distinction for a sociologist when he was invited to join the National Academy of Sciences. In 1993 he founded the Center for the Study of Urban Inequality, a permanent organization for poverty research located at the university. Wilson joined Harvard University in 1996, where he was appointed Lewis P. and Linda L. Gayser University Professor in the John F. Kennedy School of Government and later the Malcolm Wiener Professor of Social Policy.

Among his numerous publications, Wilson's *The Declining Significance of Race* (1978) and *The Truly Disadvantaged* (1987) are highly regarded by many, stimulating academic and popular debates on race and urban poverty. His book *When Work Disappears: The World of the New Urban Poor* (1996) furthers the discussion on poverty in inner cities and diagnoses and prescribes remedies for the ailments in these

areas. Wilson's views have proved controversial, as he has come out in support of national health and child care systems, work programs similar to those of the New Deal, and training programs for the poor that will allow them to gain employment.

See also BLACK STUDIES [1]; MOYNIHAN REPORT [4]; URBANIZATION [5].

REFERENCES

Newsmakers, annual edition. 1998.

Phelps, Shirelle, ed. *Contemporary Black Biography*, vol. 22. 1999.

Who's Who Among African Americans, 12th ed. 1999.

JESSIE CARNEY SMITH

Winfrey, Oprah Gail (Update) (January 29, 1954–), talk-show host, actress. During the mid-1990s, Winfrey's career continued to expand. Her talk show remained the most watched daytime show, and she also produced evening interview specials, notably an exclusive interview with the reclusive singer Michael Jackson. She began a wildly successful reading club, the Oprah Book Club, whose books she promoted on her show. In 1998, she produced and

George C. Wolfe, holding a Tony Award for Best Director. (AP/Wide World Photos)

starred in director Jonathan Demme's *Beloved*, adapted from Toni Morrison's novel. Winfrey's empire moved in a new direction with the 2000 premiere of the magazine *O: The Oprah Magazine*, dedicated to the same type of topics and coverage as her television show.

REFERENCES

Harrison, Barbara Grizutti. "The Importance of Being Oprah." *New York Times Magazine* (June 11, 1989): 28- 30.

Hine, Darlene Clark, ed. *Black Women in America*. New York, 1993.

Newcomb, Peter, and Lisa Gubernick. "The Top 40." *Forbes* (September 27, 1993): 97.

KENYA DILDAY
UPDATED BY GREG ROBINSON

Wolfe, George C. (Update)

Wolfe, George C. (Update) (September 23, 1954–), playwright and director. In 1994, Wolfe directed *Angels in America: Perestroika* on Broadway. During the following years, he concentrated his efforts on directing Public Theater productions, including several plays by Shakespeare. Two of the works he directed also went on to successful Broadway runs: the Tap Dance extravaganza *Bring on Da' Noise, Bring On Da' Funk* (1996), and the revival of the Leonard Bernstein musical *On The Town* (1998).

REFERENCES

Lubow, Arthur. "George Wolfe in Progress." *New Yorker* 69, no. 30 (1993): 48-62.

Nixon, Will. "George C. Wolfe Creates Visions of Black Culture." *American Visions* 6 (1991): 50- 52.

MICHAEL PALLER
UPDATED BY GREG ROBINSON

Timeline:
Key Events From 1444–2000

1444: Portuguese form the first slave trading company. The Portuguese learn early that slave trade proceeds best in cooperation with Africans.

1482: São Jorge de Mina (Elmina) is established. This is the first trading outpost to be built by Portugal on Africa's western coast. It is the first of many permanent trading posts initially dealing with gold and then slaves. Slaves are captured inland and then brought to the outpost. Once there they wait until a ship arrives. Slaves are traded for guns, cowrie shells, mirrors, knives, linens, silk, and beads. This castle or outpost changes ownership several times during the course of the slave trade—owners include the Portuguese, the Dutch, and the English. By the 1700s approximately 30,000 slaves would be deported from Elmina each year.

1502: Portugal brings a cargo of slaves to the Western Hemisphere.

1510: Spain begins slave trade. King Ferdinand orders the shipment of 250 African slaves from Spain to the West Indies.

1518: Spanish American Colonies are granted a license (*asiento*) for the shipment of African slaves directly from Africa to America.

1619: First African settlers arrive in North America. A Dutch ship reaches Jamestown, Virginia, carrying a cargo of twenty Africans. Fifteen are purchased as indentured servants rather than slaves.

A public school for Native Americans and blacks is established in Virginia.

1621: Dutch form the West India Company. Only members of the company are legally enabled to carry slaves or other goods from Africa to Dutch colonies or elsewhere.

1625: Virginia Court distinguishes between black servitude and black slavery.

1630: Massachusetts enacts a law to protect African slaves who escape from their owners because of abusive treatment.

Virginia restricts relations between blacks and whites.

1634: Maryland colony imports slaves.

1638: First black slave arrives in New England.

Maryland passes a law declaring that a servant convicted of running away should be executed. This is the most severe law of its kind.

Slavery is becoming the most common condition of blacks in America. Fewer are accepted as indentured servants. The de facto institution of slavery is well established.

Massachusetts is the first colony to recognize slavery as a legal institution. Virginia passes legislation that requires a servant who escapes for a second time to be branded on the cheek or shoulder with the letter R.

The New England Confederation enters into an intercolonial agreement that a simple statement of certification from any government magistrate can convict a suspected runaway slave.

Eleven blacks petition for freedom in New Netherland. This is probably the first organized black protest in America. They are freed by the Council of New Netherland because they have completed their specified years of servitude.

The first American slave ship sails from Boston. Slaving quickly becomes a major profit-making industry.

1652: Earliest statute for the suppression of slavery in the colonies is noted in the Rhode Island Records. This legislation becomes the first colonial law limiting slavery, but ironically it is never enforced.

New Netherland colony passes legislation regulating the treatment of slaves by their masters.

1655: Elizabeth Key, a slave since birth, sues for her freedom and wins. She is born the daughter of an influential Virginia planter and a slave woman. Her suit is based on three arguments: (1) her father was a free man; (2) she had been baptized, the implication being that a Christian could not be a slave for life; and (3) she had been sold to another planter even after she had served nine years.

1660: English Company of Royal Adventurers is established for trading into Africa. The Royal African will supersede it in 1672.

Maryland and Virginia colonies pass laws concerning black and white servants. White servants can buy their freedom. Black servants become slaves.

1663: First serious slave conspiracy is recorded September 13 in colonial America in Gloucester County, Virginia. The plot by white and black servants to escape from their masters is betrayed by one or more indentured servants.

1664: French West Indies Company is established.

Maryland becomes the first colony to pass legislation prohibiting marriage between black men and white women. Maryland also passes legislation

that recognizes slavery as legal. British secure control of New Amsterdam, and the status of black servants is amended to perpetual slavery. Legislation is passed condoning slavery.

1667: British pass legislation entitled "Act to Regulate the Negroes on the British Plantation" that restricts the movement and behavior of blacks.

1668: Virginia's House of Burgesses passes a law stipulating that Christian baptism does not alter a person's condition of bondage or freedom.

1669: Virginia statute is passed that declares it is not a felony for a master or overseer to kill a slave who resists punishment.

The Fundamental Constitutions of Carolina accept slavery as a legal institution.

1670: Virginia passes legislation that disallows lifelong servitude for any black person who has become a Christian before arriving in the colony. The law is passed to address the difficult moral issue raised as Christians enslave other Christians. The law further divides all non-Christian servants into two groups: those coming by sea who "shall be slaves for their lives," and those coming by land who are to serve indentured terms. Almost all Africans come by sea so they are subject to enslavement but Native Americans are not.

1671: An act is passed in Maryland declaring that a slave's conversion to Christianity does not affect his slave status.

1672: Virginia passes a new law that puts a bounty on the heads of fugitive slaves.

British Crown grants a slaving charter to a new corporation, the Royal African Company, to compete with the Dutch and the French.

1682: Movement of slaves is restricted in New York by the General Court. It forbids slaves to leave their owner's property without written permission or to buy or sell goods. Up until this time slaves in New York had been governed by the same judicial processes and criminal code that held for whites.

Slave Law passes in Virginia that prohibits slaves from possessing weapons, leaving their owner's plantations without permission, or lifting a hand against a white person, even in self-defense. Further, the slave law of 1670 is repealed, so the conversion of slaves to Christianity before arriving in the colony no longer keeps them from lifelong servitude.

1684: Slaves are imported into Philadelphia. By 1700 one in every fourteen families in Philadelphia will own slaves.

1688: Quakers pass anti-slavery resolution in Pennsylvania. On February 18, 1688 the Mennonites (Quakers) in Germantown, Pennsylvania adopt the first formal anti-slavery resolution in American history. Although the Quakers are the first religious group to denounce the slave trade and slavery, it becomes a thriving business in Pennsylvania.

1691: First law in Virginia to explicitly restrict intermarriage between blacks and whites is passed.

1692: More slave laws are enacted in Virginia. A new law imposes banishment from the colony of any free white man or woman who marries a black, mulatto, or a Native American. Later the penalty is changed to six months' imprisonment and a fine of 10 pounds. Slaves cannot keep horses, cattle, or hogs. Slaves charged with a capital offense are to be tried without a jury and can be convicted on the testimony of two witnesses under oath. Maryland, Delaware, and North Carolina later copy the Virginia laws.

1693: Philadelphia passes an ordinance restricting the movements of blacks.

1700: Pennsylvania distinguishes slaves as a separate group and laws are passed that apply only to them. Slaves can be put to death for murder, burglary, and rape, and whipped for robbing and stealing.

Judge Samuel Sewell of Massachusetts publishes a statement, entitled *The Selling of Joseph*. He becomes one of the first public officials to denounce slavery. This is the first anti-slavery tract to be distributed in the colonies.

1701: Society for the Propagation of the Gospel is founded as a vehicle to educate slaves and Native

Americans. It operates in Virginia, Maryland, North Carolina, Pennsylvania, and New Jersey.

1702: New York passes a law that imposes restraints on slaves, stipulating that no more than three slaves can assemble without the consent of their owners, and that a slave who strikes a free person could be confined for fourteen days and whipped.

1703: According to a census, as many as 43 percent of all whites in New York City own one or more slaves.

1704: Elias Neau opens one of the first schools in the colonies to enroll slaves. It is called the Catechism School for Negroes and is associated with Trinity Church.

1705: Death penalty is imposed for runaway slaves in New York.

Virginia enacts Slave Code called "Act Concerning Servants and Slaves." All existing laws dealing with blacks are collapsed into this slave code. Under this law, slaves are attached to the soil, so that the heir to a plantation is entitled to purchase the inherited interests of others in the slaves.

1706: New York passes legislation requiring that the legal status for children would be determined by the condition of the mother. A similar measure is in effect in North Carolina and Georgia, and it becomes the law in other parts of South as well.

1707: White mechanics in Philadelphia form a guild to protest unfair labor competition from black slaves.

1708: Slaves revolt in Newton, Long Island, New York. Seven whites are killed during the revolt. Three slaves and one Native American are hanged and one black woman is burned alive.

1711: Escaped slaves arm themselves and raid various plantations and farms in South Carolina. The slaves' leader is a Spanish black named Sebastian who is finally captured.

1712: New York denies slaves access to courts.

South Carolina adopts model Slave Code.

Slaves revolt in New York City on April 7. Nine whites are killed and at least twelve slaves are executed. The Catechism School for Negroes at Trinity Church is closed because slave owners believe that the French founder, Elias Neau, is inciting slaves to revolt. More restrictive slave codes are enacted.

Pennsylvania passes a law preventing the importation of slaves into the colony by imposing a duty of 20 pounds per head. However, the law is repealed in England.

1713: Quakers develop a manumission plan. Protests by Quakers seriously curtail the slave market activity in Philadelphia leading to legislative action that attempts to prohibit slavery in the colony.

1716: First slaves arrive in French Louisiana.

1717: Intermarriage is restricted in Maryland.

1720: Slaves revolt in Charleston, South Carolina. Many slaves are banished, some are hanged, and others are burned alive.

1721: The "Negro Watch" is created in Charleston, South Carolina to allay the fears of the white population of possible slave revolts. Patrols are set up to stop slaves on sight and to shoot them if they do not stop when ordered.

1722: Slave plot to kill whites is uncovered. About 200 slaves gather at a church near Rappahannock, Virginia to attack whites who had abused them. Although the plot is revealed all the slaves escape.

1723: Virginia Assembly passes legislation that disfranchises free blacks. This law is enacted as a result of the slave conspiracy. It is felt that free blacks should be punished even if they were not involved in the plot.

1724: Slave codes are enacted in Louisiana. Slave owners can legally punish runaway slaves by cutting off their ears, hamstringing them, or branding them.

1725: First Church of Colored Baptists is established. Black slaves are granted the right to have a separate Baptist church in Williamsburg, VA.

1726: Pennsylvania passes laws that further curtail the activities of slaves. Racial intermarriage is banned.

1729: Maryland passes a law that permits brutal punishments upon conviction of slaves for certain crimes. These punishments include hanging, decapitation, and severing the body into four quarters for display in public places.

1730: Marks the beginning of the high point of importation of slaves to the Americas.

Slave conspiracy is discovered in Norfolk and Princess Ann counties, VA.

1732: Slave mutiny occurs aboard a ship commanded by Captain John Major of Portsmouth, New Hampshire. The entire crew is killed. Interestingly only those uprisings resulting in the death of captain or crewmembers are documented. Little is known of uprisings that failed and of the large numbers of slaves thrown overboard.

1733: Spanish pass decree stating that any slave who escapes to Spanish territory would be considered free. Many slaves attempt to escape to Florida-especially St. Augustine.

Georgia, the last of thirteen colonies, is established. It is a haven for the indebted and oppressed. The Trustees of the colony disapprove of slavery.

1734: Slaves overtake the crew and captain of the slave ship *Dolphin*. All are killed in an explosion.

1739: Stono Rebellion — serious slave uprisings in Charleston, Stono River, and St. John's Parish, South Carolina. Groups of slaves seek freedom in St. Augustine. Many whites are killed along the route.

1740: South Carolina declares lifelong slavery for all blacks.

Fifty slaves are hanged in Charleston after alleged insurrection plots are uncovered.

1741: Soldiers from Georgia destroy an established settlement that housed fugitive slaves from South Carolina.

A series of suspicious fires and reports of slave conspiracies lead to general hysteria in New York City. According to some accounts, 13 conspirators were burned alive, 18 hanged, and 80 more deported. Another account stated that as many as 400 whites took part in the uprising and 125 blacks were arrested. It was later revealed that there was no evidence of a conspiracy or slave revolt.

1744: An Anglican missionary, Samuel Thomas, opens a school for blacks in South Carolina.

1750: Quaker abolitionist Anthony Benezet schools blacks in his home.

Georgia permits slavery so that the colony's growth will parallel that of the others.

1751: Virginia passes legislation giving the churchwardens of any parish the power to sell blacks or slaves residing one month if they had been emancipated without the consent of the governor and council.

1753: Benjamin Franklin presents the argument that "slavery is poor economic policy" in his book, *Observations Concerning the Increase of Mankind and the Peopling of Countries.*

1754: The twenty-two-year-old free black man Benjamin Banneker, considered to be the first African-American man of science, constructs the first clock made in the North American colonies. He makes the clock entirely from seasoned wood.

The Quaker abolitionist John Woolman publishes "Some Considerations on the Keeping of Negroes; Recommended to the Professors of Christianity of Every Denomination," a moral plea to other Quakers to emancipate their slaves. Fellow Quaker Anthony Benezet pens the first draft of *An Epistle of Caution and Advice, Concerning the Buying and Keeping of Slaves,* the Quakers's first official denunciation of slavery—both the slave trade and, more significantly, slaveholding.

1756: Blacks serve as scouts, wagoners, and laborers with British forces during the French and Indian War. Black militiamen serve with units from almost every colony. Many blacks receive praise for their bravery in the battles of Fort Duquesne, Fort Cumberland, and the Plains of Abraham outside Quebec City.

1758: Quakers in Philadelphia take steps to abolish slavery. They cease buying and selling slaves.

1760: "An Evening Thought: Salvation by Christ, with Penitential Cries" by the slave Jupiter Hammon is the first poem by a black person to be published in North America.

The *Narrative of the Uncommon Sufferings, and Surprizing Deliverance of Briton Hammon, A Negro Man* is the first slave narrative to be published in North America.

1763: Black chimney sweeps in Charleston form the first union-type organization. They refuse to work until the city increased their wages.

1766: Anthony Benezet, a schoolteacher from Philadelphia, writes *A Caution and Warning to Great Britain and Her Colonies, in a Sharot Representation of the Calamitous State of the Enslaved Negroes in the British Dominions.* He is one of the great pre-Revolutionary abolitionists.

1769: Thomas Jefferson tries without success to introduce a bill to the Virginia House of Burgesses that would emancipate African slaves.

1770: Crispus Attucks is the first person to be killed fighting the British at the Boston Massacre, becoming one of the first casualties of the American Revolution.

1772: Slavery is abolished in England.

1773: Phillis Wheatley, a 20-year-old slave, publishes her *Poems on Various Subjects, Religious and Moral,* making her the first African-American—and only the third American woman—to publish a volume of poetry.

Massachusetts slaves petition the legislature for freedom on January 6.

Black Baptist church is organized at Silver Bluff, South Carolina. This is probably the first black Baptist church under black leadership established in the colonies.

Caesar Hendricks of Massachusetts takes his master to court and asks to be freed. An all-white jury renders a verdict in his favor.

1774: The Society of Friends rule at their yearly meeting that Quakers who buy or sell slaves should be disowned and those who refuse to emancipate their slaves should be barred from leadership in the Society.

Connecticut, Massachusetts, and Rhode Island prohibit the importation of slaves.

Virginia Convention of 1774 passes a resolution condemning slavery.

Continental Congress pledges to end slave trade. The resolution is a powerful statement, but it proves to mean very little since the desire to gain wealth through slavery is still a potent force in America.

1775: Continental Navy recruits blacks. A recruitment poster in Newport calls for "ye able backed sailors, men white or black to volunteer for naval service in ye interest of freedom." About 2,000 blacks serve in the Continental Navy during the Revolution.

The first abolitionist society—the Society for the Relief of Free Negroes Unlawfully Held in Bondage, and for Improving the Condition of the African Race—is formed in Pennsylvania.

April 19—Blacks are among the minutemen who defeat the British at Concord. African Americans serve as minutemen before they are allowed into the regular army.

May—The Committee on Safety of the Continental Congress permits free blacks, but not slaves, to serve in the Continental Army.

June 17—Black soldiers—Salem Poor, a free black, and Peter Salem, a slave—fight the British heroically at the Battle of Bunker Hill.

July—despite the battle heroics of soldiers such as Poor and Salem, Gen. George Washington bars blacks from joining the army.

November 7—Lord Dunmore, royal governor of Virginia, issues a proclamation promising freedom to slaves willing to fight with the British. Dunmore's action will later be characterized in the Declaration of Independence as "exciting domestic insurrections."

December 31—General Washington reverses his earlier decision barring blacks from enlisting when the British start recruiting slaves for the British army.

Thomas Paine publishes *Slavery in America*—an indictment against the institution of slavery.

Benjamin Rush publishes *An Address to the Inhabitants of the British Settlements in America, Upon Slavekeeping.* He argues that blacks are not intellectually and morally inferior; that slavery is not necessary for the economic development of the South; and that slavery is not a Christian institution.

1776: New York and other colonies pass a law allowing any white man who is drafted to serve in the Continental Army to send a free black in his place. The number of whites who took advantage of this is unknown because a large number of blacks—slave and free—volunteered to serve their country.

The Declaration of Independence, written by Thomas Jefferson, himself the owner of over 175 slaves at the time, asserts that all persons "are created equal; that they are endowed by their creator with certain unalienable rights; that among these are life, liberty, and the pursuit of happiness." These words would later provide fuel for anti-slavery movements in the States.

Quakers refusing to free their slaves are disowned from the Society of Friends.

1777: Vermont becomes the first state to abolish slavery in its constitution.

Parting Ways, one of the earliest free black settlements in America, is established near Plymouth, MA. Cato Howe, a black Revolutionary War veteran, is given 94 acres of land by the town. The grant specifies that the land has to be cleared and settled by Howe and three others who participated in the war.

1778: The Continental Army enlists blacks for three-year terms. They serve in integrated units. Eventually all-black units emerge, such as the company from Connecticut referred to as the "Colonials" and a company from Boston called the "Bucks of America" whose members are slave volunteers and commanded by a black. Black soldiers, including Prince Whipple and Oliver Cromwell, were members of the regiment that crossed the Delaware River with Washington. By the end of the Revolutionary war 5,000 black soldiers and 2,000 blacks had fought bravely for their country.

First Rhode Island Regiment, an entirely black army unit, holds the line against three times as many British at Newport in the battle of August 29—the only battle fought in Rhode Island.

1779: Jean Baptiste Point Du Sable establishes the first permanent settlement at a site that would become Chicago.

November 12—twenty slaves petition the New Hampshire legislature to abolish slavery.

Rhode Island passes anti-slavery legislation including the prohibition of slave trade and the kidnapping of slaves.

1780: Pennsylvania passes the Gradual Abolition Act, the first abolition act in the United States.

Paul Cuffe and six other free blacks petition against taxation without representation. They refuse to pay their taxes because they are denied the right to vote.

The state constitution of Massachusetts effectively ends slavery in the state with the words, "All men are born free and equal, and have certain natural, essential, and unalienable rights; among which may be reckoned the right of enjoying and defending their lives and liberties."

Lemuel Haynes is commissioned to preach in the Congregational Church. He is the first black minister of this church.

James Armistead is granted permission by his owner to serve in the Continental Army. He becomes one of the most important spies of the American Revolution. Lafayette is his commander. After the war Armistead returns to being a slave. Although Lafayette writes a letter urging for his freedom, it is not until 1786 that the Virginia General Assembly intervenes and grants it.

1783: It is estimated that 20,000 blacks leave with the British troops after the Revolutionary War. Some are brought to freedom in England, Nova Scotia,

and Jamaica. Others are taken to the British West Indies and sold back into slavery.

Black populations reach one million in the colonies. More than half of all slaves reside in Virginia.

1784: Connecticut and Rhode Island pass gradual emancipation statutes.

Methodist Episcopal Churches in America denounce slavery and issue a mandate to members to free slaves. The adopted regulations are defeated and suspended a year later.

March 1—Jefferson's congressional committee proposes banning slavery everywhere in the United States after 1800. The proposal is narrowly defeated.

1785: The Rhode Island Society for Abolishing the Slave Trade is founded in Providence. Its purpose is to organize anti-slavery activities, assist free blacks in finding employment, discourage slave trade, provide education, and register deeds of manumission.

New York establishes Society for Promoting the Manumission of Slaves. It publicizes laws relating to slavery, distributes anti-slavery literature, and sponsors lectures by noted abolitionists.

Rev. Richard Allen, founder of the African Methodist Episcopal Church, is seized by a trader who makes a sworn affidavit that Allen is an escaped slave. Slavers frequently come north to kidnap freed blacks. Allen is freed after many prominent Philadelphians testify on his behalf. The slave trader is imprisoned for perjury.

Runaway slaves led by a person trained in military tactics by the British continue to harass and alarm residents of Savannah. They refer to themselves as the "King of England's soldiers."

1787: The U.S. Constitution legitimizes the institution of slavery in the laws of the United States and allows for the continuation of the African slave trade until 1808.

British establish a colony of free blacks in Sierra Leone in West Africa. Paul Cuffe, a mulatto ship captain from Massachusetts, establishes trade between the United States and Sierra Leone. He is a visible leader of the project to resettle many blacks there. The movement is continued by the American Colonization Society.

Blacks in Massachusetts, including Prince Hall, petition the General Court for funds to return to Africa. The petition is refused, but it is the first recorded effort by blacks to return to their homeland.

Richard Allen and Absalom Jones establish Philadelphia's Free African Society. The society is organized as a mutual aid society, a church, and a political structure.

Prince Hall establishes the Negro Masonic Order in the United States. This becomes the first black self-help fraternal institution in the United States.

Three-fifths Compromise is included in the U.S. Constitution. It allows the states to count three-fifths of the black population in determining political representation in the House of Representatives.

The Northwest Ordinance forbids the expansion of slavery into the area north and west of the Ohio River.

The London Society, an anti-slavery group, is organized.

New York Manumission Society establishes the African Free School. It is the first free secular school for blacks in the city.

1788: The Delaware Society for Promoting the Abolition of Slavery and for the Relief and Protection of Free Blacks and People of Colour Unlawfully Held in Bondage is organized.

New Jersey legislature passes an anti-slavery law that stipulates the confiscation of ships involved in the slave trade and prohibits the removal of slaves over twenty-one years of age rom the state.

Pennsylvania passes an act to fine slave owners 50 pounds when slave family members are separated for a distance greater than ten miles without the consent of family members.

Andrew Bryan, a slave, establishes the First African Baptist Church in Savannah, GA. He remains a slave until his owner's death when he purchases his freedom.

Free blacks in Massachusetts protest the forcible exportation of blacks from Boston to Martinique.

This prompts the Assembly to review the issue and declare slave trade illegal.

1792: Benjamin Banneker, a noted astronomer, inventor, and mathematician, becomes the first Black to publish an almanac—*Benjamin Banneker's Pennsylvania, Delaware, Maryland and Virginia Almanack and Ephemeris, for the Year of our Lord, 1792.* Banneker's heralded almanacs are published annually for the next ten years. It is the first scientific book written by a black man.

1793: Eli Whitney invents the cotton gin, a device that—by making cotton a much more profitable crop—contributes to the spread and entrenchment of slavery in the South.

The Fugitive Slave Act makes it a criminal offense to harbor a runaway slave or to interfere with the return of a slave to his or her owner.

1794: Bowdoin College is founded in Brunswick, Maine. It becomes a center for abolitionist sentiment for the Civil War.

First African Methodist Episcopal Church is founded by Richard Allen in Philadelphia.

France abolishes slavery in its colonial territories.

Amos Fortune, former slave, becomes a leading businessman in Jaffrey, New Hampshire. He founds the Jaffrey Social Library.

1795: Plans for a slave revolt in Point Coupee, Louisiana, are uncovered. Twenty-five slaves are executed.

1796: The African Methodist Episcopal Zion Church becomes the first black Methodist Church in New York City.

A grand jury in Charlotte, North Carolina accuses Quakers of inciting slave unrest and arson.

1797: First recorded anti-slavery petition to Congress. Four black slaves in North Carolina petition Congress in protest against a state law that requires illegally freed slaves to be returned to their masters. The slaves had been freed by their Quaker masters, who had purchased them for the purpose of freeing them, but this practice is illegal.

1798: Joshua Johnson, portrait painter, advertises in the Baltimore Intelligencer. He calls himself a "self taught genius." Johnson paints portraits of some of the most successful and influential white families in Maryland and Virginia.

1799: New York passes a gradual emancipation law-providing that all children born of slaves should be freed after reaching the age of twenty-eight.

1800: South Carolina becomes the clearing-house for slaves bound for plantations throughout the South. Two-fifths of the slaves who arrive in America during the early 1800s will pass through here.

Gabriel Prosser Conspiracy. On August 30 Prosser organizes 1,000 slaves and sets out to attack Richmond, Virginia with plans to establish his own government. Two house slaves betray the plot. Prosser and his family are hung on October 30 along with twenty-four other conspirators.

1801: Slave trade is reopened in the Louisiana Territory and flourishes.

Georgia passes a law with severe penalties for freeing slaves.

1802: The Ohio State Constitution prohibits slavery and involuntary servitude in the state. Blacks have the right to live in the state and receive the protection of its laws. However, they do not have the privileges of citizens.

France reinstitutes slavery.

1803: Free black settlement is established in Isle Breville, LA. Louis Metoyer, architect, designs the Melrose plantation house.

South Carolina passes legislation to reopen slave trade from South America and the West Indies.

Twenty blacks are arrested and convicted for burning eleven houses in New York City. They were planning to burn the entire city. Rioting follows their arrest.

1804: The Ohio General Assembly becomes the first in the country to enact laws intended to restricted the rights of free blacks. All blacks are required to produce certificates of freedom from a U.S. court before they can settle in the state.

1805: Virginia passes laws requiring all freed slaves to leave the state.

1806: John Parrish publishes *Remarks on the Slavery of the Black People.* This is one of the most complete treatments of slavery and the principles of democracy.

1807: George Bell, Nicholas Franklin, and Moses Liverpool, three former slaves, build the first schoolhouse for African-American children in Washington, D.C.

Congress passes a law that bars the importation of new slaves from Africa into the United States.

Louisiana legislature passes a law that defines slaves as "real estate."

1808: Federal law prohibiting the importation of new slaves into the United States goes into effect.

Louisiana court declares slave marriages illegal.

Peter Williams, Jr. publishes *An Oration on the Abolition of the Slave Trade; Delivered in The African Church, in the City of New York, January 1, 1808.* This is one of the first black anti-slavery speeches.

1809: Rev. Thomas Paul establishes the Abyssinian Baptist Church in New York City.

1810: Tom Molineaux becomes the first African American to compete for the heavyweight championship. He fights Englishman Tom Crib and is defeated after fighting thirty-nine rounds.

1811: Slave trade is reopened in the Louisiana Territory and flourishes.

Delaware passes a law that prevents free blacks from entering the state.

Pointe Coupee Revolt—five hundred slaves march toward New Orleans burning plantations on the way. Approximately 65 slaves are killed and their heads are displayed along the road from New Orleans as a deterrent to other slaves in the region.

Paul Cuffe makes his first trip to the English colony of Sierra Leone with a crew of nine black sailors. He becomes intrigued with the possibilities of beginning a three-way trade between the United States, England, and Sierra Leone.

1812: Free blacks fight in the War of 1812. At least 15 percent of all seamen during the war are black. Andrew Jackson calls upon free blacks to volunteer for the army.

Illinois Territory prohibits free blacks from immigrating into the territory.

James Forten along with Richard Allen and Absalom Jones help raise a volunteer regiment of African Americans to help defend Philadelphia from the British.

1815: Black veterans returning from the War of 1812 carry the news of freedom for blacks in Canada.

Blacks fight in the Battle of New Orleans, the last battle of the War of 1812.

1816: African Methodist Episcopal Church is established nationally.

U.S. troops attack and destroy a settlement of about three hundred fugitive slaves and about twenty Native Americans at Fort Blount on Apalachicola Bay, FL. This marks the beginning of other attacks to recapture runaway slaves.

The American Colonization Society is established to resettle free black Americans outside the territorial limits of the United States."

1817: Morris Brown is ordained a deacon in the African Methodist Episcopal Church.

Richard Allen leads blacks in Philadelphia in a protest against the efforts of the American Colonization Society.

1818: Georgia passes legislation prohibiting manumissions regardless of cause, reason, circumstance, or method in an effort to restrict or eliminate its free black populations. Other Southern states pass similar statutes.

Battle of Suwannee takes place in Florida. It is one of several battles of the First Seminole War between U.S. troops and Seminoles and blacks. Intent on both gaining territory for annexation and in setting a precedent for the destruction of runaway-slave communities as a deterrent for further defection, U.S. troops set fire to village and crops and capture Seminole Indians and Maroons.

1819: Congress passes the Anti-Slave Trade Act to curtail slave smuggling.

1820: Boston opens an elementary school for black children. Earlier Primus Hall established a separate school in his home in 1798.

The state of Maine grants the right to vote and the right to an education to all male citizens regardless of race.

U.S. Army prohibits blacks and mulattoes from enlisting.

Daniel Coker publishes his journal on procolonization, *Journal of Daniel Coker.*

Congress enacts the Missouri Compromise. This permits Missouri to enter the Union as a slave state and Maine as a free state.

1821: Alabama introduces slave-hunting patrols to prevent the escape of slaves.

The American Colonization Society purchases Cape Mesurado in Africa. It is located 225 miles south of Sierra Leone.

The Genius of Universal Emancipation begins publication in Mount Pleasant, Ohio. It is one of first abolitionist journals to be published.

Suffrage is extended to free black males in New York.

1822: Plans for one of the most elaborately planned slave revolts are uncovered—the Denmark Vesey Conspiracy. The plot reportedly involved 9,000 near Charleston, SC.

July—South Carolina State legislature passes laws to restrict the movement of free blacks. These laws are enacted in response to the Denmark Vesey affair.

James Varick is ordained as the first black bishop of the independent African Methodist Episcopal Zion Church.

1823: The U.S. Circuit Court in Washington, D.C. rules that if a slave is moved to a free state then the slave is free. The Court also rules that inhumane treatment of a slave is an indictable offense under common law.

Alexander Lucius Twilight becomes the first black to graduate from an American college.

Mississippi legislature prohibits blacks (free or slave) from congregating. It also prohibits educating blacks.

The Black Republic of Liberia is founded. The American Colonization Society believes that racial problems in America can be solved only by encouraging free blacks to emigrate.

1824: Illinois legislature rejects a proposal to establish slavery in the state.

Virginia expands its slave codes.

The Hardscrabble riots take place in Providence, Rhode Island. The riots leave black neighborhoods destroyed.

1825: Ira Aldridge, a black Shakespearean actor, appears on the London stage for the first time.

1826: Edward Jones receives a bachelor's degree from Amherst College.

John Brown Russwurm graduates from Bowdoin College.

1827: Samuel Cornish and John Brown Russwurm begin publication of the first black newspaper, Freedom's Journal.

Slavery is abolished in New York.

Publication of Nathaniel Paul's *An Address, Delivered on the Celebration of the Abolition of Slavery, in the State of New York, July, 1827,* one of the most important African-American orations regarding the abolition of slavery in New York.

Publication of Robert Roberts's *The House Servant's Directory, or a Monitor for Private Families . . . ,* the first cookbook written by an African American.

Morris Brown is ordained a deacon in the African Methodist Episcopal Church.

1828: Thomas D. Rice paints his face black and portrays a character called "Jump Jim Crow" on stage. Daniel Alexander Payne opens school for blacks in Charleston, SC.

1829: Georgia passes legislation that prohibits the education of slaves and free blacks.

Fearing the rapid growing African-American population, whites in Cincinnati insist on more rigid enforcement of the Black Laws and demand a bond payment. White mobs attack blacks who can not pay the bond. A three-day riot ensues and many blacks are killed and their communities are burned.

David Walker, a free black man, publishes a radical anti-slavery pamphlet *Appeal to the Coloured Citizens of the World.*

George Moses Horton, a poet and slave, publishes his first book of poetry.

1830: Josiah Henson escapes with his wife and family to Canada. Once there he begins working as conductor on the Underground Railroad.

Louisiana passes legislation making it a crime punishable by imprisonment or death to distribute abolitionist literature.

The first National Negro Convention, chaired by Richard Allen, meets at the Bethel AME Church in Philadelphia. Thirty-eight delegates devise ways to better their condition and respond to mob action against blacks created by colonization propaganda.

1831: Mississippi passes a law requiring freed slaves to leave the state within 90 days or be in danger of being sold back into slavery.

The first issue of William Lloyd Garrison's the Liberator is published. This is the most celebrated anti-slavery paper.

Nat Turner leads the most significant slave revolt in U.S. Turner's Rebellion claims more lives than any similar uprising. Some suggest that this uprising represents the first major battle of the long war to end slavery.

1832: A group of black women in Boston organize the African-American Female Intelligence Society for the purpose of educating "women of color."

Virginia enacts a law imposing the death penalty for both slaves and free blacks for certain offenses, including rape of a white woman, beating a white person, and inciting rebellion.

Pennsylvania rejects a petition from free blacks to admit their children to public schools.

First female anti-slavery society is organized by a group of black women in Salem, MA.

Maria Miller Stewart, abolitionist and feminist, delivers a public lecture in Boston. She is the first African-American woman to do so.

The New England Anti-Slavery Society is founded. It is first group to demand the unconditional and immediate abolition of slavery.

1833: Alabama prohibits free blacks and slaves to preach.

American Anti-Slavery Society is established.

1834: Vermont Anti-Slavery Society is formed by Quakers and others opposed to slavery.

A meeting of the American Anti-Slavery Society in New York is broken up by a proslavery mob.

Slavery is abolished throughout British colonies. Over 700,000 people are freed.

White mobs march into the black section of Philadelphia and commit acts of violence. Homes are burned, wrecked, and pulled down.

James G. Birney publishes *Letter on Colonization,* a powerful anticolonization tract.

1835: The Second Seminole War begins. During the course of the war over 1,500 American soldiers are killed and the Florida Seminoles, both Indian and black, are decimated and moved to the West.

A mob of white citizens uses oxen to pull the Noyes Academy, an integrated school, into a swamp just outside of Canaan, NH.

William Lloyd Garrison is paraded through the streets of Boston at the end of rope after a proslavery mob disrupted a meeting of the Boston Female Anti-Slavery Society. City officials are quickly denounced for the lack of protection they provide abolition meetings.

President Andrew Jackson recommends a law prohibiting the circulation of anti-slavery materials by mail.

1836: The Grimké sisters—Sarah and Angelina— both publish abolitionist tracts. Angelina wrote her *Appeal to the Christian Women of the South,* and her sister wrote *Epistle to the Clergy of the Southern States.*

Louisiana has more free black residents than any other southern state.

Alexander Lucius Twilight is elected to a one-year term in the Vermont state legislature.

The Women's Anti-Slavery Society in New York bars blacks from membership. Although the group works to abolish slavery, it is clear that the mixing of whites and blacks in public is not one of its goals.

Texas state constitution officially legalizes slavery.

Richard Hildreth publishes *The Slave: or Memoirs of Archy Moore,* the first American abolitionist novel.

1837: James McCune Smith, first African American to earn a medical degree, returns to New York and opens a medical practice.

The Weekly Advocate is first published in New York City. It is founded by Philip A. Bell and Robert Sears. Several months later Samuel Cornish takes editorial control and renames it the *Colored American.*

Cotton prices fall by nearly one-half on the New Orleans market. Many businesses fail. Since slaves are tied to cotton production, any major drop in the price of cotton forces farmers on marginal land and large plantation owners to sell their slaves in order to pay off debts.

Hosea Easton publishes *A Treatise on the Intellectual Character, and Civil and Political Condition of the Colored People of the U. States; And the Prejudice Exercised Towards Them,* the first full-length work on racial prejudice by an African American.

1838: Robert Purvis, a leading abolitionist, is given the honorary title of president of the Underground Railroad.

John C. Calhoun, advocate of states' rights, introduces resolutions in the U.S. Senate that affirm slavery as a legal institution.

The first black magazine, *Mirror of Liberty,* is published by David Ruggles.

Frederick Douglass escapes to freedom with the aid of Anna Murray, a free African-American woman.

1839: Samuel Ringgold Ward embarks on a career as an orator in abolition. He becomes known as the "black Daniel Webster."

The Amistad Mutiny occurs off the northern coast of Cuba in July. It is the best-known slave mutiny in U.S. history. The mutiny is led by a black man called Joseph Cinque.

Charles Bennet Ray becomes the editor of the *Colored American.*

Theodore Dwight Weld publishes *American Slavery As It is: Testimony of a Thousand Witnesses.* It is one of the most factual books written on the nature of slavery.

A group of moderate abolitionists form the Liberty Party in New York. Two black abolitionists Samuel Ringgold Ward and Henry Highland Garnet—are among the founders.

1840: World Anti-Slavery Convention takes place in London. Women delegates are denied seats. Charles Lenox Remond creates a sensation by chastising the assembly for their exclusionary policy and by withdrawing from the proceedings.

1841: The U.S. Supreme Court rules that African mutineer Joseph Cinque and his fellow slaves from the Amistad mutiny are free. Justice Joseph Story rules that they were kidnapped free men and thus have the same rights as other kidnapped persons.

The Liberty Party holds a national convention in New York City to reaffirm its militant anti-slavery position.

Street skirmishes in Cincinnati escalate into five days of anti-black rioting.

1842: Violence breaks out between Irish and free blacks seeking coal-mining jobs in Pennsylvania.

After five years of fighting the Second Seminole War ends.

Prigg v. Commonwealth of Pennsylvania—the U.S. Supreme Court rules that owners might recover their fugitive slaves from any state, and the states could neither help nor hinder the slaves.

Charles Lenox Remond becomes the first black to address the Massachusetts House of Representatives.

1843: Norbert Rillieux receives a patent for inventing the multiple effect vacuum pan evaporator.

The United States and Britain, according to the terms of the Webster-Ashburton Treaty, jointly agree to patrol Africa's west coast to intercept vessels involved in smuggling slaves to their territories.

The Vermont legislature blocks enforcement of the Fugitive Slave Act of 1793.

Henry Highland Garnet attends the National Convention of Colored Men and delivers his provocative "Address to the Slaves of the United States of America."

African Americans hold a state convention in Detroit, Michigan to discuss many of the problems confronting free blacks in the state. They draft a strongly worded petition against oppression and a call for blacks to defend their liberties.

1844: Macon Bolling Allen is admitted to the bar in the state of Maine, although he never practices law there.

African Americans in Boston hold mass meetings to protest segregated "Jim Crow" schools and other instances of inequality.

1845: Frederick Douglass publishes his *Narrative of the Life of Frederick Douglass,* and follows with a successful speaking of tour of Great Britain.

Florida joins the Union as a slave state and Iowa joins as a free state.

African Americans living in Massachusetts maintain a high degree of political and legal equality with whites. They are able to send their children to the public schools in Salem, New Bedford, Nantucket, Worcester, and Lowell. Only Boston maintains segregated schools.

William A. Leidesdorff is the first African American to become a diplomat. He is named vice-consul to the Mexican territory of Yerba Buena (San Francisco).

1846: The New Jersey legislature finally passes a law to abolish slavery. Blacks continue to protest the segregation of schools in Boston.

Sojourner Truth joins the anti-slavery circuit, traveling with Abby Kelly Foster, Frederick Douglass, William Lloyd Garrison, and British M.P. George Thompson.

The American Missionary Association is founded in New York. It is both a missionary and an abolitionist society.

1847: David John Peck becomes the first African American to graduate from an American medical school.

Frederick Douglass and Martin Robinson Delany begin publishing the *North Star,* an abolitionist newspaper.

1848: A posse of slavecatchers arrive in Marshall, Michigan seeking the Crosswaite family. They are jailed long enough for the fugitive slaves to flee across the border to Canada.

Ellen and William Craft make a dramatic escape to freedom. Ellen poses as a white slave owner and William as her male slave.

Charles L. Reason becomes the first black professor at a predominantly white university.

Mary Ellen Pleasant arrives in San Francisco during the Gold Rush. She opens a restaurant and boarding house where many prominent Californians stay.

John Van Surly De Grasse receives a medical degree with honors from Bowdoin College.

The legendary black explorer James Pierson Beckwourth discovers a pass in the Sierra Nevada, which is used by many pioneers to enter California, named Beckwourth Pass in his honor.

1849: Three states—Connecticut, New Jersey, and Ohio—hold conventions to discuss the conditions of free blacks and slaves.

Harriet Ross Tubman escapes from slavery, leaving behind her husband, who refused to accompany her. Shortly after her escape, Tubman becomes involved in the abolition movement and the Underground Railroad where she conducts over 300 African-American men, women, and children to freedom.

Publication of *Narrative of Henry Box Brown, Who Escaped from Slavery Enclosed in a Box 3 Feet Long and 2 Wide,* an account by an escaped slave.

Roberts v. City of Boston—court ruling that justifies the constitutionality of "Jim Crow" schools and the separate-but-equal doctrine later confirmed in Plessy v. Ferguson (1896). The case against the court's verdict was argued by abolitionist Charles Sumner and by Robert Morris, the nation's second licensed African-American lawyer.

1850: The phrase "sold down the river" becomes part of the American lexicon. During this time, slaves from older slave states could be sold to masters in the newer areas of the Cotton Belt along the Mississippi River where the living conditions were much harsher.

The narrative of Sojourner Truth is published.

Compromise of 1850 is adopted. The legislation contains five separate acts that affect African Americans. These include a new Fugitive Slave Law, the admissions of slaves into some of the new western territories, the admission of California to the Union as a free state, and the prohibition of the public sale of slaves in Washington, D.C.

Henry Walton Bibb publishes his autobiography, *Narrative of the Life and Adventures of Henry Bibb, an American Slave.*

1851: Emancipated slaves in Virginia lose or forfeit their rights if they remain in the state more than twelve months being granted their freedom.

William Cooper Nell publishes the pioneering historical work *Services of Colored Americans in the Wars of 1776 and 1812.*

The debut of Elizabeth Taylor Greenfield takes place before the Buffalo Musical Association. The Buffalo press dubs her "the Black Swan."

1852: Martin Robinson Delany publishes *The Condition, Elevation, Emancipation and Destiny of the Colored People of the United States, Politically Considered.* This work is cited for its nationalism and advocacy of emigration out of the United States.

Frederick Douglas delivers his "Independence Day Address." This is the first deliverance of a fully realized black declaration of inevitable independence.

Harriet Beecher Stowe's *Uncle Tom's Cabin* is published.

1853: Mary Ann Shadd Cary publishes the *Provincial Freeman,* a weekly Canadian newspaper.She is generally acknowledged to be the first woman newspaper publisher in Canada and the first black newspaperwoman in North America.

Publication of William Wells Brown's *Clotelle, or The President's Daugther,* the first novel published by an African American.

Sarah Mapps Douglass accepts a position with the Quaker-sponsored Institute for Colored Youth.

At Boston's Howard Athenaeum Sarah Parker Remond refuses to vacate a seat in the "whites-only" gallery during an opera. She is arrested and thrown down the stairs. She subsequently wins $500 in damages in a civil suit.

The National Council of Colored People is established.

1854: Frances Ellen Watkins Harper publishes her volume of verse, *Poems of Miscellaneous Subjects.* Many of the pieces in this volume deal with the horrors of slavery.

The Republican Party is founded, and its major goal is the abolition of slavery.

Anthony Burns, a fugitive slave, is arrested and held in jail. His arrest prompts Boston's Vigilance Committee to stage a mass protest meeting. A militant faction within meeting decides to lead an armed attack to rescue Burns. Federal troops suppress the mob. Burns is returned to his master, but his freedom is purchased the following year. This case encouraged many states to pass personal liberty acts that would block the enforcement of the Fugitive Slave Act.

Congress passes the Kansas-Nebraska Act. Settlers in these territories would be allowed to choose whether to permit slavery there.

James A. Healy is ordained a Catholic priest in Notre Dame Cathedral in Paris. He is the first black American ordained a Catholic priest.

Delegates from eleven states convene in Cleveland, Ohio to discuss and develop a national plan for black emigration. One of the most outspoken emigrationists is Martin Robinson Delany.

Frederick Douglass publishes *My Bondage and My Freedom.*

Kansas elects a proslavery legislature. Several thousand men from Missouri cross into Kansas and vote in the territorial election.

John Mercer Langston becomes one of the first African Americans elected to public office.

The governor of Massachusetts signs a bill ending "Jim Crow" schooling in Boston.

Kansas settlers opposing slavery hold a convention and petition for admission to the Union as a free state. They declare that the territorial proslavery legislature is illegal because Missourians supporting slavery voted in the election.

1855: Biddy Bridget Mason escapes from captivity and arranges to have her owner put on trial for owning slaves in California. Biddy and her family are manumitted. She settles in Los Angeles, where she works as a midwife and nurse.

1856: California's first black newspaper is founded and edited by Mifflin W. Gibbs.

James H. Adams, the governor of South Carolina, argues for the repeal of 1807 law prohibiting slave trade into the United States.

Wilberforce University is founded by the African Methodist Episcopal Church.

Bleeding Kansas—abolitionists and proslavery groups battle. Slavery supporters burn the Free State Hotel, wreck the newspaper, and ransack homes. John Brown and his followers retaliate by shooting and killing five slaveholding settlers.

Governor Daniel Woodson, a proslavery advocate, declares Kansas to be in a state of open insurrection.

1857: Disunion Convention meets in Worcester, MA. Delegates adopt the slogan "No union with slaveholders." The convention supports a split between slave states and free states.

James Buchanan is sworn in as the fifteenth president. In his inaugural speech he calls for tolerance of slavery for the purpose of keeping the states united.

Dred Scott v. Sanford—the U.S. Supreme Court rules that blacks are not citizens of the United States, thus upholding the Fugitive Slave Law and denying Congress the power to prohibit slavery in any federal territory. The Court declares that blacks have no rights that a white man is required to respect.

In response to the Dred Scott decision New Hampshire passes legislation that does not deprive any person—regardless of color—of citizenship.

Publication of Frank J. Webb's *The Garies and Their Friends,* the second novel by an African American.

1858: Voters in the Kansas Territory reject the proslavery constitution.

Arkansas requires free blacks to choose either exile or enslavement.

John Brown holds an anti-slavery convention in Chatham, Canada. The group draws up a constitution for a nation of liberated slaves to be set up in the mountains of Virginia. Brown plans to provoke a general slave uprising and lead slaves and free blacks into the mountains. His first strike is to be Harpers Ferry, VA.

Abraham Lincoln and Stephen A. Douglas complete their final debate while campaigning for the U.S. Senate. Douglas supports a state's right to choose whether or not to allow slavery, and Lincoln argues that all people are born with the right to life, liberty, and the pursuit of happiness.

William Wells Brown's *The Escape: or, A Leap for Freedom. A Drama, in Five Acts,* is the first play published by an African American.

1859: Martin R. Delany signs a treaty with the Alake of Abeokuta, in what is now western Nigeria, providing for the settlement of educated African Americans. Before the first group of settlers can leave for West Africa the Civil War breaks out.

A survey of the free black population is published in this year stating that 2,900 black men served on board whaleboats. African Americans could find work in this industry and were paid wages according to rank—not color. Integration varied from vessel to vessel.

Mississippi resolves to secede from the Union if a Republican is elected president.

"Aunt" Clara Brown journeys to Colorado with a wagon train of gold prospectors. She opens a laundry in Central City, serves as a nurse, and organizes the city's first Sunday school.

John Brown raids Harpers Ferry. He attacks and seizes arms from the United States Arsenal. He is captured and stands trial for treason. Brown is found guilty of murder and conspiring with slaves to create an insurrection.

Publication of Harriet E. Wilson's *Our Nig: or; Sketches from the Life of a Free Black in a Two-Story White House, North, Showing that Slavery's Shadows Fall Even There,* perhaps the first novel written by an African-American woman.

1860: The Republican Party nominates Abraham Lincoln as its presidential candidate.

The Democratic Party is split over the issue of slavery. It breaks into two separate political entities.

Congress adopts a set of resolutions sponsored by southern congressmen clarifying the status of slavery.

A slave conspiracy is uncovered in Plymouth, NC. The insurrection is planned by a small group of slaves who hope to encourage hundreds of others to join them. A slave betrays them.

Lincoln is elected president of the United States.

South Carolina secedes from the Union. Federal troops move to Fort Sumter several days after the secession. In response to this federal action, the South Carolina militia seizes other federal installations in Charleston.

1861: The remaining Southern states follow South Carolina in seceding from the Union and join the Confederacy.

April 12—Confederate forces open fire on Fort Sumter in Charleston harbor. This act begins the Civil War.

After the attack on Fort Sumter, President Lincoln calls for 75,000 volunteers to serve in the Union army. Although many free blacks try to enlist, they are not allowed to participate.

May 6—the Confederate Congress officially declares war on the United States.

May 23—General Benjamin Butler declares that slaves who enter his lines are "contraband." Since

Virginia claims to be a foreign country, the Fugitive Slave Act cannot be enforced. In two months' time about 900 runaway slaves seek their freedom behind his lines. Butler uses the former slaves to build roads and fortifications, unload vessels, and store provisions.

August 6—Congress passes the first Confiscation Act. Any runaway slave who has been used to aid the Confederacy can be granted freedom once under the control of the Union army.

August 30—General John C. Frémont issues a proclamation of emancipation, freeing the slaves in Missouri. On September 2, President Lincoln declares this null and void.

Mary S. Peake becomes the first teacher to be hired in the first American Missionary Association's school.

September 25—the Secretary of the Navy authorizes the enlistment of slaves to fight in the Civil War.

Harriet A. Jacobs publishes *Incidents in the Life of a Slave Girl,* the most comprehensive antebellum autobiography by an African-American woman.

1862: Lincoln meets with Frederick Douglass and other black leaders to discuss the emigration of free blacks to Central America. He asks the black leaders to recruit volunteers for a government-sponsored colonization project. Douglass is outraged by Lincoln's request. He responds, "This is our country as much as it is yours, and we will not leave it."

Jefferson Davis is elected president of the Confederacy.

Nashville becomes the first Confederate state capital to fall under the control of Union forces.

Susie Baker King Taylor joins the First South Carolina Volunteer Regiment, an all black regiment. She becomes the unit laundress and volunteer nurse.

Lincoln recommends a plan to Congress that would offer aid to any state promising gradual abolition of slavery.

Free blacks in New York organize a National Freedmen's Relief Association to help slaves adjust to their new freedom. Similar associations are established in Chicago, Cincinnati, and Philadelphia.

Penn School is established for freed slaves on St. Helena Island off South Carolina within weeks after its capture by Union troops. African Americans are trained in agriculture and home economics.

Contraband slaves and free blacks seeking protection and freedom swell the Union forces.

Slavery is abolished in the District of Columbia. Slave owners are to be compensated at the rate of $300 per slave.

New Orleans, the largest seaport in the South, falls into Union hands.

Union troops take Norfolk, Virginia, and it becomes a center for black refugees from the countryside.

The First South Carolina Volunteer Regiment is officially mustered.

Robert Smalls, a black navy pilot, is pressed into service by the Confederate government. He is made wheelsman of the steamboat the Planter. While the white crew members are on shore, Smalls seizes the opportunity to steer the ship, containing his family and a small group of other slaves, to Union lines.

President Lincoln signs a bill outlawing slavery in the territories but not in the states.

Congress authorizes an act that allows the use of blacks in the Union army.

1863: Frederick Douglass becomes a major recruiter for the Union army. After meeting several times with Lincoln, he advises blacks to join in large numbers as an expression of their patriotism. In the March issue of *Douglass' Monthly,* he publishes "Men of Color, to Arms!"—a call for black recruitment.

The first clash between officially recruited black Union troops and Confederate soldiers occurs at the Battle of Hundred Pines. The black soldiers hold their ground and repel Confederate troops.

The Emancipation Proclamation is issued. Its purpose is to deplete Southern manpower reserve in slaves. It frees only those slaves residing in the territory in rebellion. It does not abolish slavery in loyal states. Floods of fugitive slaves begin to enter Union lines in Virginia, Tennessee, and along the southern coast.

Representatives from Freedmen's Aid Societies in Boston, New York, and Philadelphia lead a missionary expedition to aid contraband slaves in Hilton Head, South Carolina.

Daniel Alexander Payne is named president of Wilberforce University, the first black-controlled college in the United States.

The U.S. War Department establishes the Bureau of Colored Troops to handle all recruitment of black regiments.

Harriet Tubman serves the Union cause as a spy and guide. She receives a formal commendation from the secretary of war for her work in the Sea Islands as a nurse and daring scout.

Draft riot erupts in New York City. The Colored Orphan Asylum is burned down, almost 100 people are killed, and many blacks flee the city. Immigrant workers vent their racial prejudices and economic fears upon the city's black population.

The Fifty-fourth Massachusetts Volunteers lead the charge against Fort Wagner, South Carolina. It is the first black regiment raised in the North, and they display extreme bravery in their assault of the fort.

Black troops protest discriminatory wages. The Fifty-fourth regiment refuses pay for eighteen months rather than accept less wages.

1864: William Walker, a black sergeant in the Third South Carolina Regiment is shot by order of a court-martial for leading a protest against unequal pay for black soldiers.

Three black regiments fight in a battle in Olustee, Florida. Three hundred of the black soldiers are killed.

Rebecca Lee graduates from the New England Female Medical College. She becomes the first African-American woman to work as a physician.

April 12 Fort Pillow in west Tennessee the site of one of the most controversial battles of the Civil War. About three hundred black troops, many of whom attempted to surrender, and their family members are massacred by the Confederate troops.

The First Kansas Colored Volunteers storm the Confederate lines at Poison Spring, Arkansas. They suffer heavy casualties. Those who are cap-

tured are murdered. African-American troops are not taken prisoner as their white counterparts are.

Black soldiers participate in the ten-month siege started in Petersburg, Virginia. Grant wants a quick engagement to cut off rail supplies to Richmond, but Lee wants to prolong the siege hoping the North will tire of the casualties and accept a peace settlement. Twelve hundred of the sixty-three hundred casualties are black soldiers. The engagement ends one week before the final Southern surrender.

The Battle for Chaffin's Farm, Richmond, VA— General Benjamin Butler uses nine black regiments in this battle. The Union forces are victorious. More than 500 black soldiers are killed or wounded, and nine receive the Congressional Medal of Honor for bravery during the battle.

A group of 150 black men hold a convention in Syracuse, New York to discuss the future of their race. Frederick Douglass is elected as their chairman. They establish the National Equal Rights League and elect John Mercer Langston as the president.

1865: Fewer than a hundred African Americans become offciers in the Union army, and not one black receives a naval commission. Major Martin Robinson Delany serves as a surgeon, as does Alexander Thomas Augusta.

By the end of the Civil War the Union army has more than 386,000 African Americans enlisted. Nearly 37,000 blacks die during the war.

The Tennessee State Convention of Negroes convenes in Nashville. A petition is submitted to the U.S. Senate protesting the seating of the Tennessee delegates in Congress until the state legislature secures the rights of blacks as freemen.

African Americans in Norfolk, Virginia hold mass meetings and demand equal rights and ballots.

The Freedman's Savings and Trust Company, the first bank for blacks, opens in Washington, D.C.

Patrick Frances Healy receives his Ph.D. from the University of Louvain in Belgium.

Illinois repeals its black laws.

John Sweat Rock becomes the first black lawyer admitted to practice before the U.S. Supreme Court.

Henry Highland Garnet is invited to deliver a memorial sermon in the U.S. House of Representatives commemorating passage of the Thirteenth Amendment.

Black troops of the Fifty-fifth Massachusetts Regiment march into Charleston, and they are greeted with the cheers of the city's black population.

Congress establishes the Bureau of Refugees, Freedmen and Abandoned Lands. It is created to help blacks adjust to their new freedom.

Jefferson Davis signs a bill authorizing the use of 300,000 slaves as soldiers in the Confederate army. The order comes too late to influence the outcome of the war.

Appomattox Courthouse—Robert E. Lee surrenders to Ulysses S. Grant. The Civil War is over.

President Johnson reveals his reconstruction plan. Reconstruction began long before the Confederacy's final surrender. Lincoln introduced a Reconstruction Plan in December of 1863.

Planters meet to fix wages and set conditions of employment regarding blacks. These meetings take place in Virginia counties and other states where black labor is plentiful.

June 19—Union forces arrive in Galveston, and the news spreads rapidly throughout the state. African Americans are declared free and celebrate emancipation on this day, known as Juneteenth.

Mississippi establishes black codes restricting the rights and movement of blacks in response to President Johnson's Restoration program. Legislatures in other southern states begin to formalize such black codes.

Committee on Reconstruction is established, and slavery is made illegal in the United States.

Fisk Free School opens in Nashville, TN. It is established by E. M. Cravath, and E. P. Smith of the American Missionary Association and John Ogden of the Freedman's Bureau to produce qualified black teachers. In 1867 it is incorporated as Fisk University.

1866: Ku Klux Klan is formed by Confederate army veterans in Pulaski, Tennessee to resist Reconstruction in Confederate states.

Sharecropping system is adopted throughout the South. Freedmen, who could not buy or rent land, were willing to work for a "share" of the crop.

Congress passes the Southern Homestead Act, which opens federal lands in Florida, Alabama, Mississippi, Louisiana, and Arkansas for homesteading. About 4,000 black families bought land, however few were able to hold on to it because they lacked capital.

A delegation of black leaders, including Frederick Douglass, meets with President Andrew Johnson. They present their views on the personal safety and protection of the rights of African Americans, and they solicit the president's views. Johnson is opposed to any federal laws to protect freed slaves and feels that the states have to solve problems within their own boundaries.

Civil Rights Bill of 1866 grants blacks the rights and privileges of American citizenship.

Race riot erupts in Memphis after a white policeman confronts a group of black men and strikes one. The policeman is then struck by a black man. News of the incident spreads through the city and a large mob of whites roam through the black community setting fires to schools, churches, and homes. Many blacks are beaten, wounded, or killed.

Eight of the former Confederate states enact laws to limit the freedom of the black labor force.

1867: Rebecca Cole becomes the second black woman to receive an M.D. and accepts an invitation to work with Elizabeth Blackwell to work in the New York Infirmary for Women and Children.

Howard University is chartered. It soon becomes an education center for free blacks.

Morehouse College is founded. It is noted for its rigorous academic standards.

Nebraska becomes the thirty-seventh state and black settlers flock because the land is cheap.

Congress passes several Reconstruction Acts to provide for political participation of blacks in southern state politics.

The Knights of the White Camellia are founded. It becomes one of the largest terrorist organizations in the Reconstruction South.

1868: Francis Lous Cardozo becomes South Carolina's secretary of state. John W. Menard of Louisiana is elected the first black congressman, but he is never seated.

South Carolina Constitutional Convention meets in Charleston. It is the first assembly of its kind to have a black majority.

Hampton Institute is founded by Samuel Chapman Armstrong. It is an agricultural and industrial college for blacks.

Pinckney B. S. Pinchback and James J. Harris become the first African-American delegates to attend a Republican convention.

Alabama, Florida, Louisiana, North Carolina, and South Carolina are readmitted to the Union.

Fourteenth Amendment is ratified—declaring blacks full citizens.

1869: George L. Ruffin becomes the first black person to earn a law degree from Harvard University.

The Union Pacific Railroad employs three hundred black workers.

President Grant appoints Ebenezer Don Carlos Bassett U.S. minister to Haiti and the Dominican Republic.

1870: Alonzo J. Ransier is elected lieutenant governor of South Carolina. He becomes the first African American to hold a high executive post in South Carolina.

Benjamin S. Turner is elected to Congress. He is the first black congressman from Alabama.

Robert Brown Elliott is elected to the House of Representatives from South Carolina. He serves on several key committees, including the Committee on Education and Labor.

James W. Smith becomes the first black student admitted to West Point. However he does not graduate. He is court-martialed and forced to leave the academy.

The *New Era* newspaper, edited by John Sella Martin, is founded.

The last of the former Confederate states are readmitted to the Union.

Jefferson Franklin Long becomes the first Georgian seated and the second African American to ever serve in the House of Representatives.

The Fifteenth Amendment, granting blacks the right to vote, is ratified.

Congress passes the first Enforcement Act to enforce the Fifteenth Amendment because terrorist tactics are being used throughout the South to keep blacks from voting.

Richard T. Greener becomes the first black to graduate from Harvard University.

Robert Carlos DeLarge is elected U.S. representative from South Carolina.

Jonathan Jasper Wright becomes the only African American to serve on a state supreme court in South Carolina during Reconstruction.

Joseph H. Rainey is elected to the House of Representatives from South Carolina. He is the first African American member of the House.

1871: A group of black farmers form the Alabama Negro Labor Union to consider the plight of black workers in the state.

Ku Klux Klan massacres thirty blacks in Meridian, MS.

The Forty-second Congress convenes with five black congressmen Joseph H. Rainey, Robert Carlos DeLarge, Robert Brown Elliott, Benjamin S. Turner, and Joseph T. Wells.

Jefferson F. Long becomes the first black to address the House. He spoke in opposition to granting leniency for ex-Confederates. "If this House removes the disabilities of disloyal men by modifying the test-oath," he warns, "I venture to prophesy you will again have trouble from the very same men who gave you trouble before."

Congress passes the Second Enforcement Act or the Ku Klux Klan Act—giving federal officers and courts control of voter registration and voting in congressional elections. The law is designed to enforce the Fifteenth Amendment.

James Milton Turner is appointed U.S. Minister to Liberia. He becomes the first black American diplomat to an African country.

Josiah Thomas Walls takes his seat in the House of Representatives to become Florida's first black Congressman.

Congress passes the Third Enforcement Act regarding Klan conspiracy as rebellion against the United States and giving broad powers to the president to suspend the writ of habeas corpus and declare martial law in rebellious areas.

The Federal government's campaign against the Klan is a success. Klansmen are convicted for murder, violence, and interfering with the rights of black and Republican voters.

P. B. S. Pinchback becomes Lieutenant governor of Louisiana.

1872: Republicans win a slate of state offices in South Carolina. Elected officials include Henry E. Hayne, Francis L. Cardozo, Henry W. Purvis, and Richard H. Gleaves.

Richard Harvey Cain is elected to the House of Representatives.

African Americans win several major offices in Louisiana including: C. C. Antoine, P. G. Deslonde, W. B. Brown.

Charlotte E. Ray graduates from Howard University's Law School, becoming the first African-American woman to receive a law degree from any law school in the nation.

Five hundred Klansmen are arrested in South Carolina as part of the anti-Klan campaign. Only fifty-five are convicted in federal court.

Congress passes the Amnesty Act that allows all but a few hundred Confederate leaders to hold elective offices.

Freedman's Bureau is closed.

James Thomas is elected to Congress. He is the second black representative from Alabama.

P. B. S. Pinchback becomes acting governor of Louisiana during the impeachment of Gov. Henry Clay Warmoth.

1873: Macon B. Allen is elected judge of the Inferior Court of Charleston, SC.

Seven African Americans are elected to the Forty-third U.S. Congress. They are Richard Harvey Cain, Alonzo J. Ransier, James Thomas Rapier,

Josiah T. Walls, and John R. Lynch. U. S. Supreme Court begins to chip away at the power of the Fourteenth Amendment in a series of decisions in the *Slaughterhouse Cases.* The court rules that the Fourteenth Amendment protects federal civil rights not the civil rights belonging exclusively to the states.

In Mississippi African Americans are elected to offices on the local and state level including lieutenant governor.

Mifflin W. Gibbs is elected city judge in Little Rock, Arkansas, thereby becoming the first African-American judge in the United States.

1874: In Louisiana after a disputed gubernatorial election, white and black factions fight for control of the government. Riots and armed confrontations break out at Liberty Place in New Orleans, at the Conshattau Massacre in Red River parish, and at the Colfax Massacre in Grant Parish—where more than sixty black men, women, and children are killed.

Edward Alexander Bouchet becomes the first black to graduate from Yale University with honors as well as election to Phi Beta Kappa national honor society.

Jeremiah Haralson is elected to the U.S Congress representing Alabama.

John A. Hyman becomes the first African American congressman from North Carolina.

Robert Smalls is elected to the U.S. Congress. Throughout his career, he made significant contributions as a soldier and politician.

Blanche K. Bruce is elected the first African-American senator from Mississippi.

Freedman's Bank fails after years of mismanagement. The bank's monetary losses are especially tragic because they represented one of the first attempts of the newly freed slaves to grasp economic security and equal citizenship.

Patrick Francis Healy is installed as president of Georgetown University.

Sixteen blacks are lynched in Tennessee.

Democrats and KKK members start a riot in Vicksburg, MS. Seventy-five blacks are killed.

1875: Oliver Lewis wins the Kentucky Derby. Black jockeys dominate horseracing at this time.

Tennessee adopts Jim Crow Laws.

Grant sends federal troops to Vicksburg, MS. White Democrats and the KKK continue to use intimidation tactics against blacks and Republicans.

Congress passes the Civil Rights act of 1875 prohibiting discrimination in public accommodations.

James Healy is named the first black Catholic Bishop of Portland Maine.

First convention of black journalists convenes in Cincinnati, Ohio. J. Stella Martin, Mifflin Gibbs, and Henry Turner are among those who attend.

Racial conflicts erupt in Mississippi in September. White Democrats and KKK members attack and kill blacks and Republicans.

November—Democrats win many state and local government elections throughout the South. Their strategy to suppress the black vote through violence, economic intimidation, and murder is successful at restoring white supremacy. The reconstruction governments in South Carolina and Louisiana are defeated.

1876: Edward Bouchet becomes the first African American to be awarded a doctorate by a major American university.

President Grant sends federal troops to South Carolina to restore order after widespread racial rioting and white terrorism erupts.

United States v. Reese—Supreme Court rules that the Fifteenth Amendment does not confer the right to suffrage but only allows the government to provide a punishment for denying the vote to anyone based on race, color, or previous condition of servitude.

Supreme Court denies punishment to the people who had broken up a black political meeting in Louisiana. In the case of the *United States v. Cruikshank,* the court decides that the right of suffrage is not a necessary attribute of citizenship and that the right to vote in the states comes from the states.

Terrorism and race riots erupt in South Carolina.

1877: The Forty-fifth Congress convenes with three African Americans Blanche K. Bruce is a senator for Mississippi and Richard Cain and Robert Smalls are representatives from South Carolina.

Frederick Douglass becomes the first black to receive a major government appointment when he is named U.S. Marshall for the District of Columbia.

Henry Ossian Flipper becomes the first black graduate of West Point.

Federal troops withdraw from Southern states.

1878: James A. Bland, a songwriter, publishes "Carry Me Back to Ole Virginny." He is considered to be one of the most successful composers of popular songs in the United States at this time.

Publication of James Monroe Trotter's *Music and Some Highly Musical People,* the first historical survey of black music by an African American.

Supreme Court overturns a Louisiana law prohibiting racial segregation in the *Hall v. De Cut* decision.

1879: Due to escalating violence thousands of blacks leave the South and migrate to the North and West.

Benjamin "Pap" Singleton organizes mass migrations to Kansas.

John M. Langston and Richard T. Greener are convinced that they should migrate to the West because the federal government will not actively support blacks in the South.

White terrorists fearing the loss of cheap labor set up a military-style blockade on the Mississippi River to prevent African Americans from migrating to Kansas.

Whites meet with African Americans throughout the South, and they promise to improve conditions for blacks in order to keep them from leaving.

Exodusters are about 20,000 southern African Americans who migrate spontaneously to Kansas from Mississippi, Louisiana, Texas, Kentucky, and Tennessee in the spring of 1879.

Mary Eliza Mahoney becomes the first African American woman to graduate from the nursing program in the United States.

1880: The first successful agricultural cooperative association settlement is established in the Sea Islands off the coast of South Carolina.

Southern University and the Agricultural and Mechanical College are chartered in New Orleans for blacks.

In *Strauder v. West,* the Supreme Court rules it unconstitutional to exclude blacks from jury duty.

1881: The Forty-seventh Congress convenes with two black representatives—Robert Smalls and John R. Lynch.

Publication of John Patterson Smapson's *Mixed Races: Their Environment, Temperament, Heredity, and Phrenology,* the first full-length study of phrenology by an African American.

Henry Highland Garnet is appointed minister to Liberia.

Tuskegee University is founded, and Booker T. Washington is recommended to organize the school.

1882: Lewis H. Latimer patents his most important invention—a carbon filament that increased the brightness and longevity of the light bulb.

A bill is proposed in the U.S. Congress to use federal lands to equalize educational opportunities for blacks and whites in the South. It is defeated.

Gray v. Cincinnati and Southern Railroad Company— a federal court rules that separation of races on trains is legal as long as accommodations are equal.

Vigilantism continues in the South—forty-nine blacks are lynched. The *Chicago Tribune* begins recording lynching.

George Washington Williams publishes his two-volume *History of the Negro Race in American, 1619–1880.* It is the first serious work in this field.

John Fox Slater creates the Slater Fund when he donates one million dollars for the schooling of former slaves and their children in the South.

1883: Isaac Murphy, a black jockey, wins a remarkable 51 out of 133 races.

Jan E. Matzaliger receives a patent for an automatic shoe laster that revolutionizes the American shoe industry.

George L. Ruffin, the first black to earn a law degree from Harvard University, is appointed city judge of the District Court of Charlestown. He is the first black to hold this position.

U. S. Supreme Court declares the Civil Rights Act of 1875 unconstitutional.

Forty-eighth Congress convenes with two African Americans James E. O'Hara of North Carolina and Robert Smalls of South Carolina.

Black citizens in Ohio meet for a State Convention to discuss continued white terrorism in the South.

1884: Benjamin Tucker Tanner establishes the *A.M.E. Church Review,* a quarterly journal focusing on African American issues.

The Medical Chirurgical Society of the District of Columbia, the first African American medical society, is established.

Black newspapers publish letters and advertisements encouraging migration to and settlement in the West.

Moses Fleetwood Walker makes his debut as a catcher on the Toledo team of the American Baseball Association. He is the first black player in major league baseball.

T. Thomas Fortune, a prominent black journalist, establishes the New York Freeman.

1885: Frank Thompson organizes the best of the all-black professional baseball teams—the Cuban Giants.

Forty-ninth Congress convenes with two black representatives—James O'Hara and Robert Smalls.

George Washington Williams is named United States minister to Haiti.

Lynching continues in Louisiana.

Augustus Tolton, the son of two escaped slaves, is ordained a Catholic priest. He is considered by some to be the first fully black ordained priest.

The Healy brothers who were ordained before him were the sons of an Irish father and a mulatto mother.

1887: Fiftieth Congress convenes with no black members.

Lynching continues in the South. Seventy are reported in this year. The black press continues to report these acts of oppression.

Granville T. Woods patents an Induction Telegraph System.

New York Age editor T. Thomas Fortune calls for the formation of the National Afro-American League. The league's goals are to seek the elimination of disfranchisement, lynching, segregation on railroads and in public accommodations, and abuse of black prisoners.

1888: Mound Bayou, Mississippi, considered by many to be the first all African American town, is founded by Isaiah Thornton Montgomery and Benjamin Green.

Henry P. Cheatham is elected to the Fifty-first Congress as a representative from North Carolina.

Sixty-nine lynchings are reported this year.

John M. Langston is elected to the U.S. Congress from Virginia but is denied his seat until 1890 when the House adjudicates in his favor.

The Capital Savings Bank of Washington, D.C. opens. It is the first African-American commercial bank.

1889: Number of lynchings reported this year escalates to ninety-four.

Charles Young graduates from West Point. He is the third African American to graduate from the military academy.

The Fifty-first Congress convenes with three black congressmen—Henry P. Cheatham, John M. Langston, and Thomas E. Miller.

1890: The "Grandfather clause" is introduced into Mississippi's constitution to keep blacks from voting. Voting is restricted to those who are descendants of persons who had voted prior to 1866. In addition a poll tax and literacy tests are adopted. This is the first attempt to eliminate black voting. By World War I almost all the ex-Confederate states had adopted some form of black disfranchisement.

Edwin P. McCabe and his wife, Sarah, move to Oklahoma and together with Charles Robbins and William L. Eagleson found Langston City, an all-black community.

The lynching of black Americans continues—eighty-five are reported this year.

T. Thomas Fortune becomes a key figure in the National Afro-American League, an early and important vehicle for civil rights agitation. He is elected secretary at the 1890 meeting.

Thomas E. Miller leaves his congressional seat. Miller's election is contested by his white opponent, and the South Carolina Supreme Court rules in the Democrat's favor.

1891: The Georgia legislature passes laws to segregate streetcars.

Lynchings continue to increase. There are 113 reported this year.

Danile Hale Williams establishes Provident Hospital in Chicago. It is the first black-owned hospital in the United States, and it has an interracial staff of doctors.

The Fifty-second Congress convenes with only one black congressman—Henry P. Cheatham, NC.

1892: William H. Lewis is the first African American selected for Walter Camp's All-American football team.

There are 161 lynchings reported this year.

Ida B. Wells-Barnett becomes editor and co-owner of the *Memphis Free Speech.*

The Baltimore Afro-American newspaper is first published. This newspaper is the oldest family-owned black publication in America.

Paul Laurence Dunbar publishes his first book, *Oak and Ivy.*

1893: Henry Ossawa Turner, painter and illustrator, begins depicting genre scenes of African-American life. His best know genre study is *The Banjo*

Lesson, which depicts an older musician teaching his art to a young boy.

The Fifty-third Congress convenes with only black member George W. Murray from South Carolina.

Daniel Hale Williams performs the first successful open-heart surgery.

1894: Harry T. Burleigh, singer and composer, becomes the baritone soloist in St. George's Episcopal Church in New York.

1895: Mary Church Terrell becomes the first African American to serve on the Washington, D.C. School Board.

Frederick Douglass, abolitionist, journalist, orator, and social reformer, dies. He fully understood and vividly personified his people's struggle from slavery to freedom, from obscurity and poverty to recognition and respectability.

W. E. B. Du Bois becomes the first African American to receive a doctorate in history at Harvard University.

Black lynchings continue—there are 113 reported this year.

Booker T. Washington delivers his famous "Atlanta Compromise" speech. It is the best single statement of Washington's philosophy of racial advancement and his political accommodation with the predominant racial ideology of this time.

South Carolina adopts a new constitution that includes an "Understanding Clause" designed to strip blacks of any remaining political rights.

Austin M. Curtis becomes the first black physician on the medical staff of Chicago's Cook County Hospital.

1896: George Washington Carver becomes the director of the agricultural department at Tuskegee Normal and Industrial Institute.

Justice John Marshall Harlan of the Supreme Court writes a dissenting opinion of the Jim Crow laws. He states that Jim Crow laws deprived black citizens of equal protection of the law.

Lynching of blacks continues—seventy-eight blacks are lynched this year.

The National Association of Colored Women is founded. Mary Church Terrell is elected the first president. The organization is mainly concerned with educational and health issues and ending the practice of lynching.

Plessy v. Ferguson—the Supreme Court upholds an 1890 Louisiana statute that required railroads to provide separate but equal accommodations for blacks and whites, and forbade persons from riding in cars not assigned to their race. This ruling gave constitutional sanction to virtually all forms of racial segregation in the United States until after World War II.

Paul Laurence Dunbar's third collection of verse, *Lyrics of Lowly Life,* is published.

1897: George Henry White is the only black congressman. He attempts to introduce the country's first anti-lynching legislation. Andrew J. Beard, inventor, receives a patent for his most important invention—a car coupler for automatically hooking railroad cars together.

One hundred and twenty-three blacks are lynched this year.

The American Negro Academy is founded to promote African American literature, science, art, and higher learning.

A Trip to Coontown, a musical comedy written by Bob Cole, is produced, directed, and managed by blacks. It runs for three years.

1898: Black troops fight in the Spanish-American War.

There are 101 lynchings reported this year.

Samuel W. Rutherford organizes the National Benefit Life Insurance Company in Washington, D.C.

Race riot erupts in Wilmington, North Carolina, and eight blacks are killed when white supremacists drive black officeholders out of office.

South Carolina passes legislation requiring racial segregation about trains.

Louisiana introduces a grandfather clause that specifies that a person could register to vote if his father or grandfather had been eligible to vote on January 1, 1867, or if he or an ancestor had served in either the Confederate army or the Union army.

1899: John Merrick and associates open the North Carolina Mutual and Provident Insurance Company.

Eight blacks are massacred in Palmetto, Georgia.

Charles W. Chesnutt publishes *The Conjure Woman,* the first book of serious fiction by an African American to garner commercial success.

W. E. B. Du Bois publishes *The Philadelphia Negro,* the most significant sociological inquiry written by an African American up to this time.

Scott Joplin releases one of his finest works, "Maple Leaf Rag."

Lynching continues—eighty-five blacks are reported lynched this year.

1900: Louis Armstrong is born in New Orleans.

Black congressman George H. White introduces the first bill in Congress that would make lynching a federal crime. It never comes to a vote.

Booker T. Washington organizes the National Negro Business League in Boston, MA.

The Black National Anthem is performed for the first time on February 12 at a celebration of Lincoln's birthday. Called "Lift Ev'ry Voice and Sing." The anthem is written by the African-American poet and political leader James Weldon Johnson with his brother John Rosamond Johnson.

Virginia passes legislation segregating trains and calls a new constitutional convention aimed at erasing Reconstruction-era civil rights gains.

One hundred six blacks are reported lynched in this year.

1901: The *Boston Guardian* is founded. Published by William Monroe Trotter and George Forbes, the newspaper is a response to the more conservative politics of Booker T. Washington.

Booker T. Washington publishes *Up From Slavery: An Autobiography.*

1902: Virginia establishes a literacy test and a poll tax that effectively disenfranchises the African-American population.

1903: W. E. B. Du Bois publishes *The Souls of Black Folk: Essays and Sketches,* which famously asserts

that "the problem of the Twentieth Century is the problem of the color line." The book also openly attacks Booker T. Washington's position that blacks should give up the right to vote and to a. liberal education in return for white friendship and support.

Maggie Lena Walker opens the St. Luke Penny Savings Bank in Richmond, Virginia, becoming the first African-American woman in America to own and operate a bank.

Boley, Oklahoma, is founded. It is one of many black towns formed in the South as a response to escalating racism.

1904: Mary McLeod Bethune establishes the Daytona Educational and Industrial Institute for girls. It is the first black school in Florida to offer education beyond the elementary grades.

George Poage, representing the Milwaukee Athletic Club is the firs African-American Olympic medalist, winning a bronze medal in the 400-meter hurdles race at the St. Louis games.

The National Liberty Party, the first nationally based black political party, is formed. They choose Iowa editor George Edwin Taylor as their presidential candidate; after he gains only a few votes, the party disappears.

Whites in Statesboro, Georgia, lynch two African-American men accused of murdering a white family. The white mob then turns on the rest of the African-American population, beating them and burning homes.

Oscar DePriest is elected to the Cook County Board of Commissioners in Chicago, Illinois.

1905: New York is the site of a race riot between the African-American community and the predominantly Irish police. The riot arises out of tensions over police brutality against African Americans.

The Chicago Defender is founded by Robert Sengstacke Abbott, a journalist and lawyer from Georgia. *The Defender,* although muckraking and sensationalistic, is mainly concerned with issues of racial justice.

The Niagara Movement, led by W.E.B. Du Bois, is formed in Fort Erie, Canada. The protest group's goal is to challenge the dominant accommodationist ideas of Booker T. Washington. Although the movement lasts for only five years, many of its goals and tactics are adopted by the National Association for the Advancement of Colored People (NAACP), which forms in 1909.

1906: The National Association for the Protection of Colored Women is founded. It addresses the problems facing the great numbers of southern African-American women who migrate to the North.

The first African-American Greek letter fraternity, Alpha Phi Alpha, is founded at Cornell University in Ithaca, New York.

In Atlanta, Georgia, a race riot erupts and lasts for several days. Gangs of white males attack African Americans in response to unsubstantiated newspaper reports of black attacks on white women. The riots leave the city's race relations tense for years to come.

In Brownsville, Texas, a racial incident occurs when suspicion falls on African American soldiers from the Twenty-fifth Infantry Division for a shooting that left one white man dead and two others wounded. President Theodore Roosevelt has three companies of African-American troops dishonorably discharged in retaliation for not giving up the guilty parties. The discharges are formally reversed in 1972 by the U.S. Army.

1907: Alain Locke becomes the first African-American Rhodes scholar. He will go on to become one of the leading figures in the Harlem Renaissance.

Oklahoma passes legislation segregating streetcars.

The U.S. Supreme Court upholds the right of railroads to segregate passengers traveling between states, even when the laws of the state in which the train is traveling do not allow segregation.

Wendell P. Dabney starts the Union, a newspaper for African Americans, in Cincinnati, Ohio.

George Henry White, a former slave and congressman, incorporates the People's Savings Bank to serve the banking needs (especially loans) of the residents of Whitesboro, New Jersey, an all-black town that White had helped found a few years earlier.

1908: At the London Olympics, John Baxter Taylor is the first African-American gold medalist, running on the 1600–meter relay team.

The first African-American sorority, Alpha Kappa Alpha, is established at Howard University in Washington, D.C., just two years after the first African-American fraternity was formed at Cornell University.

Jack Johnson becomes the first African-American heavyweight boxing champion by defeating then-champion Tommy Burns in Sydney, Australia.

In *Berea College v. Kentucky,* the U.S. Supreme Court upholds a state statute requiring segregation in private institutions.

The all-black town of Allensworth is founded in Tulare County in California by Colonel Allen Allensworth, a former slave and the highest-ranking African American in the U.S. Army. It is the westernmost such town.

Springfield, Illinois, hometown of Abraham Lincoln, is the site of a massive weeklong race riot, which begins when a white woman falsely accuses a black man of raping her. (The woman later confesses that a white man had beaten her.) The violence is so shocking that it leads to the formation of the National Association for the Advancement of Colored People (NAACP) the next year.

1909: The National Association of Colored People (NAACP) is formed in New York City in response to the violent race riot the previous year in Springfield, Illinois. The NAACP is made up of white "neo-abolitionists" and black intellectuals (led by W.E.B. Du Bois) opposed to Booker T. Washington's accommodationism.

The National Association of Colored Graduate Nurses (NACGN) is founded. At the time, African-American nurses are not allowed in the American Nurses Association and had little access to training and hospital positions.

On April 6, Matthew Henson reaches the North Pole on an expedition led by explorer Robert Peary, with whom Henson had made five previous unsuccessful attempts.

The *New York Amsterdam News,* the leading black paper in New York City for most of the twentieth century, is founded by James H. Anderson.

1910: Oklahoma introduces literacy and property qualifications for voters—effectively disfranchising blacks—but includes a grandfather clause that exempts most whites.

Sickle-cell anemia, a genetic blood disorder that affects blacks almost exclusively, is named by J.B. Herrick when he describes the bent shape of the blood cells of an anemic patient. (The name "sickle-cell disease" is now preferred to the older "sickle-cell anemia.")

Heavyweight champion Jack Johnson's defeat of the white boxer Jim Jeffries causes riots across the country when a film of the fight is shown, revealing whites' deep fears of black male power.

The first issue of W. E. B. Du Bois' *The Crisis: A Record of the Darker Races* is published.

President William Taft appoints William H. Lewis assistant attorney general of the United States, the first African American to hold this government position.

The decade begins with a reported sixty-seven lynchings of African Americans during this year.

1911: The National Urban League is founded with the merger of the National League for the Protection of Colored Women, the Committee for Improving Industrial Conditions of Negroes in New York, and the National League on Urban Conditions Among Negroes. The League provides professional social services to the black community

W.E.B. Du Bois publishes his first novel *The Quest of the Silver Fleece,* a study of the cotton industry seen through the fate of a young black couple.

1912: Claude McKay publishes his first book of poetry, *Songs of Jamaica; his second, Constab Ballads,* comes out later in the year.

W.C. Handy publishes his first blues song, the popular "Memphis Blues."

1913: James Weldon Johnson publishes—anonymously—his first and only novel, *The Autobiography of an Ex-Colored Man.* Many readers take it for a true autobiography.

Arthur A. Schomberg publishes *Racial Integrity: A Plea for the Establishment of a Chair of Negro History in our Schools and Colleges, etc.*

Rosa Parks, future civil rights leader, is born on February 4.

Harriet Tubman, an important leader of the Underground Railroad, dies on March 10.

Dr. Daniel Hale Williams becomes the first African American to become a member of the American College of Surgeons. In 1893, Williams had performed the operation for which he is best known—the first successful open-heart surgery.

1914: In Kingston, Jamaica, West Indies, Marcus Garvey founds the Universal Negro Improvement Association (UNIA), which will become incorporated in New York in 1918. Its motto is "One God, One Aim, One Destiny."

African-American inventor Garrett Morgan wins a patent for the first "gas mask," a device that allows firefighters to breath in smoke-filled buildings and protects engineers, chemists, and workers who labor near noxious fumes and dust.

The Spingarn Medal, named for former NAACP chairman Joel E. Spingarn, is instituted to honor annually the exemplary achievements of an African American man or woman.

W.C. Handy publishes the blues song for which he is best known, "St. Louis Blues."

The U.S. Supreme Court outlaws grandfather clauses in the Oklahoma case *Guinn v. United States.* Grandfather clauses were devices used by southern legislatures to limit African-American suffrage following Reconstruction.

1915: Oklahoma passes a law segregating telephone booths, the nation's first such law.

D.W. Griffith's *The Birth of a Nation* is released. The film, inspired by two overtly racist novels written by Thomas Dixon, opens to critical praise and popular success, prompting the NAACP to launch an unsuccessful campaign to have the filmed banned from theaters.

Lincoln Motion Pictures, the second black film company, is formed—partly as a protest against racist attitudes on exhibit in D.W. Griffith's hugely successful *Birth of a Nation.*

On Thanksgiving Day, in Georgia, William Joseph Simmons, along with fifteen of his friends, revives the then-dormant Ku Klux Klan.

Booker T. Washington dies on November 14 in Tuskegee, Alabama.

1916: The annual NAACP meeting having been canceled out of respect for the late Booker T. Washington (he died the year before), the Amenia Conference held in Amenia, NY brings together both the followers of Booker T. Washington and the NAACP (led by W.E.B. Du Bois) in an independent conference.

The first issue of Carter G. Woodson's *Journal of Negro History* is published.

Garrett Morgan's patented gas masks are worn when he and others enter a smoke-filled tunnel under Lake Erie to rescue workers trapped by an underground explosion.

1917: The New York City Fifth Avenue March takes place on July 28. Thousands of African Americans march in protest of lynchings and racial inequalities.

In August, a violent confrontation between the black 24th Infantry and Houston, Texas residents leads to the eventual hanging of nineteen African-American soldiers.

The U.S. Supreme Court, in *Buchanan v. Warley,* rules that laws requiring segregation of residential neighborhoods violate the Fourteenth Amendment.

The United States enters World War I. Eventually, more than 400,000 African Americans will serve in segregated units in the U.S. armed forces, mainly as laborers in the United States and France, although a small percentage will serve in two combat divisions.

During the massive spurt of black migration after the beginning of World War I, a bloody riot erupts in the wake of a failed labor strike in the steel and mining town of East St. Louis, Illinois, leaving dozens of African Americans dead and many more injured.

James Weldon Johnson publishes his first book of poetry *Fifty Years and Other Poems.*

1918: African-American filmmaker and novelist Oscar Micheaux directs his first film *The Homesteader,* based on his third novel (published in 1917).

A race riot in Philadelphia, Pennsylvania leaves four African Americans dead and many injured.

1919: The U.S. Supreme Court, in *Strauder v. West Virginia,* rules that blacks should be admitted to juries.

In rural Phillips County, Arkansas, a white deputy sheriff fires shots into a meeting of the Progressive Farmers and Householders Union, a self-help organization for African-American farmers. When union members return fire, wounding the deputy, a furious race riot breaks out and hundreds of blacks are killed. No whites are arrested for rioting, but a dozen blacks are convicted of murder at a mob-dominated trial. (Following an appeal by the NAACP, their sentences will be overturned in 1923 by the U.S. Supreme Court in *Moore v. Dempsey.*)

Delilah Beasley publishes *The Negro Trail-Blazers of California,* a meticulously researched chronicle of the role of African Americans in the Far West.

William Monroe Trotter, at the Paris Peace Conference, argues unsuccessfully that guarantees of racial equality be included in the Treaty of Versailles.

Claude Barnett founds the Associated Negro Press (ANP), the first national news service for African-American newspapers.

James Weldon Johnson coins the term "Red Summer" to describe the period during which twenty-five race riots and incidents occurred. Red Summer convinces many African Americans that their participation in the war for democracy did not mean that white domination in America would disappear.

The most serious riot of Red Summer takes place in Chicago, Illinois, starting on July 27 and lasting a week. When a black man unwittingly crosses an invisible color line in the water at Chicago's segregated Twenty-Ninth Street beach, whites stone him and he drowns. The ensuing violence leaves fifteen whites and twenty-three blacks dead; the injured number over 500. Property damage is assessed at over $1,000,000 and thousands of blacks are left homeless by the widespread bombing and arson.

The NAACP publishes its report *Thirty Years of Lynching in the United States, 1889–1918.*

A decade high of seventy-six lynchings of African Americans are reported by the end of the year.

1920: The Nineteenth Amendment to the Constitution is ratified. It enfranchises women voters.

James Weldon Johnson becomes the first African-American secretary of the NAACP.

The first international convention of Marcus Garvey's Universal Negro Improvement Association (UNIA) is held in August in Harlem.

Fritz Pollard becomes the first African-American coach in the American Professional Football Association (APFA), which would later become the National Football League (NFL). He leads his team the Akron Pros to an undefeated season and a championship win.

The National Negro Baseball League is organized by Andrew "Rube" Foster. The league is composed of six teams from midwestern cities with large African-American populations. The league enjoys great popularity until it folds in 1931 during the Great Depression.

Mamie Smith's recording of "Crazy Blues" sparks the blues craze of the 1920s upon its release.

Charles Gilpin appears on Broadway in Eugene O'Neill's *The Emperor Jones* and is named one of the ten people who had done the most for the American theater by the Drama League of New York, the first African American so honored.

1921: In an effort to disfranchise blacks, Louisiana adopts a new constitution that includes a poll tax and an "understanding clause."

On May 31, a race riot erupts in Tulsa, Oklahoma when an African-American bootblack is falsely accused of raping a white woman. Death reports range from 36 to 175, and 11,000 blacks are left homeless when the black neighborhood is leveled by bombs.

The first all-black musical, Eubie Blake and Noble Sissle's *Shuffle Along,* opens in New York City.

Lynchings of African Americans reach a decade high of fifty-nine in this year.

1922: African-American aviator Bessie Coleman receives an international pilot's license in France—the first African-American woman to do so—and returns to the United States to become an exhibition flyer known as "Brave Bessie."

Claude McKay publishes *Harlem Shadows,* which includes his acclaimed poem "If We Must Die."

The U.S. House of Representatives passes the Dyer Anti-Lynching Bill, but Republicans in the Senate vote to abandon the bill.

The first all-black professional basketball team, the Renaissance Big Five, nicknamed the Harlem Rens, is organized.

African-American inventor Garrett Morgan receives a patent for the first three-way automatic traffic signal. He will sell the invention to General Electric the following year.

1923: The first issue of the National Urban League's magazine *Opportunity,* edited by Charles Spurgeon Johnson, appears in January.

In *Moore v. Dempsey,* the U.S. Supreme Court rules that mob-dominated trials violate federal due-process guarantees. The decision overturns the death penalties of twelve African Americans convicted in the 1919 Arkansas race riot trial.

Jean Toomer's *Cane* is published, a pivotal work of the Harlem Renaissance.

Bessie Smith, considered by many to have been the greatest blues singer of all time, records her first songs, "Down Hearted Blues" and "Gulf Coast Blues."

Marcus Garvey, leader of the Universal Negro Improvement Association (UNIA), is sentenced to a five-year prison term on a single count of mail fraud. In this same year, Garvey's wife edits and publishes a volume of sayings and speeches titled *Philosophy and Opinions of Marcus Garvey.*

1924: Paul Robeson appears in his only "race" movie, Oscar Micheaux's *Body and Soul.*

At the Paris Olympics, William Dehart Hubbard wins the gold medal in the broad jump, becoming the first African American to win an Olympic gold medal.

Jessie Redmon Fauset's *There Is Confusion* is published. It is one of the earliest novels of the Harlem Renaissance.

1925: Alain Locke publishes *The New Negro,* an influential anthology that combines literature with arts and social commentary, and helps define the "New Negro" movement.

African-American entertainer Josephine Baker creates a sensation when she appears in Paris in *La Revue Negre.*

Harlem Renaissance poet Countee Cullen publishes his first book, *Color.*

Labor and civil rights leader A. Philip Randolph organizes the all-black Brotherhood of Sleeping Car Porters union to bargain with the Pullman Company. After 12 years of ignoring the Brotherhood, the Pullman Company finally recognizes it as a certified bargaining agent in 1937.

Dr. Ossian Sweet, defended by Clarence Darrow, is acquitted of murder. In self-defense, Sweet had shot and killed a man when a mob came to drive him out of the middle-class white neighborhood he had just moved into.

The National Negro Bar Association is formed in Des Moines, Iowa. (It later becomes the National Bar Association.)

1926: In February, Negro History Week is established by African-American historian Carter G. Woodson. (In the early 1970s, it will become a month-long celebration called Black History Month.)

The lavish Savoy Ballroom opens on March 12 in Harlem. Every black big band of note will eventually play at the Savoy.

Mordechai W. Johnson becomes the first African-American president of Howard University.

Black intellectuals are split in their reaction to white writer Carl Van Vechten's novel Nigger Heaven, with its incendiary title and its message that blacks' preoccupation with cultural improvement is a misguided affectation that will cost the race its vitality.

In *Corrigan v. Buckley,* the U.S. Supreme Court rejects the NAACP's challenge to restrictive covenants—provisions put in deeds to prohibit the sale of real estate to blacks—maintaining that they were private agreements and therefore did not violate the Fourteenth Amendment.

Violette Neatley Anderson becomes the first black woman admitted to practice law before the U.S. Supreme Court.

Langston Hughes publishes his first book of verse, *The Weary Blues.*

The Harlem Globetrotters basketball team is organized by Abe Saperstein in Chicago, Illinois.

1927: James Weldon Johnson publishes *God's Trombones: Seven Sermons in Verse.*

The *Cleveland Call & Post,* a black newspaper still in existence in the late 1990s, is formed by the merger of two smaller journals.

Sadie T.M. Alexander becomes the first black female graduate of the University of Pennsylvania Law School and the first African-American woman to enter the bar and practice law in Pennsylvania.

In *Nixon v. Herndon,* the U.S. Supreme Court strikes down a Texas law forbidding blacks to vote in Democratic primary elections as a violation of the Fourteenth Amendment.

After serving 33 months in a penitentiary for mail fraud, Marcus Garvey's sentence is commuted, thanks to an extensive petition campaign. Garvey is deported to Jamaica upon his release.

On December 4, Duke Ellington and his band debut at Harlem's all-white Cotton Club.

1928: Bill "Bojangles" Robinson, the most famous of all African-American tap dancers, appears on Broadway in the all-black revue, *Blackbirds of 1928,* tapping up and down a flight of stairs—a dance that would become his signature "stair dance."

Oscar DePriest of Chicago, Illinois is elected to Congress as the first African-American U.S. Representative in twenty-eight years and the first from a northern state.

The number of lynchings of African Americans drops to a low of seven.

1929: Wallace Thurman's first novel, *The Blacker the Berry,* is published. The novel deals with the problems of a dark-skinned woman who struggles with intraracial schisms caused by colorism.

A new Atlanta University is created when three historically black schools (Morehouse College, Spelman College, and Atlanta University) affiliate.

The stock market crashes on October 29, ushering in the Great Depression. Blacks will be particularly hard hit by the Depression.

1930: The NAACP successfully campaigns against President Herbert Hoover's nomination of Judge John J. Parker—a known racist who had spoken against black suffrage—to the U.S. Supreme Court.

Master W. Fard establishes the Temple of Islam in a black neighborhood in Detroit to house what he called the "Lost-Found Nation of Islam," later to be known simply as the Nation of Islam.

Paul Robeson triumphs on Broadway singing his stirring rendition of "Ol' Man River" in Jerome Kern and Oscar Hammerstein II's Show Boat.

1931: In Scottsboro, Alabama, a group of nine African-American youths traveling in a freight train are charged with raping two white women. Despite the lack of credible evidence, an all-white jury finds the nine guilty and they receive the death penalty. The U.S. Supreme Court twice overturns the death penalty convictions, but five of the nine serve long prison terms nonetheless.

In Camp Hill, Alabama, a riot erupts when a group of white farmers—led by the local sheriff—opens fire on a meeting of a black farmer's union.

1932: In *Nixon v. Condon,* the U.S. Supreme Court rules that Texas's state Democratic Party committee rules barring blacks from party primaries are unconstitutional. Texas responds by severing legal ties to the state Democratic Party convention, which subsequently votes to exclude black voters.

In one of the Scottsboro case appeals, the U.S. Supreme Court rules in *Powell v. Alabama* that defendants in capital cases must receive more than a pro forma defense. (One Scottsboro attorney had been drunk at the original trial.)

Sterling Brown's book of poems, *Southern Road,* is published.

1933: James Weldon Johnson publishes his autobiography, *Along This Way.*

Katharine Dunham dances her first leading role in Ruth Page's ballet *La Guiablesse.* She would come to be known for the "Katherine Dunham Technique," which combined African and Caribbean styles of movement with the techniques of ballet and modern dance.

Oklahoma City is segregated and martial law is established by executive order to prevent "bloodshed" when blacks move into white neighborhoods. It is a disingenuous order designed to perpetuate segregation of residential neighborhoods. The state Supreme Court reverses the order in 1935 in *Allen v. Oklahoma City.*

The NAACP holds a second Amenia Conference (the first was in 1916). The goal is to revitalize the organization, whose agenda for social advancement has been severely disrupted by the Great Depression. The meeting is later deemed a failure by many due to a lack of both real leadership and vision in the proposals.

1934: Chicago's Arthur Mitchell becomes the first black Democrat elected to Congress when he defeats black Republican Congressman Oscar DePriest.

The Southern Tenant Farmer's Association, a rare interracial labor organization, is formed in Arkansas when eleven whites and seven blacks meet to address the crisis facing tenant farmers in cotton agriculture. All agree that success against the planters can only be achieved if they preserve interracial unity.

Mary McLeod Bethune starts the National Council of Negro Women.

Elijah Muhammad establishes the national headquarters of the Nation of Islam in Chicago, with himself as the new leader. (Master Fard, the former leader of the Nation of Islam, had mysteriously disappeared.)

1935: In *Grovey v. Townsend,* the U.S. Supreme Court approves the Texas white primary, ruling that the state Democratic party is a private organization and its exclusion of black voters is not an impermissible state action.

On March 19, a riot erupts in Harlem when a false rumor spreads that a white shopkeeper had beaten a black boy for shoplifting. By the end of the riot, three blacks are dead, 200 are wounded, and damage is estimated at $2 million (mostly to white-owned property). Mayor Fiorello La Guardia appoints a biracial Mayor's Commission on Conditions in Harlem to investigate the event.

Jazz vocalist Ella Fitzgerald is discovered when she performs in an amateur competition at Harlem's Apollo Theater. Fitzgerald is hired by Chick Webb as vocalist for his band and she makes her first recording with them later that year.

In the second of the Scottsboro case appeals, Powell v. Alabama, the U.S. Supreme Court agrees with the defense argument that African Americans had been systematically excluded from Alabama juries, and returns the case to Alabama for retrial.

W. E. B. Du Bois publishes *Black Reconstruction: An Essay Toward a History of the Part Which Black Folk Played in the Attempt to Reconstruct Democracy in America, 1860–1880.*

Chemist Percy L. Julian develops physostigmine, a drug effective in the treatment of the eye disease glaucoma.

The NAACP wins an important victory in the U.S. Supreme Court decision in *Hollins v. Oklahoma,* which overturned a death-penalty rape conviction because of systematic racial prejudice in jury selection.

NAACP lawyer Charles H. Houston successfully represents Donald Murray in his suit to gain admission to the all-white University of Maryland Law School. Murray becomes the first African American in the twentieth century to integrate a state university in the South.

1936: Track-and-field athlete Jesse Owens wins four gold medals at the Berlin Olympics. Adolf Hitler refuses to shake Owens's hand.

The Nation Negro Congress (NNC) is formed, with A. Philip Randolph as its first president. The participation of the Communist Party in the NNC later became a liability, causing even Randolph to abandon the organization.

1937: William Hastie is appointed federal judge of the U.S. District Court for the Virgin Islands. Hastie is the first African American to be appointed a federal judge.

Joe Louis defeats Jim Braddock to become the boxing heavyweight champion, only the second black to become heavyweight champion and the first even permitted to fight since Jack Johnson lost the title in 1915.

Boxer Henry Armstrong holds the championship titles in the featherweight, lightweight, and welterweight divisions simultaneously, the first fighter to achieve this feat.

Sterling Brown publishes two studies of the African-American presence in American literature, *The Negro in American Fiction and Negro Poetry and Drama.*

Zora Neale Hurston publishes the novel for which she is best known, *Their Eyes Were Watching God.*

1938: In *Lane v. Wilson,* the U.S. Supreme Court invalidates Oklahoma's 1915 twelve-day voter registration limit, noting the Fifteenth Amendment forbids "sophisticated as well as simpleminded modes of discrimination."

Lionel Hampton performs with Benny Goodman's Quartet at Carnegie Hall. This famous concert, along with other engagements and recordings, solidifies his position as jazz's most influential vibraphonist.

Richard Wright's first book, *Uncle Tom's Children: Four Novellas,* is published.

Crystal Dreda Bird Fauset is elected to the Pennsylvania House of Representatives, the first African-American woman elected to a state legislature.

The U.S. Supreme Court in *Missouri* ex rel. *Gaines v. Canada* orders the University of Missouri, which has no black graduate school, to admit African-American student Lloyd Gaines, arguing that scholarships to out-of-state schools do not constitute equal admission.

1939: Hattie McDaniel becomes the first African American to win an Oscar for her performance as "Mammy" in the Civil War epic Gone with the Wind.

Opera contralto Marian Anderson is refused access (for racial reasons) to Constitution Hall for a Washington, D.C. concert by the Daughters of the American Revolution (DAR). Andersonr esponds by giving an Easter Sunday outdoor recital—introduced by Secretary of the Interior Harold Ickes—on the steps of the Lincoln Memorial before a crowd of 75,000. The scandal prompts Eleanor Roosevelt to resign her DAR membership.

Jane Bolin is named justice of the New York City Domestic Relations Court, becoming the first black woman judge in the United States.

Edward Franklin Frazier publishes his pioneering study, *The Negro Family in the United States,* which demonstrates that the internal problems of black families were socially created within and by Western civilization, not by the failure of Africans to live up to American standards.

1940: Employers and labor unions in defense-related industries are free to practice systematic and overt discrimination against African Americans during this time.

Federal antilynching legislation is introduced during the Seventy-sixth Congress but legislation is never enacted.

Virginia General Assembly selects James A. Bland's "Carry Me Back to Old Virginny" as the state song.

Roosevelt and representatives from the War and Navy departments meet with three African American leaders: A. Philip Randolph, Walter White, and T. Arnold Hill. This meeting produces a policy of giving black servicemen better treatment and greater opportunity within the confines of racial segregation.

Col. Benjamin O. Davis, Sr. receives a promotion to brigadier general and becomes the first African American to attain this rank. At the same time Col. Campbell C. Johnson becomes an aide to the director of the Selective Service System, and William H. Hastie is appointed a special advisor to the Secretary of War on matters pertaining to black soldiers.

Native Son, Richard Wright's first published novel, becomes a Book-of-the-Month selection.

The American Negro Theatre is founded by Abram Hill and Frederick O'Neal in Harlem, New York.

The Cotton Club is closed. Most of the renowned jazz performers of the period appeared at the Cotton Club including Louis Armstrong, Ethel Waters, and dancers Bill "Bojangles" Robinson, and the Nicholas Brothers.

Hansberry v. Lee—the Supreme Court declares that it is illegal for whites to bar African Americans from white neighborhoods. The plaintiff in this case is Carl Hansberry, a prominent real estate broker and father of Lorraine Hansberry, who moved his family to an all-white neighborhood. Her play A *Raisin in the Sun* is based on this incident.

The Selective Service and Training Act of 1940 is passed outlawing "discrimination against any person on account of race or color" in administering the draft. But it contains loopholes that perpetuate segregation despite the ban on discrimination.

U.S. Supreme Court rules that Edgar Smith's conviction was unconstitutional and his sentence void because blacks had been systematically excluded from jury service. Smith is released from jail in January 1941.

1941: Jesse Locker, a black Republican, is elected to the city council of Cincinnati, OH.

Joe Louis remains the undefeated world heavyweight champion. Following the Schmeling fight in 1938, Louis embarked on a remarkable string of title defenses winning seventeen fights in four years, fifteen by knockout. His only serious challenge came from Billy Conn in 1941, who outboxed the champion for twelve rounds before succumbing to Louis's knockout punch in the thirteenth.

The NAACP, the Urban League, and other organizations support A. Philip Randolph's call for a march on Washington to demand jobs and integration of the military. Randolph threatens a massive demonstration of 100,000 African Americans to be held on July 1. In response Roosevelt issues Executive Order 8802, which specifies that defense contracts bar discrimination and open training programs to minorities, and set up a Fair Employment Practice Committee to investigate violations. The march is canceled.

African-American pilots begin training at segregated facilities at Tuskegee Institute. The Tuskegee experiment produces a trained fighter unit, the 99th Pursuit Squadron, manned by African-American pilots, mechanics, and clerks.

The Golden Gate Male Quartet, a gospel group, performs at the President's Inaugural Concert at Constitution Hall in Washington, D.C. They were the only black entertainers to perform.

NAACP lobbies successfully for a Navy officer-training program for African Americans.

District of Columbia Bar Association votes to remove restrictions to the use of its library, which is housed in a federally owned building. Black lawyers, who had been prohibited from using the library, filed a suit against the association. After considering the cost of moving, the association voted to change their policy.

U.S. Supreme Court rules in *Mitchell v. United States* that segregated coach laws for interstate travel are illegal. Arthur W. Mitchell argues the case himself before the high court.

The National Urban League sponsors an hour-long national radio program to encourage equal employment opportunities for blacks in the defense program. Many famous black entertainers participate in the program.

The NAACP with the help of Aline Black and Melvin Alston, two teachers from Norfolk, Virginia, successfully challenge the constitutionality of unequal pay for teachers based on race. Black and Alston are reinstated to their positions by the city board of education.

The governor of Georgia, Eugene Talmadge, an outspoken racist, orders all public schools to ban all books on evolution, adolescence, and blacks from their libraries.

Adam Clayton Powell, Jr. is elected to the New York City Council. He is the first African American to serve on the council.

The National Negro Opera Company is established in Pittsburgh, Pennsylvania by Mary Cardwell Dawson.

Dorie Miller becomes the first African-American war hero of World War II. He shoots down four Japanese planes during the attack on Pearl Harbor.

1942: Black press launches the Double V Campaign seeking victory over tyranny abroad and racial segregation at home.

African Americans enlist in large numbers; however, all of the four major services adhere to the 10 percent black participation quota set in 1940. Blacks are primarily segregated and assigned only to certain areas.

Hugh Mulzac becomes the first of three African Americans to serve as a wartime ship's captain when he takes command of the *USS Booker T. Washington.*

William Levi Dawson is elected to the House of Representatives from Chicago, Illinois.

James Farmer becomes the first executive director of the Congress for Racial Equality.

Benjamin O. Davis, Jr. is promoted to the rank of major and is given command of the 99th Pursuit Squadron.

Chicago-based publisher John H. Johnson creates the Negro Digest. It published general articles about African-American life with an emphasis on racial progress.

Sarah Vaughan sings "Body and Soul" and wins an amateur-night contest at Harlem's Apollo Theater.

Publication of Margaret Walker's *For My People,* the first volume by an African-American woman to garner national recognition in literary competition.

1943: William H. Hastie resigns from his position as assistant to secretary of war disgusted by the Army's reluctance to lower racial barriers. Hastie decides that he can fight segregation more effectively outside the constraints of an official position.

Detroit Riot of 1943—many African Americans and whites move to Detroit seeking employment in defense industries. The city is unprepared to handle the influx, and racial tensions are exacerbated by competition for jobs and housing. Violence erupts and quickly spreads throughout the city, and military police are finally brought in to restore order. A Fact-Finding Committee blames the riots on blacks' "militant appeals for equality." However, the mayor sets up an Interracial Committee—the first of its kind in the nation—with authority to investigate complaints and to use the courts to enforce antidiscrimination laws.

The Navy admitting a shortage of 500 nurses accepts four African-American women to that specialty.

The 99th Pursuit Squadron—the first African American Army Air Corps unit—flies its first combat mission over the Mediterranean island of Pantelleria.

Paul Robeson opens in the starring role of *Othello* on Broadway.

Indifferent leadership and hatred expressed by local inhabitants contribute to riots by black soldiers at nine military bases during this year.

1944: Navy assigns predominantly black crews to man a patrol craft PC 1264 and the destroyer escort USS Mason.

Adam Clayton Powell, Jr. is elected to the U.S. House of Representatives from Harlem. He is the first African-American Congressman from the Northeast.

Smith v. Allwright—Supreme Court declares an all-white Texas Democratic primary unconstitutional. The Court states that blacks cannot be barred from voting in the Texas Democratic primaries.

Due to a shortage of troops after the casualties from the Battle of the Bulge, Lt. Gen. John C. H. Lee persuades Gen. Eisenhower to call for volunteers among the predominantly black service units to retrain as riflemen. Forty-five hundred African Americans sign up, undergo training, and serve in sixty-man platoons that join two-hundred-man white rifle companies. This improvised racial policy integrates the fighting but not the army.

1945: Colonel Benjamin O. Davis, Jr. is appointed commander of the 477th Composite Group.

The premier issue of *Ebony* magazine is published. It becomes the largest circulation African-American periodical.

Benjamin Quarles has an essay accepted by the Mississippi Valley Historical Review. It is the first from a black historian to appear in a major historical journal.

1946: Alabama passes the Boswell amendment requiring prospective voters to be able to "interpret" the state constitution.

Race riots break out in Alabama, Tennessee, and Pennsylvania—nearly 100 blacks are injured.

Sugar Ray Robinson wins the world welterweight boxing title in a fifteen-round decision over Tommy Bell.

The NAACP Legal Defense and Education Fund brings a series of cases before the Supreme Court— *Sipuel Board of Regents of the University of Oklahoma, McLaurin v. Oklahoma,* and *Sweatt v. Painter.*

Harry S. Truman appoints a national committee on civil rights to investigate racial injustices and recommend action.

Morgan v. Virginia—Supreme Court prohibits segregation in interstate bus travel.

Jackie Robinson joins the Montreal Royals of the International League, the top farm club in the Dodger system. He breaks the color line when he moves to the Dodgers in 1947. He becomes the first African American to play major league baseball.

1947: Charles S. Johnson becomes the first black president of Fisk University.

Larry Doby becomes the second African American to play major league baseball. He is recruited by the Cleveland Indians—making him the first black player in the American League.

The Congress of Racial Equality (CORE) decides to test the Morgan decision with the Journey of Reconciliation—sixteen men (eight white and eight black) travel by bus through the region challenging segregated seating arrangements that relegated blacks to the back of the bus. The arrest of four of the protesters in Chapel Hill, North Carolina catapults CORE and the Journey of Reconciliation to national attention.

Truman appoints Edith S. Sampson as an alternate to the United Nations, making her the first black U.S. delegate to the organization.

1948: Ralph J. Bunche is appointed acting mediator for the U.N. Special Commission on Palestine after the assassination of Folke Bernadotte by Jewish militants. Bunche negotiates with both sides and arranges an armistice. His actions earn him the 1950 Nobel Prize for Peace.

Roy Campanella joins Jackie Robinson on the Brooklyn Dodgers. He becomes the major league's first African-American catcher.

The Supreme Court of California declares the state law prohibiting interracial marriages unconstitutional.

The Supreme Court rules in *Sipuel v. University of Oklahoma* that a state must provide legal education for blacks at the same time it is offered to whites.

Shelley v. Kramer—Supreme Court rules that courts cannot enforce restrictive housing covenants, that restricted certain homes or tracts of land from use and occupancy by blacks.

President Truman issues Executive Order 9981 to end discrimination in the armed forces.

Satchel Paige becomes the first black baseball player to pitch for the American League.

Nat King Cole becomes the first African American to have his own network radio show.

1949: Wesley A. Brown becomes the first African American to graduate from the U.S. Naval Academy.

William H. Hastie leaves his position of governor of the Virgin Islands to take a seat as judge on the Third Circuit Court of Appeals.

President Truman signs an order banning federal housing aid in areas where racial or religious bias is found.

Robert McFerrin, Sr. performs in William Grant Still's *Troubled Island* with the New York City Opera Company.

1950: The Korean War begins. Segregation still persists. The largest African-American combat unit, the 24th Infantry, which traces its regimental lineage to the post-Civil War reorganization of the Army, goes to war in July 1950. Black troops share in the first American victory.

Prolific writer Gwendolyn Brooks is awarded the Pulitzer Prize for poetry. She is the first African American to win a Pulitzer Prize.

Ralph Bunche, scholar and United Nations diplomat, is awarded the Nobel Peace Prize for his brilliant negotiation of an armistice in the Arab-Israeli War of 1948.

The University of Texas is ordered by the U.S. Supreme Court to admit Heman Sweatt to its law school. In *Sweatt vs. Painter,* Thurgood Marshall argues the speciousness of the separate-but-equal doctrine. The decision weakens segregation generally.

1951: Paul Robeson and William L. Patterson present a petition to the United Nations, charging the U.S. government with genocide. It charges the United States with genocide by "deliberately inflicting on [African Americans] conditions of life calculated to bring about their physical destruction" through executions, lynchings, and terrorism.

Sugar Ray Robinson knocks out Jake La Motta and becomes the middleweight champion.

In Washington, D.C., Mary Church Turrell, a prominent civil rights and women's rights activist for fifty years, joins the sit-ins challenging racial segregation in restaurants and public accommodations. Partially as a result of this, the Municipal Court of Appeals outlaws segregation in restaurants in the District of Columbia.

Governor Adlai Stevenson of Illinois dispatches the National Guard to quell a race riot in Cicero, Illinois. More than 3,000 whites were protesting a black family's residence at a home in an all-white community.

1952: For the first time, no lynchings of blacks are reported in the United States.

The University of Tennessee admits its first black student.

Dorothy Maynor becomes the first black artist to perform commercially in Constitution Hall.

Boxer Archie Moore wins the light heavyweight crown.

Ralph Ellison publishes his novel *Invisible Man,* which receives the National Book Award the following year.

1953: James Baldwin publishes his first novel Go Tell It on the Mountain.

Earl Warren becomes Chief Justice of the United States Supreme Court. The "Warren Court" era begins.

Percy Lavon Julian, chemist and educator, founds Julian Laboratories, Inc., a pharmaceutical company. It is successful. When he retires, he holds more than 130 chemical patents.

Rufus Early Clement is elected to the Atlanta Board of Education by a sweeping majority making him the first African American to be elected to public office in Atlanta since Reconstruction.

Hulin Edwin Jack is elected Manhattan borough president. He is the first black to hold this office.

1954: The case of the century, *Brown v. Board of Education of Topeka.* It is actually five similar (school desegregation) cases, which the Supreme Court decides to hear as one. The trial lasts about one year. Going against the advice of some of his colleagues, Thurgood Marshall uses "sociological evidence" and argues that separate-but-equal is the psychological abuse of black youngsters. On May 17 Chief Justice Earl Warren reads the famous verdict, saying, "In the field of public education, separate but equal has no place. "The verdict precipitates a backlash, and the formation of a wave of defensive groups who denounce the decision. Many Southern leaders and communities are defiant.

Benjamin O. Davis, Jr., is appointed general in the U.S. Air Force making him the first African American to hold this rank.

Charles C. Diggs, Jr. is elected to the U.S. House of Representatives from Michigan. He is the first black Congressman from the state.

The U.S. Supreme Court rules in *District of Columbia v. John R. Thompson Co., Inc.* that discrimination in Washington, D.C. restaurants is illegal.

1955: A. Philip Randolph becomes a vice-president of the newly merged AFL-CIO.

Emmett Till, a fourteen-year old black adolescent who allegedly made sexual advances toward a white woman, is kidnapped and murdered. Two white men tried for his murder are acquitted. The trial, receiving national attention, highlights the unequal administration of justice.

In Montgomery, Alabama, Rosa Parks refuses to give up her seat on a segregated bus and provokes the Montgomery Bus Boycott. More than fifty thousand African Americans participate in the boycott, which is led by the twenty-six-year old Martin Luther King, Jr.

Roy Wilkins becomes executive secretary of the NAACP.

The Interstate Commerce Commission prohibits segregation in public vehicles operating in interstate travel.

Marian Anderson appears at the Metropolitan Opera.

Ray Charles releases his breakthrough hit "I've Got a Woman."

1956: Autherine Lucy enters the University of Alabama. Lucy is accepted by the University of Alabama in 1952; however, her acceptance is rescinded when the school administration discovers she is not white. Three years go by. In the wake of the U.S. Supreme Court *Brown* decision, the university is ordered by a federal District Court to admit her. There are protests. She is suspended from the school on the grounds that her own safety is in jeopardy. The NAACP protests the suspension, and the federal court orders that the school reinstate her as well as undertake measures to protect her. Shortly thereafter, Lucy is expelled from the university on the grounds that she has maligned its officials by taking them to court. The NAACP, this time around, feeling that further legal action is pointless, does not contest this decision. In 1992 the University of Alabama names an endowed fellowship in her honor.

Sammy Davis, Jr. appears in the lead role in *Mr. Wonderful* on Broadway.

Nat King Cole gets his own television show. (The program was canceled, however, because of difficulty in finding sponsors for it.)

Floyd Patterson knocks out forty-three-year-old champion Archie Moore to take the light-heaveyweight crown.

In some quarters white resistance to school integration grows. Segregationists use a variety of stratagems to circumvent court-ordered desegregation, including shutting down schools and the formation of private schools.

1957: Hank Aaron is named the National League's Most Valuable Player.

Federal troops escort nine black students to class in Little Rock, Arkansas. Governor Orval Faubus of Arkansas, using the Arkansas National Guard and under pretense of maintaining order, obstructs the integration of the city's Central High School. Supreme Court justices and others are shocked at his blatant defiance of a Supreme Court decision. President Eisenhower orders one thousand federal troops into Little Rock, to halt the obstruction of desegregation and to protect the nine black teenagers who wish to attend Central High.

The Southern Christian Leadership Conference, a network of nonviolent civil rights activists drawn mainly from black churches, is formed.

Senator Strom Thurmond of South Carolina speaks against the pending civil rights bill and sets a record for filibuster.

The Civil Rights Act of 1957 becomes law. President Eisenhower signs the first civil rights act since reconstruction. The act creates a commission to monitor civil rights violations and authorizes the Justice Department to guard black voting rights through litigation against discriminatory voter registrars.

Althea Gibson becomes the first black to win the Wimbledon and the U.S. singles.

1958: Governor J.P. Coleman of Mississippi proclaims that blacks in Mississippi are not ready to vote.

NAACP Youth Council chapters in Wichita and Oklahoma City stage "sit-downs" at lunch-counters.

The state of Alabama imposes a $100,000 fine on the already financially strapped NAACP, for refusing to provide its membership lists to an Alabama judge. It is a clear attempt to undermine and even bring to a halt civil rights progress in the state. Through legal maneuvers, the NAACP is kept out of Alabama until 1964.

Alvin Ailey starts his own dance theater company. The Alvin Ailey American Dance Theater begins as repertory company of seven dancers devoted to both modern dance classics and new works created by Ailey.

The Supreme Court unanimously rejects an appeal by the Little Rock school board for a delay in the racial integration of Central High School.

1959: School desegregation is getting mixed reviews and having mixed results. Whites continue to use various ploys to thwart integration. In some places school districts open their desegregated public schools without any disturbance.

Lorriane Hansberry's *A Raisin in the Sun* is produced and is a huge critical and commercial success. She wins the New York Drama Critics Circle Award and other awards.

Berry Gordy, Jr., forms Motown Records.

1960: Black college students attempting to integrate a Woolworth lunch counter in Greensboro, North Carolina spearhead a sit-in movement that spreads rapidly throughout the South. Reacting to this upsurge in student activism, Ella Baker, Southern Christian Leadership Conference official, invites student protest leaders to an Easter weekend conference in Raleigh, NC. The student leaders, believing that existing civil rights organizations are overly cautious, agree to form a new group, the Student Non-Violent Coordinating Committee (SNCC). Marion S. Berry, Jr. is elected as chairman.

Black Americans at the Olympics in Rome win medals in major events: Cassius Clay, Willie McClure, and Eddie Crooks bring home gold; Wilma Rudolph wins three gold medals in track; and Rafer Johnson wins gold for the decathlon.

Martin Luther King, Jr., is arrested at a student initiated protest in Atlanta. Presidential candidate John F. Kennedy intervenes to secure his release from jail.

A. Philip Randolph forms the Negro American Labor Council as a vehicle through which to pressure the labor federation to act against segregated and discriminatory unions.

Wilma Rudolph is chosen as the United Press Athlete of the Year, and the next year is designated Woman Athlete of the Year by the Associated Press.

Six years after the Supreme Court prohibited segregation in the schools only a small percentage of the schools in the South have begun to integrate.

President Eisenhower signs the Voting Rights Act. This law is sometimes called the Civil Rights Act of 1960.

Dionne Warwick meets Burt Bacharach and Hal David and begins her solo career.

A major race riot erupts after blacks move onto a section of the Biloxi beach reserved for whites only. City officials blame the NAACP for inciting the violence.

A federal court ends restrictions against black voting in Fayette Country, TN.

Harry Belafonte wins an Emmy for his television special "Tonight with Harry Belafonte." He becomes the first African American to win an Emmy.

W. E. B. Du Bois visits Ghana for the inauguration of Kwame Nkrumah as its first president. He accepts an invitation from Nkrumah to return and start work on an Encyclopedia Africana.

Gomillion v. Lightfoot—the Supreme Court rules that the Fifteenth Amendment rights of Tuskegee blacks had been violated when the Alabama legislature redefined the city limits to exclude blacks and give whites political control. This is a major triumph over segregationists who tried to crush the political power of the black population.

1961: President Kennedy appoints Thurgood Marshall as judge of the Second U.S. Circuit Court of Appeals.

Adam Clayton Powell, Jr. becomes the chairman of the powerful House Education and Labor Committee.

Oscar Robertson is voted NBA Rookie of the Year. He averaged 30.5 points per game in this first season in the National Basketball Association.

Robert Weaver is appointed director of the U.S. Housing and Home Finance Agency, at the time the highest federal position ever held by an African American.

President Kennedy appoints Clifton R. Wharton, Sr. U.S. ambassador to Norway. He is the first black to attain this position by rising through the ranks of the foreign service.

Whitney Young, Jr. is selected to be executive director of the National Urban League.

Congress of Racial Equality mounts its most militant challenge to segregation—the Freedom Rides. The Freedom Rides are protests against segregated interstate buses and terminals in the South. Seven white and six black activists including James Farmer participate in the Freedom Rides.

Jackie Robinson is inducted into the Baseball Hall of Fame. He becomes the first black member.

1962: The Albany Movement is organized to abolish discrimination in all public facilities in Albany,

Georgia. It is supported by the Southern Christian Leadership Conference, the Student Non-Violent Coordinating Committee, NAACP, and the Congress of Racial Equality and led by Martin Luther King, Jr. Many of the demonstrators are beaten and jailed, including Dr. King who leaves Albany without a victory.

Edward W. Brooke III is elected attorney general for the state of Massachusetts. He becomes the highest-ranking African-American official in New England.

Wilt Chamberlain scores 100 points in a single game against the New York Knickerbockers.

Marvin Gaye releases his debut solo album on Motown.

Augustus Hawkins is elected to the House of Representatives. He is the first black representative from California.

Leroy Johnson is elected to the Georgia Senate. He becomes the first black legislator in Georgia since Reconstruction.

James Meredith tries to enroll at the University of Mississippi but his admission is blocked by the governor. The Kennedy administration dispatches federal marshals to escort Meredith to classes. To quell subsequent rioting, U.S. troops police the campus. They remain there until 1963 when Meredith graduates.

Carl Stokes becomes the first black Democrat elected to the Ohio House of Representatives.

Mal Goode is selected as news commentator on ABC-TV. He is the first African American on network television news.

Sonny Liston wins the world heavyweight boxing championship from Floyd Patterson.

President John F. Kennedy signs an executive order prohibiting racial discrimination in housing built or purchased with federal assistance.

1963: W. E. B. DuBois renounces his U.S. citizenship and officially becomes a citizen of Ghana.

Thomas Bradley is elected to the Los Angeles city council. He is the first black official in Los Angeles.

Elston Howard of the New York Yankees becomes the first black player in the American League to win the Most Valuable Player award.

President Kennedy declares the black struggle for civil rights a "moral issue." He calls on Congress to strengthen voting rights and create job opportunities for African Americans.

Sidney Poitier becomes the first African American to win an Academy Award for best actor for his performance in *Lilies of the Field*.

Bayard Rustin coordinates the March on Washington.

The U.S. Supreme Court rules in several cases that help bolster the civil rights movement. It rules that segregation in courtrooms is unconstitutional; state and local governments cannot interfere with peaceful sit-ins for racial integration of public places of business; and the court prohibits an indefinite delay in the desegregation of public schools.

Medgar Evers, NAACP field secretary, is murdered in the doorway of his home in Jackson, MS. His alleged assailant is acquitted by a hung jury.

The March on Washington is held to advance the civil rights bill then before Congress. Several hundred thousand African Americans and whites attend. They gather on the steps of the Lincoln Memorial and listen to Martin Luther King, Jr. deliver his "I Have a Dream" speech.

Four young black girls are killed when a bomb explodes in the Sixteenth Street Baptist Church. Martin Luther King, Jr., gives a eulogy at a joint funeral for three of the girls and urges African Americans to keep up their struggle despite the murders.

1964: Congress passes the Civil Rights Act of 1964. President Johnson signs the bill in the presence of Martin Luther King, Jr.

Congress passes the Economic Opportunity Act. Some of the programs in this legislative package include Head Start, Upward Bound, and college work-study educational programs.

John Conyers, Jr. is elected to Congress as a representative from Michigan.

John Hope Franklin is selected to chair the department of history at the University of Chicago.

The Mississppi Freedom Democratic Party is established to serve as an alternative party that will allow black and white Mississippians to be in a party that shares the same views as the national organization.

Malcolm X breaks with the Black Muslim movement. No longer bound by Elijah Muhammad's religious structures, he is free to develop his own philosophy of the black freedom struggle.

Constance Baker Motley is elected to the New York State Senate. She is the first African American elected to this body.

Martin Luther King, Jr. receives the Nobel Peace Prize.

Race riots occur throughout the country. In Harlem violence erupts over police brutality. The rebellion continues for four nights and spreads to Brooklyn's Bedford-Stuyvesant neighborhood. Race riots also erupt in Chicago, Jersey City, Rochester, and Philadelphia.

Carl T. Rowan is appointed director of the United States Information Service by President Johnson. He is the first black to hold this post.

The Twenty-fourth Amendment to the U.S. Constitution is ratified. The amendment eliminates poll-tax requirement in national elections.

Cassius Clay wins the world heavyweight championship by defeating Sonny Liston.

Three young men who had been working on black voter registration are declared missing and presumed murdered in Mississippi. They are James E. Chaney, Michael Schwerner, and Andrew Goodman. President Johnson sends 200 naval personnel to assist in the search for the missing men. Their bodies are found buried near Philadelphia, MS.

Bob Hayes is awarded a gold medal at the Olympic Games in Tokyo for the 100-meter dash.

1965: Julian Bond is denied his seat in the Georgia House of Representatives because he opposes the U.S. involvement in Vietnam. The Supreme Court orders Bond seated in December of 1966.

President Johnson names Thurgood Marshall to be solicitor general of the United States. This is the highest judicial position ever held by an African American.

Bill Cosby becomes the first African American to star in a television series, *I Spy*.

President Johnson creates a cabinet-level Council on Equal Opportunity.

James Earl Jones receives an Obie for his performance in the title role of *Othello* at the New York Shakespeare Festival.

President Johnson appoints Robert C. Weaver to head the Department of Housing and Urban Development. He is the first African American to become a Cabinet member.

Martin Luther King, Jr. leads a successful voting rights campaign in Selma, AL. Demonstrations had begun early in 1965 and reached a turning point on March 7, when a group of demonstrators began a march from Selma to the state capitol in Montgomery. State troopers attack the marchers with tear gas and clubs on the outskirts of Selma. The police assault on the marchers increases national support. President Johnson reacts by introducing the Voting Rights Act of 1965.

Malcolm X is shot down by assassins as he speaks at the Audubon Ballroom in Harlem.

Patricia Roberts Harris is appointed U.S. ambassador to Luxembourg. She becomes the first African-American woman to be an ambassador of the United States.

Muhammad Ali defeats Floyd Patterson for the world heavyweight boxing title.

1966: Arthur Ashe becomes the first black man to win one of the preeminent Grand Slam titles in tennis.

Emmett Ashford begins his first year in the major leagues officiating at the opening-day game in Washington, D.C. He is the first African American to umpire in the major leagues.

Huey P. Newton and Bobby Seale found the Black Panther Party for Self-Defense. The party expanded from its base in Oakland, California to become a national organization.

Stokely Carmichael is elected SNCC chairman. He proffers an outspoken, militant stance that helps distance SNCC from the moderate leadership of competing civil rights organizations. He is the chief architect and spokesperson for the new Black Power ideology.

President Lyndon B. Johnson names Andrew F. Brimmer to the Board of Governors of the Federal Reserve Bank.

Edward W. Brooke, III is elected U.S. Senator from Massachusetts. He is the first popularly elected African-American member of the Senate.

Yvonne Brathwaite Burke is elected to the first of her three two-year terms in the California State Assembly. She is the first black assemblywoman in California.

Barbara Jordan becomes the first black since 1883 elected to the Texas Senate.

Samuel Proctor Massie, Jr. becomes the first African American to join the faculty of the U.S. Naval Academy at Annapolis.

Frank Robinson wins the American League's Most Valuable Player award—making him the first player to win the award in both major leagues.

Floyd B. McKissick becomes national director of CORE.

Constance Baker Motley, first African-American woman to be elected to the New York State Senate and to be elected borough president of Manhattan, becomes the first black woman to be appointed as a federal judge.

James Meredith sets out on a "walk against fear" from Memphis to Jackson, MS. On the second day out he is shot by an assailant and wounded. His attack sparks outrage and the major civil rights organizations carry on the march to Jackson. This procession is marked by Stokely Carmichael's call for black power and a resulting rift between the moderate and militant wings of the movement.

1967: The Black Power Conference is held in Newark, NJ. It is an assembly of over 1,000 delegates who meet to discuss the most pressing issues of the day.

Morgan Freeman makes his Broadway debut in an all-black production of *Hello Dolly*.

Nineteen men are indicted in the murders of civil rights workers James C. Chaney, Michael Schwerner, and Andrew Goodman who were slain in 1964. Twelve are acquitted.

Major Robert Lawrence is selected for the Department of Defense's Manned Orbital Laboratory program. He dies six months later in a plane crash.

There are urban riots in Newark and Detroit.

Thurgood Marshall becomes the first black Supreme Court Justice.

Carl Burton Stokes is elected mayor of Cleveland, Ohio. He is the first elected black mayor of a major American city.

Adam Clayton Powell, Jr. is expelled from the House of Representatives. It is the first time since 1919 that the House had expelled one of its members. Powell vows to fight the case all the way to the Supreme Court. However, he wins a special election to fill his own vacant seat.

H. Rap Brown becomes Stokely Carmichael's successor as National Chairman of SNCC where he continues a militant stance.

Supreme Court rules that states cannot interfere with or prevent interracial marriages.

The Organziation of Black-American Culture (OBAC) is founded. In its most dramatic public statement members of the visual arts workshop paint the Wall of Respect, a Black Power mural depicting various historical and contemporary black heroes such as Muhammad Ali, W. E. B. Du Bois, Malcolm, Marcus Garvey, Nina Simone, Amiri Baraka, and Gwendolyn Brooks.

1968: William Lacy Clay wins a congressional election to become the first black congressman from Missouri.

In his second term President Johnson appoints more blacks to federal positions than any previous president.

Eartha Kitt criticizes the war in Vietnam at a White House luncheon. As a result she loses bookings and is vilified by conservatives.

Former Congressman Adam Clayton powell, Jr. goes on a speaking tour of college campuses rallying black and white students to fight for equality and end the American involvement in Vietnam.

The Kerner Report—the result of a seven-month study by the National Commission on Civil Disorders to pinpoint the cause of racial violence in American cities in the late 1960s—is released to President Johnson. Stating that discrimination and segregation are deeply embedded in American society, the reports warns that America is "moving toward two societies, one black, one white—separate and unequal."

Eldridge Leroy Cleaver publishes Soul on Ice. It is a collection of autobiographical and political essays that articulate the sense of alienation that many black nationalists feel.

Dr. Martin Luther King, Jr. goes to Memphis to take part in a strike by black sanitation workers and he is assassinated as he stands on the balcony of the Lorraine Motel. Rioting breaks out in different parts of the city as blacks expressed their rage in the streets.

The Rev. Ralph Abernathy is unanimously elected to succeed Martin Luther King, Jr. as head of SCLC.

Arthur R. Ashe, Jr. wins the U.S. amateur men's singles championship and the U.S. Open championship.

Huey Newton is convicted on manslaughter charges and sentenced to two to fifteen years in prison. His conviction is later overturned by the Court of Appeals because of procedural errors.

Wyomia Tyus wins a gold medal in the 100-meter race in the 1968 Olympics making her the first person to win this race in two consecutive Olympics.

Tommie Smith and John Carlos, medal winner sprinters, offer the Black Power salute during the playing of the U.S. national anthem at the 1968 Summer Olympics in Mexico.

1969: James Charles Evers gains national prominence when he is elected mayor of Fayette, MS. Evers's victory helped open the way for many black candidates who desired political office.

James Earl Jones wins the Tony award for The Great White Hope.

The U.S. Department of Justice sues the state of Georgia for its refusal to desegregate schools.

Arhutr Mitchell forms the Dance Theatre of Harlem.

Moneta Street becomes the first African American to win the Pulitzer Prize in photography.

Alexander v. Holmes—Supreme Court rules that Mississippi's continued operation of segregated schools is unconstitutional. It also rejects the Nixon administration's appeal to delay desegregating thirty Mississippi schools districts.

The Black Panther Party's clashes with police decimate its leadership. Cleaver leaves for exile to avoid returning to prison. Bobby Seale is arrested for conspiracy to incite rioting at the 1968 Democratic Convention in Chicago. In May Connecticut officials charge Seale and seven other Panthers with murder in the slaying of party member Alex Rackley. In New York twenty-one Panthers are charged with plotting to assassinate policemen and blow up buildings. Nearly all the charges brought against Panther members either do not result in convictions or are overturned on appeal. The prosecutions absorbed much of the party's resources.

1970: Civil rights groups clash with President Richard Nixon. In a report, the U.S. Commission on Civil Rights reprimands President Nixon for being overly cautious about ending de facto segregation in northern states. Also, the NAACP denounces Nixon's nomination of G. Harold Carswell of Florida, whom they believe to be racist, as an associate justice of the Supreme Court. His nomination is defeated. Later in the year the NAACP denounces the Nixon administration as "anti-Negro."

Marxist philosopher Angela Davis is placed on the FBI's Ten Most Wanted List. In San Rafael, California, three Soledad Prison inmates are being tried for the murder of a prison guard. The brother of one of the defendants enters the courtroom and, holding the room at gunpoint, distributes weapons to the three defendants. There is a dramatic shootout resulting in four deaths. During the investigation several of the guns are traced to Davis. Distrustful of the judicial system, Davis goes into hiding.

A serious effort to collect and preserve forgotten music scores by black composers begins at the Music Library of Indiana University at Bloomington.

The first celebration of Martin Luther King, Jr., Day. Public schools are closed in many cities. (It is not yet a national holiday.) .

Essence: The Magazine for Today's Black Woman appears and is successful almost immediately.

1971: Jesse Jackson founds People United to Save Humanity (Operation PUSH). As head of PUSH he undertakes an agenda of negotiating black employment agreements with white businesses. Jackson also articulates the organization's other agenda—to promote black educational excellence and black self-esteem.

Swann v. Charlotte-Mecklenburg. The U.S. Supreme Court votes unanimously to direct school authorities in North Carolina to achieve "the greatest possible degree of actual desegregation." In effect, the Supreme Court rules in favor of busing to achieve integration.

The Attica Prison Uprising. Starting in early summer 1971, prisoners at the Attica Correctional Facility in upstate New York have been organizing and demanding more humane prison conditions. In September more than 1,200 black and Latino inmates seize control of the prison. Governor Nelson Rockefeller authorizes a raid. State police retake the prison, killing ten hostages and twenty-nine prisoners.

Shaft, representative of the blaxploitation film genre, opens in theaters.

1972: Barbara Jordan of Texas is elected to the U.S. House of Representatives, becoming the first African-American woman elected to Congress from the South.

Eight thousand African Americans from every region of the Unites States attend the first National Black Political Convention in Gary, Indiana. The convention approves a platform that demands reparations for slavery, proportional congressional representation for blacks, the elimination of capital punishment, increased federal spending to combat drug trafficking, a reduced military budget, and a guaranteed income of $6,500 for a family of four.

President Nixon proposes a moratorium on all court-ordered busing.

National People's Action (NPA) is established from a coalition of community-based organizations. Its purpose is to focus national attention on redlining and other housing discrimination policies, in part by identifying discriminatory lenders.

NPA, assisted by the NAACP and the National Urban League, attempts to form partnerships (with government and the private sector) dedicated to the eradication of discrimination in lending practices.

1973: The secretary of the U.S. Army rescinds the dishonorable discharges given to 167 African-American soldiers after the Bronwsville, Texas, incident of 1906. Soldiers of the Twenty-fifth Infantry had been involved in a riot with city police and merchants, during which some 250 rounds of ammunition were fired into several Brownsville buildings. One man was killed and two were wounded. President Theodore Roosevelt had discharged the soldiers without trial. The Army finds that this action had been improper. Only one of the soldiers is still alive.

Forty years of medical experimentation on human subjects comes to light and becomes the worst medical scandal in U.S. history. The Tuskegee Syphilis Experiment (1932–1972) was a study conducted by the U.S. Public Health Service. It involved observing the effects of untreated syphilis on several hundred black men living in rural Alabama. The study proceeded without the informed consent of the participants. The study is still ongoing in 1972 when a whistle-blower inside the PHS leaks the story to the press. Health officials try to defend their actions but public outrage silences them as they agree to end the experiment.

Coleman Young is elected mayor of Detroit and becomes one of the most powerful leaders in the state.

Thomas Bradley is elected mayor of Los Angeles, America's third largest city.

Marian Wright Edelman, who started her career as a lawyer working with the poor in Mississippi, founds the Children's Defense Fund, an advocacy organization for children.

1974: Julius Erving, the "greatest slam dunker of all time," is selected the Most Valuable Player by the American Basketball Association.

In Boston, violence erupts between supporters and opponents of public school desegregation. As court-ordered busing of black students to white schools in South Boston begins, whites riot outside the schools and attack black students. Boston becomes a national symbol of resistance to busing.

In Kansas City, in tribute to the city's historical role as a regional political and cultural center, civil rights activist Horace Peterson III opens an archives/museum, the Black Archives of Mid-America.

The Kentucky state legislature passes a law that makes victims of discrimination eligible for financial compensation for embarrassment and/or humiliation.

1975: Physicist Shirley Ann Jackson is a visiting scientist at the European Center for Nuclear Research (CERN), where she concentrates on theories of strongly interacting elementary particles.

Elijah Muhammad dies. Wallace Deen Muhammad is named his father's successor as supreme minister of the Nation of Islam. In short order Wallace shocks the movement by announcing an end to its racial doctrines and black-nationalist teachings. He disbands the Fruit of Islam and the Muslim Girls Training, elite internal organizations, and moves his followers toward orthodox Sunni Islam.

WGPR-TV in Detroit, the first black-owned television station, goes on the air for the first time.

The Voting Rights Act of 1975, an expansion of the voting rights act of ten years prior, passed by Congress and signed by President Ford, abolishes all literacy requirements for voting.

1976: At the Montreal Summer Olympics Edwin Moses wins the 400-meter hurdles in world-record time.

President Gerald Ford presents the Medal of Freedom to Jesse Owens, for his "inspirational life" and for his contribution to the ideals of freedom and democracy. Owens won four gold medals at the 1936 Olympic Games in Berlin, upsetting his Nazi hosts (as well as racists on both sides of the Atlantic), and disputing Adolf Hitler's belief in Aryan racial superiority.

The Afro-American Historical and Cultural Museum opens in Philadelphia.

The federal courts order the Omaha (Nebraska) Public School Districts to use busing to integrate their schools.

President-elect Jimmy Carter appoints Andrew Young as the United States Ambassador to the United Nations.

1977: Alberta Hunter, one of the best-known blues singers of the 1920s and a popular band singer throughout the World War II era, is coaxed back to the nightclub circuit after three decades of hiatus. She becomes a hit all over again, in New York City.

Toni Morrison publishes *Song of Solomon* and becomes generally known as a novelist.

Roots, the television miniseries dramatization of Alex Haley's novel of black history, is one of the greatest successes in the history of television. Close to 130 million Americans follow the 300-year saga chronicling the travails of African Americans in their trajectory from Africa to Emancipation.

Filmmaker William Miles releases his first film, Men of Bronze, launching his career as a filmmaker. The film demonstrates his passion for uncovering the history of forgotten black Americans through archival film footage and historic photographs.

Reggie Jackson, in the sixth game of the 1977 World Series against the Los Angeles Dodgers, hits three consecutive homeruns thrown by three different pitchers, all on the first pitch.

The Congressional Black Caucus establishes TransAfrica. Headed by Randall Robinson, TransAfrica becomes the major lobbying body in Washington on behalf of the Anti-Apartheid Movement in South Africa.

1978: Warrington Hudlin, George Cunningham, and Alric Nembhard, Yale classmates, found a non-profit organization, the Black Filmmakers Foundation. Based in New York City, the organization provides administrative and networking support to black filmmakers, and publishes a semiannual journal on black film, Black Face. The foundation distributes the early films of such notable filmmakers as Spike Lee, Bill Duke, and John Singleton.

Louis Farrakhan, who had expected to be chosen as Elijah Muhammad's successor, leads a schis-matic group and resurrects the old Nation of Islam. Farrakhan's Nation retains the black-nationalist and separatist doctrines that were part of the teachings of Elijah Muhammad.

U.S. Representative Augustus Freeman Hawkins coauthors with Hubert Humphrey the Humphrey-Hawkins Full Employment and Balanced Growth Act. In its original form, the legislation requires that the federal government provide jobs for all people who cannot find work in the private sector. The bill that passes, however, has considerably weaker language and provisions.

The U.S. Supreme Court rules in a 5 to 4 decision, in Regents of the University of *California v. Bakke,* that the University of California must admit Allan Bakke to its medical school. Bakke had charged that he was rejected because preference was given to minority students with lower scores. The Court rules that race CAN be considered in admissions decisions, but that schools cannot apply rigid quotas for minorities.

1979: Patricia Harris is chosen by President Jimmy Carter to become Secretary of Health, Education, and Welfare—renamed the Department of Health and Human Services in 1980. She serves until 1981.

Segregation of schools is still widespread. The United States Commission on Civil Rights issues a report stating that 46 percent of the nation's minority students still attend segregated schools. The report also states that only token integration has been implemented in historically segregated areas.

The Congressional Black Caucus sets up an "action alert communications network." The network is designed to exert pressure on white congressional representatives of select areas to vote with the Caucus.

Andrew Young resigns his position as Ambassador to the United Nations after it is reported that he has held unauthorized talks with representatives of the Palestine Liberation Organization.

1980: In *Mobile v. Bolden,* the U.S. Supreme Court rules that electoral failure of black candidates is insufficient proof of voting discrimination.

In *Rome v. United States,* the U.S. Supreme Court rules that the Voting Rights Act's preclearance strictures apply even to measures which unintentionally lead to discrimination.

In May, rioting erupts in Miami, Florida when four Dade County policemen—with extensive histories of citizen complaints and internal review probes—are acquitted by an all-white, all-male jury of the shooting death of Arthur McDuffie, a black motorist. After two days of rioting, eighteen are dead (eight whites and ten blacks) and property damage is estimated at $80 million.

Vernon E. Jordan, Jr, executive director of the National Urban League, is shot in the back. One suspect is tried in relation to the shooting—charged with violating Jordan's civil rights, not attempted murder—but is acquitted. Vernon resigns in 1981.

Maruice "Maury" Wills is named manager of the Seattle Mariners, becoming only the third black manager in major league baseball.

At the height of his popularity, comedy great Richard Pryor sets himself on fire while freebasing cocaine and nearly dies.

The U.S. Civil Rights Commission endorses racially based employment quotas in a report entitled "Civil Rights in the 1980s: Dismantling the Process of Discrimination."

Earvin "Magic" Johnson, Jr. leads the Los Angeles Lakers to the National Basketball Association (NBA) Championship, the first of five championship wins in the decade.

Willie Brown makes a successful bid to become speaker of the California state assembly. He is the first African American to hold this position.

1981: Samuel Pierce becomes secretary of Housing and Urban Development (HUD) under President Ronald Reagan, the only African American in Reagan's cabinet. Pierce would have an undistinguished tenure in the position and, though Pierce himself would not be charged with any wrongdoing, several of his close associates would serve prison terms for fraud, bribery, and lying to Congress.

Pam Johnson becomes publisher of the *Ithaca Journal* in upstate New York. She is the first African-American woman to control a mainstream daily newspaper.

The Reagan administration fights vigorously against a third extension of the Voting Rights Act of 1965. Nevertheless, the Act is not only extended, but it is also amended to address the wide range of strategies designed to circumvent it, effectively nullifying the Mobile decision of 1980.

Acquired Immune Deficiency Syndrome (AIDS) first receives national media attention. Although the disease is widely regarded to be a disease affecting mainly white gay men, it would become clear by the end of the decade that African Americans could no longer deny the extent to which it was affecting their community. (Cultural taboos against homosexuality are often cited as the reason for the denial among blacks.)

1982: President Ronald Reagan restores the federal tax exemptions for segregated private schools that had been ended in 1970. The next year, the U.S. Supreme Court would overturn this decision, ruling that it violated the Civil Rights Act of 1964.

Voting Rights Act is extended twenty-five years. States are required to eliminate procedures with discriminatory effect and to draw electoral district lines to maximize minority voting strength. Numerous black-majority electoral districts will be created in succeeding years.

Andrew Young is elected mayor of Atlanta, Georgia.

Michael Jackson releases his album *Thriller,* which sells more than 40 million copies, making it the best-selling album of all time.

Charles Fuller wins the Pulitzer Prize for Drama (along with a host of other awards) for *A Soldier's Play,* about the investigation of a black sergeant's murder at an army base in Louisiana during World War II.

Clarence Thomas is appointed chair of the Equal Employment Opportunity Commission. Known for his conservative views, Thomas would go on to be confirmed as a justice of the Supreme Court in 1991 after controversial confirmation hearings in which a former assistant Anita Hill would charge that Thomas had sexually harassed her when she had worked for him.

Baseball great Frank Robinson is inducted into the Baseball Hall of Fame. Robinson holds the distinction of being the only player to be named Most Valuable Player in both the National League and the American League.

1983: The U.S. Supreme Court rules that private schools that discriminate on the basis of race are not eligible for tax-exempt status.

Guion Stewart Bluford becomes the first African American in space when he joins the eighth Challenger shuttle flight in August.

Alice Walker's *The Color Purple* wins both the Pulitzer Prize and the National Book Award.

Gloria Naylor's novel *The Women of Brewster Place,* about the lives of seven black women who live on one ghetto street, wins the American Book Award for best first novel.

Lou Gossett, Jr wins the Best Supporting Actor Academy Award for his role as a drill sergeant in *An Officer and a Gentleman.* He is only the third black actor to win an Oscar.

Harold Washington is elected mayor of Chicago, the city's first African-American mayor.

Vanessa Williams is the first African American to be crowned Miss America. She will be stripped of her crown when nude photographs that she posed for surface during her reign.

Jesse Jackson announces on the television program "60 Minutes" that he will run for the Democratic nomination for the Presidency. He will garner an impressive 3.3 million votes out of the approximately 18 million cast.

President Ronald Reagan signs into law a bill making Martin Luther King, Jr.'s birthday a national holiday.

Harvey Gantt, W. Wilson Goode, and James A. Sharp, Jr. become the first black mayors of Charlotte, North Carolina, Philadelphia, Pennsylvania, and Flint, Michigan, respectively.

1984: Track-and-field athlete Carl Lewis wins four gold medals in the Olympic Games, the first Olympic athlete to win four gold medals in track and field since Jesse Owens in 1936.

Benjamin Hooks, executive director of the NAACP, leads a 125,000-person March on Washington to protest the "legal lynching" of civil rights by the Reagan administration.

Rap artists Run D.M.C. release the first gold rap album, the eponymously named Run D.M.C.

Recording artist Prince produces, writes, scores, and stars in the film *Purple Rain.* The soundtrack wins an Oscar for best original music score, as well as three Grammys and three American Music Awards.

On April 1, Motown superstar Marvin Gaye is shot to death by his father in Los Angeles.

"The Cosby Show" premieres on NBC in the fall. The show, which features Bill Cosby as Cliff Huxtable, an obstetrician living with his wife and four children in a brownstone in New York City, breaks new ground by representing the daily lives of an African-American upper-middle-class family, which had been rarely seen on American television.

Michael Jordan, playing for the Chicago Bulls, is named the National Basketball Association's Rookie of the Year.

In November, Randall Robinson and other activists begin an anti-apartheid vigil in front of the South African embassy in Washington, D.C. The vigil, which raises awareness about the evils of apartheid and expresses opposition to President Reagan's policy of constructive engagement, lasts over fifty-three weeks.

1985: A constitutional amendment to grant full voting privileges to residents of District of Columbia fails to achieve ratification by the required three-quarters of states.

Popular talk-show host Oprah Winfrey is nominated for a Best Supporting Actress Oscar for her performance in Steven Spielberg's adaptation of the Alice Walker novel, *The Color Purple.*

In a final showdown with police, eleven members of the countercultural group MOVE are killed when a bomb is dropped on their headquarters in Philadelphia. MOVE's philosophy—rejecting the "man-made" or "unnatural" and refusing to subscribe to "man's laws"—brought its members into conflict with social workers concerned over children and neighbors who complained of garbage and fecal odors and rat infestations.

1986: African-American scientist-astronaut Ronald McNair is killed when the ill-fated space shuttle *Challenger* explodes shortly after liftoff on January 28. In February, the Massachusetts Institute of

Technology names the building that houses its Center for Space Research after McNair.

A mob of white men attack three black men in Howard Beach, a predominantly white neighborhood in Queens, New York.

Mike Tyson wins the World Boxing Council heavyweight title in Las Vegas, Nevada, becoming the youngest heavyweight champion in history.

August Wilson's play *Fences* receives the Pulitzer Prize. (The play wins the Tony Award for best play in 1987.) Set in 1957, the play is about the frustrations felt by a garbage collector who was once a star player in the Negro Leagues before Jackie Robinson broke baseball's color line. Wilson will win a second Pulitzer in 1990 for his play *The Piano Lesson.*

1987: Rita Dove wins the Pulitzer Prize in Poetry for her book *Thomas and Beulah.* In 1993, Dove would have the distinction of becoming the first African-American woman Poet Laureate of the United States.

Kurt Schmoke becomes the first black mayor of Baltimore, Maryland.

In Wappingers Falls, New York, fifteen-year-old Tawana Brawley claims that she has been kidnapped, sexually assaulted, physically defiled, and verbally abused by four white men—two off-duty policemen, a New York assistant prosecutor, and a utility worker. Her supporters include Alton Maddox, Jr., and C. Vernon Mason, her lawyers, and the Rev. Al Sharpton. A grand jury report later concludes that the entire incident was a hoax.

1988: At the Seoul Olympic Games, track-and-field athlete Florence Griffith Joyner, popularly known as "Flo Jo," wins three gold medals, tying Wilma Rudolph's 1960 record. Her sister-in-law Jackie Joyner-Kersee wins the gold medal in the heptathlon—the most demanding event in women's track and field—making her "America's best all-around female athlete."

Ice skater Debi Thomas is the first African American to win a medal in a Winter Olympics at Calgary, winning the bronze medal.

Novelist Toni Morrison wins the Pulitzer prize for Beloved, a novel that deals with the legacy of slavery in the years following the Civil War.

Jesse Jackson makes a strong showing in the Democratic presidential primaries, coming in either first or second in thirty-one out of thirty-six primaries, and accruing almost seven million votes out of a total of twenty-three million cast.

Donald Payne of Newark becomes New Jersey's first African-American congressman.

1989: Having led the Washington Redskins to a victory over the Denver Broncos, Doug Williams is named Most Valuable Player in Super Bowl XXII. He is the first African American ever to start as quarterback in a Super Bowl game.

Barbara Harris becomes the first female bishop (and the first female African-American bishop) of the Protestant Episcopal Church.

Ronald Brown is chosen to be chairman of the Democratic National Committee, the first African American to chair a major political party.

African-American men in Boston, Massachusetts are randomly searched and intimidated by the police after a white man Charles Stuart falsely claims that his pregnant wife was murdered by a young black man. Stuart would later commit suicide when he became a suspect in the case.

Bill White is named president of the National Baseball League, the first African American to head a major professional sports league.

Colin Powell, a newly promoted four star general, is nominated by President George Bush to become the first African-American chairman of the Joint Chiefs of Staff, the highest military position in the armed forces. Powell becomes a national hero after the successful conclusion of the war in the Persian Gulf in 1991.

In the predominantly white neighborhood of Bensonhurst, New York, a group of whites shoots and kills black sixteen-year-old Yusuf Hawkins who has come to the neighborhood to look at a used car. Protest marches in the wake of the incident are plagued by violence between protesters and hostile residents of the neighborhood. Five whites are eventually convicted and sentenced for the killing.

David Dinkins wins the New York City Democratic mayoral primary against incumbent Edward

Koch and then defeats Republican Rudolph Giuliani to become the city's first African-American mayor.

Douglas Wilder is elected governor of Virginia, the first African-American state governor.

Spike Lee releases his controversial and highly successful film *Do the Right Thing.* The film explores the tensions between an Italian-American family that owns a pizzeria in the Bedford-Stuyvesant neighborhood of Brooklyn and the economically depressed black community that patronizes it.

When Alvin Ailey dies in December leaving his American Dance Theater without an artistic director, former Ailey dancer Judith Jamison is chosen for the position.

The Centers for Disease Control report that—in the United States—African Americans are twice as likely as whites to contract AIDS; that more than one-half of all women with the disease are African American; that about 70 percent of babies born with the disease are African American; and that nearly one-fourth of all males with the disease are African American.

1990: The Medger Evers murder case is reopened. Bryon De La Beckwith, a white supremacist who had been tried twice before for the murder, is brought to trial again and convicted.

Floyd Flake, U.S. representative of New York is indicted on charges of misappropriating thousands of dollars from a federally subsidized housing complex built by his church. He is also charged with evading taxes. Flake is subsequently cleared of all wrongdoing.

Gary Franks becomes the first black Republican to win a House seat in Connecticut in fifty years.

Conrad Harper is elected president of the New York City Bar Association.

James Usry, the mayor of Atlantic City, is indicted on charges of bribery and corruption associated with the gaming resort. Usry is the first black mayor of Atlantic City. He pleads not guilty to all charges.

President Bush names Arthur Fletcher to head the Civil Rights Commission.

Leander Jay Shaw, Jr. is appointed chief justice of the Florida Supreme Court. He becomes the first black to attain this position in the state.

Walter Mosley publishes *Devil in a Blue Dress,* the first of his "Easy Rawlins" detective novels.

John Edgar Wideman wins the P.E.N./Faulkner Award for the second time for his novel *Philadelphia Fire.* He received his first award for *Sent for You Yesterday* in 1984. He is the first author to twice receive this prestigious award.

Marion S. Barry, Jr., mayor of Washington D.C., is convicted of cocaine possession and serves a six-month prison sentence.

Lee Patrick Brown becomes the first black commissioner of the New York Police Department.

Denzel Washington receives an Academy Award for his performance in *Glory.*

The U.S. Senate passes the Civil Rights Bill of 1990, but President Bush vetoes the bill because it is a "quota" bill. The Senate fails by one vote to overturn Bush's veto.

Maxine Moore Waters is elected to represent a wide area of South Central Los Angeles in the U.S. House of Representatives.

Amid charges that it had not given the community sufficient notice, the federal government closes Freedom National Bank. The bank had been losing money for several years.

Itabari Njeri is awarded the American Book Award for her book *Every Good-bye Ain't Gone.*

Whoopi Goldberg wins an Academy for Best Supporting Actress in *Ghost.*

1991: Rickey Henderson becomes the all-time stolen base leader when he breaks Lou Brock's mark of 938 career steals.

President Bush nominates Clarence Thomas, a conservative, to replace Thurgood Marshall on the Supreme Court. Thomas's confirmation hearings are acrimonious. Many national organizations including the NAACP and the Congressional Black Caucus voice opposition to his nomination. The Senate Judiciary Committee is deadlocked on his nomination and sends it to the Senate floor without a recommendation. Shortly thereafter information is leaked to the media about the testimony of Anita Hill, a former assistant of Thomas, who claimed that he had sexually harassed her. The committee reopens hearings and the questioning of becomes a national television event. Despite the damaging allegations, Thomas is confirmed.

Miles Davis, one of the most influential jazz musicians in America during the 1950s and 1960s, dies.

Quincy Jones wins six Grammy awards for his album Back on the Block.

Police officers in Los Angeles stop a car driven by an African American named Rodney King. The four officers proceed to kick and beat him with clubs, fracturing his skull and one of his legs. A witness records King's beating on videotape. The tape is broadcast throughout the country. Within two weeks the police officers are indicted on charges that include assault with a deadly weapon.

While excavating a site for a new office building, workers discover an African American Burial Ground in Manhattan. The cemetery is one of the oldest and largest black cemeteries known in the United States.

Willy T. Ribbs becomes the first African American to qualify for the Indy 500.

The National Civil Rights Museum opens at the Lorraine Motel in Memphis, the site of the assassination of Martin Luther King, Jr.

Robert L. Johnson offers shares in Black Entertainment Television. The initial public offering on the New York Stock Exchanges sells 4.2 million shares.

Magic Johnson retires from professional basketball after testing positive for HIV.

Riots break out between blacks and Jews in Crown Heights, Brooklyn when young black boy is killed by a car driven by a Jewish driver.

1992: Gregory hines receives a Tony award for best actor in a Broadway musical for *Jelly's Last Jam.*

Carol Moseley-Braun becomes the first black woman to hold a seat in the U.S. Senate.

Riots break out in Los Angeles after the four white police officers who had beaten Rodney King are acquitted.

Terry McMillan publishes *Waiting to Exhale.* It becomes a bestseller within the first week of its release.

Arthur Ashe reveals that he is suffering from AIDS, which he contracted through blood transfusions.

Mike Tyson is found guilty of raping a young woman and is sentenced to serve six years in the Indiana Youth Center.

Michael Jordan is named the NBA's Most Valuable Player.

The Federal Reserve issues its second annual report on lending discrimination, stating that mortgage applications from blacks and Hispanic Americans are rejected about twice as often as those from whites and Asian Americans.

Spike Lee releases his film *Malcolm X,* which is based on Alex Haley's biography of the slain civil rights leader.

1993: Hazel Rollins O'Leary is confirmed as secretary of energy in the Clinton administration. She becomes the first woman ever to hold this post. Clinton also appoints Clifton R. Wharton, Jr. as Deputy Secretary of State, Mike Espy as head of the Agriculture Department, Ron Brown as Secretary of Commerce, Jesse Brown as Veterans Affairs Secretary, and Joycelyn Elders as Surgeon General.

Maya Angelou writes a poem for President Clinton's inauguration.

Thurgood Marshall, Supreme Court Justice for twenty-four years, dies. His extraordinary contributions to American life are memorialized in an outpouring of popular grief and adulation greater than that expressed for any previous justice.

Michael Jordan announces his retirement from basketball.

Benjamin Chavis is named the seventh director of the NAACP.

Police Sergeant Stacey C. Koon and Officer Laurence M. Powell are found guilty of violating Rodney King's civil rights after being tried again in federal court.

Toni Morrison becomes the first African American to win a Nobel Prize for literature.

Senator Carol Moseley-Braun is one of two women elected to the Senate Judiciary Committee. Braun was inspired to run partly as a result of angry feelings over the Anita Hill-Clarence Thomas Hearings in 1991.

Colin Powell retires from the Army at the end of his second term as chairman of the Joint Chiefs of Staff.

David Dinkins is defeated by Rudolph Giuliani in his bid for reelection.

David Satcher is appointed director of the federal Centers for Disease Control.

1994: The Florida legislature agrees to pay up to $150,000 to each survivor of the Rosewood Massacre. On New Year's Day in 1923 a white woman claimed that she had been assaulted by a black man. A white mob marched to the small, black community of Rosewood in search of the man. Failing to find him they proceeded to burn nearly every house. Many people fled the violence.

Joycelyn Elders resigns as U.S. Surgeon General after making controversial statements on sex education and drug use.

Benjamin Franklin Chavis joins the Nation of Islam as an organizer and close adviser to Minister Louis Farrakhan after resigning from the NAACP.

Stanley Crouch wins the prestigious Guggenheim "genius" award.

Carl McCall is elected New York Stare Comptroller.

1995: Mike Tyson is released after serving three years in prison.

O. J. Simpson is acquitted of the murder of his ex-wife Nicole Brown Simpson and her friend Ron Goldman. The lasted over eight months.

Bob Watson is hired to be the General Manager of the New York Yankees. He is the first African American to hold this position.

Colin Powell publishes his memoir *My American Journey.*

The Million Man March — Louis Farrakhan of the Nation of Islam organizes this march as an opportunity for black men to take responsibility for their lives and communities. Many turn out for the march. It stimulates black voter registration and political activism.

Eubie Blake is featured on a U.S. postage stamp.

1996: Arthur Ashe is honored in his native Richmond by the erection of a statue on Monument Avenue, the city's central thoroughfare.

Nikki McCray dominates the women's basketball competition at the 1996 Olympics.

Harry Belafonte produces and stars in a television special "Harry Belafonte and Friends."

Ron Brown and his party are killed in an airplane crash while on a trip to Croatia.

Kweisi Mfume is sworn in as the head of the NAACP.

Carl Lewis wins the long jump in the 1996 Olympics, thus tying an Olympic record with nine gold medals.

1997: Debbie Allen fulfills a decades-long dream by producing Steven Spielberg's film Amistad.

Mike Tyson is suspended from boxing for biting Evander Holyfield's ears during a boxing match.

Bill Cosby's life is shattered when his son Ennis is robbed and murdered in Los Angeles. Later this year he becomes the target of an extortion plot by Autumn Jackson, who threatens to reveal that Cosby is her father unless he pays her. Cosby admits to an extramarital affair with Jackson's mother, but he denies that he is her father. DNA testing confirms his assertion.

Tiger Woods, a twenty-one-year-old African American, astounds the golf world by shooting a record low score to win the Masters Tournament.

Betty Shabazz is badly burned in a fire set by her grandson. She dies three weeks later.

Lee Brown is elected mayor of Houston.

1998: Julian Bond is elected Chair of the Board of the NAACP.

Mike Tyson's boxing suspension is lifted.

Charles Burnett directs *The Wedding,* a television adaptations of Dorothy West's novel.

Vernon Jordan testifies before a grand jury investigating Clinton's relationship with Monica Lewinsky.

James Byrd, Jr. is beaten and dragged to his death in Jasper, Texas by two white supremacists. The horror of his death shocks the country.

Kwame Tuore (Stokely Carmichael) dies of prostate cancer. He spent the last thirty years of his life in Guinea where he continued his work in political education and promoting the goal of a unified socialist Africa.

Ruby Dee and Ossie Davis celebrate their fiftieth wedding anniversary by publishing a joint memoir, *With Ossie and Rudy Dee: In This Life Together.*

Richard Pryor becomes the first recipient of the Kennedy Center's Mark Twain prize for humor.

1999: Michael Jordan retires from basketball for a second and final time after leading the Bulls to their sixth NBA championship.

Stanley Hill announces his retirement eleven weeks after taking a leave of absence from his longtime position as the executive director of District Council 17. He was being investigated for allegations of embezzlement, kickbacks, and vote fraud by the Manhattan District Attorney's office.

A long-lost poem by Phillis Wheatley, "Ocean," is read publicly for the first time in 226 years.

President Clinton grants Henry O. Flipper a presidential pardon fifty-nine years after his death. Flipper was court-martialed in 1881 on thievery charges that were trumped up.

February—Amadou Diallo, a young African immigrant, is shot and killed by four New York City policemen in the doorway of his Bronx apartment building. Forty-one shots are fired. Local residents protest over police brutality. Rallies are held everyday outside of police headquarters until the police officers are indicted for murder. Many prominent citizens are arrested daily, including: David Dinkins, Carl McCall, Ossie Davis, Ruby Dee, and Susan Sarandon.

The federal government investigates the New Jersey State Police and New York City Police department for their policies of "racial profiling."

Maurice Ashley becomes the first African-American Grandmaster chess player. An estimated 600 players worldwide hold the Grandmaster title—approximately forty-five are U.S. players.

April—a protest led by the relatives of victims of police brutality from across the country is held in Washington, D.C. The protesters intend to mobilize and organize to fight for social, economic, and racial justice.

Louis Farrakhan is seriously ill with cancer and is hospitalized.

Lincoln Center celebrates Duke Ellington's 100th birthday with a centennial year tribute honoring his contributions to jazz and classical music.

2000: South Carolina Governor Jim Hodges signed a bill that officially instituted a Martin Luther King, Jr. holiday for state workers in South Carolina, the last state in the nation to commemorate the event as a state holiday.

L. A. Reid took over as president and CEO of Arista Records.

Tennis player, Venus Williams won the Women's singles at Wimbledon, making her only the second African-American to do so.

Denzel Washington wins the Golden Globe award for Best Performance by an Actor in a Dramatic Motion Picture for *The Hurricane.*

Tiger Woods becomes the youngest player to win all four major golf championships (the British Open, the Masters, the PGA Championship, and the U.S. Open).

Gustavas A. McLeod becomes the first man to pilot an open-cockpit plane to the North Pole.

Christopher Paul Curtis wins the Newbery Medal and the Coretta Scott King Author award for his book, *Bud, Not Buddy.* This marks the first time that one book has won both awards. This is also the first time since 1976 that a black writer has won the Newbury award.

Three sisters, Joetta Clark-Diggs, Hazel Clark, and Jearl Miles-Clark, become the first family to win all three spots on the U.S. Olympic team for the womens' 800 meter track event.

The South Carolina Senate votes to remove the Confederate flag from the dome of the State Capitol Building.

INDEX

Q

Quadroons, 1655, 1995
Quaker Oats Company, 22
Quakers. *See* Society of Friends
Quality Education for Minorities Network, 2403
Quamino, "Dutchess," 897
Quammnie, John, 2704
Quarles, Benjamin, 572, 1285, 1382, **2245–2246,** S:ix
Quarles, Frank, 2542
Quarles, John F., 1588
Quarles, Norma, 1507
Quarles, Ralph, 1574
Quarry, Jerry, 97, 419
Quarterman, Lloyd A., 2406
Queen Charlotte Island Coal Company, 1104
Queenie Pie (Ellington), 2058
Queen Latifah, *S:227,* **S:227–228**
Queens County, New York, black income, 590
Queen: The Story of an American Family (Haley), 1173–1174
Queen Vee Records, 2554
"Question of Color, A" (television documentary), 2449
Quest of the Silver Fleece, The (Du Bois), 808, 1202
Quicksand (Larsen), 1213, 1578, 1631
Quiet One, The (film), 965
"Quiet storm" (radio style), 2256–2257
Quigley, Elijah, 1708
Quilt making, 991–992, 997, **2246–2247**
    Africanisms, 61
    Hunter, Clementine, 1329
    story quilts, 2342
Quincy (comic strip), 625
Quinichette, Paul, 281
Quinland, William Samuel, 1617, **2247**
Quinn, William Paul, 63, 823, 1357, **2247–2248**
Quotas. *See* Affirmative action
Qwest Productions, 1485

R

Race
    anatomical differences, 130
    anthropologic studies, 144–145, 602
    brain size, 130, 1255–1256, 2232, 2400
    epidemiology, 910
    eugenics, 916–917
    genetic inferiority theory, 364
    health surveys, use of, 1258
    IQ tests, 395, 917, 2234, 2401
    male genitalia size, 2421
    photographic studies, 2142
    runaway slave causation, 2232
    scientific theories of, **2252–2253,** **2398–2400**
    sexual attraction and skin color, 2108

    skin pigmentation, 2448
    skull shape, 399
    sociologists, 2522
    syphilis infection, 2685–2686, 2687
Race Adjustments (Miller), 689
Race and Economics (Sowell), 2648
Race and History (Franklin), 1040
Race, caste, and class, **2249–2251**
    anthropologic studies, 147
    Cox (Oliver Cromwell) studies, 670–671
    Creoles, 672–674
    crime, 675–679
    draft, 2741
    feminist perspective, 681, 683, 686
    free blacks, 1062
    lynchings, 1670–1671
    Mexico, 1768
    mutual aid society membership, 1043
    passing for white, 2105–2108
    race relations studies, 2522–2524, 2525
    urban community divisions, 1784
    See also Black identity; Skin color
Race, Caste and Class (Cox), 2250
Race records (music), 387, 1753, 2493, 2497
Race relations. *See* Race, caste, and class
Race riots. *See* Urban riots and rebellions; specific cities
Race: Science and Politics (Benedict), 144
Races of Mankind, The (Benedict), 144
Race Traits and Tendencies of the American Negro (Hoffman), 335
Rachel (play), 790, 1150
Racial Isolation in the Public Schools (Commission on Civil Rights), 861–862, 2710
Racial passing. *See* Passing
Rackley, Alex, 362
Radical Lecture Forum, 1230
Radical Republicans, 2205, 2275–2276, 2280, 2281–2283, 2284, 2318
    Fourteenth Amendment, 1035
    land redisribution, 1032–1033
Radio, **2253–2257**
    Amos 'n'Andy, 128
    Apollo Theater amateur night, 658
    Apostolic ministries, 167
    black advertising, 26–27
    blues shows, 389
    comedies, 2616
    disco music, 2290
    gospel music, 1123, 2864–2865
    Horn, Rosa Artimus, 1300
    Jack Benny program, 131
    Jackson, Mahalia, 1412
    jive parlance, 2266
    Mammy and Sambo stereotypes, 2566, 2567
    Michaux, Elder (Lightfoot Solomon) broadcasts, 1772
    Miller (George Frazier) sermons, 1798

    music publishers, 2287
    rating books, 27
    recording industry, 2287, 2288, 2289–2290
    Sutton (Percy Ellis) station ownership, 2598
    talk format, 2256
    urban contemporary, 2256–2257, 2290
    See also Disc jockeys; Television
Rae, M., 124
Ragsdale, William, 2701
Ragtime, 1827, 1894, **2257–2259**
    Blake, James Hubert "Eubie," 377–378
    Harlem Renaissance and, 1201
    as jazz precursor, 1430
    Joplin, Scott, 1486
    Kansas City, Mo., 1522
    music collections, 1912
    Scott, James Sylvester, 2408
    slave tradition, 1891
    St. Louis, Mo., 2380
    stride transformation, 1458–1459
    Walker, Aida Overton, 2759
    Wilson, Arthur Eric "Dooley," 2858
Rahaman, Abdul (African Muslim), 77, 1397, 1398
Rahn, Muriel, 633, 2056
Railroad Porter, The (film), 961
Railroads
    black employment, 438–441, 832
    inventions, 294, 1731
Railway Act of 1934, 440
Rainbow Coalition, 1406, 1407
Rainbow Commission for Fairness, 279
Rainbow Tribe, 232
Raines, Franklin D., *S:229,* **S:229–230**
Rainey, Gertrude Pridgett "Ma," *387,* 779, 1096, 1618, **2260**
    blues origins, 386
    lesbianism, 1602, 1603
    Smith (Bessie) friendship, 2492–2493
Rainey, Joseph Hayne, 1164, *2175,* **2260**
Raisin in the Sun (play), 793–795, 797, 1187, 1632, 2332
Raitt, Bonnie, 2770
Raleigh, North Carolina, 566
Ralston, James, 643
RAM. *See* Revolutionary Action Movement
Ramos, Arthur, 207
Ram, Samuel "Buck," 2160–2161
Ramsey, Henry, Jr., 1589
Ram's Horn (newspaper), 1288, **2261**
Ranavalon III, queen of Madagascar, 2273
Randall, Dudley Felker, 434, 713, 1550, **2261**
Randall, Herbert, 2147
Randall, Tony, 204
Randle, Eddie, 721
Randol, George, 964